Defect
Detect

Linux Debugging⁴

Accelerated

Dmitry Vostokov
Software Diagnostics Services

Published by OpenTask, Republic of Ireland

OpenTask books and magazines are available through booksellers and distributors worldwide. For further information or comments, send requests to press@opentask.com.

A CIP catalog record for this book is available from the British Library.

ISBN-13: 978-1912636-71-6 (Paperback)

Revision 1.02 (April 2025)

Contents

About the Author

Dmitry Vostokov is an internationally recognized expert, speaker, educator, scientist, inventor, and author. He founded the pattern-oriented software diagnostics, forensics, and prognostics discipline (Systematic Software Diagnostics) and Software Diagnostics Institute (DA+TA: DumpAnalysis.org + TraceAnalysis.org). Vostokov has also authored over 50 books on software diagnostics, anomaly detection and analysis, software and memory forensics, root cause analysis and problem solving, memory dump analysis, debugging, software trace and log analysis, reverse engineering, and malware analysis. He has over 30 years of experience in software architecture, design, development, and maintenance in various industries, including leadership, technical, and people management roles. Dmitry founded OpenTask Iterative and Incremental Publishing (OpenTask.com) and Software Diagnostics Technology and Services (former Memory Dump Analysis Services) PatternDiagnostics.com. In his spare time, he explores Software Narratology and Quantum Software Diagnostics. His interest areas are theoretical software diagnostics and its mathematical and computer science foundations, application of formal logic, semiotics, artificial intelligence, machine learning, and data mining to diagnostics and anomaly detection, software diagnostics engineering and diagnostics-driven development, diagnostics workflow and interaction. Recent interest areas also include functional programming, cloud native computing, monitoring, observability, visualization, security, automation, applications of category theory to software diagnostics, development and big data, and diagnostics of artificial intelligence.

Presentation Slides and Transcript

Linux
Debugging^4
Accelerated

Dmitry Vostokov
Software Diagnostics Services

Hello, everyone, my name is Dmitry Vostokov, and I teach this training course. In the beginning, we go through a few introductory slides.

Prerequisites

GDB Commands
We use these boxes to introduce GDB commands used in practice exercises

WinDbg Commands
We use these boxes to introduce WinDbg commands used in practice exercises

- Debugging at source code level

LLDB Commands
We use these boxes to introduce LLDB commands used in practice exercises

or

- Basic crash dump analysis

To get most of this training, you are expected to have basic debugging or crash dump analysis experience. The ability to read assembly language has some advantages but is not really necessary for this training because we review assembly language basics.

GDB & LLDB, but Why WinDbg?

- The latest choice of a live debugger for Linux

- Second pair of eyes

- Debugging cross platform code

- WSL

Training Goals

- ⊚ Review fundamentals

- ⊚ Learn live debugging techniques

- ⊚ See how software diagnostics is used during debugging

Our primary goal is to learn live debugging in an accelerated fashion. So, first, we review the essential fundamentals necessary for Linux debugging using GDB, LLDB, and WinDbg. Then, we learn how to debug different scenarios and, in the process, learn how pattern-oriented software diagnostics is used and influences the choice of various debugging techniques.

Training Principles

- Talk only about what I can show

- Lots of pictures

- Lots of examples

- Original content and examples

There were many training formats to consider, and I decided that the best way is to concentrate on hands-on exercises. Specifically, for this training, I developed more than 20 of them.

Course Idea

1. Chemistry[3]: Introducing Inorganic, Organic, and Physical Chemistry book
2. Accelerated Windows Debugging[3] and Accelerated Windows Debugging[4]

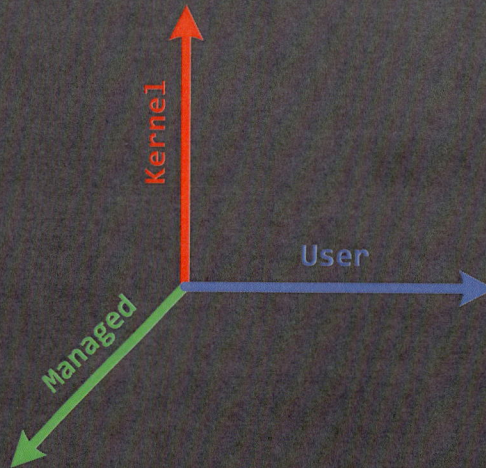

I took the course idea from the book **Chemistry[3]**, which I bought in 2012, to refresh my knowledge. I quickly realized the potential of the same multidimensional format to cover all different debugging spaces to show their interrelationship. My first professional education was in Chemistry. The idea was initially implemented as the Accelerated Windows Debugging 3D course and later became the 4D course. After developing the Linux core dump analysis course, I realized a similar Linux live debugging course is required.

Part 1: Fundamentals

Now, I show you some diagrams.

Memory Space[3]

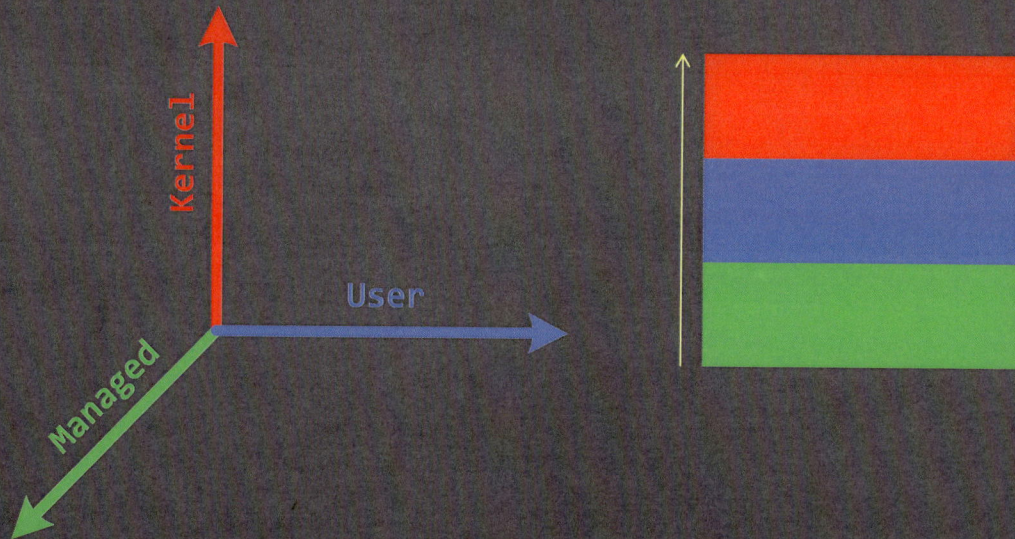

We divided memory space into 3 areas: kernel, process user space, and managed space. Managed space is a fictitious space. It is a part of the process user space, but we consider it a separate space due to analysis differences. Abstractly, we can see it as Linux .NET code (from managed space), Python runtime, or JVM that uses Linux API.

Execution Mode[3]

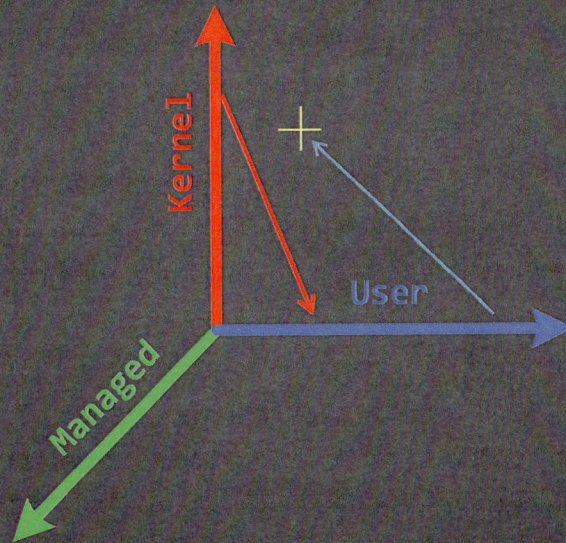

Please note that the CPU execution mode differs from the memory space partition. We can have kernel drivers accessing user space in kernel mode, for example, when they need application buffers to write data to a disk.

Code³

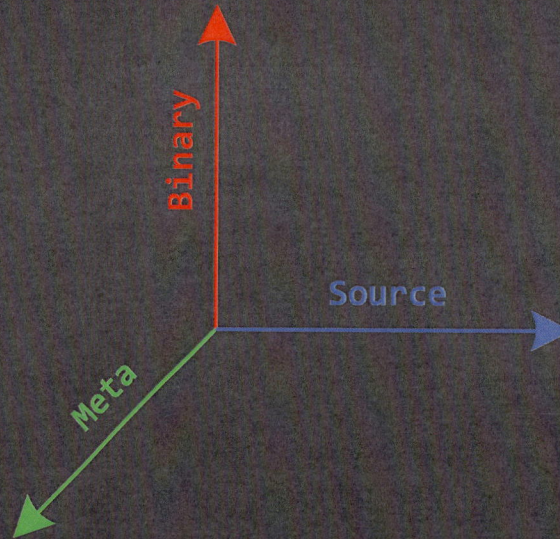

Debugging is usually considered as fixing source code defects. However, it is also important that some problems can be fixed by adjusting code generation parameters (which we call meta-code), especially when porting legacy code or due to a platform change. We would see that in one of our exercises.

Live Debugging Technique^3

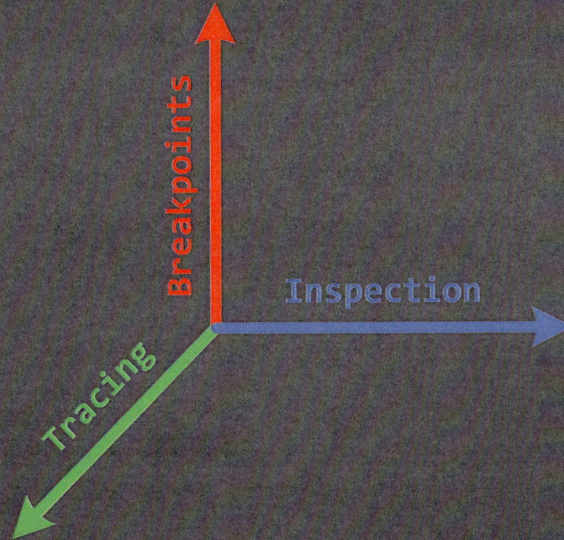

In this training, we also cover 3 important debugging techniques: setting appropriate data and code breakpoints, tracing source code, and inspecting data either structured by source code symbol files or just binary.

Pattern^3

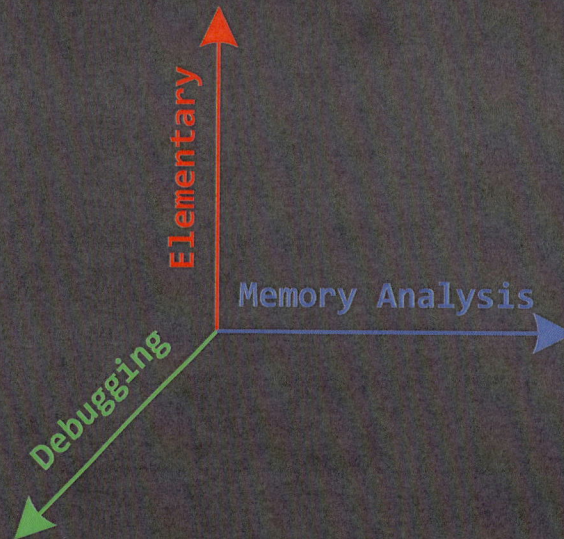

Here is a diagram for the pattern catalogs we use in this training. There are many different catalogs, and we selected only three: **Elementary Software Diagnostics** patterns, **Memory Analysis** patterns, and **Debugging Implementation** patterns. Their difference is explained in one of the next slides.

Debugging Paradigm^3

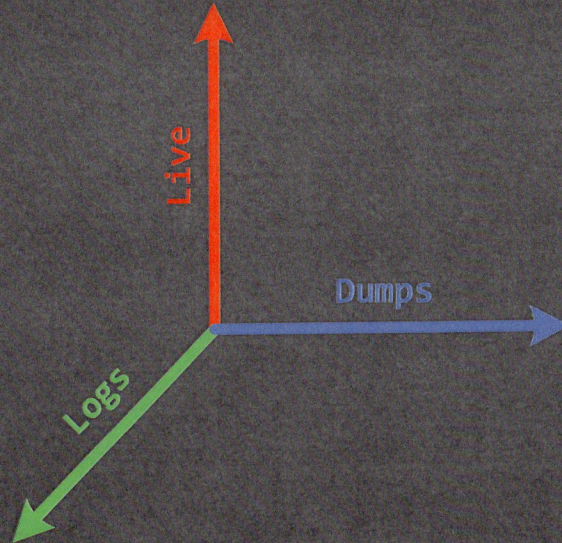

Traditionally, there are three debugging paradigms: dumps (postmortem debugging), logs, and live (debugging).

Debugging Paradigm^4

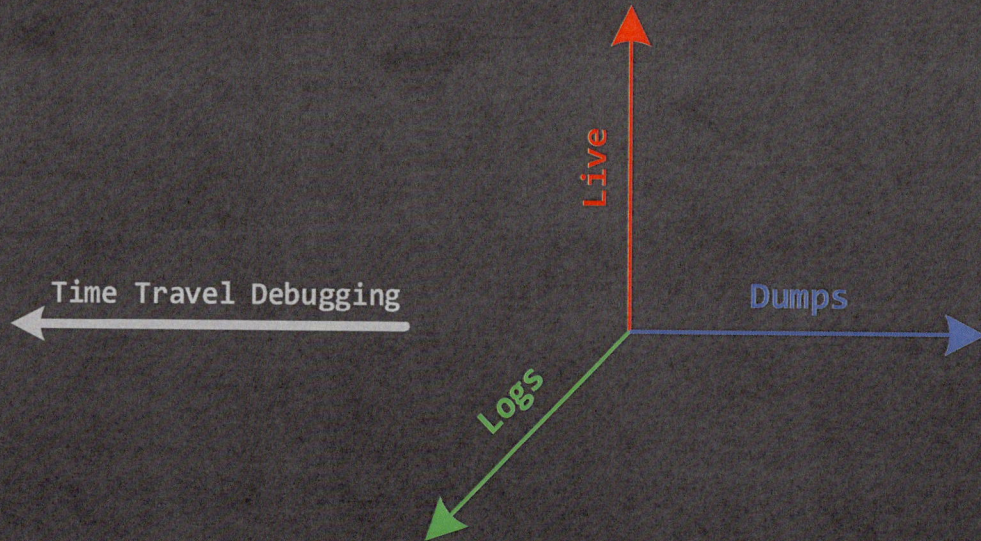

To them, we add the 4th paradigm, time travel debugging (TTD).

Memory Spacetime

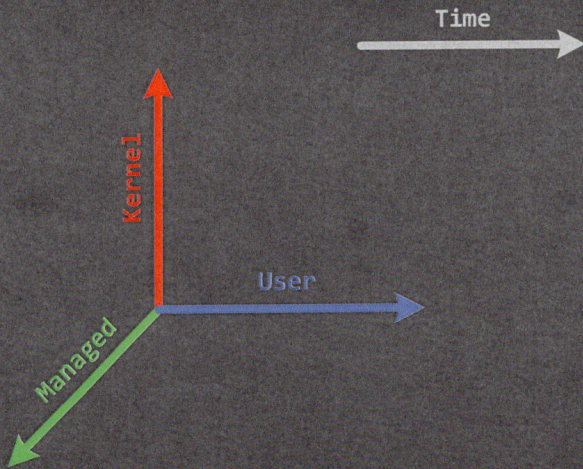

We can also apply the metaphor of spacetime from relativity theories in physics to memory spaces and their changes in time. Both TDD and memory spacetime inspired the Debugging[4] or Debugging 4D course title.

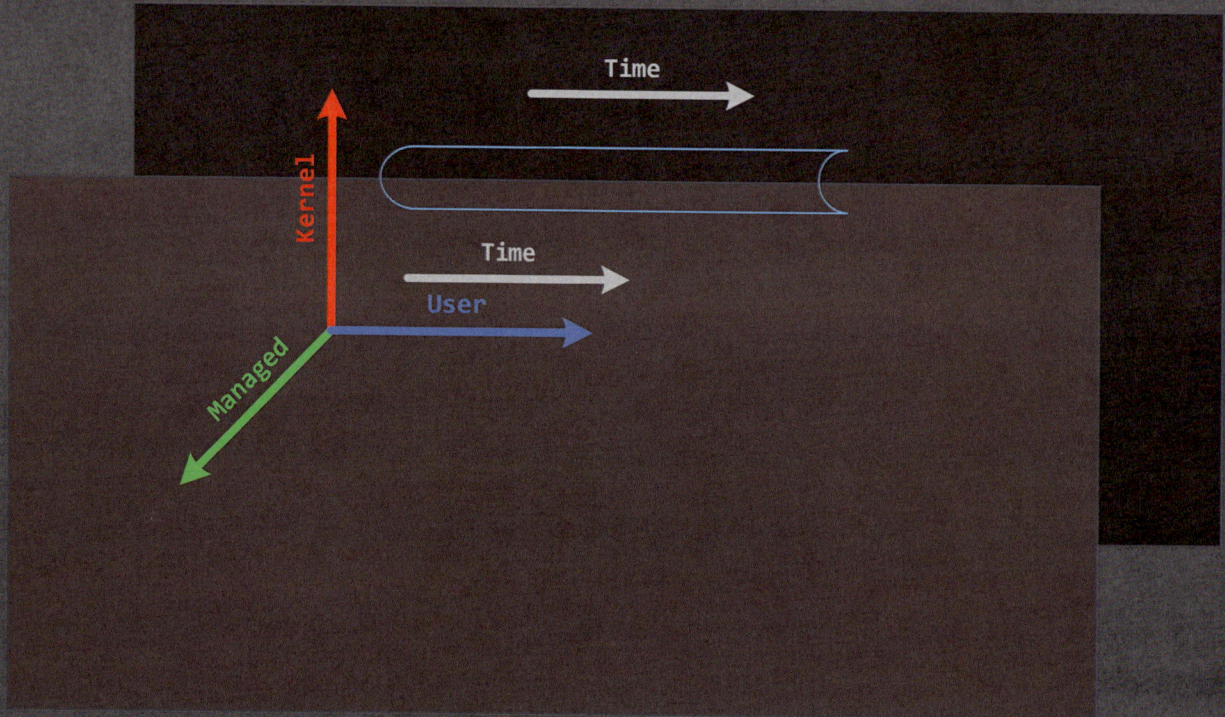

Debugging Paradigm[5]

Idea: Kaluza-Klein Theory of a microscopic 5th dimension

Because we can do kernel debugging of guest VM 4D space from the separate host machine 4D space, we can also apply the metaphor of a microscopic 5th dimension.

Kaluza-Klein Theory

https://en.wikipedia.org/wiki/Kaluza%E2%80%93Klein_theory

Pattern Mapping

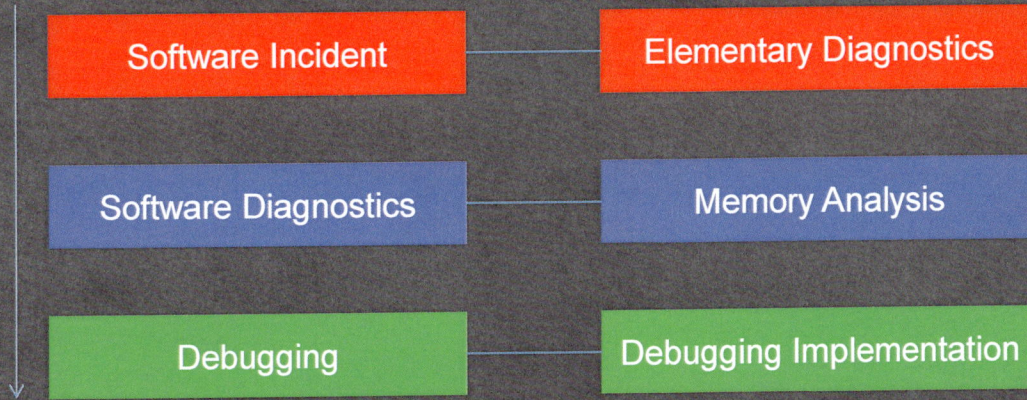

Software Incident — Elementary Diagnostics

Software Diagnostics — Memory Analysis

Debugging — Debugging Implementation

Upon a software incident described by elementary software diagnostics patterns, we perform some software diagnostics activities such as memory analysis (be it live memory or postmortem memory dump analysis or software trace and log analysis) and finally come to some debugging strategy covered by debugging implementation patterns.

Elementary Diagnostics

- ◉ Functional
  - Use-case Deviation

- ◉ Non-functional
  - Crash
  - Hang (includes delays)
  - Counter Value (includes resource leaks, CPU spikes)
  - Error Message

What are **Elementary Software Diagnostics** patterns? These are patterns of abnormal software behavior that affect software users and trigger the application of pattern-oriented software diagnostics and debugging if necessary. On this slide, you see the initial list of relevant elementary patterns we cover in this training.

Analysis Patterns

⊚ <u>Memory Analysis catalog</u>

⊚ <u>Software Trace and Log Analysis catalog</u>

Analysis patterns allow us to reuse memory dump and software trace and log analysis pattern catalogs from the Software Diagnostics Library[1]. In this training, we only cover relevant memory analysis patterns. At the end of this training, I put a slide with links to their description and additional examples.

Memory Analysis catalog
https://www.dumpanalysis.org/blog/index.php/crash-dump-analysis-patterns/

Software Trace and Log Analysis catalog
https://www.dumpanalysis.org/blog/index.php/trace-analysis-patterns/

---

[1] Also available in **Memory Dump Analysis Anthology (Diagnomicon)** volumes, **Encyclopedia of Crash Dump Analysis Patterns**, and **Trace, Log, Text, Narrative, Data** books.

Pattern-Oriented Diagnostic Analysis

Diagnostic Pattern: a common recurrent identifiable problem together with a set of recommendations and possible solutions to apply in a specific context.

Diagnostic Problem: a set of indicators (symptoms, signs) describing a problem.

Diagnostic Analysis Pattern: a common recurrent analysis technique and method of diagnostic pattern identification in a specific context.

Diagnostics Pattern Language: common names of diagnostic and diagnostic analysis patterns. The same language for any operating system: Windows, Mac OS X, Linux, ...

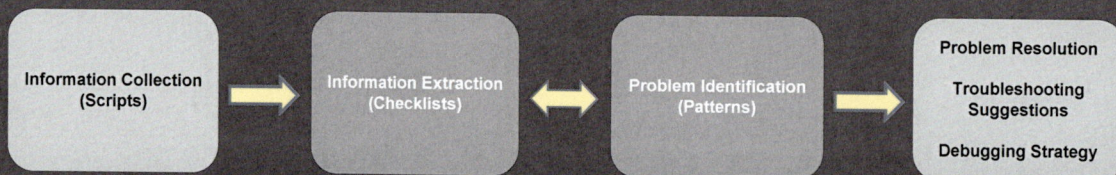

Information Collection (Scripts) → Information Extraction (Checklists) ↔ Problem Identification (Patterns) → Problem Resolution / Troubleshooting Suggestions / Debugging Strategy

A few words about logs, checklists, and patterns: memory analysis is usually an analysis of a text for the presence of patterns. We run commands, they output text, and then we look at that textual output, and when we find something suspicious, we execute more commands. Here, checklists can be very useful. In some cases (such as physical memory), it is beneficial to collect information into one log file by running several commands at once (like a script) and then doing the first-order analysis.

Unified Debugging Patterns

- Analysis (software diagnostics)

- Architecture/Design of debugging

- Implementation of debugging

- Usage/presentation of debugging (for example, Watch dialog)

Debugging Implementation patterns come from a unified debugging pattern approach[2] like the pattern-oriented approach in software construction with its architecture and design phases, implementation, usage, and presentation patterns[3]. In this training, we only cover implementation patterns as they are basically core debugging techniques.

---

[2] Memory Dump Analysis Anthology, Volume 6, and Volume 7
[3] See also **Pattern-Oriented Debugging Process**: https://www.dumpanalysis.org/pattern-oriented-debugging-process

Full Debugging Patterns Catalog

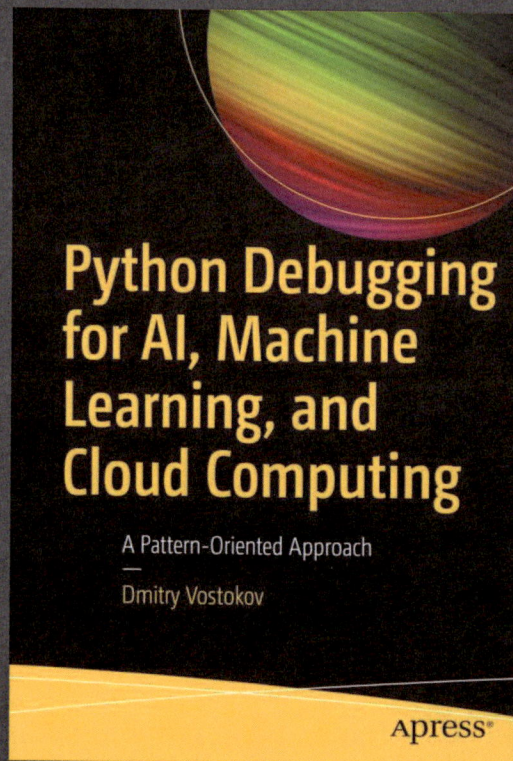

The full unified pattern stack is described in **Python Debugging for AI, Machine Learning, and Cloud Computing: A Pattern-Oriented Approach**[4] book.

---

[4] https://link.springer.com/book/10.1007/978-1-4842-9745-2

Space Review (x64)

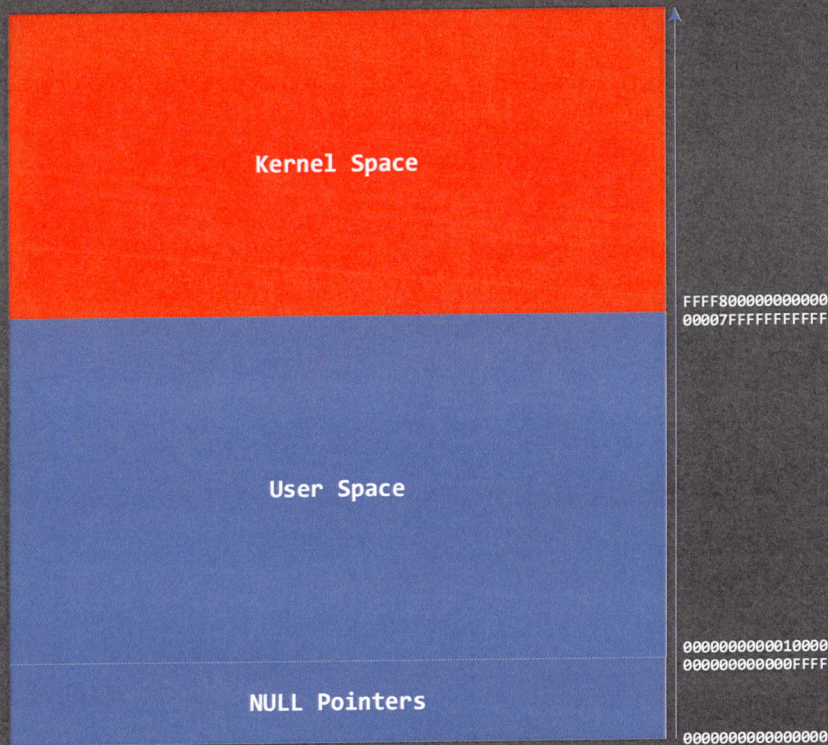

Kernel Space

FFFF800000000000
00007FFFFFFFFFFF

User Space

0000000000010000
000000000000FFFF

NULL Pointers

0000000000000000

If you come from a Windows or macOS background, you find the fundamentals almost the same. For every process, the Linux memory range is divided into the kernel and user space parts and an inaccessible part for catching null pointers[5]. This non-accessible region is different from macOS, where it is 1 GB. I follow the long tradition of using red for the kernel and blue for the user part. Please note that there is a difference between space and mode. The mode is the execution privilege attribute; for example, code running in kernel space has a higher execution privilege than code running in user space. However, kernel code can access user space and access data there. We say that such code is running in kernel mode. On the contrary, the application code from user space is running in user mode, and because of its lower privilege, it cannot access kernel space. This division prevents accidental kernel modifications. Otherwise, you could easily crash your system. I put addresses on the right. This uniform memory space is called virtual process space because it is an abstraction that allows us to analyze process memory without thinking about how it is all organized in physical memory. When we look at process execution, we are concerned with virtual space only.

---

[5] On my Debian system it is 0xFFFF, as seen from /proc/sys/vm/mmap_min_addr value.

App/Process/Library

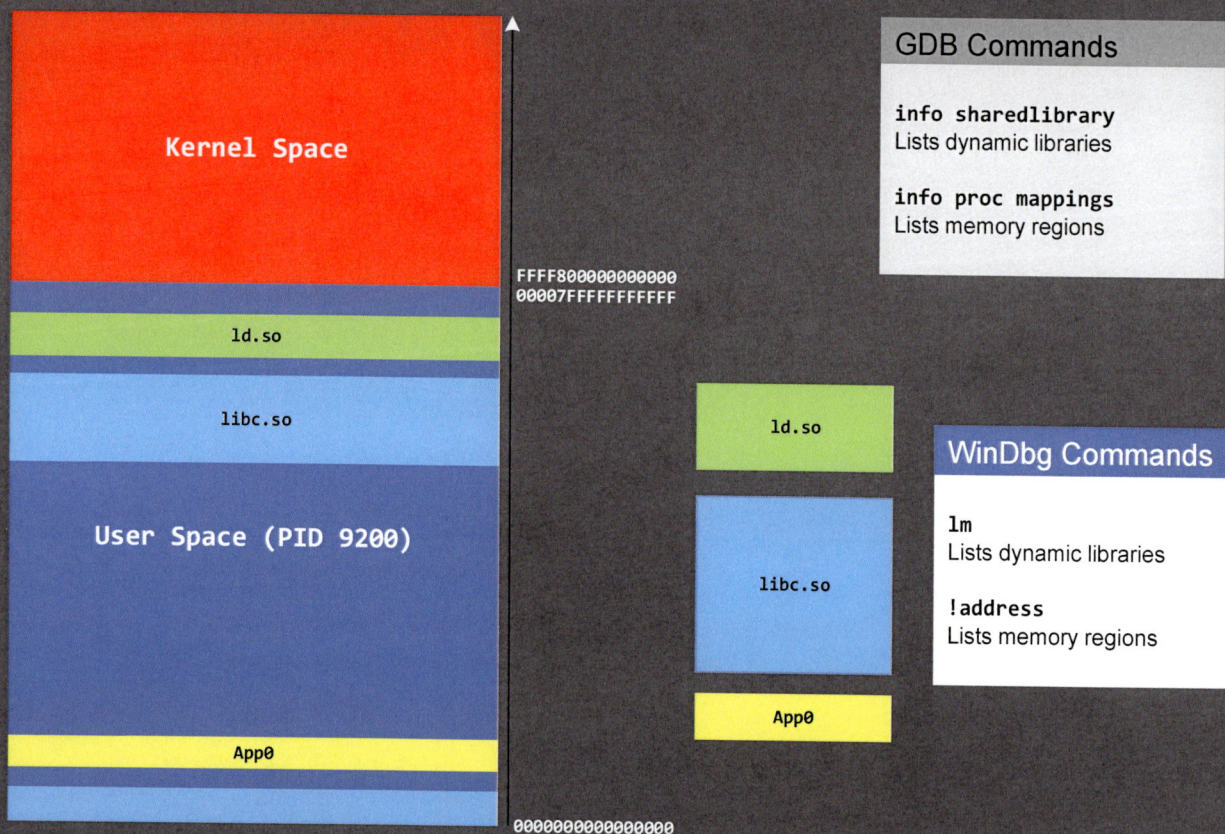

Kernel Space

FFFF800000000000
00007FFFFFFFFFFF

`ld.so`

`libc.so`

User Space (PID 9200)

App0

0000000000000000

GDB Commands

`info sharedlibrary`
Lists dynamic libraries

`info proc mappings`
Lists memory regions

`ld.so`

`libc.so`

App0

WinDbg Commands

`lm`
Lists dynamic libraries

`!address`
Lists memory regions

When an app is loaded, all its referenced dynamic libraries are mapped to virtual memory space. Different sections of the same file (like code and data) may be mapped into a different portion of memory. In contrast, modules in Windows are organized sequentially in virtual memory space. A process is then set up for running, and a process ID is assigned to it. If you run another such app, it has a different virtual memory space.

Lightweight Processes (Threads)

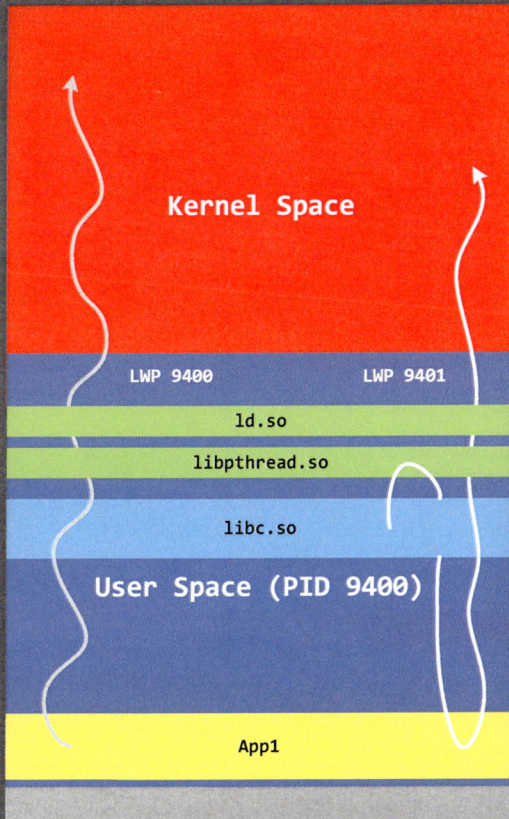

GDB Commands

`info threads`
Lists threads

`thread <n>`
Switches between threads

`thread apply all bt`
Lists stack traces from all threads

WinDbg Commands

`~*k`
Lists stack traces from all threads

`~<n>s`
Switches between threads

© 2024 Software Diagnostics Services

Now, we come to another important fundamental concept in Linux debugging: a thread or lightweight process (LWP). It is basically a unit of execution, and there can be many threads (LWPs) for a given process (all of them share the same process space). Every thread just executes some code and performs various tasks. Every thread has its ID (LWP ID). In this training, we also learn how to navigate between process threads. Note that threads transition to kernel space via *libc* dynamic library similar to *ntdll* on Windows and *libsystem_kernel* in macOS. Threads additional to the main thread (POSIX Threads) originate from *libc* and *libpthread* dynamic libraries similar to *libsystem_c* in macOS.

33

Thread Stack Raw Data

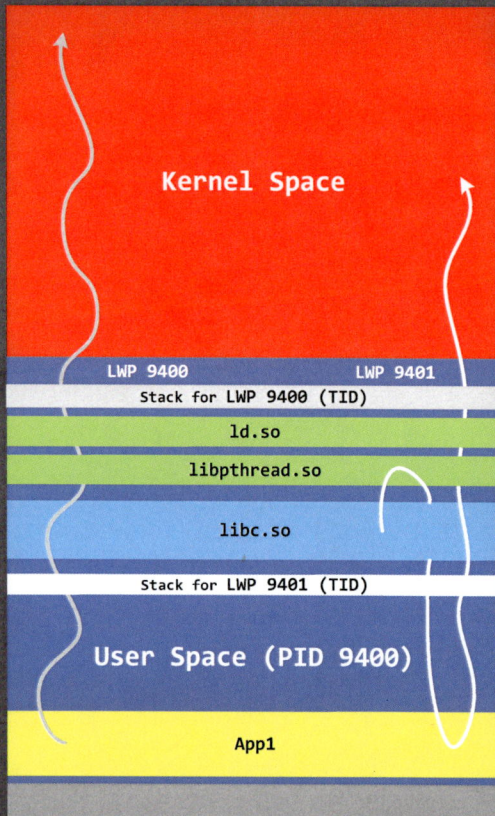

Every thread needs a temporary memory region to store its execution history and temporary data. This region is called a thread stack. Please note that the stack region is just any other memory region, and you can use any GDB data dumping commands there. We also learn how to get the address range of a thread stack region. Examining raw stack data can hint at the past process and kernel behavior: the so-called **Execution Residue** pattern.

Thread Stack Trace

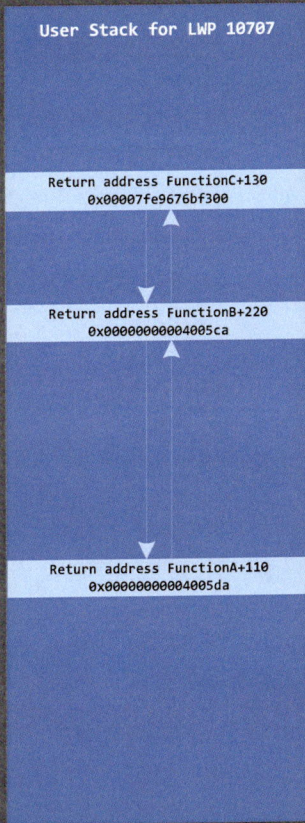

```
User Stack for LWP 10707




      Return address FunctionC+130
            0x00007fe9676bf300




      Return address FunctionB+220
            0x00000000004005ca




      Return address FunctionA+110
            0x00000000004005da
```

```
FunctionA()
{
  ...
  FunctionB();
  ...
}
FunctionB()
{
  ...
  FunctionC();
  ...
}
FunctionC()
{
  ...
  FunctionD();
  ...
}
```

GDB Commands

```
(gdb) bt
#0 0x00007fe9676bf48d in FunctionD ()
#1 0x00007fe9676bf300 in FunctionC ()
#2 0x00000000004005ca in FunctionB ()
#3 0x00000000004005da in FunctionA ()
```

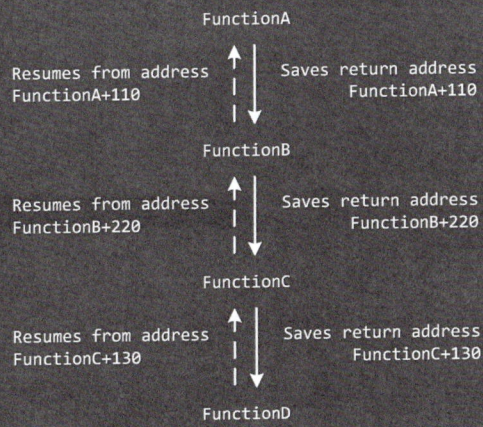

```
                           FunctionA
                              ↑  |
Resumes from address          |  |   Saves return address
FunctionA+110                 |  ↓         FunctionA+110
                           FunctionB
                              ↑  |
Resumes from address          |  |   Saves return address
FunctionB+220                 |  ↓         FunctionB+220
                           FunctionC
                              ↑  |
Resumes from address          |  |   Saves return address
FunctionC+130                 |  ↓         FunctionC+130
                           FunctionD
```

© 2024 Software Diagnostics Services

Now, we explain thread stack traces. Suppose we have source code where *FunctionA* calls *FunctionB* at some point, *FunctionB* calls *FunctionC*, and so on. This sequence is called a thread of execution. If *FunctionA* calls *FunctionB*, you expect the execution thread to return to the same place where it left, and to resume from there. This goal is achieved by saving a return address in the thread stack region. So every return address is saved and then restored during the course of thread execution. Although the memory addresses grow from top to bottom in this picture, return addresses are saved from bottom to top: the stack grows from higher to lower addresses. This picture might seem counter-intuitive to all previous pictures, but this is how you see the output from GDB commands. What GDB does when you instruct it to dump a backtrace from a given thread is to analyze the thread raw stack data and figure out return addresses, map them to a symbolic form according to symbol files and show them from top to bottom. Note that *FunctionD* is not present in the raw stack data on the left because it is a currently executing function called from *FunctionC*. However, *FunctionC* called *FunctionD*, and the return address of *FunctionC* was saved. In the box on the right, we see the result of the GDB **bt** command.

GDB vs. WinDbg vs. LLDB

GDB Commands

```
(gdb) bt
#0 0x00007fe9676bf48d in FunctionD ()
#1 0x00007fe9676bf300 in FunctionC ()
#2 0x00000000004005ca in FunctionB ()
#3 0x00000000004005da in FunctionA ()
```

WinDbg Commands

```
0:000> k
00 00007fe9676bf300 Module!FunctionD+offset
01 00000000004005ca Module!FunctionC+130
02 00000000004005da AppA!FunctionB+220
03 0000000000000000 AppA!FunctionA+110
```

LLDB Commands

```
(lldb) bt
frame #0: 0x000000020328982a Module`FunctionD + offset
frame #1: 0x0000000203288a9c Module`FunctionC + 130
frame #2: 0x0000000104da3ea9 AppA`FunctionB + 220
frame #3: 0x0000000104da3edb AppA`FunctionA + 110
```

The difference from WinDbg (from Debugging Tools for Windows) here is that the return address is on the same line for the function to return (except for *FunctionD*, where the address is the next instruction to execute), whereas, in WinDbg, it is for the function on the next line.

Thread Stack Trace (no symbols)

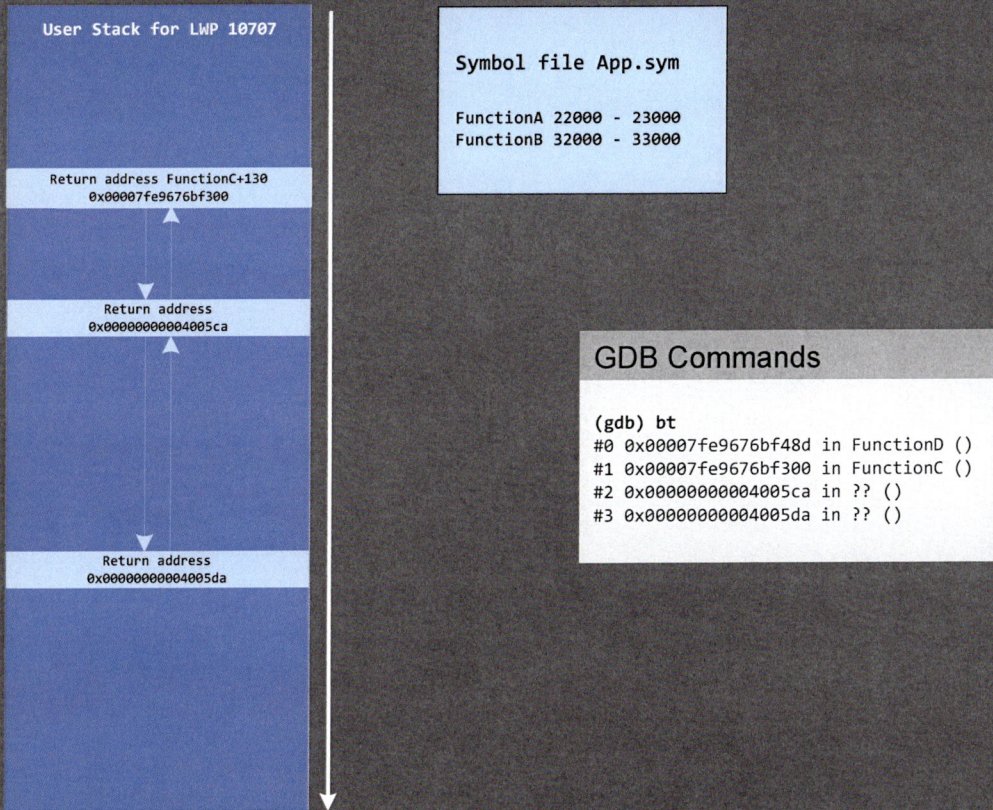

```
User Stack for LWP 10707



Return address FunctionC+130
   0x00007fe9676bf300



   Return address
0x00000000004005ca



   Return address
0x00000000004005da
```

```
Symbol file App.sym

FunctionA 22000 - 23000
FunctionB 32000 - 33000
```

GDB Commands

```
(gdb) bt
#0 0x00007fe9676bf48d in FunctionD ()
#1 0x00007fe9676bf300 in FunctionC ()
#2 0x00000000004005ca in ?? ()
#3 0x00000000004005da in ?? ()
```

Here, I'd like to show you why symbol files are important and what stack traces you get without them. Symbol files just provide mappings between memory address ranges and associated symbol names, like the table of contents in a book. So, in the absence of symbols, we are left with bare addresses that are saved in a dump. For example, without App symbols, we have the output shown in the box on the right.

Exceptions (Seg Fault)

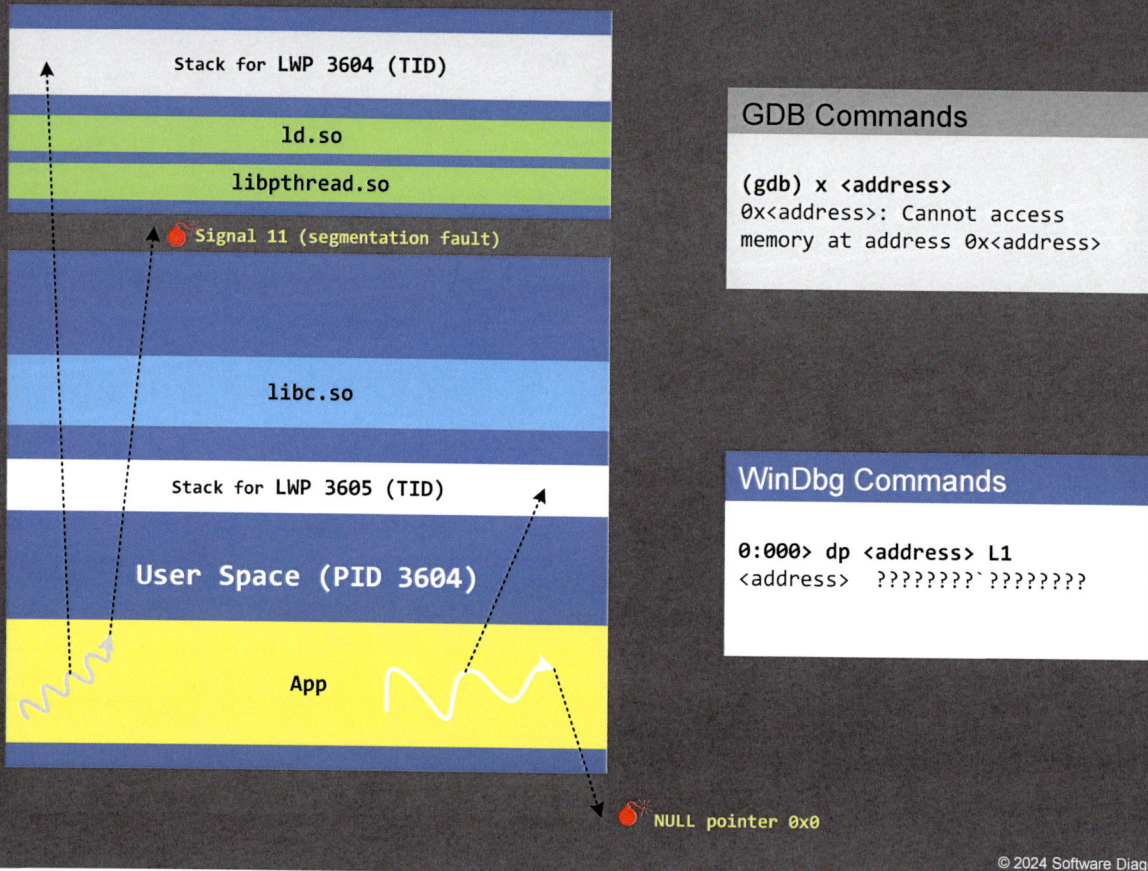

Now we talk about seg fault exceptions. During the thread execution, it accesses various memory addresses doing reads and writes. Sometimes, memory is not present due to gaps in virtual address space or different protection levels like read-only or no-execute memory regions. If a thread tries to violate that, we get an exception that is also translated to a traditional UNIX signal. Certain regions are forbidden to read and write, such as the first 64KB. If we have such an access violation there, then it is called NULL pointer access. Note that any thread can have an exception (a victim thread in macOS). It is also sometimes the case that code can catch these exceptions, preventing a user from seeing error messages. Such exceptions can contribute to corruption, and we call them hidden.

Exceptions (Runtime)

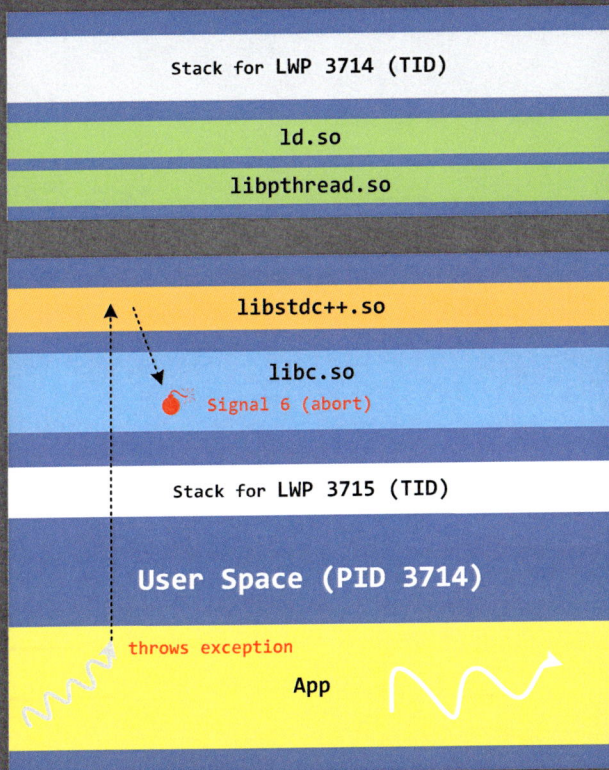

However, not all exceptions happen from invalid access. Many exceptions are generated by the code itself when it checks for some condition and it is not satisfied, for example, when the code checks a buffer or an array to verify whether it is full before trying to add more data. If it finds it is already full, the code throws an exception translated to SIGABRT. We would see that in one of our practice examples when C++ code throws a C++ exception. Such exceptions are usually called runtime exceptions.

Thread Raw Stack Data

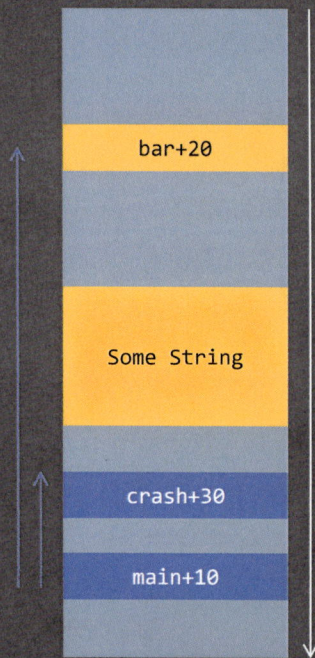

```
void main()
{
    foo();
    crash();
}

void foo()
{
    char sz[256] = "Some String";
    bar();
}

void bar()
{
    do();
}

void crash()
{
    // ...
}
```

```
(gdb) bt
crash+30
main+10
```

Stack memory regions (top to bottom): bar+20, Some String, crash+30, main+10

Each thread of execution has its own region in user space called a stack. We also call it raw stack to differentiate it from the stack trace. Every function call stores a return address. Sometimes, such return addresses are overwritten by subsequent execution, and sometimes they survive. We call this the **Execution Residue** pattern. We can also see ASCII and UNICODE string fragments there if they survived. For example, in the output of the GDB **bt** command on the right after the *crash()* function execution that calls exception processing code, we see a stack trace, but there is also surviving execution residue of the *bar()* because of a pre-allocated buffer. Please note again that the stack grows towards lower addresses during function calls, as shown by blue arrows on the left of the stack memory region box.

Review of x64 Disassembly (GDB, LLDB)

Part 2: x64 Disassembly GDB, LLDB

Now, we come to a brief overview of relevant x64 disassembly. We only cover what we would see in the exercises.

CPU Registers (x64)

- RAX ⊃ EAX ⊃ AX ⊇ {AH, AL} | **RAX 64-bit** | **EAX 32-bit** |

- ALU: **RAX**, **RDX**

- Counter: **RCX**

- Memory copy: **RSI** (src), **RDI** (dst)

- Stack: **RSP**, **RBP**

- Next instruction: **RIP**

- New: **R8** – **R15**, **Rx(D|W|L)**

GDB Commands

```
info registers
```

WinDbg Commands

```
r
```

There are usual 32-bit CPU register names, such as **EAX,** that are extended to 64-bit names, such as **RAX**. Most of them are traditionally specialized, such as ALU, counter, and memory copy registers. Although, now they all can be used as general-purpose registers. There is, of course, a stack pointer, **RSP**, and, additionally, a frame pointer, **RBP**, that are used to address local variables and saved parameters. They can be used for backtrace reconstruction. In some compiler code generation implementations, **RBP** is also used as a general-purpose register, with **RSP** taking the role of a frame pointer. An instruction pointer RIP is saved in the stack memory region with every function call, then restored on return from the called function. In addition, the x64 platform features another eight general-purpose registers, from **R8** to **R15**.

Instructions: registers (x64)

- Opcode SRC, DST # default AT&T flavour

- Examples:

```
mov    $0x10, %rax        # 0x10 → RAX
mov    %rsp, %rbp         # RSP → RBP
add    $0x10, %r10        # R10 + 0x10 → R10
imul   %ecx, %edx         # ECX * EDX → EDX
callq  *%rdx              # RDX already contains
                         #     the address of func (&func)
                         # PUSH RIP; &func → RIP
sub    $0x30, %rsp        # RSP-0x30 → RSP
                         # make a room for local variables
```

This slide shows a few examples of CPU instructions involving operations with registers, such as moving a value and doing arithmetic. The direction of operands is opposite to the Intel x64 disassembly flavor if you are accustomed to WinDbg on Windows. It is possible to use the Intel disassembly flavor in GDB, but we opted for the default AT&T flavor in line with our book **Foundations of Linux Debugging, Disassembly, and Reversing**.

Memory and Stack Addressing

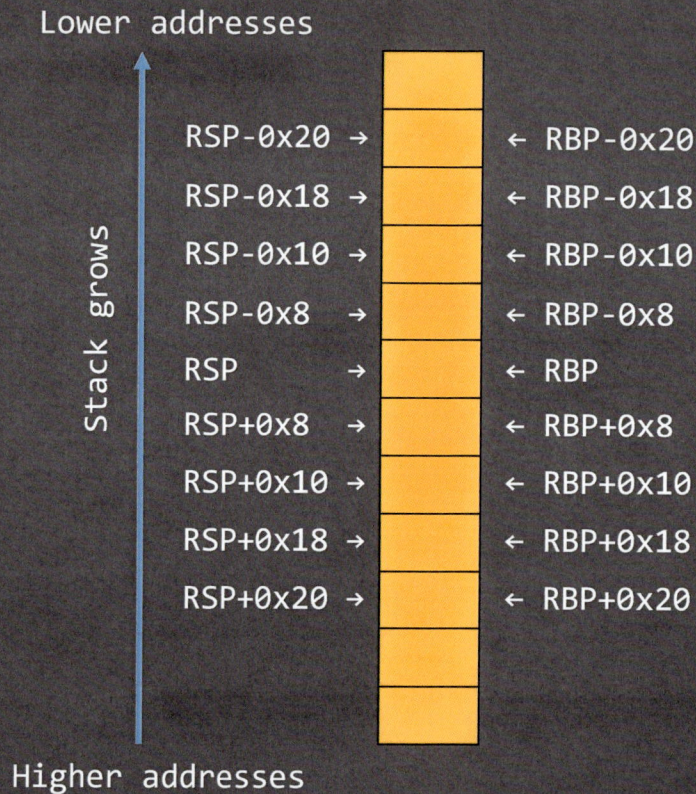

Lower addresses

Stack grows

RSP-0x20 →	← RBP-0x20
RSP-0x18 →	← RBP-0x18
RSP-0x10 →	← RBP-0x10
RSP-0x8 →	← RBP-0x8
RSP →	← RBP
RSP+0x8 →	← RBP+0x8
RSP+0x10 →	← RBP+0x10
RSP+0x18 →	← RBP+0x18
RSP+0x20 →	← RBP+0x20

Higher addresses

Before we look at operations with memory, let's look at a graphical representation of memory addressing. A thread stack is just any other memory region, so instead of **RSP** and **RBP,** any other register can be used. Please note that the stack grows towards lower addresses, so to access the previously pushed values, you need to use positive offsets from **RSP**.

46

Instructions: memory load (x64)

- Opcode Offset(SRC), DST

- Opcode DST

- Examples:

```
mov    0x10(%rsp), %rax      # value at address RSP+0x10 → RAX
mov    -0x10(%rbp), %rcx     # value at address RBP-0x10 → RCX
add    (%rax), %rdx          # RDX + value at address RAX → RDX
pop    %rdi                  # value at address RSP → RDI
                            # RSP + 8 → RSP
lea    0x20(%rbp), %r8       # address RBP+0x20 → R8
```

Constants are encoded in instructions, but if we need arbitrary values, we must get them from memory.
Round brackets show memory access relative to an address stored in some register.

Instructions: memory store (x64)

- Opcode SRC, Offset(DST)

- Opcode SRC|DST

- Examples:

```
mov    %rcx, -0x20(%rbp)        # RCX → value at address RBP-0x20
addl   $1, (%rax)               # 1 + 32-bit value at address RAX →
                                #      32-bit value at address RAX
push   %rsi                     # RSP - 8 → RSP
                                # RSI → value at address RSP
inc    (%rcx)                   # 1 + value at address RCX →
                                #      value at address RCX
```

Storing is similar to loading.

Instructions: flow (x64)

- Opcode DST

- Examples:

```
jmp     0x10493fc1c        # 0x10493fc1c → RIP
                           # (goto 0x10493fc1c)


call    0x10493ff74        # RSP – 8 → RSP
0x10493fc14:               # 0x10493fc14 → value at address RSP
                           # 0x10493ff74 → RIP
                           # (goto 0x10493ff74)
```

Goto (an unconditional jump) is implemented via the **JMP** instruction. Function calls are implemented via **CALL** instruction. For conditional branches, please look at the official documentation provided in the References slide. We don't use these instructions in our exercises.

x64 Function Parameters

- foo(...);

- **Left to right** via `RDI, RSI, RDX, RCX, R8, R9, stack`

On x64 Linux, the first 6 function parameters are passed via registers, and the rest – via the stack locations.

Review of ARM64 Disassembly

Part 3: A64 Disassembly

Now, we come to a brief overview of relevant ARM64 disassembly. We only cover what we would see in the exercises.

CPU Registers (A64)

- **X0 – X28, W0 – W28**

X 64-bit	W 32-bit

- Stack: **SP**, **X29** (**FP**)

- Next instruction: **PC**

GDB Commands

```
info registers
```

- Link register: **X30** (**LR**)

WinDbg Commands

```
r
```

- Zero register: **XZR**, **WZR**

- 64-bit floating point registers **D0 – D31**

There are 31 general registers from **X0** and **X30**, with some delegated to specific tasks such as addressing stack frames (Frame Pointer, **FP**, **X29**) and return addresses, the so-called Link Register (**LR**, **X30**). When you call a function, the return address of a caller is saved in **LR**, not on the stack as in Intel/AMD x64. The return instruction in a callee uses the address in **LR** to assign it to **PC** and resume execution. But if a callee calls other functions, the current **LR** needs to be manually saved somewhere, usually on the stack. There's Stack Pointer, **SP**, of course. To get zero values, there's the so-called Zero Register, **XZR**. All **X** registers are 64-bit, and 32-bit lower parts are addressed via the **W** prefix. The References slide provides links to the ARM64 instruction set architecture. Next, we briefly look at some aspects related to our exercises.

Instructions: registers (A64)

⊙ Opcode DST, SRC, SRC$_2$

⊙ Examples:

```
mov    x0, #16              // X0 ← 16 (0x10)
mov    x29, sp              // X29 ← SP
add    x1, x2, #16          // X1 ← X2+16 (0x10)
mul    x1, x2, x3           // X1 ← X2*X3
blr    x8                   // X8 already contains
                            //    the address of func (&func)
                            // LR ← PC+4; PC ← &func
sub    sp, sp, #48          // SP ← SP-48 (-0x30)
                            // make a room for local variables
```

This slide shows a few examples of CPU instructions that involve operations with registers, for example, moving a value and doing arithmetic. The direction of operands is the same as in the Intel x64 disassembly flavor if you are accustomed to WinDbg on Windows. It is equivalent to an assignment. **BLR** is a call of some function whose address is in the register. **BL** means Branch and Link.

Memory and Stack Addressing

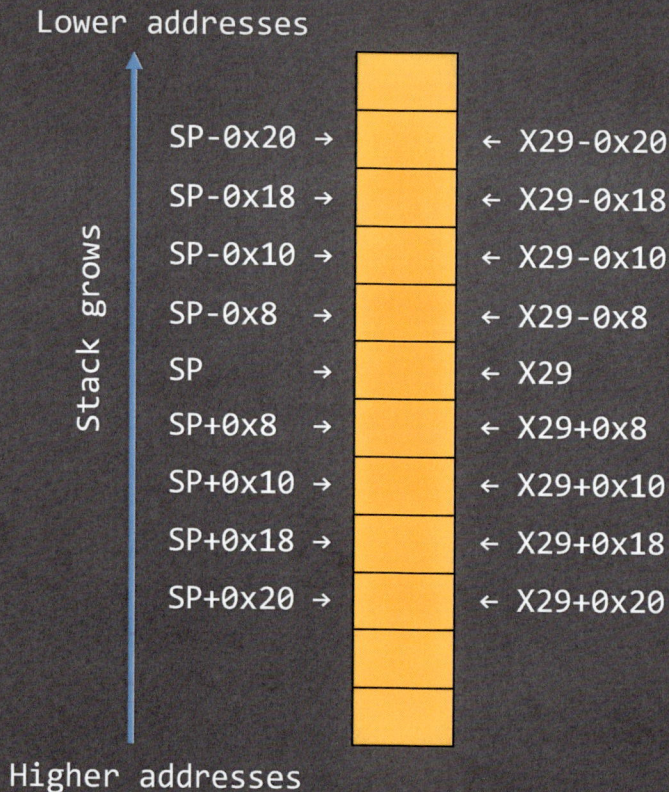

Lower addresses

Stack grows

SP-0x20 →	← X29-0x20
SP-0x18 →	← X29-0x18
SP-0x10 →	← X29-0x10
SP-0x8 →	← X29-0x8
SP →	← X29
SP+0x8 →	← X29+0x8
SP+0x10 →	← X29+0x10
SP+0x18 →	← X29+0x18
SP+0x20 →	← X29+0x20

Higher addresses

Before we look at operations with memory, let's look at a graphical representation of memory addressing. A thread stack is just any other memory region, so instead of **SP** and **X29 (FP)**, any other register can be used. Please note that the stack grows towards lower addresses, so to access the previously pushed values, you need to use positive offsets from **SP**.

Instructions: memory load (A64)

- Opcode DST, DST$_2$, [SRC, Offset]

- Opcode DST, DST$_2$, [SRC], Offset // Postincrement

- Examples:

```
ldr    x0, [sp]             // X0 ← value at address SP+0
ldr    x0, [x29, #-8]       // X0 ← value at address X29-0x8
ldp    x29, x30, [sp, #32]  // X29 ← value at address SP+32 (0x20)
                            // X30 ← value at address SP+40 (0x28)

ldp    x29, x30, [sp], #16  // X29 ← value at address SP+0
                            // X30 ← value at address SP+8
                            // SP ← SP+16 (0x10)
```

Constants are encoded in instructions, but if we need arbitrary values, we must get them from memory. Square brackets are used to show memory access relative to an address stored in some register. There's also an option to adjust the value of the register after load, the so-called **Postincrement**, which can be negative. As we see later, loading pairs of registers can be useful.

Instructions: memory store (A64)

- Opcode SRC, SRC$_2$, [DST, Offset]

- Opcode SRC, SRC$_2$, [DST, Offset]! // Preincrement

- Examples:

```
str    x0, [sp, #16]          // x0 → value at address SP+16 (0x10)
str    x0, [x29, #-8]         // x0 → value at address X29-8
stp    x29, x30, [sp, #32]    // x29 → value at address SP+32 (0x20)
                              // x30 → value at address SP+40 (0x28)
stp    x29, x30, [sp, #-16]!  // SP ← SP-16 (-0x10)
                              // x29 → set value at address SP
                              // x30 → set value at address SP+8
```

Storing operand order goes in the other direction compared to other instructions. There's a possibility to **Preincrement** the destination register before storing values.

Instructions: flow (A64)

- Opcode DST, SRC

- Examples:

```
adrp  x0, 0x420000       // x0 ← 0x420000

b     0x10493fc1c        // PC ← 0x10493fc1c
                         // (goto 0x10493fc1c)
br    x17                // PC ← the value of X17


0x10493fc14:             // PC == 0x10493fc14
bl    0x10493ff74        // LR ← PC+4 (0x10493fc18)
                         // PC ← 0x10493ff74
                         // (goto 0x10493ff74)
```

Because the size of every instruction is 4 bytes (32 bits), it is only possible to encode a part of a large 4GB address range, either as a relative offset to the current **PC** or via **ADRP** instruction. Goto (an unconditional branch) is implemented via the **B** instruction. Function calls are implemented via the **BL** (Branch and Link) instruction. For conditional branches, please look at the official documentation provided in the References slide. We don't use these instructions in our exercises.

A64 Function Parameters

- foo(…);

- Left to right via X0 – X7, [SP], [SP+8], [SP+16], ...

On ARM64 Linux, the first 8 function parameters are passed via registers, and the rest – via the stack locations.

Review of x64 Disassembly (WinDbg)

Part 4: x64 Disassembly WinDbg

This section provides an overview of disassembly for the x64 platform. Linux developers who know the x64 assembly language may benefit because we use a different flavor than the default in Linux GDB.

CPU Registers (x64)

- **RAX** ⊃ **EAX** ⊃ **AX** ⊇ {**AH**, **AL**} | **RAX 64-bit** | **EAX 32-bit** |

- ALU: **RAX**, **RDX**

- Counter: **RCX**

- Memory copy: **RSI** (src), **RDI** (dst)

- Stack: **RSP**, **RBP**

- Next instruction: **RIP**

- New: **R8 – R15**, **Rx(D|W|B)**

There are familiar 32-bit CPU register names, such as **EAX,** that are extended to 64-bit names, such as **RAX**. Most of them are traditionally specialized, such as ALU, counter, and memory copy registers. Although, now they all can be used as general-purpose registers. There is, of course, a stack pointer, **RSP**, and, additionally, a frame pointer, **RBP**, that are used to address local variables and saved parameters. They can be used for stack reconstruction. In some compiler code generation implementations, **RBP** is also used as a general-purpose register, with **RSP** taking the role of a frame pointer. An instruction pointer **RIP** is saved in the stack memory region with every function call, then restored on return from the called function. In addition, the x64 platform features another eight general-purpose registers, from **R8** to **R15**.

Instructions and Registers (x64)

- ⊙ Opcode DST, SRC

- ⊙ Examples:

```
mov    rax, 10h          ; RAX ← 0x10
mov    r13, rdx          ; R13 ← RDX
add    r10, 10h          ; R10 ← R10 + 0x10
imul   edx, ecx          ; EDX ← EDX * ECX
call   rdx               ; RDX already contains
                         ;    the address of func (&func)
                         ; PUSH RIP; RIP ← &func

sub    rsp, 30h          ; RSP ← RSP−0x30
                         ; make room for local variables
```

This slide shows a few examples of CPU instructions involving operations with registers, such as moving a value and doing arithmetic. The direction of operands is opposite to the AT&T x64 disassembly flavor if you are accustomed to default GDB disassembly on Linux.

Memory and Stack Addressing

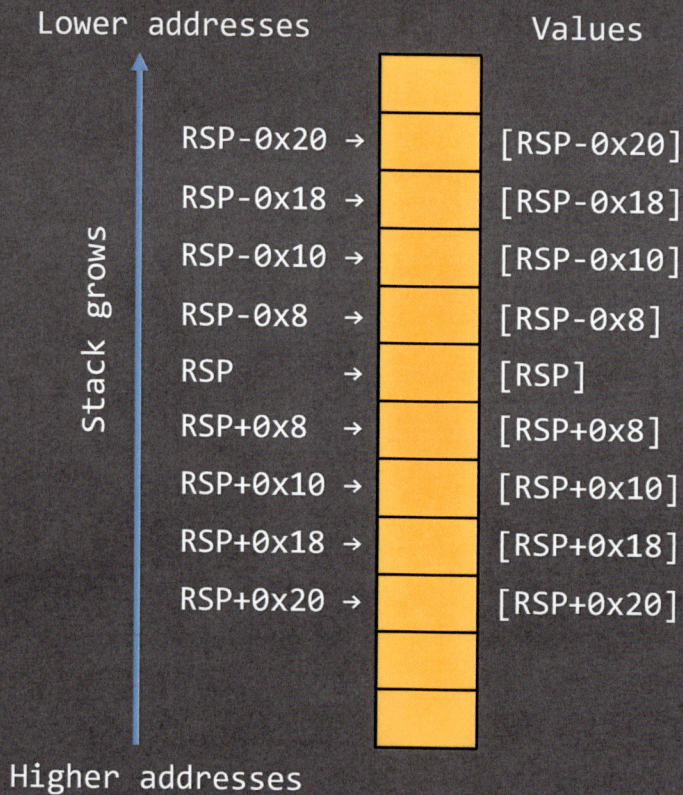

Lower addresses   Values

Stack grows →

RSP-0x20 → [RSP-0x20]

RSP-0x18 → [RSP-0x18]

RSP-0x10 → [RSP-0x10]

RSP-0x8 → [RSP-0x8]

RSP   → [RSP]

RSP+0x8 → [RSP+0x8]

RSP+0x10 → [RSP+0x10]

RSP+0x18 → [RSP+0x18]

RSP+0x20 → [RSP+0x20]

Higher addresses

Before we look at operations with memory, let's look at a graphical representation of memory addressing where, for simplicity, I use 64-bit (or 8-byte) memory cells. A thread stack is just any other memory region, so instead of **RSP,** any other register can be used. Please note that the stack grows towards lower addresses, so to access the previously pushed values, you need to use positive offsets from **RSP**.

Memory Cell Sizes

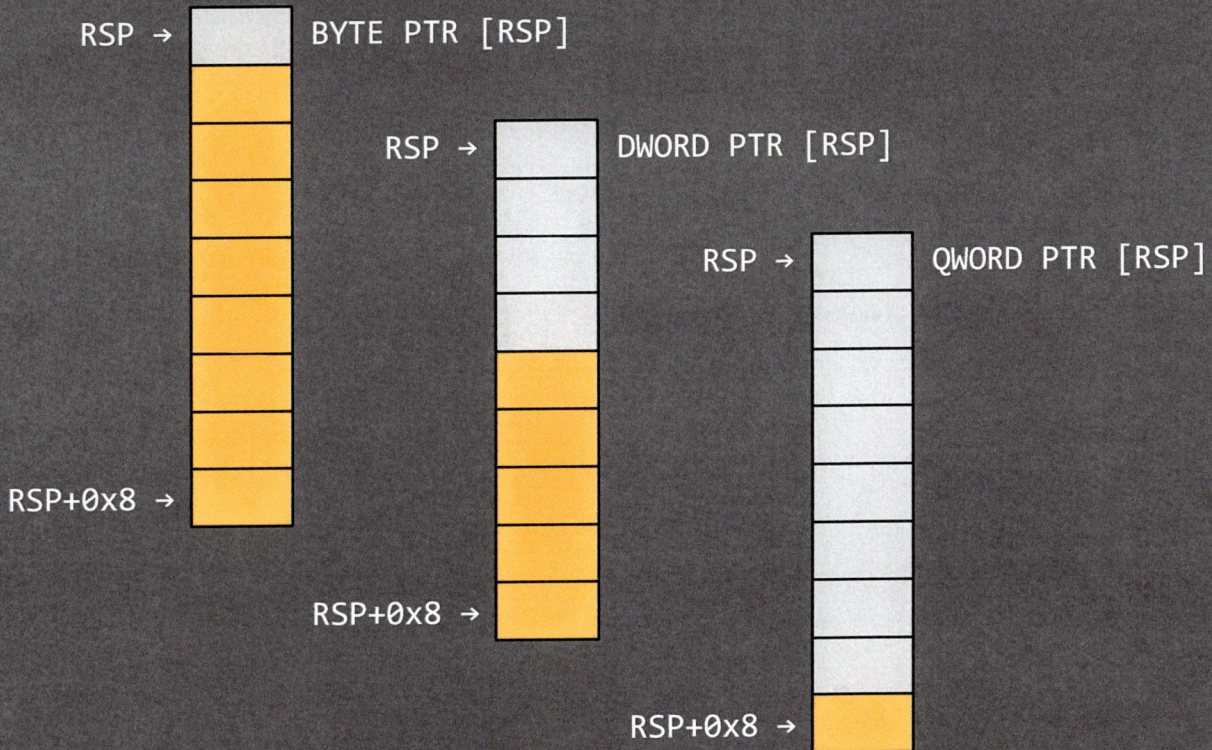

RSP → BYTE PTR [RSP]

RSP → DWORD PTR [RSP]

RSP → QWORD PTR [RSP]

RSP+0x8 →

RSP+0x8 →

RSP+0x8 →

Here, each memory cell is 8-bit (or one byte). When we have a register pointing to memory, and we want to work with the value at that address, we need to specify the size of memory cells to work with, for example, **BYTE PTR** if we want to work with a byte, **DWORD PTR** if we want to work with 32-bit double words, and **QWORD PTR** if we want to work with 64-bit quad words. There's also **WORD PTR** for 16-bit values. This notation is different from Linux GDB, where we have bytes, half-words, words, and double words.

Memory Load Instructions (x64)

- Opcode DST, PTR [SRC+Offset]

- Opcode DST

- Examples:

```
mov    rax, qword ptr [rsp+10h] ; RAX ←
                                ; 64-bit value at address RSP+0x10
mov    ecx, dword ptr [20]      ; ECX ←
                                ; 32-bit value at address 0x20
pop    rdi                      ; RDI ← value at address RSP
                                ; RSP ← RSP + 8
lea    r8, [rsp+20h]            ; R8 ← address RSP+0x20
```

Constants are encoded in instructions, but if we need arbitrary values, we must get them from memory. Square brackets show memory access relative to an address stored in a register.

Memory Store Instructions (x64)

- Opcode PTR [DST+Offset], SRC

- Opcode DST|SRC

- Examples:

```
mov    qword ptr [rbp-20h], rcx  ; 64-bit value at address RBP-0x20
                                 ;    ← RCX
mov    byte ptr [0], 1           ; 8-bit value at address 0 ← 1
push   rsi                       ; RSP ← RSP - 8
                                 ; value at address RSP ← RSI
inc    dword ptr [rcx]           ; 32-bit value at address RCX ←
                                 ;    1 + 32-bit value at address RCX
```

Storing is similar to loading.

Flow Instructions (x64)

- Opcode DST

- Opcode PTR [DST]

- Examples:

```
jmp    00007ff6`9ef2f008    ; RIP ← 0x7ff69ef2f008
                            ; (goto 0x7ff69ef2f008)
jmp    qword ptr [rax+10h]  ; RIP ← value at address RAX+0x10
call   00007ff6`9ef21400    ; RSP ← RSP - 8
00007ff6`9ef21057:          ; value at address RSP ← 0x7ff69ef21057
                            ; RIP ← 0x7ff69ef21400
                            ; (goto 0x7ff69ef21400)
```

Goto (an unconditional jump) is implemented via the **JMP** instruction. Function calls are implemented via **CALL** instruction. For conditional branches, please look at the official Intel documentation. We don't use these instructions in our exercises.

Function Parameters (x64)

- foo(…);

- Left to right via RDI, RSI, RDX, RCX, R8, R9, stack

Args to Child are not parameters

WinDbg Commands

```
0:000> kv
 # Child-SP    RetAddr   : Args to Child   : Call Site
 ...
```

On x64 Linux, the first 6 function parameters are passed via registers, and the rest – via the stack locations. Also, in WinDbg, the **kv** command doesn't show valid function arguments compared to x86 code since the 4 arguments are passed via registers, not stack, so the values shown in the output are just random values taken from the stack region.

Practice Exercises

Part 5: Practice Exercises

Now we come to practice. The goal is to show you important commands and techniques and how they help in live debugging.

Links

- ### Applications:

  Download links are in every exercise.

- ### Exercise Transcripts:

  Included in this book.

Warning

Because of live debugging, due to differences in actual systems and ASLR (Address Space Layout Randomization), when you launch applications, actual addresses and even the number and order of threads in WinDbg, GDB, and LLDB command output may differ from those shown in exercise transcripts.

Here is just a warning if you see the differences in the output on your system and what is shown in exercise transcripts.

Exercise UD0

- **Goal:** Download and verify GDB, LLDB, and WinDbg installations

- **Memory Analysis Patterns:** Stack Trace

- \ALD4\Exercise-Linux-UD0.pdf

Goal: Download and verify GDB, LLDB, and WinDbg installations.

Memory Analysis Patterns: Stack Trace.

1.   Download and install the version of GDB available for your distribution. For x64 WSL2 Debian and A64 Ubuntu, we used the following commands:

```
$ sudo apt install build-essential
$ sudo apt install gdb
$ sudo apt install gdbserver
```

2.   Verify that GDB is accessible and then exit it (**q** command):

```
$ gdb
GNU gdb (Debian 8.2.1-2+b3) 8.2.1
Copyright (C) 2018 Free Software Foundation, Inc.
License GPLv3+: GNU GPL version 3 or later <http://gnu.org/licenses/gpl.html>
This is free software: you are free to change and redistribute it.
There is NO WARRANTY, to the extent permitted by law.
Type "show copying" and "show warranty" for details.
This GDB was configured as "x86_64-linux-gnu".
Type "show configuration" for configuration details.
For bug reporting instructions, please see:
<http://www.gnu.org/software/gdb/bugs/>.
Find the GDB manual and other documentation resources online at:
    <http://www.gnu.org/software/gdb/documentation/>.

For help, type "help".
Type "apropos word" to search for commands related to "word".

(gdb) q
$
```

3.   Download and install the version of LLDB available for your distribution. For x64 WSL2 Debian and A64 Ubuntu, we used the following commands:

```
$ sudo apt install lldb
```

4.   Verify that LLDB is accessible and then exit it (**q** command):

```
$ lldb
(lldb) q
$
```

5.   Install WinDbg (or upgrade existing WinDbg Preview) from https://learn.microsoft.com/en-gb/windows-hardware/drivers/debugger. Run WinDbg.

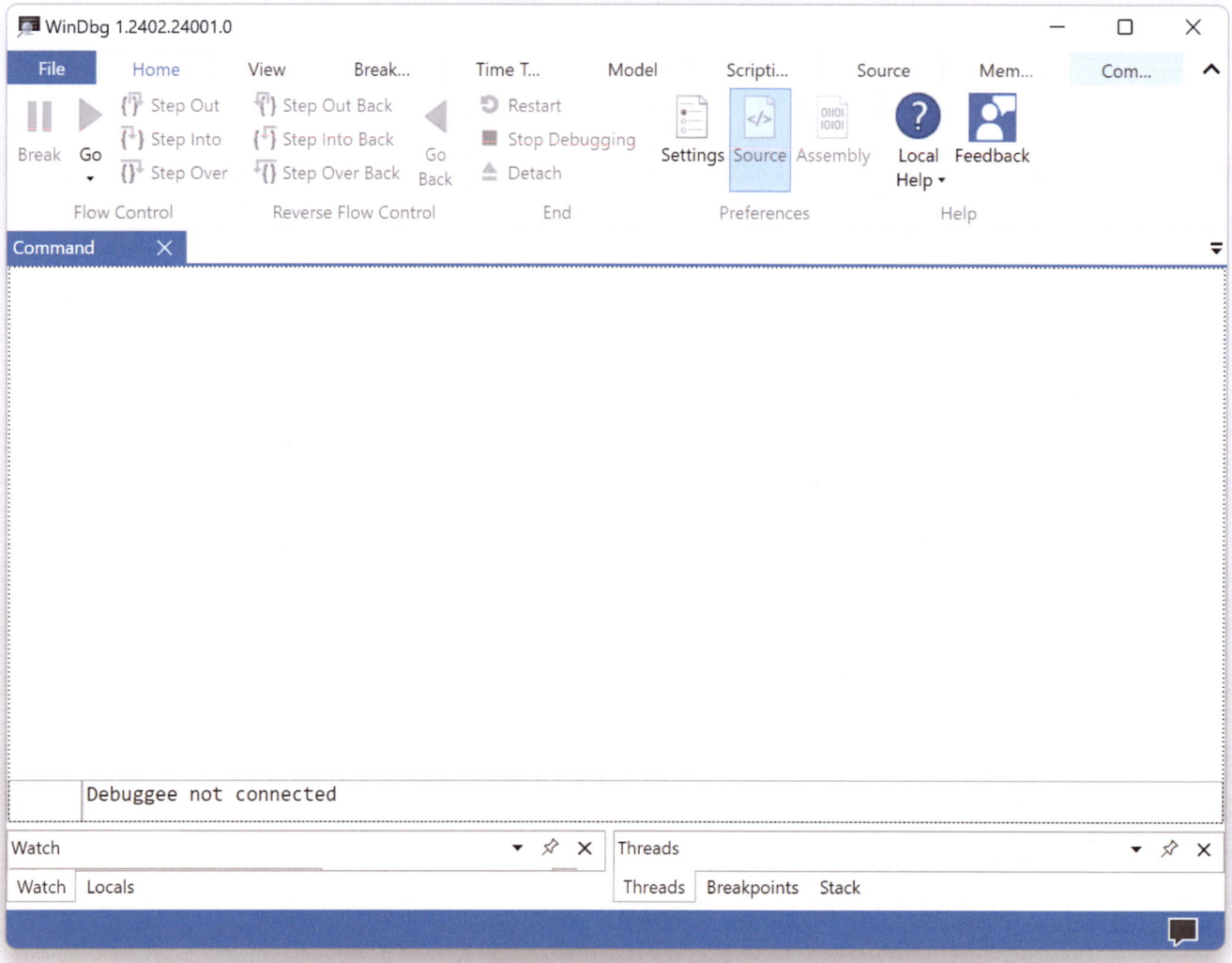

6.   Create a new bash process and attach the **gdbserver** to it:

```
$ gdbserver localhost:1234 bash
Process bash created; pid = 6854
Listening on port 1234
```

7.   Choose *File \ Connect to remote debugger* menu option:

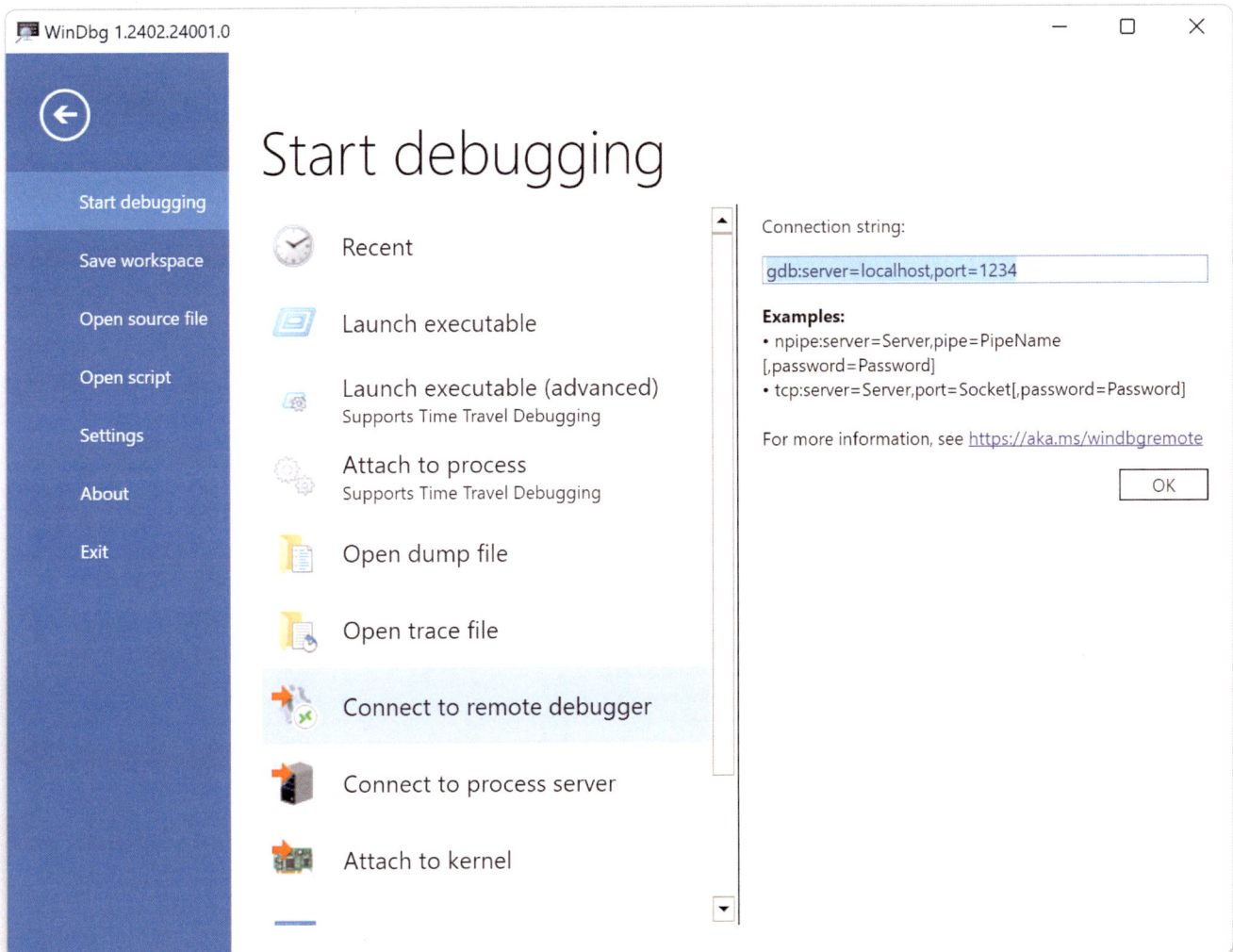

8.   You get the WinDbg debugger attached to the newly created *bash* process:

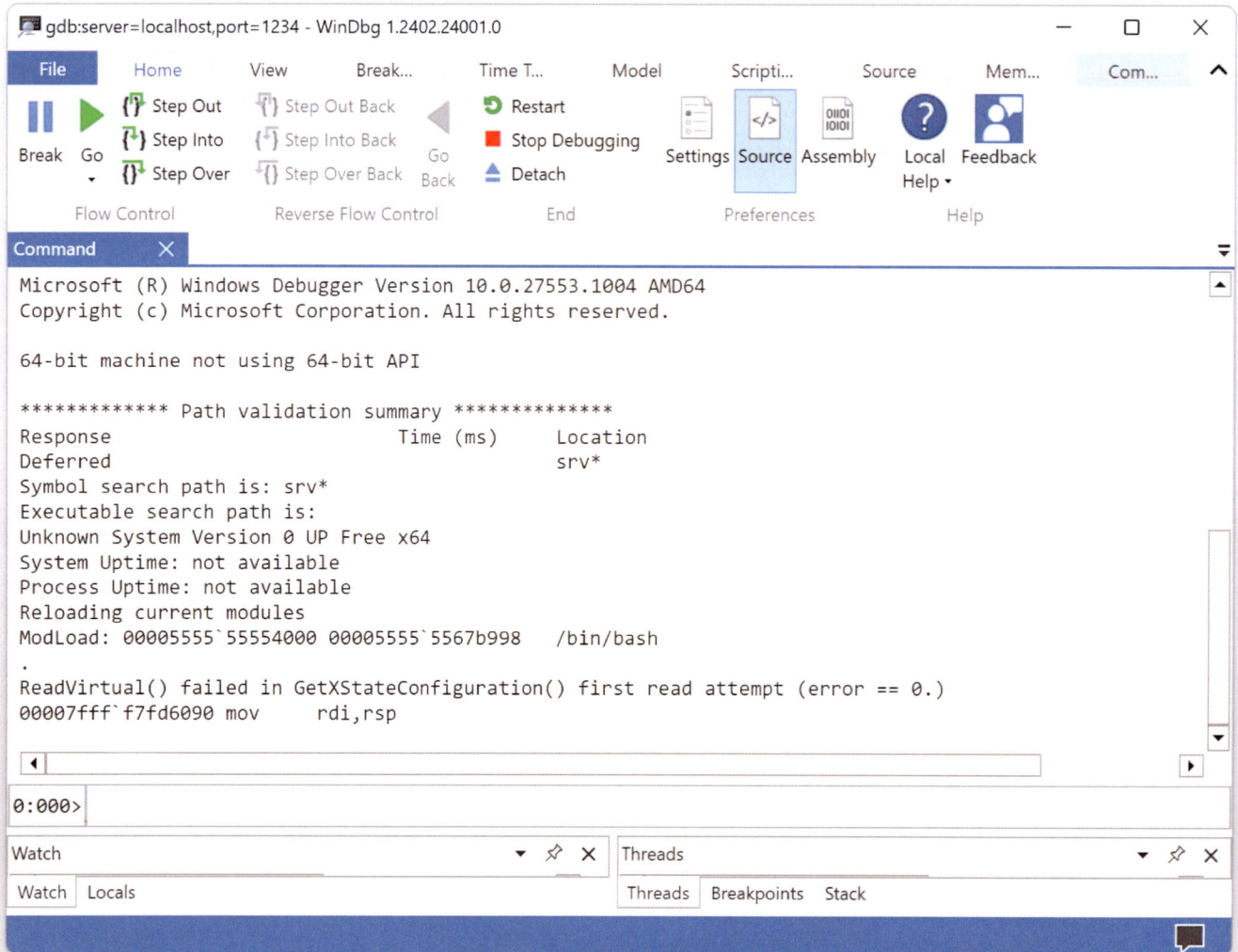

9.   Type the **k** command to verify the absence of the stack trace:

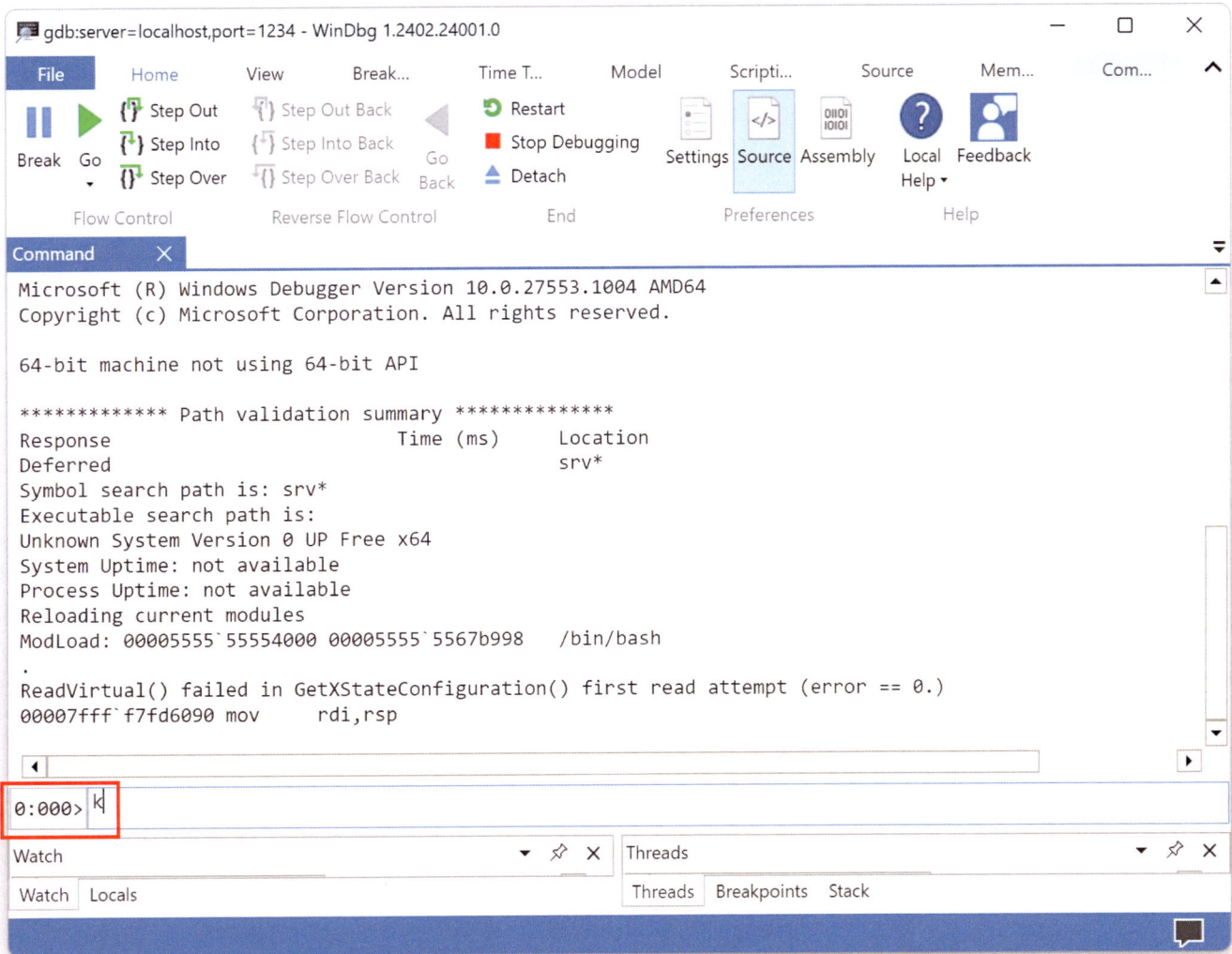

10.   We get the following output:

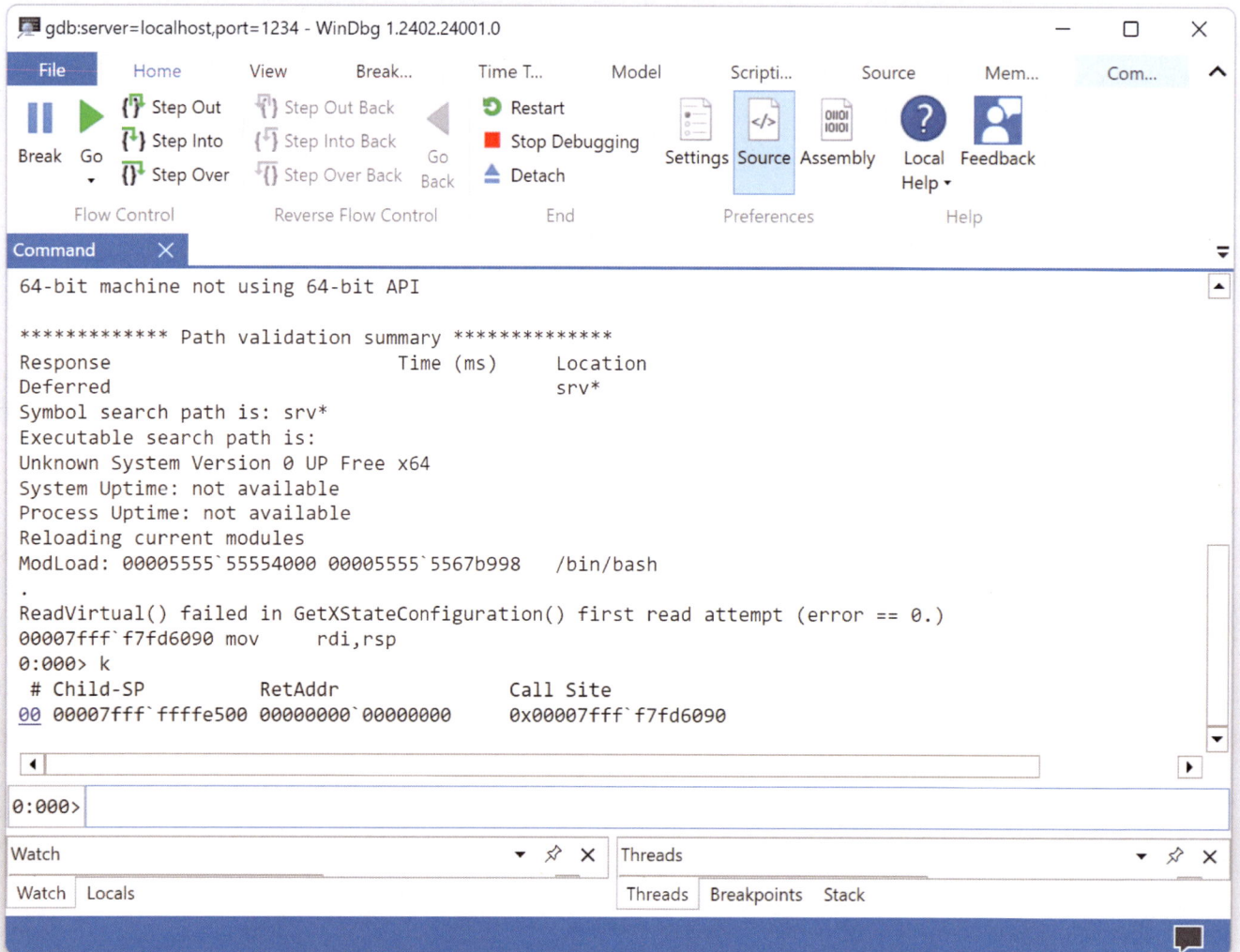

11.   The output of the command should be similar to this:

```
0:000> k
 # Child-SP          RetAddr           Call Site
00 00007fff`ffffe500 00000000`00000000     0x00007fff`f7fd6090
```

We run a few **g** commands until we get the *Debuggee is running...* message:

```
0:000> g
ModLoad: 00007fff`f7fd3000 00007fff`f7fd3000   linux-vdso.so.1
ModLoad: 00007fff`f7f94000 00007fff`f7fc1980   /lib/x86_64-linux-gnu/libtinfo.so.6
ModLoad: 00007fff`f7f8f000 00007fff`f7f93110   /lib/x86_64-linux-gnu/libdl.so.2
ModLoad: 00007fff`f7dcf000 00007fff`f7f8e800   /lib/x86_64-linux-gnu/libc.so.6
ModLoad: 00007fff`f7fd5000 00007fff`f7ffe190   /lib64/ld-linux-x86-64.so.2
ModLoad: 00007fff`f7ac7000 00007fff`f7adb738   /lib/x86_64-linux-gnu/libnss_files.so.2


************* Path validation summary **************
Response                       Time (ms)     Location
Deferred                                     srv*
Symbol search path is: srv*
Executable search path is:
```

84

```
Unable to load image /lib/x86_64-linux-gnu/libc.so.6, Win32 error 0n2
*** WARNING: Unable to verify timestamp for /lib/x86_64-linux-gnu/libc.so.6
Unable to load image /bin/bash, Win32 error 0n2
*** WARNING: Unable to verify timestamp for /bin/bash
libc_so!_libc_fork+0x4e:
00007fff`f7e9565e cmp     rax,0FFFFFFFFFFFFF000h

0:000> g
(1ac6.1ac6): Signal SIGCHLD code CLD_EXITED (Child has exited) at 0x7ffff7e06b8d originating
from PID 1ac6
First chance exceptions are reported before any exception handling.
This exception may be expected and handled.
libc_so!sigprocmask+0xd:
00007fff`f7e06b8d cmp     rax,0FFFFFFFFFFFFF000h

0:000> g
```

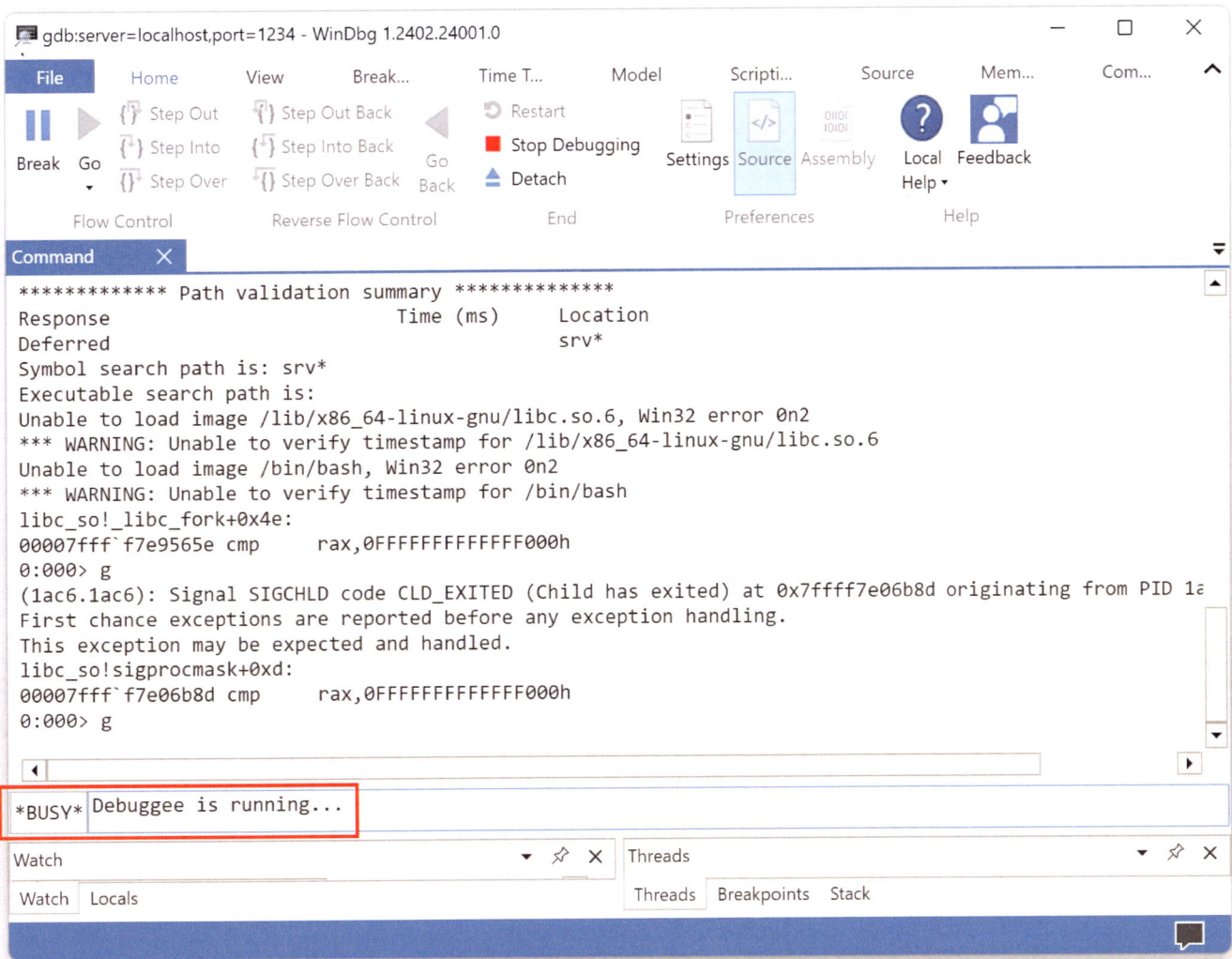

12.   Break into the running process:

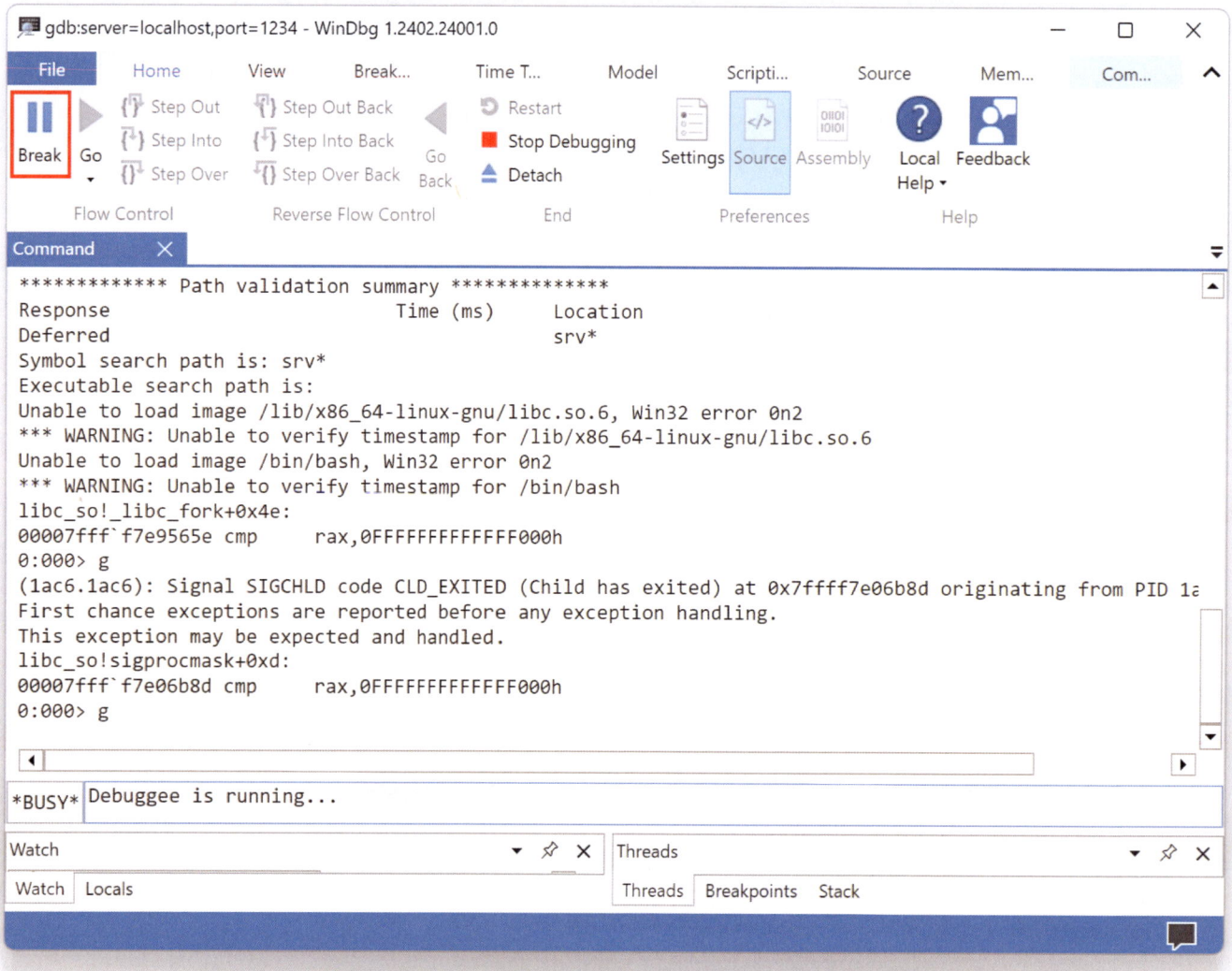

13.   We get the following output:

```
0:000> g
(1ac6.1ac6): Signal SIGINT code SI_USER (Sent by kill, sigsend, raise) at 0x7ffff7ebfc89
originating from PID 1ac6
First chance exceptions are reported before any exception handling.
This exception may be expected and handled.
libc_so!pselect+0x59:
00007fff`f7ebfc89 cmp        rax,0FFFFFFFFFFFFF000h
```

14.   Check the current thread stack trace:

```
0:000> k
 # Child-SP          RetAddr           Call Site
00 00007fff`ffffd110 00005555`55622784   libc_so!pselect+0x59
01 00007fff`ffffd190 00005555`55623065   bash!rl_getc+0xa4
02 00007fff`ffffd260 00005555`55609a12   bash!rl_read_key+0x135
03 00007fff`ffffd270 00005555`5560a225   bash!readline_internal_char+0x62
04 00007fff`ffffd290 00005555`55584de2   bash!readline+0x45
05 00007fff`ffffd2a0 00005555`555871d0   bash!pretty_print_loop+0x422
06 00007fff`ffffd2c0 00005555`5558a79a   bash!decode_prompt_string+0xf90
```

```
07 00007fff`ffffd310 00005555`5558e0d8    bash!read_secondary_line+0x2d6a
08 00007fff`ffffd3a0 00005555`55584476    bash!yyparse+0x3f8
09 00007fff`ffffe250 00005555`55584584    bash!parse_command+0x36
0a 00007fff`ffffe270 00005555`55584798    bash!read_command+0x54
0b 00007fff`ffffe2a0 00005555`55583104    bash!reader_loop+0x128
0c 00007fff`ffffe2d0 00007fff`f7df309b    bash!main+0x12d4
0d 00007fff`ffffe430 00005555`5558365a    libc_so!_libc_start_main+0xeb
0e 00007fff`ffffe4f0 ffffffff`ffffffff    bash!start+0x2a
0f 00007fff`ffffe4f8 00000000`00000000    0xffffffff`ffffffff
```

15.   If you want to stop debugging the process, resume its execution in WinDbg (the **g** command) and choose *Stop Debugging*:

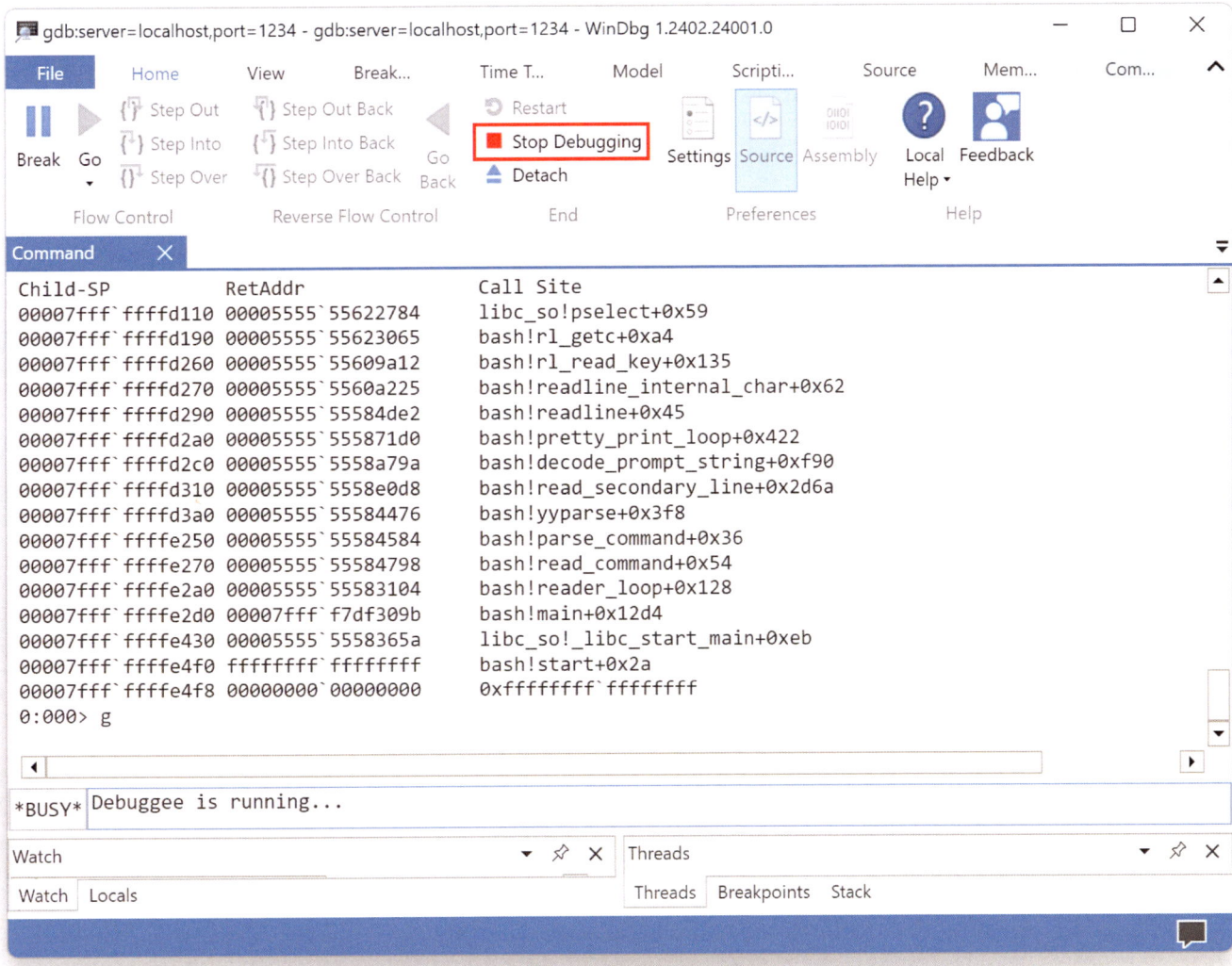

16.   Switch to your WSL2 instance and type Ctrl-D:

```
client connection closed ^D
exit
Child exited with status 0
```

17.   Close the WinDbg. To avoid confusion, unless otherwise stated, we recommend exiting WinDbg after each exercise.

User Mode Debugging

Exercises UD1 – UD7

Exercise UD1

- **Goal:** Learn how code generation parameters can influence process execution behavior

- **Elementary Diagnostics Patterns:** Crash

- **Memory Analysis Patterns:** Exception Stack Trace; NULL Pointer (Code); Constant Subtrace

- **Debugging Implementation Patterns:** Break-in; Scope; Variable Value; Type Structure; Code Breakpoint

- \ALD4\Exercise-Linux-UD1.pdf

Exercise UD1 (WinDbg)

Goal: Learn how code generation parameters can influence process execution behavior.

Elementary Diagnostics Patterns: Crash.

Memory Analysis Patterns: Exception Stack Trace; NULL Pointer (Code); Constant Subtrace.

Debugging Implementation Patterns: Break-in; Scope; Variable Value; Type Structure; Code Breakpoint.

1. The source code and the *Makefile* to build executables and libraries can be found in the *ud1* directory:

```
$ git clone https://bitbucket.org/softwarediagnostics/ald4
```

2. Launch the *ud1a* executable under the *gdbserver*:

```
/mnt/c/ALD4/ud1$ LD_LIBRARY_PATH=. gdbserver localhost:1234 ud1a
Process /mnt/c/ALD4/ud1/ud1a created; pid = 3652
Listening on port 1234
```

3. Connect WinDbg to the remote debugger:

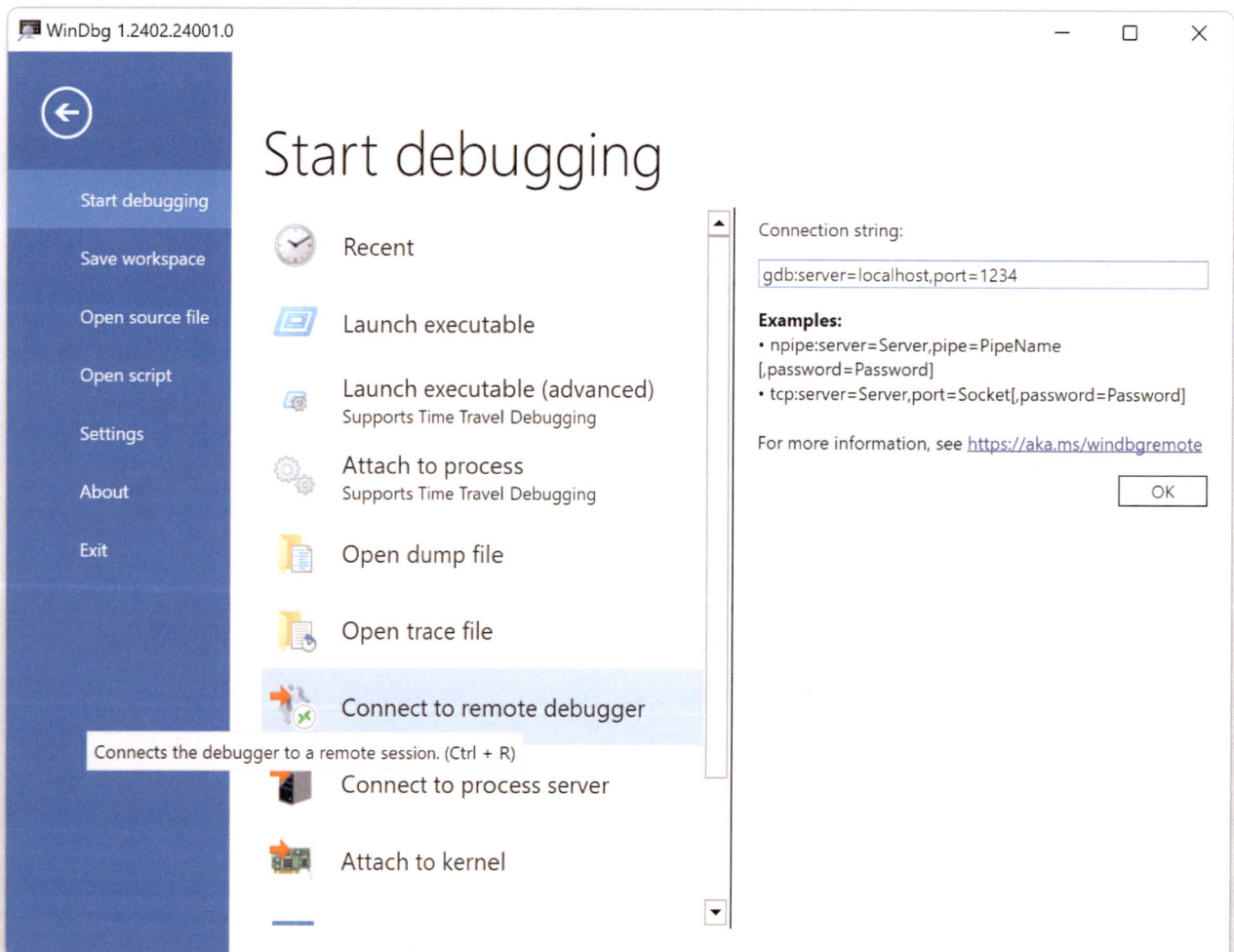

4.   We get ready for a debugging session:

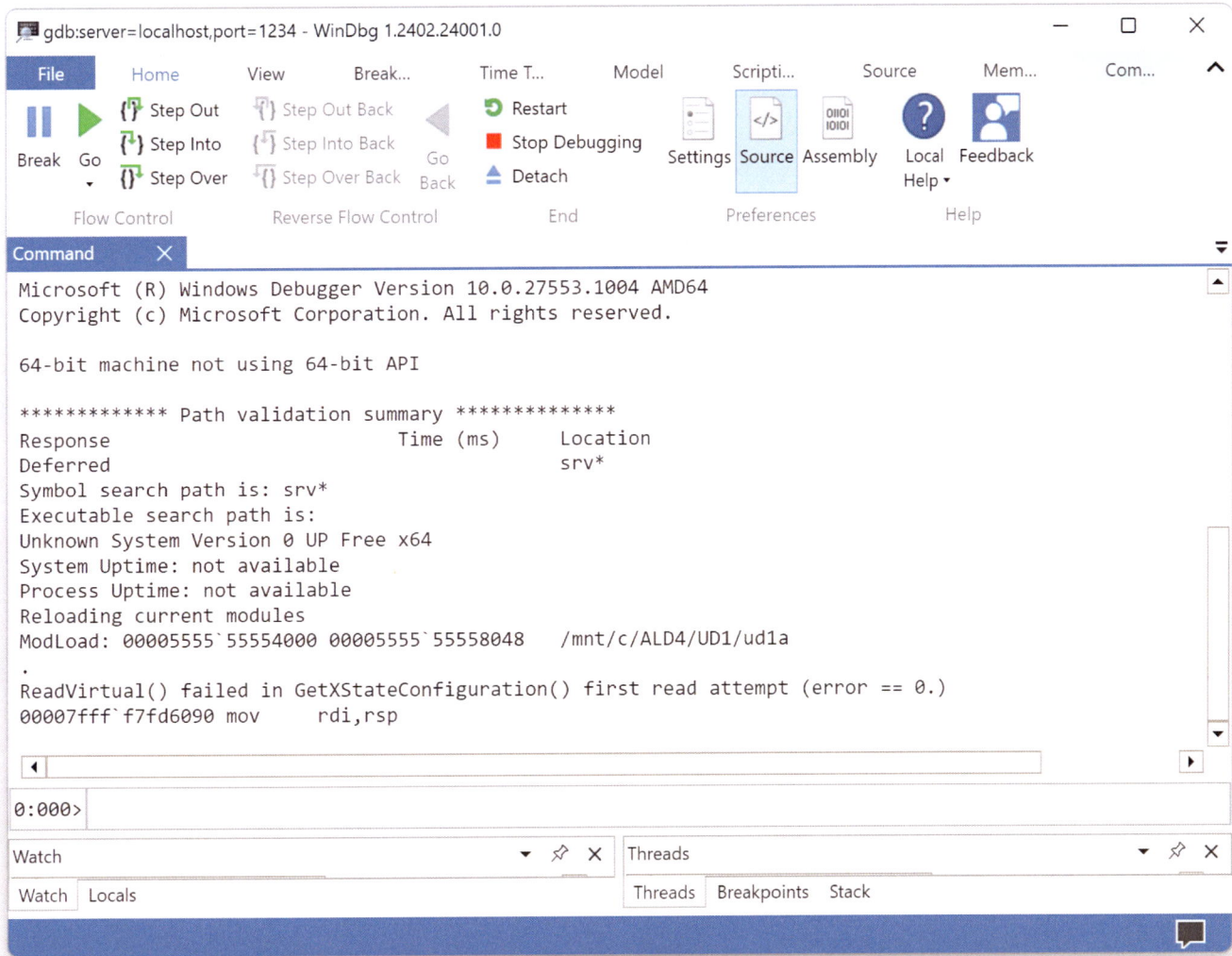

From now on, we only show the output from the command window unless we need another view.

```
Microsoft (R) Windows Debugger Version 10.0.27553.1004 AMD64
Copyright (c) Microsoft Corporation. All rights reserved.

64-bit machine not using 64-bit API

************* Path validation summary **************
Response                        Time (ms)      Location
Deferred                                       srv*
Symbol search path is: srv*
Executable search path is:
Unknown System Version 0 UP Free x64
System Uptime: not available
Process Uptime: not available
Reloading current modules
ModLoad: 00005555`55554000 00005555`55558048    /mnt/c/ALD4/ud1/ud1a
.
ReadVirtual() failed in GetXStateConfiguration() first read attempt (error == 0.)
00007fff`f7fd6090 mov      rdi,rsp
```

5.   Open a log file (useful when the output doesn't fit into the buffer and we need to search for something):

```
0:000> .logopen C:\ALD4\ud1a.log
Opened log file 'C:\ALD4\ud1a.log'
```

6.   The **lm** command lists loaded modules and their addresses (it also shows whether symbols files are loaded):

```
0:000> lm
start              end                module name
00005555`55554000  00005555`55558048  ud1a       (deferred)
```

7.   We continue process execution using the **g** command until we get a segmentation fault:

```
0:000> g
ModLoad: 00007fff`f7fd3000 00007fff`f7fd3000   linux-vdso.so.1
ModLoad: 00007fff`f7fc8000 00007fff`f7fcc048   ./libwindows.so
ModLoad: 00007fff`f7dfd000 00007fff`f7fbc800   /lib/x86_64-linux-gnu/libc.so.6
ModLoad: 00007fff`f7fd5000 00007fff`f7ffe190   /lib64/ld-linux-x86-64.so.2
(e44.e44): Signal SIGSEGV (Segmentation fault) code SEGV_MAPERR (Address not mapped to object)
at 0x5555 originating from PID 70fb
First chance exceptions are reported before any exception handling.
This exception may be expected and handled.
Unable to load image ./libwindows.so, Win32 error 0n2
*** WARNING: Unable to verify timestamp for ./libwindows.so
00000000`00005555 ???
```

```
0:000> lm
start              end                module name
00005555`55554000  00005555`55558048  ud1a     T (service symbols: DWARF Private Symbols)
C:\Users\dmitr\AppData\Local\Temp\srcD37D.tmp
00007fff`f7dfd000  00007fff`f7fbc800  libc_so  T (service symbols: ELF Export Symbols)
C:\Users\dmitr\AppData\Local\Temp\srcD880.tmp
00007fff`f7fc8000  00007fff`f7fcc048  libwindows T (service symbols: DWARF Private Symbols)
C:\Users\dmitr\AppData\Local\Temp\srcD12B.tmp
00007fff`f7fd3000  00007fff`f7fd3000  linux_vdso_so    (deferred)
00007fff`f7fd5000  00007fff`f7ffe190  ld_linux_x86_64_so    (deferred)
```

There, we see that the crash happens in the **libwindows** module with the following CPU state:

```
0:000> k
 # Child-SP          RetAddr             Call Site
00 00007fff`ffffe318 00007fff`f7fc926c   0x5555
01 00007fff`ffffe320 00005555`555551ef   libwindows!dispatch_message+0x28
[/mnt/c/ALD4/ud1/windows.c @ 81]
02 00007fff`ffffe340 00007fff`f7e2109b   ud1a!main+0x88 [/mnt/c/ALD4/ud1/ud1.c @ 36]
03 00007fff`ffffe3e0 00005555`5555509a   libc_so!_libc_start_main+0xeb
04 00007fff`ffffe4a0 ffffffff`ffffffff   ud1a!start+0x2a
05 00007fff`ffffe4a8 00000000`00000000   0xffffffff`ffffffff
```

```
0:000> r
rax=0000000000005555 rbx=0000000000000000 rcx=00007ffff7ec3594
rdx=00007fffffffe3a0 rsi=00007fffffffe2a0 rdi=00007fffffffe3a0
rip=0000000000005555 rsp=00007fffffffe318 rbp=00007fffffffe330
 r8=00007ffff7fb8d80  r9=00007ffff7fb8d80 r10=fffffffffffff429
r11=00007ffff7fc9244 r12=0000555555555070 r13=00007fffffffe4b0
r14=0000000000000000 r15=0000000000000000
iopl=0         nv up ei pl nz na po nc
cs=0033  ss=002b  ds=0000  es=0000  fs=0000  gs=0000        efl=00010206
00000000`00005555 ???
```

8. We switch to the *libwindows* thread stack frame #1 and set the source code location:

```
0:000> kn
 # Child-SP          RetAddr           Call Site
00 00007fff`ffffe318 00007fff`f7fc926c 0x5555
01 00007fff`ffffe320 00005555`555551ef libwindows!dispatch_message+0x28
[/mnt/c/ALD4/ud1/windows.c @ 81]
02 00007fff`ffffe340 00007fff`f7e2109b ud1a!main+0x88 [/mnt/c/ALD4/ud1/ud1.c @ 36]
03 00007fff`ffffe3e0 00005555`5555509a libc_so!_libc_start_main+0xeb
04 00007fff`ffffe4a0 ffffffff`ffffffff ud1a!start+0x2a
05 00007fff`ffffe4a8 00000000`00000000 0xffffffff`ffffffff

0:000> .frame 1
01 00007fff`ffffe320 00005555`555551ef libwindows!dispatch_message+0x28
[/mnt/c/ALD4/ud1/windows.c @ 81]

0:000> .srcpath+ C:\ALD4\ud1
Source search path is: SRV*;C:\ALD4\ud1

************* Path validation summary **************
Response                    Time (ms)       Location
Deferred                                    SRV*
OK                                          C:\ALD4\ud1
```

Note: We see a source code window immediately to the left of the command window:

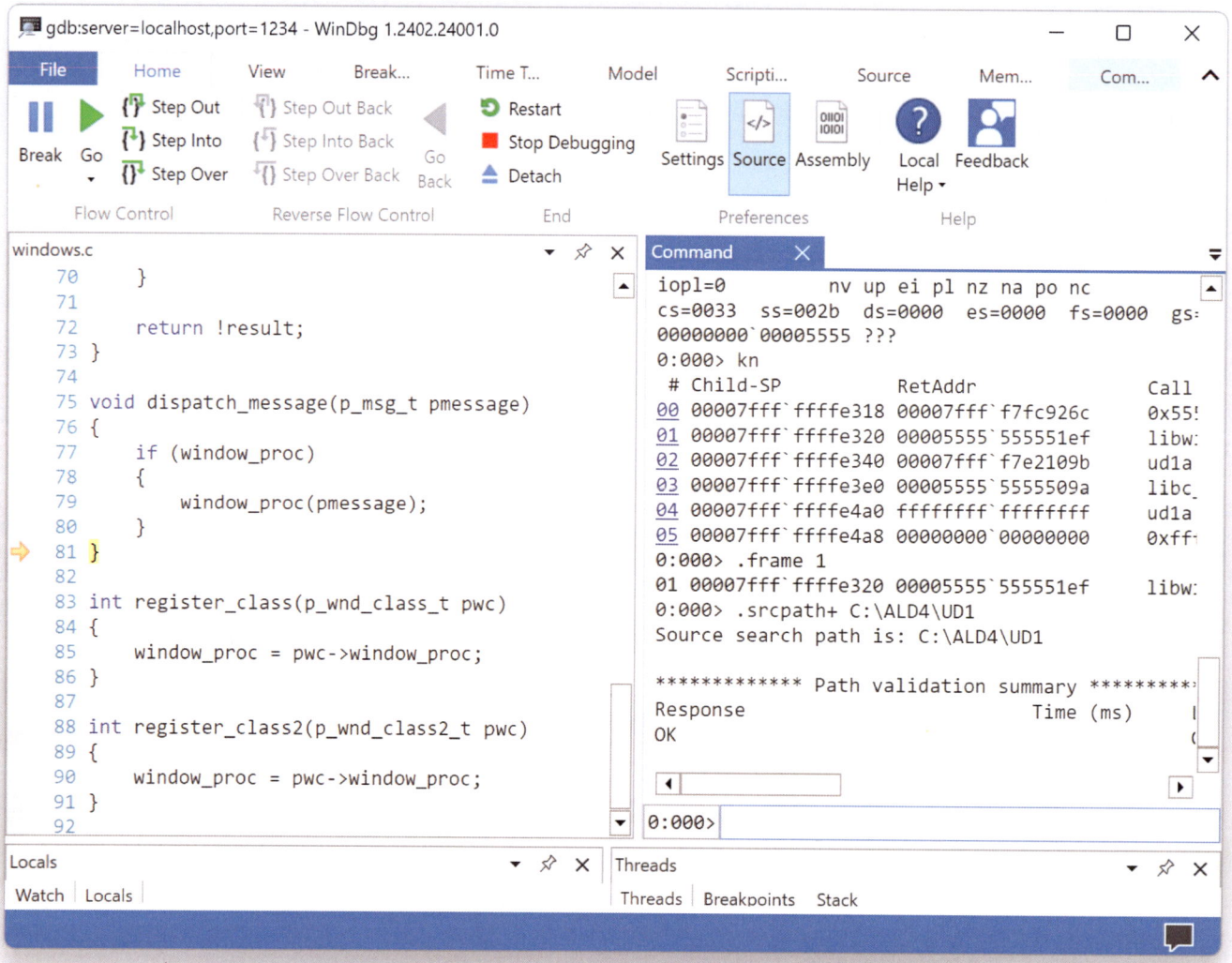

9.   We see that the *window_proc* pointer is invalid, so we need to investigate when it is set in the *register_class* function below. First, we set the next frame where the *dispatch_message* was called:

```
0:000> dp libwindows!window_proc L1
00007fff`f7fcc040   00000000`00005555

0:000> kn
 # Child-SP          RetAddr               Call Site
00 00007fff`ffffe318 00007fff`f7fc926c     0x5555
01 00007fff`ffffe320 00005555`555551ef     libwindows!dispatch_message+0x28
[/mnt/c/ALD4/ud1/windows.c @ 81]
02 00007fff`ffffe340 00007fff`f7e2109b     ud1a!main+0x88 [/mnt/c/ALD4/ud1/ud1.c @ 36]
03 00007fff`ffffe3e0 00005555`5555509a     libc_so!_libc_start_main+0xeb
04 00007fff`ffffe4a0 ffffffff`ffffffff     ud1a!start+0x2a
05 00007fff`ffffe4a8 00000000`00000000     0xffffffff`ffffffff

0:000> .frame 2
02 00007fff`ffffe340 00007fff`f7e2109b     ud1a!main+0x88 [/mnt/c/ALD4/ud1/ud1.c @ 36]
```

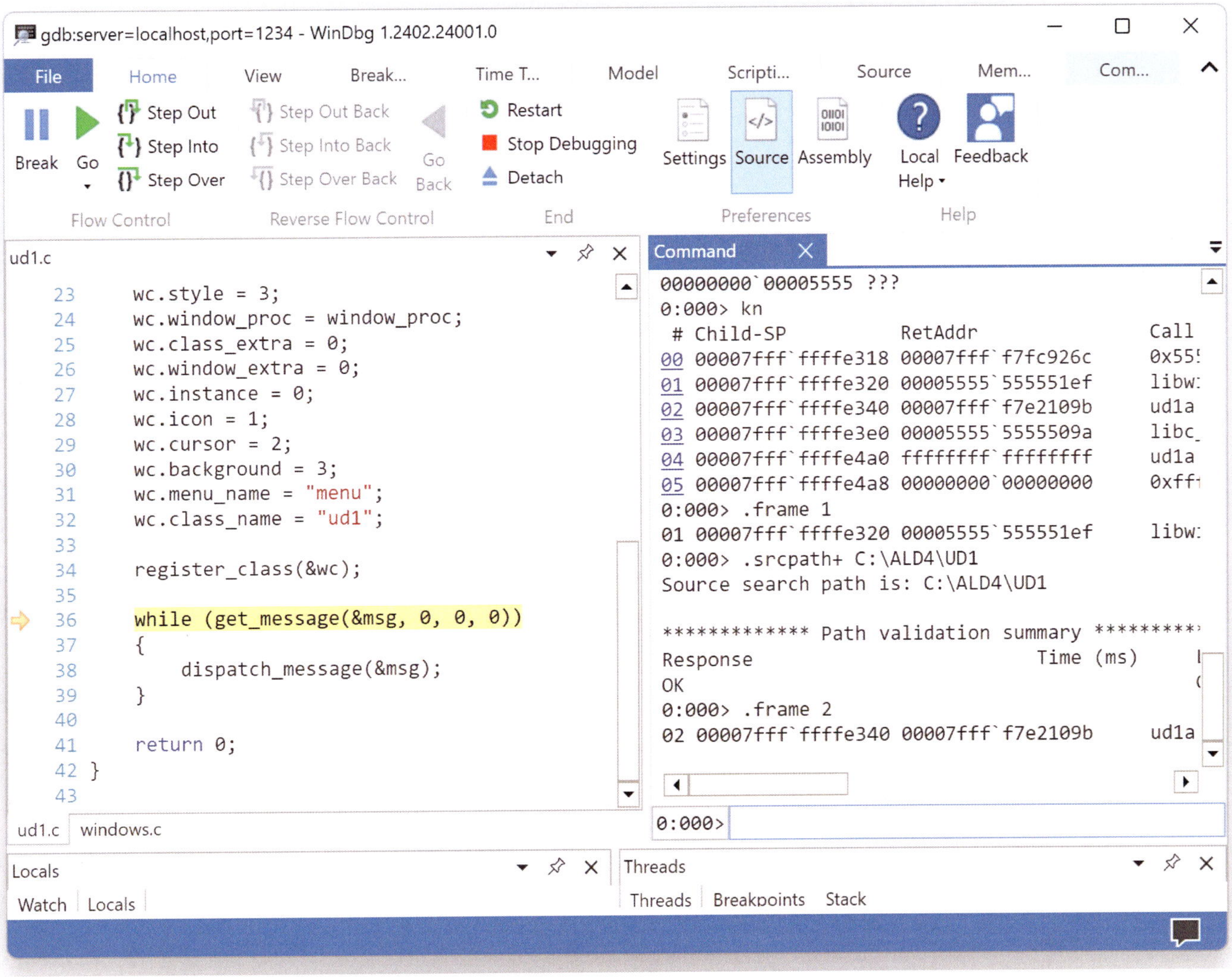
gdb:server=localhost,port=1234 - WinDbg 1.2402.24001.0
File
Home
View
Break...
Time T...
Model
Scripti...
Source
Mem...
Com...
Break
Go
Step Out
Step Into
Step Over
Step Out Back
Step Into Back
Step Over Back
Go Back
Restart
Stop Debugging
Detach
Settings
Source
Assembly
Local Help
Feedback
Flow Control
Reverse Flow Control
End
Preferences
Help
ud1.c
23 wc.style = 3;
24 wc.window_proc = window_proc;
25 wc.class_extra = 0;
26 wc.window_extra = 0;
27 wc.instance = 0;
28 wc.icon = 1;
29 wc.cursor = 2;
30 wc.background = 3;
31 wc.menu_name = "menu";
32 wc.class_name = "ud1";
34 register_class(&wc);
36 while (get_message(&msg, 0, 0, 0))
37 {
38 dispatch_message(&msg);
39 }
41 return 0;
42 }
ud1.c
windows.c
Command
00000000`00005555 ???
0:000> kn
Child-SP RetAddr Call
00 00007fff`ffffe318 00007fff`f7fc926c 0x555
01 00007fff`ffffe320 00005555`555551ef libw
02 00007fff`ffffe340 00007fff`f7e2109b ud1a
03 00007fff`ffffe3e0 00005555`5555509a libc_
04 00007fff`ffffe4a0 ffffffff`ffffffff ud1a
05 00007fff`ffffe4a8 00000000`00000000 0xff
0:000> .frame 1
01 00007fff`ffffe320 00005555`555551ef libw
0:000> .srcpath+ C:\ALD4\UD1
Source search path is: C:\ALD4\UD1
************* Path validation summary *********
Response Time (ms)
OK
0:000> .frame 2
02 00007fff`ffffe340 00007fff`f7e2109b ud1a
0:000>
Locals
Watch
Locals
Threads
Threads
Breakpoints
Stack

10. We can now expand local structures in the *Locals* window (for example, *wc*):

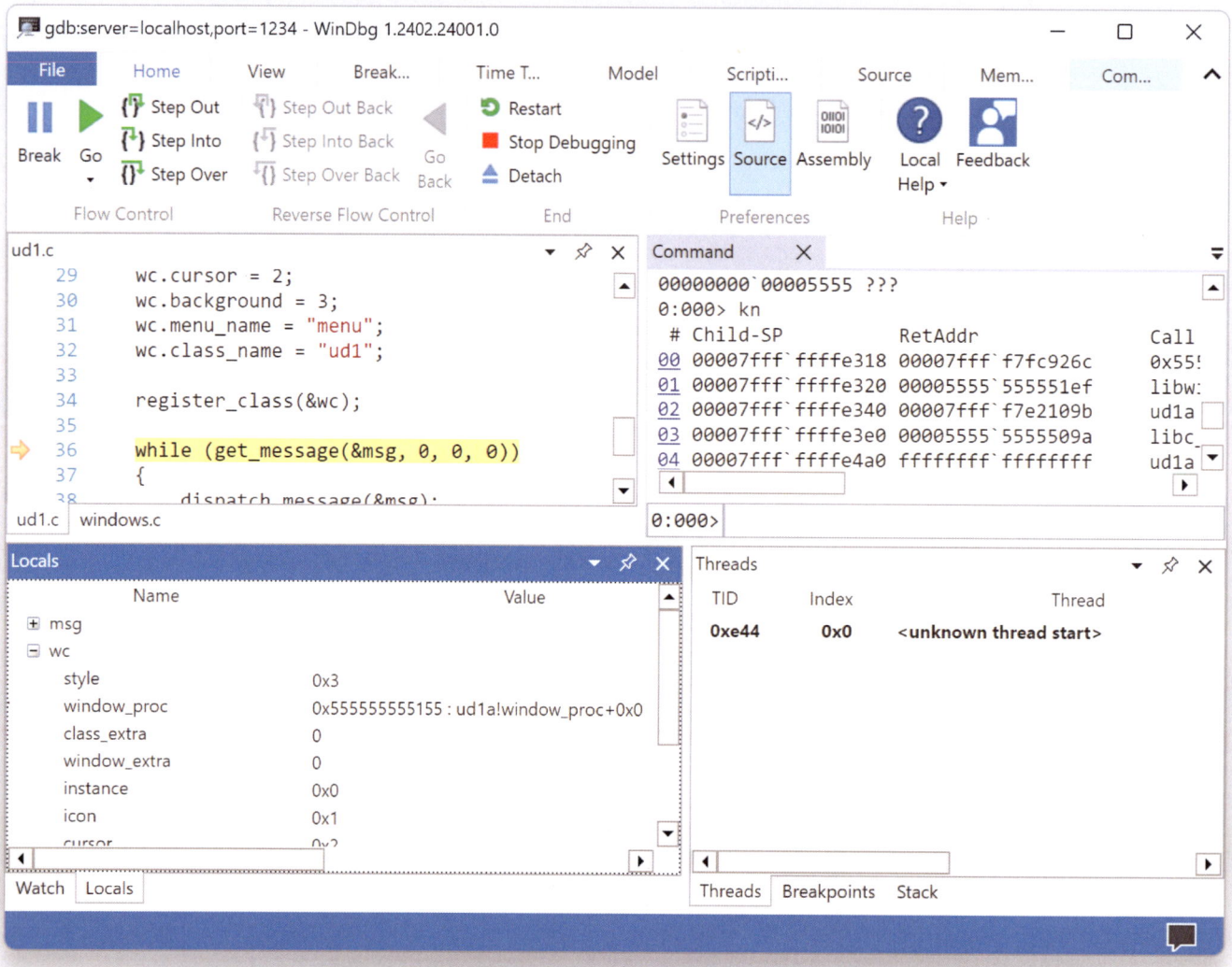

We can also dump this variable using type information:

```
0:000> dt wc
Local var @ 0x7ffffffe350 Type wnd_class_t
   +0x000 style        : 3
   +0x004 window_proc  : 0x00005555`55555155     void  ud1a!window_proc+0
   +0x00c class_extra  : 0n0
   +0x010 window_extra : 0n0
   +0x014 instance     : 0
   +0x01c icon         : 1
   +0x024 cursor       : 2
   +0x02c background   : 3
   +0x034 menu_name    : 0x00005555`55556004    "menu"
   +0x03c class_name   : 0x00005555`55556009    "ud1"
```

11. We need to make sure that *libwindows* is loaded before we put a breakpoint on the *register_class* function. To do that, we determine the *main* function address to set the breakpoint there first once we restart the debugged process. Then, on break-in we set our *register_class* breakpoint since the library is already loaded.

```
0:000> ln main
Browse module
Set bu breakpoint

 [/mnt/c/ALD4/ud1/ud1.c @ 19] (00005555`55555167)    ud1a!main
Exact matches:
    ud1a!main (int, char **)
```

12.	Now, we finish the process (the **g** command) and see WinDbg disconnected. Then we start the **gdbserver** again and reattach WinDbg to the remote debugger.

```
/mnt/c/ALD4/ud1$ LD_LIBRARY_PATH=. gdbserver localhost:1234 ud1a
Process /mnt/c/ALD4/ud1/ud1a created; pid = 34
Listening on port 1234


Microsoft (R) Windows Debugger Version 10.0.27553.1004 AMD64
Copyright (c) Microsoft Corporation. All rights reserved.

64-bit machine not using 64-bit API

************* Path validation summary **************
Response                        Time (ms)       Location
Deferred                                        srv*
Symbol search path is: srv*
Executable search path is:
Unknown System Version 0 UP Free x64
System Uptime: not available
Process Uptime: not available
Reloading current modules
ModLoad: 00005555`55554000 00005555`55558048    /mnt/c/ALD4/ud1/ud1a
.
ReadVirtual() failed in GetXStateConfiguration() first read attempt (error == 0.)
00007fff`f7fd6090 mov        rdi,rsp
```

13.	We put a breakpoint on the main function address we determined previously and resume execution until it is hit:

```
0:000> bp 00005555`55555167

0:000> g
ModLoad: 00007fff`f7fd3000 00007fff`f7fd3000    linux-vdso.so.1
ModLoad: 00007fff`f7fc8000 00007fff`f7fcc048    ./libwindows.so
ModLoad: 00007fff`f7dfd000 00007fff`f7fbc800    /lib/x86_64-linux-gnu/libc.so.6
ModLoad: 00007fff`f7fd5000 00007fff`f7ffe190    /lib64/ld-linux-x86-64.so.2
Breakpoint 0 hit
Unable to load image /lib/x86_64-linux-gnu/libc.so.6, Win32 error 0n2
*** WARNING: Unable to verify timestamp for /lib/x86_64-linux-gnu/libc.so.6
ud1a!main:
00005555`55555167 push       rbp
```

14.   We now put a breakpoint on the call to the *register_class* function (F9) and resume execution:

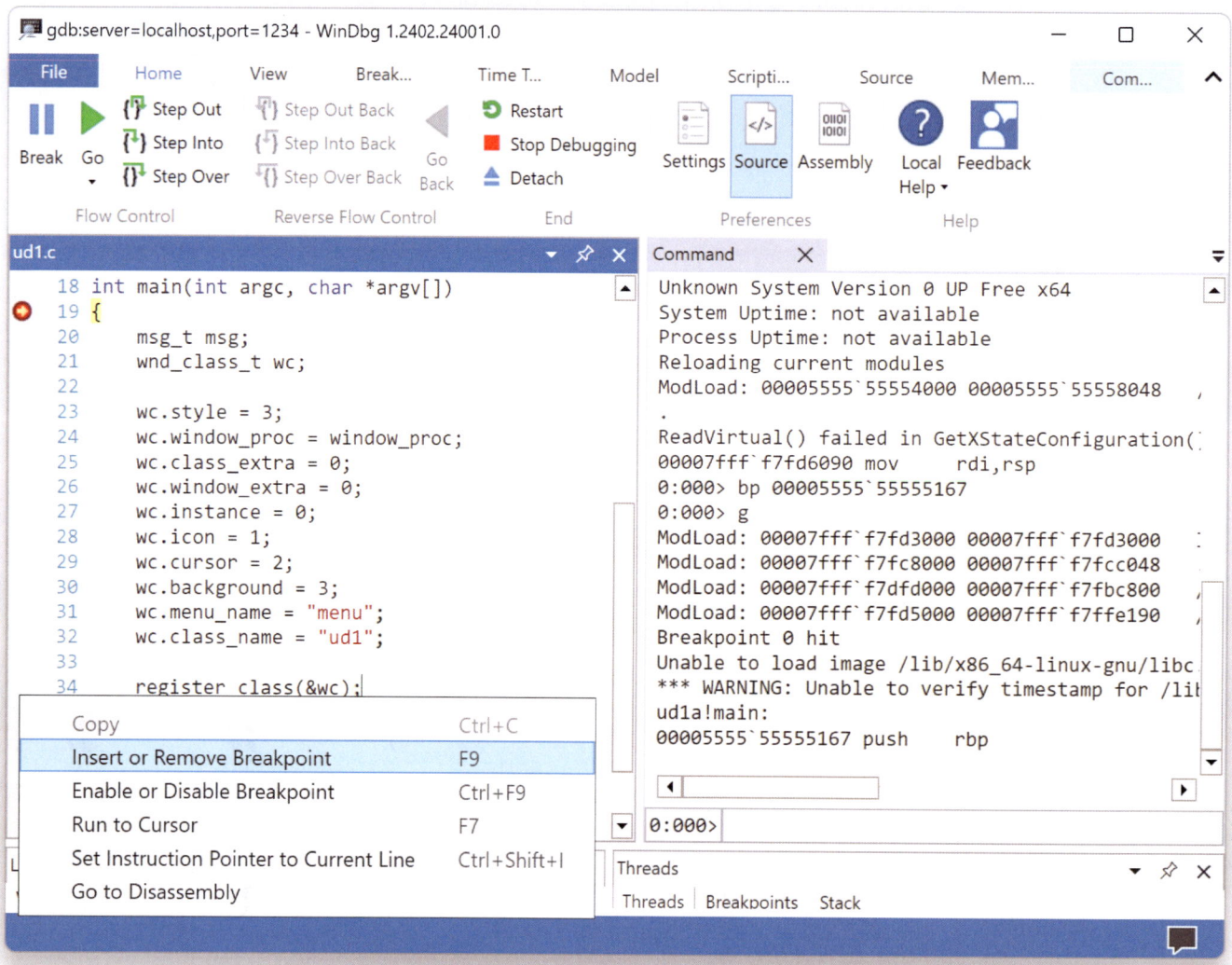

```
0:000> g
Breakpoint 1 hit
ud1a!main+0x6e:
00005555`555551d5 lea     rax,[rbp-80h]

0:000> dt ud1a!wc
Local var @ 0x7fffffffe350 Type wnd_class_t
   +0x000 style           : 3
   +0x004 window_proc     : 0x00005555`55555155     void  ud1a!window_proc+0
   +0x00c class_extra     : 0n0
   +0x010 window_extra    : 0n0
   +0x014 instance        : 0
   +0x01c icon            : 1
   +0x024 cursor          : 2
   +0x02c background      : 3
   +0x034 menu_name       : 0x00005555`55556004  "menu"
   +0x03c class_name      : 0x00005555`55556009  "ud1"
```

15. Then, we put a breakpoint inside the *register_class* function and resume execution:

```
0:000> bp libwindows!register_class
Unable to load image ./libwindows.so, Win32 error 0n2
*** WARNING: Unable to verify timestamp for ./libwindows.so

0:000> bp libwindows!register_class
breakpoint 2 redefined

0:000> g
Breakpoint 2 hit
libwindows!register_class:
00007fff`f7fc926f push      rbp
```

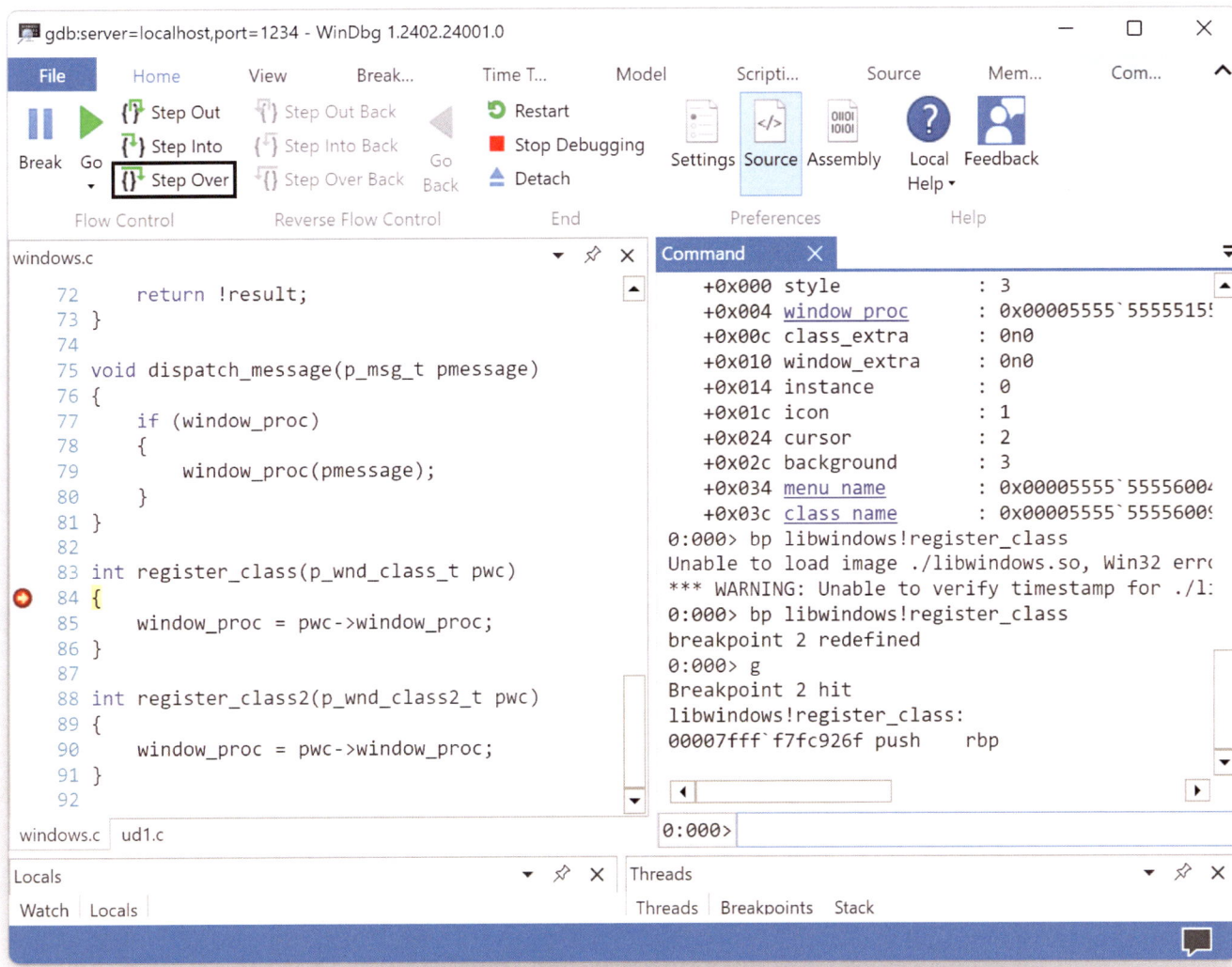

16. Do one step over to have the parameter initialized and inspect it:

```
0:000> p
libwindows!register_class+0x8:
00007fff`f7fc9277 mov       rax,qword ptr [rbp-8] ss:00007fff`ffffe328=00007fffffffe350
```

```
0:000> dt pwc
Local var @ 0x7fffffffe328 Type p_wnd_class_t
0x00007fff`ffffe350
   +0x000 style           : 3
   +0x008 window_proc     : 0x00000000`00005555      void  +5555
   +0x010 class_extra     : 0n0
   +0x014 window_extra    : 0n0
   +0x018 instance        : 0x00000001`00000000
   +0x020 icon            : 0x00000002`00000000
   +0x028 cursor          : 0x00000003`00000000
   +0x030 background      : 0x55556004`00000000
   +0x038 menu_name       : 0x55556009`00005555   "--- memory read error at address
0x55556009`00005555 ---"
   +0x040 class_name      : 0x00000000`00005555   "--- memory read error at address
0x00000000`00005555 ---"

0:000> dt libwindows!p_wnd_class_t
Ptr64    +0x000 style            : Uint4B
   +0x008 window_proc     : Ptr64       void
   +0x010 class_extra     : Int4B
   +0x014 window_extra    : Int4B
   +0x018 instance        : Uint8B
   +0x020 icon            : Uint8B
   +0x028 cursor          : Uint8B
   +0x030 background      : Uint8B
   +0x038 menu_name       : Ptr64 Char
   +0x040 class_name      : Ptr64 Char
```

17.   But if we look at the *ud1a* structure variant, we see its members have different offsets:

```
0:000> dt ud1a!wnd_class_t
   +0x000 style           : Uint4B
   +0x004 window_proc     : Ptr64       void
   +0x00c class_extra     : Int4B
   +0x010 window_extra    : Int4B
   +0x014 instance        : Uint8B
   +0x01c icon            : Uint8B
   +0x024 cursor          : Uint8B
   +0x02c background      : Uint8B
   +0x034 menu_name       : Ptr64 Char
   +0x03c class_name      : Ptr64 Char
```

18.   These discrepancies explain the crash. Looking at the *Makefile*, we can see that *ud1a* was compiled with the *-fpack-struct* setting. The *ud1b* executable was compiled without it and runs fine. Also, the problem was coincidentally fixed without changing alignment by using a different, bigger *wnd_class2_t* structure in the *ud1c* executable that adds another 32-bit field that makes both alignments identical.

19.   We continue execution (**g**) to have the remote process finished and then close WinDbg.

Exercise UD1 (GDB)

Goal: Learn how code generation parameters can influence process execution behavior.

Elementary Diagnostics Patterns: Crash.

Memory Analysis Patterns: Exception Stack Trace; NULL Pointer (Code); Constant Subtrace.

Debugging Implementation Patterns: Break-in; Scope; Variable Value; Type Structure; Code Breakpoint.

1.   The source code and the *Makefile* to build executables and libraries can be found in the *ud1* directory:

```
$ git clone https://bitbucket.org/softwarediagnostics/ald4
```

2.   When we launch the *ud1a* executable, it crashes:

```
/mnt/c/ALD4/ud1$ LD_LIBRARY_PATH=. ./ud1a
Segmentation fault
```

3.   We run the executable under GDB until it shows a segmentation fault:

```
/mnt/c/ALD4/ud1$ LD_LIBRARY_PATH=. gdb ./ud1a
GNU gdb (Debian 8.2.1-2+b3) 8.2.1
...
Reading symbols from ./ud1a...done.

(gdb) r
Starting program: /mnt/c/ALD4/ud1/ud1a

Program received signal SIGSEGV, Segmentation fault.
0x0000000000005555 in ?? ()
```

4.   The **info proc mappings** and **info sharedlibrary** commands list loaded modules and their addresses and show if symbols are available:

```
(gdb) info proc mappings
process 14581
Mapped address spaces:

          Start Addr           End Addr       Size     Offset objfile
      0x555555554000     0x555555555000     0x1000        0x0 /mnt/c/ALD4/ud1/ud1a
      0x555555555000     0x555555556000     0x1000     0x1000 /mnt/c/ALD4/ud1/ud1a
      0x555555556000     0x555555557000     0x1000     0x2000 /mnt/c/ALD4/ud1/ud1a
      0x555555557000     0x555555558000     0x1000     0x2000 /mnt/c/ALD4/ud1/ud1a
      0x555555558000     0x555555559000     0x1000     0x3000 /mnt/c/ALD4/ud1/ud1a
      0x7ffff7dfa000     0x7ffff7dfd000     0x3000        0x0
      0x7ffff7dfd000     0x7ffff7e1f000    0x22000        0x0 /lib/x86_64-linux-gnu/libc-2.28.so
      0x7ffff7e1f000     0x7ffff7f66000   0x147000    0x22000 /lib/x86_64-linux-gnu/libc-2.28.so
      0x7ffff7f66000     0x7ffff7fb2000    0x4c000   0x169000 /lib/x86_64-linux-gnu/libc-2.28.so
      0x7ffff7fb2000     0x7ffff7fb3000     0x1000   0x1b5000 /lib/x86_64-linux-gnu/libc-2.28.so
      0x7ffff7fb3000     0x7ffff7fb7000     0x4000   0x1b5000 /lib/x86_64-linux-gnu/libc-2.28.so
      0x7ffff7fb7000     0x7ffff7fb9000     0x2000   0x1b9000 /lib/x86_64-linux-gnu/libc-2.28.so
      0x7ffff7fb9000     0x7ffff7fbd000     0x4000        0x0
      0x7ffff7fc8000     0x7ffff7fc9000     0x1000        0x0 /mnt/c/ALD4/ud1/libwindows.so
      0x7ffff7fc9000     0x7ffff7fca000     0x1000     0x1000 /mnt/c/ALD4/ud1/libwindows.so
      0x7ffff7fca000     0x7ffff7fcb000     0x1000     0x2000 /mnt/c/ALD4/ud1/libwindows.so
```

```
        0x7ffff7fcb000     0x7ffff7fcc000     0x1000     0x2000 /mnt/c/ALD4/ud1/libwindows.so
        0x7ffff7fcc000     0x7ffff7fcd000     0x1000     0x3000 /mnt/c/ALD4/ud1/libwindows.so
        0x7ffff7fcd000     0x7ffff7fcf000     0x2000        0x0
        0x7ffff7fcf000     0x7ffff7fd3000     0x4000        0x0 [vvar]
        0x7ffff7fd3000     0x7ffff7fd5000     0x2000        0x0 [vdso]
        0x7ffff7fd5000     0x7ffff7fd6000     0x1000        0x0 /lib/x86_64-linux-gnu/ld-2.28.so
        0x7ffff7fd6000     0x7ffff7ff4000    0x1e000     0x1000 /lib/x86_64-linux-gnu/ld-2.28.so
        0x7ffff7ff4000     0x7ffff7ffc000     0x8000    0x1f000 /lib/x86_64-linux-gnu/ld-2.28.so
        0x7ffff7ffc000     0x7ffff7ffd000     0x1000    0x26000 /lib/x86_64-linux-gnu/ld-2.28.so
        0x7ffff7ffd000     0x7ffff7ffe000     0x1000    0x27000 /lib/x86_64-linux-gnu/ld-2.28.so
        0x7ffff7ffe000     0x7ffff7fff000     0x1000        0x0
        0x7ffffffde000     0x7ffffffff000    0x21000        0x0 [stack]
```

(gdb) **info sharedlibrary**

From	To	Syms Read	Shared Object Library
0x00007ffff7fd6090	0x00007ffff7ff3b50	Yes	/lib64/ld-linux-x86-64.so.2
0x00007ffff7fc9050	0x00007ffff7fc92a3	Yes	./libwindows.so
0x00007ffff7e1f320	0x00007ffff7f6514b	Yes	/lib/x86_64-linux-gnu/libc.so.6

5.   We see that the crash happens in the libwindows module with the following CPU state:

```
(gdb) bt
#0  0x0000000000005555 in ?? ()
#1  0x00007ffff7fc926c in dispatch_message (pmessage=0x7fffffffe380) at windows.c:76
#2  0x00005555555551ef in main (argc=1, argv=0x7fffffffe498) at ud1.c:35
```

```
(gdb) info r
rax            0x5555                21845
rbx            0x0                   0
rcx            0x7ffff7ec3594        140737352840596
rdx            0x7fffffffe3b0        140737488348080
rsi            0x7fffffffe2b0        140737488347824
rdi            0x7fffffffe3b0        140737488348080
rbp            0x7fffffffe340        0x7fffffffe340
rsp            0x7fffffffe328        0x7fffffffe328
r8             0x7ffff7fb8d80        140737353846144
r9             0x7ffff7fb8d80        140737353846144
r10            0xfffffffffffff429    -3031
r11            0x7ffff7fc9244        140737353912900
r12            0x555555555070        93824992235632
r13            0x7fffffffe4c0        140737488348352
r14            0x0                   0
r15            0x0                   0
rip            0x5555                0x5555
eflags         0x10206               [ PF IF RF ]
cs             0x33                  51
ss             0x2b                  43
ds             0x0                   0
es             0x0                   0
fs             0x0                   0
gs             0x0                   0
```

6.   We switch to stack frame #1 and check the source code:

```
(gdb) frame 1
#1  0x00007ffff7fc926c in dispatch_message (pmessage=0x7fffffffe3b0) at windows.c:76
76                  window_proc(pmessage);
```

```
(gdb) list
71
72          void dispatch_message(p_msg_t pmessage)
73          {
74              if (window_proc)
75              {
76                  window_proc(pmessage);
77              }
78          }
79
80          int register_class(p_wnd_class_t pwc)

(gdb) p window_proc
$1 = (void (*)(p_msg_t)) 0x5555

(gdb) list 83
78              {
79                  window_proc(pmessage);
80              }
81          }
82
83          int register_class(p_wnd_class_t pwc)
84          {
85              window_proc = pwc->window_proc;
86          }
87
```

7.   We see that the *window_proc* pointer is invalid, so we need to investigate when it is set in the *register_class* function below. First, we set the next frame where the *dispatch_message* was called:

```
(gdb) bt
#0  0x0000000000005555 in ?? ()
#1  0x00007ffff7fc926c in dispatch_message (pmessage=0x7fffffffe3b0) at windows.c:76
#2  0x00005555555551ef in main (argc=1, argv=0x7fffffffe4c8) at ud1.c:35

(gdb) frame 2
#2  0x00005555555551ef in main (argc=1, argv=0x7fffffffe4c8) at ud1.c:35
35                  dispatch_message(&msg);

(gdb) list
30
31                  register_class(&wc);
32
33                  while (get_message(&msg, 0, 0, 0))
34                  {
35                      dispatch_message(&msg);
36                  }
37
38              return 0;
39          }
```

8.   We can now check local variables and their structures (for example, *wc*):

```
(gdb) info locals
msg = {hwnd = 0, message = 275, param1 = 1, param2 = 140737353912581, time = 72844112, pt = {x
= 156, y = 327},
  priv = 0}
```

```
wc = {style = 3, window_proc = 0x555555555155 <window_proc>, class_extra = 0, window_extra = 0,
instance = 0,
  icon = 1, cursor = 2, background = 3, menu_name = 0x555555556004 "menu", class_name =
0x555555556009 "ud1"}
```

```
(gdb) ptype /o wc
type = struct {
/*      0      |       4 */      uint32_t style;
/*      4      |       8 */      void (*window_proc)(p_msg_t);
/*     12      |       4 */      int32_t class_extra;
/*     16      |       4 */      int32_t window_extra;
/*     20      |       8 */      uint64_t instance;
/*     28      |       8 */      uint64_t icon;
/*     36      |       8 */      uint64_t cursor;
/*     44      |       8 */      uint64_t background;
/*     52      |       8 */      char *menu_name;
/*     60      |       8 */      char *class_name;

                                 /* total size (bytes):   68 */
                             }
```

9.   We put a breakpoint on the *main* function and resume execution until it is hit:

```
(gdb) c
Continuing.

Program terminated with signal SIGSEGV, Segmentation fault.
The program no longer exists.

(gdb) break main
Breakpoint 1 at 0x55555555517f: file ud1.c, line 20.

(gdb) r
Starting program: /mnt/c/ALD4/ud1/ud1a

Breakpoint 1, main (argc=1, argv=0x7fffffffe4c8) at ud1.c:20
20              wc.style = 3;
```

10.   We now put a breakpoint on the call to the *register_class* function and resume execution to inspect the passed value of the *wc* structure:

```
(gdb) list 27, 40
27              wc.background = 3;
28              wc.menu_name = "menu";
29              wc.class_name = "ud1";
30
31              register_class(&wc);
32
33              while (get_message(&msg, 0, 0, 0))
34              {
35                  dispatch_message(&msg);
36              }
37
38          return 0;
39      }
```

```
(gdb) break ud1.c:31
Breakpoint 2 at 0x5555555551d5: file ud1.c, line 31.

(gdb) c
Continuing.

Breakpoint 2, main (argc=1, argv=0x7fffffffe4c8) at ud1.c:31
31              register_class(&wc);

(gdb) p wc
$1 = {style = 3, window_proc = 0x555555555155 <window_proc>, class_extra = 0, window_extra = 0,
instance = 0,
   icon = 1, cursor = 2, background = 3, menu_name = 0x555555556004 "menu", class_name =
0x555555556009 "ud1"}

(gdb) ptype /o wc
type = struct {
/*     0      |     4 */    uint32_t style;
/*     4      |     8 */    void (*window_proc)(p_msg_t);
/*    12      |     4 */    int32_t class_extra;
/*    16      |     4 */    int32_t window_extra;
/*    20      |     8 */    uint64_t instance;
/*    28      |     8 */    uint64_t icon;
/*    36      |     8 */    uint64_t cursor;
/*    44      |     8 */    uint64_t background;
/*    52      |     8 */    char *menu_name;
/*    60      |     8 */    char *class_name;

                           /* total size (bytes):   68 */
                         }
```

11.   Then, we put a breakpoint inside the *register_class* function, resume execution, and inspect the parameter:

```
(gdb) break register_class
Breakpoint 3 at 0x7ffff7fc9277: file windows.c, line 82.

(gdb) c
Continuing.

Breakpoint 3, register_class (pwc=0x7fffffffe360) at windows.c:82
82              window_proc = pwc->window_proc;

(gdb) p pwc
$2 = (p_wnd_class_t) 0x7fffffffe360

(gdb) ptype /o pwc
type = struct {
/*     0      |     4 */    uint32_t style;
/* XXX   4-byte hole */
/*     8      |     8 */    void (*window_proc)(p_msg_t);
/*    16      |     4 */    int32_t class_extra;
/*    20      |     4 */    int32_t window_extra;
/*    24      |     8 */    uint64_t instance;
/*    32      |     8 */    uint64_t icon;
/*    40      |     8 */    uint64_t cursor;
/*    48      |     8 */    uint64_t background;
/*    56      |     8 */    char *menu_name;
```

105

```
/*    64      |      8 */    char *class_name;

                             /* total size (bytes):    72 */
                        } *
```

```
(gdb) p *pwc
$3 = {style = 3, window_proc = 0x5555, class_extra = 0, window_extra = 0, instance =
4294967296, icon = 8589934592,
  cursor = 12884901888, background = 6148926436540416000,
  menu_name = 0x5555600900005555 <error: Cannot access memory at address 0x5555600900005555>,
  class_name = 0x5555 <error: Cannot access memory at address 0x5555>}
```

12.   But if we compare the structure inside the function with the structure variant outside (see step #10), we see its members have different offsets:

```
type = struct {
/*     0      |      4 */    uint32_t style;
/*     4      |      8 */    void (*window_proc)(p_msg_t);
/*    12      |      4 */    int32_t class_extra;
/*    16      |      4 */    int32_t window_extra;
/*    20      |      8 */    uint64_t instance;
/*    28      |      8 */    uint64_t icon;
/*    36      |      8 */    uint64_t cursor;
/*    44      |      8 */    uint64_t background;
/*    52      |      8 */    char *menu_name;
/*    60      |      8 */    char *class_name;

                             /* total size (bytes):    68 */
                        }
```

13.   These discrepancies explain the crash. Looking at the *Makefile*, we can see that *ud1a* was compiled with the *-fpack-struct* setting. The *ud1b* executable was compiled without it and runs fine. Also, the problem was coincidentally fixed without changing alignment by using a different, bigger *wnd_class2_t* structure in the *ud1c* executable that adds another 32-bit field that makes both alignments identical.

14.   We continue the execution and then quit GDB.

```
(gdb) c
Continuing.

Program received signal SIGSEGV, Segmentation fault.
0x0000000000005555 in ?? ()

(gdb) c
Continuing.

Program terminated with signal SIGSEGV, Segmentation fault.
The program no longer exists.

(gdb) q
```

106

Exercise UD1 (LLDB)

Goal: Learn how code generation parameters can influence process execution behavior.

Elementary Diagnostics Patterns: Crash.

Memory Analysis Patterns: Exception Stack Trace; NULL Pointer (Code); Constant Subtrace.

Debugging Implementation Patterns: Break-in; Scope; Variable Value; Type Structure; Code Breakpoint.

1.   The source code and the *Makefile* to build executables and libraries can be found in the *ud1* directory:

```
$ git clone https://bitbucket.org/softwarediagnostics/ald4
```

2.   When we launch the *ud1a* executable, it crashes:

```
/mnt/c/ALD4/ud1$ LD_LIBRARY_PATH=. ./ud1a
Segmentation fault
```

3.   We run the executable under LLDB until it shows a segmentation fault:

```
/mnt/c/ALD4/ud1$ LD_LIBRARY_PATH=. lldb ./ud1a
(lldb) target create "./ud1a"
Current executable set to './ud1a' (x86_64).

(lldb) r
Process 112 launched: '/mnt/c/ALD4/ud1/ud1a' (x86_64)
Process 112 stopped
* thread #1, name = 'ud1a', stop reason = signal SIGSEGV: invalid address (fault address:
0x5555)
    frame #0: 0x0000000000005555
error: memory read failed for 0x5400
```

4.   The **image list** command lists loaded modules and their addresses:

```
(lldb) image list
[  0] 2C8F3A74-A0FC-977F-6362-C129A1E426DA-25DA9B99              /mnt/c/ALD4/ud1/ud1a
[  1] 6005CB75-A439-321F-212E-2B1164734DFC-13352DF7              /mnt/c/ALD4/ud1/libwindows.so
[  2] 83743DDD-4258-A7D1-38A2-8C4F2032D17A-D92A15B5              /lib/x86_64-linux-gnu/ld-2.28.so
       /usr/lib/debug/.build-id/83/743ddd4258a7d138a28c4f2032d17ad92a15b5.debug
[  3] 6F3490CE-A127-50C7-4A4F-D33AC3B6CAAA-2ACE115B 0x00007ffff7fd3000 [vdso] (0x00007ffff7fd3000)
[  4] C7AA9A1E-121F-E239-5F38-40F3F0213146-046D9FE3              /lib/x86_64-linux-gnu/libc.so.6
       /usr/lib/debug/.build-id/c7/aa9a1e121fe2395f3840f3f0213146046d9fe3.debug
```

5.   We see that the crash happens in the libwindows module with the following CPU state:

```
(lldb) bt
* thread #1, name = 'ud1a', stop reason = signal SIGSEGV: invalid address (fault address: 0x5555)
  * frame #0: 0x0000000000005555
    frame #1: 0x00007ffff7fc926c libwindows.so`dispatch_message(pmessage=0x00007fffffffe3b0) at windows.c:76
    frame #2: 0x00005555555551ef ud1a`main(argc=1, argv=0x00007fffffffe4c8) at ud1.c:35
    frame #3: 0x00007ffff7e2109b libc.so.6`__libc_start_main(main=(ud1a`main at ud1.c:16), argc=1,
argv=0x00007fffffffe4c8, init=<unavailable>, fini=<unavailable>, rtld_fini=<unavailable>,
stack_end=0x00007fffffffe4b8) at libc-start.c:308
    frame #4: 0x000055555555509a ud1a`_start + 42
```

```
(lldb) register read
General Purpose Registers:
       rax = 0x0000000000005555
       rbx = 0x0000000000000000
       rcx = 0x00007ffff7ec3594  libc.so.6`__GI___nanosleep + 20 at nanosleep.c:28
       rdx = 0x00007fffffffe3b0
       rdi = 0x00007fffffffe3b0
       rsi = 0x00007fffffffe2b0
       rbp = 0x00007fffffffe340
       rsp = 0x00007fffffffe328
        r8 = 0x00007ffff7fb8d80  libc.so.6`initial
        r9 = 0x00007ffff7fb8d80  libc.so.6`initial
       r10 = 0xffffffffffffff429
       r11 = 0x00007ffff7fc9244  libwindows.so`dispatch_message at windows.c:76
       r12 = 0x0000555555555070  ud1a`_start
       r13 = 0x00007fffffffe4c0
       r14 = 0x0000000000000000
       r15 = 0x0000000000000000
       rip = 0x0000000000005555
    rflags = 0x0000000000010206
        cs = 0x0000000000000033
        fs = 0x0000000000000000
        gs = 0x0000000000000000
        ss = 0x000000000000002b
        ds = 0x0000000000000000
        es = 0x0000000000000000
```

6.   We switch to stack frame #1 and check the source code:

```
(lldb) frame select 1
frame #1: 0x00007ffff7fc926c libwindows.so`dispatch_message(pmessage=0x00007fffffffe3b0) at
windows.c:76
   73   {
   74       if (window_proc)
   75       {
-> 76           window_proc(pmessage);
   77       }
   78   }
   79
```

```
(lldb) p window_proc
(void (*)(p_msg_t)) $0 = 0x0000000000005555
```

```
(lldb) list 80
   80   int register_class(p_wnd_class_t pwc)
   81   {
   82       window_proc = pwc->window_proc;
   83   }
   84
   85   int register_class2(p_wnd_class2_t pwc)
   86   {
   87       window_proc = pwc->window_proc;
   88   }
```

7.   We see that the *window_proc* pointer is invalid, so we need to investigate when it is set in the *register_class*
function below. First, we set the next frame where the *dispatch_message* was called:

```
(lldb) bt
* thread #1, name = 'ud1a', stop reason = signal SIGSEGV: invalid address (fault address: 0x5555)
    frame #0: 0x0000000000005555
  * frame #1: 0x00007ffff7fc926c libwindows.so`dispatch_message(pmessage=0x00007fffffffe3b0) at windows.c:76
    frame #2: 0x00005555555551ef ud1a`main(argc=1, argv=0x00007fffffffe4c8) at ud1.c:35
    frame #3: 0x00007ffff7e2109b libc.so.6`__libc_start_main(main=(ud1a`main at ud1.c:16), argc=1,
argv=0x00007fffffffe4c8, init=<unavailable>, fini=<unavailable>, rtld_fini=<unavailable>,
stack_end=0x00007fffffffe4b8) at libc-start.c:308
    frame #4: 0x000055555555509a ud1a`_start + 42


(lldb) frame select 2
frame #2: 0x00005555555551ef ud1a`main(argc=1, argv=0x00007fffffffe4c8) at ud1.c:35
   32
   33              while (get_message(&msg, 0, 0, 0))
   34              {
-> 35                  dispatch_message(&msg);
   36              }
   37
   38          return 0;


(lldb) list 30
   30
   31              register_class(&wc);
   32
   33              while (get_message(&msg, 0, 0, 0))
   34              {
   35                  dispatch_message(&msg);
   36              }
   37
   38          return 0;
   39      }
```

8.   We can now check local variables and their structures (for example, *wc*):

```
(lldb) frame variable
(int) argc = 1
(char **) argv = 0x00007fffffffe4c8
(msg_t) msg = {
  hwnd = 0
  message = 275
  param1 = 1
  param2 = 140737353912581
  time = 72844112
  pt = (x = 156, y = 327)
  priv = 0
}
(wnd_class_t) wc = {
  style = 3
  window_proc = 0x0000555555555155 (ud1a`window_proc at ud1.c:11)
  class_extra = 0
  window_extra = 0
  instance = 0
  icon = 1
  cursor = 2
  background = 3
  menu_name = 0x0000555555556004 "menu"
  class_name = 0x0000555555556009 "ud1"
}
(lldb) p &wc
(wnd_class_t *) $1 = 0x00007fffffffe360
```

```
(lldb) memory read 0x00007fffffffe360
0x7fffffffe360: 03 00 00 00 55 51 55 55 55 55 55 00 00 00 00 00 00   ....UQUUUU......
0x7fffffffe370: 00 00 00 00 00 00 00 00 00 00 00 00 01 00 00 00   ................
```

9.   We put a breakpoint on the *main* function and resume execution until it is hit:

```
(lldb) c
Process 112 resuming
Process 112 exited with status = 11 (0x0000000b)

(lldb) breakpoint set -name main
Breakpoint 1: where = ud1a`main + 24 at ud1.c:20, address = 0x000055555555517f

(lldb) r
Process 176 launched: '/mnt/c/ALD4/ud1/ud1a' (x86_64)
Process 176 stopped
* thread #1, name = 'ud1a', stop reason = breakpoint 1.1
    frame #0: 0x000055555555517f ud1a`main(argc=1, argv=0x00007fffffffe4c8) at ud1.c:20
   20          msg_t msg;
   21          wnd_class_t wc;
   22
-> 23          wc.style = 3;
   24          wc.window_proc = window_proc;
   25          wc.class_extra = 0;
   26          wc.window_extra = 0;
```

10.   We now put a breakpoint on the call to the *register_class* function and resume execution to inspect the passed value of the *wc* structure:

```
(lldb) list 27
   27          wc.background = 3;
   28          wc.menu_name = "menu";
   29          wc.class_name = "ud1";
   30
   31              register_class(&wc);
   32
   33          while (get_message(&msg, 0, 0, 0))
   34          {
   35              dispatch_message(&msg);
   36          }

(lldb) breakpoint set -line 31
Breakpoint 2: where = ud1a`main + 110 at ud1.c:31, address = 0x00005555555551d5

(lldb) c
Process 176 resuming
Process 176 stopped
* thread #1, name = 'ud1a', stop reason = breakpoint 2.1
    frame #0: 0x00005555555551d5 ud1a`main(argc=1, argv=0x00007fffffffe4c8) at ud1.c:31
   28          wc.menu_name = "menu";
   29          wc.class_name = "ud1";
   30
-> 31              register_class(&wc);
   32
```

```
    33            while (get_message(&msg, 0, 0, 0))
    34            {
```

```
(lldb) p wc
(wnd_class_t) $3 = {
  style = 3
  window_proc = 0x0000555555555155 (ud1a`window_proc at ud1.c:11)
  class_extra = 0
  window_extra = 0
  instance = 0
  icon = 1
  cursor = 2
  background = 3
  menu_name = 0x0000555555556004 "menu"
  class_name = 0x0000555555556009 "ud1"
}
```

```
(lldb) memory read &wc
0x7fffffffe360: 03 00 00 00 55 51 55 55 55 55 00 00 00 00 00 00   ....UQUUUU......
0x7fffffffe370: 00 00 00 00 00 00 00 00 00 00 00 00 01 00 00 00   ...............
```

```
(lldb) p &wc.window_proc
(void (**)(p_msg_t)) $10 = 0x00007fffffffe364
```

11.   Then, we put a breakpoint inside the *register_class* function, resume execution, and inspect the parameter:

```
(lldb) breakpoint set -name register_class
Breakpoint 3: where = libwindows.so`register_class + 8 at windows.c:82, address =
0x00007ffff7fc9277
```

```
(lldb) c
Process 176 resuming
Process 176 stopped
* thread #1, name = 'ud1a', stop reason = breakpoint 3.1
    frame #0: 0x00007ffff7fc9277 libwindows.so`register_class(pwc=0x00007fffffffe360) at
windows.c:82
    79
    80   int register_class(p_wnd_class_t pwc)
    81   {
->  82       window_proc = pwc->window_proc;
    83   }
    84
    85   int register_class2(p_wnd_class2_t pwc)
```

```
(lldb) p pwc
(p_wnd_class_t) $5 = 0x00007fffffffe360
```

```
(lldb) memory read pwc
0x7fffffffe360: 03 00 00 00 55 51 55 55 55 55 00 00 00 00 00 00   ....UQUUUU......
0x7fffffffe370: 00 00 00 00 00 00 00 00 00 00 00 00 01 00 00 00   ...............
```

```
(lldb) p &pwc->window_proc
(void (**)(p_msg_t)) $10 = 0x00007fffffffe368
```

```
(lldb) p *pwc
((anonymous struct)) $8 = {
  style = 3
  window_proc = 0x0000000000005555
```

```
      class_extra = 0
      window_extra = 0
      instance = 4294967296
      icon = 8589934592
      cursor = 12884901888
      background = 6148926436540416000
      menu_name = 0x5555600900005555 <no value available>
      class_name = 0x0000000000005555 <no value available>
}
```

12.   So, if we compare the structure field address inside the function with the structure variant outside (see step #10), we see its members have different offsets:

```
(lldb) p &wc.window_proc
(void (**)(p_msg_t)) $10 = 0x00007fffffffe364
```

13.   These discrepancies explain the crash. Looking at the *Makefile*, we can see that *ud1a* was compiled with the -*fpack-struct* setting. The *ud1b* executable was compiled without it and runs fine. Also, the problem was coincidentally fixed without changing alignment by using a different, bigger *wnd_class2_t* structure in the *ud1c* executable that adds another 32-bit field that makes both alignments identical.

14.   We continue the execution and then quit LLDB.

```
(lldb) c
Process 176 resuming
Process 176 stopped
* thread #1, name = 'ud1a', stop reason = signal SIGSEGV: invalid address (fault address:
0x5555)
    frame #0: 0x0000000000005555
error: memory read failed for 0x5400

(lldb) c
Process 176 resuming
Process 176 exited with status = 11 (0x0000000b)

(lldb) q
```

Code Breakpoints

GDB Commands

```
break <name>
info break
delete break <number>
```

WinDbg Commands

```
bp <name>
bl
bc <number>
```

LLDB Commands

```
break set -name <name>
break list
break delete <number>
```

Exercise UD2

- **Goal:** Learn how to use hardware breakpoints to catch data corruption

- **Elementary Diagnostics Patterns:** Counter Value

- **Memory Analysis Patterns:** Unloaded Module; Memory Leak (Process Heap); Corrupt Structure; Abnormal Value (*from trace analysis patterns*)

- **Debugging Implementation Patterns:** Break-in; Code Breakpoint; Scope; Variable Value; Data Breakpoint

- \ALD4\Exercise-Linux-UD2.pdf

Exercise UD2 (GDB)

Goal: Learn how to use hardware breakpoints to catch data corruption.

Elementary Diagnostics Patterns: Counter Value.

Memory Analysis Patterns: Unloaded Module; Memory Leak (Process Heap); Corrupt Structure; Abnormal Value *(from trace analysis patterns)*.

Debugging Implementation Patterns: Break-in; Code Breakpoint; Scope; Variable Value; Data Breakpoint.

1.   The source code and the *Makefile* to build executables and libraries can be found in the *ud2* directory:

```
$ git clone https://bitbucket.org/softwarediagnostics/ald4
```

2.   Problem history:

An application *ud2* starts consuming memory after some time. We want to find out the root cause.

3.   Run the *ud2* executable. Using the *top*, we initially see approximately this memory consumption:

```
/mnt/c/ALD4/ud2$ ./ud2 &
[1] 8071

top - 12:46:37 up  9:30,  0 users,  load average: 0.00, 0.00, 0.00
Tasks:   1 total,   0 running,   1 sleeping,   0 stopped,   0 zombie
%Cpu(s):  0.0 us,  0.0 sy,  0.0 ni,100.0 id,  0.0 wa,  0.0 hi,  0.0 si,  0.0 st
MiB Mem :   7904.1 total,   7112.2 free,    301.4 used,    490.4 buff/cache
MiB Swap:   2048.0 total,   2048.0 free,      0.0 used.   7375.6 avail Mem

  PID USER      PR  NI    VIRT    RES    SHR S  %CPU  %MEM     TIME+ COMMAND
 8071 coredump   20   0  100780   1228   1120 S   0.0   0.0   0:00.00 ud2
```

4.   After a minute, memory starts growing:

```
top - 12:48:11 up  9:31,  0 users,  load average: 0.00, 0.00, 0.00
Tasks:   1 total,   0 running,   1 sleeping,   0 stopped,   0 zombie
%Cpu(s):  0.0 us,  0.0 sy,  0.0 ni,100.0 id,  0.0 wa,  0.0 hi,  0.0 si,  0.0 st
MiB Mem :   7904.1 total,   7109.2 free,    304.4 used,    490.4 buff/cache
MiB Swap:   2048.0 total,   2048.0 free,      0.0 used.   7372.7 avail Mem

  PID USER      PR  NI    VIRT    RES    SHR S  %CPU  %MEM     TIME+ COMMAND
 8071 coredump   20   0  100780   3196   1244 S   0.0   0.0   0:00.02 ud2
```

5.   Wait for another 2-3 minutes more, and then we attach GDB to the process:

```
top - 12:50:02 up  9:33,  0 users,  load average: 0.00, 0.00, 0.00
Tasks:   1 total,   0 running,   1 sleeping,   0 stopped,   0 zombie
%Cpu(s):  0.0 us,  0.0 sy,  0.0 ni,100.0 id,  0.0 wa,  0.0 hi,  0.0 si,  0.0 st
MiB Mem :   7904.1 total,   7092.6 free,    321.0 used,    490.4 buff/cache
MiB Swap:   2048.0 total,   2048.0 free,      0.0 used.   7356.0 avail Mem

  PID USER      PR  NI    VIRT    RES    SHR S  %CPU  %MEM     TIME+ COMMAND
```

```
 8071 coredump  20   0  166296  20272   1232 S   0.0   0.3   0:00.08 ud2
```

```
/mnt/c/ALD4/ud2$ gdb -p 8071
GNU gdb (Debian 8.2.1-2+b3) 8.2.1
Copyright (C) 2018 Free Software Foundation, Inc.
License GPLv3+: GNU GPL version 3 or later <http://gnu.org/licenses/gpl.html>
This is free software: you are free to change and redistribute it.
There is NO WARRANTY, to the extent permitted by law.
Type "show copying" and "show warranty" for details.
This GDB was configured as "x86_64-linux-gnu".
Type "show configuration" for configuration details.
For bug reporting instructions, please see:
<http://www.gnu.org/software/gdb/bugs/>.
Find the GDB manual and other documentation resources online at:
    <http://www.gnu.org/software/gdb/documentation/>.

For help, type "help".
Type "apropos word" to search for commands related to "word".
Attaching to process 8071
[New LWP 8073]
[New LWP 8074]
[New LWP 8075]
[Thread debugging using libthread_db enabled]
Using host libthread_db library "/lib/x86_64-linux-gnu/libthread_db.so.1".
0x00007f988c93d5c0 in __GI___nanosleep (requested_time=requested_time@entry=0x7ffc2b14bc50,
    remaining=remaining@entry=0x7ffc2b14bc50) at ../sysdeps/unix/sysv/linux/nanosleep.c:28
28      ../sysdeps/unix/sysv/linux/nanosleep.c: No such file or directory.
(gdb)
```

6.   There are 4 threads, and the current one, #1 (numbering starts from 1), is the main thread:

```
(gdb) info thread
  Id   Target Id                          Frame
* 1    Thread 0x7f988c874740 (LWP 8071) "ud2" 0x00007f988c93d5c0 in __GI___nanosleep (
   requested_time=requested_time@entry=0x7ffc2b14bc50,
remaining=remaining@entry=0x7ffc2b14bc50)
    at ../sysdeps/unix/sysv/linux/nanosleep.c:28
  2    Thread 0x7f988c072700 (LWP 8073) "ud2" 0x00007f988c93d5c0 in __GI___nanosleep (
   requested_time=requested_time@entry=0x7f988c071ea0,
remaining=remaining@entry=0x7f988c071ea0)
    at ../sysdeps/unix/sysv/linux/nanosleep.c:28
  3    Thread 0x7f988b871700 (LWP 8074) "ud2" 0x00007f988c93d5c0 in __GI___nanosleep (
   requested_time=requested_time@entry=0x7f988b870eb0, remaining=remaining@entry=0x0)
    at ../sysdeps/unix/sysv/linux/nanosleep.c:28
  4    Thread 0x7f988b070700 (LWP 8075) "ud2" 0x00007f988c93d5c0 in __GI___nanosleep (
   requested_time=requested_time@entry=0x7f988b06fea0,
remaining=remaining@entry=0x7f988b06fea0)
    at ../sysdeps/unix/sysv/linux/nanosleep.c:28
```

```
(gdb) bt
#0  0x00007f988c93d5c0 in __GI___nanosleep (requested_time=requested_time@entry=0x7ffc2b14bc50,
    remaining=remaining@entry=0x7ffc2b14bc50) at ../sysdeps/unix/sysv/linux/nanosleep.c:28
#1  0x00007f988c93d4ca in __sleep (seconds=0) at ../sysdeps/posix/sleep.c:55
#2  0x000055bb388bd23b in main () at ud2.c:43
```

7.   We can list all threads' backtraces using this command:

```
(gdb) thread apply * bt

Thread 1 (Thread 0x7f988c874740 (LWP 8071)):
#0  0x00007f988c93d5c0 in __GI___nanosleep (requested_time=requested_time@entry=0x7ffc2b14bc50,
     remaining=remaining@entry=0x7ffc2b14bc50) at ../sysdeps/unix/sysv/linux/nanosleep.c:28
#1  0x00007f988c93d4ca in __sleep (seconds=0) at ../sysdeps/posix/sleep.c:55
#2  0x000055bb388bd23b in main () at ud2.c:43

Thread 2 (Thread 0x7f988c072700 (LWP 8073)):
#0  0x00007f988c93d5c0 in __GI___nanosleep (requested_time=requested_time@entry=0x7f988c071ea0,
     remaining=remaining@entry=0x7f988c071ea0) at ../sysdeps/unix/sysv/linux/nanosleep.c:28
#1  0x00007f988c93d4ca in __sleep (seconds=0) at ../sysdeps/posix/sleep.c:55
#2  0x000055bb388bd255 in thread_proc_a (_=0x0) at ud2.c:50
#3  0x00007f988ca3efa3 in start_thread (arg=<optimized out>) at pthread_create.c:486
#4  0x00007f988c97006f in clone () at ../sysdeps/unix/sysv/linux/x86_64/clone.S:95

Thread 3 (Thread 0x7f988b871700 (LWP 8074)):
#0  0x00007f988c93d5c0 in __GI___nanosleep (requested_time=requested_time@entry=0x7f988b870eb0,
     remaining=remaining@entry=0x0) at ../sysdeps/unix/sysv/linux/nanosleep.c:28
#1  0x00007f988c968414 in usleep (useconds=<optimized out>) at ../sysdeps/posix/usleep.c:32
#2  0x000055bb388bd284 in thread_proc_b (_=0x0) at ud2.c:59
#3  0x00007f988ca3efa3 in start_thread (arg=<optimized out>) at pthread_create.c:486
#4  0x00007f988c97006f in clone () at ../sysdeps/unix/sysv/linux/x86_64/clone.S:95

Thread 4 (Thread 0x7f988b070700 (LWP 8075)):
#0  0x00007f988c93d5c0 in __GI___nanosleep (requested_time=requested_time@entry=0x7f988b06fea0,
     remaining=remaining@entry=0x7f988b06fea0) at ../sysdeps/unix/sysv/linux/nanosleep.c:28
#1  0x00007f988c93d4ca in __sleep (seconds=0) at ../sysdeps/posix/sleep.c:55
#2  0x000055bb388bd2cf in thread_proc_c (_=0x0) at ud2.c:73
#3  0x00007f988ca3efa3 in start_thread (arg=<optimized out>) at pthread_create.c:486
#4  0x00007f988c97006f in clone () at ../sysdeps/unix/sysv/linux/x86_64/clone.S:95
```

8.   The following command lists currently loaded shared libraries:

```
(gdb) info sharedlibrary
From                To                  Syms Read   Shared Object Library
0x00007f988ca59130  0x00007f988ca59eb5  Yes         /lib/x86_64-linux-gnu/libdl.so.2
0x00007f988ca3d5b0  0x00007f988ca4b641  Yes         /lib/x86_64-linux-gnu/libpthread.so.0
0x00007f988c899320  0x00007f988c9df14b  Yes         /lib/x86_64-linux-gnu/libc.so.6
0x00007f988ca6b090  0x00007f988ca88b50  Yes         /lib64/ld-linux-x86-64.so.2
```

9.   We suspect process heap leak and print memory information:

```
(gdb) info proc mappings
process 8071
Mapped address spaces:

          Start Addr          End Addr      Size    Offset objfile
       0x55bb388bc000    0x55bb388bd000    0x1000       0x0 /mnt/c/ALD4/ud2/ud2
       0x55bb388bd000    0x55bb388be000    0x1000    0x1000 /mnt/c/ALD4/ud2/ud2
       0x55bb388be000    0x55bb388bf000    0x1000    0x2000 /mnt/c/ALD4/ud2/ud2
       0x55bb388bf000    0x55bb388c0000    0x1000    0x2000 /mnt/c/ALD4/ud2/ud2
       0x55bb388c0000    0x55bb388c1000    0x1000    0x3000 /mnt/c/ALD4/ud2/ud2
       0x55bb388fb000    0x55bb3891c000   0x21000       0x0 [heap]
       0x7f987c000000    0x7f987c021000   0x21000       0x0
```

```
0x7f987c021000    0x7f9880000000    0x3fdf000         0x0
0x7f9884000000    0x7f9885cbb000    0x1cbb000         0x0
0x7f9885cbb000    0x7f9888000000    0x2345000         0x0
0x7f988a870000    0x7f988a871000     0x1000           0x0
0x7f988a871000    0x7f988b071000    0x800000          0x0
0x7f988b071000    0x7f988b072000     0x1000           0x0
0x7f988b072000    0x7f988b872000    0x800000          0x0
0x7f988b872000    0x7f988b873000     0x1000           0x0
0x7f988b873000    0x7f988c073000    0x800000          0x0
0x7f988c073000    0x7f988c074000     0x1000           0x0
0x7f988c074000    0x7f988c877000    0x803000          0x0
0x7f988c877000    0x7f988c899000    0x22000           0x0 /lib/x86_64-linux-gnu/libc-2.28.so
0x7f988c899000    0x7f988c9e0000    0x147000      0x22000 /lib/x86_64-linux-gnu/libc-2.28.so
0x7f988c9e0000    0x7f988ca2c000    0x4c000      0x169000 /lib/x86_64-linux-gnu/libc-2.28.so
0x7f988ca2c000    0x7f988ca2d000     0x1000      0x1b5000 /lib/x86_64-linux-gnu/libc-2.28.so
0x7f988ca2d000    0x7f988ca31000     0x4000      0x1b5000 /lib/x86_64-linux-gnu/libc-2.28.so
0x7f988ca31000    0x7f988ca33000     0x2000      0x1b9000 /lib/x86_64-linux-gnu/libc-2.28.so
0x7f988ca33000    0x7f988ca37000     0x4000           0x0
0x7f988ca37000    0x7f988ca3d000     0x6000           0x0 /lib/x86_64-linux-gnu/libpthread-2.28.so
0x7f988ca3d000    0x7f988ca4c000     0xf000       0x6000 /lib/x86_64-linux-gnu/libpthread-2.28.so
0x7f988ca4c000    0x7f988ca52000     0x6000      0x15000 /lib/x86_64-linux-gnu/libpthread-2.28.so
0x7f988ca52000    0x7f988ca53000     0x1000      0x1a000 /lib/x86_64-linux-gnu/libpthread-2.28.so
0x7f988ca53000    0x7f988ca54000     0x1000      0x1b000 /lib/x86_64-linux-gnu/libpthread-2.28.so
0x7f988ca54000    0x7f988ca58000     0x4000           0x0
0x7f988ca58000    0x7f988ca59000     0x1000           0x0 /lib/x86_64-linux-gnu/libdl-2.28.so
0x7f988ca59000    0x7f988ca5a000     0x1000       0x1000 /lib/x86_64-linux-gnu/libdl-2.28.so
0x7f988ca5a000    0x7f988ca5b000     0x1000       0x2000 /lib/x86_64-linux-gnu/libdl-2.28.so
0x7f988ca5b000    0x7f988ca5c000     0x1000       0x2000 /lib/x86_64-linux-gnu/libdl-2.28.so
0x7f988ca5c000    0x7f988ca5d000     0x1000       0x3000 /lib/x86_64-linux-gnu/libdl-2.28.so
0x7f988ca5d000    0x7f988ca5f000     0x2000           0x0
0x7f988ca6a000    0x7f988ca6b000     0x1000           0x0 /lib/x86_64-linux-gnu/ld-2.28.so
0x7f988ca6b000    0x7f988ca89000    0x1e000       0x1000 /lib/x86_64-linux-gnu/ld-2.28.so
0x7f988ca89000    0x7f988ca91000     0x8000      0x1f000 /lib/x86_64-linux-gnu/ld-2.28.so
0x7f988ca91000    0x7f988ca92000     0x1000      0x26000 /lib/x86_64-linux-gnu/ld-2.28.so
0x7f988ca92000    0x7f988ca93000     0x1000      0x27000 /lib/x86_64-linux-gnu/ld-2.28.so
0x7f988ca93000    0x7f988ca94000     0x1000           0x0
0x7ffc2b12d000    0x7ffc2b14e000    0x21000           0x0 [stack]
0x7ffc2b1f1000    0x7ffc2b1f5000     0x4000           0x0 [vvar]
0x7ffc2b1f5000    0x7ffc2b1f7000     0x2000           0x0 [vdso]
```

Then we resume, wait for 2-3 minutes, break-in, and print memory info again:

```
(gdb) c
Continuing.
^C
Thread 1 "ud2" received signal SIGINT, Interrupt.
0x00007f988c93d5c0 in __GI___nanosleep (requested_time=requested_time@entry=0x7ffc2b14bc50,
    remaining=remaining@entry=0x7ffc2b14bc50) at ../sysdeps/unix/sysv/linux/nanosleep.c:28
28        in ../sysdeps/unix/sysv/linux/nanosleep.c


(gdb) info proc mappings
process 8071
Mapped address spaces:

          Start Addr         End Addr       Size   Offset objfile
      0x55bb388bc000    0x55bb388bd000     0x1000      0x0 /mnt/c/ALD4/ud2/ud2
      0x55bb388bd000    0x55bb388be000     0x1000   0x1000 /mnt/c/ALD4/ud2/ud2
      0x55bb388be000    0x55bb388bf000     0x1000   0x2000 /mnt/c/ALD4/ud2/ud2
      0x55bb388bf000    0x55bb388c0000     0x1000   0x2000 /mnt/c/ALD4/ud2/ud2
      0x55bb388c0000    0x55bb388c1000     0x1000   0x3000 /mnt/c/ALD4/ud2/ud2
      0x55bb388fb000    0x55bb3891c000    0x21000      0x0 [heap]
      0x7f987c000000    0x7f987c021000    0x21000      0x0
```

```
0x7f987c021000      0x7f9880000000   0x3fdf000         0x0
0x7f9884000000      0x7f98878c7000   0x38c7000         0x0
0x7f98878c7000      0x7f9888000000   0x739000          0x0
0x7f988a870000      0x7f988a871000    0x1000           0x0
0x7f988a871000      0x7f988b071000   0x800000          0x0
0x7f988b071000      0x7f988b072000    0x1000           0x0
0x7f988b072000      0x7f988b872000   0x800000          0x0
0x7f988b872000      0x7f988b873000    0x1000           0x0
0x7f988b873000      0x7f988c073000   0x800000          0x0
0x7f988c073000      0x7f988c074000    0x1000           0x0
0x7f988c074000      0x7f988c877000   0x803000          0x0
0x7f988c877000      0x7f988c899000   0x22000           0x0 /lib/x86_64-linux-gnu/libc-2.28.so
0x7f988c899000      0x7f988c9e0000  0x147000       0x22000 /lib/x86_64-linux-gnu/libc-2.28.so
0x7f988c9e0000      0x7f988ca2c000   0x4c000      0x169000 /lib/x86_64-linux-gnu/libc-2.28.so
0x7f988ca2c000      0x7f988ca2d000    0x1000      0x1b5000 /lib/x86_64-linux-gnu/libc-2.28.so
0x7f988ca2d000      0x7f988ca31000    0x4000      0x1b5000 /lib/x86_64-linux-gnu/libc-2.28.so
0x7f988ca31000      0x7f988ca33000    0x2000      0x1b9000 /lib/x86_64-linux-gnu/libc-2.28.so
0x7f988ca33000      0x7f988ca37000    0x4000           0x0
0x7f988ca37000      0x7f988ca3d000    0x6000           0x0 /lib/x86_64-linux-gnu/libpthread-2.28.so
0x7f988ca3d000      0x7f988ca4c000    0xf000        0x6000 /lib/x86_64-linux-gnu/libpthread-2.28.so
0x7f988ca4c000      0x7f988ca52000    0x6000       0x15000 /lib/x86_64-linux-gnu/libpthread-2.28.so
0x7f988ca52000      0x7f988ca53000    0x1000       0x1a000 /lib/x86_64-linux-gnu/libpthread-2.28.so
0x7f988ca53000      0x7f988ca54000    0x1000       0x1b000 /lib/x86_64-linux-gnu/libpthread-2.28.so
0x7f988ca54000      0x7f988ca58000    0x4000           0x0
0x7f988ca58000      0x7f988ca59000    0x1000           0x0 /lib/x86_64-linux-gnu/libdl-2.28.so
0x7f988ca59000      0x7f988ca5a000    0x1000        0x1000 /lib/x86_64-linux-gnu/libdl-2.28.so
0x7f988ca5a000      0x7f988ca5b000    0x1000        0x2000 /lib/x86_64-linux-gnu/libdl-2.28.so
0x7f988ca5b000      0x7f988ca5c000    0x1000        0x2000 /lib/x86_64-linux-gnu/libdl-2.28.so
0x7f988ca5c000      0x7f988ca5d000    0x1000        0x3000 /lib/x86_64-linux-gnu/libdl-2.28.so
0x7f988ca5d000      0x7f988ca5f000    0x2000           0x0
0x7f988ca6a000      0x7f988ca6b000    0x1000           0x0 /lib/x86_64-linux-gnu/ld-2.28.so
0x7f988ca6b000      0x7f988ca89000   0x1e000        0x1000 /lib/x86_64-linux-gnu/ld-2.28.so
0x7f988ca89000      0x7f988ca91000    0x8000       0x1f000 /lib/x86_64-linux-gnu/ld-2.28.so
0x7f988ca91000      0x7f988ca92000    0x1000       0x26000 /lib/x86_64-linux-gnu/ld-2.28.so
0x7f988ca92000      0x7f988ca93000    0x1000       0x27000 /lib/x86_64-linux-gnu/ld-2.28.so
0x7f988ca93000      0x7f988ca94000    0x1000           0x0
0x7ffc2b12d000      0x7ffc2b14e000   0x21000           0x0 [stack]
0x7ffc2b1f1000      0x7ffc2b1f5000    0x4000           0x0 [vvar]
0x7ffc2b1f5000      0x7ffc2b1f7000    0x2000           0x0 [vdso]
```

Then we resume again, wait for 2-3 minutes, break-in, and print memory info again:

```
(gdb) c
Continuing.
^C
Thread 1 "ud2" received signal SIGINT, Interrupt.
0x00007f988c93d5c0 in __GI___nanosleep (requested_time=requested_time@entry=0x7ffc2b14bc50,
    remaining=remaining@entry=0x7ffc2b14bc50) at ../sysdeps/unix/sysv/linux/nanosleep.c:28
28        in ../sysdeps/unix/sysv/linux/nanosleep.c

(gdb) info proc mappings
process 8071
Mapped address spaces:

          Start Addr         End Addr      Size   Offset objfile
       0x55bb388bc000   0x55bb388bd000    0x1000      0x0 /mnt/c/ALD4/ud2/ud2
       0x55bb388bd000   0x55bb388be000    0x1000   0x1000 /mnt/c/ALD4/ud2/ud2
       0x55bb388be000   0x55bb388bf000    0x1000   0x2000 /mnt/c/ALD4/ud2/ud2
       0x55bb388bf000   0x55bb388c0000    0x1000   0x2000 /mnt/c/ALD4/ud2/ud2
       0x55bb388c0000   0x55bb388c1000    0x1000   0x3000 /mnt/c/ALD4/ud2/ud2
       0x55bb388fb000   0x55bb3891c000   0x21000      0x0 [heap]
       0x7f987c000000   0x7f987c021000   0x21000      0x0
       0x7f987c021000   0x7f9880000000  0x3fdf000      0x0
```

```
0x7f9880000000      0x7f98814de000   0x14de000       0x0
0x7f98814de000      0x7f9884000000   0x2b22000       0x0
0x7f9884000000      0x7f9887ffe000   0x3ffe000       0x0
0x7f9887ffe000      0x7f9888000000    0x2000         0x0
0x7f988a870000      0x7f988a871000    0x1000         0x0
0x7f988a871000      0x7f988b071000   0x800000        0x0
0x7f988b071000      0x7f988b072000    0x1000         0x0
0x7f988b072000      0x7f988b872000   0x800000        0x0
0x7f988b872000      0x7f988b873000    0x1000         0x0
0x7f988b873000      0x7f988c073000   0x800000        0x0
0x7f988c073000      0x7f988c074000    0x1000         0x0
0x7f988c074000      0x7f988c877000   0x803000        0x0
0x7f988c877000      0x7f988c899000   0x22000         0x0 /lib/x86_64-linux-gnu/libc-2.28.so
0x7f988c899000      0x7f988c9e0000   0x147000     0x22000 /lib/x86_64-linux-gnu/libc-2.28.so
0x7f988c9e0000      0x7f988ca2c000   0x4c000     0x169000 /lib/x86_64-linux-gnu/libc-2.28.so
0x7f988ca2c000      0x7f988ca2d000    0x1000     0x1b5000 /lib/x86_64-linux-gnu/libc-2.28.so
0x7f988ca2d000      0x7f988ca31000    0x4000     0x1b5000 /lib/x86_64-linux-gnu/libc-2.28.so
0x7f988ca31000      0x7f988ca33000    0x2000     0x1b9000 /lib/x86_64-linux-gnu/libc-2.28.so
0x7f988ca33000      0x7f988ca37000    0x4000         0x0
0x7f988ca37000      0x7f988ca3d000    0x6000         0x0 /lib/x86_64-linux-gnu/libpthread-2.28.so
0x7f988ca3d000      0x7f988ca4c000    0xf000      0x6000 /lib/x86_64-linux-gnu/libpthread-2.28.so
0x7f988ca4c000      0x7f988ca52000    0x6000     0x15000 /lib/x86_64-linux-gnu/libpthread-2.28.so
0x7f988ca52000      0x7f988ca53000    0x1000     0x1a000 /lib/x86_64-linux-gnu/libpthread-2.28.so
0x7f988ca53000      0x7f988ca54000    0x1000     0x1b000 /lib/x86_64-linux-gnu/libpthread-2.28.so
0x7f988ca54000      0x7f988ca58000    0x4000         0x0
0x7f988ca58000      0x7f988ca59000    0x1000         0x0 /lib/x86_64-linux-gnu/libdl-2.28.so
0x7f988ca59000      0x7f988ca5a000    0x1000      0x1000 /lib/x86_64-linux-gnu/libdl-2.28.so
0x7f988ca5a000      0x7f988ca5b000    0x1000      0x2000 /lib/x86_64-linux-gnu/libdl-2.28.so
0x7f988ca5b000      0x7f988ca5c000    0x1000      0x2000 /lib/x86_64-linux-gnu/libdl-2.28.so
0x7f988ca5c000      0x7f988ca5d000    0x1000      0x3000 /lib/x86_64-linux-gnu/libdl-2.28.so
0x7f988ca5d000      0x7f988ca5f000    0x2000         0x0
0x7f988ca6a000      0x7f988ca6b000    0x1000         0x0 /lib/x86_64-linux-gnu/ld-2.28.so
0x7f988ca6b000      0x7f988ca89000   0x1e000      0x1000 /lib/x86_64-linux-gnu/ld-2.28.so
0x7f988ca89000      0x7f988ca91000    0x8000     0x1f000 /lib/x86_64-linux-gnu/ld-2.28.so
0x7f988ca91000      0x7f988ca92000    0x1000     0x26000 /lib/x86_64-linux-gnu/ld-2.28.so
0x7f988ca92000      0x7f988ca93000    0x1000     0x27000 /lib/x86_64-linux-gnu/ld-2.28.so
0x7f988ca93000      0x7f988ca94000    0x1000         0x0
0x7ffc2b12d000      0x7ffc2b14e000   0x21000         0x0 [stack]
0x7ffc2b1f1000      0x7ffc2b1f5000    0x4000         0x0 [vvar]
0x7ffc2b1f5000      0x7ffc2b1f7000    0x2000         0x0 [vdso]
```

Note: We definitely see an increase in process heap memory usage.

10.   Let's put a breakpoint on the *malloc* function (usually, even if we use *new* in C++, allocations go through that function) and inspect a backtrace when the breakpoint is hit:

```
(gdb) break malloc
Breakpoint 1 at 0x7f988c8fb510: malloc. (2 locations)

(gdb) c
Continuing.
[Switching to Thread 0x7f988b871700 (LWP 8074)]

Thread 3 "ud2" hit Breakpoint 1, __GI___libc_malloc (bytes=17740) at malloc.c:3036
3036    malloc.c: No such file or directory.

(gdb) bt
#0  __GI___libc_malloc (bytes=17740) at malloc.c:3036
#1  0x000055bb388bd273 in thread_proc_b (_=0x0) at ud2.c:58
#2  0x00007f988ca3efa3 in start_thread (arg=<optimized out>) at pthread_create.c:486
#3  0x00007f988c97006f in clone () at ../sysdeps/unix/sysv/linux/x86_64/clone.S:95
```

120

11.   Let's now switch to the appropriate frame that calls *malloc*:

```
(gdb) frame 1
#1  0x000055bb388bd273 in thread_proc_b (_=0x0) at ud2.c:58
58                      alloc_manager.alloc_data = (uint8_t *)malloc(alloc_manager.alloc_size);
```

12.   Let's examine our source code fragments related to using *malloc* and *free*:

```
typedef struct
{
        uint32_t alloc_size;
        uint8_t keep;
        uint8_t *alloc_data;
} ALLOCMGR;

ALLOCMGR alloc_manager;

void start_modeling (void)
{
        alloc_manager.alloc_size = 64;
        alloc_manager.keep = 0;
...
}

void *thread_proc_b (void *_)
{
        while (1)
        {
                alloc_manager.alloc_data = (uint8_t *)malloc(alloc_manager.alloc_size);
                usleep(100000);     // do some work
                if (!alloc_manager.keep)
                {
                        free(alloc_manager.alloc_data);
                }
        }

        return 0;
}
```

According to the source code, every allocation should be freed after some work.

13.   Let's now examine the *alloc_manager* structure:

```
(gdb) p alloc_manager
$1 = {alloc_size = 17740, keep = 65 'A', alloc_data = 0x7f98814d98d0 ""}

(gdb) x/4w &alloc_manager
0x55bb388c0080 <alloc_manager>: 17740    19265    -2125621040       32664

(gdb) x/16c &alloc_manager
0x55bb388c0080 <alloc_manager>: 76 'L'  69 'E'  0 '\000'        0 '\000'        65 'A'  75 'K'
0 '\000'        0 '\000'
0x55bb388c0088 <alloc_manager+8>:               -48 '\320'      -104 '\230'     77 'M'  -127 '\201'
-104 '\230'     127 '\177'      0 '\000'        0 '\000'
```

Note: We see the corruption effect: *alloc_size* is no longer 64 (0x40), *keep* is no longer 0, and the latter prevents *free* according to the source code.

121

14. To catch the moment of corruption, we need to restart debugging the process and put a hardware memory write breakpoint (we also remove our *malloc* breakpoint after the first hit):

```
(gdb) r
The program being debugged has been started already.
Start it from the beginning? (y or n) y
Starting program: /mnt/c/ALD4/ud2/ud2

Breakpoint 1, malloc (n=1433) at dl-minimal.c:50
50        dl-minimal.c: No such file or directory.

(gdb) p &alloc_manager
$1 = (ALLOCMGR *) 0x555555558080 <alloc_manager>

(gdb) watch *0x555555558080
Hardware watchpoint 2: *0x555555558080

(gdb) info break
Num     Type           Disp Enb Address            What
1       breakpoint     keep y   0x00007ffff7fedda0 in malloc at dl-minimal.c:50
        breakpoint already hit 1 time
2       hw watchpoint  keep y                      *0x555555558080

(gdb) delete breakpoints 1

(gdb) info break
Num     Type           Disp Enb Address            What
2       hw watchpoint  keep y                      *0x555555558080
```

15. Now we resume execution:

```
(gdb) c
Continuing.
[Thread debugging using libthread_db enabled]
Using host libthread_db library "/lib/x86_64-linux-gnu/libthread_db.so.1".
[New Thread 0x7ffff7dd8700 (LWP 16877)]

Thread 1 "ud2" hit Hardware watchpoint 2: *0x555555558080

Old value = 0
New value = 64
start_modeling () at ud2.c:80
80                  alloc_manager.keep = 0;
```

Note: the first hit is normal as it is related to structure initialization.

```
(gdb) c
Continuing.
[New Thread 0x7ffff75d7700 (LWP 16890)]
[New Thread 0x7ffff6dd6700 (LWP 16891)]
[New Thread 0x7ffff65d5700 (LWP 16892)]
[Switching to Thread 0x7ffff7dd8700 (LWP 16877)]

Thread 2 "ud2" hit Hardware watchpoint 2: *0x555555558080

Old value = 64
New value = 17740
```

```
__memmove_avx_unaligned_erms () at ../sysdeps/x86_64/multiarch/memmove-vec-unaligned-erms.S:329
329      ../sysdeps/x86_64/multiarch/memmove-vec-unaligned-erms.S: No such file or directory.
```

```
(gdb) p alloc_manager
$3 = {alloc_size = 17740, keep = 0 '\000', alloc_data = 0x7ffff0000b20 ""}
```

```
(gdb) bt
#0  __memmove_avx_unaligned_erms () at ../sysdeps/x86_64/multiarch/memmove-vec-unaligned-
erms.S:329
#1  0x00007ffff7fcb179 in thread_proc_d () from ./liblib.so
#2  0x00007ffff7fa3fa3 in start_thread (arg=<optimized out>) at pthread_create.c:486
#3  0x00007ffff7ed506f in clone () at ../sysdeps/unix/sysv/linux/x86_64/clone.S:95
```

Note: We see corruption going on and originating from *liblib.so* code.

16.   We can even modify the structure contents to eliminate the leak:

```
(gdb) c
Continuing.
[Thread 0x7ffff7dd8700 (LWP 16877) exited]
^C
Thread 1 "ud2" received signal SIGINT, Interrupt.
[Switching to Thread 0x7ffff7dd9740 (LWP 16798)]
0x00007ffff7ea25c0 in __GI___nanosleep (requested_time=requested_time@entry=0x7fffffffe390,
    remaining=remaining@entry=0x7fffffffe390) at ../sysdeps/unix/sysv/linux/nanosleep.c:28
28      ../sysdeps/unix/sysv/linux/nanosleep.c: No such file or directory.
```

```
(gdb) set alloc_manager.keep=0
```

```
(gdb) set alloc_manager.alloc_size=64
```

```
(gdb) p alloc_manager
$4 = {alloc_size = 64, keep = 0 '\000', alloc_data = 0x7ffff00f7dd0 ""}
```

Note: If we continue execution, we won't see any leaks anymore. We quit our debugging session.

```
(gdb) c
Continuing.
^C
Thread 1 "ud2" received signal SIGINT, Interrupt.
0x00007ffff7ea25c0 in __GI___nanosleep (requested_time=requested_time@entry=0x7fffffffe390,
    remaining=remaining@entry=0x7fffffffe390) at ../sysdeps/unix/sysv/linux/nanosleep.c:28
28      in ../sysdeps/unix/sysv/linux/nanosleep.c
```

```
(gdb) q
A debugging session is active.

        Inferior 1 [process 16798] will be killed.

Quit anyway? (y or n) y
[1]+  Killed                  ./ud2
```

Exercise UD2 (LLDB)

Goal: Learn how to use hardware breakpoints to catch data corruption.

Elementary Diagnostics Patterns: Counter Value.

Memory Analysis Patterns: Unloaded Module; Memory Leak (Process Heap); Corrupt Structure; Abnormal Value *(from trace analysis patterns).*

Debugging Implementation Patterns: Break-in; Code Breakpoint; Scope; Variable Value; Data Breakpoint.

1.   The source code and the *Makefile* to build executables and libraries can be found in the *ud2* directory:

```
$ git clone https://bitbucket.org/softwarediagnostics/ald4
```

2.   Problem history:

An application *ud2* starts consuming memory after some time. We want to find out the root cause.

3.   Run the *ud2* executable and wait 2-3 minutes. Attach LLDB to it.

```
/mnt/c/ALD4/ud2$ ./ud2 &
[1] 13106

/mnt/c/ALD4/ud2$ lldb -p 13106
Process 13106 stopped
* thread #1, name = 'ud2', stop reason = signal SIGSTOP
    frame #0: 0x00007f348a46b5c0 libc.so.6`__GI___nanosleep(requested_time=0x00007ffcc4de39c0,
remaining=0x00007ffcc4de39c0) at nanosleep.c:28
  thread #2, name = 'ud2', stop reason = signal SIGSTOP
    frame #0: 0x00007f348a46b5c0 libc.so.6`__GI___nanosleep(requested_time=0x00007f3489b9fea0,
remaining=0x00007f3489b9fea0) at nanosleep.c:28
  thread #3, name = 'ud2', stop reason = signal SIGSTOP
    frame #0: 0x00007f348a46b5c0 libc.so.6`__GI___nanosleep(requested_time=0x00007f348939eeb0,
remaining=0x0000000000000000) at nanosleep.c:28
  thread #4, name = 'ud2', stop reason = signal SIGSTOP
    frame #0: 0x00007f348a46b5c0 libc.so.6`__GI___nanosleep(requested_time=0x00007f3488b9dea0,
remaining=0x00007f3488b9dea0) at nanosleep.c:28

Executable module set to "/mnt/c/ALD4/ud2/ud2".
Architecture set to: x86_64-pc-linux-gnu.
```

4.   There are 4 threads, and the current one, #1 (numbering starts from 1), is the main thread:

```
(lldb) bt
* thread #1, name = 'ud2', stop reason = signal SIGSTOP
  * frame #0: 0x00007f348a46b5c0 libc.so.6`__GI___nanosleep(requested_time=0x00007ffcc4de39c0,
remaining=0x00007ffcc4de39c0) at nanosleep.c:28
    frame #1: 0x00007f348a46b4ca libc.so.6`__sleep(seconds=0) at sleep.c:55
    frame #2: 0x0000556f1ad3724b ud2`main at ud2.c:43
    frame #3: 0x00007f348a3c909b libc.so.6`__libc_start_main(main=(ud2`main at ud2.c:25),
argc=1, argv=0x00007ffcc4de3af8, init=<unavailable>, fini=<unavailable>,
rtld_fini=<unavailable>, stack_end=0x00007ffcc4de3ae8) at libc-start.c:308
    frame #4: 0x0000556f1ad3710a ud2`_start + 42
```

5.	We can list all threads' backtraces using this command:

```
(lldb) bt all
* thread #1, name = 'ud2', stop reason = signal SIGSTOP
  * frame #0: 0x00007f348a46b5c0 libc.so.6`__GI___nanosleep(requested_time=0x00007ffcc4de39c0,
remaining=0x00007ffcc4de39c0) at nanosleep.c:28
    frame #1: 0x00007f348a46b4ca libc.so.6`__sleep(seconds=0) at sleep.c:55
    frame #2: 0x0000556f1ad3724b ud2`main at ud2.c:43
    frame #3: 0x00007f348a3c909b libc.so.6`__libc_start_main(main=(ud2`main at ud2.c:25),
argc=1, argv=0x00007ffcc4de3af8, init=<unavailable>, fini=<unavailable>,
rtld_fini=<unavailable>, stack_end=0x00007ffcc4de3ae8) at libc-start.c:308
    frame #4: 0x0000556f1ad3710a ud2`_start + 42
  thread #2, name = 'ud2', stop reason = signal SIGSTOP
    frame #0: 0x00007f348a46b5c0 libc.so.6`__GI___nanosleep(requested_time=0x00007f3489b9fea0,
remaining=0x00007f3489b9fea0) at nanosleep.c:28
    frame #1: 0x00007f348a46b4ca libc.so.6`__sleep(seconds=0) at sleep.c:55
    frame #2: 0x0000556f1ad37265 ud2`thread_proc_a(_=0x0000000000000000) at ud2.c:50
    frame #3: 0x00007f348a56cfa3 libpthread.so.0`start_thread(arg=<unavailable>) at
pthread_create.c:486
    frame #4: 0x00007f348a49e06f libc.so.6`__GI___clone at clone.S:95
  thread #3, name = 'ud2', stop reason = signal SIGSTOP
    frame #0: 0x00007f348a46b5c0 libc.so.6`__GI___nanosleep(requested_time=0x00007f348939eeb0,
remaining=0x0000000000000000) at nanosleep.c:28
    frame #1: 0x00007f348a496414 libc.so.6`usleep(useconds=<unavailable>) at usleep.c:32
    frame #2: 0x0000556f1ad37294 ud2`thread_proc_b(_=0x0000000000000000) at ud2.c:59
    frame #3: 0x00007f348a56cfa3 libpthread.so.0`start_thread(arg=<unavailable>) at
pthread_create.c:486
    frame #4: 0x00007f348a49e06f libc.so.6`__GI___clone at clone.S:95
  thread #4, name = 'ud2', stop reason = signal SIGSTOP
    frame #0: 0x00007f348a46b5c0 libc.so.6`__GI___nanosleep(requested_time=0x00007f3488b9dea0,
remaining=0x00007f3488b9dea0) at nanosleep.c:28
    frame #1: 0x00007f348a46b4ca libc.so.6`__sleep(seconds=0) at sleep.c:55
    frame #2: 0x0000556f1ad372df ud2`thread_proc_c(_=0x0000000000000000) at ud2.c:73
    frame #3: 0x00007f348a56cfa3 libpthread.so.0`start_thread(arg=<unavailable>) at
pthread_create.c:486
    frame #4: 0x00007f348a49e06f libc.so.6`__GI___clone at clone.S:95
```

6.	The following command lists currently loaded shared libraries:

```
(lldb) image list
[  0] 48E933E9-5D0A-597B-0CA7-5CFE3638514F-ABE17CF1                /mnt/c/ALD4/ud2/ud2
[  1] 6F3490CE-A127-50C7-4A4F-D33AC3B6CAAA-2ACE115B 0x00007ffcc4df5000 [vdso]
(0x00007ffcc4df5000)
[  2] E0A26233-ADBE-AA08-DE07-D76DBAACD9C3-FF5B18F9                /lib/x86_64-linux-
gnu/libdl.so.2
      /usr/lib/debug/.build-id/e0/a26233adbeaa08de07d76dbaacd9c3ff5b18f9.debug
[  3] 48041452-AEF9-3DDB-2366-CA0FA49DA8F3-2684A9C8                /lib/x86_64-linux-
gnu/libpthread.so.0
      /usr/lib/debug/.build-id/48/041452aef93ddb2366ca0fa49da8f32684a9c8.debug
[  4] C7AA9A1E-121F-E239-5F38-40F3F0213146-046D9FE3                /lib/x86_64-linux-
gnu/libc.so.6
      /usr/lib/debug/.build-id/c7/aa9a1e121fe2395f3840f3f0213146046d9fe3.debug
[  5] 83743DDD-4258-A7D1-38A2-8C4F2032D17A-D92A15B5                /lib64/ld-linux-x86-
64.so.2
      /usr/lib/debug/.build-id/83/743ddd4258a7d138a28c4f2032d17ad92a15b5.debug
```

7.   Since we suspect a process heap memory leak, let's put a breakpoint on the *malloc* function (usually, even if we use *new* in C++, allocations go through that function) and inspect a backtrace when the breakpoint is hit:

```
(lldb) breakpoint set --name malloc
Breakpoint 1: 2 locations.
```

```
(lldb) breakpoint list
Current breakpoints:
1: name = 'malloc', locations = 2, resolved = 2, hit count = 0
  1.1: where = libc.so.6`__GI___libc_malloc at malloc.c:3031, address = 0x00007f348a429510,
resolved, hit count = 0
  1.2: where = ld-linux-x86-64.so.2`malloc at dl-minimal.c:50, address = 0x00007f348a5b0da0,
resolved, hit count = 0
```

```
(lldb) c
Process 13106 resuming
Process 13106 stopped
* thread #3, name = 'ud2', stop reason = breakpoint 1.1
    frame #0: 0x00007f348a429510 libc.so.6`__GI___libc_malloc(bytes=17740) at malloc.c:3031
```

```
(lldb) bt
* thread #3, name = 'ud2', stop reason = breakpoint 1.1
  * frame #0: 0x00007f348a429510 libc.so.6`__GI___libc_malloc(bytes=17740) at malloc.c:3031
    frame #1: 0x0000556f1ad37283 ud2`thread_proc_b(_=0x0000000000000000) at ud2.c:58
    frame #2: 0x00007f348a56cfa3 libpthread.so.0`start_thread(arg=<unavailable>) at
pthread_create.c:486
    frame #3: 0x00007f348a49e06f libc.so.6`__GI___clone at clone.S:95
```

8.   Let's now switch to the appropriate frame that calls *malloc*:

```
(lldb) frame select 1
frame #1: 0x0000556f1ad37283 ud2`thread_proc_b(_=0x0000000000000000) at ud2.c:58
   55   {
   56           while (1)
   57           {
-> 58                   alloc_manager.alloc_data = (uint8_t *)malloc(alloc_manager.alloc_size);
   59                   usleep(100000); // do some work
   60                   if (!alloc_manager.keep)
   61                   {
```

9.   Let's examine our source code fragments related to using *malloc* and *free*:

```
typedef struct
{
        uint32_t alloc_size;
        uint8_t keep;
        uint8_t *alloc_data;
} ALLOCMGR;

ALLOCMGR alloc_manager;

void start_modeling (void)
{
        alloc_manager.alloc_size = 64;
        alloc_manager.keep = 0;
...
}
```

```
void *thread_proc_b (void *_)
{
        while (1)
        {
                alloc_manager.alloc_data = (uint8_t *)malloc(alloc_manager.alloc_size);
                usleep(100000);      // do some work
                if (!alloc_manager.keep)
                {
                        free(alloc_manager.alloc_data);
                }
        }

        return 0;
}
```

According to the source code, every allocation should be freed after some work.

10.   Let's now examine the *alloc_manager* structure:

```
(lldb) p alloc_manager
(ALLOCMGR) $0 = (alloc_size = 17740, keep = 'A', alloc_data = <no value available>)

(lldb) x/4w &alloc_manager
0x556f1ad3a090: 0x0000454c 0x00004b41 0x852b3970 0x00007f34

(lldb) x/16b &alloc_manager
0x556f1ad3a090: LE\0\0AK\0\0p9+\x854\x7f\0\0
```

Note: We see the corruption effect: *alloc_size* is no longer 64 (0x40), *keep* is no longer 0, and the latter prevents *free* according to the source code.

11.   To catch the moment of corruption, we need to restart debugging the process and put a hardware memory write breakpoint (we also remove our *malloc* breakpoint after the first hit):

```
(lldb) r
There is a running process, detach from it and restart?: [Y/n] Y
Process 13106 detached
1 location added to breakpoint 1
Process 13320 launched: '/mnt/c/ALD4/ud2/ud2' (x86_64)
Process 13320 stopped
* thread #1, name = 'ud2', stop reason = breakpoint 1.1
    frame #0: 0x00007ffff7e60510 libc.so.6`__GI___libc_malloc(bytes=32) at malloc.c:3031

(lldb) p &alloc_manager
error: libdl.so.2 0xffffffff000148c7: adding range [0x1558-0x155a) which has a base that is
less than the function's low PC 0x1930. Please file a bug and attach the file at the start of
this error message
error: libdl.so.2 0xffffffff000148c7: adding range [0x155e-0x1571) which has a base that is
less than the function's low PC 0x1950. Please file a bug and attach the file at the start of
this error message
(ALLOCMGR *) $4 = 0x0000555555558090

(lldb) watchpoint set expression -- 0x0000555555558090
Watchpoint created: Watchpoint 1: addr = 0x555555558090 size = 8 state = enabled type = w
    new value: 0
```

```
(lldb) breakpoint list
Current breakpoints:
1: name = 'malloc', locations = 3, resolved = 1, hit count = 2
  1.1: where = libc.so.6`__GI___libc_malloc at malloc.c:3031, address = 0x00007ffff7e60510,
resolved, hit count = 2
  1.2: where = ld-linux-x86-64.so.2`malloc at dl-minimal.c:50, address = ld-linux-x86-
64.so.2[0x0000000000018da0], unresolved, hit count = 0
  1.3: where = ld-2.28.so`malloc at dl-minimal.c:50, address = 0x00007ffff7fedda0, unresolved,
hit count = 0

(lldb) break delete 1
1 breakpoints deleted; 0 breakpoint locations disabled.

(lldb) breakpoint list
No breakpoints currently set.
```

12.   Now we resume execution:

```
(lldb) c
Process 13320 resuming

Watchpoint 1 hit:
old value: 0
new value: 64
Process 13320 stopped
* thread #1, name = 'ud2', stop reason = watchpoint 1
    frame #0: 0x00005555555552f3 ud2`start_modeling at ud2.c:80
   77   void start_modeling (void)
   78   {
   79           alloc_manager.alloc_size = 64;
-> 80           alloc_manager.keep = 0;
   81
   82           pthread_t thread;
   83         if (pthread_create(&thread, NULL, thread_proc_a, NULL))
```

Note: the first hit is normal as it is related to structure initialization.

```
(lldb) c
Process 13320 resuming

Watchpoint 1 hit:
old value: 64
new value: 17740

Watchpoint 1 hit:
old value: 17740
new value: 17740
Process 13320 stopped
* thread #1, name = 'ud2', stop reason = watchpoint 1
    frame #0: 0x00005555555552fa ud2`start_modeling at ud2.c:83
   80           alloc_manager.keep = 0;
   81
   82           pthread_t thread;
-> 83         if (pthread_create(&thread, NULL, thread_proc_a, NULL))
   84         {
   85           exit(1);
   86         }
  thread #2, name = 'ud2', stop reason = watchpoint 1
```

```
    frame #0: 0x00007ffff7f3850e libc.so.6`__memmove_avx_unaligned_erms at memmove-vec-
unaligned-erms.S:329

(lldb) bt all
* thread #1, name = 'ud2', stop reason = watchpoint 1
  * frame #0: 0x00005555555552fa ud2`start_modeling at ud2.c:83
    frame #1: 0x0000555555555241 ud2`main at ud2.c:41
    frame #2: 0x00007ffff7e0009b libc.so.6`__libc_start_main(main=(ud2`main at ud2.c:25),
argc=1, argv=0x00007fffffffe4e8, init=<unavailable>, fini=<unavailable>,
rtld_fini=<unavailable>, stack_end=0x00007fffffffe4d8) at libc-start.c:308
    frame #3: 0x000055555555510a ud2`_start + 42
  thread #2, name = 'ud2'
    frame #0: 0x00007ffff7ea25c0 libc.so.6`__GI___nanosleep(requested_time=0x00007ffff7dd7ea0,
remaining=0x00007ffff7dd7ea0) at nanosleep.c:28
    frame #1: 0x00007ffff7ea24ca libc.so.6`__sleep(seconds=0) at sleep.c:55
    frame #2: 0x00007ffff7fcb15b liblib.so`thread_proc_d + 22
    frame #3: 0x00007ffff7fa3fa3 libpthread.so.0`start_thread(arg=<unavailable>) at
pthread_create.c:486
    frame #4: 0x00007ffff7ed506f libc.so.6`__GI___clone at clone.S:95
```

Note: We see *liblib.so* is present in parallel while corruption is going on and check its *thread_proc_d*. Sometimes, results are unreliable, and we need to repeat restart/watchpoint again (don't forget to add the initial breakpoint). In such a case, we may be able to get a good backtrace at the moment of corruption, for example:

```
(lldb) c
Process 22317 resuming

Watchpoint 1 hit:
old value: 64
new value: 17740
Process 22317 stopped
* thread #2, name = 'ud2', stop reason = watchpoint 1
    frame #0: 0x00007ffff7f3850e libc.so.6`__memmove_avx_unaligned_erms at memmove-vec-
unaligned-erms.S:329

(lldb) bt
* thread #2, name = 'ud2', stop reason = watchpoint 1
  * frame #0: 0x00007ffff7f3850e libc.so.6`__memmove_avx_unaligned_erms at memmove-vec-
unaligned-erms.S:329
    frame #1: 0x00007ffff7fcb179 liblib.so`thread_proc_d + 52
    frame #2: 0x00007ffff7fa3fa3 libpthread.so.0`start_thread(arg=<unavailable>) at
pthread_create.c:486
    frame #3: 0x00007ffff7ed506f libc.so.6`__GI___clone at clone.S:95
```

13.   We can even modify the structure contents to eliminate the leak:

```
(lldb) c
Process 13320 resuming
^C
Process 13320 stopped
* thread #1, name = 'ud2', stop reason = signal SIGSTOP
    frame #0: 0x00007ffff7ea25c0 libc.so.6`__GI___nanosleep(requested_time=0x00007fffffffe3b0,
remaining=0x00007fffffffe3b0) at nanosleep.c:28

(lldb) memory write &alloc_manager.alloc_size 0x40

(lldb) memory write &alloc_manager.keep 0
```

129

```
(lldb) p alloc_manager
(ALLOCMGR) $15 = (alloc_size = 64, keep = '\0', alloc_data = <no value available>)
```

Note: If we continue execution, we won't see any leaks anymore. Sometimes, a memory write may be only partial. We quit our debugging session.

```
(lldb) c
Process 13320 resuming
^C
Process 13320 stopped
* thread #1, name = 'ud2', stop reason = signal SIGSTOP
    frame #0: 0x00007ffff7ea25c0 libc.so.6`__GI___nanosleep(requested_time=0x00007fffffffe3b0,
remaining=0x00007fffffffe3b0) at nanosleep.c:28

(lldb) q
Quitting LLDB will kill one or more processes. Do you really want to proceed: [Y/n] Y
```

Note: We also kill any residue processes.

```
/mnt/c/ALD4/ud2$ ps
  PID TTY          TIME CMD
13106 pts/0    00:00:00 ud2
13496 pts/0    00:00:00 ps
23427 pts/0    00:00:00 bash

/mnt/c/ALD4/ud2$ kill 13106
[1]+  Terminated              ./ud2
```

Data Breakpoints

GDB Commands

```
watch *<address>
info break
delete break <number>
```

LLDB Commands

```
watch set expression -- <address>
watch list
watch delete <number>
```

Exercise UD3

- **Goal:** Learn how to navigate parameters, static and local variables, and data structures

- **Elementary Diagnostics Patterns:** Crash

- **Memory Analysis Patterns:** Exception Stack Trace; Stack Overflow (User Mode); String Parameter; Module Variable

- **Debugging Implementation Patterns:** Break-in; Scope; Variable Value; Type Structure

- \ALD4\Exercise-Linux-UD3.pdf

Exercise UD3 (WinDbg)

Goal: Learn how to navigate parameters, static and local variables, and data structures.

Elementary Diagnostics Patterns: Crash.

Memory Analysis Patterns: Exception Stack Trace; Stack Overflow (User Mode); String Parameter; Module Variable.

Debugging Implementation Patterns: Break-in; Scope; Variable Value; Type Structure.

1.   The source code and the *Makefile* to build executables and libraries can be found in the *ud3* directory:

```
$ git clone https://bitbucket.org/softwarediagnostics/ald4
```

2.   Launch the *ud3* executable under the *gdbserver*:

```
/mnt/c/ALD4/ud3$ gdbserver localhost:1234 ud3
Process /mnt/c/ALD4/ud3/ud3 created; pid = 31148
Listening on port 1234
```

3.   Connect WinDbg to the remote debugger:

```
Microsoft (R) Windows Debugger Version 10.0.27553.1004 AMD64
Copyright (c) Microsoft Corporation. All rights reserved.

64-bit machine not using 64-bit API

************* Path validation summary **************
Response                    Time (ms)      Location
Deferred                                   srv*
Symbol search path is: srv*
Executable search path is:
Unknown System Version 0 UP Free x64
System Uptime: not available
Process Uptime: not available
Reloading current modules
ModLoad: 00005555`55554000 00005555`5555d438   /mnt/c/ALD4/ud3/ud3
.
ReadVirtual() failed in GetXStateConfiguration() first read attempt (error == 0.)
00007fff`f7fd6090 mov     rdi,rsp
```

4.   Open a log file (useful when the output doesn't fit into the buffer and we need to search for something):

```
0:000> .logopen C:\ALD4\ud3.log
Opened log file 'C:\ALD4\ud3.log'
```

5.   If we continue execution using the **g** command, we get a segmentation fault:

```
0:000> g
ModLoad: 00007fff`f7fd3000 00007fff`f7fd3000   linux-vdso.so.1
ModLoad: 00007fff`f7e3e000 00007fff`f7fc1020   /usr/lib/x86_64-linux-gnu/libstdc++.so.6
ModLoad: 00007fff`f7cbb000 00007fff`f7e3d148   /lib/x86_64-linux-gnu/libm.so.6
ModLoad: 00007fff`f7ca1000 00007fff`f7cba430   /lib/x86_64-linux-gnu/libgcc_s.so.1
ModLoad: 00007fff`f7ae1000 00007fff`f7ca0800   /lib/x86_64-linux-gnu/libc.so.6
```

```
ModLoad: 00007fff`f7fd5000 00007fff`f7ffe190   /lib64/ld-linux-x86-64.so.2
(79ac.79ac): Signal SIGSEGV (Segmentation fault) code SEGV_MAPERR (Address not mapped to
object) at 0x555555555aa9 originating from PID 79ac
First chance exceptions are reported before any exception handling.
This exception may be expected and handled.
Unable to load image /mnt/c/ALD4/ud3/ud3, Win32 error 0n2
*** WARNING: Unable to verify timestamp for /mnt/c/ALD4/ud3/ud3
ud3!bar+0xb:
00005555`55555aa9 mov      dword ptr [rbp-404h],edi ss:00007fff`ff7fefcc=????????
```

Note: From the disassembly and source code, it looks like the problem happened before the memory copy when saving parameters:

```
0:000> uf ud3!bar
ud3!bar [/mnt/c/ALD4/ud3/ud3.cpp @ 171]:
  171 00005555`55555a9e push     rbp
  171 00005555`55555a9f mov      rbp,rsp
  171 00005555`55555aa2 sub      rsp,410h
  171 00005555`55555aa9 mov      dword ptr [rbp-404h],edi
  171 00005555`55555aaf mov      qword ptr [rbp-410h],rsi
  172 00005555`55555ab6 mov      rax,6863206C61636F4Ch
  172 00005555`55555ac0 mov      rdx,2072657463617261h
  172 00005555`55555aca mov      qword ptr [rbp-400h],rax
  172 00005555`55555ad1 mov      qword ptr [rbp-3F8h],rdx
  172 00005555`55555ad8 mov      rax,7961727261h
  172 00005555`55555ae2 mov      edx,0
  172 00005555`55555ae7 mov      qword ptr [rbp-3F0h],rax
  172 00005555`55555aee mov      qword ptr [rbp-3E8h],rdx
  172 00005555`55555af5 lea      rdx,[rbp-3E0h]
  172 00005555`55555afc mov      eax,0
  172 00005555`55555b01 mov      ecx,7Ch
  172 00005555`55555b06 mov      rdi,rdx
  172 00005555`55555b09 rep stos qword ptr [rdi]
  174 00005555`55555b0c cmp      dword ptr [rbp-404h],0
  174 00005555`55555b13 je       ud3!bar+0x95 (00005555`55555b33)   Branch

ud3!bar+0x77 [/mnt/c/ALD4/ud3/ud3.cpp @ 175]:
  175 00005555`55555b15 add      dword ptr [rbp-404h],1
  175 00005555`55555b1c mov      rdx,qword ptr [rbp-410h]
  175 00005555`55555b23 mov      eax,dword ptr [rbp-404h]
  175 00005555`55555b29 mov      rsi,rdx
  175 00005555`55555b2c mov      edi,eax
  175 00005555`55555b2e call     ud3!bar (00005555`55555a9e)

ud3!bar+0x95 [/mnt/c/ALD4/ud3/ud3.cpp @ 176]:
  176 00005555`55555b33 nop
  176 00005555`55555b34 leave
  176 00005555`55555b35 ret
```

```
void bar(int param1, const char *param2)
{
        char local[1024] = "Local character array";

        if (param1)
                bar(++param1, param2);
}
```

6.   If we try to see a stack trace, we get only 4,096 frames for this stack overflow:

```
0:000> k
 # Child-SP          RetAddr               Call Site
00 00007fff`ff7fefc0 00005555`55555b33   ud3!bar+0xb [/mnt/c/ALD4/ud3/ud3.cpp @ 171]
01 00007fff`ff7ff3e0 00005555`55555b33   ud3!bar+0x95 [/mnt/c/ALD4/ud3/ud3.cpp @ 176]
02 00007fff`ff7ff800 00005555`55555b33   ud3!bar+0x95 [/mnt/c/ALD4/ud3/ud3.cpp @ 176]
03 00007fff`ff7ffc20 00005555`55555b33   ud3!bar+0x95 [/mnt/c/ALD4/ud3/ud3.cpp @ 176]
04 00007fff`ff800040 00005555`55555b33   ud3!bar+0x95 [/mnt/c/ALD4/ud3/ud3.cpp @ 176]
05 00007fff`ff800460 00005555`55555b33   ud3!bar+0x95 [/mnt/c/ALD4/ud3/ud3.cpp @ 176]
06 00007fff`ff800880 00005555`55555b33   ud3!bar+0x95 [/mnt/c/ALD4/ud3/ud3.cpp @ 176]
07 00007fff`ff800ca0 00005555`55555b33   ud3!bar+0x95 [/mnt/c/ALD4/ud3/ud3.cpp @ 176]
08 00007fff`ff8010c0 00005555`55555b33   ud3!bar+0x95 [/mnt/c/ALD4/ud3/ud3.cpp @ 176]
09 00007fff`ff8014e0 00005555`55555b33   ud3!bar+0x95 [/mnt/c/ALD4/ud3/ud3.cpp @ 176]
0a 00007fff`ff801900 00005555`55555b33   ud3!bar+0x95 [/mnt/c/ALD4/ud3/ud3.cpp @ 176]
0b 00007fff`ff801d20 00005555`55555b33   ud3!bar+0x95 [/mnt/c/ALD4/ud3/ud3.cpp @ 176]
0c 00007fff`ff802140 00005555`55555b33   ud3!bar+0x95 [/mnt/c/ALD4/ud3/ud3.cpp @ 176]
0d 00007fff`ff802560 00005555`55555b33   ud3!bar+0x95 [/mnt/c/ALD4/ud3/ud3.cpp @ 176]
0e 00007fff`ff802980 00005555`55555b33   ud3!bar+0x95 [/mnt/c/ALD4/ud3/ud3.cpp @ 176]
0f 00007fff`ff802da0 00005555`55555b33   ud3!bar+0x95 [/mnt/c/ALD4/ud3/ud3.cpp @ 176]
10 00007fff`ff8031c0 00005555`55555b33   ud3!bar+0x95 [/mnt/c/ALD4/ud3/ud3.cpp @ 176]
[...]
fee 00007fff`ffc1a580 00005555`55555b33   ud3!bar+0x95 [/mnt/c/ALD4/ud3/ud3.cpp @ 176]
fef 00007fff`ffc1a9a0 00005555`55555b33   ud3!bar+0x95 [/mnt/c/ALD4/ud3/ud3.cpp @ 176]
ff0 00007fff`ffc1adc0 00005555`55555b33   ud3!bar+0x95 [/mnt/c/ALD4/ud3/ud3.cpp @ 176]
ff1 00007fff`ffc1b1e0 00005555`55555b33   ud3!bar+0x95 [/mnt/c/ALD4/ud3/ud3.cpp @ 176]
ff2 00007fff`ffc1b600 00005555`55555b33   ud3!bar+0x95 [/mnt/c/ALD4/ud3/ud3.cpp @ 176]
ff3 00007fff`ffc1ba20 00005555`55555b33   ud3!bar+0x95 [/mnt/c/ALD4/ud3/ud3.cpp @ 176]
ff4 00007fff`ffc1be40 00005555`55555b33   ud3!bar+0x95 [/mnt/c/ALD4/ud3/ud3.cpp @ 176]
ff5 00007fff`ffc1c260 00005555`55555b33   ud3!bar+0x95 [/mnt/c/ALD4/ud3/ud3.cpp @ 176]
ff6 00007fff`ffc1c680 00005555`55555b33   ud3!bar+0x95 [/mnt/c/ALD4/ud3/ud3.cpp @ 176]
ff7 00007fff`ffc1caa0 00005555`55555b33   ud3!bar+0x95 [/mnt/c/ALD4/ud3/ud3.cpp @ 176]
ff8 00007fff`ffc1cec0 00005555`55555b33   ud3!bar+0x95 [/mnt/c/ALD4/ud3/ud3.cpp @ 176]
ff9 00007fff`ffc1d2e0 00005555`55555b33   ud3!bar+0x95 [/mnt/c/ALD4/ud3/ud3.cpp @ 176]
ffa 00007fff`ffc1d700 00005555`55555b33   ud3!bar+0x95 [/mnt/c/ALD4/ud3/ud3.cpp @ 176]
ffb 00007fff`ffc1db20 00005555`55555b33   ud3!bar+0x95 [/mnt/c/ALD4/ud3/ud3.cpp @ 176]
ffc 00007fff`ffc1df40 00005555`55555b33   ud3!bar+0x95 [/mnt/c/ALD4/ud3/ud3.cpp @ 176]
ffd 00007fff`ffc1e360 00005555`55555b33   ud3!bar+0x95 [/mnt/c/ALD4/ud3/ud3.cpp @ 176]
ffe 00007fff`ffc1e780 00005555`55555b33   ud3!bar+0x95 [/mnt/c/ALD4/ud3/ud3.cpp @ 176]
```

7.   Let's increase the number of shown frames:

```
0:000> .kframes 0xffff
Default stack trace depth is 0n65535 frames

0:000> k
 # Child-SP          RetAddr               Call Site
00 00007fff`ff7fefc0 00005555`55555b33   ud3!bar+0xb [/mnt/c/ALD4/ud3/ud3.cpp @ 171]
01 00007fff`ff7ff3e0 00005555`55555b33   ud3!bar+0x95 [/mnt/c/ALD4/ud3/ud3.cpp @ 176]
02 00007fff`ff7ff800 00005555`55555b33   ud3!bar+0x95 [/mnt/c/ALD4/ud3/ud3.cpp @ 176]
03 00007fff`ff7ffc20 00005555`55555b33   ud3!bar+0x95 [/mnt/c/ALD4/ud3/ud3.cpp @ 176]
04 00007fff`ff800040 00005555`55555b33   ud3!bar+0x95 [/mnt/c/ALD4/ud3/ud3.cpp @ 176]
05 00007fff`ff800460 00005555`55555b33   ud3!bar+0x95 [/mnt/c/ALD4/ud3/ud3.cpp @ 176]
06 00007fff`ff800880 00005555`55555b33   ud3!bar+0x95 [/mnt/c/ALD4/ud3/ud3.cpp @ 176]
07 00007fff`ff800ca0 00005555`55555b33   ud3!bar+0x95 [/mnt/c/ALD4/ud3/ud3.cpp @ 176]
08 00007fff`ff8010c0 00005555`55555b33   ud3!bar+0x95 [/mnt/c/ALD4/ud3/ud3.cpp @ 176]
09 00007fff`ff8014e0 00005555`55555b33   ud3!bar+0x95 [/mnt/c/ALD4/ud3/ud3.cpp @ 176]
0a 00007fff`ff801900 00005555`55555b33   ud3!bar+0x95 [/mnt/c/ALD4/ud3/ud3.cpp @ 176]
```

```
0b 00007fff`ff801d20 00005555`55555b33    ud3!bar+0x95 [/mnt/c/ALD4/ud3/ud3.cpp @ 176]
0c 00007fff`ff802140 00005555`55555b33    ud3!bar+0x95 [/mnt/c/ALD4/ud3/ud3.cpp @ 176]
0d 00007fff`ff802560 00005555`55555b33    ud3!bar+0x95 [/mnt/c/ALD4/ud3/ud3.cpp @ 176]
0e 00007fff`ff802980 00005555`55555b33    ud3!bar+0x95 [/mnt/c/ALD4/ud3/ud3.cpp @ 176]
0f 00007fff`ff802da0 00005555`55555b33    ud3!bar+0x95 [/mnt/c/ALD4/ud3/ud3.cpp @ 176]
10 00007fff`ff8031c0 00005555`55555b33    ud3!bar+0x95 [/mnt/c/ALD4/ud3/ud3.cpp @ 176]
[...]
1ef8 00007fff`ffffaec0 00005555`55555b33    ud3!bar+0x95 [/mnt/c/ALD4/ud3/ud3.cpp @ 176]
1ef9 00007fff`ffffb2e0 00005555`55555b33    ud3!bar+0x95 [/mnt/c/ALD4/ud3/ud3.cpp @ 176]
1efa 00007fff`ffffb700 00005555`55555b33    ud3!bar+0x95 [/mnt/c/ALD4/ud3/ud3.cpp @ 176]
1efb 00007fff`ffffbb20 00005555`55555b33    ud3!bar+0x95 [/mnt/c/ALD4/ud3/ud3.cpp @ 176]
1efc 00007fff`ffffbf40 00005555`55555b33    ud3!bar+0x95 [/mnt/c/ALD4/ud3/ud3.cpp @ 176]
1efd 00007fff`ffffc360 00005555`55555b33    ud3!bar+0x95 [/mnt/c/ALD4/ud3/ud3.cpp @ 176]
1efe 00007fff`ffffc780 00005555`55555b33    ud3!bar+0x95 [/mnt/c/ALD4/ud3/ud3.cpp @ 176]
1eff 00007fff`ffffcba0 00005555`55555b33    ud3!bar+0x95 [/mnt/c/ALD4/ud3/ud3.cpp @ 176]
1f00 00007fff`ffffcfc0 00005555`55555b33    ud3!bar+0x95 [/mnt/c/ALD4/ud3/ud3.cpp @ 176]
1f01 00007fff`ffffd3e0 00005555`55555b33    ud3!bar+0x95 [/mnt/c/ALD4/ud3/ud3.cpp @ 176]
1f02 00007fff`ffffd800 00005555`55555b33    ud3!bar+0x95 [/mnt/c/ALD4/ud3/ud3.cpp @ 176]
1f03 00007fff`ffffdc20 00005555`55555a9b    ud3!bar+0x95 [/mnt/c/ALD4/ud3/ud3.cpp @ 176]
1f04 00007fff`ffffe040 00005555`555559ce    ud3!foo+0x4f [/mnt/c/ALD4/ud3/ud3.cpp @ 168]
1f05 00007fff`ffffe090 00005555`555552ae    ud3!start_modeling+0xfc [/mnt/c/ALD4/ud3/ud3.cpp @
154]
1f06 00007fff`ffffe3f0 00007fff`f7b0509b    ud3!main+0x9 [/mnt/c/ALD4/ud3/ud3.cpp @ 20]
1f07 00007fff`ffffe400 00005555`555551ea    libc_so!__libc_start_main+0xeb
1f08 00007fff`ffffe4c0 ffffffff`ffffffff    ud3!start+0x2a
1f09 00007fff`ffffe4c8 00000000`00000000    0xffffffff`ffffffff
```

8.   Since our goal is data navigation, we switch into each frame one by one and inspect data there. Let's start with frame **1f03**:

```
0:000> .frame 1f03
1f03 00007fff`ffffdc20 00005555`55555a9b    ud3!bar+0x95 [/mnt/c/ALD4/ud3/ud3.cpp @ 176]
```

```
0:000> dv /i /V
prv param   00007fff`ffffdc2c @rbp-0x0404        param1 = 0n2
prv param   00007fff`ffffdc20 @rbp-0x0410        param2 = 0x00005555`55559019 "Hello World!"
prv local   00007fff`ffffdc30 @rbp-0x0400         local = char [1024] "--- memory read error at
address 0x00007fff`ffffdc30 ---"
```

Notice the large offsets. This is because of the large local array, and its space was allocated on stack by the **sub** instruction. Also, despite parameters being passed by **edi** and **rsi** registers (the first was passed by 32-bit **edi** and not by 64-bit **rdi** because it is a 32-bit **int** parameter), they were saved on the stack, and this is why we are able to get them:

```
0:000> uf ud3!bar
ud3!bar [/mnt/c/ALD4/ud3/ud3.cpp @ 171]:
  171 00005555`55555a9e push    rbp
  171 00005555`55555a9f mov     rbp,rsp
  171 00005555`55555aa2 sub     rsp,410h
[...]
```

Note: If everything is very slow then reduce the number of frames by 10, rebuild the app and repeat from the beginning. The number of frames can be reduced by making the local variable larger, for example:

```
void bar(int param1, const char *param2)
{
        char local[10*1024] = "Local character array";

        if (param1)
                bar(++param1, param2);
}
```

9.   Let's look at two variables:

```
prv param   00007fff`ffffdc2c @rbp-0x0404            param1 = 0n2
prv param   00007fff`ffffdc20 @rbp-0x0410            param2 = 0x00005555`55559019 "Hello World!"
```

Green numbers are the stack region addresses where they are located. The first one is an integer and can be directly inspected by the simple data dumping command **dd**:

```
0:000> dd param1 L1
00007fff`ffffdc2c  00000002

0:000> dd 000000ee`68cff640 L1
00007fff`ffffdc2c  00000002
```

10.   For **param2**, the stack region contains pointer values. We can use a character dumping command for ASCII strings (**da**):

```
0:000> dq param2 L1
00007fff`ffffdc20  00005555`55559019

0:000> dc 00005555`55559019
00005555`55559019  6c6c6548 6f57206f 21646c72 656e6f00  Hello World!.one
00005555`55559029  6f777400 72687400 6d006565 74732079  .two.three.my st
00005555`55559039  676e6972 63657600 3a726f74 5f4d5f3a  ring.vector::_M_
00005555`55559049  6c616572 5f636f6c 65736e69 9a007472  realloc_insert..
00005555`55559059  99999999 9a3ff199 99999999 66400199  ......?.......@f
00005555`55559069  66666666 31400a66 5f796d33 63627573  fffff.@13my_subc
00005555`55559079  7373616c 3100745f 5f796d30 73616c63  lass_t.10my_clas
00005555`55559089  00745f73 01000000 b43b031b d5000006  s_t.......;.....

0:000> da 00005555`55559019
00005555`55559019  "Hello World!"
```

Note: Here, we can also use dumping commands for pointers, such as **dpa**:

```
0:000> dpa param2 L1
00007fff`ffffdc20  00005555`55559019 "Hello World!"
```

Note: We can also use a C++ evaluation operator **??** and **dx** command. The latter displays a C++ expression using the NatVis extension model:

```
0:000> ?? param1
int 0n2

0:000> ?? param2
char * 0x00005555`55559019
 "Hello World!"
```

```
0:000> ?? local
char [1024] 0x00007fff`ffffdc30
0x4c 'L'
```

```
0:000> dx param1
param1            : 2 [Type: int]
```

```
0:000> dx param2
param2                : 0x555555559019 : "Hello World!" [Type: char *]
    72 'H' [Type: char]
```

```
0:000> dx local
local                : "Local character array" [Type: char [1024]]
```

11.   Let's now move to the next frame **1f04**:

```
0:000> .frame 1f04
1f04 00007fff`ffffe040 00005555`555559ce    ud3!foo+0x4f [/mnt/c/ALD4/ud3/ud3.cpp @ 168]
```

The associated source code:

```
void foo(my_struct_t& ref_struct, my_struct_t *p_struct, const my_class_t& ref_class,
my_class_t *p_class, my_subclass_t& ref_subclass, my_subclass_t *p_subclass)
{
        const char *str = p_class->get_data().p_string;

        bar(1, str);
}
```

```
0:000> dv /i /V
prv param   00007fff`ffffe068 @rbp-0x0018         ref_struct = 0x00007fff`ffffe0c0
prv param   00007fff`ffffe060 @rbp-0x0020           p_struct = 0x00005555`5556fe70
prv param   00007fff`ffffe058 @rbp-0x0028          ref_class = 0x00007fff`ffffe0b0
prv param   00007fff`ffffe050 @rbp-0x0030            p_class = 0x00005555`55573ad0
prv param   00007fff`ffffe048 @rbp-0x0038       ref_subclass = 0x00007fff`ffffe090
prv param   00007fff`ffffe040 @rbp-0x0040         p_subclass = 0x00005555`55573ca0
prv local   00007fff`ffffe078 @rbp-0x0008                str = 0x00005555`55559019 "Hello
World!"
```

Note: We are interested in 6 parameters, either references or pointers to structures and C++ classes. Remember that in C++, structures are the same as classes regarding their data layout. Also, even if a variable is passed as a reference, it is internally passed as a pointer:

```
0:000> ?? ref_struct
my_struct_t * 0x00007fff`ffffe0c0
   +0x000 p_string         : 0x00005555`55559019  "Hello World!"
   +0x008 uarray           : [10] 0
   +0x030 p_uarray         : [10] 0x00005555`55571370  -> 0
   +0x080 pp_uarray        : [10] 0x00005555`555716c0  -> 0x00005555`55571720  -> 0
   +0x0d0 uarray2          : [10] [10] 0
   +0x260 p_substruct      : 0x00007fff`ffffe328 my_substruct
   +0x268 substruct        : my_substruct
   +0x2e8 p_list           : 0x00005555`55571660 my_dlist
```

```
0:000> dx ref_struct
ref_struct                      [Type: my_struct_t]
    [+0x000] p_string            : 0x555555559019 : "Hello World!" [Type: char *]
    [+0x008] uarray             [Type: uint32_t [10]]
    [+0x030] p_uarray           [Type: uint32_t * [10]]
    [+0x080] pp_uarray          [Type: uint32_t * * [10]]
    [+0x0d0] uarray2            [Type: uint32_t [10][10]]
    [+0x260] p_substruct         : 0x7fffffffe328 [Type: my_substruct_t *]
    [+0x268] substruct          [Type: my_substruct_t]
    [+0x2e8] p_list              : 0x555555571660 [Type: p_my_dlist_t]

0:000> ?? p_struct
my_struct_t * 0x00005555`5556fe70
    +0x000 p_string            : 0x00005555`55559019  "Hello World!"
    +0x008 uarray              : [10] 0
    +0x030 p_uarray            : [10] 0x00005555`55572720  -> 0
    +0x080 pp_uarray           : [10] 0x00005555`55572a70  -> 0x00005555`55572ad0  -> 0
    +0x0d0 uarray2             : [10] [10] 0
    +0x260 p_substruct         : 0x00005555`555700d8 my_substruct
    +0x268 substruct           : my_substruct
    +0x2e8 p_list              : 0x00005555`55572a10 my_dlist

0:000> dx p_struct
p_struct                        : 0x55555556fe70 [Type: my_struct_t *]
    [+0x000] p_string            : 0x555555559019 : "Hello World!" [Type: char *]
    [+0x008] uarray             [Type: uint32_t [10]]
    [+0x030] p_uarray           [Type: uint32_t * [10]]
    [+0x080] pp_uarray          [Type: uint32_t * * [10]]
    [+0x0d0] uarray2            [Type: uint32_t [10][10]]
    [+0x260] p_substruct         : 0x5555555700d8 [Type: my_substruct_t *]
    [+0x268] substruct          [Type: my_substruct_t]
    [+0x2e8] p_list              : 0x555555572a10 [Type: p_my_dlist_t]
```

The associated source code:

```
typedef struct
{
        const char *p_string;
        uint32_t uarray[10];
        uint32_t *p_uarray[10];
        uint32_t **pp_uarray[10];
        uint32_t uarray2[10][10];
        my_substruct_t *p_substruct;
        my_substruct_t substruct;
        p_my_dlist_t p_list;
} my_struct_t;
```

```
0:000> ?? ref_class
my_class_t * 0x00007fff`ffffe0b0
    +0x000 _vptr.my_class_t : 0x00005555`5555cd88  -> 0x00005555`55555cee       int
ud3!my_class_t::~my_class_t+0
    +0x008 ref_my_struct      : 0x00007fff`ffffe0c0 <unnamed-tag>

0:000> dx ref_class
ref_class                       [Type: my_class_t]
    [+0x000] _vptr.my_class_t : 0x55555555cd88 [Type: int (__cdecl**)()]
    [+0x008] ref_my_struct      : 0x7fffffffe0c0 [Type: my_struct_t &]
```

```
0:000> ?? p_class
my_class_t * 0x00005555`55573ad0
    +0x000 _vptr.my_class_t : 0x00005555`5555cd88  -> 0x00005555`55555cee     int
ud3!my_class_t::~my_class_t+0
    +0x008 ref_my_struct    : 0x00005555`5556fe70 <unnamed-tag>

0:000> dx p_class
p_class                      : 0x555555573ad0 [Type: my_class_t *]
    [+0x000] _vptr.my_class_t : 0x55555555cd88 [Type: int (__cdecl**)()]
    [+0x008] ref_my_struct    : 0x55555556fe70 [Type: my_struct_t &]
```

The associated source code:

```
class my_class_t
{
public:
        my_class_t(my_struct_t& _ref_my_struct) : ref_my_struct(_ref_my_struct) {}

        virtual ~my_class_t() {}
        virtual my_struct_t& get_data() { return ref_my_struct; }

private:
        my_struct_t& ref_my_struct;
};
```

```
0:000> ?? ref_subclass
my_subclass_t * 0x00007fff`ffffe090
    +0x000 _vptr.my_class_t : 0x00005555`5555cd60  -> 0x00005555`555586fa     int
ud3!my_subclass_t::~my_subclass_t+0
    +0x008 ref_my_struct    : 0x00007fff`ffffe0c0 <unnamed-tag>
    +0x010 name             : 0x00005555`5555900b "Derived Class"

0:000> dx ref_subclass
ref_subclass                 [Type: my_subclass_t]
    [+0x000] _vptr.my_class_t : 0x55555555cd60 [Type: int (__cdecl**)()]
    [+0x008] ref_my_struct    : 0x7fffffffe0c0 [Type: my_struct_t &]
    [+0x010] name             : 0x55555555900b : "Derived Class" [Type: char *]

0:000> ?? p_subclass
my_subclass_t * 0x00005555`55573ca0
    +0x000 _vptr.my_class_t : 0x00005555`5555cd60  -> 0x00005555`555586fa     int
ud3!my_subclass_t::~my_subclass_t+0
    +0x008 ref_my_struct    : 0x00005555`5556fe70 <unnamed-tag>
    +0x010 name             : 0x00005555`5555900b "Derived Class"

0:000> dx p_subclass
p_subclass                   : 0x555555573ca0 [Type: my_subclass_t *]
    [+0x000] _vptr.my_class_t : 0x55555555cd60 [Type: int (__cdecl**)()]
    [+0x008] ref_my_struct    : 0x55555556fe70 [Type: my_struct_t &]
    [+0x010] name             : 0x55555555900b : "Derived Class" [Type: char *]
```

The associated source code:

```
class my_subclass_t : public my_class_t
{
public:
        my_subclass_t(my_struct_t& _ref_my_struct) : my_class_t(_ref_my_struct) { name =
"Derived Class"; }
```

```
private:
        const char *name;
};
```

12.   We can also check any member of a structure or a class (you need to use **->** for **??** and . for **dx**):

```
0:000> ?? ref_struct->p_substruct
my_substruct_t * 0x00007fff`ffffe328
   +0x000 ivec                 : std::vector<int, std::allocator<int> >
   +0x018 str                  : std::__cxx11::basic_string<char, std::char_traits<char>,
std::allocator<char> >
   +0x038 slist                : std::__cxx11::list<std::__cxx11::basic_string<char,
std::char_traits<char>, std::allocator<char> >, std::allocator<std::__cxx11::basic_string<char,
std::char_traits<char>, std::allocator<char> > > >
   +0x050 ismap                : std::map<int, std::__cxx11::basic_string<char,
std::char_traits<char>, std::allocator<char> >, std::less<int>, std::allocator<std::pair<int
const, std::__cxx11::basic_string<char, std::char_traits<char>, std::allocator<char> > > > >

0:000> dx ref_struct.p_substruct
ref_struct.p_substruct                    : 0x7ffffffffe328 [Type: my_substruct_t *]
    [+0x000] ivec              [Type: std::vector<int, std::allocator<int> >]
    [+0x018] str               [Type: std::__cxx11::string]
    [+0x038] slist             [Type: std::__cxx11::list<std::__cxx11::basic_string<char,
std::char_traits<char>, std::allocator<char> >, std::allocator<std::__cxx11::basic_string<char,
std::char_traits<char>, std::allocator<char> > > >]
    [+0x050] ismap             [Type: std::map<int, std::__cxx11::basic_string<char,
std::char_traits<char>, std::allocator<char> >, std::less<int>, std::allocator<std::pair<int
const, std::__cxx11::basic_string<char, std::char_traits<char>, std::allocator<char> > > > >]
```

The associated source code:

```
typedef struct my_substruct
{
        std::vector<int> ivec;
        std::string str;
        std::list<std::string> slist;
        std::map<int, std::string> ismap;
} my_substruct_t;
```

```
0:000> ?? ref_struct->p_list
p_my_dlist_t 0x00005555`55571660
   +0x000 data                 : 1.1000000000000000888
   +0x008 p_next               : 0x00005555`55571680 my_dlist
   +0x010 p_prev               : (null)

0:000> dx ref_struct.p_list
ref_struct.p_list                    : 0x555555571660 [Type: p_my_dlist_t]
    [+0x000] data              : 1.100000 [Type: double]
    [+0x008] p_next            : 0x555555571680 [Type: my_dlist *]
    [+0x010] p_prev            : 0x0 [Type: my_dlist *]
```

The associated source code:

```
typedef struct my_dlist
{
        double data;
        struct my_dlist *p_next;
        struct my_dlist *p_prev;
```

141

```
} my_dlist_t, *p_my_dlist_t;
```

```
0:000> ?? ref_class->ref_my_struct
my_struct_t * 0x00007fff`ffffe0c0
   +0x000 p_string       : 0x00005555`55559019  "Hello World!"
   +0x008 uarray         : [10] 0
   +0x030 p_uarray       : [10] 0x00005555`55571370  -> 0
   +0x080 pp_uarray      : [10] 0x00005555`555716c0  -> 0x00005555`55571720  -> 0
   +0x0d0 uarray2        : [10] [10] 0
   +0x260 p_substruct    : 0x00007fff`ffffe328 my_substruct
   +0x268 substruct      : my_substruct
   +0x2e8 p_list         : 0x00005555`55571660 my_dlist
```

```
0:000> dx ref_class.ref_my_struct
ref_class.ref_my_struct                    [Type: my_struct_t]
    [+0x000] p_string       : 0x555555559019 : "Hello World!" [Type: char *]
    [+0x008] uarray         [Type: uint32_t [10]]
    [+0x030] p_uarray       [Type: uint32_t * [10]]
    [+0x080] pp_uarray      [Type: uint32_t * * [10]]
    [+0x0d0] uarray2        [Type: uint32_t [10][10]]
    [+0x260] p_substruct    : 0x7fffffffe328 [Type: my_substruct_t *]
    [+0x268] substruct      [Type: my_substruct_t]
    [+0x2e8] p_list         : 0x555555571660 [Type: p_my_dlist_t]
```

```
0:000> ?? ref_struct->uarray2[3][3]
unsigned int 9
```

```
0:000> dx ref_struct.uarray2[3][3]
ref_struct.uarray2[3][3] : 0x9 [Type: uint32_t]
```

Note: There is also a global variable that can be found by examining symbols using a pattern:

```
0:000> x *!*my_struct
00005555`5555d120 ud3!g_my_struct = my_struct_t
00000000`00000000 ud3!ref_my_struct = <Memory access error>
00005555`555558b7 ud3!initialize_my_struct (my_struct_t *, my_struct_t *, my_class_t *,
my_class_t *, my_subclass_t *, my_subclass_t *)
00005555`555552ba ud3!initialize_my_struct (my_struct_t *, my_struct_t *, my_class_t *,
my_class_t *, my_subclass_t *, my_subclass_t *)
```

```
0:000> ?? g_my_struct
my_struct_t
   +0x000 p_string       : 0x00005555`55559019  "Hello World!"
   +0x008 uarray         : [10] 0
   +0x030 p_uarray       : [10] 0x00005555`55570170  -> 0
   +0x080 pp_uarray      : [10] 0x00005555`55570310  -> 0x00005555`55570370  -> 0
   +0x0d0 uarray2        : [10] [10] 0
   +0x260 p_substruct    : 0x00005555`5555d388 my_substruct
   +0x268 substruct      : my_substruct
   +0x2e8 p_list         : 0x00005555`555702b0 my_dlist
```

```
0:000> dx g_my_struct
g_my_struct                    [Type: my_struct_t]
    [+0x000] p_string       : 0x555555559019 : "Hello World!" [Type: char *]
    [+0x008] uarray         [Type: uint32_t [10]]
    [+0x030] p_uarray       [Type: uint32_t * [10]]
    [+0x080] pp_uarray      [Type: uint32_t * * [10]]
    [+0x0d0] uarray2        [Type: uint32_t [10][10]]
```

```
[+0x260] p_substruct        : 0x55555555d388 [Type: my_substruct_t *]
[+0x268] substruct          [Type: my_substruct_t]
[+0x2e8] p_list             : 0x5555555702b0 [Type: p_my_dlist_t]
```

Note: In case there are similar names in different modules, use module qualification:

```
0:000> ?? ud3!g_my_struct.p_string
char * 0x00005555`55559019
 "Hello World!

0:000> dx ud3!g_my_struct.p_string
ud3!g_my_struct.p_string                  : 0x555555559019 : "Hello World!" [Type: char *]
    72 'H' [Type: char]
```

13.   We can also check for data types and associated variables that exist globally using the **dt** command. Since the output is very big, we restrict it to "**my**" structures and classes:

```
0:000> dt ud3!*my*
          ud3!my_dlist
          ud3!p_my_dlist_t
          ud3!my_substruct
          ud3!my_substruct_t
          ud3!my_struct_t
          ud3!my_class_t
          ud3!my_subclass_t
000005555555d120  ud3!g_my_struct
000005555555d410  ud3!g_my_class
000005555555d420  ud3!g_my_subclass
0000555555558724  ud3!my_subclass_t::~my_subclass_t
00005555555586fa  ud3!my_subclass_t::~my_subclass_t
0000555555555f24  ud3!my_struct_t::~my_struct_t
00005555555558b7  ud3!initialize_my_struct
00005555555552ba  ud3!initialize_my_struct
0000555555555f02  ud3!my_struct_t::my_struct_t
0000555555555eb6  ud3!my_substruct::~my_substruct
0000555555555e6a  ud3!my_substruct::my_substruct
0000555555555d46  ud3!my_subclass_t::my_subclass_t
0000555555555d34  ud3!my_class_t::get_data
0000555555555d08  ud3!my_class_t::~my_class_t
0000555555555cee  ud3!my_class_t::~my_class_t
0000555555555cc4  ud3!my_class_t::my_class_t
```

14.   With the **dt** command, we can see a bigger picture:

```
0:000> dt ud3!my_struct_t
   +0x000 p_string          : Ptr64 Char
   +0x008 uarray            : [10] Uint4B
   +0x030 p_uarray          : [10] Ptr64 Uint4B
   +0x080 pp_uarray         : [10] Ptr64 Ptr64 Uint4B
   +0x0d0 uarray2           : [10] [10] Uint4B
   +0x260 p_substruct       : Ptr64 my_substruct
   +0x268 substruct         : my_substruct
   +0x2e8 p_list            : Ptr64 my_dlist
```

```
0:000> dt ud3!my_subclass_t
   +0x000 _vptr.my_class_t : Ptr64 Ptr64      int
   +0x008 ref_my_struct    : Ptr64 <unnamed-tag>
   +0x010 name             : Ptr64 Char
```

Note: With the **-v** switch, we can get more information, including associated constructors and destructors for C++:

```
0:000> dt -v ud3!my_struct_t
struct <unnamed-tag>, 8 elements, 0x2f0 bytes
   +0x000 p_string         : Ptr64 to Char
   +0x008 uarray           : [10] Uint4B
   +0x030 p_uarray         : [10] Ptr64 to Uint4B
   +0x080 pp_uarray        : [10] Ptr64 to Ptr64 to Uint4B
   +0x0d0 uarray2          : [10] [10] Uint4B
   +0x260 p_substruct      : Ptr64 to struct my_substruct, 4 elements, 0x80 bytes
   +0x268 substruct        : struct my_substruct, 4 elements, 0x80 bytes
   +0x2e8 p_list           : Ptr64 to struct my_dlist, 3 elements, 0x18 bytes

0:000> dt -v ud3!my_subclass_t
struct my_subclass_t, 2 elements, 0x18 bytes
   +0x000 __BaseClass struct my_class_t, 2 elements, 0x10 bytes
   +0x000 _vptr.my_class_t : Ptr64 to Ptr64 to      int
   +0x008 ref_my_struct    : Ptr64 to struct <unnamed-tag>, 8 elements, 0x2f0 bytes
   +0x010 name             : Ptr64 to Char
```

Note: To print substructures and subclasses, we can use the **-r** (recursion) switch:

```
0:000> dt -r ud3!my_struct_t
   +0x000 p_string      : Ptr64 Char
   +0x008 uarray        : [10] Uint4B
   +0x030 p_uarray      : [10] Ptr64 Uint4B
   +0x080 pp_uarray     : [10] Ptr64 Ptr64 Uint4B
   +0x0d0 uarray2       : [10] [10] Uint4B
   +0x260 p_substruct   : Ptr64 my_substruct
      +0x000 ivec           : std::vector<int, std::allocator<int> >
         +0x000 _M_impl         : std::_Vector_base<int, std::allocator<int> >::_Vector_impl
      +0x018 str            : std::__cxx11::basic_string<char, std::char_traits<char>, std::allocator<char> >
         +0x000 _M_dataplus     : std::__cxx11::basic_string<char, std::char_traits<char>, std::allocator<char> >::_Alloc_hider
         +0x008 _M_string_length : Uint8B
         +0x010 _M_local_buf    : [16] Char
         +0x010 _M_allocated_capacity : Uint8B
      +0x038 slist          : std::__cxx11::list<std::__cxx11::basic_string<char, std::char_traits<char>, std::allocator<char> >,
std::allocator<std::__cxx11::basic_string<char, std::char_traits<char>, std::allocator<char> > > >
         +0x000 _M_impl         : std::__cxx11::_List_base<std::__cxx11::basic_string<char, std::char_traits<char>, std::allocator<char> >,
std::allocator<std::__cxx11::basic_string<char, std::char_traits<char>, std::allocator<char> > > >::_List_impl
      +0x050 ismap          : std::map<int, std::__cxx11::basic_string<char, std::char_traits<char>, std::allocator<char> >, std::less<int>,
std::allocator<std::pair<int const, std::__cxx11::basic_string<char, std::char_traits<char>, std::allocator<char> > > > >
         +0x000 _M_t            : std::_Rb_tree<int, std::pair<int const, std::__cxx11::basic_string<char, std::char_traits<char>, std::allocator<char> > >,
std::_Select1st<std::pair<int const, std::__cxx11::basic_string<char, std::char_traits<char>, std::allocator<char> > > >, std::less<int>,
std::allocator<std::pair<int const, std::__cxx11::basic_string<char, std::char_traits<char>, std::allocator<char> > > > >
   +0x268 substruct     : my_substruct
      +0x000 ivec           : std::vector<int, std::allocator<int> >
         +0x000 _M_impl         : std::_Vector_base<int, std::allocator<int> >::_Vector_impl
      +0x018 str            : std::__cxx11::basic_string<char, std::char_traits<char>, std::allocator<char> >
         +0x000 _M_dataplus     : std::__cxx11::basic_string<char, std::char_traits<char>, std::allocator<char> >::_Alloc_hider
         +0x008 _M_string_length : Uint8B
         +0x010 _M_local_buf    : [16] Char
         +0x010 _M_allocated_capacity : Uint8B
      +0x038 slist          : std::__cxx11::list<std::__cxx11::basic_string<char, std::char_traits<char>, std::allocator<char> >,
std::allocator<std::__cxx11::basic_string<char, std::char_traits<char>, std::allocator<char> > > >
         +0x000 _M_impl         : std::__cxx11::_List_base<std::__cxx11::basic_string<char, std::char_traits<char>, std::allocator<char> >,
std::allocator<std::__cxx11::basic_string<char, std::char_traits<char>, std::allocator<char> > > >::_List_impl
      +0x050 ismap          : std::map<int, std::__cxx11::basic_string<char, std::char_traits<char>, std::allocator<char> >, std::less<int>,
std::allocator<std::pair<int const, std::__cxx11::basic_string<char, std::char_traits<char>, std::allocator<char> > > > >
         +0x000 _M_t            : std::_Rb_tree<int, std::pair<int const, std::__cxx11::basic_string<char, std::char_traits<char>, std::allocator<char> > >,
std::_Select1st<std::pair<int const, std::__cxx11::basic_string<char, std::char_traits<char>, std::allocator<char> > > >, std::less<int>,
std::allocator<std::pair<int const, std::__cxx11::basic_string<char, std::char_traits<char>, std::allocator<char> > > > >
   +0x2e8 p_list        : Ptr64 my_dlist
      +0x000 data           : Float
      +0x008 p_next         : Ptr64 my_dlist
         +0x000 data           : Float
         +0x008 p_next         : Ptr64 my_dlist
         +0x010 p_prev         : Ptr64 my_dlist
      +0x010 p_prev         : Ptr64 my_dlist
         +0x000 data           : Float
         +0x008 p_next         : Ptr64 my_dlist
         +0x010 p_prev         : Ptr64 my_dlist
```

```
0:000> dt -r ud3!my_subclass_t
   +0x000 _vptr.my_class_t : Ptr64 Ptr64     int
   +0x008 ref_my_struct   : Ptr64 <unnamed-tag>
      +0x000 p_string         : Ptr64 Char
      +0x008 uarray           : [10] Uint4B
      +0x030 p_uarray         : [10] Ptr64 Uint4B
      +0x080 pp_uarray        : [10] Ptr64 Ptr64 Uint4B
      +0x0d0 uarray2          : [10] [10] Uint4B
      +0x260 p_substruct      : Ptr64 my_substruct
         +0x000 ivec             : std::vector<int, std::allocator<int> >
         +0x018 str              : std::__cxx11::basic_string<char, std::char_traits<char>, std::allocator<char> >
         +0x038 slist            : std::__cxx11::list<std::__cxx11::basic_string<char, std::char_traits<char>, std::allocator<char> >,
std::allocator<std::__cxx11::basic_string<char, std::char_traits<char>, std::allocator<char> > >
         +0x050 ismap            : std::map<int, std::__cxx11::basic_string<char, std::char_traits<char>, std::allocator<char> >, std::less<int>,
std::allocator<std::pair<int const, std::__cxx11::basic_string<char, std::char_traits<char>, std::allocator<char> > > > >
      +0x268 substruct        : my_substruct
         +0x000 ivec             : std::vector<int, std::allocator<int> >
         +0x018 str              : std::__cxx11::basic_string<char, std::char_traits<char>, std::allocator<char> >
         +0x038 slist            : std::__cxx11::list<std::__cxx11::basic_string<char, std::char_traits<char>, std::allocator<char> >,
std::allocator<std::__cxx11::basic_string<char, std::char_traits<char>, std::allocator<char> > >
         +0x050 ismap            : std::map<int, std::__cxx11::basic_string<char, std::char_traits<char>, std::allocator<char> >, std::less<int>,
std::allocator<std::pair<int const, std::__cxx11::basic_string<char, std::char_traits<char>, std::allocator<char> > > > >
      +0x2e8 p_list           : Ptr64 my_dlist
         +0x000 data             : Float
         +0x008 p_next           : Ptr64 my_dlist
         +0x010 p_prev           : Ptr64 my_dlist
   +0x010 name            : Ptr64 Char
```

15.   We can supply a variable address to the **dt** command as well, for example:

```
00005555`5555d120 ud3!g_my_struct = my_struct_t * from the previous x output above
```

```
0:000> dt -r my_struct_t 00005555`5555d120
ud3!my_struct_t
   +0x000 p_string         : 0x00005555`55559019  "Hello World!"
   +0x008 uarray           : [10] 0
   +0x030 p_uarray         : [10] 0x00005555`55570170  -> 0
   +0x080 pp_uarray        : [10] 0x00005555`55570310  -> 0x00005555`55570370  -> 0
   +0x0d0 uarray2          : [10] [10] 0
   +0x260 p_substruct      : 0x00005555`5555d388 my_substruct
      +0x000 ivec             : std::vector<int, std::allocator<int> >
         +0x000 _M_impl          : std::_Vector_base<int, std::allocator<int> >::_Vector_impl
      +0x018 str              : std::__cxx11::basic_string<char, std::char_traits<char>, std::allocator<char> >
         +0x000 _M_dataplus      : std::__cxx11::basic_string<char, std::char_traits<char>, std::allocator<char> >::_Alloc_hider
         +0x008 _M_string_length : 9
         +0x010 _M_local_buf     : [16]  "my string"
         +0x010 _M_allocated_capacity : 0x6e697274`7320796d
      +0x038 slist            : std::__cxx11::list<std::__cxx11::basic_string<char, std::char_traits<char>, std::allocator<char> >,
std::allocator<std::__cxx11::basic_string<char, std::char_traits<char>, std::allocator<char> > >
         +0x000 _M_impl          : std::__cxx11::_List_base<std::__cxx11::basic_string<char, std::char_traits<char>, std::allocator<char> >,
std::allocator<std::__cxx11::basic_string<char, std::char_traits<char>, std::allocator<char> > > >::_List_impl
      +0x050 ismap            : std::map<int, std::__cxx11::basic_string<char, std::char_traits<char>, std::allocator<char> >, std::less<int>,
std::allocator<std::pair<int const, std::__cxx11::basic_string<char, std::char_traits<char>, std::allocator<char> > > > >
         +0x000 _M_t             : std::_Rb_tree<int, std::pair<int const, std::__cxx11::basic_string<char, std::char_traits<char>, std::allocator<char> > >,
std::_Select1st<std::pair<int const, std::__cxx11::basic_string<char, std::char_traits<char>, std::allocator<char> > > >, std::less<int>,
std::allocator<std::pair<int const, std::__cxx11::basic_string<char, std::char_traits<char>, std::allocator<char> > > > >
   +0x268 substruct        : my_substruct
      +0x000 ivec             : std::vector<int, std::allocator<int> >
         +0x000 _M_impl          : std::_Vector_base<int, std::allocator<int> >::_Vector_impl
      +0x018 str              : std::__cxx11::basic_string<char, std::char_traits<char>, std::allocator<char> >
         +0x000 _M_dataplus      : std::__cxx11::basic_string<char, std::char_traits<char>, std::allocator<char> >::_Alloc_hider
         +0x008 _M_string_length : 9
         +0x010 _M_local_buf     : [16]  "my string"
         +0x010 _M_allocated_capacity : 0x6e697274`7320796d
      +0x038 slist            : std::__cxx11::list<std::__cxx11::basic_string<char, std::char_traits<char>, std::allocator<char> >,
std::allocator<std::__cxx11::basic_string<char, std::char_traits<char>, std::allocator<char> > >
         +0x000 _M_impl          : std::__cxx11::_List_base<std::__cxx11::basic_string<char, std::char_traits<char>, std::allocator<char> >,
std::allocator<std::__cxx11::basic_string<char, std::char_traits<char>, std::allocator<char> > > >::_List_impl
      +0x050 ismap            : std::map<int, std::__cxx11::basic_string<char, std::char_traits<char>, std::allocator<char> >, std::less<int>,
std::allocator<std::pair<int const, std::__cxx11::basic_string<char, std::char_traits<char>, std::allocator<char> > > > >
         +0x000 _M_t             : std::_Rb_tree<int, std::pair<int const, std::__cxx11::basic_string<char, std::char_traits<char>, std::allocator<char> > >,
std::_Select1st<std::pair<int const, std::__cxx11::basic_string<char, std::char_traits<char>, std::allocator<char> > > >, std::less<int>,
std::allocator<std::pair<int const, std::__cxx11::basic_string<char, std::char_traits<char>, std::allocator<char> > > > >
   +0x2e8 p_list           : 0x00005555`555702b0 my_dlist
      +0x000 data             : 1.1000000000000000888
      +0x008 p_next           : 0x00005555`555702d0 my_dlist
         +0x000 data             : 2.2000000000000001776
         +0x008 p_next           : 0x00005555`555702f0 my_dlist
         +0x010 p_prev           : 0x00005555`555702d0 my_dlist
      +0x010 p_prev           : (null)
```

16. We can also view local variables and parameters in the *Locals* tab (you may need to set the source code path via **.srcpath**):

Name	Value	Type	Location
⊞ str	0x555555559019 : "Hello World!"	char *	
⊞ p_class	0x555555573ad0	my_class_t *	
⊟ p_struct	0x555555556fe70	my_struct_t *	
⊞ p_string	0x555555559019 : "Hello World!"	char *	
⊞ uarray		uint32_t [10]	Address 0x55555556fe78
⊞ p_uarray		uint32_t * [10]	Address 0x55555556fea0
⊞ pp_uarray		uint32_t * * [10]	Address 0x55555556fef0
⊞ uarray2		uint32_t [10][10]	Address 0x55555556ff40
⊞ p_substruct	0x5555555700d8	my_substruct_t *	
⊞ substruct		my_substruct_t	Address 0x5555555700d8
⊟ p_list	0x555555572a10	p_my_dlist_t	
data	1.100000	double	
⊟ p_next	0x555555572a30	my_dlist *	
data	2.200000	double	
⊞ p_next	0x555555572a50	my_dlist *	
⊞ p_prev	0x555555572a30	my_dlist *	
p_prev	0x0	my_dlist *	
⊞ p_subclass	0x555555573ca0	my_subclass_t *	
⊞ ref_class	0x7fffffffe0b0	my_class_t &	
⊞ ref_struct	0x7fffffffe0c0	my_struct_t &	
⊞ ref_subclass	0x7fffffffe090	my_subclass_t &	

Name	Value	Type	Location
⊞ p_string	0x555555559019 : "Hello World!"	char *	
⊞ uarray		uint32_t [10]	Address 0x55555556fe78
⊞ p_uarray		uint32_t * [10]	Address 0x55555556fea0
⊞ pp_uarray		uint32_t * * [10]	Address 0x55555556fef0
⊟ uarray2		uint32_t [10][10]	Address 0x55555556ff40
⊞ [0]		uint32_t [10]	Address 0x55555556ff40
⊞ [1]		uint32_t [10]	Address 0x55555556ff68
⊞ [2]		uint32_t [10]	Address 0x55555556ff90
⊟ [3]		uint32_t [10]	Address 0x55555556ffb8
[0]	0x0	uint32_t	
[1]	0x3	uint32_t	
[2]	0x6	uint32_t	
[3]	0x9	uint32_t	
[4]	0xc	uint32_t	
[5]	0xf	uint32_t	
[6]	0x12	uint32_t	
[7]	0x15	uint32_t	
[8]	0x18	uint32_t	
[9]	0x1b	uint32_t	
⊞ [4]		uint32_t [10]	Address 0x55555556ffe0
⊞ [5]		uint32_t [10]	Address 0x555555570008
⊞ [6]		uint32_t [10]	Address 0x555555570030
⊞ [7]		uint32_t [10]	Address 0x555555570058

Note: We can convert any data displayed as hexadecimal to other formats, for example:

```
0:000> ? 1b
Evaluate expression: 27 = 00000000`0000001b
```

```
0:000> ? 0n27
Evaluate expression: 27 = 00000000`0000001b

0:000> .formats 1b
Evaluate expression:
  Hex:        00000000`0000001b
  Decimal:    27
  Octal:      0000000000000000000033
  Binary:     00000000 00000000 00000000 00000000 00000000 00000000 00000000 00011011
  Chars:      ........
  Time:       Wed Dec 31 16:00:27 1969
  Float:      low 3.78351e-044 high 0
  Double:     1.33398e-322
```

17.   If we go two frames up (towards higher stack addresses), we can see locals from our window procedure:

```
0:000> .frame 1e5
1e5 000000ee`68cff680 00007ff6`21761851   AppD3!StartModeling+0x191 [C:\AWD3\AppD3\AppD3\AppD3.cpp @ 332]

0:000> .frame 1e6
1e6 000000ee`68cffa30 00007ff9`54148241   AppD3!WndProc+0xb1 [C:\AWD3\AppD3\AppD3\AppD3.cpp @ 153]

0:000> dv /i /V
prv param  000000ee`68cffaf0 @rsp+0x00c0            hWnd = 0x00000000`003917ee
prv param  000000ee`68cffaf8 @rsp+0x00c8         message = 0x111
prv param  000000ee`68cffb00 @rsp+0x00d0          wParam = 0x8003
prv param  000000ee`68cffb08 @rsp+0x00d8          lParam = 0n0
prv local  000000ee`68cffa68 @rsp+0x0038            wmId = 0n32771
prv local  000000ee`68cffa6c @rsp+0x003c         wmEvent = 0n0
prv local  000000ee`68cffa80 @rsp+0x0050              ps = struct tagPAINTSTRUCT
prv local  000000ee`68cffa70 @rsp+0x0040             hdc = 0x00000000`00000000
```

18.   There is also a possibility to watch variables during program tracing via the *Watch* tab:

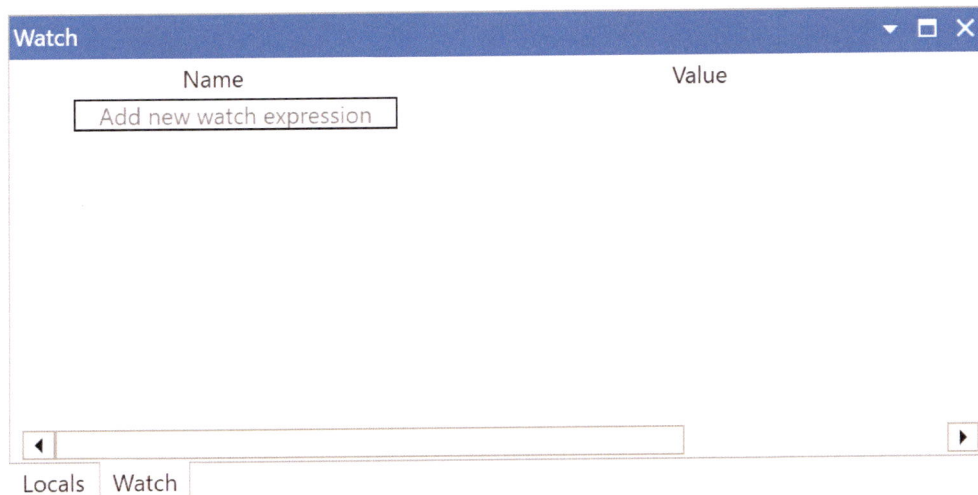

To try this out, we finish the process (the **g** command), choose *Stop Debugging*, and see WinDbg disconnected. Then we start the gdbserver again and reattach WinDbg to the remote debugger.

```
/mnt/c/ALD4/ud3$ gdbserver localhost:1234 ud3
Process /mnt/c/ALD4/ud3/ud3 created; pid = 32236
Listening on port 1234
```

```
Microsoft (R) Windows Debugger Version 10.0.27553.1004 AMD64
Copyright (c) Microsoft Corporation. All rights reserved.

64-bit machine not using 64-bit API

************* Path validation summary *************
Response                           Time (ms)     Location
Deferred                                         srv*
Symbol search path is: srv*
Executable search path is:
Unknown System Version 0 UP Free x64
System Uptime: not available
Process Uptime: not available
Reloading current modules
ModLoad: 00005555`55554000 00005555`5555d438    /mnt/c/ALD4/ud3/ud3
.
ReadVirtual() failed in GetXStateConfiguration() first read attempt (error == 0.)
00007fff`f7fd6090 mov      rdi,rsp
```

Then, we put a breakpoint on the *start_modeling* function:

```
0:009> bp ud3!start_modeling
```

We can see breakpoints in the *Breakpoints* tab:

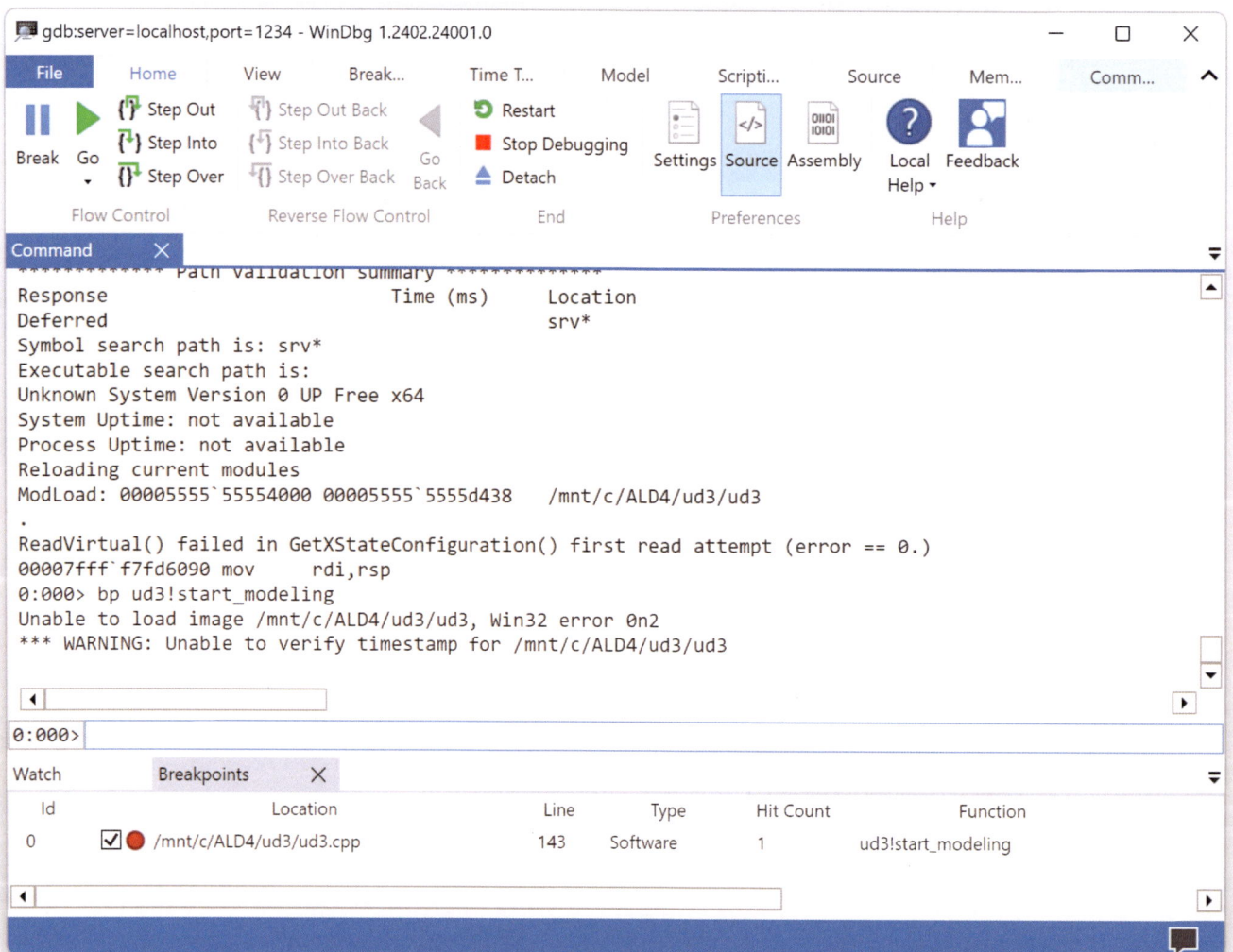

```
0:000> bl
0 e 00005555`555558d2 [/mnt/c/ALD4/ud3/ud3.cpp @ 143]     0001 (0001)  0:**** ud3!start_modeling
```

```
0:000> g
ModLoad: 00007fff`f7fd3000 00007fff`f7fd3000   linux-vdso.so.1
ModLoad: 00007fff`f7e3e000 00007fff`f7fc1020   /usr/lib/x86_64-linux-gnu/libstdc++.so.6
ModLoad: 00007fff`f7cbb000 00007fff`f7e3d148   /lib/x86_64-linux-gnu/libm.so.6
ModLoad: 00007fff`f7ca1000 00007fff`f7cba430   /lib/x86_64-linux-gnu/libgcc_s.so.1
ModLoad: 00007fff`f7ae1000 00007fff`f7ca0800   /lib/x86_64-linux-gnu/libc.so.6
ModLoad: 00007fff`f7fd5000 00007fff`f7ffe190   /lib64/ld-linux-x86-64.so.2
Breakpoint 0 hit
ud3!start_modeling:
00005555`555558d2 push    rbp
```

We then add *ud3!g_my_struct* to the *Watch* tab (*Add new watch expression*):

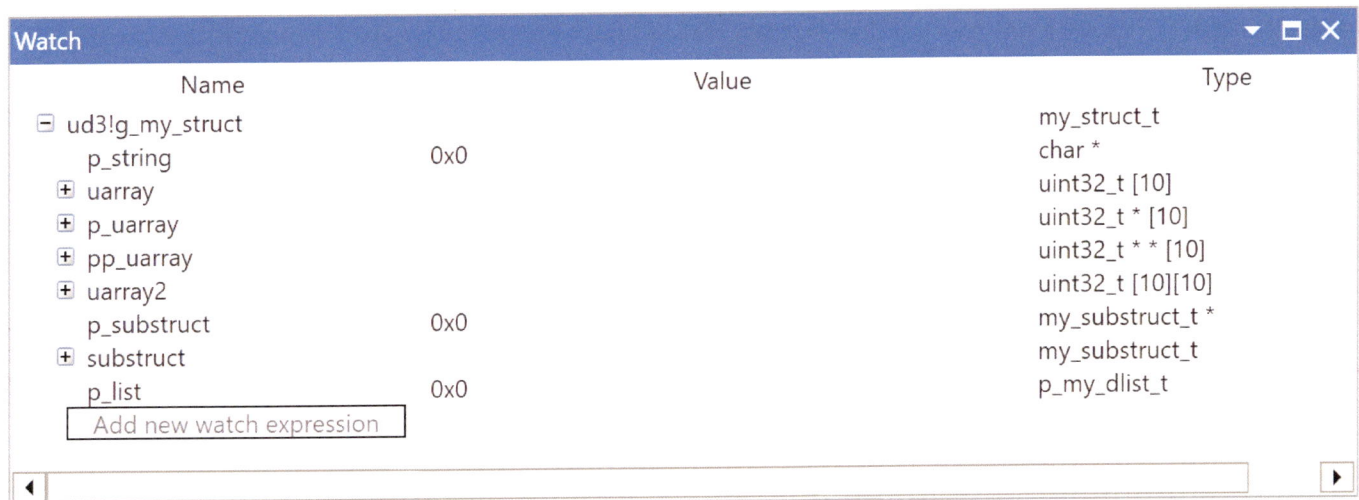

Name	Value	Type
⊟ ud3!g_my_struct		my_struct_t
p_string	0x0	char *
⊞ uarray		uint32_t [10]
⊞ p_uarray		uint32_t * [10]
⊞ pp_uarray		uint32_t * * [10]
⊞ uarray2		uint32_t [10][10]
p_substruct	0x0	my_substruct_t *
⊞ substruct		my_substruct_t
p_list	0x0	p_my_dlist_t
Add new watch expression		

We also add source code location from WinDbg perspective:

```
0:000> .srcpath C:\ALD4\ud3
Source search path is: C:\ALD4\ud3
```

```
************ Path validation summary **************
Response                  Time (ms)    Location
OK                                     C:\ALD4\ud3
```

We then step (*Step Over*) through source code (**p** command, also F10 key) until we pass over *g_my_struct* initialization (please note that the trace **t** command (*Step Into*) may enter into a function and even into a hidden function such as a constructor if you do that accidentally then you need to do *Step Out*, **gu** or Shift-F11 key):

```
0:000> p
Unable to load image /lib/x86_64-linux-gnu/libc.so.6, Win32 error 0n2
*** WARNING: Unable to verify timestamp for /lib/x86_64-linux-gnu/libc.so.6
ud3!start_modeling+0x1b:
00005555`555558ed mov     edi,2F0h
```

```
0:000> t
ud3!Znwm$plt:
00005555`555550f0 jmp     qword ptr [ud3!GLOBAL_OFFSET_TABLE_+0x78 (00005555`5555d078)]
ds:00005555`5555d078=00005555555550f6
```

149

```
0:000> t
ud3!Znwm$plt+0x6:
00005555`555550f6 push    0Ch

0:000> t
ud3!Znwm$plt+0xb:
00005555`555550fb jmp     ud3+0x1020 (00005555`55555020)

0:000> t
ud3+0x1020:
00005555`55555020 push    qword ptr [ud3!GLOBAL_OFFSET_TABLE_+0x8 (00005555`5555d008)]
ds:00005555`5555d008=00007ffff7ffe190

0:000> t
ud3+0x1026:
Unable to load image /lib64/ld-linux-x86-64.so.2, Win32 error 0n2
*** WARNING: Unable to verify timestamp for /lib64/ld-linux-x86-64.so.2
00005555`55555026 jmp     qword ptr [ud3!GLOBAL_OFFSET_TABLE_+0x10 (00005555`5555d010)]
ds:00005555`5555d010=00007ffff7fea510

0:000> t
ld_linux_x86_64_so!dl_find_dso_for_object+0x2ab0:
00007fff`f7fea510 push    rbx

0:000> gu
ud3!start_modeling+0x25:
00005555`555558f7 mov     rbx,rax

0:000> p
ud3!start_modeling+0x34:
00005555`55555906 lea     rdi,[ud3!g_my_struct (00005555`5555d120)]

0:000> p
ud3!start_modeling+0x40:
00005555`55555912 lea     rax,[rbp-320h]
```

The associated source code and *Watch* tab:

```
void start_modeling(void)
{
        my_struct_t my_struct;
        my_struct_t *p_my_struct = new my_struct_t;

        initialize_my_struct(&g_my_struct);
>>>     initialize_my_struct(&my_struct);
        initialize_my_struct(p_my_struct);

        my_class_t my_class(my_struct);
        my_class_t *p_my_class = new my_class_t(*p_my_struct);

        my_subclass_t my_subclass(my_struct);
        my_subclass_t *p_my_subclass = new my_subclass_t(*p_my_struct);

        foo(my_struct, p_my_struct, my_class, p_my_class, my_subclass, p_my_subclass);
}
```

```
ud3.cpp                                              ▼ ◻ ✕

    142 void start_modeling(void)
  ● 143 {
    144     my_struct_t my_struct;
    145     my_struct_t *p_my_struct = new my_struct_t;
    146
    147     initialize_my_struct(&g_my_struct);
 ⇨  148     initialize_my_struct(&my_struct);
    149     initialize_my_struct(p_my_struct);
    150
```

```
Watch                                                ▼ ◻ ✕

        Name                    Value                         Type
 ⊟ ud3!g_my_struct                                      my_struct_t
   ⊞ uarray                                             uint32_t [10]
   ⊞ p_uarray                                           uint32_t * [10]
   ⊞ pp_uarray                                          uint32_t * * [10]
   ⊞ uarray2                                            uint32_t [10][10]
   ⊞ substruct                                          my_substruct_t
   ⊞ p_string           0x555555559019 : "Hello World!"  char *
   ⊞ p_substruct        0x55555555d388                  my_substruct_t *
   ⊞ p_list             0x5555555702b0                  p_my_dlist_t
      Add new watch expression
```

19.   We finish the process (the **g** command twice), choose *Stop Debugging*, and see the WinDbg disconnected. We exit WinDbg.

Exercise UD3 (GDB)

Goal: Learn how to navigate parameters, static and local variables, and data structures.

Elementary Diagnostics Patterns: Crash.

Memory Analysis Patterns: Exception Stack Trace; Stack Overflow (User Mode); String Parameter; Module Variable.

Debugging Implementation Patterns: Break-in; Scope; Variable Value; Type Structure.

1.   The source code and the *Makefile* to build executables and libraries can be found in the *ud3* directory:

```
$ git clone https://bitbucket.org/softwarediagnostics/ald4
```

2.   Launch the *ud3* executable under GDB:

```
/mnt/c/ALD4/ud3$ gdb ud3
GNU gdb (Debian 8.2.1-2+b3) 8.2.1
Copyright (C) 2018 Free Software Foundation, Inc.
License GPLv3+: GNU GPL version 3 or later <http://gnu.org/licenses/gpl.html>
This is free software: you are free to change and redistribute it.
There is NO WARRANTY, to the extent permitted by law.
Type "show copying" and "show warranty" for details.
This GDB was configured as "x86_64-linux-gnu".
Type "show configuration" for configuration details.
For bug reporting instructions, please see:
<http://www.gnu.org/software/gdb/bugs/>.
Find the GDB manual and other documentation resources online at:
    <http://www.gnu.org/software/gdb/documentation/>.

For help, type "help".
Type "apropos word" to search for commands related to "word"...
Reading symbols from ud3...done.
(gdb)
```

3.   If we continue execution using the **g** command, we get a segmentation fault:

```
(gdb) r
Starting program: /mnt/c/ALD4/ud3/ud3

Program received signal SIGSEGV, Segmentation fault.
0x0000555555555aa9 in bar (param1=<error reading variable: Cannot access memory at address
0x7fffff7fefac>,
    param2=<error reading variable: Cannot access memory at address 0x7fffff7fefa0>) at
ud3.cpp:171
171         {

(gdb) list 171
166
167                 bar(1, str);
168         }
169
170      void bar(int param1, const char *param2)
171         {
172                 char local[1024] = "Local character array";
```

```
173
174                if (param1)
175                    bar(++param1, param2);
```

Note: From the disassembly and source code, it looks like the problem happened before the memory copy when saving parameters:

```
(gdb) disassemble bar
Dump of assembler code for function bar(int, char const*):
   0x0000555555555a9e <+0>:     push   %rbp
   0x0000555555555a9f <+1>:     mov    %rsp,%rbp
   0x0000555555555aa2 <+4>:     sub    $0x410,%rsp
=> 0x0000555555555aa9 <+11>:    mov    %edi,-0x404(%rbp)
   0x0000555555555aaf <+17>:    mov    %rsi,-0x410(%rbp)
   0x0000555555555ab6 <+24>:    movabs $0x6863206c61636f4c,%rax
   0x0000555555555ac0 <+34>:    movabs $0x2072657463617261,%rdx
   0x0000555555555aca <+44>:    mov    %rax,-0x400(%rbp)
   0x0000555555555ad1 <+51>:    mov    %rdx,-0x3f8(%rbp)
   0x0000555555555ad8 <+58>:    movabs $0x7961727261,%rax
   0x0000555555555ae2 <+68>:    mov    $0x0,%edx
   0x0000555555555ae7 <+73>:    mov    %rax,-0x3f0(%rbp)
   0x0000555555555aee <+80>:    mov    %rdx,-0x3e8(%rbp)
   0x0000555555555af5 <+87>:    lea    -0x3e0(%rbp),%rdx
   0x0000555555555afc <+94>:    mov    $0x0,%eax
   0x0000555555555b01 <+99>:    mov    $0x7c,%ecx
   0x0000555555555b06 <+104>:   mov    %rdx,%rdi
   0x0000555555555b09 <+107>:   rep stos %rax,%es:(%rdi)
   0x0000555555555b0c <+110>:   cmpl   $0x0,-0x404(%rbp)
   0x0000555555555b13 <+117>:   je     0x555555555b33 <bar(int, char const*)+149>
   0x0000555555555b15 <+119>:   addl   $0x1,-0x404(%rbp)
   0x0000555555555b1c <+126>:   mov    -0x410(%rbp),%rdx
   0x0000555555555b23 <+133>:   mov    -0x404(%rbp),%eax
   0x0000555555555b29 <+139>:   mov    %rdx,%rsi
   0x0000555555555b2c <+142>:   mov    %eax,%edi
   0x0000555555555b2e <+144>:   callq  0x555555555a9e <bar(int, char const*)>
   0x0000555555555b33 <+149>:   nop
   0x0000555555555b34 <+150>:   leaveq
--Type <RET> for more, q to quit, c to continue without paging--
   0x0000555555555b35 <+151>:   retq
End of assembler dump.
```

```
void bar(int param1, const char *param2)
{
    char local[1024] = "Local character array";

    if (param1)
        bar(++param1, param2);
}
```

4.   If we try to see a stack trace, we see endless frames for this stack overflow:

```
(gdb) bt
#0  0x0000555555555aa9 in bar (param1=<error reading variable: Cannot access memory at address
0x7fffff7fefac>,
    param2=<error reading variable: Cannot access memory at address 0x7fffff7fefa0>) at ud3.cpp:171
#1  0x0000555555555b33 in bar (param1=7940, param2=0x555555559019 "Hello World!") at ud3.cpp:175
#2  0x0000555555555b33 in bar (param1=7939, param2=0x555555559019 "Hello World!") at ud3.cpp:175
#3  0x0000555555555b33 in bar (param1=7938, param2=0x555555559019 "Hello World!") at ud3.cpp:175
```

```
#4  0x0000555555555b33 in bar (param1=7937, param2=0x555555559019 "Hello World!") at ud3.cpp:175
#5  0x0000555555555b33 in bar (param1=7936, param2=0x555555559019 "Hello World!") at ud3.cpp:175
#6  0x0000555555555b33 in bar (param1=7935, param2=0x555555559019 "Hello World!") at ud3.cpp:175
#7  0x0000555555555b33 in bar (param1=7934, param2=0x555555559019 "Hello World!") at ud3.cpp:175
#8  0x0000555555555b33 in bar (param1=7933, param2=0x555555559019 "Hello World!") at ud3.cpp:175
#9  0x0000555555555b33 in bar (param1=7932, param2=0x555555559019 "Hello World!") at ud3.cpp:175
#10 0x0000555555555b33 in bar (param1=7931, param2=0x555555559019 "Hello World!") at ud3.cpp:175
#11 0x0000555555555b33 in bar (param1=7930, param2=0x555555559019 "Hello World!") at ud3.cpp:175
#12 0x0000555555555b33 in bar (param1=7929, param2=0x555555559019 "Hello World!") at ud3.cpp:175
#13 0x0000555555555b33 in bar (param1=7928, param2=0x555555559019 "Hello World!") at ud3.cpp:175
#14 0x0000555555555b33 in bar (param1=7927, param2=0x555555559019 "Hello World!") at ud3.cpp:175
#15 0x0000555555555b33 in bar (param1=7926, param2=0x555555559019 "Hello World!") at ud3.cpp:175
#16 0x0000555555555b33 in bar (param1=7925, param2=0x555555559019 "Hello World!") at ud3.cpp:175
#17 0x0000555555555b33 in bar (param1=7924, param2=0x555555559019 "Hello World!") at ud3.cpp:175
#18 0x0000555555555b33 in bar (param1=7923, param2=0x555555559019 "Hello World!") at ud3.cpp:175
#19 0x0000555555555b33 in bar (param1=7922, param2=0x555555559019 "Hello World!") at ud3.cpp:175
#20 0x0000555555555b33 in bar (param1=7921, param2=0x555555559019 "Hello World!") at ud3.cpp:175
#21 0x0000555555555b33 in bar (param1=7920, param2=0x555555559019 "Hello World!") at ud3.cpp:175
#22 0x0000555555555b33 in bar (param1=7919, param2=0x555555559019 "Hello World!") at ud3.cpp:175
#23 0x0000555555555b33 in bar (param1=7918, param2=0x555555559019 "Hello World!") at ud3.cpp:175
#24 0x0000555555555b33 in bar (param1=7917, param2=0x555555559019 "Hello World!") at ud3.cpp:175
#25 0x0000555555555b33 in bar (param1=7916, param2=0x555555559019 "Hello World!") at ud3.cpp:175
#26 0x0000555555555b33 in bar (param1=7915, param2=0x555555559019 "Hello World!") at ud3.cpp:175
#27 0x0000555555555b33 in bar (param1=7914, param2=0x555555559019 "Hello World!") at ud3.cpp:175
--Type <RET> for more, q to quit, c to continue without paging--
#28 0x0000555555555b33 in bar (param1=7913, param2=0x555555559019 "Hello World!") at ud3.cpp:175
#29 0x0000555555555b33 in bar (param1=7912, param2=0x555555559019 "Hello World!") at ud3.cpp:175
#30 0x0000555555555b33 in bar (param1=7911, param2=0x555555559019 "Hello World!") at ud3.cpp:175
#31 0x0000555555555b33 in bar (param1=7910, param2=0x555555559019 "Hello World!") at ud3.cpp:175
#32 0x0000555555555b33 in bar (param1=7909, param2=0x555555559019 "Hello World!") at ud3.cpp:175
#33 0x0000555555555b33 in bar (param1=7908, param2=0x555555559019 "Hello World!") at ud3.cpp:175
#34 0x0000555555555b33 in bar (param1=7907, param2=0x555555559019 "Hello World!") at ud3.cpp:175
#35 0x0000555555555b33 in bar (param1=7906, param2=0x555555559019 "Hello World!") at ud3.cpp:175
#36 0x0000555555555b33 in bar (param1=7905, param2=0x555555559019 "Hello World!") at ud3.cpp:175
#37 0x0000555555555b33 in bar (param1=7904, param2=0x555555559019 "Hello World!") at ud3.cpp:175
#38 0x0000555555555b33 in bar (param1=7903, param2=0x555555559019 "Hello World!") at ud3.cpp:175
#39 0x0000555555555b33 in bar (param1=7902, param2=0x555555559019 "Hello World!") at ud3.cpp:175
#40 0x0000555555555b33 in bar (param1=7901, param2=0x555555559019 "Hello World!") at ud3.cpp:175
#41 0x0000555555555b33 in bar (param1=7900, param2=0x555555559019 "Hello World!") at ud3.cpp:175
#42 0x0000555555555b33 in bar (param1=7899, param2=0x555555559019 "Hello World!") at ud3.cpp:175
#43 0x0000555555555b33 in bar (param1=7898, param2=0x555555559019 "Hello World!") at ud3.cpp:175
#44 0x0000555555555b33 in bar (param1=7897, param2=0x555555559019 "Hello World!") at ud3.cpp:175
#45 0x0000555555555b33 in bar (param1=7896, param2=0x555555559019 "Hello World!") at ud3.cpp:175
#46 0x0000555555555b33 in bar (param1=7895, param2=0x555555559019 "Hello World!") at ud3.cpp:175
#47 0x0000555555555b33 in bar (param1=7894, param2=0x555555559019 "Hello World!") at ud3.cpp:175
#48 0x0000555555555b33 in bar (param1=7893, param2=0x555555559019 "Hello World!") at ud3.cpp:175
#49 0x0000555555555b33 in bar (param1=7892, param2=0x555555559019 "Hello World!") at ud3.cpp:175
#50 0x0000555555555b33 in bar (param1=7891, param2=0x555555559019 "Hello World!") at ud3.cpp:175
#51 0x0000555555555b33 in bar (param1=7890, param2=0x555555559019 "Hello World!") at ud3.cpp:175
#52 0x0000555555555b33 in bar (param1=7889, param2=0x555555559019 "Hello World!") at ud3.cpp:175
#53 0x0000555555555b33 in bar (param1=7888, param2=0x555555559019 "Hello World!") at ud3.cpp:175
#54 0x0000555555555b33 in bar (param1=7887, param2=0x555555559019 "Hello World!") at ud3.cpp:175
#55 0x0000555555555b33 in bar (param1=7886, param2=0x555555559019 "Hello World!") at ud3.cpp:175
#56 0x0000555555555b33 in bar (param1=7885, param2=0x555555559019 "Hello World!") at ud3.cpp:175
--Type <RET> for more, q to quit, c to continue without paging--
#57 0x0000555555555b33 in bar (param1=7884, param2=0x555555559019 "Hello World!") at ud3.cpp:175
#58 0x0000555555555b33 in bar (param1=7883, param2=0x555555559019 "Hello World!") at ud3.cpp:175
#59 0x0000555555555b33 in bar (param1=7882, param2=0x555555559019 "Hello World!") at ud3.cpp:175
#60 0x0000555555555b33 in bar (param1=7881, param2=0x555555559019 "Hello World!") at ud3.cpp:175
#61 0x0000555555555b33 in bar (param1=7880, param2=0x555555559019 "Hello World!") at ud3.cpp:175
#62 0x0000555555555b33 in bar (param1=7879, param2=0x555555559019 "Hello World!") at ud3.cpp:175
#63 0x0000555555555b33 in bar (param1=7878, param2=0x555555559019 "Hello World!") at ud3.cpp:175
#64 0x0000555555555b33 in bar (param1=7877, param2=0x555555559019 "Hello World!") at ud3.cpp:175
#65 0x0000555555555b33 in bar (param1=7876, param2=0x555555559019 "Hello World!") at ud3.cpp:175
#66 0x0000555555555b33 in bar (param1=7875, param2=0x555555559019 "Hello World!") at ud3.cpp:175
```

```
#67 0x0000555555555b33 in bar (param1=7874, param2=0x555555559019 "Hello World!") at ud3.cpp:175
#68 0x0000555555555b33 in bar (param1=7873, param2=0x555555559019 "Hello World!") at ud3.cpp:175
#69 0x0000555555555b33 in bar (param1=7872, param2=0x555555559019 "Hello World!") at ud3.cpp:175
#70 0x0000555555555b33 in bar (param1=7871, param2=0x555555559019 "Hello World!") at ud3.cpp:175
#71 0x0000555555555b33 in bar (param1=7870, param2=0x555555559019 "Hello World!") at ud3.cpp:175
#72 0x0000555555555b33 in bar (param1=7869, param2=0x555555559019 "Hello World!") at ud3.cpp:175
#73 0x0000555555555b33 in bar (param1=7868, param2=0x555555559019 "Hello World!") at ud3.cpp:175
#74 0x0000555555555b33 in bar (param1=7867, param2=0x555555559019 "Hello World!") at ud3.cpp:175
#75 0x0000555555555b33 in bar (param1=7866, param2=0x555555559019 "Hello World!") at ud3.cpp:175
#76 0x0000555555555b33 in bar (param1=7865, param2=0x555555559019 "Hello World!") at ud3.cpp:175
#77 0x0000555555555b33 in bar (param1=7864, param2=0x555555559019 "Hello World!") at ud3.cpp:175
#78 0x0000555555555b33 in bar (param1=7863, param2=0x555555559019 "Hello World!") at ud3.cpp:175
#79 0x0000555555555b33 in bar (param1=7862, param2=0x555555559019 "Hello World!") at ud3.cpp:175
#80 0x0000555555555b33 in bar (param1=7861, param2=0x555555559019 "Hello World!") at ud3.cpp:175
#81 0x0000555555555b33 in bar (param1=7860, param2=0x555555559019 "Hello World!") at ud3.cpp:175
#82 0x0000555555555b33 in bar (param1=7859, param2=0x555555559019 "Hello World!") at ud3.cpp:175
#83 0x0000555555555b33 in bar (param1=7858, param2=0x555555559019 "Hello World!") at ud3.cpp:175
#84 0x0000555555555b33 in bar (param1=7857, param2=0x555555559019 "Hello World!") at ud3.cpp:175
#85 0x0000555555555b33 in bar (param1=7856, param2=0x555555559019 "Hello World!") at ud3.cpp:175
--Type <RET> for more, q to quit, c to continue without paging--q
```

5.   Fortunately, in GDB, we can list backtraces from the bottom frames:

```
(gdb) bt -10
#7933 0x0000555555555b33 in bar (param1=8, param2=0x555555559019 "Hello World!") at ud3.cpp:175
#7934 0x0000555555555b33 in bar (param1=7, param2=0x555555559019 "Hello World!") at ud3.cpp:175
#7935 0x0000555555555b33 in bar (param1=6, param2=0x555555559019 "Hello World!") at ud3.cpp:175
#7936 0x0000555555555b33 in bar (param1=5, param2=0x555555559019 "Hello World!") at ud3.cpp:175
#7937 0x0000555555555b33 in bar (param1=4, param2=0x555555559019 "Hello World!") at ud3.cpp:175
#7938 0x0000555555555b33 in bar (param1=3, param2=0x555555559019 "Hello World!") at ud3.cpp:175
#7939 0x0000555555555b33 in bar (param1=2, param2=0x555555559019 "Hello World!") at ud3.cpp:175
#7940 0x0000555555555a9b in foo (ref_struct=..., p_struct=0x55555556fe70, ref_class=...,
p_class=0x555555573ad0,
    ref_subclass=..., p_subclass=0x555555573ca0) at ud3.cpp:167
#7941 0x00005555555559ce in start_modeling () at ud3.cpp:157
#7942 0x00005555555552ae in main () at ud3.cpp:18
```

6.   Since our goal is data navigation, we switch into each frame one by one and inspect data there. Let's start with frame **#7939**:

```
(gdb) frame 7939
#7939 0x0000555555555b33 in bar (param1=2, param2=0x555555559019 "Hello World!") at ud3.cpp:175
175                         bar(++param1, param2);

(gdb) info locals
local = "Local character array", '\000' <repeats 1002 times>

(gdb) info args
param1 = 2
param2 = 0x555555559019 "Hello World!"

(gdb) info frame
Stack level 7939, frame at 0x7fffffffe020:
 rip = 0x555555555b33 in bar (ud3.cpp:175); saved rip = 0x555555555a9b
 called by frame at 0x7fffffffe070, caller of frame at 0x7fffffffdc00
 source language c++.
 Arglist at 0x7fffffffe010, args: param1=2, param2=0x555555559019 "Hello World!"
 Locals at 0x7fffffffe010, Previous frame's sp is 0x7fffffffe020
 Saved registers:
  rbp at 0x7fffffffe010, rip at 0x7fffffffe018
```

Notice the large difference between the caller and callee frames. This is because of the large local array, and its space was allocated on stack by the *sub* instruction. Also, despite parameters being passed by **edi** and **rsi** registers (the first was passed by 32-bit **edi** and not by 64-bit **rdi** because it is a 32-bit **int** parameter), they were saved on the stack, and this is why we are able to get them:

```
(gdb) disassemble bar
Dump of assembler code for function bar(int, char const*):
   0x0000555555555a9e <+0>:     push   %rbp
   0x0000555555555a9f <+1>:     mov    %rsp,%rbp
   0x0000555555555aa2 <+4>:     sub    $0x410,%rsp
[...]
```

7.   Let's look at two variables. The first one is an integer and can be directly inspected by the simple data dumping command:

```
(gdb) x/w &param1
0x7fffffffdc0c: 2
```

8.   For **param2**, the stack region contains a pointer value. We can use character and string dumping formats:

```
(gdb) x/gx &param2
0x7fffffffdc00: 0x0000555555559019
```

```
(gdb) x/a &param2
0x7fffffffdc00: 0x555555559019
```

```
(gdb) x/20c param2
0x555555559019: 72 'H'   101 'e' 108 'l' 108 'l' 111 'o' 32 ' '   87 'W'   111 'o'
0x555555559021: 114 'r'  108 'l' 100 'd' 33 '!'  0 '\000'         111 'o' 110 'n' 101 'e'
0x555555559029: 0 '\000'         116 't' 119 'w' 111 'o'
```

```
(gdb) x/s param2
0x555555559019: "Hello World!"
```

Note: We can also use the **print** and **ptype** commands:

```
(gdb) p param2
$3 = 0x555555559019 "Hello World!"
```

```
(gdb) ptype param2
type = const char *
```

9.   Let's now move to the next frame, **#7940**:

```
(gdb) frame 7940
#7940 0x0000555555555a9b in foo (ref_struct=..., p_struct=0x55555556fe70, ref_class=...,
p_class=0x555555573ad0,
    ref_subclass=..., p_subclass=0x555555573ca0) at ud3.cpp:167
167             bar(1, str);
```

The associated source code:

```
void foo(my_struct_t& ref_struct, my_struct_t *p_struct, const my_class_t& ref_class,
my_class_t *p_class, my_subclass_t& ref_subclass, my_subclass_t *p_subclass)
{
        const char *str = p_class->get_data().p_string;
```

```
      bar(1, str);
}

(gdb) info locals
str = 0x555555559019 "Hello World!"

(gdb) info args
ref_struct = @0x7fffffffe0a0: {p_string = 0x555555559019 "Hello World!", uarray = {0, 1, 2, 3,
4, 5, 6, 7, 8, 9},
  p_uarray = {0x555555571370, 0x555555571540, 0x555555571560, 0x555555571580, 0x5555555715a0,
0x5555555715c0,
    0x5555555715e0, 0x555555571600, 0x555555571620, 0x555555571640}, pp_uarray =
{0x5555555716c0, 0x555555571860,
    0x555555571a00, 0x555555571ba0, 0x555555571d40, 0x555555571ee0, 0x555555572080,
0x555555572220, 0x5555555723c0,
    0x555555572560}, uarray2 = {{0, 0, 0, 0, 0, 0, 0, 0, 0, 0}, {0, 1, 2, 3, 4, 5, 6, 7, 8, 9},
{0, 2, 4, 6, 8, 10,
    12, 14, 16, 18}, {0, 3, 6, 9, 12, 15, 18, 21, 24, 27}, {0, 4, 8, 12, 16, 20, 24, 28, 32,
36}, {0, 5, 10, 15, 20,
    25, 30, 35, 40, 45}, {0, 6, 12, 18, 24, 30, 36, 42, 48, 54}, {0, 7, 14, 21, 28, 35, 42,
49, 56, 63}, {0, 8, 16,
    24, 32, 40, 48, 56, 64, 72}, {0, 9, 18, 27, 36, 45, 54, 63, 72, 81}}, p_substruct =
0x7fffffffe308, substruct = {
    ivec = std::vector of length 3, capacity 4 = {1, 2, 3}, str = "my string", slist =
std::__cxx11::list = {
      [0] = "one", [1] = "two", [2] = "three"}, ismap = std::map with 3 elements = {[1] =
"one", [2] = "two",
      [3] = "three"}}, p_list = 0x555555571660}
p_struct = 0x55555556fe70
ref_class = @0x7fffffffe090: {_vptr.my_class_t = 0x55555555cd88 <vtable for my_class_t+16>,
  ref_my_struct = @0x7fffffffe0a0}
p_class = 0x555555573ad0
ref_subclass = @0x7fffffffe070: {<my_class_t> = {_vptr.my_class_t = 0x55555555cd60 <vtable for
my_subclass_t+16>,
    ref_my_struct = @0x7fffffffe0a0}, name = 0x55555555900b "Derived Class"}
p_subclass = 0x555555573ca0

(gdb) info frame
Stack level 7940, frame at 0x7fffffffe070:
 rip = 0x555555555a9b in foo (ud3.cpp:167); saved rip = 0x5555555559ce
 called by frame at 0x7fffffffe3d0, caller of frame at 0x7fffffffe020
 source language c++.
 Arglist at 0x7fffffffe060, args: ref_struct=..., p_struct=0x55555556fe70, ref_class=...,
p_class=0x555555573ad0,
    ref_subclass=..., p_subclass=0x555555573ca0
 Locals at 0x7fffffffe060, Previous frame's sp is 0x7fffffffe070
 Saved registers:
  rbp at 0x7fffffffe060, rip at 0x7fffffffe068
```

Note: We are interested in 6 parameters (args), either references or pointers to structures and C++ classes. We also see that reference structure and class values are printed with fields. Remember that in C++, structures are the same as classes regarding their data layout. Also, even if a variable is passed as a reference, it is internally passed as a pointer:

```
(gdb) ptype ref_struct
type = struct my_struct_t {
    const char *p_string;
    uint32_t uarray[10];
    uint32_t *p_uarray[10];
    uint32_t **pp_uarray[10];
    uint32_t uarray2[10][10];
    my_substruct_t *p_substruct;
    my_substruct_t substruct;
    p_my_dlist_t p_list;
} &
(gdb) ptype p_struct
type = struct my_struct_t {
    const char *p_string;
    uint32_t uarray[10];
    uint32_t *p_uarray[10];
    uint32_t **pp_uarray[10];
    uint32_t uarray2[10][10];
    my_substruct_t *p_substruct;
    my_substruct_t substruct;
    p_my_dlist_t p_list;
} *

(gdb) p *p_struct
$6 = {p_string = 0x555555559019 "Hello World!", uarray = {0, 1, 2, 3, 4, 5, 6, 7, 8, 9},
p_uarray = {0x555555572720,
    0x5555555728f0, 0x555555572910, 0x555555572930, 0x555555572950, 0x555555572970,
0x555555572990, 0x5555555729b0,
    0x5555555729d0, 0x5555555729f0}, pp_uarray = {0x555555572a70, 0x555555572c10,
0x555555572db0, 0x555555572f50,
    0x5555555730f0, 0x555555573290, 0x555555573430, 0x5555555735d0, 0x555555573770,
0x555555573910}, uarray2 = {{0, 0,
    0, 0, 0, 0, 0, 0, 0, 0}, {0, 1, 2, 3, 4, 5, 6, 7, 8, 9}, {0, 2, 4, 6, 8, 10, 12, 14, 16,
18}, {0, 3, 6, 9, 12,
    15, 18, 21, 24, 27}, {0, 4, 8, 12, 16, 20, 24, 28, 32, 36}, {0, 5, 10, 15, 20, 25, 30,
35, 40, 45}, {0, 6, 12,
    18, 24, 30, 36, 42, 48, 54}, {0, 7, 14, 21, 28, 35, 42, 49, 56, 63}, {0, 8, 16, 24, 32,
40, 48, 56, 64, 72}, {0,
    9, 18, 27, 36, 45, 54, 63, 72, 81}}, p_substruct = 0x5555555700d8, substruct = {
    ivec = std::vector of length 3, capacity 4 = {1, 2, 3}, str = "my string", slist =
std::__cxx11::list = {
    [0] = "one", [1] = "two", [2] = "three"}, ismap = std::map with 3 elements = {[1] =
"one", [2] = "two",
    [3] = "three"}}, p_list = 0x555555572a10}
```

The associated source code:

```
typedef struct
{
    const char *p_string;
    uint32_t uarray[10];
    uint32_t *p_uarray[10];
    uint32_t **pp_uarray[10];
    uint32_t uarray2[10][10];
    my_substruct_t *p_substruct;
    my_substruct_t substruct;
    p_my_dlist_t p_list;
} my_struct_t;
```

```
(gdb) ptype ref_class
type = const class my_class_t {
  private:
    my_struct_t &ref_my_struct;

  public:
    my_class_t(my_struct_t &);
    ~my_class_t();
    virtual my_struct_t & get_data(void);
} &

(gdb) ptype p_class
type = class my_class_t {
  private:
    my_struct_t &ref_my_struct;

  public:
    my_class_t(my_struct_t &);
    ~my_class_t();
    virtual my_struct_t & get_data(void);
} *

(gdb) p *p_class
$7 = {_vptr.my_class_t = 0x55555555cd88 <vtable for my_class_t+16>, ref_my_struct =
@0x55555556fe70}
```

The associated source code:

```
class my_class_t
{
public:
      my_class_t(my_struct_t& _ref_my_struct) : ref_my_struct(_ref_my_struct) {}

      virtual ~my_class_t() {}
      virtual my_struct_t& get_data() { return ref_my_struct; }

private:
      my_struct_t& ref_my_struct;
};
```

```
(gdb) ptype ref_subclass
type = class my_subclass_t : public my_class_t {
  private:
    const char *name;

  public:
    my_subclass_t(my_struct_t &);
} &

(gdb) ptype p_subclass
type = class my_subclass_t : public my_class_t {
  private:
    const char *name;

  public:
    my_subclass_t(my_struct_t &);
} *
```

159

```
(gdb) p *p_subclass
$8 = {<my_class_t> = {_vptr.my_class_t = 0x55555555cd60 <vtable for my_subclass_t+16>,
    ref_my_struct = @0x55555556fe70}, name = 0x55555555900b "Derived Class"}
```

The associated source code:

```
class my_subclass_t : public my_class_t
{
public:
        my_subclass_t(my_struct_t& _ref_my_struct) : my_class_t(_ref_my_struct) { name =
"Derived Class"; }

private:
        const char *name;
};
```

10.   We can also check any member of a structure or a class:

```
(gdb) ptype ref_struct.p_substruct
type = struct my_substruct {
    std::vector<int> ivec;
    std::__cxx11::string str;
    std::list<std::string> slist;
    std::map<int, std::string> ismap;
} *
```

```
(gdb) p *ref_struct.p_substruct
$12 = {ivec = std::vector of length 3, capacity 4 = {1, 2, 3}, str = "my string", slist =
std::__cxx11::list = {
    [0] = "one", [1] = "two", [2] = "three"}, ismap = std::map with 3 elements = {[1] = "one",
[2] = "two",
    [3] = "three"}}
```

The associated source code:

```
typedef struct my_substruct
{
        std::vector<int> ivec;
        std::string str;
        std::list<std::string> slist;
        std::map<int, std::string> ismap;
} my_substruct_t;
```

```
(gdb) ptype ref_struct.p_list
type = struct my_dlist {
    double data;
    my_dlist *p_next;
    my_dlist *p_prev;
} *
```

```
(gdb) p *ref_struct.p_list
$13 = {data = 1.1000000000000001, p_next = 0x555555571680, p_prev = 0x0}
```

The associated source code:

```
typedef struct my_dlist
{
        double data;
```

160

```
        struct my_dlist *p_next;
        struct my_dlist *p_prev;
} my_dlist_t, *p_my_dlist_t;

(gdb) ptype ref_class.ref_my_struct
type = struct my_struct_t {
    const char *p_string;
    uint32_t uarray[10];
    uint32_t *p_uarray[10];
    uint32_t **pp_uarray[10];
    uint32_t uarray2[10][10];
    my_substruct_t *p_substruct;
    my_substruct_t substruct;
    p_my_dlist_t p_list;
} &

(gdb) p ref_class.ref_my_struct
$14 = (my_struct_t &) @0x7fffffffe0a0: {p_string = 0x555555559019 "Hello World!", uarray = {0,
1, 2, 3, 4, 5, 6, 7, 8,
    9}, p_uarray = {0x555555571370, 0x555555571540, 0x555555571560, 0x555555571580,
0x5555555715a0, 0x5555555715c0,
    0x5555555715e0, 0x555555571600, 0x555555571620, 0x555555571640}, pp_uarray =
{0x5555555716c0, 0x555555571860,
    0x555555571a00, 0x555555571ba0, 0x555555571d40, 0x555555571ee0, 0x555555572080,
0x555555572220, 0x5555555723c0,
    0x555555572560}, uarray2 = {{0, 0, 0, 0, 0, 0, 0, 0, 0, 0}, {0, 1, 2, 3, 4, 5, 6, 7, 8, 9},
{0, 2, 4, 6, 8, 10,
      12, 14, 16, 18}, {0, 3, 6, 9, 12, 15, 18, 21, 24, 27}, {0, 4, 8, 12, 16, 20, 24, 28, 32,
36}, {0, 5, 10, 15, 20,
      25, 30, 35, 40, 45}, {0, 6, 12, 18, 24, 30, 36, 42, 48, 54}, {0, 7, 14, 21, 28, 35, 42,
49, 56, 63}, {0, 8, 16,
      24, 32, 40, 48, 56, 64, 72}, {0, 9, 18, 27, 36, 45, 54, 63, 72, 81}}, p_substruct =
0x7fffffffe308, substruct = {
    ivec = std::vector of length 3, capacity 4 = {1, 2, 3}, str = "my string", slist =
std::__cxx11::list = {
      [0] = "one", [1] = "two", [2] = "three"}, ismap = std::map with 3 elements = {[1] =
"one", [2] = "two",
      [3] = "three"}}, p_list = 0x555555571660}

(gdb) ptype ref_struct.uarray2[3][3]
type = unsigned int

(gdb) p ref_struct.uarray2[3][3]
$15 = 9
```

Note: There is also a global variable that can be found by examining symbols using a pattern:

```
(gdb) info variables .*my_struct.*
All variables matching regular expression ".*my_struct.*":

File ud3.cpp:
73:     my_struct_t g_my_struct;

(gdb) ptype g_my_struct
type = struct my_struct_t {
    const char *p_string;
    uint32_t uarray[10];
    uint32_t *p_uarray[10];
```

```
    uint32_t **pp_uarray[10];
    uint32_t uarray2[10][10];
    my_substruct_t *p_substruct;
    my_substruct_t substruct;
    p_my_dlist_t p_list;
}
```

```
(gdb) p g_my_struct
$16 = {p_string = 0x555555559019 "Hello World!", uarray = {0, 1, 2, 3, 4, 5, 6, 7, 8, 9},
p_uarray = {0x555555570170,
    0x555555570190, 0x5555555701b0, 0x5555555701d0, 0x5555555701f0, 0x555555570210,
0x555555570230, 0x555555570250,
    0x555555570270, 0x555555570290}, pp_uarray = {0x555555570310, 0x5555555704b0,
0x555555570650, 0x5555555707f0,
    0x555555570990, 0x555555570b30, 0x555555570cd0, 0x555555570e70, 0x555555571010,
0x5555555711b0}, uarray2 = {{0, 0,
    0, 0, 0, 0, 0, 0, 0, 0}, {0, 1, 2, 3, 4, 5, 6, 7, 8, 9}, {0, 2, 4, 6, 8, 10, 12, 14, 16,
18}, {0, 3, 6, 9, 12,
    15, 18, 21, 24, 27}, {0, 4, 8, 12, 16, 20, 24, 28, 32, 36}, {0, 5, 10, 15, 20, 25, 30,
35, 40, 45}, {0, 6, 12,
    18, 24, 30, 36, 42, 48, 54}, {0, 7, 14, 21, 28, 35, 42, 49, 56, 63}, {0, 8, 16, 24, 32,
40, 48, 56, 64, 72}, {0,
    9, 18, 27, 36, 45, 54, 63, 72, 81}}, p_substruct = 0x55555555d388 <g_my_struct+616>,
substruct = {
    ivec = std::vector of length 3, capacity 4 = {1, 2, 3}, str = "my string", slist =
std::__cxx11::list = {
      [0] = "one", [1] = "two", [2] = "three"}, ismap = std::map with 3 elements = {[1] =
"one", [2] = "two",
      [3] = "three"}}, p_list = 0x5555555702b0}
```

11.   We can also check for data types and associated variables that exist globally using the **dt** command. Since the output is very big, we restrict it to "**my**" structures and classes:

```
(gdb) info functions .*my_struct.*
All functions matching regular expression ".*my_struct.*":

File ud3.cpp:
162:    void foo(my_struct_t&, my_struct_t*, my_class_t const&, my_class_t*, my_subclass_t&,
my_subclass_t*);
77:     void initialize_my_struct(my_struct_t&);
135:    void initialize_my_struct(my_struct_t*);
55:     void my_class_t::my_class_t(my_struct_t&);
50:     void my_struct_t::my_struct_t();
50:     void my_struct_t::~my_struct_t();
67:     void my_subclass_t::my_subclass_t(my_struct_t&);
```

```
(gdb) info types .*my_struct.*
All types matching regular expression ".*my_struct.*":

File ud3.cpp:
41:     my_struct_t;
50:     typedef my_struct_t my_struct_t;
```

12.   We finish the process (the **c** command) and quit GDB.

Exercise UD4

- **Goal:** Learn how to use conditional breakpoints to log behavior

- **Elementary Diagnostics Patterns:** Use-case Deviation

- **Memory Analysis Patterns:** -

- **Debugging Implementation Patterns:** Break-in; Code Breakpoint; Breakpoint Action

- \ALD4\Exercise-Linux-UD4.pdf

Exercise UD4 (WinDbg)

Goal: Learn how to use conditional breakpoints to log behavior.

Elementary Diagnostics Patterns: Use-case Deviation.

Memory Analysis Patterns: -

Debugging Implementation Patterns: Break-in; Code Breakpoint; Breakpoint Action.

1.   Run the *bash* executable.

```
/mnt/c/ALD4$ ps
  PID TTY          TIME CMD
21423 pts/8    00:00:00 bash
29917 pts/8    00:00:00 ps

/mnt/c/ALD4$ bash

/mnt/c/ALD4$ ps
  PID TTY          TIME CMD
21423 pts/8    00:00:00 bash
29918 pts/8    00:00:00 bash
29920 pts/8    00:00:00 ps
```

2.   Open a different terminal and run gdbserver as a process server:

```
/mnt/c/ALD4$ sudo gdbserver --multi localhost:1234
Listening on port 1234
```

3.   Connect WinDbg to the process server:

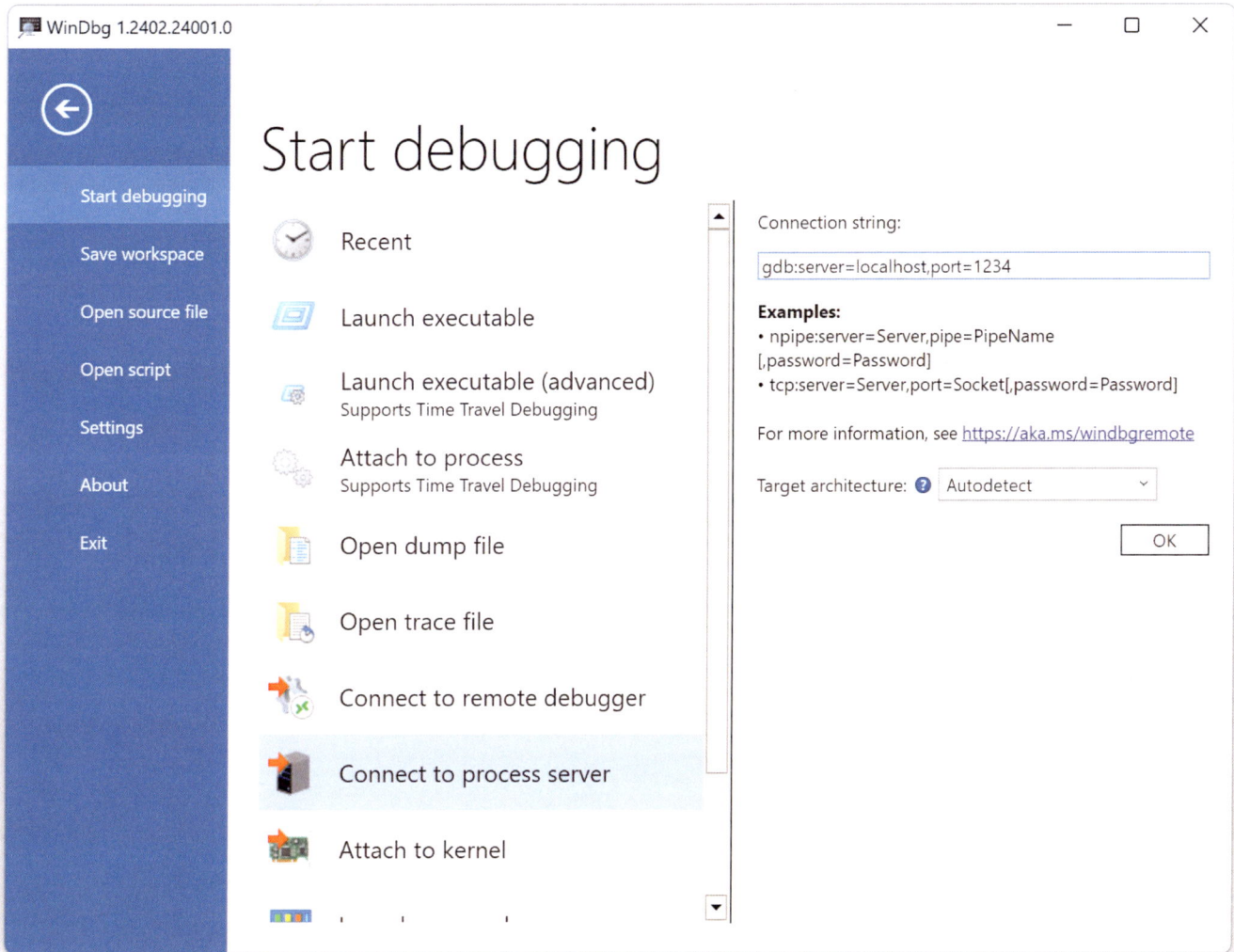

4.   Select *Attach to process* and choose our *bash* process:

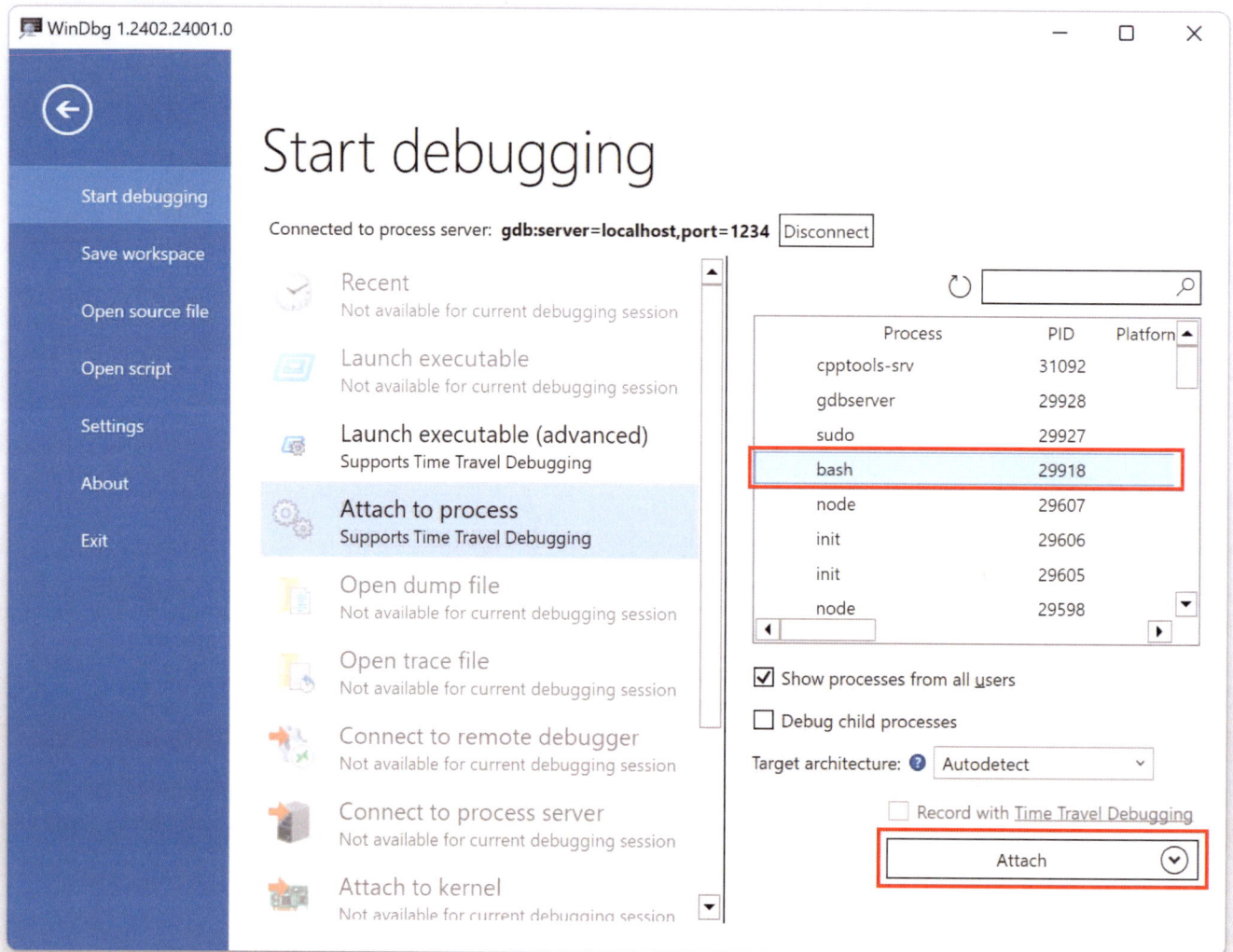

```
Microsoft (R) Windows Debugger Version 10.0.27553.1004 AMD64
Copyright (c) Microsoft Corporation. All rights reserved.

64-bit machine not using 64-bit API

************* Path validation summary **************
Response                        Time (ms)       Location
Deferred                                        srv*
Symbol search path is: srv*
Executable search path is:
Unknown System Version 0 UP Free x64
System Uptime: not available
Process Uptime: not available
Reloading current modules
ModLoad: 00005615`7cbf6000 00005615`7cd1d998   /bin/bash
ModLoad: 00007ffe`c3ee2000 00007ffe`c3ee2000   linux-vdso.so.1
ModLoad: 00007fd7`39543000 00007fd7`39570980   /lib/x86_64-linux-gnu/libtinfo.so.6
ModLoad: 00007fd7`3953e000 00007fd7`39542110   /lib/x86_64-linux-gnu/libdl.so.2
ModLoad: 00007fd7`3937e000 00007fd7`3953d800   /lib/x86_64-linux-gnu/libc.so.6
ModLoad: 00007fd7`3957e000 00007fd7`395a7190   /lib64/ld-linux-x86-64.so.2
ModLoad: 00007fd7`39076000 00007fd7`3908a738   /lib/x86_64-linux-gnu/libnss_files.so.2
```

```
.......
ReadVirtual() failed in GetXStateConfiguration() first read attempt (error == 0.)
Unable to load image /lib/x86_64-linux-gnu/libc.so.6, Win32 error 0n2
*** WARNING: Unable to verify timestamp for /lib/x86_64-linux-gnu/libc.so.6
Unable to load image /bin/bash, Win32 error 0n2
*** WARNING: Unable to verify timestamp for /bin/bash
libc_so!pselect+0x59:
00007fd7`3946ec89 cmp     rax,0FFFFFFFFFFFFF000h
```

5.   Open a log file (useful when the output doesn't fit into the buffer and we need to search for something):

```
0:000> .logopen C:\ALD4\ud4.log
Opened log file 'C:\ALD4\ud4.log'
```

6.   Our task is to log any characters that can be typed inside the bash. For this, we need to put a breakpoint on the *read* function and specify a breakpoint action to execute after each hit. For example, we want to show a backtrace and continue:

```
0:000> bp libc_so!read "k; gc"
```

```
0:000> bl
     0 e Disable Clear  00007fd7`39468300     0001 (0001)  0:**** libc_so!_read "k; gc"
```

7.   When we continue and switch to another terminal where the debugged *bash* process is running and type *Hello* we get the following GDB output:

```
0:000> g
 # Child-SP         RetAddr            Call Site
00 00007ffe`c3e13a08 00005615`7ccc4867  libc_so!_read
01 00007ffe`c3e13a10 00005615`7ccc5065  bash!rl_getc+0x187
02 00007ffe`c3e13ae0 00005615`7ccaba12  bash!rl_read_key+0x135
03 00007ffe`c3e13af0 00005615`7ccac225  bash!readline_internal_char+0x62
04 00007ffe`c3e13b10 00005615`7cc26de2  bash!readline+0x45
05 00007ffe`c3e13b20 00005615`7cc291d0  bash!pretty_print_loop+0x422
06 00007ffe`c3e13b40 00005615`7cc2c79a  bash!decode_prompt_string+0xf90
07 00007ffe`c3e13b90 00005615`7cc300d8  bash!read_secondary_line+0x2d6a
08 00007ffe`c3e13c20 00005615`7cc26476  bash!yyparse+0x3f8
09 00007ffe`c3e14ad0 00005615`7cc26584  bash!parse_command+0x36
0a 00007ffe`c3e14af0 00005615`7cc26798  bash!read_command+0x54
0b 00007ffe`c3e14b20 00005615`7cc25104  bash!reader_loop+0x128
0c 00007ffe`c3e14b50 00007fd7`393a209b  bash!main+0x12d4
0d 00007ffe`c3e14cb0 00005615`7cc2565a  libc_so!_libc_start_main+0xeb
0e 00007ffe`c3e14d70 ffffffff`ffffffff  bash!start+0x2a
0f 00007ffe`c3e14d78 00000000`00000000  0xffffffff`ffffffff
 # Child-SP         RetAddr            Call Site
00 00007ffe`c3e13a08 00005615`7ccc4867  libc_so!_read
01 00007ffe`c3e13a10 00005615`7ccc5065  bash!rl_getc+0x187
02 00007ffe`c3e13ae0 00005615`7ccaba12  bash!rl_read_key+0x135
03 00007ffe`c3e13af0 00005615`7ccac225  bash!readline_internal_char+0x62
04 00007ffe`c3e13b10 00005615`7cc26de2  bash!readline+0x45
05 00007ffe`c3e13b20 00005615`7cc291d0  bash!pretty_print_loop+0x422
06 00007ffe`c3e13b40 00005615`7cc2c79a  bash!decode_prompt_string+0xf90
07 00007ffe`c3e13b90 00005615`7cc300d8  bash!read_secondary_line+0x2d6a
08 00007ffe`c3e13c20 00005615`7cc26476  bash!yyparse+0x3f8
09 00007ffe`c3e14ad0 00005615`7cc26584  bash!parse_command+0x36
0a 00007ffe`c3e14af0 00005615`7cc26798  bash!read_command+0x54
```

```
0b 00007ffe`c3e14b20 00005615`7cc25104   bash!reader_loop+0x128
0c 00007ffe`c3e14b50 00007fd7`393a209b   bash!main+0x12d4
0d 00007ffe`c3e14cb0 00005615`7cc2565a   libc_so!_libc_start_main+0xeb
0e 00007ffe`c3e14d70 ffffffff`ffffffff   bash!start+0x2a
0f 00007ffe`c3e14d78 00000000`00000000   0xffffffff`ffffffff
 # Child-SP          RetAddr              Call Site
00 00007ffe`c3e13a08 00005615`7ccc4867   libc_so!_read
01 00007ffe`c3e13a10 00005615`7ccc5065   bash!rl_getc+0x187
02 00007ffe`c3e13ae0 00005615`7ccaba12   bash!rl_read_key+0x135
03 00007ffe`c3e13af0 00005615`7ccac225   bash!readline_internal_char+0x62
04 00007ffe`c3e13b10 00005615`7cc26de2   bash!readline+0x45
05 00007ffe`c3e13b20 00005615`7cc291d0   bash!pretty_print_loop+0x422
06 00007ffe`c3e13b40 00005615`7cc2c79a   bash!decode_prompt_string+0xf90
07 00007ffe`c3e13b90 00005615`7cc300d8   bash!read_secondary_line+0x2d6a
08 00007ffe`c3e13c20 00005615`7cc26476   bash!yyparse+0x3f8
09 00007ffe`c3e14ad0 00005615`7cc26584   bash!parse_command+0x36
0a 00007ffe`c3e14af0 00005615`7cc26798   bash!read_command+0x54
0b 00007ffe`c3e14b20 00005615`7cc25104   bash!reader_loop+0x128
0c 00007ffe`c3e14b50 00007fd7`393a209b   bash!main+0x12d4
0d 00007ffe`c3e14cb0 00005615`7cc2565a   libc_so!_libc_start_main+0xeb
0e 00007ffe`c3e14d70 ffffffff`ffffffff   bash!start+0x2a
0f 00007ffe`c3e14d78 00000000`00000000   0xffffffff`ffffffff
 # Child-SP          RetAddr              Call Site
00 00007ffe`c3e13a08 00005615`7ccc4867   libc_so!_read
01 00007ffe`c3e13a10 00005615`7ccc5065   bash!rl_getc+0x187
02 00007ffe`c3e13ae0 00005615`7ccaba12   bash!rl_read_key+0x135
03 00007ffe`c3e13af0 00005615`7ccac225   bash!readline_internal_char+0x62
04 00007ffe`c3e13b10 00005615`7cc26de2   bash!readline+0x45
05 00007ffe`c3e13b20 00005615`7cc291d0   bash!pretty_print_loop+0x422
06 00007ffe`c3e13b40 00005615`7cc2c79a   bash!decode_prompt_string+0xf90
07 00007ffe`c3e13b90 00005615`7cc300d8   bash!read_secondary_line+0x2d6a
08 00007ffe`c3e13c20 00005615`7cc26476   bash!yyparse+0x3f8
09 00007ffe`c3e14ad0 00005615`7cc26584   bash!parse_command+0x36
0a 00007ffe`c3e14af0 00005615`7cc26798   bash!read_command+0x54
0b 00007ffe`c3e14b20 00005615`7cc25104   bash!reader_loop+0x128
0c 00007ffe`c3e14b50 00007fd7`393a209b   bash!main+0x12d4
0d 00007ffe`c3e14cb0 00005615`7cc2565a   libc_so!_libc_start_main+0xeb
0e 00007ffe`c3e14d70 ffffffff`ffffffff   bash!start+0x2a
0f 00007ffe`c3e14d78 00000000`00000000   0xffffffff`ffffffff
 # Child-SP          RetAddr              Call Site
00 00007ffe`c3e13a08 00005615`7ccc4867   libc_so!_read
01 00007ffe`c3e13a10 00005615`7ccc5065   bash!rl_getc+0x187
02 00007ffe`c3e13ae0 00005615`7ccaba12   bash!rl_read_key+0x135
03 00007ffe`c3e13af0 00005615`7ccac225   bash!readline_internal_char+0x62
04 00007ffe`c3e13b10 00005615`7cc26de2   bash!readline+0x45
05 00007ffe`c3e13b20 00005615`7cc291d0   bash!pretty_print_loop+0x422
06 00007ffe`c3e13b40 00005615`7cc2c79a   bash!decode_prompt_string+0xf90
07 00007ffe`c3e13b90 00005615`7cc300d8   bash!read_secondary_line+0x2d6a
08 00007ffe`c3e13c20 00005615`7cc26476   bash!yyparse+0x3f8
09 00007ffe`c3e14ad0 00005615`7cc26584   bash!parse_command+0x36
0a 00007ffe`c3e14af0 00005615`7cc26798   bash!read_command+0x54
0b 00007ffe`c3e14b20 00005615`7cc25104   bash!reader_loop+0x128
0c 00007ffe`c3e14b50 00007fd7`393a209b   bash!main+0x12d4
0d 00007ffe`c3e14cb0 00005615`7cc2565a   libc_so!_libc_start_main+0xeb
0e 00007ffe`c3e14d70 ffffffff`ffffffff   bash!start+0x2a
0f 00007ffe`c3e14d78 00000000`00000000   0xffffffff`ffffffff
```

8.   If we want to log the *read* function parameters instead, we should specify a different list of commands:

```
<Break>
(74de.74de): Signal SIGINT code SI_USER (Sent by kill, sigsend, raise) at 0x7fd73946ec89
originating from PID 74de
First chance exceptions are reported before any exception handling.
This exception may be expected and handled.
libc_so!pselect+0x59:
00007fd7`3946ec89 cmp       rax,0FFFFFFFFFFFFF000hd

0:000> bp libc_so!read "r rdi,rsi,rdx; gc"
breakpoint 0 redefined
```

After we continue and resume typing, we get the new output:

```
0:000> g
rdi=0000000000000000 rsi=00007ffec3e13a1f rdx=0000000000000001
rdi=0000000000000000 rsi=00007ffec3e13a1f rdx=0000000000000001
rdi=0000000000000000 rsi=00007ffec3e13a1f rdx=0000000000000001
rdi=0000000000000000 rsi=00007ffec3e13a1f rdx=0000000000000001
rdi=0000000000000000 rsi=00007ffec3e13a1f rdx=0000000000000001
```

Note: The first parameter (rdi) is 0 – stdin, the second (rsi) is the buffer address, and the third (rdx) – is the number of characters read.

9.   We can dereference the buffer's first byte and print typed characters instead:

```
<Break>
(74de.74de): Signal SIGINT code SI_USER (Sent by kill, sigsend, raise) at 0x7fd73946ec89
originating from PID 74de
First chance exceptions are reported before any exception handling.
This exception may be expected and handled.
libc_so!pselect+0x59:
00007fd7`3946ec89 cmp       rax,0FFFFFFFFFFFFF000h

0:000> bp libc_so!read "db rsi L1; gc"
breakpoint 0 redefined

0:000> g
00007ffe`c3e13a1f  00                                               .
00007ffe`c3e13a1f  00                                               .
00007ffe`c3e13a1f  00                                               .
00007ffe`c3e13a1f  00                                               .
00007ffe`c3e13a1f  00                                               .
```

Note: However, we see that the buffer contents are 0. This is because we just entered the *read* function. We need to read the buffer when we return from it.

10.   We change the commands appropriately to log the buffer on return:

```
<Break>
(74de.74de): Signal SIGINT code SI_USER (Sent by kill, sigsend, raise) at 0x7fd73946ec89
originating from PID 74de
First chance exceptions are reported before any exception handling.
```

```
This exception may be expected and handled.
libc_so!pselect+0x59:
00007fd7`3946ec89 cmp     rax,0FFFFFFFFFFFFF000h
```

```
0:000> bp libc_so!read "gu; db rsi L1; gc"
breakpoint 0 redefined
```

```
0:000> g
Some commands were skipped because previous commands caused target execution inside an event
handler.Some commands were skipped because previous commands caused target execution inside an
event handler.Some commands were skipped because previous commands caused target execution
inside an event handler.Some commands were skipped because previous commands caused target
execution inside an event handler.Some commands were skipped because previous commands caused
target execution inside an event handler.
```

Note: Unfortunately, the **gu** (Step Out) command doesn't work, and there is no continuation.

11.   We rectify this situation by putting the breakpoint on the return address, specifying commands for it instead, and deleting the original first breakpoint:

```
<Break>
First chance exceptions are reported before any exception handling.
This exception may be expected and handled.
libc_so!pselect+0x59:
00007fd7`3946ec89 cmp     rax,0FFFFFFFFFFFFF000h
```

Note: We take the return address from the backtrace we got previously:

```
# Child-SP          RetAddr            Call Site
00 00007ffe`c3e13a08 00005615`7ccc4867  libc_so!_read
01 00007ffe`c3e13a10 00005615`7ccc5065  bash!rl_getc+0x187
02 00007ffe`c3e13ae0 00005615`7ccaba12  bash!rl_read_key+0x135
03 00007ffe`c3e13af0 00005615`7ccac225  bash!readline_internal_char+0x62
04 00007ffe`c3e13b10 00005615`7cc26de2  bash!readline+0x45
05 00007ffe`c3e13b20 00005615`7cc291d0  bash!pretty_print_loop+0x422
06 00007ffe`c3e13b40 00005615`7cc2c79a  bash!decode_prompt_string+0xf90
07 00007ffe`c3e13b90 00005615`7cc300d8  bash!read_secondary_line+0x2d6a
08 00007ffe`c3e13c20 00005615`7cc26476  bash!yyparse+0x3f8
09 00007ffe`c3e14ad0 00005615`7cc26584  bash!parse_command+0x36
0a 00007ffe`c3e14af0 00005615`7cc26798  bash!read_command+0x54
0b 00007ffe`c3e14b20 00005615`7cc25104  bash!reader_loop+0x128
0c 00007ffe`c3e14b50 00007fd7`393a209b  bash!main+0x12d4
0d 00007ffe`c3e14cb0 00005615`7cc2565a  libc_so!_libc_start_main+0xeb
0e 00007ffe`c3e14d70 ffffffff`ffffffff  bash!start+0x2a
0f 00007ffe`c3e14d78 00000000`00000000  0xffffffff`ffffffff
0:000> bp 00005615`7ccc4867 "db rsi L1; gc"
```

```
0:000> bc 0
```

```
0:000> bl
     1 e Disable Clear  00005615`7ccc4867     0001 (0001)  0:**** bash!rl_getc+0x187 "db rsi L1; gc"
```

```
0:000> g
00007ffe`c3e13a1f  48                                                          H
00007ffe`c3e13a1f  65                                                          e
00007ffe`c3e13a1f  6c                                                          l
```

```
00007ffe`c3e13a1f  6c                                                    l
00007ffe`c3e13a1f  6f                                                    o
```

12.   If we want just to output characters, we can set the different command list:

```
<Break>
(74de.74de): Signal SIGINT code SI_USER (Sent by kill, sigsend, raise) at 0x7fd73946ec89
originating from PID 74de
First chance exceptions are reported before any exception handling.
This exception may be expected and handled.
libc_so!pselect+0x59:
00007fd7`3946ec89 cmp     rax,0FFFFFFFFFFFFF000h

0:000> bp 00005615`7ccc4867 "r $t0 = poi(@rsi) & 0xFF; .printf \"%c\", @$t0; gc"
breakpoint 0 redefined

0:000> g
Hello
```

Note: We get the first byte from the memory RSI points to and assign it to a pseudo-register $t0 variable, and then we print the $t0 value. We use the @ sign to tell WinDbg that $t0 is not a symbol (this speeds up the lookup).

13.   We detach in WinDbg and exit, then switch to the *gdbserver* terminal and break via ^C. We also exit our *bash*.

Goal: Learn how to use conditional breakpoints to log behavior.

Elementary Diagnostics Patterns: Use-case Deviation.

Memory Analysis Patterns: -

Debugging Implementation Patterns: Break-in; Code Breakpoint; Breakpoint Action.

1.   Run the *bash* executable.


```
/mnt/c/ALD4$ ps
  PID TTY          TIME CMD
15648 pts/0    00:00:00 bash
17442 pts/0    00:00:00 ps

/mnt/c/ALD4$ bash

/mnt/c/ALD4$ ps
  PID TTY          TIME CMD
15648 pts/0    00:00:00 bash
17446 pts/0    00:00:00 bash
17448 pts/0    00:00:00 ps
```

2.   Open another terminal and attach GDB to the new *bash* process:


```
/mnt/c/ALD4$ gdb -p 17446
GNU gdb (Debian 8.2.1-2+b3) 8.2.1
Copyright (C) 2018 Free Software Foundation, Inc.
License GPLv3+: GNU GPL version 3 or later <http://gnu.org/licenses/gpl.html>
This is free software: you are free to change and redistribute it.
There is NO WARRANTY, to the extent permitted by law.
Type "show copying" and "show warranty" for details.
This GDB was configured as "x86_64-linux-gnu".
Type "show configuration" for configuration details.
For bug reporting instructions, please see:
<http://www.gnu.org/software/gdb/bugs/>.
Find the GDB manual and other documentation resources online at:
    <http://www.gnu.org/software/gdb/documentation/>.

For help, type "help".
Type "apropos word" to search for commands related to "word".
Attaching to process 17446
Reading symbols from /bin/bash...(no debugging symbols found)...done.
Reading symbols from /lib/x86_64-linux-gnu/libtinfo.so.6...(no debugging symbols found)...done.
Reading symbols from /lib/x86_64-linux-gnu/libdl.so.2...Reading symbols from
/usr/lib/debug/.build-id/e0/a26233adbeaa08de07d76dbaacd9c3ff5b18f9.debug...done.
done.
Reading symbols from /lib/x86_64-linux-gnu/libc.so.6...Reading symbols from
/usr/lib/debug/.build-id/c7/aa9a1e121fe2395f3840f3f0213146046d9fe3.debug...done.
done.
Reading symbols from /lib64/ld-linux-x86-64.so.2...Reading symbols from /usr/lib/debug/.build-
id/83/743ddd4258a7d138a28c4f2032d17ad92a15b5.debug...done.
done.
```

```
Reading symbols from /lib/x86_64-linux-gnu/libnss_files.so.2...Reading symbols from
/usr/lib/debug/.build-id/d7/cfd27ca5fda4bde8f71998d7384810ae8406af.debug...done.
done.
0x00007ff3ff9b6c89 in __pselect (nfds=1, readfds=0x7fff742049b0, writefds=0x0, exceptfds=0x0,
timeout=<optimized out>,
    sigmask=0x55b3fc377840 <_rl_orig_sigset>) at ../sysdeps/unix/sysv/linux/pselect.c:69
69      ../sysdeps/unix/sysv/linux/pselect.c: No such file or directory.
(gdb)
```

3.   Our task is to log any characters that can be typed inside the *bash*. For this, we need to put a breakpoint on the *read* function:

```
(gdb) break read
Breakpoint 1 at 0x7ff3ff9b0300: file ../sysdeps/unix/sysv/linux/read.c, line 26.
```

4.   Next, we specify a breakpoint action to execute after each hit. For example, we want to show a backtrace and continue:

```
(gdb) commands 1
Type commands for breakpoint(s) 1, one per line.
End with a line saying just "end".
>bt
>continue
>end
(gdb)
```

5.   When we continue and switch to another terminal where the debugged *bash* process is running and type *Hello* we get the following GDB output:

```
(gdb) c
Continuing.

Breakpoint 1, __GI___libc_read (fd=0, buf=0x7fff742049af, nbytes=1) at
../sysdeps/unix/sysv/linux/read.c:26
26       ../sysdeps/unix/sysv/linux/read.c: No such file or directory.
#0  __GI___libc_read (fd=0, buf=0x7fff742049af, nbytes=1) at
../sysdeps/unix/sysv/linux/read.c:26
#1  0x000055b3fc31e867 in rl_getc ()
#2  0x000055b3fc31f065 in rl_read_key ()
#3  0x000055b3fc305a12 in readline_internal_char ()
#4  0x000055b3fc306225 in readline ()
#5  0x000055b3fc280de2 in ?? ()
#6  0x000055b3fc2831d0 in ?? ()
#7  0x000055b3fc28679a in ?? ()
#8  0x000055b3fc28a0d8 in yyparse ()
#9  0x000055b3fc280476 in parse_command ()
#10 0x000055b3fc280584 in read_command ()
#11 0x000055b3fc280798 in reader_loop ()
#12 0x000055b3fc27f104 in main ()

Breakpoint 1, __GI___libc_read (fd=0, buf=0x7fff742049af, nbytes=1) at
../sysdeps/unix/sysv/linux/read.c:26
26        in ../sysdeps/unix/sysv/linux/read.c
#0  __GI___libc_read (fd=0, buf=0x7fff742049af, nbytes=1) at
../sysdeps/unix/sysv/linux/read.c:26
#1  0x000055b3fc31e867 in rl_getc ()
```

```
#2   0x000055b3fc31f065 in rl_read_key ()
#3   0x000055b3fc305a12 in readline_internal_char ()
#4   0x000055b3fc306225 in readline ()
#5   0x000055b3fc280de2 in ?? ()
#6   0x000055b3fc2831d0 in ?? ()
#7   0x000055b3fc28679a in ?? ()
#8   0x000055b3fc28a0d8 in yyparse ()
#9   0x000055b3fc280476 in parse_command ()
--Type <RET> for more, q to quit, c to continue without paging--q
#10 0x000055b3fc280584 in read_command ()
#11 0x000055b3fc280798 in reader_loop ()
#12 0x000055b3fc27f104 in main ()

Breakpoint 1, __GI___libc_read (fd=0, buf=0x7fff7420494f, nbytes=1) at
../sysdeps/unix/sysv/linux/read.c:26
26      in ../sysdeps/unix/sysv/linux/read.c
#0   __GI___libc_read (fd=0, buf=0x7fff7420494f, nbytes=1) at
../sysdeps/unix/sysv/linux/read.c:26
#1   0x000055b3fc31e867 in rl_getc ()
#2   0x000055b3fc31f065 in rl_read_key ()
#3   0x000055b3fc32253a in rl_insert ()
#4   0x000055b3fc3054d9 in _rl_dispatch_subseq ()
#5   0x000055b3fc305a5c in readline_internal_char ()
#6   0x000055b3fc306225 in readline ()
#7   0x000055b3fc280de2 in ?? ()
#8   0x000055b3fc2831d0 in ?? ()
#9   0x000055b3fc28679a in ?? ()
#10 0x000055b3fc28a0d8 in yyparse ()
#11 0x000055b3fc280476 in parse_command ()
#12 0x000055b3fc280584 in read_command ()
#13 0x000055b3fc280798 in reader_loop ()
#14 0x000055b3fc27f104 in main ()

Breakpoint 1, __GI___libc_read (fd=0, buf=0x7fff742049af, nbytes=1) at
../sysdeps/unix/sysv/linux/read.c:26
26      in ../sysdeps/unix/sysv/linux/read.c
#0   __GI___libc_read (fd=0, buf=0x7fff742049af, nbytes=1) at
../sysdeps/unix/sysv/linux/read.c:26
#1   0x000055b3fc31e867 in rl_getc ()
#2   0x000055b3fc31f065 in rl_read_key ()
#3   0x000055b3fc305a12 in readline_internal_char ()
#4   0x000055b3fc306225 in readline ()
--Type <RET> for more, q to quit, c to continue without paging--q
#5   0x000055b3fc280de2 in ?? ()
#6   0x000055b3fc2831d0 in ?? ()
#7   0x000055b3fc28679a in ?? ()
#8   0x000055b3fc28a0d8 in yyparse ()
#9   0x000055b3fc280476 in parse_command ()
#10 0x000055b3fc280584 in read_command ()
#11 0x000055b3fc280798 in reader_loop ()
#12 0x000055b3fc27f104 in main ()

Breakpoint 1, __GI___libc_read (fd=0, buf=0x7fff742049af, nbytes=1) at
../sysdeps/unix/sysv/linux/read.c:26
26      in ../sysdeps/unix/sysv/linux/read.c
#0   __GI___libc_read (fd=0, buf=0x7fff742049af, nbytes=1) at
../sysdeps/unix/sysv/linux/read.c:26
#1   0x000055b3fc31e867 in rl_getc ()
#2   0x000055b3fc31f065 in rl_read_key ()
```

```
#3  0x000055b3fc305a12 in readline_internal_char ()
#4  0x000055b3fc306225 in readline ()
#5  0x000055b3fc280de2 in ?? ()
#6  0x000055b3fc2831d0 in ?? ()
#7  0x000055b3fc28679a in ?? ()
#8  0x000055b3fc28a0d8 in yyparse ()
#9  0x000055b3fc280476 in parse_command ()
#10 0x000055b3fc280584 in read_command ()
#11 0x000055b3fc280798 in reader_loop ()
#12 0x000055b3fc27f104 in main ()
```

6.   If we want to log the *read* function parameters instead, we should specify a different list of commands:

```
^C
Program received signal SIGINT, Interrupt.
0x00007ff3ff9b6c89 in __pselect (nfds=1, readfds=0x7fff742049b0, writefds=0x0, exceptfds=0x0,
timeout=<optimized out>,
    sigmask=0x55b3fc377840 <_rl_orig_sigset>) at ../sysdeps/unix/sysv/linux/pselect.c:69
69      ../sysdeps/unix/sysv/linux/pselect.c: No such file or directory.

(gdb) commands 1
Type commands for breakpoint(s) 1, one per line.
End with a line saying just "end".
>silent
>info r rdi rsi rdx
>c
>end
(gdb)
```

Note: For an A64 system, you need to specify X0, X1, and X2.

After we continue and resume typing, we get the new output:

```
(gdb) c
Continuing.
rdi            0x0                 0
rsi            0x7fff742049af      140735141661103
rdx            0x1                 1
rdi            0x0                 0
rsi            0x7fff742049af      140735141661103
rdx            0x1                 1
rdi            0x0                 0
rsi            0x7fff742049af      140735141661103
rdx            0x1                 1
rdi            0x0                 0
rsi            0x7fff742049af      140735141661103
rdx            0x1                 1
rdi            0x0                 0
rsi            0x7fff742049af      140735141661103
rdx            0x1                 1
```

Note: The first parameter (rdi) is 0 – stdin, the second (rsi) is the buffer address, and the third (rdx) – is the number of characters read.

7.   We can dereference the buffer's first byte and print typed characters instead:

```
^C
Program received signal SIGINT, Interrupt.
0x00007ff3ff9b6c89 in __pselect (nfds=1, readfds=0x7fff742049b0, writefds=0x0, exceptfds=0x0,
timeout=<optimized out>,
     sigmask=0x55b3fc377840 <_rl_orig_sigset>) at ../sysdeps/unix/sysv/linux/pselect.c:69
69         in ../sysdeps/unix/sysv/linux/pselect.c

(gdb) commands 1
Type commands for breakpoint(s) 1, one per line.
End with a line saying just "end".
>silent
>x/c $rsi
>c
>end
(gdb)

(gdb) c
Continuing.
0x7fff742049af: 0 '\000'
0x7fff742049af: 0 '\000'
0x7fff742049af: 0 '\000'
0x7fff742049af: 0 '\000'
0x7fff742049af: 0 '\000'
```

Note: However, we see that the buffer contents are 0. This is because we just entered the *read* function. We need to read the buffer when we return from it.

8.   We change the commands appropriately to log the buffer on return:

```
^C
Program received signal SIGINT, Interrupt.
0x00007ff3ff9b6c89 in __pselect (nfds=1, readfds=0x7fff742049b0, writefds=0x0, exceptfds=0x0,
timeout=<optimized out>,
     sigmask=0x55b3fc377840 <_rl_orig_sigset>) at ../sysdeps/unix/sysv/linux/pselect.c:69
69         ../sysdeps/unix/sysv/linux/pselect.c: No such file or directory.

(gdb) commands 1
Type commands for breakpoint(s) 1, one per line.
End with a line saying just "end".
>silent
>finish
>x/c $rsi
>c
>end

(gdb) c
Continuing.
0x000055b3fc31e867 in rl_getc ()
Value returned is $2 = 1
```

Note: Unfortunately, the *finish* command breaks, and there is no continuation.

9.   We rectify this situation by putting the breakpoint on the current return address, specifying commands for it instead, and deleting the original first breakpoint:

```
(gdb) break
Breakpoint 2 at 0x55b3fc31e867

(gdb) commands 2
Type commands for breakpoint(s) 2, one per line.
End with a line saying just "end".
>silent
>x/c $rsi
>c
>end

(gdb) del break 1

(gdb) c
Continuing.
0x7fff742049af: 72 'H'
0x7fff742049af: 101 'e'
0x7fff742049af: 108 'l'
0x7fff742049af: 108 'l'
0x7fff742049af: 111 'o'
```

10.   If we want just to output characters, we can set the different command list:

```
^C
Program received signal SIGINT, Interrupt.
0x00007ff3ff9b6c89 in __pselect (nfds=1, readfds=0x7fff742049b0, writefds=0x0, exceptfds=0x0,
timeout=<optimized out>,
    sigmask=0x55b3fc377840 <_rl_orig_sigset>) at ../sysdeps/unix/sysv/linux/pselect.c:69
69      ../sysdeps/unix/sysv/linux/pselect.c: No such file or directory.

(gdb) commands 2
Type commands for breakpoint(s) 2, one per line.
End with a line saying just "end".
>silent
>printf "%c", *$rsi
>c
>end

(gdb) c
Continuing.
Hello
```

11.   We quit our debugging session and also exit the *bash* process in another terminal.

```
^C
Program received signal SIGINT, Interrupt.
0x00007ff3ff9b6c89 in __pselect (nfds=1, readfds=0x7fff742049b0, writefds=0x0, exceptfds=0x0,
timeout=<optimized out>,
    sigmask=0x55b3fc377840 <_rl_orig_sigset>) at ../sysdeps/unix/sysv/linux/pselect.c:69
69      ../sysdeps/unix/sysv/linux/pselect.c: No such file or directory.

(gdb) q
A debugging session is active.

        Inferior 1 [process 17446] will be detached.
Quit anyway? (y or n) y
Detaching from program: /bin/bash, process 17446
[Inferior 1 (process 17446) detached]
```

Exercise UD4 (LLDB)

Goal: Learn how to use conditional breakpoints to log behavior.

Elementary Diagnostics Patterns: Use-case Deviation.

Memory Analysis Patterns: -

Debugging Implementation Patterns: Break-in; Code Breakpoint; Breakpoint Action.

1.   Run the *bash* executable.

```
/mnt/c/ALD4$ ps
   PID TTY          TIME CMD
15648 pts/0     00:00:00 bash
28081 pts/0     00:00:00 ps

/mnt/c/ALD4$ bash

/mnt/c/ALD4$ ps
   PID TTY          TIME CMD
15648 pts/0     00:00:00 bash
28921 pts/0     00:00:00 bash
28084 pts/0     00:00:00 ps
```

2.   Open another terminal and attach LLDB to the new *bash* process:

```
/mnt/c/ALD4$ lldb -p 28921
Process 28921 stopped
* thread #1, name = 'bash', stop reason = signal SIGSTOP
    frame #0: 0x00007f8fdebdec89 libc.so.6`__pselect(nfds=1, readfds=0x00007ffe037bffd0,
writefds=0x0000000000000000, exceptfds=0x0000000000000000, timeout=<unavailable>,
sigmask=0x00005593503b9840) at pselect.c:69

Executable module set to "/bin/bash".
Architecture set to: x86_64-pc-linux-gnu.
(lldb)
```

3.   Our task is to log any characters that can be typed inside the *bash*. For this, we need to put a breakpoint on the *read* function:

```
(lldb) break set -name read
Breakpoint 1: where = libc.so.6`__GI___libc_read at read.c:26, address = 0x00007f8fdebd8300
```

4.   Next, we specify a breakpoint action to execute after each hit. For example, we want to show a backtrace and continue:

```
(lldb) break command add 1
Enter your debugger command(s).  Type 'DONE' to end.
> bt
> c
> DONE
(lldb)
```

5.   When we continue and switch to another terminal where the debugged *bash* process is running and type *Hello* we get the following LLDB output:

```
(lldb) c
Process 28921 resuming
(lldb)  bt
* thread #1, name = 'bash', stop reason = breakpoint 1.1
  * frame #0: 0x00007f8fdebd8300 libc.so.6`__GI___libc_read(fd=0, buf=0x00007ffe037bffcf,
nbytes=1) at read.c:26
    frame #1: 0x0000559350360867 bash`rl_getc + 391
    frame #2: 0x0000559350361065 bash`rl_read_key + 309
    frame #3: 0x0000559350347a12 bash`readline_internal_char + 98
    frame #4: 0x0000559350348225 bash`readline + 69
    frame #5: 0x00005593502c2de2 bash`___lldb_unnamed_symbol25$$bash + 162
    frame #6: 0x00005593502c51d0 bash`___lldb_unnamed_symbol37$$bash + 384
    frame #7: 0x00005593502c879a bash`___lldb_unnamed_symbol42$$bash + 90
    frame #8: 0x00005593502cc0d8 bash`yyparse + 1016
    frame #9: 0x00005593502c2476 bash`parse_command + 54
    frame #10: 0x00005593502c2584 bash`read_command + 84
    frame #11: 0x00005593502c2798 bash`reader_loop + 296
    frame #12: 0x00005593502c1104 bash`main + 4820
    frame #13: 0x00007f8fdeb1209b libc.so.6`__libc_start_main(main=(bash`main), argc=1,
argv=0x00007ffe037c1338, init=<unavailable>, fini=<unavailable>, rtld_fini=<unavailable>,
stack_end=0x00007ffe037c1328) at libc-start.c:308
    frame #14: 0x00005593502c165a bash`_start + 42


(lldb)  c
Process 28921 resuming

Command #2 'c' continued the target.
(lldb)  bt
* thread #1, name = 'bash', stop reason = breakpoint 1.1
  * frame #0: 0x00007f8fdebd8300 libc.so.6`__GI___libc_read(fd=0, buf=0x00007ffe037bffcf,
nbytes=1) at read.c:26
    frame #1: 0x0000559350360867 bash`rl_getc + 391
    frame #2: 0x0000559350361065 bash`rl_read_key + 309
    frame #3: 0x0000559350347a12 bash`readline_internal_char + 98
    frame #4: 0x0000559350348225 bash`readline + 69
    frame #5: 0x00005593502c2de2 bash`___lldb_unnamed_symbol25$$bash + 162
    frame #6: 0x00005593502c51d0 bash`___lldb_unnamed_symbol37$$bash + 384
    frame #7: 0x00005593502c879a bash`___lldb_unnamed_symbol42$$bash + 90
    frame #8: 0x00005593502cc0d8 bash`yyparse + 1016
    frame #9: 0x00005593502c2476 bash`parse_command + 54
    frame #10: 0x00005593502c2584 bash`read_command + 84
    frame #11: 0x00005593502c2798 bash`reader_loop + 296
    frame #12: 0x00005593502c1104 bash`main + 4820
    frame #13: 0x00007f8fdeb1209b libc.so.6`__libc_start_main(main=(bash`main), argc=1,
argv=0x00007ffe037c1338, init=<unavailable>, fini=<unavailable>, rtld_fini=<unavailable>,
stack_end=0x00007ffe037c1328) at libc-start.c:308
    frame #14: 0x00005593502c165a bash`_start + 42


(lldb)  c
Process 28921 resuming

Command #2 'c' continued the target.
(lldb)  bt
```

```
* thread #1, name = 'bash', stop reason = breakpoint 1.1
  * frame #0: 0x00007f8fdebd8300 libc.so.6`__GI___libc_read(fd=0, buf=0x00007ffe037bffcf,
nbytes=1) at read.c:26
    frame #1: 0x0000559350360867 bash`rl_getc + 391
    frame #2: 0x0000559350361065 bash`rl_read_key + 309
    frame #3: 0x0000559350347a12 bash`readline_internal_char + 98
    frame #4: 0x0000559350348225 bash`readline + 69
    frame #5: 0x00005593502c2de2 bash`___lldb_unnamed_symbol25$$bash + 162
    frame #6: 0x00005593502c51d0 bash`___lldb_unnamed_symbol37$$bash + 384
    frame #7: 0x00005593502c879a bash`___lldb_unnamed_symbol42$$bash + 90
    frame #8: 0x00005593502cc0d8 bash`yyparse + 1016
    frame #9: 0x00005593502c2476 bash`parse_command + 54
    frame #10: 0x00005593502c2584 bash`read_command + 84
    frame #11: 0x00005593502c2798 bash`reader_loop + 296
    frame #12: 0x00005593502c1104 bash`main + 4820
    frame #13: 0x00007f8fdeb1209b libc.so.6`__libc_start_main(main=(bash`main), argc=1,
argv=0x00007ffe037c1338, init=<unavailable>, fini=<unavailable>, rtld_fini=<unavailable>,
stack_end=0x00007ffe037c1328) at libc-start.c:308
    frame #14: 0x00005593502c165a bash`_start + 42

(lldb)  c
Process 28921 resuming

Command #2 'c' continued the target.
(lldb)  bt
* thread #1, name = 'bash', stop reason = breakpoint 1.1
  * frame #0: 0x00007f8fdebd8300 libc.so.6`__GI___libc_read(fd=0, buf=0x00007ffe037bffcf,
nbytes=1) at read.c:26
    frame #1: 0x0000559350360867 bash`rl_getc + 391
    frame #2: 0x0000559350361065 bash`rl_read_key + 309
    frame #3: 0x0000559350347a12 bash`readline_internal_char + 98
    frame #4: 0x0000559350348225 bash`readline + 69
    frame #5: 0x00005593502c2de2 bash`___lldb_unnamed_symbol25$$bash + 162
    frame #6: 0x00005593502c51d0 bash`___lldb_unnamed_symbol37$$bash + 384
    frame #7: 0x00005593502c879a bash`___lldb_unnamed_symbol42$$bash + 90
    frame #8: 0x00005593502cc0d8 bash`yyparse + 1016
    frame #9: 0x00005593502c2476 bash`parse_command + 54
    frame #10: 0x00005593502c2584 bash`read_command + 84
    frame #11: 0x00005593502c2798 bash`reader_loop + 296
    frame #12: 0x00005593502c1104 bash`main + 4820
    frame #13: 0x00007f8fdeb1209b libc.so.6`__libc_start_main(main=(bash`main), argc=1,
argv=0x00007ffe037c1338, init=<unavailable>, fini=<unavailable>, rtld_fini=<unavailable>,
stack_end=0x00007ffe037c1328) at libc-start.c:308
    frame #14: 0x00005593502c165a bash`_start + 42

(lldb)  c
Process 28921 resuming

Command #2 'c' continued the target.
(lldb)  bt
* thread #1, name = 'bash', stop reason = breakpoint 1.1
  * frame #0: 0x00007f8fdebd8300 libc.so.6`__GI___libc_read(fd=0, buf=0x00007ffe037bffcf,
nbytes=1) at read.c:26
    frame #1: 0x0000559350360867 bash`rl_getc + 391
    frame #2: 0x0000559350361065 bash`rl_read_key + 309
    frame #3: 0x0000559350347a12 bash`readline_internal_char + 98
    frame #4: 0x0000559350348225 bash`readline + 69
    frame #5: 0x00005593502c2de2 bash`___lldb_unnamed_symbol25$$bash + 162
    frame #6: 0x00005593502c51d0 bash`___lldb_unnamed_symbol37$$bash + 384
```

```
    frame #7: 0x00005593502c879a bash`___lldb_unnamed_symbol142$$bash + 90
    frame #8: 0x00005593502cc0d8 bash`yyparse + 1016
    frame #9: 0x00005593502c2476 bash`parse_command + 54
    frame #10: 0x00005593502c2584 bash`read_command + 84
    frame #11: 0x00005593502c2798 bash`reader_loop + 296
    frame #12: 0x00005593502c1104 bash`main + 4820
    frame #13: 0x00007f8fdeb1209b libc.so.6`__libc_start_main(main=(bash`main), argc=1,
argv=0x00007ffe037c1338, init=<unavailable>, fini=<unavailable>, rtld_fini=<unavailable>,
stack_end=0x00007ffe037c1328) at libc-start.c:308
    frame #14: 0x00005593502c165a bash`_start + 42

(lldb)  c
Process 28921 resuming

Command #2 'c' continued the target.
(lldb)
```

6.   If we want to log the *read* function parameters instead, we should specify a different list of commands:

```
^C
Process 28921 stopped
* thread #1, name = 'bash', stop reason = signal SIGSTOP
    frame #0: 0x00007f8fdebdec89 libc.so.6`__pselect(nfds=1, readfds=0x00007ffe037bffd0,
writefds=0x0000000000000000, exceptfds=0x0000000000000000, timeout=<unavailable>,
sigmask=0x00005593503b9840) at pselect.c:69

(lldb) break command add 1
Enter your debugger command(s).  Type 'DONE' to end.
> register read rdi rsi rdx
> c
> DONE
(lldb)
```

Note: For an A64 system, you need to specify X0, X1, and X2.

After we continue and resume typing, we get the new output:

```
(lldb) c
Process 28921 resuming
(lldb)  register read rdi rsi rdx
     rdi = 0x0000000000000000
     rsi = 0x00007ffe037bffcf
     rdx = 0x0000000000000001

(lldb)  c
Process 28921 resuming
Command #2 'c' continued the target.
(lldb)  register read rdi rsi rdx
     rdi = 0x0000000000000000
     rsi = 0x00007ffe037bffcf
     rdx = 0x0000000000000001

(lldb)  c
Process 28921 resuming
Command #2 'c' continued the target.
(lldb)  register read rdi rsi rdx
     rdi = 0x0000000000000000
```

```
        rsi = 0x00007ffe037bffcf
        rdx = 0x0000000000000001

(lldb)  c
Process 28921 resuming
Command #2 'c' continued the target.
(lldb)  register read rdi rsi rdx
        rdi = 0x0000000000000000
        rsi = 0x00007ffe037bffcf
        rdx = 0x0000000000000001

(lldb)  c
Process 28921 resuming
Command #2 'c' continued the target.
(lldb)  register read rdi rsi rdx
        rdi = 0x0000000000000000
        rsi = 0x00007ffe037bffcf
        rdx = 0x0000000000000001

(lldb)  c
Process 28921 resuming
Command #2 'c' continued the target.
(lldb)
```

Note: The first parameter (rdi) is 0 – stdin, the second (rsi) is the buffer address, and the third (rdx) – is the number of characters read.

7.   We can dereference the buffer's first byte and print typed characters instead:

```
^C
Process 28921 stopped
* thread #1, name = 'bash', stop reason = signal SIGSTOP
    frame #0: 0x00007f8fdebdec89 libc.so.6`__pselect(nfds=1, readfds=0x00007ffe037bffd0,
writefds=0x0000000000000000, exceptfds=0x0000000000000000, timeout=<unavailable>,
sigmask=0x00005593503b9840) at pselect.c:69

(lldb) break command add 1
Enter your debugger command(s).  Type 'DONE' to end.
> x/b $rsi
> c
> DONE
(lldb)

(lldb) c
Process 28921 resuming
(lldb)  x/b $rsi
0x7ffe037bffcf: '\0'

(lldb)  c
Process 28921 resuming
Command #2 'c' continued the target.
(lldb)  x/b $rsi
0x7ffe037bffcf: '\0'

(lldb)  c
Process 28921 resuming
Command #2 'c' continued the target.
```

```
(lldb)  x/b $rsi
0x7ffe037bffcf: '\0'

(lldb)  c
Process 28921 resuming
Command #2 'c' continued the target.
(lldb)  x/b $rsi
0x7ffe037bffcf: '\0'

(lldb)  c
Process 28921 resuming
Command #2 'c' continued the target.
(lldb)  x/b $rsi
0x7ffe037bffcf: '\0'

(lldb)  c
Process 28921 resuming
Command #2 'c' continued the target.
(lldb)
```

Note: However, we see that the buffer contents are 0. This is because we just entered the *read* function. We need to read the buffer when we return from it.

8.   We change the commands appropriately to log the buffer on return:

```
^C
Process 28921 stopped
* thread #1, name = 'bash', stop reason = signal SIGSTOP
    frame #0: 0x00007f8fdebdec89 libc.so.6`__pselect(nfds=1, readfds=0x00007ffe037bffd0,
writefds=0x0000000000000000, exceptfds=0x0000000000000000, timeout=<unavailable>,
sigmask=0x00005593503b9840) at pselect.c:69

(lldb) break command add 1
Enter your debugger command(s).  Type 'DONE' to end.
> finish
> x/c $rsi
> c
> DONE

(lldb) c
Process 28921 resuming
(lldb)  finish
error: Aborting reading of commands after command #1: 'finish' continued the target.
Process 28921 stopped
* thread #1, name = 'bash', stop reason = step out
Return value: (ssize_t) $10 = 1

    frame #0: 0x0000559350360867 bash`rl_getc + 391
bash`rl_getc:
->  0x559350360867 <+391>: cmpl   $0x1, %eax
    0x55935036086a <+394>: je     0x5593503608d0            ; <+496>
    0x55935036086c <+396>: testl  %eax, %eax
    0x55935036086e <+398>: jne    0x55935036078c            ; <+172>
```

Note: Unfortunately, the *finish* command breaks, and there is no continuation.

9.   We rectify this situation by putting the breakpoint on the current return address, specifying commands for it instead, and deleting the original first breakpoint:

```
(lldb) break set -a 0x559350360867
Breakpoint 2: where = bash`rl_getc + 391, address = 0x0000559350360867

(lldb) break command add 2
Enter your debugger command(s).  Type 'DONE' to end.
> x/c $rsi
> c
> DONE

(lldb) break delete 1
1 breakpoints deleted; 0 breakpoint locations disabled.

(lldb) c
Process 28921 resuming
Command #2 'c' continued the target.
(lldb)  x/b $rsi
0x7ffe037bffcf: 'H'

(lldb)  c
Process 28921 resuming
Command #2 'c' continued the target.
(lldb)  x/b $rsi
0x7ffe037bffcf: 'e'

(lldb)  c
Process 28921 resuming
Command #2 'c' continued the target.
(lldb)  x/b $rsi
0x7ffe037bffcf: 'l'

(lldb)  c
Process 28921 resuming
Command #2 'c' continued the target.
(lldb)  x/b $rsi
0x7ffe037bffcf: 'l'

(lldb)  c
Process 28921 resuming
Command #2 'c' continued the target.
(lldb)  x/b $rsi
0x7ffe037bffcf: 'o'

(lldb)  c
Process 28921 resuming
Command #2 'c' continued the target.
```

10.   We quit our debugging session and also exit the *bash* process in another terminal.

```
(lldb) q
Quitting LLDB will detach from one or more processes. Do you really want to proceed: [Y/n] y
```

Exercise UD5

- ⊙ **Goal:** Learn how to debug multiple processes and their deadlock

- ⊙ **Elementary Diagnostics Patterns:** Crash; Hang

- ⊙ **Memory Analysis Patterns:** Exception Stack Trace; Constant Subtrace; NULL Pointer (Data); Main Thread; Execution Residue (Unmanaged Space, User); C++ Exception; Hidden Exception (User Space); Handled Exception (User Space); Wait Chain (Mutex Objects); Deadlock (Objects, User Space); Coincidental Symbolic Information; Function Pointer

- ⊙ **Debugging Implementation Patterns:** Break-in

- ⊙ \ALD4\Exercise-Linux-UD5.pdf

Exercise UD5 (WinDbg)

Goal: Learn how to debug multiple processes and their deadlock.

Elementary Diagnostics Patterns: Crash; Hang.

Memory Analysis Patterns: Exception Stack Trace; Constant Subtrace; NULL Pointer (Data); Main Thread; Execution Residue (Unmanaged Space, User); C++ Exception; Hidden Exception (User Space); Handled Exception (User Space); Wait Chain (Mutex Objects); Deadlock (Objects, User Space); Coincidental Symbolic Information; Function Pointer.

Debugging Implementation Patterns: Break-in.

1.   The source code and the *Makefile* to build executables and libraries can be found in the *ud5* directory:

```
$ git clone https://bitbucket.org/softwarediagnostics/ald4
```

2.   Run the *ud5a* executable.

```
/mnt/c/ALD4/ud5$ ./ud5a
```

3.   Open a different terminal and run the *ud5b* executable.

```
/mnt/c/ALD4/ud5$ ./ud5b
```

4.   Both applications do not exit for almost 30 seconds. This is normal expected behavior (from these applications) as they mutually wait while doing some work (modeled by the *sleep* function call). The source code for the *ud5a* part:

```
void start_modeling()
{
        sem_t *sem_a = sem_open("ud5_sem_a", O_CREAT, 0644, 1);
        if (sem_a == SEM_FAILED) exit(EXIT_FAILURE);

        sem_wait(sem_a);

        sleep(20); // some work

        sem_t *sem_b = sem_open("ud5_sem_b", 0);
        if (sem_b == SEM_FAILED) exit(EXIT_FAILURE);

        sem_wait(sem_b);

        sleep(10); // some more work

        sem_post(sem_b);
        sem_post(sem_a);

        sem_close(sem_b);
        sem_close(sem_a);
```

```
        sem_unlink("ud5_sem_a");
}
```

The source code for the *ud5b* part:

```
void start_modeling()
{
        sem_t *sem_b = sem_open("ud5_sem_b", O_CREAT, 0644, 1);
        if (sem_b == SEM_FAILED) exit(EXIT_FAILURE);

        sem_wait(sem_b);

        sleep(10); // some work

        sem_post(sem_b);

        sem_t *sem_a = sem_open("ud5_sem_a", 0);
        if (sem_a == SEM_FAILED) exit(EXIT_FAILURE);

        sem_wait(sem_a);

        sleep(10); // some more work

        sem_post(sem_a);

        sem_close(sem_a);
        sem_close(sem_b);

        sem_unlink("ud5_sem_b");
}
```

Note: Although we have 2 synchronization objects, the code is deadlock-free as we acquire and release them in ABBA and BBAA orders and hold their ownership for a limited time.

5.   Run the *ud5a* again, then run the *ud5bv2* in a different terminal. The new feature was added to the *ud5b* (now version 2):

```
void start_modeling()
{
        sem_t *sem_b = sem_open("ud5_sem_b", O_CREAT, 0644, 1);
        if (sem_b == SEM_FAILED) exit(EXIT_FAILURE);

        sem_wait(sem_b);

        sleep(10); // some work

        new_feature();

        sem_post(sem_b);
```

```
sem_t *sem_a = sem_open("ud5_sem_a", 0);
if (sem_a == SEM_FAILED) exit(EXIT_FAILURE);

sem_wait(sem_a);

sleep(10); // some more work

sem_post(sem_a);

sem_close(sem_a);
sem_close(sem_b);

sem_unlink("ud5_sem_b");
}
```

We see that in about 10 seconds, the *ud5bv2* is aborted:

```
/mnt/c/ALD4/ud5$ ./ud5bv2
terminate called after throwing an instance of 'int'
Aborted
```

6.   After waiting more than 30 seconds, we see that the *ud5a* is never finished. To debug it, we check its PID and launch the process server in another terminal:

```
/mnt/c/ALD4/ud5$ ps -a | grep ud5a
16178 pts/5    00:00:00 ud5a
```

```
/mnt/c/ALD4/ud5$ sudo gdbserver --multi localhost:1234
Listening on port 1234
```

7.   Connect WinDbg to the process server and attach it to the *ud5a* process:

```
Microsoft (R) Windows Debugger Version 10.0.27553.1004 AMD64
Copyright (c) Microsoft Corporation. All rights reserved.

64-bit machine not using 64-bit API

************* Path validation summary **************
Response                        Time (ms)     Location
Deferred                                      srv*
Symbol search path is: srv*
Executable search path is:
Unknown System Version 0 UP Free x64
System Uptime: not available
Process Uptime: not available
Reloading current modules
ModLoad: 0000562d`91b02000 0000562d`91b06068   /mnt/c/ALD4/ud5/ud5a
ModLoad: 00007ffd`a2cfd000 00007ffd`a2cfd000   linux-vdso.so.1
ModLoad: 00007f1b`38fbe000 00007f1b`38fde4c0   /lib/x86_64-linux-gnu/libpthread.so.0
ModLoad: 00007f1b`38e3a000 00007f1b`38fbd020   /usr/lib/x86_64-linux-gnu/libstdc++.so.6
ModLoad: 00007f1b`38cb7000 00007f1b`38e39148   /lib/x86_64-linux-gnu/libm.so.6
ModLoad: 00007f1b`38c9d000 00007f1b`38cb6430   /lib/x86_64-linux-gnu/libgcc_s.so.1
ModLoad: 00007f1b`38add000 00007f1b`38c9c800   /lib/x86_64-linux-gnu/libc.so.6
```

```
ModLoad: 00007f1b`38fec000 00007f1b`39015190   /lib64/ld-linux-x86-64.so.2
........
ReadVirtual() failed in GetXStateConfiguration() first read attempt (error == 0.)
Unable to load image /lib/x86_64-linux-gnu/libpthread.so.0, Win32 error 0n2
*** WARNING: Unable to verify timestamp for /lib/x86_64-linux-gnu/libpthread.so.0
libpthread_so!do_futex_wait.constprop.1+0x36:
00007f1b`38fce896 cmp      rax,0FFFFFFFFFFFFF000h
```

8.   Open a log file (useful when the output doesn't fit into the buffer and we need to search for something).

```
0:000> .logopen C:\ALD4\ud5.log
Opened log file 'C:\ALD4\ud5.log'
```

9.   We examine the backtrace:

```
0:000> k
Unable to load image /mnt/c/ALD4/ud5/ud5a, Win32 error 0n2
*** WARNING: Unable to verify timestamp for /mnt/c/ALD4/ud5/ud5a
Unable to load image /lib/x86_64-linux-gnu/libc.so.6, Win32 error 0n2
*** WARNING: Unable to verify timestamp for /lib/x86_64-linux-gnu/libc.so.6
 # Child-SP          RetAddr             Call Site
00 00007ffd`a2cc20c0 00007f1b`38fce988 libpthread_so!do_futex_wait.constprop.1+0x36
01 00007ffd`a2cc20f0 0000562d`91b0323b libpthread_so!_new_sem_wait_slow.constprop.0+0x98
02 00007ffd`a2cc2150 0000562d`91b031aa ud5a!start_modeling+0x8a [/mnt/c/ALD4/ud5/ud5a.cpp @ 36]
03 00007ffd`a2cc2170 00007f1b`38b0109b ud5a!main+0x15 [/mnt/c/ALD4/ud5/ud5a.cpp @ 19]
04 00007ffd`a2cc2180 0000562d`91b030da libc_so!__libc_start_main+0xeb
05 00007ffd`a2cc2240 ffffffff`ffffffff ud5a!start+0x2a
06 00007ffd`a2cc2248 00000000`00000000 0xffffffff`ffffffff
```

We see that the thread is waiting for a semaphore that is implemented as a fast userspace mutex. We now switch to frame **2** after setting the source code location:

```
0:000> .srcpath C:\ALD4\ud5
Source search path is: C:\ALD4\ud5

************* Path validation summary **************
Response                    Time (ms)      Location
OK                                         C:\ALD4\ud5

0:000> .frame 2
02 00007ffd`a2cc2150 0000562d`91b031aa   ud5a!start_modeling+0x8a [/mnt/c/ALD4/ud5/ud5a.cpp @ 36]
```

Source code should also be highlighted:

```
ud5a.cpp                                            ▾ ☐ ✕
   21
   22 void start_modeling()
   23 {
   24      sem_t *sem_a = sem_open("ud5_sem_a", O_CREAT, 0644, 1);
   25      if (sem_a == SEM_FAILED) exit(EXIT_FAILURE);
   26
   27      sem_wait(sem_a);
   28
   29      sleep(20); // some work
   30
   31      sem_t *sem_b = sem_open("ud5_sem_b", 0);
   32      if (sem_b == SEM_FAILED) exit(EXIT_FAILURE);
   33
   34      sem_wait(sem_b);
   35
⇨  36      sleep(10); // some more work
   37
   38      sem_post(sem_b);
   39      sem_post(sem_a);
   40
   41      sem_close(sem_b);
```

Note: We see that the *ud5a* is waiting for the *sem_b* semaphore created in the aborted *ud5bv2* process.

10.   Now we continue execution (**g**), disconnect from the process server, quit WinDbg, quit the process server (**^C**), and the *ud5a* process (**^C**).

11.   An inexperienced developer tried to fix the problem in the *ud5bv2* by enclosing a portion of the code into a *try/catch* block and produced *ud5bv3*:

```
void start_modeling()
{
        sem_t *sem_b = sem_open("ud5_sem_b", O_CREAT, 0644, 1);
        if (sem_b == SEM_FAILED) exit(EXIT_FAILURE);

        sem_wait(sem_b);

        sleep(10); // some work

        try
        {
                new_feature();

                sem_post(sem_b);
        }
        catch (...)
        {
                // ignore
        }

        sem_t *sem_a = sem_open("ud5_sem_a", 0);
        if (sem_a == SEM_FAILED) exit(EXIT_FAILURE);
```

190

```
    sem_wait(sem_a);

    sleep(10); // some more work

    sem_post(sem_a);

    sem_close(sem_a);
    sem_close(sem_b);

    sem_unlink("ud5_sem_b");
}
```

12.   We run *ud5a* and *ud5bv3* (in a different terminal). After waiting more than a minute we see that both processes still hang. To debug *ud5bv3*, we launch the process server in another terminal and attach WinDbg to *ud5bv3*:

```
Microsoft (R) Windows Debugger Version 10.0.27553.1004 AMD64
Copyright (c) Microsoft Corporation. All rights reserved.

64-bit machine not using 64-bit API

************* Path validation summary **************
Response                        Time (ms)    Location
Deferred                                     srv*
Symbol search path is: srv*
Executable search path is:
Unknown System Version 0 UP Free x64
System Uptime: not available
Process Uptime: not available
Reloading current modules
ModLoad: 00005564`99d57000 00005564`99d5b090   /mnt/c/ALD4/ud5/ud5bv3
ModLoad: 00007fff`29bde000 00007fff`29bde000   linux-vdso.so.1
ModLoad: 00007f73`e4891000 00007f73`e48b14c0   /lib/x86_64-linux-gnu/libpthread.so.0
ModLoad: 00007f73`e470d000 00007f73`e4890020   /usr/lib/x86_64-linux-gnu/libstdc++.so.6
ModLoad: 00007f73`e458a000 00007f73`e470c148   /lib/x86_64-linux-gnu/libm.so.6
ModLoad: 00007f73`e4570000 00007f73`e4589430   /lib/x86_64-linux-gnu/libgcc_s.so.1
ModLoad: 00007f73`e43b0000 00007f73`e456f800   /lib/x86_64-linux-gnu/libc.so.6
ModLoad: 00007f73`e48bf000 00007f73`e48e8190   /lib64/ld-linux-x86-64.so.2
........
ReadVirtual() failed in GetXStateConfiguration() first read attempt (error == 0.)
Unable to load image /lib/x86_64-linux-gnu/libpthread.so.0, Win32 error 0n2
*** WARNING: Unable to verify timestamp for /lib/x86_64-linux-gnu/libpthread.so.0
libpthread_so!do_futex_wait.constprop.1+0x36:
00007f73`e48a1896 cmp       rax,0FFFFFFFFFFFFF000h
```

We examine its backtrace and the corresponding frame:

```
0:000> k
Unable to load image /mnt/c/ALD4/ud5/ud5bv3, Win32 error 0n2
*** WARNING: Unable to verify timestamp for /mnt/c/ALD4/ud5/ud5bv3
Unable to load image /lib/x86_64-linux-gnu/libc.so.6, Win32 error 0n2
*** WARNING: Unable to verify timestamp for /lib/x86_64-linux-gnu/libc.so.6
 # Child-SP          RetAddr           Call Site
00 00007fff`29bccd90 00007f73`e48a1988 libpthread_so!do_futex_wait.constprop.1+0x36
01 00007fff`29bccdc0 00005564`99d5828c libpthread_so!_new_sem_wait_slow.constprop.0+0x98
02 00007fff`29bcce20 00005564`99d581ea ud5bv3!start_modeling+0x9b [/mnt/c/ALD4/ud5/ud5bv3.cpp @ 48]
03 00007fff`29bcce40 00007f73`e43d409b ud5bv3!main+0x15 [/mnt/c/ALD4/ud5/ud5bv3.cpp @ 20]
```

```
04 00007fff`29bcce50 00005564`99d5811a   libc_so!_libc_start_main+0xeb
05 00007fff`29bccf10 ffffffff`ffffffff   ud5bv3!start+0x2a
06 00007fff`29bccf18 00000000`00000000   0xffffffff`ffffffff
```

```
0:000> .frame 2
02 00007fff`29bcce20 00005564`99d581ea   ud5bv3!start_modeling+0x9b [/mnt/c/ALD4/ud5/ud5bv3.cpp @ 48]
```

ud5bv3.cpp   ▾ ☐ ✕

```cpp
23  void start_modeling()
24  {
25      sem_t *sem_b = sem_open("ud5_sem_b", O_CREAT, 0644, 1);
26      if (sem_b == SEM_FAILED) exit(EXIT_FAILURE);
27
28      sem_wait(sem_b);
29
30      sleep(10); // some work
31
32      try
33      {
34          new_feature();
35
36          sem_post(sem_b);
37      }
38      catch (...)
39      {
40          // ignore
41      }
42
43      sem_t *sem_a = sem_open("ud5_sem_a", 0);
44      if (sem_a == SEM_FAILED) exit(EXIT_FAILURE);
45
46      sem_wait(sem_a);
47
48      sleep(10); // some more work
49
50      sem_post(sem_a);
51
52      sem_close(sem_a);
53      sem_close(sem_b);
54
55      sem_unlink("ud5_sem_b");
56  }
```

Since we do not expect a wait (we assume *new_feature* code is complex), we look at raw stack data to find any anomalies, such as hidden and handled exceptions. This is done by dumping the stack region (**dps**) and looking for relevant symbol references:

```
0:000> k
 # Child-SP          RetAddr               Call Site
00 00007fff`29bccd90 00007f73`e48a1988   libpthread_so!do_futex_wait.constprop.1+0x36
01 00007fff`29bccdc0 00005564`99d5828c   libpthread_so!_new_sem_wait_slow.constprop.0+0x98
02 00007fff`29bcce20 00005564`99d581ea   ud5bv3!start_modeling+0x9b [/mnt/c/ALD4/ud5/ud5bv3.cpp @ 48]
03 00007fff`29bcce40 00007f73`e43d409b   ud5bv3!main+0x15 [/mnt/c/ALD4/ud5/ud5bv3.cpp @ 20]
04 00007fff`29bcce50 00005564`99d5811a   libc_so!_libc_start_main+0xeb
05 00007fff`29bccf10 ffffffff`ffffffff   ud5bv3!start+0x2a
06 00007fff`29bccf18 00000000`00000000   0xffffffff`ffffffff
```

```
0:000> dps 00007fff`29bcc000 00007fff`29bcce50
00007fff`29bcc000  00000000`00000006
00007fff`29bcc008  00000000`000055b2
00007fff`29bcc010  00000003`00000000
00007fff`29bcc018  00007f73`e48b33f0
00007fff`29bcc020  00005564`99d57607 ud5bv3!+0x10f
00007fff`29bcc028  00007f73`e48e8160 ld_linux_x86_64_so!r_debug
00007fff`29bcc030  00000000`00000820
00007fff`29bcc038  00007f73`e48c86fc ld_linux_x86_64_so!dl_rtld_di_serinfo+0x34c
00007fff`29bcc040  00000000`00000001
00007fff`29bcc048  00000000`00000333
00007fff`29bcc050  00007f73`e48b3410
00007fff`29bcc058  00000000`00000001
00007fff`29bcc060  00007f73`e43b27a0 libc_so!_h_errno+0x272c
00007fff`29bcc068  00007f73`e48c8b04 ld_linux_x86_64_so!dl_rtld_di_serinfo+0x754
00007fff`29bcc070  00000000`00000333
00007fff`29bcc078  00007f73`e43c1cd8 libc_so!_h_errno+0x11c64
00007fff`29bcc080  00007f73`e48b3410
00007fff`29bcc088  00007fff`29bcc108
00007fff`29bcc090  00007fff`29bcc104
00007fff`29bcc098  00007f73`e48c886e ld_linux_x86_64_so!dl_rtld_di_serinfo+0x4be
00007fff`29bcc0a0  00000000`00000000
00007fff`29bcc0a8  00007f73`e43c1cd8 libc_so!_h_errno+0x11c64
00007fff`29bcc0b0  00007f73`e43b3fb0 libc_so!_h_errno+0x3f3c
00007fff`29bcc0b8  00007f73`e4571d2a libgcc_s_so!+0x1d2a
00007fff`29bcc0c0  00000000`1c93bb9d
00007fff`29bcc0c8  00007f73`e45707e8 libgcc_s_so!+0x7e8
00007fff`29bcc0d0  00000000`00724eee
00007fff`29bcc0d8  00007fff`29bcc1d0
00007fff`29bcc0e0  00007fff`29bcc1c0
00007fff`29bcc0e8  00007fff`29bcc108
00007fff`29bcc0f0  00007f73`e48b3a60
00007fff`29bcc0f8  00000000`00000007
00007fff`29bcc100  00000000`00000001
00007fff`29bcc108  00000000`00000000
00007fff`29bcc110  00007fff`00000000
00007fff`29bcc118  00000000`1c93bb9d
00007fff`29bcc120  00007f73`e48b3270
00007fff`29bcc128  00007fff`29bcc268
00007fff`29bcc130  00007f73`e48b2f10
00007fff`29bcc138  00000000`00000000
00007fff`29bcc140  00007f73`e43ae7e0
00007fff`29bcc148  00007f73`e48c939f ld_linux_x86_64_so!dl_rtld_di_serinfo+0xfef
00007fff`29bcc150  00000000`00000005
00007fff`29bcc158  00007f73`e43ae7e0
00007fff`29bcc160  00000000`00000001
00007fff`29bcc168  00000000`00000000
00007fff`29bcc170  00000000`00000001
00007fff`29bcc178  00007f73`e48c86fc ld_linux_x86_64_so!dl_rtld_di_serinfo+0x34c
00007fff`29bcc180  00007f73`e4571d2a libgcc_s_so!+0x1d2a
00007fff`29bcc188  00000000`0000005c
00007fff`29bcc190  00007f73`e48b2f10
00007fff`29bcc198  00000000`00000001
00007fff`29bcc1a0  00007f73`e4570618 libgcc_s_so!+0x618
00007fff`29bcc1a8  00007f73`e48c8b04 ld_linux_x86_64_so!dl_rtld_di_serinfo+0x754
00007fff`29bcc1b0  00000000`0000005c
00007fff`29bcc1b8  00007f73`e4571778 libgcc_s_so!+0x1778
00007fff`29bcc1c0  00007f73`e48b2f10
00007fff`29bcc1c8  00007fff`29bcc248
00007fff`29bcc1d0  00007fff`29bcc244
00007fff`29bcc1d8  00007f73`e48c886e ld_linux_x86_64_so!dl_rtld_di_serinfo+0x4be
00007fff`29bcc1e0  00007f73`00000000
00007fff`29bcc1e8  00007f73`e4571778 libgcc_s_so!+0x1778
00007fff`29bcc1f0  00007f73`e4570758 libgcc_s_so!+0x758
00007fff`29bcc1f8  00007f73`e4737c99 libstdc___so!std::__once_callable+0x2ac81
```

```
00007fff`29bcc200  00000000`919221fd
00007fff`29bcc208  00007f73`e4716350 libstdc___so!std::__once_callable+0x9338
00007fff`29bcc210  00000000`02464887
00007fff`29bcc218  00007fff`29bcc310
00007fff`29bcc220  00007fff`29bcc300
00007fff`29bcc228  00007fff`29bcc248
00007fff`29bcc230  00007f73`e48b3a60
00007fff`29bcc238  00000000`00000007
00007fff`29bcc240  00000000`00000001
00007fff`29bcc248  00000000`00000000
00007fff`29bcc250  00000000`00000001
00007fff`29bcc258  00000000`919221fd
00007fff`29bcc260  00007f73`e48b2870
00007fff`29bcc268  00007fff`29bcc3a8
00007fff`29bcc270  00007f73`e48b2510
00007fff`29bcc278  00000000`00000000
00007fff`29bcc280  00007f73`e43ae420
00007fff`29bcc288  00007f73`e48c939f ld_linux_x86_64_so!dl_rtld_di_serinfo+0xfef
00007fff`29bcc290  00000000`00000004
00007fff`29bcc298  00007f73`e43ae420
00007fff`29bcc2a0  00000000`00000001
00007fff`29bcc2a8  00000000`00000000
00007fff`29bcc2b0  00000000`00000001
00007fff`29bcc2b8  00007f73`e48b2510
00007fff`29bcc2c0  00007f73`e4737c99 libstdc___so!std::__once_callable+0x2ac81
00007fff`29bcc2c8  00000001`29bcc348
00007fff`29bcc2d0  00007fff`29bcc300
00007fff`29bcc2d8  00007fff`29bcc310
00007fff`29bcc2e0  00007f73`e48b2870
00007fff`29bcc2e8  00000000`00000000
00007fff`29bcc2f0  00007f73`e4892080 libpthread_so!
00007fff`29bcc2f8  00007f73`e4571dc5 libgcc_s_so!+0x1dc5
00007fff`29bcc300  00000000`ffffffff
00007fff`29bcc308  00007f73`e4570890 libgcc_s_so!+0x890
00007fff`29bcc310  00007f73`e4570ff8 libgcc_s_so!+0xff8
00007fff`29bcc318  00007f73`e48b2f10
00007fff`29bcc320  00007fff`29bcc400
00007fff`29bcc328  00007fff`29bcc348
00007fff`29bcc330  00007f73`e48b3a60
00007fff`29bcc338  00007f73`e48c86fc ld_linux_x86_64_so!dl_rtld_di_serinfo+0x34c
00007fff`29bcc340  00000000`ffffffff
00007fff`29bcc348  00000000`00000041
00007fff`29bcc350  00007f73`e48b2f10
00007fff`29bcc358  00007f73`e488c900 libstdc___so!vtable for std::messages_byname<wchar_t>+0x2c10
00007fff`29bcc360  00005564`99d582c8 ud5bv3!start_modeling+0xd7 [/mnt/c/ALD4/ud5/ud5bv3.cpp @ 38]
00007fff`29bcc368  00005564`9aa62f30
00007fff`29bcc370  00000000`00000001
00007fff`29bcc378  00000000`00000003
00007fff`29bcc380  00000000`00000000
00007fff`29bcc388  00007f73`e48cdb10 ld_linux_x86_64_so!dl_rtld_di_serinfo+0x5760
00007fff`29bcc390  00000000`00000001
00007fff`29bcc398  00000000`00000000
00007fff`29bcc3a0  00000000`00000000
00007fff`29bcc3a8  00007f73`e4570ff8 libgcc_s_so!+0xff8
00007fff`29bcc3b0  00007fff`29bcc760
00007fff`29bcc3b8  00007f73`e48d458a ld_linux_x86_64_so!dl_find_dso_for_object+0x2b2a
00007fff`29bcc3c0  00000000`00000008
00007fff`29bcc3c8  00007fff`29bccdb0
00007fff`29bcc3d0  00000000`00000001
00007fff`29bcc3d8  00005564`99d582c8 ud5bv3!start_modeling+0xd7 [/mnt/c/ALD4/ud5/ud5bv3.cpp @ 38]
00007fff`29bcc3e0  00007fff`29bccb30
00007fff`29bcc3e8  00007fff`29bccb30
00007fff`29bcc3f0  00000000`00000150
00007fff`29bcc3f8  00000000`00000007
00007fff`29bcc400  00000000`ffffffff
```

```
00007fff`29bcc408    00000000`00000000
00007fff`29bcc410    00007f73`e4893778 libpthread_so!+0x16f8
00007fff`29bcc418    0000ffff`00001f80
00007fff`29bcc420    00007f73`e48b2870
00007fff`29bcc428    00007fff`29bcc568
00007fff`29bcc430    00007f73`e48b2510
00007fff`29bcc438    00007f73`e48c86fc ld_linux_x86_64_so!dl_rtld_di_serinfo+0x34c
00007fff`29bcc440    00007f73`e43ae4e0
00007fff`29bcc448    00000000`0000006e
00007fff`29bcc450    00007f73`e48b2f10
00007fff`29bcc458    00000000`00000001
00007fff`29bcc460    00007f73`e4570660 libgcc_s_so!+0x660
00007fff`29bcc468    00007f73`e48c8b04 ld_linux_x86_64_so!dl_rtld_di_serinfo+0x754
00007fff`29bcc470    00000000`0000006e
00007fff`29bcc478    00007f73`e4571778 libgcc_s_so!+0x1778
00007fff`29bcc480    00007f73`e48b2f10
00007fff`29bcc488    00007fff`29bcc508
00007fff`29bcc490    00007fff`29bcc504
00007fff`29bcc498    00007fff`29bcc4d0
00007fff`29bcc4a0    00000000`00000000
00007fff`29bcc4a8    00000000`00000000
00007fff`29bcc4b0    000000ff`00000000
00007fff`29bcc4b8    0000ffff`00000000
00007fff`29bcc4c0    00000000`00000000
00007fff`29bcc4c8    00000000`00000000
00007fff`29bcc4d0    00000000`00000000
00007fff`29bcc4d8    00005564`99d582dc ud5bv3!new_feature [/mnt/c/ALD4/ud5/new_feature.cpp @ 2]
00007fff`29bcc4e0    40000000`00000000
00007fff`29bcc4e8    00000000`00000000
00007fff`29bcc4f0    00000000`00000000
00007fff`29bcc4f8    00000000`00000000
00007fff`29bcc500    00000000`00000000
00007fff`29bcc508    00000000`00000000
00007fff`29bcc510    00007fff`29bccdd0
00007fff`29bcc518    00007fff`29bccdd8
00007fff`29bcc520    5f6d6573`5f356475
00007fff`29bcc528    65735f35`64750062
00007fff`29bcc530    00000000`00000000
00007fff`29bcc538    00000000`00000000
00007fff`29bcc540    00000000`00000000
00007fff`29bcc548    00000000`00000000
00007fff`29bcc550    00000000`00000000
00007fff`29bcc558    00000000`00000000
00007fff`29bcc560    00000000`00000000
00007fff`29bcc568    00000000`00000000
00007fff`29bcc570    00000000`00000000
00007fff`29bcc578    00000000`00000000
00007fff`29bcc580    00000000`00000000
00007fff`29bcc588    00000000`00000000
00007fff`29bcc590    00000000`00000000
00007fff`29bcc598    00000000`00000000
00007fff`29bcc5a0    00007f73`e48b3270
00007fff`29bcc5a8    00000000`00000000
00007fff`29bcc5b0    00000000`00000150
00007fff`29bcc5b8    ffff0000`00000000
00007fff`29bcc5c0    00000000`ffffffff
00007fff`29bcc5c8    00000000`0000ff00
00007fff`29bcc5d0    00007f73`e45711a8 libgcc_s_so!+0x11a8
00007fff`29bcc5d8    00007f73`e48b2f10
00007fff`29bcc5e0    2f2f2f2f`2f2f2f2f
00007fff`29bcc5e8    2f2f2f2f`2f2f2f2f
00007fff`29bcc5f0    00000000`00000000
00007fff`29bcc5f8    00000000`00000000
00007fff`29bcc600    00000000`00000002
00007fff`29bcc608    80000000`00000006
```

```
00007fff`29bcc610    00000000`00000000
00007fff`29bcc618    00000000`00000000
00007fff`29bcc620    00000000`00000000
00007fff`29bcc628    00000000`00000000
00007fff`29bcc630    00000000`00000000
00007fff`29bcc638    00000000`00000000
00007fff`29bcc640    00007fff`29bcc790
00007fff`29bcc648    00007f73`e4582517 libgcc_s_so!Unwind_Backtrace+0xc27
00007fff`29bcc650    00000000`00000001
00007fff`29bcc658    00000000`00000000
00007fff`29bcc660    00005564`99d59068 ud5bv3!
00007fff`29bcc668    00000000`00000008
00007fff`29bcc670    00000000`000000eb
00007fff`29bcc678    00007f73`e48d458a ld_linux_x86_64_so!dl_find_dso_for_object+0x2b2a
00007fff`29bcc680    00000000`00000006
00007fff`29bcc688    00000000`0000000b
00007fff`29bcc690    00005564`9aa62f50
00007fff`29bcc698    00005564`99d591d8 ud5bv3!
00007fff`29bcc6a0    00007fff`29bccb30
00007fff`29bcc6a8    00007fff`29bcc700
00007fff`29bcc6b0    00000000`00000008
00007fff`29bcc6b8    00007f73`e48e7060 ld_linux_x86_64_so!rtld_global
00007fff`29bcc6c0    00007fff`29bccb30
00007fff`29bcc6c8    00000000`00000000
00007fff`29bcc6d0    00007f73`e48e8190
00007fff`29bcc6d8    00007f73`e44e3973 libc_so!dl_iterate_phdr+0x193
00007fff`29bcc6e0    5f6d6573`5f356475
00007fff`29bcc6e8    65735f35`00000001
00007fff`29bcc6f0    00007f73`e45820b0 libgcc_s_so!Unwind_Backtrace+0x7c0
00007fff`29bcc6f8    00007fff`29bcc790
00007fff`29bcc700    00005564`99d57000 ud5bv3!
00007fff`29bcc708    00007f73`e48e8728
00007fff`29bcc710    00005564`99d57040 ud5bv3!+0x40
00007fff`29bcc718    00007fff`29bc000b
00007fff`29bcc720    00000000`00000008
00007fff`29bcc728    00000000`00000000
00007fff`29bcc730    00000000`00000000
00007fff`29bcc738    00000000`00000000
00007fff`29bcc740    00000000`00000000
00007fff`29bcc748    2495fa01`d3f21300
00007fff`29bcc750    00007fff`29bccdf8
00007fff`29bcc758    00007fff`29bccb30
00007fff`29bcc760    00007fff`29bccb30
00007fff`29bcc768    00007f73`e48b2510
00007fff`29bcc770    00000000`0000031d
00007fff`29bcc778    00007f73`e479f118 libstdc___so!_gxx_personality_v0+0xb8
00007fff`29bcc780    00005564`99d58248 ud5bv3!start_modeling+0x57 [/mnt/c/ALD4/ud5/ud5bv3.cpp @ 34]
00007fff`29bcc788    00005564`9aa62f30
00007fff`29bcc790    00000006`01d58248
00007fff`29bcc798    00000000`00000000
00007fff`29bcc7a0    00005564`99d591d8 ud5bv3!
00007fff`29bcc7a8    00007fff`29bcc701
00007fff`29bcc7b0    00005564`99d59130 ud5bv3!+0xc8
00007fff`29bcc7b8    00005564`00000001
00007fff`29bcc7c0    00000000`00000000
00007fff`29bcc7c8    00005564`99d59145 ud5bv3!+0xdd
00007fff`29bcc7d0    00005564`99d59145 ud5bv3!+0xdd
00007fff`29bcc7d8    00000000`29bccb30
00007fff`29bcc7e0    00000000`00000000
00007fff`29bcc7e8    00000000`0000001b
00007fff`29bcc7f0    00007fff`29bcc880
00007fff`29bcc7f8    00007f73`e48c86fc ld_linux_x86_64_so!dl_rtld_di_serinfo+0x34c
00007fff`29bcc800    00000000`00000000
00007fff`29bcc808    00000000`00000895
00007fff`29bcc810    00007f73`e48b2510
```

```
00007fff`29bcc818  00000000`00000001
00007fff`29bcc820  00007f73`e47122c0 libstdc___so!std::__once_callable+0x52a8
00007fff`29bcc828  00007f73`e48c8b04 ld_linux_x86_64_so!dl_rtld_di_serinfo+0x754
00007fff`29bcc830  00000000`00000895
00007fff`29bcc838  00007f73`e48c86fc ld_linux_x86_64_so!dl_rtld_di_serinfo+0x34c
00007fff`29bcc840  00007f73`e48b2510
00007fff`29bcc848  00000000`00000929
00007fff`29bcc850  00007f73`e48b3410
00007fff`29bcc858  00000000`00000001
00007fff`29bcc860  00007f73`e43b3f78 libc_so!h_errno+0x3f04
00007fff`29bcc868  00007f73`e48c8b04 ld_linux_x86_64_so!dl_rtld_di_serinfo+0x754
00007fff`29bcc870  00000000`00000929
00007fff`29bcc878  00007f73`e43c1cd8 libc_so!h_errno+0x11c64
00007fff`29bcc880  00007f73`e48b3410
00007fff`29bcc888  00007fff`29bcc908
00007fff`29bcc890  00007fff`29bcc904
00007fff`29bcc898  00007f73`e48c886e ld_linux_x86_64_so!dl_rtld_di_serinfo+0x4be
00007fff`29bcc8a0  00007fff`00000000
00007fff`29bcc8a8  00007f73`e43c1cd8 libc_so!h_errno+0x11c64
00007fff`29bcc8b0  00007f73`e43b3fb0 libc_so!h_errno+0x3f3c
00007fff`29bcc8b8  00007f73`e47378f8 libstdc___so!std::__once_callable+0x2a8e0
00007fff`29bcc8c0  00000000`7c96f087
00007fff`29bcc8c8  00007f73`e4715c48 libstdc___so!std::__once_callable+0x8c30
00007fff`29bcc8d0  00000000`01f25bc2
00007fff`29bcc8d8  00007fff`29bcc9d0
00007fff`29bcc8e0  00007fff`29bcc9c0
00007fff`29bcc8e8  00007fff`29bcc908
00007fff`29bcc8f0  00007f73`e48b3a60
00007fff`29bcc8f8  00000000`00000007
00007fff`29bcc900  00000000`e43ae2a0
00007fff`29bcc908  00000000`00000000
00007fff`29bcc910  00000000`00000002
00007fff`29bcc918  00000000`7c96f087
00007fff`29bcc920  00007f73`e48b2870
00007fff`29bcc928  00007fff`29bcca68
00007fff`29bcc930  00007f73`e48b2510
00007fff`29bcc938  00000000`00000000
00007fff`29bcc940  00007f73`e43ae3f0
00007fff`29bcc948  00007f73`e48c939f ld_linux_x86_64_so!dl_rtld_di_serinfo+0xfef
00007fff`29bcc950  00000000`00000005
00007fff`29bcc958  00007f73`e43ae3f0
00007fff`29bcc960  00000000`00000001
00007fff`29bcc968  00000000`00000000
00007fff`29bcc970  00000000`00000001
00007fff`29bcc978  00007f73`e48b2510
00007fff`29bcc980  00007f73`e47378f8 libstdc___so!std::__once_callable+0x2a8e0
00007fff`29bcc988  00000001`00000001
00007fff`29bcc990  00007fff`29bcc9c0
00007fff`29bcc998  00007fff`29bcc9d0
00007fff`29bcc9a0  00007f73`e48b2870
00007fff`29bcc9a8  00000000`00000000
00007fff`29bcc9b0  00000000`00000006
00007fff`29bcc9b8  00000000`00000000
00007fff`29bcc9c0  00000000`ffffffff
00007fff`29bcc9c8  00005564`99d582db ud5bv3!start_modeling+0xea [/mnt/c/ALD4/ud5/ud5bv3.cpp @ 56]
00007fff`29bcc9d0  00007f73`e43c1b88 libc_so!h_errno+0x11b14
00007fff`29bcc9d8  00007f73`e48b3410
00007fff`29bcc9e0  00007fff`29bcce30
00007fff`29bcc9e8  00005564`99d580f0 ud5bv3!start
00007fff`29bcc9f0  00007fff`29bccf20
00007fff`29bcc9f8  00000000`00000000
00007fff`29bcca00  00000000`00000000
00007fff`29bcca08  00007f73`e48cdb10 ld_linux_x86_64_so!dl_rtld_di_serinfo+0x5760
00007fff`29bcca10  00000000`00000001
00007fff`29bcca18  00007f73`e488ba10 libstdc___so!vtable for std::messages_byname<wchar_t>+0x1d20
```

```
00007fff`29bcca20  00007fff`29bcce30
00007fff`29bcca28  00005564`99d580f0  ud5bv3!start
00007fff`29bcca30  00007fff`29bccf20
00007fff`29bcca38  00000000`00000000
00007fff`29bcca40  00000000`00000000
00007fff`29bcca48  00007f73`e48cdb10  ld_linux_x86_64_so!dl_rtld_di_serinfo+0x5760
00007fff`29bcca50  00000000`00000001
00007fff`29bcca58  00000000`00000000
00007fff`29bcca60  00000000`00000001
00007fff`29bcca68  00007f73`e43c1b88  libc_so!_h_errno+0x11b14
00007fff`29bcca70  00007fff`29bcce00
00007fff`29bcca78  00007f73`e48d458a  ld_linux_x86_64_so!dl_find_dso_for_object+0x2b2a
00007fff`29bcca80  00000000`00000018
00007fff`29bcca88  00000000`00000000
00007fff`29bcca90  00000000`00000007
00007fff`29bcca98  00000000`00000020
00007fff`29bccaa0  00005564`00000002
00007fff`29bccaa8  00005564`9aa51010
00007fff`29bccab0  00000000`0000000f
00007fff`29bccab8  00000000`00000040
00007fff`29bccac0  ffffffff`ffffff90
00007fff`29bccac8  00000000`00000000
00007fff`29bccad0  00000030`00000002
00007fff`29bccad8  00000000`00000000
00007fff`29bccae0  00000077`0000005b
00007fff`29bccae8  00000000`00000000
00007fff`29bccaf0  0000006e`0000007c
00007fff`29bccaf8  00000000`00000000
00007fff`29bccb00  00000000`00000004
00007fff`29bccb08  00000000`0000000f
00007fff`29bccb10  00000000`00000018
00007fff`29bccb18  00000000`00000000
00007fff`29bccb20  ffffffff`ffffff90
00007fff`29bccb28  00000000`00000000
00007fff`29bccb30  00000000`00000000
00007fff`29bccb38  00007f73`e44345a3  libc_so!_libc_malloc+0x93
00007fff`29bccb40  00000077`0000005b
00007fff`29bccb48  00005564`9aa62eb0
00007fff`29bccb50  00000000`ffffffff
00007fff`29bccb58  00007f73`e48b14b0  libpthread_so!_sem_mappings
00007fff`29bccb60  00000000`00000000
00007fff`29bccb68  00007f73`e44a51c4  libc_so!tsearch+0x134
00007fff`29bccb70  00005564`9aa62eb8
00007fff`29bccb78  00005564`9aa62fa0
00007fff`29bccb80  00005564`9aa62f60
00007fff`29bccb88  00007f73`e48a10f0  libpthread_so!_sem_search
00007fff`29bccb90  00007fff`29bccbd0
00007fff`29bccb98  00007f73`e48bd000
00007fff`29bccba0  00007fff`29bcccf0
00007fff`29bccba8  00000000`0000000a
00007fff`29bccbb0  00000000`00000003
00007fff`29bccbb8  00005564`99d5900e  ud5bv3!IO_stdin_used+0xe
00007fff`29bccbc0  00005564`9aa62f60
00007fff`29bccbc8  00007f73`e48a103e  libpthread_so!check_add_mapping+0x21e
00007fff`29bccbd0  00000000`00000043
00007fff`29bccbd8  00000000`0000001a
00007fff`29bccbe0  5f6d6573`5f356475
00007fff`29bccbe8  65735f35`64750062
00007fff`29bccbf0  5f6d6573`5f356475
00007fff`29bccbf8  00000000`00000061
00007fff`29bccc00  00000000`00000000
00007fff`29bccc08  00007f73`e48a0e63  libpthread_so!check_add_mapping+0x43
00007fff`29bccc10  00000000`00000000
00007fff`29bccc18  00000000`00000000
00007fff`29bccc20  00000000`00000043
```

```
00007fff`29bccc28    00000000`0000001a
00007fff`29bccc30    00000000`00000001
00007fff`29bccc38    000003e8`000081a4
00007fff`29bccc40    00000000`000003e8
00007fff`29bccc48    00000000`00000000
00007fff`29bccc50    00000000`00000020
00007fff`29bccc58    00000000`00001000
00007fff`29bccc60    00000000`00000008
00007fff`29bccc68    00000000`666db2cb
00007fff`29bccc70    00000000`30930d4d
00007fff`29bccc78    00000000`666db2cb
00007fff`29bccc80    00000000`30930d4d
00007fff`29bccc88    00000000`666db2cb
00007fff`29bccc90    00000000`30930d4d
00007fff`29bccc98    00000000`00000000
00007fff`29bccca0    00000000`00000000
00007fff`29bccca8    00000000`00000000
00007fff`29bcccb0    00000000`00000000
00007fff`29bcccb8    2495fa01`d3f21300
00007fff`29bcccc0    00000000`00000002
00007fff`29bcccc8    00005564`99d5900e ud5bv3!IO_stdin_used+0xe
00007fff`29bcccd0    00000000`0000000a
00007fff`29bcccd8    00000000`00000000
00007fff`29bccce0    00000000`00000000
00007fff`29bccce8    00000001`00000001
00007fff`29bcccf0    00007fff`29bcce10
00007fff`29bcccf8    00007f73`e48a153e libpthread_so!sem_open+0x41e
00007fff`29bccd00    6d68732f`7665642f
00007fff`29bccd08    3564752e`6d65732f
00007fff`29bccd10    0000615f`6d65735f
00007fff`29bccd18    00007f73`e48a11b1 libpthread_so!sem_open+0x91
00007fff`29bccd20    ffffffff`fffffff8
00007fff`29bccd28    00007fff`29bccd00
00007fff`29bccd30    00000000`00000000
00007fff`29bccd38    00000000`00000000
00007fff`29bccd40    00000000`00000000
00007fff`29bccd48    ffffffff`ffffff60
00007fff`29bccd50    00000000`00000006
00007fff`29bccd58    00000000`00000000
00007fff`29bccd60    00000000`00000009
00007fff`29bccd68    00005564`99d582db ud5bv3!start_modeling+0xea [/mnt/c/ALD4/ud5/ud5bv3.cpp @ 56]
00007fff`29bccd70    00007f73`e479f060 libstdc___so!_gxx_personality_v0
00007fff`29bccd78    ffffffff`fffffff8
00007fff`29bccd80    00000000`00000001
00007fff`29bccd88    00007f73`e48a1873 libpthread_so!do_futex_wait.constprop.1+0x13
00007fff`29bccd90    00000000`00011b1b
00007fff`29bccd98    00000000`00000000
00007fff`29bccda0    00007f73`e48bd000
00007fff`29bccda8    00000000`00000000
00007fff`29bccdb0    00007fff`29bccdc0
00007fff`29bccdb8    00007f73`e48a1988 libpthread_so!_new_sem_wait_slow.constprop.0+0x98
00007fff`29bccdc0    00007f73`e48a1850 libpthread_so!_sem_wait_cleanup
00007fff`29bccdc8    00007f73`e48bd000
00007fff`29bccdd0    00000000`00000000
00007fff`29bccdd8    00000000`00000000
00007fff`29bccde0    00007fff`29bcce30
00007fff`29bccde8    2495fa01`d3f21300
00007fff`29bccdf0    00005564`99d580f0 ud5bv3!start
00007fff`29bccdf8    00000000`00000000
00007fff`29bcce00    00007fff`29bcce30
00007fff`29bcce08    00005564`99d580f0 ud5bv3!start
00007fff`29bcce10    00007fff`29bccf20
00007fff`29bcce18    00005564`99d5828c ud5bv3!start_modeling+0x9b [/mnt/c/ALD4/ud5/ud5bv3.cpp @ 48]
00007fff`29bcce20    00007f73`e48bd000
00007fff`29bcce28    00007f73`e48be000
```

```
00007fff`29bcce30  00007fff`29bcce40
00007fff`29bcce38  00005564`99d581ea ud5bv3!main+0x15 [/mnt/c/ALD4/ud5/ud5bv3.cpp @ 20]
00007fff`29bcce40  00005564`99d58310 ud5bv3!_libc_csu_init
00007fff`29bcce48  00007f73`e43d409b libc_so!_libc_start_main+0xeb
00007fff`29bcce50  ffffffff`ffffff90
```

Note: If you see that the region is too short or doesn't include interesting symbolic references, try to decrease the lower region bound, for example, `00007fff`29bcb000`.

Note: We see some symbolic references in the past stack region addresses (highlighted in blue) related to stack unwinding during exceptions and functions from the *ud5bv3*. The stack region related to the current stack trace is highlighted in green.

13.   Let's examine the selected symbolic references:

```
0:000> u 00005564`99d58248
ud5bv3!start_modeling+0x57 [/mnt/c/ALD4/ud5/ud5bv3.cpp @ 34]:
00005564`99d58248 add     byte ptr [rax-75h],cl
00005564`99d5824b clc
00005564`99d5824d mov     rdi,rax
00005564`99d58250 call    ud5bv3!sem_post$plt (00005564`99d58070)
00005564`99d58255 mov     esi,0
00005564`99d5825a lea     rdi,[ud5bv3!IO_stdin_used+0xe (00005564`99d5900e)]
00005564`99d58261 mov     eax,0
00005564`99d58266 call    ud5bv3!sem_open$plt (00005564`99d58030)

0:000> ub 00005564`99d58248
                          ^ Unable to find valid previous instruction for 'ub
00005564`99d58248 '
```

Note: The reference above seems coincidental since neither forward nor backward disassembly shows valid code.

```
0:000> u 00007f73`e45820b0
libgcc_s_so!Unwind_Backtrace+0x7c0:
00007f73`e45820b0 push    r15
00007f73`e45820b2 push    r14
00007f73`e45820b4 push    r13
00007f73`e45820b6 push    r12
00007f73`e45820b8 push    rbp
00007f73`e45820b9 push    rbx
00007f73`e45820ba sub     rsp,58h
00007f73`e45820be mov     ecx,dword ptr [rdx+28h]

0:000> ub 00007f73`e45820b0
libgcc_s_so!Unwind_Backtrace+0x7a7:
00007f73`e4582097 pop     rbp
00007f73`e4582098 pop     r12
00007f73`e458209a pop     r13
00007f73`e458209c pop     r14
00007f73`e458209e pop     r15
00007f73`e45820a0 ret
00007f73`e45820a1 nop     word ptr cs:[rax+rax]
00007f73`e45820ac nop     dword ptr [rax]
```

Note: The forward disassembly of the reference above looks like a valid function (it is also possible to do full function disassembly using **uf**), so it may have been a function pointer.

```
0:000> u 00007f73`e4582517
libgcc_s_so!Unwind_Backtrace+0xc27:
00007f73`e4582517 movsxd  r10,dword ptr [r14]
00007f73`e458251a mov     rax,qword ptr [rsp+20h]
00007f73`e458251f add     r10,rbx
00007f73`e4582522 add     rax,r10
00007f73`e4582525 cmp     qword ptr [rbp],rax
00007f73`e4582529 jae     libgcc_s_so!Unwind_Backtrace+0xc3f (00007f73`e458252f)
00007f73`e458252b mov     qword ptr [rbp+20h],r12
00007f73`e458252f mov     qword ptr [rbp+18h],r10
```

```
0:000> ub 00007f73`e4582517
libgcc_s_so!Unwind_Backtrace+0xc0b:
00007f73`e45824fb idiv    bh
00007f73`e45824fd inc     dword ptr [rcx+rcx*4-11h]
00007f73`e4582501 lea     rcx,[rsp+20h]
00007f73`e4582506 xor     esi,esi
00007f73`e4582508 mov     eax,eax
00007f73`e458250a and     edi,0Fh
00007f73`e458250d lea     rdx,[r12+rax+8]
00007f73`e4582512 call    libgcc_s_so!Unwind_Backtrace+0x320 (00007f73`e4581c10)
```

Note: The symbolic reference above looks like a valid saved return address according to the backwards disassembly.

```
0:000> u 00005564`99d582dc
ud5bv3!new_feature [/mnt/c/ALD4/ud5/new_feature.cpp @ 2]:
00005564`99d582dc push    rbp
00005564`99d582dd mov     rbp,rsp
00005564`99d582e0 mov     edi,4
00005564`99d582e5 call    ud5bv3!_cxa_allocate_exception$plt (00005564`99d58050)
00005564`99d582ea mov     dword ptr [rax],0
00005564`99d582f0 mov     edx,0
00005564`99d582f5 lea     rsi,[ud5bv3!ZTIiCXXABI_1.3 (00005564`99d5ada0)]
00005564`99d582fc mov     rdi,rax
```

```
0:000> ub 00005564`99d582dc
ud5bv3!start_modeling+0xd0 [/mnt/c/ALD4/ud5/ud5bv3.cpp @ 55]:
00005564`99d582c1 call    ud5bv3!sem_unlink$plt (00005564`99d580c0)
00005564`99d582c6 jmp     ud5bv3!start_modeling+0xe9 (00005564`99d582da)
00005564`99d582c8 mov     rdi,rax
00005564`99d582cb call    ud5bv3!_cxa_begin_catch$plt (00005564`99d58040)
00005564`99d582d0 call    ud5bv3!_cxa_end_catch$plt (00005564`99d580b0)
00005564`99d582d5 jmp     ud5bv3!start_modeling+0x64 (00005564`99d58255)
00005564`99d582da leave
00005564`99d582db ret
```

Note: The symbolic reference above looks like a valid function pointer (forward disassembly).

```
0:000> u 00005564`99d582c8
ud5bv3!start_modeling+0xd7 [/mnt/c/ALD4/ud5/ud5bv3.cpp @ 38]:
00005564`99d582c8 mov     rdi,rax
00005564`99d582cb call    ud5bv3!_cxa_begin_catch$plt (00005564`99d58040)
00005564`99d582d0 call    ud5bv3!_cxa_end_catch$plt (00005564`99d580b0)
00005564`99d582d5 jmp     ud5bv3!start_modeling+0x64 (00005564`99d58255)
00005564`99d582da leave
```

```
00005564`99d582db ret
ud5bv3!new_feature [/mnt/c/ALD4/ud5/new_feature.cpp @ 2]:
00005564`99d582dc push    rbp
00005564`99d582dd mov     rbp,rsp

0:000> ub 00005564`99d582c8
ud5bv3!start_modeling+0xb5 [/mnt/c/ALD4/ud5/ud5bv3.cpp @ 52]:
00005564`99d582a6 mov     rdi,rax
00005564`99d582a9 call    ud5bv3!sem_close$plt (00005564`99d580a0)
00005564`99d582ae mov     rax,qword ptr [rbp-8]
00005564`99d582b2 mov     rdi,rax
00005564`99d582b5 call    ud5bv3!sem_close$plt (00005564`99d580a0)
00005564`99d582ba lea     rdi,[ud5bv3!IO_stdin_used+0x4 (00005564`99d59004)]
00005564`99d582c1 call    ud5bv3!sem_unlink$plt (00005564`99d580c0)
00005564`99d582c6 jmp     ud5bv3!start_modeling+0xe9 (00005564`99d582da)
```

Note: The forward disassembly looks like the beginning of a catch block.

14.   We continue execution (**g**), disconnect from the process server, quit WinDbg, quit the process server (**^C**), and the *ud5a* and *ud5bv3* processes (**^C**).

Exercise UD5 (GDB)

Goal: Learn how to debug multiple processes and their deadlock.

Elementary Diagnostics Patterns: Crash; Hang.

Memory Analysis Patterns: Exception Stack Trace; Constant Subtrace; NULL Pointer (Data); Main Thread; Execution Residue (Unmanaged Space, User); C++ Exception; Hidden Exception (User Space); Handled Exception (User Space); Wait Chain (Mutex Objects); Deadlock (Objects, User Space); Coincidental Symbolic Information; Function Pointer.

Debugging Implementation Patterns: Break-in.

1.   The source code and the *Makefile* to build executables and libraries can be found in the *ud5* directory:

```
$ git clone https://bitbucket.org/softwarediagnostics/ald4
```

2.   Run the *ud5a* executable.

```
/mnt/c/ALD4/ud5$ ./ud5a
```

3.   Open a different terminal and run the *ud5b* executable.

```
/mnt/c/ALD4/ud5$ ./ud5b
```

4.   Both applications do not exit for almost 30 seconds. This is normal expected behavior (from these applications) as they mutually wait while doing some work (modeled by the *sleep* function call). The source code for the *ud5a* part:

```
void start_modeling()
{
      sem_t *sem_a = sem_open("ud5_sem_a", O_CREAT, 0644, 1);
if (sem_a == SEM_FAILED) exit(EXIT_FAILURE);

      sem_wait(sem_a);

      sleep(20); // some work

      sem_t *sem_b = sem_open("ud5_sem_b", 0);
      if (sem_b == SEM_FAILED) exit(EXIT_FAILURE);

      sem_wait(sem_b);

      sleep(10); // some more work

      sem_post(sem_b);
      sem_post(sem_a);

      sem_close(sem_b);
      sem_close(sem_a);
```

```
        sem_unlink("ud5_sem_a");
}
```

The source code for the *ud5b* part:

```
void start_modeling()
{
        sem_t *sem_b = sem_open("ud5_sem_b", O_CREAT, 0644, 1);
        if (sem_b == SEM_FAILED) exit(EXIT_FAILURE);

        sem_wait(sem_b);

        sleep(10); // some work

        sem_post(sem_b);

        sem_t *sem_a = sem_open("ud5_sem_a", 0);
        if (sem_a == SEM_FAILED) exit(EXIT_FAILURE);

        sem_wait(sem_a);

        sleep(10); // some more work

        sem_post(sem_a);

sem_close(sem_a);
        sem_close(sem_b);

        sem_unlink("ud5_sem_b");
}
```

Note: Although we have 2 synchronization objects, the code is deadlock-free as we acquire and release them in ABBA and BBAA orders and hold their ownership for a limited time.

5.   Run the *ud5a* again, then run the *ud5bv2* in a different terminal. The new feature was added to the *ud5b* (now version 2):

```
void start_modeling()
{
        sem_t *sem_b = sem_open("ud5_sem_b", O_CREAT, 0644, 1);
        if (sem_b == SEM_FAILED) exit(EXIT_FAILURE);

        sem_wait(sem_b);

        sleep(10); // some work

        new_feature();

        sem_post(sem_b);
```

```c
    sem_t *sem_a = sem_open("ud5_sem_a", 0);
    if (sem_a == SEM_FAILED) exit(EXIT_FAILURE);

    sem_wait(sem_a);

    sleep(10); // some more work

    sem_post(sem_a);

sem_close(sem_a);
    sem_close(sem_b);

    sem_unlink("ud5_sem_b");
}
```

We see that in about 10 seconds, the *ud5bv2* is aborted:

```
/mnt/c/ALD4/ud5$ ./ud5bv2
terminate called after throwing an instance of 'int'
Aborted
```

6.   After waiting more than 30 seconds, we see that the *ud5a* is never finished. To debug it, we check its PID and attach GDB to it in another terminal:

```
/mnt/c/ALD4/ud5$ ps -a | grep ud5a
19521 pts/5    00:00:00 ud5a

/mnt/c/ALD4/ud5$ gdb -p 19521
GNU gdb (Debian 8.2.1-2+b3) 8.2.1
Copyright (C) 2018 Free Software Foundation, Inc.
License GPLv3+: GNU GPL version 3 or later <http://gnu.org/licenses/gpl.html>
This is free software: you are free to change and redistribute it.
There is NO WARRANTY, to the extent permitted by law.
Type "show copying" and "show warranty" for details.
This GDB was configured as "x86_64-linux-gnu".
Type "show configuration" for configuration details.
For bug reporting instructions, please see:
<http://www.gnu.org/software/gdb/bugs/>.
Find the GDB manual and other documentation resources online at:
    <http://www.gnu.org/software/gdb/documentation/>.

For help, type "help".
Type "apropos word" to search for commands related to "word".
Attaching to process 19521
Reading symbols from /mnt/c/ALD4/ud5/ud5a...done.
Reading symbols from /lib/x86_64-linux-gnu/libpthread.so.0...Reading symbols from
/usr/lib/debug/.build-id/48/041452aef93ddb2366ca0fa49da8f32684a9c8.debug...done.
done.
[Thread debugging using libthread_db enabled]
Using host libthread_db library "/lib/x86_64-linux-gnu/libthread_db.so.1".
Reading symbols from /usr/lib/x86_64-linux-gnu/libstdc++.so.6...(no debugging symbols
found)...done.
```

```
Reading symbols from /lib/x86_64-linux-gnu/libm.so.6...Reading symbols from
/usr/lib/debug/.build-id/1c/a5f623620c7885aa34446bf372be6c01f27042.debug...done.
done.
Reading symbols from /lib/x86_64-linux-gnu/libgcc_s.so.1...(no debugging symbols found)...done.
Reading symbols from /lib/x86_64-linux-gnu/libc.so.6...Reading symbols from
/usr/lib/debug/.build-id/c7/aa9a1e121fe2395f3840f3f0213146046d9fe3.debug...done.
done.
Reading symbols from /lib64/ld-linux-x86-64.so.2...Reading symbols from /usr/lib/debug/.build-
id/83/743ddd4258a7d138a28c4f2032d17ad92a15b5.debug...done.
done.
futex_abstimed_wait_cancelable (private=128, abstime=0x0, expected=0,
futex_word=0x7f7e79426000) at ../sysdeps/unix/sysv/linux/futex-internal.h:205
205       ../sysdeps/unix/sysv/linux/futex-internal.h: No such file or directory.
```

7.   We examine the backtrace:

```
(gdb) bt
#0  futex_abstimed_wait_cancelable (private=128, abstime=0x0, expected=0, futex_word=0x7f7e79426000)
    at ../sysdeps/unix/sysv/linux/futex-internal.h:205
#1  do_futex_wait (sem=sem@entry=0x7f7e79426000, abstime=0x0) at sem_waitcommon.c:111
#2  0x00007f7e7940a988 in __new_sem_wait_slow (sem=0x7f7e79426000, abstime=0x0) at sem_waitcommon.c:181
#3  0x0000555dd000f23b in start_modeling () at ud5a.cpp:34
#4  0x0000555dd000f1aa in main () at ud5a.cpp:17
```

We see that the thread is waiting for a semaphore that is implemented as a fast userspace mutex. We now switch to frame **3**:

```
(gdb) frame 3
#3  0x0000555dd000f23b in start_modeling () at ud5a.cpp:34
34              sem_wait(sem_b);
```

Note: We see that the *ud5a* is waiting for the *sem_b* semaphore created in the aborted *ud5bv2* process.

8.   Now, we quit GDB (**q**) and the *ud5a* process (**^C**).

9.   An inexperienced developer tried to fix the problem in the *ud5bv2* by enclosing a portion of the code into a *try/catch* block and produced *ud5bv3*:

```
void start_modeling()
{
        sem_t *sem_b = sem_open("ud5_sem_b", O_CREAT, 0644, 1);
        if (sem_b == SEM_FAILED) exit(EXIT_FAILURE);

        sem_wait(sem_b);

        sleep(10); // some work

        try
        {
                new_feature();

                sem_post(sem_b);
        }
        catch (...)
        {
                // ignore
```

```
        }

        sem_t *sem_a = sem_open("ud5_sem_a", 0);
        if (sem_a == SEM_FAILED) exit(EXIT_FAILURE);

sem_wait(sem_a);

        sleep(10); // some more work

        sem_post(sem_a);

        sem_close(sem_a);
        sem_close(sem_b);

        sem_unlink("ud5_sem_b");
}
```

10.   We run *ud5a* and *ud5bv3* (in a different terminal). After waiting more than a minute we see that both processes still hang. To debug *ud5bv3*, we attach WinDbg to it:

```
/mnt/c/ALD4/ud5$ ps -a | grep ud5bv3
19952 pts/1    00:00:00 ud5bv3

/mnt/c/ALD4/ud5$ gdb -p 19952
GNU gdb (Debian 8.2.1-2+b3) 8.2.1
Copyright (C) 2018 Free Software Foundation, Inc.
License GPLv3+: GNU GPL version 3 or later <http://gnu.org/licenses/gpl.html>
This is free software: you are free to change and redistribute it.
There is NO WARRANTY, to the extent permitted by law.
Type "show copying" and "show warranty" for details.
This GDB was configured as "x86_64-linux-gnu".
Type "show configuration" for configuration details.
For bug reporting instructions, please see:
<http://www.gnu.org/software/gdb/bugs/>.
Find the GDB manual and other documentation resources online at:
    <http://www.gnu.org/software/gdb/documentation/>.

For help, type "help".
Type "apropos word" to search for commands related to "word".
Attaching to process 19952
Reading symbols from /mnt/c/ALD4/ud5/ud5bv3...done.
Reading symbols from /lib/x86_64-linux-gnu/libpthread.so.0...Reading symbols from
/usr/lib/debug/.build-id/48/041452aef93ddb2366ca0fa49da8f32684a9c8.debug...done.
done.
[Thread debugging using libthread_db enabled]
Using host libthread_db library "/lib/x86_64-linux-gnu/libthread_db.so.1".
Reading symbols from /usr/lib/x86_64-linux-gnu/libstdc++.so.6...(no debugging symbols
found)...done.
Reading symbols from /lib/x86_64-linux-gnu/libm.so.6...Reading symbols from
/usr/lib/debug/.build-id/1c/a5f623620c7885aa34446bf372be6c01f27042.debug...done.
done.
Reading symbols from /lib/x86_64-linux-gnu/libgcc_s.so.1...(no debugging symbols found)...done.
Reading symbols from /lib/x86_64-linux-gnu/libc.so.6...Reading symbols from
/usr/lib/debug/.build-id/c7/aa9a1e121fe2395f3840f3f0213146046d9fe3.debug...done.
done.
Reading symbols from /lib64/ld-linux-x86-64.so.2...Reading symbols from /usr/lib/debug/.build-
id/83/743ddd4258a7d138a28c4f2032d17ad92a15b5.debug...done.
done.
```

```
futex_abstimed_wait_cancelable (private=128, abstime=0x0, expected=0,
futex_word=0x7f838957e000) at ../sysdeps/unix/sysv/linux/futex-internal.h:205
205     ../sysdeps/unix/sysv/linux/futex-internal.h: No such file or directory.
```

11.   We examine its backtrace and the corresponding frame:

```
(gdb) bt
#0  futex_abstimed_wait_cancelable (private=128, abstime=0x0, expected=0, futex_word=0x7f838957e000)
    at ../sysdeps/unix/sysv/linux/futex-internal.h:205
#1  do_futex_wait (sem=sem@entry=0x7f838957e000, abstime=0x0) at sem_waitcommon.c:111
#2  0x00007f8389562988 in __new_sem_wait_slow (sem=0x7f838957e000, abstime=0x0) at sem_waitcommon.c:181
#3  0x00005598d1acc28c in start_modeling () at ud5bv3.cpp:46
#4  0x00005598d1acc1ea in main () at ud5bv3.cpp:18

(gdb) frame 3
#3  0x00005598d1acc28c in start_modeling () at ud5bv3.cpp:46
46              sem_wait(sem_a);
```

12.   Since we do not expect a wait (we assume *new_feature* code is complex), we look at raw stack data to find any anomalies, such as hidden and handled exceptions. This is done by dumping the stack region and looking for relevant symbol references:

```
(gdb) frame 4
#4  0x00005598d1acc1ea in main () at ud5bv3.cpp:18
18              start_modeling();

(gdb) info r rsp
rsp             0x7fff3e4a1a90      0x7fff3e4a1a90

(gdb) frame 0
#0  futex_abstimed_wait_cancelable (private=128, abstime=0x0, expected=0,
futex_word=0x7f838957e000)
    at ../sysdeps/unix/sysv/linux/futex-internal.h:205
205     ../sysdeps/unix/sysv/linux/futex-internal.h: No such file or directory.

(gdb) info r rsp
rsp             0x7fff3e4a19e0      0x7fff3e4a19e0

(gdb) x/1024a 0x7fff3e4a0000
0x7fff3e4a0000: 0x0     0x0
0x7fff3e4a0010: 0x0     0x0
0x7fff3e4a0020: 0x0     0x0
0x7fff3e4a0030: 0x0     0x0
0x7fff3e4a0040: 0x0     0x0
0x7fff3e4a0050: 0x0     0x0
0x7fff3e4a0060: 0x0     0x0
0x7fff3e4a0070: 0x0     0x0
0x7fff3e4a0080: 0x0     0x0
0x7fff3e4a0090: 0x0     0x0
0x7fff3e4a00a0: 0x0     0x0
0x7fff3e4a00b0: 0x0     0x0
0x7fff3e4a00c0: 0x0     0x0
0x7fff3e4a00d0: 0x0     0x0
0x7fff3e4a00e0: 0x0     0x0
0x7fff3e4a00f0: 0x0     0x0
0x7fff3e4a0100: 0x0     0x0
0x7fff3e4a0110: 0x0     0x0
```

```
0x7fff3e4a0120: 0x0      0x0
0x7fff3e4a0130: 0x0      0x0
0x7fff3e4a0140: 0x0      0x0
0x7fff3e4a0150: 0x0      0x0
0x7fff3e4a0160: 0x0      0x0
0x7fff3e4a0170: 0x0      0x0
0x7fff3e4a0180: 0x0      0x0
0x7fff3e4a0190: 0x0      0x0
0x7fff3e4a01a0: 0x0      0x0
0x7fff3e4a01b0: 0x0      0x0
0x7fff3e4a01c0: 0x0      0x0
0x7fff3e4a01d0: 0x0      0x0
0x7fff3e4a01e0: 0x0      0x0
0x7fff3e4a01f0: 0x0      0x0
0x7fff3e4a0200: 0x0      0x0
0x7fff3e4a0210: 0x0      0x0
0x7fff3e4a0220: 0x0      0x0
0x7fff3e4a0230: 0x0      0x0
0x7fff3e4a0240: 0x0      0x0
0x7fff3e4a0250: 0x0      0x0
0x7fff3e4a0260: 0x0      0x0
0x7fff3e4a0270: 0x0      0x0
0x7fff3e4a0280: 0x0      0x0
--Type <RET> for more, q to quit, c to continue without paging--
0x7fff3e4a0290: 0x0      0x0
0x7fff3e4a02a0: 0x0      0x0
0x7fff3e4a02b0: 0x0      0x0
0x7fff3e4a02c0: 0x0      0x0
0x7fff3e4a02d0: 0x0      0x0
0x7fff3e4a02e0: 0x0      0x0
0x7fff3e4a02f0: 0x0      0x0
0x7fff3e4a0300: 0x0      0x0
0x7fff3e4a0310: 0x0      0x0
0x7fff3e4a0320: 0x0      0x0
0x7fff3e4a0330: 0x0      0x0
0x7fff3e4a0340: 0x0      0x0
0x7fff3e4a0350: 0x0      0x0
0x7fff3e4a0360: 0x0      0x0
0x7fff3e4a0370: 0x0      0x0
0x7fff3e4a0380: 0x0      0x0
0x7fff3e4a0390: 0x0      0x0
0x7fff3e4a03a0: 0x0      0x0
0x7fff3e4a03b0: 0x0      0x0
0x7fff3e4a03c0: 0x0      0x0
0x7fff3e4a03d0: 0x0      0x0
0x7fff3e4a03e0: 0x0      0x0
0x7fff3e4a03f0: 0x0      0x0
0x7fff3e4a0400: 0x0      0x0
0x7fff3e4a0410: 0x0      0x0
0x7fff3e4a0420: 0x0      0x0
0x7fff3e4a0430: 0x0      0x0
0x7fff3e4a0440: 0x0      0x0
0x7fff3e4a0450: 0x0      0x0
0x7fff3e4a0460: 0x0      0x0
0x7fff3e4a0470: 0x0      0x0
0x7fff3e4a0480: 0x0      0x0
0x7fff3e4a0490: 0x0      0x0
0x7fff3e4a04a0: 0x0      0x0
0x7fff3e4a04b0: 0x0      0x0
```

```
0x7fff3e4a04c0: 0x0        0x0
0x7fff3e4a04d0: 0x0        0x0
0x7fff3e4a04e0: 0x0        0x0
0x7fff3e4a04f0: 0x0        0x0
0x7fff3e4a0500: 0x0        0x0
0x7fff3e4a0510: 0x0        0x0
--Type <RET> for more, q to quit, c to continue without paging--
0x7fff3e4a0520: 0x0        0x0
0x7fff3e4a0530: 0x0        0x0
0x7fff3e4a0540: 0x0        0x0
0x7fff3e4a0550: 0x0        0x0
0x7fff3e4a0560: 0x0        0x0
0x7fff3e4a0570: 0x0        0x0
0x7fff3e4a0580: 0x0        0x0
0x7fff3e4a0590: 0x0        0x0
0x7fff3e4a05a0: 0x0        0x0
0x7fff3e4a05b0: 0x0        0x0
0x7fff3e4a05c0: 0x0        0x0
0x7fff3e4a05d0: 0x0        0x0
0x7fff3e4a05e0: 0x0        0x0
0x7fff3e4a05f0: 0x0        0x0
0x7fff3e4a0600: 0x0        0x0
0x7fff3e4a0610: 0x0        0x0
0x7fff3e4a0620: 0x0        0x0
0x7fff3e4a0630: 0x0        0x0
0x7fff3e4a0640: 0x0        0x0
0x7fff3e4a0650: 0x0        0x0
0x7fff3e4a0660: 0x0        0x0
0x7fff3e4a0670: 0x0        0x0
0x7fff3e4a0680: 0x0        0x0
0x7fff3e4a0690: 0x0        0x0
0x7fff3e4a06a0: 0x0        0x0
0x7fff3e4a06b0: 0x0        0x0
0x7fff3e4a06c0: 0x0        0x0
0x7fff3e4a06d0: 0x0        0x0
0x7fff3e4a06e0: 0x0        0x0
0x7fff3e4a06f0: 0x0        0x0
0x7fff3e4a0700: 0x0        0x0
0x7fff3e4a0710: 0x0        0x0
0x7fff3e4a0720: 0x0        0x0
0x7fff3e4a0730: 0x0        0x0
0x7fff3e4a0740: 0x0        0x0
0x7fff3e4a0750: 0x0        0x0
0x7fff3e4a0760: 0x0        0x0
0x7fff3e4a0770: 0x0        0x0
0x7fff3e4a0780: 0x0        0x0
0x7fff3e4a0790: 0x0        0x0
0x7fff3e4a07a0: 0x0        0x0
--Type <RET> for more, q to quit, c to continue without paging--
0x7fff3e4a07b0: 0x0        0x0
0x7fff3e4a07c0: 0x0        0x0
0x7fff3e4a07d0: 0x0        0x0
0x7fff3e4a07e0: 0x0        0x0
0x7fff3e4a07f0: 0x0        0x0
0x7fff3e4a0800: 0x0        0x0
0x7fff3e4a0810: 0x0        0x0
0x7fff3e4a0820: 0x0        0x0
0x7fff3e4a0830: 0x0        0x0
0x7fff3e4a0840: 0x0        0x0
```

```
0x7fff3e4a0850: 0x0      0x0
0x7fff3e4a0860: 0x0      0x0
0x7fff3e4a0870: 0x0      0x0
0x7fff3e4a0880: 0x0      0x0
0x7fff3e4a0890: 0x0      0x0
0x7fff3e4a08a0: 0x0      0x0
0x7fff3e4a08b0: 0x0      0x0
0x7fff3e4a08c0: 0x0      0x0
0x7fff3e4a08d0: 0x0      0x0
0x7fff3e4a08e0: 0x0      0x0
0x7fff3e4a08f0: 0x0      0x0
0x7fff3e4a0900: 0x0      0x0
0x7fff3e4a0910: 0x0      0x0
0x7fff3e4a0920: 0x0      0x0
0x7fff3e4a0930: 0x0      0x0
0x7fff3e4a0940: 0x0      0x0
0x7fff3e4a0950: 0x0      0x0
0x7fff3e4a0960: 0x0      0x0
0x7fff3e4a0970: 0x0      0x0
0x7fff3e4a0980: 0x0      0x7f8389574410
0x7fff3e4a0990: 0x7fff3e4a0d40   0x7fff3e4a0a50
0x7fff3e4a09a0: 0x7fff3e4a0e28   0x4
0x7fff3e4a09b0: 0x820    0x7f8389586b12 <_dl_map_object_from_fd+3634>
0x7fff3e4a09c0: 0x0      0x22000
0x7fff3e4a09d0: 0x21438 0x21438
0x7fff3e4a09e0: 0x0      0x1
0x7fff3e4a09f0: 0x22000 0x169000
0x7fff3e4a0a00: 0x168f88         0x168f88
0x7fff3e4a0a10: 0x22000 0x5
0x7fff3e4a0a20: 0x169000         0x1b5000
0x7fff3e4a0a30: 0x1b4a50         0x1b4a50
--Type <RET> for more, q to quit, c to continue without paging--
0x7fff3e4a0a40: 0x169000         0x7fff00000001
0x7fff3e4a0a50: 0x1b6000         0x1bc000
0x7fff3e4a0a60: 0x1bb860         0x1bf800
0x7fff3e4a0a70: 0x1b5000         0x3
0x7fff3e4a0a80: 0x2850   0x2850
0x7fff3e4a0a90: 0x0      0x1
0x7fff3e4a0aa0: 0x3000   0x14000
0x7fff3e4a0ab0: 0x13c39 0x13c39
0x7fff3e4a0ac0: 0x3000   0x5
0x7fff3e4a0ad0: 0x14000 0x17000
0x7fff3e4a0ae0: 0x16f28 0x16f28
0x7fff3e4a0af0: 0x14000 0x1
0x7fff3e4a0b00: 0x18000 0x1a000
0x7fff3e4a0b10: 0x19178 0x19430
0x7fff3e4a0b20: 0x17000 0x3
0x7fff3e4a0b30: 0x18213c         0x182148
0x7fff3e4a0b40: 0x180000         0x3
0x7fff3e4a0b50: 0x0      0x0
0x7fff3e4a0b60: 0x0      0x0
0x7fff3e4a0b70: 0x0      0x0
0x7fff3e4a0b80: 0x0      0x7f838958b4f3 <_dl_new_object+675>
0x7fff3e4a0b90: 0x0      0x7f83895743f0
0x7fff3e4a0ba0: 0x2f00000000     0x20
0x7fff3e4a0bb0: 0xa      0x5598d1acb607
0x7fff3e4a0bc0: 0x2f000004a8     0x0
0x7fff3e4a0bd0: 0x7fff3e4a0d40   0x7f838958b1de <_dl_add_to_namespace_list+30>
0x7fff3e4a0be0: 0x7f8389574410   0x7fff3e4a0d40
```

```
0x7fff3e4a0bf0: 0x37ffff1a8      0x7f83895867a2 <_dl_map_object_from_fd+2754>
0x7fff3e4a0c00: 0x7f8389573f10    0x7fff3e4a09c0
0x7fff3e4a0c10: 0x7f8389230800    0x1bf800
0x7fff3e4a0c20: 0x7fff3e4a09c0    0x7fff3e4a0c00
0x7fff3e4a0c30: 0x7f8300000003    0x0
0x7fff3e4a0c40: 0x7fff00000003    0x7fff3e4a0de0
0x7fff3e4a0c50: 0x6      0x55b2
0x7fff3e4a0c60: 0x300000000       0x7f83895743f0
0x7fff3e4a0c70: 0x5598d1acb607    0x7f83895896fc <check_match+316>
0x7fff3e4a0c80: 0x820    0x333
0x7fff3e4a0c90: 0x7f8389574410    0x1
0x7fff3e4a0ca0: 0x7f83890737a0    0x7f8389589b04 <do_lookup_x+932>
0x7fff3e4a0cb0: 0x333    0x7f8389082cd8
0x7fff3e4a0cc0: 0x7f8389574410    0x7fff3e4a0d48
--Type <RET> for more, q to quit, c to continue without paging--
0x7fff3e4a0cd0: 0x7fff3e4a0d44    0x7f838958986e <do_lookup_x+270>
0x7fff3e4a0ce0: 0x0      0x7f8389082cd8
0x7fff3e4a0cf0: 0x7f8389074fb0    0x7f8389232d2a
0x7fff3e4a0d00: 0x1c93bb9d        0x7f83892317e8
0x7fff3e4a0d10: 0x724eee          0x7fff3e4a0e10
0x7fff3e4a0d20: 0x7fff3e4a0e00    0x7fff3e4a0d48
0x7fff3e4a0d30: 0x7f8389574a60    0x7
0x7fff3e4a0d40: 0x0      0x0
0x7fff3e4a0d50: 0x100000001       0x1c93bb9d
0x7fff3e4a0d60: 0x7f8389574270    0x7fff3e4a0ea8
0x7fff3e4a0d70: 0x7f8389573f10    0x0
0x7fff3e4a0d80: 0x7f838906f7e0    0x7f838958a39f <_dl_lookup_symbol_x+335>
0x7fff3e4a0d90: 0x5      0x7f838906f7e0
0x7fff3e4a0da0: 0x1      0x0
0x7fff3e4a0db0: 0x1      0x7f83895896fc <check_match+316>
0x7fff3e4a0dc0: 0x7f8389232d2a    0x5c
0x7fff3e4a0dd0: 0x7f8389573f10    0x1
0x7fff3e4a0de0: 0x7f8389231618    0x7f8389589b04 <do_lookup_x+932>
0x7fff3e4a0df0: 0x5c     0x7f8389232778
0x7fff3e4a0e00: 0x7f8389573f10    0x7fff3e4a0e88
0x7fff3e4a0e10: 0x7fff3e4a0e84    0x7f838958986e <do_lookup_x+270>
0x7fff3e4a0e20: 0x7f8300000000    0x7f8389232778
0x7fff3e4a0e30: 0x7f8389231758    0x7f83893f8c99
0x7fff3e4a0e40: 0x919221fd        0x7f83893d7350
0x7fff3e4a0e50: 0x2464887         0x7fff3e4a0f50
0x7fff3e4a0e60: 0x7fff3e4a0f40    0x7fff3e4a0e88
0x7fff3e4a0e70: 0x7f8389574a60    0x7
0x7fff3e4a0e80: 0x1      0x0
0x7fff3e4a0e90: 0x1      0x919221fd
0x7fff3e4a0ea0: 0x7f8389573870    0x7fff3e4a0fe8
0x7fff3e4a0eb0: 0x7f8389573510    0x0
0x7fff3e4a0ec0: 0x7f838906f420    0x7f838958a39f <_dl_lookup_symbol_x+335>
0x7fff3e4a0ed0: 0x4      0x7f838906f420
0x7fff3e4a0ee0: 0x1      0x0
0x7fff3e4a0ef0: 0x1      0x7f8389573510
0x7fff3e4a0f00: 0x7f83893f8c99    0x13e4a0f88
0x7fff3e4a0f10: 0x7fff3e4a0f40    0x7fff3e4a0f50
0x7fff3e4a0f20: 0x7f8389573870    0x0
0x7fff3e4a0f30: 0x7f8389553080    0x7f8389232dc5
0x7fff3e4a0f40: 0xffffffff        0x7f8389231890
0x7fff3e4a0f50: 0x7f8389231ff8    0x7f8389573f10
--Type <RET> for more, q to quit, c to continue without paging--
0x7fff3e4a0f60: 0x7fff3e4a1040    0x7fff3e4a0f88
0x7fff3e4a0f70: 0x7f8389574a60    0x7f83895896fc <check_match+316>
```

```
0x7fff3e4a0f80: 0xffffffff        0x57
0x7fff3e4a0f90: 0x7f8389573f10   0x7f838954d900 <_Unwind_SetIP@got.plt>
0x7fff3e4a0fa0: 0x5598d1acc2c8 <start_modeling()+215>    0x5598d2cf0f30
0x7fff3e4a0fb0: 0x1      0x3
0x7fff3e4a0fc0: 0x0      0x7f838958eb10 <_dl_fixup+208>
0x7fff3e4a0fd0: 0x1      0x0
0x7fff3e4a0fe0: 0x7f83892315ac   0x7f8389231ff8
0x7fff3e4a0ff0: 0x7fff3e4a13b0   0x7f838959558a <_dl_runtime_resolve_xsavec+122>
0x7fff3e4a1000: 0x8      0x7fff3e4a1a00
0x7fff3e4a1010: 0x1      0x5598d1acc2c8 <start_modeling()+215>
0x7fff3e4a1020: 0x7fff3e4a1780   0x7fff3e4a1780
0x7fff3e4a1030: 0x150    0x7f83893f8cc7
0x7fff3e4a1040: 0xfbf1759d       0x7f83893d6f90
0x7fff3e4a1050: 0x3efc5d6        0xffff00001f80
0x7fff3e4a1060: 0x7fff3e4a1140   0x7fff3e4a1088
0x7fff3e4a1070: 0x7f8389574a60   0x7f83895896fc <check_match+316>
0x7fff3e4a1080: 0x8906f420       0x6e
0x7fff3e4a1090: 0x7f8389573f10   0x1
0x7fff3e4a10a0: 0x7f8389231660   0x7f8389589b04 <do_lookup_x+932>
0x7fff3e4a10b0: 0x6e     0x7f8389232778
0x7fff3e4a10c0: 0x7f8389573f10   0x7fff3e4a1148
0x7fff3e4a10d0: 0x7fff3e4a1144   0x7f838906f4e0
0x7fff3e4a10e0: 0x0      0x0
0x7fff3e4a10f0: 0xff00000000     0xffff00000000
0x7fff3e4a1100: 0x0      0x0
0x7fff3e4a1110: 0x0      0x5598d1acc2dc <new_feature()>
0x7fff3e4a1120: 0x4000000000000000       0x0
0x7fff3e4a1130: 0x0      0x0
0x7fff3e4a1140: 0x0      0x0
0x7fff3e4a1150: 0x7fff3e4a1a20   0x7fff3e4a1a28
0x7fff3e4a1160: 0x5f6d65735f356475       0x65735f3564750062
0x7fff3e4a1170: 0x0      0x0
0x7fff3e4a1180: 0x0      0x0
0x7fff3e4a1190: 0x0      0x0
0x7fff3e4a11a0: 0x0      0x0
0x7fff3e4a11b0: 0x0      0x0
0x7fff3e4a11c0: 0x0      0x0
0x7fff3e4a11d0: 0x0      0x0
0x7fff3e4a11e0: 0x7f8389574270   0x0
--Type <RET> for more, q to quit, c to continue without paging--
0x7fff3e4a11f0: 0x7fff3e4a1580   0x7f838959558a <_dl_runtime_resolve_xsavec+122>
0x7fff3e4a1200: 0xffffffff       0x7
0x7fff3e4a1210: 0x7f83892321a8   0x7f8389573f10
0x7fff3e4a1220: 0x7fff3e4a1780   0x7fff3e4a1780
0x7fff3e4a1230: 0x150    0x0
0x7fff3e4a1240: 0x2      0x8000000000000006
0x7fff3e4a1250: 0x0      0x0
0x7fff3e4a1260: 0x0      0x0
0x7fff3e4a1270: 0x0      0x0
0x7fff3e4a1280: 0x0      0x5598d1acd018
0x7fff3e4a1290: 0x7fff3e4a13e0   0x7f8389243517
0x7fff3e4a12a0: 0x0      0x7f83892321a8
0x7fff3e4a12b0: 0x5598d1acd068   0x8
0x7fff3e4a12c0: 0xeb     0xb
0x7fff3e4a12d0: 0x5598d2cf0f50   0x5598d1acd1d8
0x7fff3e4a12e0: 0x7fff3e4a1780   0x0
0x7fff3e4a12f0: 0x80     0x7fff3e4a1350
0x7fff3e4a1300: 0x8      0x7f83895a8060 <_rtld_global>
0x7fff3e4a1310: 0x7fff3e4a1780   0x0
```

```
0x7fff3e4a1320: 0x7f83895a9190   0x7f83891a4973 <__GI___dl_iterate_phdr+403>
0x7fff3e4a1330: 0x0        0x1
0x7fff3e4a1340: 0x7f83892430b0   0x7fff3e4a13e0
0x7fff3e4a1350: 0x5598d1acb000   0x7f83895a9728
0x7fff3e4a1360: 0x5598d1acb040   0x7fff3e4a000b
0x7fff3e4a1370: 0x8        0x0
0x7fff3e4a1380: 0x0        0x0
0x7fff3e4a1390: 0x0        0x17e30f990797b00
0x7fff3e4a13a0: 0x7fff3e4a1a48   0x7fff3e4a1780
0x7fff3e4a13b0: 0x7fff3e4a1780   0x7f8389573510
0x7fff3e4a13c0: 0x31d      0x7f8389460118 <__gxx_personality_v0+184>
0x7fff3e4a13d0: 0x5598d1acc248 <start_modeling()+87>     0x5598d2cf0f30
0x7fff3e4a13e0: 0x601acc248     0x0
0x7fff3e4a13f0: 0x5598d1acd1d8   0x7fff3e4a1401
0x7fff3e4a1400: 0x5598d1acd130   0x559800000001
0x7fff3e4a1410: 0x0        0x5598d1acd145
0x7fff3e4a1420: 0x5598d1acd145   0x3e4a1780
0x7fff3e4a1430: 0x0        0x1b
0x7fff3e4a1440: 0x7fff3e4a14d0   0x7f8389240d00
0x7fff3e4a1450: 0x0        0x9b00000000
0x7fff3e4a1460: 0x5598d1acd129   0x7fff3e4a1478
0x7fff3e4a1470: 0x7fff3e4a14d0   0x7f83895896fc <check_match+316>
--Type <RET> for more, q to quit, c to continue without paging--
0x7fff3e4a1480: 0x7fff3e4a14d0   0x929
0x7fff3e4a1490: 0x7f8389574410   0x1
0x7fff3e4a14a0: 0x7f8389074f78   0x7f8389589b04 <do_lookup_x+932>
0x7fff3e4a14b0: 0x929      0x7f8389082cd8
0x7fff3e4a14c0: 0x7f8389574410   0x7fff3e4a1548
0x7fff3e4a14d0: 0x7fff3e4a1544   0x7f838958986e <do_lookup_x+270>
0x7fff3e4a14e0: 0x0        0x7f8389082cd8
0x7fff3e4a14f0: 0x7f8389074fb0   0x7f83893f88f8
0x7fff3e4a1500: 0x7c96f087      0x7f83893d6c48
0x7fff3e4a1510: 0x1f25bc2       0x7f8389460060 <__gxx_personality_v0>
0x7fff3e4a1520: 0x7fff3e4a1600   0x7fff3e4a1548
0x7fff3e4a1530: 0x7f8389574a60   0x7
0x7fff3e4a1540: 0x0        0x0
0x7fff3e4a1550: 0x0        0x7c96f087
0x7fff3e4a1560: 0x7f8389573870   0x7fff3e4a16a8
0x7fff3e4a1570: 0x7f8389573510   0x0
0x7fff3e4a1580: 0x7f838906f3f0   0x7f838958a39f <_dl_lookup_symbol_x+335>
0x7fff3e4a1590: 0x5        0x7f838906f3f0
0x7fff3e4a15a0: 0x1        0x0
0x7fff3e4a15b0: 0x1        0x7f8389573510
0x7fff3e4a15c0: 0x7f83893f88f8   0x100000000
0x7fff3e4a15d0: 0x7fff3e4a1600   0x7fff3e4a1610
0x7fff3e4a15e0: 0x7f8389573870   0x0
0x7fff3e4a15f0: 0x0        0x10
0x7fff3e4a1600: 0xffffffff      0x0
0x7fff3e4a1610: 0x7f8389082b88   0x7f8389574410
0x7fff3e4a1620: 0x7f8389460060 <__gxx_personality_v0>    0xfffffffffffffff8
0x7fff3e4a1630: 0x1        0x10
0x7fff3e4a1640: 0x11b1b    0x0
0x7fff3e4a1650: 0x5598d2cf0f30   0x7f838954ca10 <free@got.plt>
0x7fff3e4a1660: 0x7fff3e4a1a80   0x5598d1acc0f0 <_start>
0x7fff3e4a1670: 0x7fff3e4a1b70   0x0
0x7fff3e4a1680: 0x0        0x7f838958eb10 <_dl_fixup+208>
0x7fff3e4a1690: 0x1        0x0
0x7fff3e4a16a0: 0x0        0x7f8389082b88
0x7fff3e4a16b0: 0x7fff3e4a1a50   0x7f838959558a <_dl_runtime_resolve_xsavec+122>
```

```
0x7fff3e4a16c0: 0x5598d2cf0e60   0x1
0x7fff3e4a16d0: 0x18      0x0
0x7fff3e4a16e0: 0x7       0x20
0x7fff3e4a16f0: 0x7fff00000002   0x5598d2cdf010
0x7fff3e4a1700: 0xf       0x40
--Type <RET> for more, q to quit, c to continue without paging--
0x7fff3e4a1710: 0xffffffffffffff90        0x0
0x7fff3e4a1720: 0x3000000002     0x0
0x7fff3e4a1730: 0x770000005b     0x0
0x7fff3e4a1740: 0x6e0000007c     0x0
0x7fff3e4a1750: 0x4       0xf
0x7fff3e4a1760: 0x18      0x0
0x7fff3e4a1770: 0xffffffffffffff90        0x0
0x7fff3e4a1780: 0x0       0x7f83890f55a3 <__GI___libc_malloc+147>
0x7fff3e4a1790: 0x770000005b     0x5598d2cf0eb0
0x7fff3e4a17a0: 0xffffffff       0x7f83895724b0 <__sem_mappings>
0x7fff3e4a17b0: 0x0       0x7f83891661c4 <__GI___tsearch+308>
0x7fff3e4a17c0: 0x5598d2cf0eb8   0x5598d2cf0fa0
0x7fff3e4a17d0: 0x5598d2cf0f60   0x7f83895620f0 <__sem_search>
0x7fff3e4a17e0: 0x7fff3e4a1820   0x7f838957e000
0x7fff3e4a17f0: 0x7fff3e4a1940   0xa
0x7fff3e4a1800: 0x3       0x5598d1acd00e
0x7fff3e4a1810: 0x5598d2cf0f60   0x7f838956203e <check_add_mapping+542>
0x7fff3e4a1820: 0x43      0x1e
0x7fff3e4a1830: 0x0       0x0
0x7fff3e4a1840: 0x5f6d65735f356475        0x61
0x7fff3e4a1850: 0x0       0x7f8389561e63 <check_add_mapping+67>
0x7fff3e4a1860: 0x0       0x0
0x7fff3e4a1870: 0x43      0x1e
0x7fff3e4a1880: 0x1       0x3e8000081a4
0x7fff3e4a1890: 0x3e8     0x0
0x7fff3e4a18a0: 0x20      0x1000
0x7fff3e4a18b0: 0x8       0x666ee735
0x7fff3e4a18c0: 0x21e2e1d9        0x666ee735
0x7fff3e4a18d0: 0x21e2e1d9        0x666ee735
0x7fff3e4a18e0: 0x21e2e1d9        0x0
0x7fff3e4a18f0: 0x0       0x0
0x7fff3e4a1900: 0x2       0x17e30f990797b00
0x7fff3e4a1910: 0x0       0x5598d1acd00e
0x7fff3e4a1920: 0xa       0x0
0x7fff3e4a1930: 0x0       0x100000001
0x7fff3e4a1940: 0x7fff3e4a1a60   0x7f838956253e <sem_open+1054>
0x7fff3e4a1950: 0x6d68732f7665642f        0x3564752e6d65732f
0x7fff3e4a1960: 0x615f6d65735f     0x7f83895621b1 <sem_open+145>
0x7fff3e4a1970: 0xfffffffffffffff8        0x7fff3e4a1950
0x7fff3e4a1980: 0x0       0x0
0x7fff3e4a1990: 0x0       0xffffffffffffff60
--Type <RET> for more, q to quit, c to continue without paging--
0x7fff3e4a19a0: 0x6       0x0
0x7fff3e4a19b0: 0x9       0x5598d1acc2db <start_modeling()+234>
0x7fff3e4a19c0: 0x7f8389460060 <__gxx_personality_v0>     0xfffffffffffffff8
0x7fff3e4a19d0: 0x1       0x7f8389562873 <do_futex_wait+19>
0x7fff3e4a19e0: 0x11b1b 0x0
0x7fff3e4a19f0: 0x7f838957e000   0x0
0x7fff3e4a1a00: 0x7fff3e4a1a10   0x7f8389562988 <__new_sem_wait_slow+152>
0x7fff3e4a1a10: 0x7f8389562850 <__sem_wait_cleanup>       0x7f838957e000
0x7fff3e4a1a20: 0x0       0x0
0x7fff3e4a1a30: 0x7fff3e4a1a80   0x17e30f990797b00
0x7fff3e4a1a40: 0x5598d1acc0f0 <_start> 0x0
```
215

```
0x7fff3e4a1a50: 0x7fff3e4a1a80   0x5598d1acc0f0 <_start>
0x7fff3e4a1a60: 0x7fff3e4a1b70   0x5598d1acc28c <start_modeling()+155>
0x7fff3e4a1a70: 0x7f838957e000   0x7f838957f000
0x7fff3e4a1a80: 0x7fff3e4a1a90   0x5598d1acc1ea <main()+21>
0x7fff3e4a1a90: 0x5598d1acc310 <__libc_csu_init>        0x7f838909509b <__libc_start_main+235>
0x7fff3e4a1aa0: 0xffffffffffffff90      0x7fff3e4a1b78
0x7fff3e4a1ab0: 0x1894899e0       0x5598d1acc1d5 <main()>
0x7fff3e4a1ac0: 0x0       0x801498e3bb17f13a
0x7fff3e4a1ad0: 0x5598d1acc0f0 <_start> 0x7fff3e4a1b70
0x7fff3e4a1ae0: 0x0       0x0
0x7fff3e4a1af0: 0xd4db472e0877f13a         0xd42229a89d91f13a
0x7fff3e4a1b00: 0x0       0x0
0x7fff3e4a1b10: 0x0       0x7fff3e4a1b88
0x7fff3e4a1b20: 0x7f83895a9190   0x7f838958f486 <_dl_init+118>
0x7fff3e4a1b30: 0x0       0x0
0x7fff3e4a1b40: 0x5598d1acc0f0 <_start> 0x7fff3e4a1b70
0x7fff3e4a1b50: 0x0       0x5598d1acc11a <_start+42>
0x7fff3e4a1b60: 0x7fff3e4a1b68   0x1c
0x7fff3e4a1b70: 0x1       0x7fff3e4a2408
0x7fff3e4a1b80: 0x0       0x7fff3e4a2411
0x7fff3e4a1b90: 0x7fff3e4a2421   0x7fff3e4a2435
0x7fff3e4a1ba0: 0x7fff3e4a244d   0x7fff3e4a2469
0x7fff3e4a1bb0: 0x7fff3e4a2480   0x7fff3e4a2495
0x7fff3e4a1bc0: 0x7fff3e4a24a9   0x7fff3e4a24ba
0x7fff3e4a1bd0: 0x7fff3e4a2522   0x7fff3e4a2536
0x7fff3e4a1be0: 0x7fff3e4a2547   0x7fff3e4a2567
0x7fff3e4a1bf0: 0x7fff3e4a2b49   0x7fff3e4a2b63
0x7fff3e4a1c00: 0x7fff3e4a2bd9   0x7fff3e4a2bf8
0x7fff3e4a1c10: 0x7fff3e4a2c0c   0x7fff3e4a2c1a
0x7fff3e4a1c20: 0x7fff3e4a2c61   0x7fff3e4a2c6c
--Type <RET> for more, q to quit, c to continue without paging--
0x7fff3e4a1c30: 0x7fff3e4a2c74   0x7fff3e4a2caa
0x7fff3e4a1c40: 0x7fff3e4a2cd0   0x7fff3e4a2d07
0x7fff3e4a1c50: 0x7fff3e4a2d8e   0x7fff3e4a2f22
0x7fff3e4a1c60: 0x7fff3e4a2f32   0x7fff3e4a2f5a
0x7fff3e4a1c70: 0x7fff3e4a2f6e   0x7fff3e4a2fcd
0x7fff3e4a1c80: 0x7fff3e4a2fe4   0x0
0x7fff3e4a1c90: 0x21      0x7fff3e4e8000
0x7fff3e4a1ca0: 0x33      0x6f0
0x7fff3e4a1cb0: 0x10      0x1f8bfbff
0x7fff3e4a1cc0: 0x6       0x1000
...
```

Note: If you see that the region is too short (no zeros at the beginning) or doesn't include interesting symbolic references, try to decrease the lower region bound, for example, `0x7fff3e490000`. Alternatively, we could dump the whole stack region:

```
(gdb) info proc mappings
process 19952
Mapped address spaces:

          Start Addr         End Addr       Size     Offset objfile
      0x5598d1acb000   0x5598d1acc000     0x1000        0x0 /mnt/c/ALD4/ud5/ud5bv3
      0x5598d1acc000   0x5598d1acd000     0x1000     0x1000 /mnt/c/ALD4/ud5/ud5bv3
      0x5598d1acd000   0x5598d1ace000     0x1000     0x2000 /mnt/c/ALD4/ud5/ud5bv3
      0x5598d1ace000   0x5598d1acf000     0x1000     0x2000 /mnt/c/ALD4/ud5/ud5bv3
      0x5598d1acf000   0x5598d1ad0000     0x1000     0x3000 /mnt/c/ALD4/ud5/ud5bv3
      0x5598d2cdf000   0x5598d2d00000    0x21000        0x0 [heap]
      0x7f838906c000   0x7f8389071000     0x5000        0x0
      0x7f8389071000   0x7f8389093000    0x22000        0x0 /lib/x86_64-linux-gnu/libc-2.28.so
```

216

```
0x7f8389093000    0x7f83891da000    0x147000     0x22000 /lib/x86_64-linux-gnu/libc-2.28.so
0x7f83891da000    0x7f8389226000     0x4c000    0x169000 /lib/x86_64-linux-gnu/libc-2.28.so
0x7f8389226000    0x7f8389227000      0x1000    0x1b5000 /lib/x86_64-linux-gnu/libc-2.28.so
0x7f8389227000    0x7f838922b000      0x4000    0x1b5000 /lib/x86_64-linux-gnu/libc-2.28.so
0x7f838922b000    0x7f838922d000      0x2000    0x1b9000 /lib/x86_64-linux-gnu/libc-2.28.so
0x7f838922d000    0x7f8389231000      0x4000        0x0
0x7f8389231000    0x7f8389234000      0x3000        0x0 /lib/x86_64-linux-gnu/libgcc_s.so.1
0x7f8389234000    0x7f8389245000     0x11000     0x3000 /lib/x86_64-linux-gnu/libgcc_s.so.1
0x7f8389245000    0x7f8389248000      0x3000    0x14000 /lib/x86_64-linux-gnu/libgcc_s.so.1
0x7f8389248000    0x7f8389249000      0x1000    0x17000 /lib/x86_64-linux-gnu/libgcc_s.so.1
0x7f8389249000    0x7f838924a000      0x1000    0x17000 /lib/x86_64-linux-gnu/libgcc_s.so.1
0x7f838924a000    0x7f838924b000      0x1000    0x18000 /lib/x86_64-linux-gnu/libgcc_s.so.1
0x7f838924b000    0x7f8389258000      0xd000        0x0 /lib/x86_64-linux-gnu/libm-2.28.so
0x7f8389258000    0x7f83892f7000     0x9f000     0xd000 /lib/x86_64-linux-gnu/libm-2.28.so
0x7f83892f7000    0x7f83893cc000     0xd5000    0xac000 /lib/x86_64-linux-gnu/libm-2.28.so
0x7f83893cc000    0x7f83893cd000      0x1000   0x180000 /lib/x86_64-linux-gnu/libm-2.28.so
0x7f83893cd000    0x7f83893ce000      0x1000   0x181000 /lib/x86_64-linux-gnu/libm-2.28.so
0x7f83893ce000    0x7f8389457000     0x89000        0x0 /usr/lib/x86_64-linux-gnu/libstdc++.so.6.0.25
0x7f8389457000    0x7f8389503000     0xac000    0x89000 /usr/lib/x86_64-linux-gnu/libstdc++.so.6.0.25
0x7f8389503000    0x7f8389541000     0x3e000   0x135000 /usr/lib/x86_64-linux-gnu/libstdc++.so.6.0.25
0x7f8389541000    0x7f8389542000      0x1000   0x173000 /usr/lib/x86_64-linux-gnu/libstdc++.so.6.0.25
0x7f8389542000    0x7f838954c000      0xa000   0x173000 /usr/lib/x86_64-linux-gnu/libstdc++.so.6.0.25
0x7f838954c000    0x7f838954e000      0x2000   0x17d000 /usr/lib/x86_64-linux-gnu/libstdc++.so.6.0.25
0x7f838954e000    0x7f8389552000      0x4000        0x0
0x7f8389552000    0x7f8389558000      0x6000        0x0 /lib/x86_64-linux-gnu/libpthread-2.28.so
0x7f8389558000    0x7f8389567000      0xf000     0x6000 /lib/x86_64-linux-gnu/libpthread-2.28.so
0x7f8389567000    0x7f838956d000      0x6000    0x15000 /lib/x86_64-linux-gnu/libpthread-2.28.so
0x7f838956d000    0x7f838956e000      0x1000    0x1a000 /lib/x86_64-linux-gnu/libpthread-2.28.so
0x7f838956e000    0x7f838956f000      0x1000    0x1b000 /lib/x86_64-linux-gnu/libpthread-2.28.so
--Type <RET> for more, q to quit, c to continue without paging--
0x7f838956f000    0x7f8389575000      0x6000        0x0
0x7f838957e000    0x7f838957f000      0x1000        0x0 /dev/shm/sem.ud5_sem_a
0x7f838957f000    0x7f8389580000      0x1000        0x0 /dev/shm/8LrDDa (deleted)
0x7f8389580000    0x7f8389581000      0x1000        0x0 /lib/x86_64-linux-gnu/ld-2.28.so
0x7f8389581000    0x7f838959f000     0x1e000     0x1000 /lib/x86_64-linux-gnu/ld-2.28.so
0x7f838959f000    0x7f83895a7000      0x8000    0x1f000 /lib/x86_64-linux-gnu/ld-2.28.so
0x7f83895a7000    0x7f83895a8000      0x1000    0x26000 /lib/x86_64-linux-gnu/ld-2.28.so
0x7f83895a8000    0x7f83895a9000      0x1000    0x27000 /lib/x86_64-linux-gnu/ld-2.28.so
0x7f83895a9000    0x7f83895aa000      0x1000        0x0
0x7fff3e482000    0x7fff3e4a3000     0x21000        0x0 [stack]
0x7fff3e4e4000    0x7fff3e4e8000      0x4000        0x0 [vvar]
0x7fff3e4e8000    0x7fff3e4ea000      0x2000        0x0 [vdso]
```

(gdb) **x/16896a** 0x7fff3e482000
[...]

Note: 16896 is 0x2100/8 (0x4200) in decimal.

Note: We see some symbolic references in the past stack region addresses (highlighted in blue) related to stack unwinding during exceptions and functions from the *ud5bv3*. The stack region related to the current stack trace is highlighted in green.

13.   Let's examine the selected symbolic references:

(gdb) **x/a** 0x7f838954d900
0x7f838954d900 <_Unwind_SetIP@got.plt>: 0x7f838923ffd0 <_Unwind_SetIP>

Note: The reference above is a function pointer.

(gdb) **disassemble** 0x5598d1acc2c8
Dump of assembler code for function start_modeling():
   0x00005598d1acc1f1 <+0>:   push   %rbp
   0x00005598d1acc1f2 <+1>:   mov   %rsp,%rbp
   0x00005598d1acc1f5 <+4>:   sub $0x10,%rsp

```
   0x00005598d1acc1f9 <+8>:      mov     $0x1,%ecx
   0x00005598d1acc1fe <+13>:     mov     $0x1a4,%edx
   0x00005598d1acc203 <+18>:     mov     $0x40,%esi
   0x00005598d1acc208 <+23>:     lea     0xdf5(%rip),%rdi        # 0x5598d1acd004
   0x00005598d1acc20f <+30>:     mov     $0x0,%eax
   0x00005598d1acc214 <+35>:     callq   0x5598d1acc030 <sem_open@plt>
   0x00005598d1acc219 <+40>:     mov     %rax,-0x8(%rbp)
   0x00005598d1acc21d <+44>:     cmpq    $0x0,-0x8(%rbp)
   0x00005598d1acc222 <+49>:     jne     0x5598d1acc22e <start_modeling()+61>
   0x00005598d1acc224 <+51>:     mov     $0x1,%edi
   0x00005598d1acc229 <+56>:     callq   0x5598d1acc090 <exit@plt>
   0x00005598d1acc22e <+61>:     mov     -0x8(%rbp),%rax
   0x00005598d1acc232 <+65>:     mov     %rax,%rdi
   0x00005598d1acc235 <+68>:     callq   0x5598d1acc080 <sem_wait@plt>
   0x00005598d1acc23a <+73>:     mov     $0xa,%edi
   0x00005598d1acc23f <+78>:     callq   0x5598d1acc060 <sleep@plt>
   0x00005598d1acc244 <+83>:     callq   0x5598d1acc2dc <new_feature()>
   0x00005598d1acc249 <+88>:     mov     -0x8(%rbp),%rax
   0x00005598d1acc24d <+92>:     mov     %rax,%rdi
   0x00005598d1acc250 <+95>:     callq   0x5598d1acc070 <sem_post@plt>
   0x00005598d1acc255 <+100>:    mov     $0x0,%esi
   0x00005598d1acc25a <+105>:    lea     0xdad(%rip),%rdi        # 0x5598d1acd00e
   0x00005598d1acc261 <+112>:    mov     $0x0,%eax
   0x00005598d1acc266 <+117>:    callq   0x5598d1acc030 <sem_open@plt>
   0x00005598d1acc26b <+122>:    mov     %rax,-0x10(%rbp)
   0x00005598d1acc26f <+126>:    cmpq    $0x0,-0x10(%rbp)
   0x00005598d1acc274 <+131>:    jne     0x5598d1acc280 <start_modeling()+143>
   0x00005598d1acc276 <+133>:    mov     $0x1,%edi
   0x00005598d1acc27b <+138>:    callq   0x5598d1acc090 <exit@plt>
   0x00005598d1acc280 <+143>:    mov     -0x10(%rbp),%rax
   0x00005598d1acc284 <+147>:    mov     %rax,%rdi
   0x00005598d1acc287 <+150>:    callq   0x5598d1acc080 <sem_wait@plt>
   0x00005598d1acc28c <+155>:    mov     $0xa,%edi
   0x00005598d1acc291 <+160>:    callq   0x5598d1acc060 <sleep@plt>
   0x00005598d1acc296 <+165>:    mov     -0x10(%rbp),%rax
   0x00005598d1acc29a <+169>:    mov     %rax,%rdi
   0x00005598d1acc29d <+172>:    callq   0x5598d1acc070 <sem_post@plt>
--Type <RET> for more, q to quit, c to continue without paging--
   0x00005598d1acc2a2 <+177>:    mov     -0x10(%rbp),%rax
   0x00005598d1acc2a6 <+181>:    mov     %rax,%rdi
   0x00005598d1acc2a9 <+184>:    callq   0x5598d1acc0a0 <sem_close@plt>
   0x00005598d1acc2ae <+189>:    mov     -0x8(%rbp),%rax
   0x00005598d1acc2b2 <+193>:    mov     %rax,%rdi
   0x00005598d1acc2b5 <+196>:    callq   0x5598d1acc0a0 <sem_close@plt>
   0x00005598d1acc2ba <+201>:    lea     0xd43(%rip),%rdi        # 0x5598d1acd004
   0x00005598d1acc2c1 <+208>:    callq   0x5598d1acc0c0 <sem_unlink@plt>
   0x00005598d1acc2c6 <+213>:    jmp     0x5598d1acc2da <start_modeling()+233>
   0x00005598d1acc2c8 <+215>:    mov     %rax,%rdi
   0x00005598d1acc2cb <+218>:    callq   0x5598d1acc040 <__cxa_begin_catch@plt>
   0x00005598d1acc2d0 <+223>:    callq   0x5598d1acc0b0 <__cxa_end_catch@plt>
   0x00005598d1acc2d5 <+228>:    jmpq    0x5598d1acc255 <start_modeling()+100>
   0x00005598d1acc2da <+233>:    leaveq
   0x00005598d1acc2db <+234>:    retq
End of assembler dump.
```

Note: The disassembly points to the beginning of a catch block..

```
(gdb) disassemble 0x5598d1acc2dc
Dump of assembler code for function new_feature():
   0x00005598d1acc2dc <+0>:     push   %rbp
   0x00005598d1acc2dd <+1>:     mov    %rsp,%rbp
   0x00005598d1acc2e0 <+4>:     mov    $0x4,%edi
   0x00005598d1acc2e5 <+9>:     callq  0x5598d1acc050 <__cxa_allocate_exception@plt>
   0x00005598d1acc2ea <+14>:    movl   $0x0,(%rax)
   0x00005598d1acc2f0 <+20>:    mov    $0x0,%edx
   0x00005598d1acc2f5 <+25>:    lea    0x2aa4(%rip),%rsi        # 0x5598d1aceda0
<_ZTIi@@CXXABI_1.3>
   0x00005598d1acc2fc <+32>:    mov    %rax,%rdi
   0x00005598d1acc2ff <+35>:    callq  0x5598d1acc0d0 <__cxa_throw@plt>
End of assembler dump.
```

Note: The stack address of a symbolic reference above is a function pointer.

```
(gdb) x/i 0x5598d1acc248
   0x5598d1acc248 <start_modeling()+87>:        add    %cl,-0x75(%rax)
```

```
(gdb) disassemble 0x5598d1acc248
Dump of assembler code for function start_modeling():
   0x00005598d1acc1f1 <+0>:     push   %rbp
   0x00005598d1acc1f2 <+1>:     mov    %rsp,%rbp
   0x00005598d1acc1f5 <+4>:     sub    $0x10,%rsp
   0x00005598d1acc1f9 <+8>:     mov    $0x1,%ecx
   0x00005598d1acc1fe <+13>:    mov    $0x1a4,%edx
   0x00005598d1acc203 <+18>:    mov    $0x40,%esi
   0x00005598d1acc208 <+23>:    lea    0xdf5(%rip),%rdi         # 0x5598d1acd004
   0x00005598d1acc20f <+30>:    mov    $0x0,%eax
   0x00005598d1acc214 <+35>:    callq  0x5598d1acc030 <sem_open@plt>
   0x00005598d1acc219 <+40>:    mov    %rax,-0x8(%rbp)
   0x00005598d1acc21d <+44>:    cmpq   $0x0,-0x8(%rbp)
   0x00005598d1acc222 <+49>:    jne    0x5598d1acc22e <start_modeling()+61>
   0x00005598d1acc224 <+51>:    mov    $0x1,%edi
   0x00005598d1acc229 <+56>:    callq  0x5598d1acc090 <exit@plt>
   0x00005598d1acc22e <+61>:    mov    -0x8(%rbp),%rax
   0x00005598d1acc232 <+65>:    mov    %rax,%rdi
   0x00005598d1acc235 <+68>:    callq  0x5598d1acc080 <sem_wait@plt>
   0x00005598d1acc23a <+73>:    mov    $0xa,%edi
   0x00005598d1acc23f <+78>:    callq  0x5598d1acc060 <sleep@plt>
   0x00005598d1acc244 <+83>:    callq  0x5598d1acc2dc <new_feature()>
   0x00005598d1acc249 <+88>:    mov    -0x8(%rbp),%rax
   0x00005598d1acc24d <+92>:    mov    %rax,%rdi
   0x00005598d1acc250 <+95>:    callq  0x5598d1acc070 <sem_post@plt>
   0x00005598d1acc255 <+100>:   mov    $0x0,%esi
   0x00005598d1acc25a <+105>:   lea    0xdad(%rip),%rdi         # 0x5598d1acd00e
   0x00005598d1acc261 <+112>:   mov    $0x0,%eax
   0x00005598d1acc266 <+117>:   callq  0x5598d1acc030 <sem_open@plt>
   0x00005598d1acc26b <+122>:   mov    %rax,-0x10(%rbp)
   0x00005598d1acc26f <+126>:   cmpq   $0x0,-0x10(%rbp)
   0x00005598d1acc274 <+131>:   jne    0x5598d1acc280 <start_modeling()+143>
   0x00005598d1acc276 <+133>:   mov    $0x1,%edi
   0x00005598d1acc27b <+138>:   callq  0x5598d1acc090 <exit@plt>
   0x00005598d1acc280 <+143>:   mov    -0x10(%rbp),%rax
   0x00005598d1acc284 <+147>:   mov    %rax,%rdi
   0x00005598d1acc287 <+150>:   callq  0x5598d1acc080 <sem_wait@plt>
   0x00005598d1acc28c <+155>:   mov    $0xa,%edi
   0x00005598d1acc291 <+160>:   callq  0x5598d1acc060 <sleep@plt>
```

```
0x00005598d1acc296 <+165>:    mov     -0x10(%rbp),%rax
0x00005598d1acc29a <+169>:    mov     %rax,%rdi
0x00005598d1acc29d <+172>:    callq   0x5598d1acc070 <sem_post@plt>
--Type <RET> for more, q to quit, c to continue without paging--
0x00005598d1acc2a2 <+177>:    mov     -0x10(%rbp),%rax
0x00005598d1acc2a6 <+181>:    mov     %rax,%rdi
0x00005598d1acc2a9 <+184>:    callq   0x5598d1acc0a0 <sem_close@plt>
0x00005598d1acc2ae <+189>:    mov     -0x8(%rbp),%rax
0x00005598d1acc2b2 <+193>:    mov     %rax,%rdi
0x00005598d1acc2b5 <+196>:    callq   0x5598d1acc0a0 <sem_close@plt>
0x00005598d1acc2ba <+201>:    lea     0xd43(%rip),%rdi        # 0x5598d1acd004
0x00005598d1acc2c1 <+208>:    callq   0x5598d1acc0c0 <sem_unlink@plt>
0x00005598d1acc2c6 <+213>:    jmp     0x5598d1acc2da <start_modeling()+233>
0x00005598d1acc2c8 <+215>:    mov     %rax,%rdi
0x00005598d1acc2cb <+218>:    callq   0x5598d1acc040 <__cxa_begin_catch@plt>
0x00005598d1acc2d0 <+223>:    callq   0x5598d1acc0b0 <__cxa_end_catch@plt>
0x00005598d1acc2d5 <+228>:    jmpq    0x5598d1acc255 <start_modeling()+100>
0x00005598d1acc2da <+233>:    leaveq
0x00005598d1acc2db <+234>:    retq
End of assembler dump.
```

Note: The address above doesn't belong to the valid disassembly code. Most likely, this is coincidental.

14.   We quit GDB, the *ud5a* and *ud5bv3* processes (**^C**).

Expected Behavior

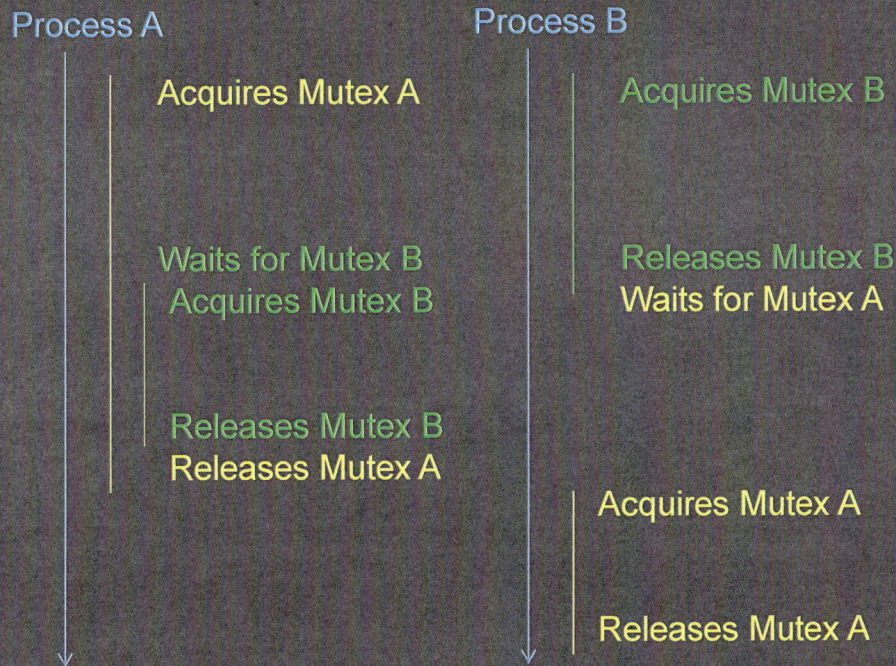

Process A	Process B
Acquires Mutex A	Acquires Mutex B
Waits for Mutex B Acquires Mutex B	Releases Mutex B Waits for Mutex A
Releases Mutex B Releases Mutex A	Acquires Mutex A
	Releases Mutex A

The diagram shows the expected behavior for *ud5a* and *ud5b* applications.

Deadlock

Process A	Process B
Acquires Mutex A	Acquires Mutex B
	new_feature()
Waits for Mutex B	Waits for Mutex A

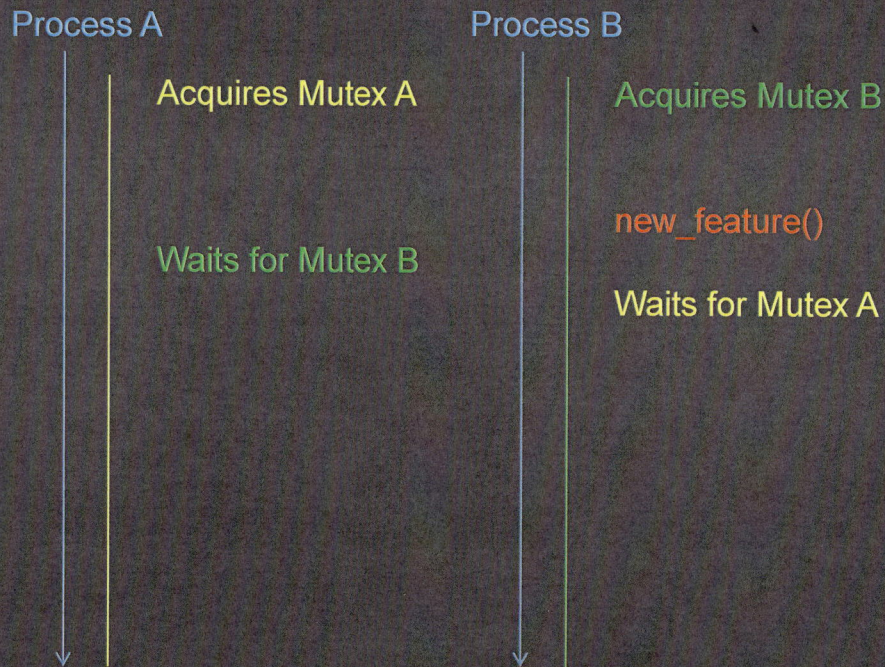

The diagram shows the abnormal behavior for *ud5bv3* after the problem new feature was introduced in *ud5bv2* and incorrectly fixed.

Exercise UD6

- **Goal:** Learn how to recognize when we need kernel-level debugging

- **Elementary Diagnostics Patterns:** Hang; Counter Value

- **Memory Analysis Patterns:** Abnormal Value (*from trace analysis patterns*); Spiking Thread

- **Debugging Implementation Patterns:** Break-in; Code Breakpoint; Data Breakpoint; Code Trace

- \ALD4\Exercise-Linux-UD6.pdf

Exercise UD6 (GDB)

Goal: Learn how to recognize when we need kernel-level debugging.

Elementary Diagnostics Patterns: Hang; Counter Value.

Memory Analysis Patterns: Abnormal Value (*from trace analysis patterns*); Spiking Thread.

Debugging Implementation Patterns: Break-in; Code Breakpoint; Data Breakpoint; Code Trace.

1.   The source code and the *Makefile* to build executables and libraries can be found in the *ud6* directory:

```
$ git clone https://bitbucket.org/softwarediagnostics/ald4
```

2.   Run the *ud6* executable and wait approximately 30 seconds until it finishes:

```
/mnt/c/ALD4/ud6$ ./ud6
```

3.   Here's the source code:

```
void start_modeling()
{
        volatile unsigned int *p_int = NULL;

        allocate_storage(&p_int); // allocates a memory for p_int

        *p_int = 5000;

        sleep(30);

        while (--(*p_int))
        {
                sleep(0); // do some work
        }

        deallocate_storage(p_int);
}
```

The application is not supposed to hang after 30 seconds and, subsequently, shouldn't have CPU consumption.

4.   Now run the *ud6* executable again and, **in less than 30 seconds**, launch *../driver_emulator/driver_emulator* in another terminal. Wait for about 30 seconds until *ud6* starts consuming CPU:

PID	USER	PR	NI	VIRT	RES	SHR	S	%CPU	%MEM	TIME+	COMMAND
5025	coredump	20	0	2332	796	708	R	10.7	0.0	0:04.44	ud6
73	coredump	20	0	11.3g	181408	52424	S	2.7	2.2	1:06.12	node
24	coredump	20	0	1334196	106592	43612	S	0.7	1.3	0:52.38	node
93	coredump	20	0	1115780	60808	40232	S	0.7	0.8	0:04.09	node
36	root	20	0	2520	128	0	S	0.3	0.0	0:00.38	Relay(37)
37	coredump	20	0	999588	54724	37192	S	0.3	0.7	0:01.52	node
244	coredump	20	0	90896	33712	11736	S	0.3	0.4	0:03.48	cpptools
1	root	20	0	2476	1716	1600	S	0.0	0.0	0:00.02	init(Debian)
5	root	20	0	2476	4	0	S	0.0	0.0	0:00.00	init
12	root	20	0	2484	116	0	S	0.0	0.0	0:00.00	SessionLeader

```
    13 root        20   0    2500     124        0 S   0.0   0.0   0:00.00 Rel
```

5.   We attach *gdb* to the process:

```
/mnt/c/ALD4/driver_emulator$ gdb -p 5025
GNU gdb (Debian 8.2.1-2+b3) 8.2.1
Copyright (C) 2018 Free Software Foundation, Inc.
License GPLv3+: GNU GPL version 3 or later <http://gnu.org/licenses/gpl.html>
This is free software: you are free to change and redistribute it.
There is NO WARRANTY, to the extent permitted by law.
Type "show copying" and "show warranty" for details.
This GDB was configured as "x86_64-linux-gnu".
Type "show configuration" for configuration details.
For bug reporting instructions, please see:
<http://www.gnu.org/software/gdb/bugs/>.
Find the GDB manual and other documentation resources online at:
    <http://www.gnu.org/software/gdb/documentation/>.

For help, type "help".
Type "apropos word" to search for commands related to "word".
Attaching to process 5025
Reading symbols from /mnt/c/ALD4/ud6/ud6...done.
Reading symbols from /lib/x86_64-linux-gnu/librt.so.1...Reading symbols from
/usr/lib/debug/.build-id/c8/899aec85ac923281dfa7ad96e261b772c0be85.debug...done.
done.
Reading symbols from /lib/x86_64-linux-gnu/libc.so.6...Reading symbols from
/usr/lib/debug/.build-id/c7/aa9a1e121fe2395f3840f3f0213146046d9fe3.debug...done.
done.
Reading symbols from /lib/x86_64-linux-gnu/libpthread.so.0...Reading symbols from
/usr/lib/debug/.build-id/48/041452aef93ddb2366ca0fa49da8f32684a9c8.debug...done.
done.
[Thread debugging using libthread_db enabled]
Using host libthread_db library "/lib/x86_64-linux-gnu/libthread_db.so.1".
Reading symbols from /lib64/ld-linux-x86-64.so.2...Reading symbols from /usr/lib/debug/.build-
id/83/743ddd4258a7d138a28c4f2032d17ad92a15b5.debug...done.
done.
0x00007f22756ab594 in __GI___nanosleep (requested_time=0x7fff219e18f0,
remaining=0x7fff219e18f0) at ../sysdeps/unix/sysv/linux/nanosleep.c:28
28      ../sysdeps/unix/sysv/linux/nanosleep.c: No such file or directory.
(gdb)
```

6.   List the backtrace, select frame #2, and then inspect the value of **p_int*:

```
(gdb) bt
#0  0x00007f22756ab594 in __GI___nanosleep (requested_time=0x7fff219e18f0,
remaining=0x7fff219e18f0) at ../sysdeps/unix/sysv/linux/nanosleep.c:28
#1  0x00007f22756ab4ca in __sleep (seconds=0) at ../sysdeps/posix/sleep.c:55
#2  0x0000559b176c41f6 in start_modeling () at ud6.c:33
#3  0x0000559b176c41b3 in main () at ud6.c:13

(gdb) frame 2
#2  0x0000559b176c41f6 in start_modeling () at ud6.c:33
33                        sleep(0); // do some work

(gdb) p *p_int
$1 = 4292692614
```

Note: Its value is not the expected 0 or less than 5000.

7. To find when it is changed, we quit our GDB session (**q**) and *ud6* (**^C**) and launch *ud6* again under GDB:

```
/mnt/c/ALD4/ud6$ gdb ./ud6
GNU gdb (Debian 8.2.1-2+b3) 8.2.1
Copyright (C) 2018 Free Software Foundation, Inc.
License GPLv3+: GNU GPL version 3 or later <http://gnu.org/licenses/gpl.html>
This is free software: you are free to change and redistribute it.
There is NO WARRANTY, to the extent permitted by law.
Type "show copying" and "show warranty" for details.
This GDB was configured as "x86_64-linux-gnu".
Type "show configuration" for configuration details.
For bug reporting instructions, please see:
<http://www.gnu.org/software/gdb/bugs/>.
Find the GDB manual and other documentation resources online at:
    <http://www.gnu.org/software/gdb/documentation/>.

For help, type "help".
Type "apropos word" to search for commands related to "word"...
Reading symbols from ./ud6...done.
(gdb)
```

8. We put a breakpoint on the *start_modeling* function and run the program:

```
(gdb) break start_modeling
Breakpoint 1 at 0x11c2: file ud6.c, line 23.

(gdb) r
Starting program: /mnt/c/ALD4/ud6/ud6
[Thread debugging using libthread_db enabled]
Using host libthread_db library "/lib/x86_64-linux-gnu/libthread_db.so.1".

Breakpoint 1, start_modeling () at ud6.c:23
23              volatile unsigned int *p_int = NULL;
```

9. We then step over until the storage for the *p_int* variable is allocated:

```
(gdb) next
25              allocate_storage(&p_int); // allocates a memory for p_int

(gdb) next
27              *p_int = 5000;
```

10. We now put a write hardware breakpoint for 4 bytes (int) on the value of *p_int*:

```
(gdb) p p_int
$1 = (volatile unsigned int *) 0x12340000

(gdb) watch *0x12340000
Hardware watchpoint 2: *0x12340000
```

11. If we continue, we get the first hit where we change the value to 5000 as expected:

```
(gdb) c
Continuing.
```

226

```
Hardware watchpoint 2: *0x12340000

Old value = -2325480
New value = 5000
start_modeling () at ud6.c:29
29              sleep(30);
```

12.   We then continue and run *driver_emulator* again (we have no more than 30 seconds to do that!) and wait:

```
(gdb) c
Continuing.

Hardware watchpoint 2: *0x12340000

Old value = 5000
New value = -2
0x0000555555555201 in start_modeling () at ud6.c:31
31              while (--(*p_int))

(gdb) bt
#0  0x0000555555555201 in start_modeling () at ud6.c:31
#1  0x00005555555551b3 in main () at ud6.c:13
```

Note: Unfortunately, the next hit only happened when we started the loop, which modifies *p_int* in each iteration, and we were unable to catch the moment when the variable value was changed from 5000 to 0xffffffff. We try to debug such corruption in kernel mode debugging.

13.   We quit our GDB session (**q**).

227

Exercise UD7

- **Goal:** Learn how to manipulate threads to debug race conditions

- **Elementary Diagnostics Patterns:** Crash

- **Memory Analysis Patterns:** Exception Stack Trace; NULL Pointer (Code)

- **Debugging Implementation Patterns:** Frozen Thread

- \ALD4\Exercise-Linux-UD7.pdf

Goal: Learn how to manipulate threads to debug race conditions.

Elementary Diagnostics Patterns: Crash.

Memory Analysis Patterns: Exception Stack Trace; NULL Pointer (Code).

Debugging Implementation Patterns: Frozen Thread.

1.   The source code and the *Makefile* to build executables and libraries can be found in the *ud7* directory:

$ **git** clone https://bitbucket.org/softwarediagnostics/ald4

2.   Problem history:

The application *ud7* crashes shortly after it starts. We want to find out the root cause.

3.   We run *ud7* under GDB:

```
/mnt/c/ALD4/ud7$ gdb ./ud7
GNU gdb (Debian 8.2.1-2+b3) 8.2.1
Copyright (C) 2018 Free Software Foundation, Inc.
License GPLv3+: GNU GPL version 3 or later <http://gnu.org/licenses/gpl.html>
This is free software: you are free to change and redistribute it.
There is NO WARRANTY, to the extent permitted by law.
Type "show copying" and "show warranty" for details.
This GDB was configured as "x86_64-linux-gnu".
Type "show configuration" for configuration details.
For bug reporting instructions, please see:
<http://www.gnu.org/software/gdb/bugs/>.
Find the GDB manual and other documentation resources online at:
    <http://www.gnu.org/software/gdb/documentation/>.

For help, type "help".
Type "apropos word" to search for commands related to "word"...
Reading symbols from ./ud7...done.

(gdb) r
Starting program: /mnt/c/ALD4/ud7/ud7
[Thread debugging using libthread_db enabled]
Using host libthread_db library "/lib/x86_64-linux-gnu/libthread_db.so.1".
[New Thread 0x7ffff7ddd700 (LWP 17262)]
[New Thread 0x7ffff75dc700 (LWP 17263)]
[New Thread 0x7ffff6ddb700 (LWP 17281)]
[Thread 0x7ffff6ddb700 (LWP 17281) exited]
[Thread 0x7ffff7ddd700 (LWP 17262) exited]
[Thread 0x7ffff75dc700 (LWP 17263) exited]
```

Note: We see that it doesn't crash. So, it looks like the GDB debugger influenced program behavior.

4.   Let's look at the source code of the *start_modeling* function:

```
void start_modeling (void)
{
```

```
    pthread_t thread;
    if (pthread_create(&thread, NULL, thread_proc_a, NULL))
    {
      exit(1);
    }
    pthread_detach(thread);

    if (pthread_create(&thread, NULL, thread_proc_b, NULL))
    {
      exit(1);
    }
    pthread_detach(thread);
}
```

5.   We want to put breakpoints when we run the *ud7* again, so we quit GDB. Then, we run the *ud7* under the GDB again.

```
^C
Thread 1 "ud7" received signal SIGINT, Interrupt.
0x00007ffff7ea75c0 in __GI___nanosleep (requested_time=requested_time@entry=0x7fffffffe020,
remaining=remaining@entry=0x7fffffffe020)
    at ../sysdeps/unix/sysv/linux/nanosleep.c:28
28      ../sysdeps/unix/sysv/linux/nanosleep.c: No such file or directory.

(gdb) q
A debugging session is active.

        Inferior 1 [process 17258] will be killed.

Quit anyway? (y or n) y

/mnt/c/ALD4/ud7$ gdb ./ud7
GNU gdb (Debian 8.2.1-2+b3) 8.2.1
Copyright (C) 2018 Free Software Foundation, Inc.
License GPLv3+: GNU GPL version 3 or later <http://gnu.org/licenses/gpl.html>
This is free software: you are free to change and redistribute it.
There is NO WARRANTY, to the extent permitted by law.
Type "show copying" and "show warranty" for details.
This GDB was configured as "x86_64-linux-gnu".
Type "show configuration" for configuration details.
For bug reporting instructions, please see:
<http://www.gnu.org/software/gdb/bugs/>.
Find the GDB manual and other documentation resources online at:
    <http://www.gnu.org/software/gdb/documentation/>.

For help, type "help".
Type "apropos word" to search for commands related to "word"...
Reading symbols from ./ud7...done.

(gdb) break thread_proc_a
Breakpoint 1 at 0x1253: file ud7.c, line 36.

(gdb) break thread_proc_b
Breakpoint 2 at 0x1288: file ud7.c, line 46.
```

6.   We also enable non-stop mode, run the execution, and then break in (**^C**):

```
(gdb) set non-stop on
```

```
(gdb) r
Starting program: /mnt/c/ALD4/ud7/ud7
[Thread debugging using libthread_db enabled]
Using host libthread_db library "/lib/x86_64-linux-gnu/libthread_db.so.1".
[New Thread 0x7ffff7ddd700 (LWP 18818)]

Thread 2 "ud7" hit Breakpoint 1, thread_proc_a (_=0x0) at ud7.c:36
36              usleep(100000); // some work
(gdb) [New Thread 0x7ffff75dc700 (LWP 18819)]

Thread 3 "ud7" hit Breakpoint 2, thread_proc_b (_=0x0) at ud7.c:46
46              simulate_delay(); // some work
^C
Quit

(gdb) info threads
  Id   Target Id                          Frame
* 1    Thread 0x7ffff7dde740 (LWP 18808) "ud7" (running)
  2    Thread 0x7ffff7ddd700 (LWP 18818) "ud7" thread_proc_a (_=0x0) at ud7.c:36
  3    Thread 0x7ffff75dc700 (LWP 18819) "ud7" thread_proc_b (_=0x0) at ud7.c:46
```

7.   We then continue thread #3:

```
(gdb) thread 3
[Switching to thread 3 (Thread 0x7ffff75dc700 (LWP 18819))]
#0  thread_proc_b (_=0x0) at ud7.c:46
46              simulate_delay(); // some work

(gdb) c
Continuing.
[New Thread 0x7ffff6ddb700 (LWP 19696)]

Thread 4 "ud7" received signal SIGSEGV, Segmentation fault.
0x0000000000000000 in ?? ()

(gdb) info threads
  Id   Target Id                          Frame
  1    Thread 0x7ffff7dde740 (LWP 18808) "ud7" (running)
  2    Thread 0x7ffff7ddd700 (LWP 18818) "ud7" thread_proc_a (_=0x0) at ud7.c:36
* 3    Thread 0x7ffff75dc700 (LWP 18819) "ud7" (running)
  4    Thread 0x7ffff6ddb700 (LWP 19696) "ud7" 0x0000000000000000 in ?? ()
(gdb) [Thread 0x7ffff75dc700 (LWP 18819) exited]

The current thread <Thread ID 3> has terminated.  See `help thread'.
```

Note: The backtrace shows that another newly created thread was called with the NULL thread function:

```
(gdb) thread 4
[Switching to thread 4 (Thread 0x7ffff6ddb700 (LWP 19696))]
#0  0x0000000000000000 in ?? ()

(gdb) bt
#0  0x0000000000000000 in ?? ()
#1  0x00007ffff7fa8fa3 in start_thread (arg=<optimized out>) at pthread_create.c:486
#2  0x00007ffff7eda06f in clone () at ../sysdeps/unix/sysv/linux/x86_64/clone.S:95
```

Note: Source code inspection shows a race condition with initialization of *my_shared_data.p_proc,* which under debugger was masked by the extra delay in *simulate_delay*:

```c
void *thread_proc_a (void *_)
{
        usleep(100000);      // some work
        my_shared_data.p_proc = thread_proc_c;
        sleep(10);
        return 0;
}

void *thread_proc_b (void *_)
{
        pthread_t thread;

        simulate_delay(); // some work

        if (pthread_create(&thread, NULL, my_shared_data.p_proc, NULL))
        {
                return (void *)1;
        }
                pthread_detach(thread);

        sleep(10);
        return 0;
}
```

8.   We now exit the GDB.

Exercise UD7 (LLDB)

Goal: Learn how to manipulate threads to debug race conditions.

Elementary Diagnostics Patterns: Crash.

Memory Analysis Patterns: Exception Stack Trace; NULL Pointer (Code).

Debugging Implementation Patterns: Frozen Thread.

1.   The source code and the *Makefile* to build executables and libraries can be found in the *ud7* directory:

```
$ git clone https://bitbucket.org/softwarediagnostics/ald4
```

2.   Problem history:

The application *ud7* crashes shortly after it starts. We want to find out the root cause.

3.   We run *ud7* under LLDB:

```
/mnt/c/ALD4/ud7$ lldb ./ud7
(lldb) target create "./ud7"
Current executable set to './ud7' (x86_64).

(lldb) r
Process 25213 launched: '/mnt/c/ALD4/ud7/ud7' (x86_64)
```

Note: We see that it doesn't crash. So, it looks like the LLDB debugger influenced program behavior.

4.   Let's look at the source code of the *start_modeling* function:

```
void start_modeling (void)
{
        pthread_t thread;
        if (pthread_create(&thread, NULL, thread_proc_a, NULL))
        {
          exit(1);
        }
        pthread_detach(thread);

        if (pthread_create(&thread, NULL, thread_proc_b, NULL))
        {
          exit(1);
        }
        pthread_detach(thread);
}
```

5.   We want to put breakpoints when we run the *ud7* again, so we quit LLDB. Then, we run the *ud7* under the LLDB again.

```
^C
Process 25213 stopped
* thread #1, name = 'ud7', stop reason = signal SIGSTOP
```

```
        frame #0: 0x00007ffff7ea75c0 libc.so.6`__GI___nanosleep(requested_time=0x00007fffffffe050,
remaining=0x00007fffffffe050) at nanosleep.c:28

(lldb) q
Quitting LLDB will kill one or more processes. Do you really want to proceed: [Y/n] y

/mnt/c/ALD4/ud7$ lldb ./ud7
(lldb) target create "./ud7"
Current executable set to './ud7' (x86_64).

(lldb) break set -name thread_proc_a
Breakpoint 1: where = ud7`thread_proc_a + 12 at ud7.c:36, address = 0x0000000000001253

(lldb) break set -name thread_proc_b
Breakpoint 2: where = ud7`thread_proc_b + 12 at ud7.c:46, address = 0x0000000000001288
```

6.   We run the execution until the first breakpoint is hit:

```
(lldb) r
Process 25625 stopped
* thread #2, name = 'ud7', stop reason = breakpoint 1.1
    frame #0: 0x0000555555555253 ud7`thread_proc_a(_=0x0000000000000000) at ud7.c:36
   33
   34   void *thread_proc_a (void *_)
   35   {
-> 36           usleep(100000); // some work
   37           my_shared_data.p_proc = thread_proc_c;
   38           sleep(10);
   39           return 0;

(lldb) thread list
Process 25625 stopped
  thread #1: tid = 25625, 0x00007ffff7eda061 libc.so.6`__GI___clone at clone.S:78, name = 'ud7'
* thread #2: tid = 25721, 0x0000555555555253 ud7`thread_proc_a(_=0x0000000000000000) at
ud7.c:36, name = 'ud7', stop reason = breakpoint 1.1
```

7.   We then continue thread #1 to allow the second breakpoint hit:

```
(lldb) thread select 1
* thread #1, name = 'ud7'
    frame #0: 0x00007ffff7eda061 libc.so.6`__GI___clone at clone.S:78

(lldb) thread continue 1
Resuming thread: 1 in process 25625
Process 25625 resuming
Process 25625 stopped
* thread #2, name = 'ud7', stop reason = breakpoint 1.1
    frame #0: 0x0000555555555253 ud7`thread_proc_a(_=0x0000000000000000) at ud7.c:36
   33
   34   void *thread_proc_a (void *_)
   35   {
-> 36           usleep(100000); // some work
   37           my_shared_data.p_proc = thread_proc_c;
   38           sleep(10);
   39           return 0;
  thread #3, name = 'ud7', stop reason = breakpoint 2.1
    frame #0: 0x0000555555555288 ud7`thread_proc_b(_=0x0000000000000000) at ud7.c:46
   43   {
```

```
   44            pthread_t thread;
   45
-> 46            simulate_delay(); // some work
   47
   48        if (pthread_create(&thread, NULL, my_shared_data.p_proc, NULL))
   49            {
```

```
(lldb) thread list
Process 25625 stopped
  thread #1: tid = 25625, 0x00007ffff7ea7490 libc.so.6`__sleep(seconds=1) at sleep.c:34, name =
'ud7'
* thread #2: tid = 25721, 0x0000555555555253 ud7`thread_proc_a(_=0x0000000000000000) at
ud7.c:36, name = 'ud7', stop reason = breakpoint 1.1
  thread #3: tid = 26367, 0x0000555555555288 ud7`thread_proc_b(_=0x0000000000000000) at
ud7.c:46, name = 'ud7', stop reason = breakpoint 2.1
```

8.   We then continue thread #3:

```
(lldb) thread select 3
* thread #3, name = 'ud7', stop reason = breakpoint 2.1
    frame #0: 0x0000555555555288 ud7`thread_proc_b(_=0x0000000000000000) at ud7.c:46
   43    {
   44            pthread_t thread;
   45
-> 46            simulate_delay(); // some work
   47
   48        if (pthread_create(&thread, NULL, my_shared_data.p_proc, NULL))
   49            {
```

```
(lldb) thread continue 3
Resuming thread: 3 in process 25625
Process 25625 resuming
Process 25625 stopped
* thread #2, name = 'ud7', stop reason = breakpoint 1.1
    frame #0: 0x0000555555555253 ud7`thread_proc_a(_=0x0000000000000000) at ud7.c:36
   33
   34    void *thread_proc_a (void *_)
   35    {
-> 36            usleep(100000); // some work
   37            my_shared_data.p_proc = thread_proc_c;
   38            sleep(10);
   39            return 0;
  thread #4, name = 'ud7', stop reason = signal SIGSEGV: invalid address (fault address: 0x0)
    frame #0: 0x0000000000000000
error: memory read failed for 0x0
```

```
(lldb) thread list
Process 25625 stopped
  thread #1: tid = 25625, 0x00007ffff7ea7490 libc.so.6`__sleep(seconds=1) at sleep.c:34, name =
'ud7'
* thread #2: tid = 25721, 0x0000555555555253 ud7`thread_proc_a(_=0x0000000000000000) at
ud7.c:36, name = 'ud7', stop reason = breakpoint 1.1
  thread #3: tid = 26367, 0x00007ffff7ea75c0
libc.so.6`__GI___nanosleep(requested_time=0x00007ffff75dbe90, remaining=0x00007ffff75dbe90) at
nanosleep.c:28, name = 'ud7'
  thread #4: tid = 26523, 0x0000000000000000, name = 'ud7', stop reason = signal SIGSEGV:
invalid address (fault address: 0x0)
    frame #2: 0x00007ffff7eda06f libc.so.6`__GI___clone at clone.S:95
```

Note: The backtrace shows that another newly created thread was called with the NULL thread function:

```
(lldb) thread select 4
* thread #4, name = 'ud7', stop reason = signal SIGSEGV: invalid address (fault address: 0x0)
    frame #0: 0x0000000000000000
error: memory read failed for 0x0
```

```
(lldb) bt
* thread #4, name = 'ud7', stop reason = signal SIGSEGV: invalid address (fault address: 0x0)
  * frame #0: 0x0000000000000000
    frame #1: 0x00007ffff7fa8fa3 libpthread.so.0`start_thread(arg=<unavailable>) at
pthread_create.c:486
```

Note: Source code inspection shows a race condition with initialization of *my_shared_data.p_proc,* which under debugger was masked by the extra delay in *simulate_delay*:

```
void *thread_proc_a (void *_)
{
        usleep(100000);      // some work
        my_shared_data.p_proc = thread_proc_c;
        sleep(10);
        return 0;
}

void *thread_proc_b (void *_)
{
        pthread_t thread;

        simulate_delay(); // some work

        if (pthread_create(&thread, NULL, my_shared_data.p_proc, NULL))
        {
                return (void *)1;
        }
                pthread_detach(thread);

        sleep(10);
        return 0;
}
```

9.   We now exit the LLDB.

Kernel Mode Debugging

Exercises KD8, KD10

I use Ubuntu 22.04 LTS under Hyper-V.

Goal: Set up Hyper-V kernel debugging environment.

1. You should have already set up Hyper-V with Windows 11. For these book edition exercises, we use Hyper-V Ubuntu 22.04 LTS:

2.   *Edit settings...* to expand the default 12GB hard drive to 40GB or more.

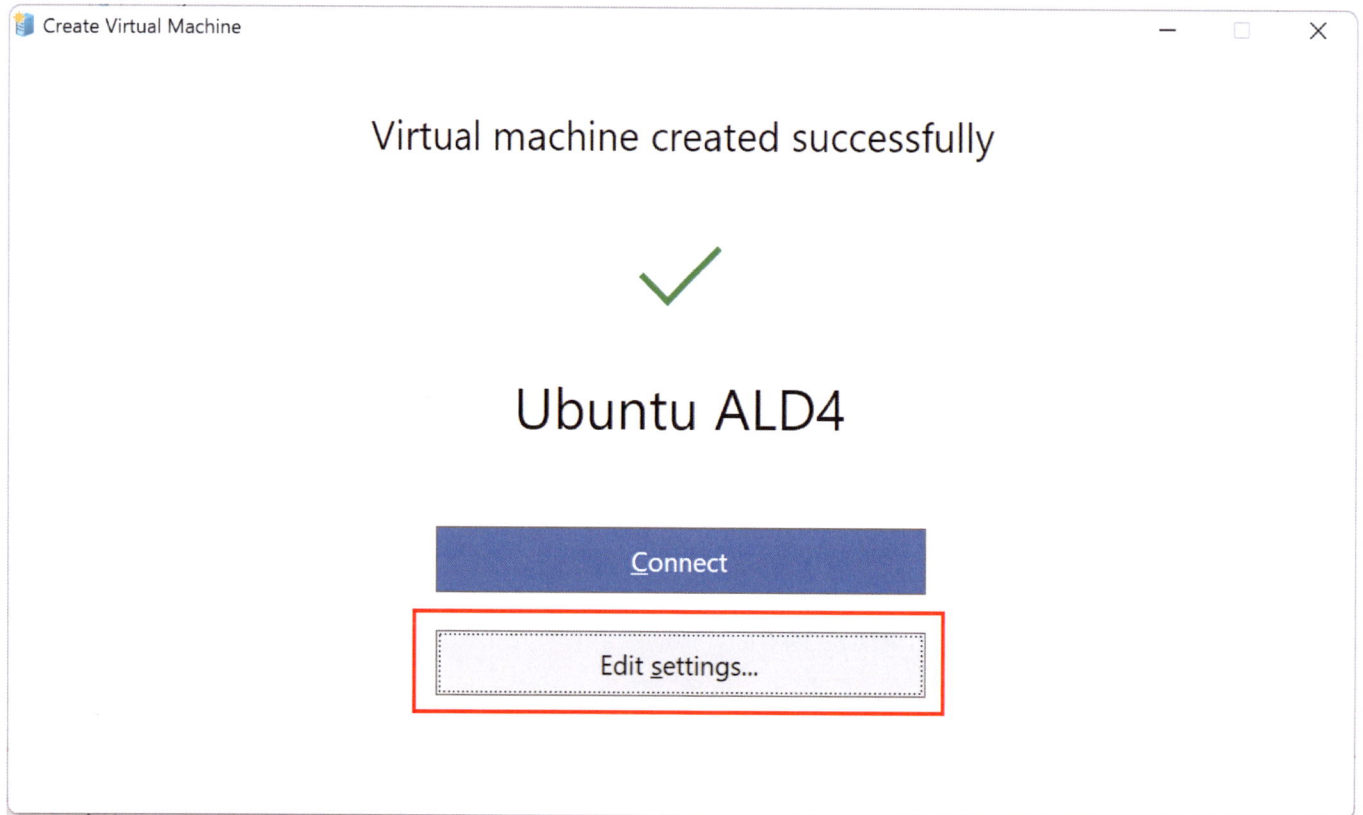

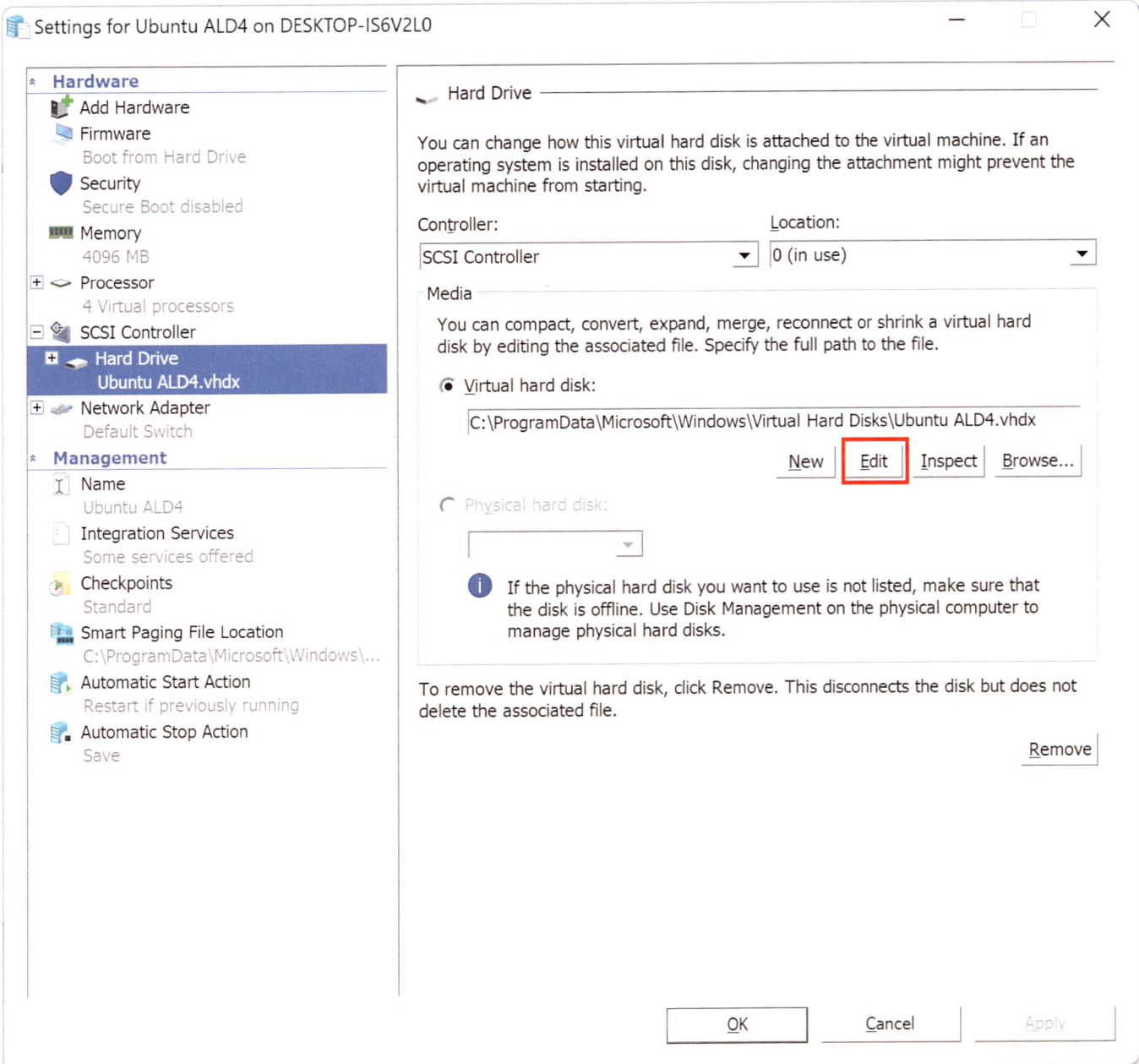

Settings for Ubuntu ALD4 on DESKTOP-IS6V2L0 — ☐ ✕

Hardware
- 🖥️ **Add Hardware**
- 💽 **Firmware**
  - Boot from Hard Drive
- 🛡️ **Security**
  - Secure Boot disabled
- ▥ **Memory**
  - 4096 MB
- ⊞ ⌁ **Processor**
  - 4 Virtual processors
- ⊟ 🖧 **SCSI Controller**
  - ⊞ 🖴 **Hard Drive**
    - **Ubuntu ALD4.vhdx**
  - ⊞ 🖧 **Network Adapter**
    - Default Switch

Management
- ⌶ **Name**
  - Ubuntu ALD4
- **Integration Services**
  - Some services offered
- 📁 **Checkpoints**
  - Standard
- 🖳 **Smart Paging File Location**
  - C:\ProgramData\Microsoft\Windows\...
- 🖥️ **Automatic Start Action**
  - Restart if previously running
- 🖥️ **Automatic Stop Action**
  - Save

Hard Drive

You can change how this virtual hard disk is attached to the virtual machine. If an operating system is installed on this disk, changing the attachment might prevent the virtual machine from starting.

Controller: Location:

| SCSI Controller ▼ | 0 (in use) ▼ |

Media

You can compact, convert, expand, merge, reconnect or shrink a virtual hard disk by editing the associated file. Specify the full path to the file.

◉ Virtual hard disk:

C:\ProgramData\Microsoft\Windows\Virtual Hard Disks\Ubuntu ALD4.vhdx

| New | **Edit** | Inspect | Browse... |

○ Physical hard disk:

[▼]

ⓘ If the physical hard disk you want to use is not listed, make sure that the disk is offline. Use Disk Management on the physical computer to manage physical hard disks.

To remove the virtual hard disk, click Remove. This disconnects the disk but does not delete the associated file.

Remove

| OK | Cancel | Apply |

Edit Virtual Hard Disk Wizard ✕

Locate Virtual Hard Disk

Before You Begin
Locate Disk
Choose Action
Summary

Where is the virtual hard disk file located?

Location: `C:\ProgramData\Microsoft\Windows\Virtual Hard Disks\Ubuntu ALD4.vhdx` Browse...

⚠ Editing the following types of virtual hard disks might result in data loss:

Virtual hard disks in a differencing disk chain that have child virtual hard disks associated with them.

Virtual hard disks (.avhd/.avhdx) associated with virtual machine checkpoints.

Virtual hard disks associated with a virtual machine that has replication enabled and is currently involved in initial replication, resynchronization, test failover, or failover.

< Previous   Next >   Finish   Cancel

Edit Virtual Hard Disk Wizard ✕

✎ Choose Action

Before You Begin
Locate Disk
Choose Action
   Configure Disk
Summary

What do you want to do to the virtual hard disk?

○ Compact

This option compacts the file size of a virtual hard disk. The storage capacity of the virtual hard disk remains the same.

○ Convert

This option converts a virtual hard disk by copying the contents to a new virtual hard disk. The new virtual hard disk can use a different type and format than the original virtual hard disk.

● Expand

This option expands the capacity of the virtual hard disk.

< Previous   Next >   Finish   Cancel

Edit Virtual Hard Disk Wizard ✕

Expand Virtual Hard Disk

Before You Begin

Locate Disk

Choose Action

Configure Disk

Summary

What size do you want to make the virtual hard disk?

Current size is 12 GB.

New size: 40 GB (Maximum: 64 TB)

< Previous   Next >   Finish   Cancel

Edit Virtual Hard Disk Wizard

✕

🖊 **Completing the Edit Virtual Hard Disk Wizard**

Before You Begin

Locate Disk

Choose Action

   Configure Disk

Summary

You have successfully completed the Edit Virtual Hard Disk Wizard. You are about to make the following changes.

Description:

Virtual Hard Disk:	Ubuntu ALD4.vhdx (VHDX, dynamically expanding)
Action:	Expand
Configuration:	New virtual disk size: 40 GB

To complete the action and close the wizard, click Finish.

< Previous   Next >   **Finish**   Cancel

Settings for Ubuntu ALD4 on DESKTOP-IS6V2L0

Hardware
- **Add Hardware**
- **Firmware**
  - Boot from Hard Drive
- **Security**
  - Secure Boot disabled
- **Memory**
  - 4096 MB
- **Processor**
  - 4 Virtual processors
- **SCSI Controller**
  - **Hard Drive**
    - Ubuntu ALD4.vhdx
- **Network Adapter**
  - Default Switch

Management
- **Name**
  - Ubuntu ALD4
- **Integration Services**
  - Some services offered
- **Checkpoints**
  - Standard
- **Smart Paging File Location**
  - C:\ProgramData\Microsoft\Windows\...
- **Automatic Start Action**
  - Restart if previously running
- **Automatic Stop Action**
  - Save

Hard Drive

You can change how this virtual hard disk is attached to the virtual machine. If an operating system is installed on this disk, changing the attachment might prevent the virtual machine from starting.

Controller: Location:
[SCSI Controller ▼]   [0 (in use) ▼]

Media

You can compact, convert, expand, merge, reconnect or shrink a virtual hard disk by editing the associated file. Specify the full path to the file.

◉ Virtual hard disk:

[C:\ProgramData\Microsoft\Windows\Virtual Hard Disks\Ubuntu ALD4.vhdx]

[New] [Edit] [Inspect] [Browse...]

○ Physical hard disk:

[▼]

ⓘ If the physical hard disk you want to use is not listed, make sure that the disk is offline. Use Disk Management on the physical computer to manage physical hard disks.

To remove the virtual hard disk, click Remove. This disconnects the disk but does not delete the associated file.

[Remove]

[OK] [Cancel] [Apply]

246

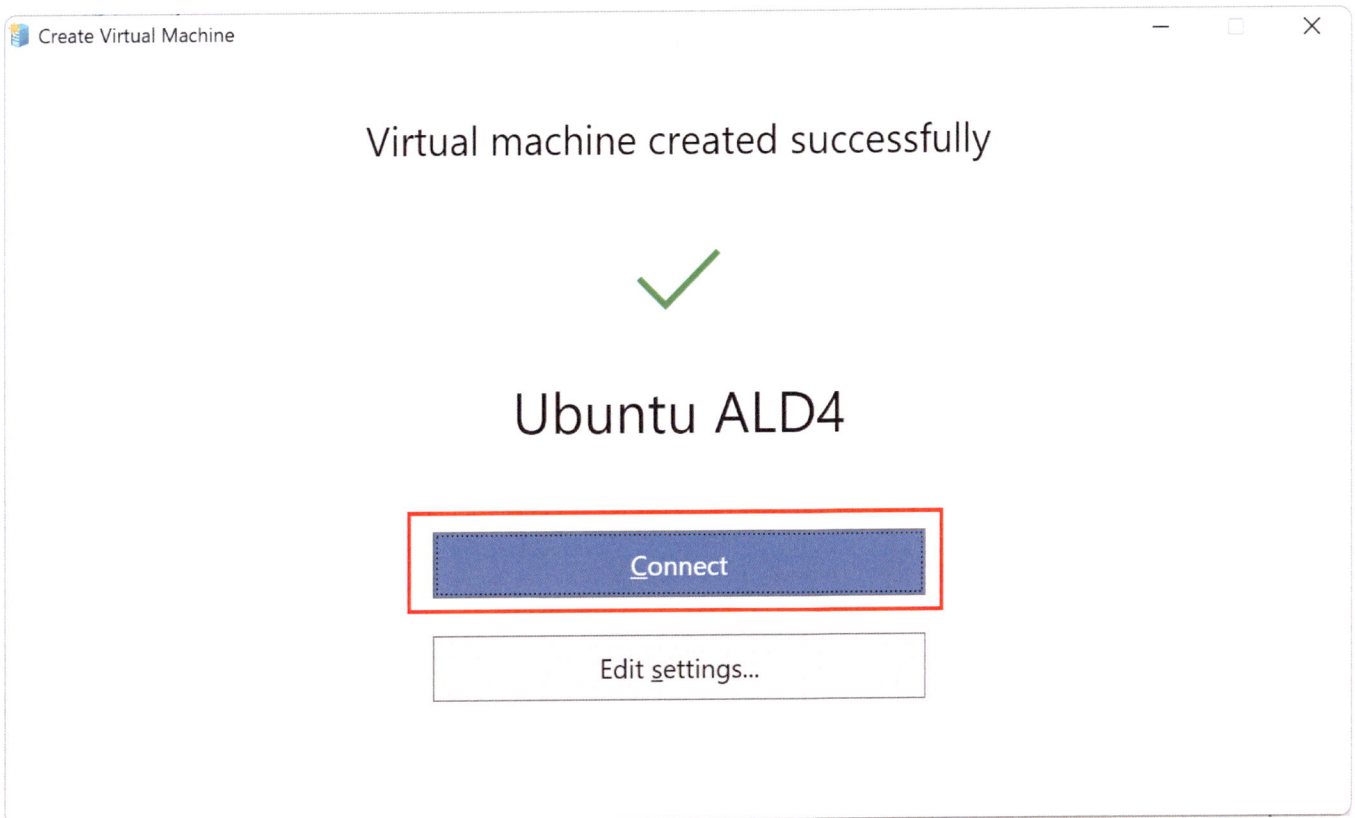

3. Connect to the virtual machine and finish setup. Select *Require my password to log in*.

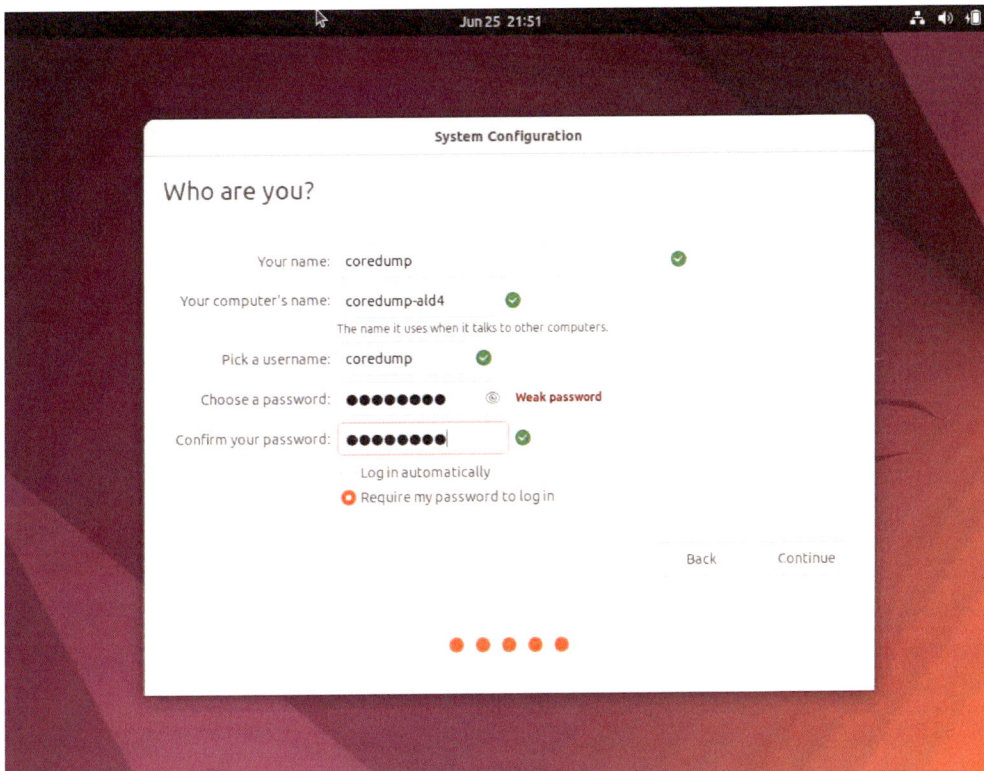

4. Resize the partition after installation is complete:

```
$ sudo apt install cloud-guest-utils
```

```
$ df -h
Filesystem      Size  Used Avail Use% Mounted on
tmpfs           393M  1.6M  391M   1% /run
/dev/sda1        12G  6.0G  5.5G  53% /
tmpfs           2.0G     0  2.0G   0% /dev/shm
tmpfs           5.0M  4.0K  5.0M   1% /run/lock
/dev/sda15      105M  5.3M  100M   5% /boot/efi
tmpfs           393M   76K  393M   1% /run/user/127
tmpfs           393M  156K  393M   1% /run/user/1000
```

```
$ sudo growpart /dev/sda 1
CHANGED: partition=1 start=227328 old: size=24938463 end=25165791 new: size=83658719
end=83886047
```

```
$ sudo resize2fs /dev/sda1
resize2fs 1.46.5 (30-Dec-2021)
Filesystem at /dev/sda1 is mounted on /; on-line resizing required
old_desc_blocks = 2, new_desc_blocks = 5
The filesystem on /dev/sda1 is now 10457339 (4k) blocks long.
```

```
$ df -h
Filesystem      Size  Used Avail Use% Mounted on
tmpfs           393M  1.6M  391M   1% /run
/dev/sda1        40G  6.1G   34G  15% /
tmpfs           2.0G     0  2.0G   0% /dev/shm
tmpfs           5.0M  4.0K  5.0M   1% /run/lock
/dev/sda15      105M  5.3M  100M   5% /boot/efi
tmpfs           393M   76K  393M   1% /run/user/127
tmpfs           393M  160K  393M   1% /run/user/1000
```

5. On the host, open the PowerShell and enable the first serial port for Ubuntu ALD4 VM:

```
PS > Set-VMComPort "Ubuntu ALD4" 1 \\.\pipe\kdbpipe
```

```
PS > Get-VMComPort "Ubuntu ALD4"

VMName      Name  Path
------      ----  ----
Ubuntu ALD4 COM 1 \\.\pipe\kdbpipe
Ubuntu ALD4 COM 2
```

6. Shutdown Ubuntu ALD4 VM, start it, and connect to it again.

7. On the Host, create a shared folder with an Administrator-type user and password. We share C:\ALD4 with the *coredump* user. Install CIFS on Ubuntu:

```
$ sudo apt install cifs-utils
```

8. On the Host computer, run Command Prompt and note the IP4 address of the *Default Switch* (it may be different and change with every new Hyper-V start after the Host restart):

```
> ipconfig
Windows IP Configuration
[...]
Ethernet adapter vEthernet (Default Switch):
   Connection-specific DNS Suffix  . :
   Link-local IPv6 Address . . . . . : [...]
   IPv4 Address. . . . . . . . . . . : 172.23.112.1
   Subnet Mask . . . . . . . . . . . : 255.255.240.0
   Default Gateway . . . . . . . . . :
[...]
```

9. Mount the previously created share to the */mnt/c/ALD4* folder:

```
$ sudo mkdir -p /mnt/c/ALD4

$ sudo mount -t cifs //172.23.112.1/ALD4 /mnt/c/ALD4 -o
noperm,mfsymlinks,username=coredump,password=<...>
```

10. Check that the kernel debugger is enabled:

```
$ grep CONFIG_KGDB /boot/config-$(uname -r)
CONFIG_KGDB=y
CONFIG_KGDB_HONOUR_BLOCKLIST=y
CONFIG_KGDB_SERIAL_CONSOLE=y
# CONFIG_KGDB_TESTS is not set
CONFIG_KGDB_LOW_LEVEL_TRAP=y
CONFIG_KGDB_KDB=y
```

11. Then, set appropriate permissions and enable the kernel debugger over the first serial port:

```
$ sudo chmod 666 /proc/sysrq-trigger

$ sudo chmod 666 /sys/module/kgdboc/parameters/kgdboc

$ echo "ttyS0" >/sys/module/kgdboc/parameters/kgdboc
```

12. On the host, install PuTTY. Run PuTTY, open a serial session, and wait for the connection:

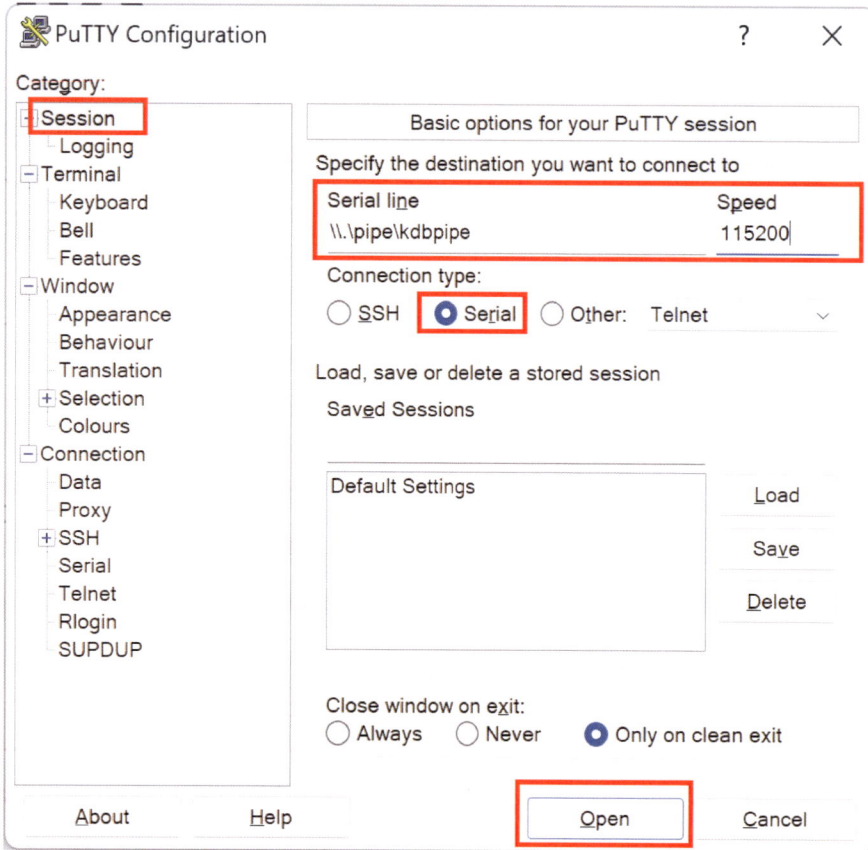

13.   On Ubuntu VM, trigger the kernel debugger:

```
$ sudo echo g >/proc/sysrq-trigger
```

Note: The current terminal freezes now (but you can continue with other tasks).

14.   On the host, PuTTY now shows a kernel debugger interface:

15.   We can now enter kernel debugger commands, for example, print the backtrace for the current PID:

```
[0]kdb> bt
Stack traceback for pid 2114
0xffff89782d821980      2114      2113  1    0    R    0xffff89782d822e80 *echo
CPU: 0 PID: 2114 Comm: echo Not tainted 6.5.0-1022-azure #23~22.04.1-Ubuntu
Hardware name: Microsoft Corporation Virtual Machine/Virtual Machine, BIOS Hyper-V UEFI Release
v4.1 04/06/2022
Call Trace:
 <TASK>
 dump_stack_lvl+0x37/0x50
 dump_stack+0x10/0x20
 kdb_dump_stack_on_cpu+0xb1/0x130
 kdb_show_stack+0x82/0x90
 kdb_bt1+0xc1/0x140
 kdb_bt+0x34b/0x3b0
 kdb_parse+0x2ed/0x560
 kdb_local.constprop.0+0x2ed/0x840
 kdb_main_loop+0xf1/0x220
 ? queued_spin_unlock+0x50/0x70
 kdb_stub+0x1b7/0x400
 kgdb_cpu_enter+0x3a0/0xb60
 ? printk_get_next_message+0x83/0x300
 kgdb_handle_exception+0xc2/0x120
```

```
 __kgdb_notify+0x34/0xd0
 kgdb_ll_trap+0x46/0x60
 do_int3+0x30/0x90
 exc_int3+0x93/0xd0
 asm_exc_int3+0x3a/0x40
RIP: 0010:kgdb_breakpoint+0x14/0x30
Code: 00 00 0f 1f 40 00 90 90 90 90 90 90 90 90 90 90 90 90 90 90 90 90 0f 1f 44 00 00 55 48 89
e5 f0 ff 05 48 3c 4a 03 0f ae f8 cc <0f> ae f8 f0 ff 0d 3a 3c 4a 03 5d c3 cc cc cc cc 66 66 2e
0f 1f 84
RSP: 0018:ffff98c4878ffd60 EFLAGS: 00000202
RAX: 0000000000000001 RBX: ffffffff88a2aec0 RCX: 0000000000000000
RDX: 0000000000000000 RSI: ffff897903c1f680 RDI: 0000000000000067
RBP: ffff98c4878ffd60 R08: 0000000000000003 R09: 0000000000000000
R10: 0000000000000000 R11: 44203a7172737973 R12: 0000000000000000
R13: 0000000000000067 R14: 0000000000000000 R15: 0000000000000004
 ? kgdb_breakpoint+0x14/0x30
 sysrq_handle_dbg+0x26/0x80
 __handle_sysrq+0xde/0x270
 ? apparmor_file_permission+0x7e/0x180
 write_sysrq_trigger+0x28/0x40
 proc_reg_write+0x5e/0xa0
 ? __cond_resched+0x1a/0x50
 vfs_write+0xef/0x3c0
 ? __count_memcg_events+0x60/0xe0
 ? __cond_resched+0x1a/0x50
 ksys_write+0x67/0xf0
 __x64_sys_write+0x19/0x20
 x64_sys_call+0x1613/0x1ff0
 do_syscall_64+0x56/0x80
 ? irqentry_exit_to_user_mode+0x19/0x30
 ? irqentry_exit+0x1d/0x30
 ? exc_page_fault+0x80/0x160
 entry_SYSCALL_64_after_hwframe+0x73/0xdd
RIP: 0033:0x72854ab14887
Code: 10 00 f7 d8 64 89 02 48 c7 c0 ff ff ff ff eb b7 0f 1f 00 f3 0f 1e fa 64 8b 04 25 18 00 00
00 85 c0 75 10 b8 01 00 00 00 0f 05 <48> 3d 00 f0 ff ff 77 51 c3 48 83 ec 28 48 89 54 24 18 48
89 74 24
RSP: 002b:00007fffe664c108 EFLAGS: 00000246 ORIG_RAX: 0000000000000001
RAX: ffffffffffffffda RBX: 0000000000000002 RCX: 000072854ab14887
RDX: 0000000000000002 RSI: 000060cf96fea440 RDI: 0000000000000001
RBP: 000060cf96fea440 R08: 0000000000000000 R09: 000060cf96fea440
R10: 0000000000000077 R11: 0000000000000246 R12: 0000000000000002
R13: 000072854ac1b780 R14: 000072854ac17600 R15: 000072854ac16a00
 </TASK>
[0]kdb>
```

16.   To resume Ubuntu execution, use the **go** command:

```
[0]kdb> go
Stack traceback for pid 2114
0xffff89782d821980     2114     2113  1    0    R    0xffff89782d822e80 *echo
CPU: 0
```

Note: The current terminal now unfreezes.

17.   We can now quit PuTTY and continue using Ubuntu.

Exercise KD8

- **Goal:** Learn how to navigate kernel space using KDB

- **Elementary Diagnostics Patterns:** -

- **Memory Analysis Patterns:** Stack Trace; Stack Trace Collection (Unmanaged Space); Stack Trace Collection (CPUs); Module Collection; Execution Residue (Unmanaged Space, Kernel)

- **Debugging Implementation Patterns:** Code Breakpoint

- \ALD4\Exercise-Linux-KD8.pdf

Exercise KD8

Goal: Learn how to navigate kernel space using KDB.

Memory Analysis Patterns: Stack Trace; Stack Trace Collection (Unmanaged Space); Stack Trace Collection (CPUs); Module Collection; Execution Residue (Unmanaged Space, Kernel).

Debugging Implementation Patterns: Code Breakpoint.

1.   The source code and the *Makefile* to build executables and libraries can be found in the *kd8* directory:

```
$ git clone https://bitbucket.org/softwarediagnostics/ald4
```

2.   Exercise KD0 is a prerequisite. If you rebooted the VM after it, you need to set appropriate permissions and enable the kernel debugger over the first serial port again (you may want to create a shell script for that if you do these reboots often):

```
$ sudo chmod 666 /proc/sysrq-trigger
```

```
$ sudo chmod 666 /sys/module/kgdboc/parameters/kgdboc
```

```
$ echo "ttyS0" >/sys/module/kgdboc/parameters/kgdboc
```

3.   Run PuTTY, open a serial session, and wait for the connection. On Ubuntu VM, trigger the kernel debugger:

```
$ sudo echo g >/proc/sysrq-trigger
```

Note: The current terminal now freezes, but you can continue with other tasks, if any.

4.   On the host, PuTTY now shows a kernel debugger interface:

```
Entering kdb (current=0xffff9d0496001980, pid 2299) on processor 2 due to NonMaskable Interrupt
@ 0xffffffffb8621394
[2]kdb>
```

5.   The **help** command shows all available commands:

```
[2]kdb> help
Command         Usage               Description
------------------------------------------------------------
md              <vaddr>             Display Memory Contents, also mdWcN, e.g. md8c1
mdr             <vaddr> <bytes>     Display Raw Memory
mdp             <paddr> <bytes>     Display Physical Memory
mds             <vaddr>             Display Memory Symbolically
mm              <vaddr> <contents>  Modify Memory Contents
go              [<vaddr>]           Continue Execution
rd                                  Display Registers
rm              <reg> <contents>    Modify Registers
ef              <vaddr>             Display exception frame
bt              [<vaddr>]           Stack traceback
btp             <pid>               Display stack for process <pid>
bta             [<state_chars>|A]   Backtrace all processes whose state matches
```

```
btc                                        Backtrace current process on each cpu
btt                <vaddr>                 Backtrace process given its struct task address
env                                        Show environment variables
set                                        Set environment variables
help                                       Display Help Message
?                                          Display Help Message
cpu                <cpunum>                Switch to new cpu
kgdb                                       Enter kgdb mode
ps                 [<state_chars>|A]       Display active task list
pid                <pidnum>                Switch to another task
reboot                                     Reboot the machine immediately
lsmod                                      List loaded kernel modules
sr                 <key>                   Magic SysRq key
dmesg              [lines]                 Display syslog buffer
defcmd             name "usage" "help"     Define a set of commands, down to endefcmd
kill               <-signal> <pid>         Send a signal to a process
summary                                    Summarize the system
per_cpu            <sym> [<bytes>] [<cpu>]
                                           Display per_cpu variables
grephelp                                   Display help on | grep
bp                 [<vaddr>]               Set/Display breakpoints
bl                 [<vaddr>]               Display breakpoints
bc                 <bpnum>                 Clear Breakpoint
be                 <bpnum>                 Enable Breakpoint
bd                 <bpnum>                 Disable Breakpoint
ss                                         Single Step
bph                [<vaddr>]               [datar [length]|dataw [length]]   Set hw brk
dumpcommon                                 Common kdb debugging
dumpall                                    First line debugging
dumpcpu                                    Same as dumpall but only tasks on cpus
ftdump             [skip_#entries] [cpu]
                                           Dump ftrace log; -skip dumps last #entries
```

6.   The current thread (task) backtrace on the current CPU, including user space registers at the moment of the transition to the kernel space, can be listed using the **bt** command:

```
[2]kdb> bt
Stack traceback for pid 2299
0xffff9d0496001980      2299    2298  1    2   R   0xffff9d0496002e80 *echo
CPU: 2 PID: 2299 Comm: echo Tainted: G           L     6.5.0-1023-azure #24~22.04.1-Ubuntu
Hardware name: Microsoft Corporation Virtual Machine/Virtual Machine, BIOS Hyper-V UEFI Release
v4.1 04/06/2022
Call Trace:
 <TASK>
 dump_stack_lvl+0x37/0x50
 dump_stack+0x10/0x20
 kdb_dump_stack_on_cpu+0xb1/0x130
 kdb_show_stack+0x82/0x90
 kdb_bt1+0xc1/0x140
 kdb_bt+0x34b/0x3b0
 kdb_parse+0x2ed/0x560
 kdb_local.constprop.0+0x2ed/0x840
 kdb_main_loop+0xf1/0x220
 ? queued_spin_unlock+0x50/0x70
 kdb_stub+0x1b7/0x400
 kgdb_cpu_enter+0x3a0/0xb60
 ? printk_get_next_message+0x83/0x300
```

```
  kgdb_handle_exception+0xc2/0x120
  __kgdb_notify+0x34/0xd0
  ? _prb_read_valid+0x62/0xc0
  kgdb_ll_trap+0x46/0x60
  do_int3+0x30/0x90
  exc_int3+0x93/0xd0
  asm_exc_int3+0x3a/0x40
RIP: 0010:kgdb_breakpoint+0x14/0x30
Code: 00 00 0f 1f 40 00 90 90 90 90 90 90 90 90 90 90 90 90 90 90 90 90 0f 1f 44 00 00 55 48 89
e5 f0 ff 05 48 3c 4a 03 0f ae f8 cc <0f> ae f8 f0 ff 0d 3a 3c 4a 03 5d c3 cc cc cc cc 66 66 2e
0f 1f 84
RSP: 0018:ffffc15346a43d28 EFLAGS: 00000202
RAX: 0000000000000001 RBX: fffffffffb962aec0 RCX: 0000000000000000
RDX: 0000000000000000 RSI: ffff9d0483d1f680 RDI: 0000000000000067
RBP: ffffc15346a43d28 R08: 0000000000000003 R09: 0000000000000000
R10: 0000000000000000 R11: 44203a7172737973 R12: 0000000000000000
R13: 0000000000000067 R14: 0000000000000000 R15: 0000000000000004
  ? kgdb_breakpoint+0x14/0x30
  sysrq_handle_dbg+0x26/0x80
  __handle_sysrq+0xde/0x270
  ? apparmor_file_permission+0x7e/0x180
  write_sysrq_trigger+0x28/0x40
  proc_reg_write+0x5e/0xa0
  ? __cond_resched+0x1a/0x50
  vfs_write+0xef/0x3c0
  ? __handle_mm_fault+0x306/0x6b0
  ? __cond_resched+0x1a/0x50
  ksys_write+0x67/0xf0
  __x64_sys_write+0x19/0x20
  x64_sys_call+0x1613/0x1ff0
  do_syscall_64+0x56/0x80
  ? exit_to_user_mode_prepare+0x49/0x100
  ? irqentry_exit_to_user_mode+0x19/0x30
  ? irqentry_exit+0x1d/0x30
  ? exc_page_fault+0x80/0x160
  entry_SYSCALL_64_after_hwframe+0x73/0xdd
RIP: 0033:0x763df0b14a37
Code: 10 00 f7 d8 64 89 02 48 c7 c0 ff ff ff ff eb b7 0f 1f 00 f3 0f 1e fa 64 8b 04 25 18 00 00
00 85 c0 75 10 b8 01 00 00 00 0f 05 <48> 3d 00 f0 ff ff 77 51 c3 48 83 ec 28 48 89 54 24 18 48
89 74 24
RSP: 002b:00007ffde8131218 EFLAGS: 00000246 ORIG_RAX: 0000000000000001
RAX: ffffffffffffffda RBX: 0000000000000002 RCX: 0000763df0b14a37
RDX: 0000000000000002 RSI: 00005caff8c7b440 RDI: 0000000000000001
RBP: 00005caff8c7b440 R08: 0000000000000000 R09: 00005caff8c7b440
R10: 0000000000000077 R11: 0000000000000246 R12: 0000000000000002
R13: 0000763df0c1a780 R14: 0000763df0c16600 R15: 0000763df0c15a00
  </TASK>
```

Note: Since the system was interrupted, the current thread shows the *sysrq* processing for the *echo* process and subsequent *kdb* processing.

7.   To list all existent tasks (processes) there is the **ps** command. It first shows current tasks on each CPU and then the list of tasks sorted by PID:

```
[2]kdb> ps
83 sleeping system daemon (state [ims]) processes suppressed,
use 'ps A' to see all.
```

```
Task Addr              Pid    Parent [*] cpu State Thread              Command
0xffffffffba40fbc0       0        0   1    0    R   0xffffffffba4110c0  swapper/0
   Error: no saved data for this cpu
0xffff9d038710e600     555        2   1    1    R   0xffff9d038710fb00  kworker/1:3
   Error: no saved data for this cpu
0xffff9d0496001980    2299     2298   1    2    R   0xffff9d0496002e80  *echo
0xffff9d04802f9980       0        0   1    3    R   0xffff9d04802fae80  swapper/3
   Error: no saved data for this cpu

0xffff9d048028cc80       1        0   0    0    D   0xffff9d048028e180  systemd
0xffff9d0480323300      21        2   0    2    R   0xffff9d0480324800  migration/2
0xffff9d0480353300      27        2   0    1    R   0xffff9d0480354800  migration/1
0xffff9d0480396600      28        2   0    1    R   0xffff9d0480397b00  ksoftirqd/1
0xffff9d0480b86600      47        2   0    0    D   0xffff9d0480b87b00  khugepaged
0xffff9d0480ba1980      51        2   0    2    R   0xffff9d0480ba2e80  kworker/2:1
0xffff9d0382116600     233        1   0    3    D   0xffff9d0382117b00  systemd-journal
0xffff9d0475b04c80     249        2   0    1    R   0xffff9d0475b06180  kworker/1:2
0xffff9d0475b0e600     290        1   0    0    S   0xffff9d0475b0fb00  systemd-udevd
0xffff9d03815a4c80     339        1   0    0    S   0xffff9d03815a6180  hv_kvp_daemon
0xffff9d03814de600     447        1   0    0    S   0xffff9d03814dfb00  systemd-oomd
0xffff9d03814db300     448        1   0    0    S   0xffff9d03814dc800  systemd-resolve
0xffff9d03814d9980     449        1   0    0    S   0xffff9d03814dae80  systemd-timesyn
0xffff9d03814dcc80     451        1   0    1    S   0xffff9d03814de180  sd-resolve
0xffff9d0381134c80     487        1   0    3    S   0xffff9d0381136180  acpid
0xffff9d0381133300     490        1   0    0    S   0xffff9d0381134800  avahi-daemon
0xffff9d0475b0b300     491        1   0    3    S   0xffff9d0475b0c800  dbus-daemon
0xffff9d0475b09980     494        1   0    0    S   0xffff9d0475b0ae80  NetworkManager
0xffff9d0475b2e600     557        1   0    0    S   0xffff9d0475b2fb00  gmain
0xffff9d0386410000     559        1   0    0    S   0xffff9d0386411500  gdbus
0xffff9d0386f3e600     500        1   0    0    S   0xffff9d0386f3fb00  hv_vss_daemon
0xffff9d0386413300     503        1   0    0    S   0xffff9d0386414800  irqbalance
0xffff9d0381129980     528        1   0    1    S   0xffff9d038112ae80  gmain
0xffff9d0386416600     507        1   0    1    S   0xffff9d0386417b00  networkd-dispat
0xffff9d0386411980     509        1   0    3    S   0xffff9d0386412e80  polkitd
0xffff9d038112e600     530        1   0    2    S   0xffff9d038112fb00  gmain
0xffff9d0475b2b300     554        1   0    3    S   0xffff9d0475b2c800  gdbus
0xffff9d0387108000     510        1   0    3    S   0xffff9d0387109500  power-profiles-
0xffff9d0381663300     541        1   0    3    S   0xffff9d0381664800  gmain
0xffff9d0381664c80     553        1   0    3    S   0xffff9d0381666180  gdbus
0xffff9d0387109980     511        1   0    0    S   0xffff9d038710ae80  rsyslogd
0xffff9d0382110000     548        1   0    2    S   0xffff9d0382111500  in:imuxsock
0xffff9d0382114c80     549        1   0    3    S   0xffff9d0382116180  in:imklog
0xffff9d0386f3cc80     550        1   0    3    S   0xffff9d0386f3e180  rs:main Q:Reg
0xffff9d0381666600     520        1   0    1    S   0xffff9d0381667b00  snapd
0xffff9d039e424c80     669        1   0    0    S   0xffff9d039e426180  snapd
0xffff9d039e420000     674        1   0    3    S   0xffff9d039e421500  snapd
0xffff9d039e423300     675        1   0    0    S   0xffff9d039e424800  snapd
0xffff9d0385d8b300     676        1   0    0    S   0xffff9d0385d8c800  snapd
0xffff9d0386af6600     677        1   0    0    S   0xffff9d0386af7b00  snapd
0xffff9d0385d8cc80     682        1   0    0    S   0xffff9d0385d8e180  snapd
0xffff9d0385ca4c80     684        1   0    0    S   0xffff9d0385ca6180  snapd
0xffff9d038212cc80     686        1   0    1    S   0xffff9d038212e180  snapd
0xffff9d038212b300     707        1   0    0    S   0xffff9d038212c800  snapd
0xffff9d03cc60e600    1479        1   0    3    S   0xffff9d03cc60fb00  snapd
0xffff9d038710b300     522        1   0    3    S   0xffff9d038710c800  accounts-daemon
0xffff9d0475b28000     571        1   0    3    S   0xffff9d0475b29500  gmain
0xffff9d0387066600     573        1   0    3    S   0xffff9d0387067b00  gdbus
0xffff9d0475b00000     529        1   0    2    S   0xffff9d0475b01500  cron
0xffff9d038112cc80     531        1   0    3    S   0xffff9d038112e180  switcheroo-cont
```

```
0xffff9d0386414c80    575      1   0    1   S   0xffff9d0386416180   gmain
0xffff9d038212e600    577      1   0    2   S   0xffff9d038212fb00   gdbus
0xffff9d038710cc80    533      1   0    3   S   0xffff9d038710e180   systemd-logind
0xffff9d0475b06600    540      1   0    0   S   0xffff9d0475b07b00   udisksd
0xffff9d0381e23300    562      1   0    2   S   0xffff9d0381e24800   gmain
0xffff9d0387061980    574      1   0    2   S   0xffff9d0387062e80   gdbus
0xffff9d039e529980    620      1   0    3   S   0xffff9d039e52ae80   probing-thread
0xffff9d0475b18000    637      1   0    0   S   0xffff9d0475b19500   cleanup
0xffff9d0475b2cc80    542      1   0    0   S   0xffff9d0475b2e180   wpa_supplicant
0xffff9d0381660000    547    490   0    2   S   0xffff9d0381661500   avahi-daemon
0xffff9d038710e600    555      2   1    1   R   0xffff9d038710fb00   kworker/1:3
    Error: no saved data for this cpu
0xffff9d0385ca1980    580      1   0    2   S   0xffff9d0385ca2e80   cupsd
0xffff9d0385ca0000    583      1   0    1   S   0xffff9d0385ca1500   ModemManager
0xffff9d0382111980    610      1   0    0   S   0xffff9d0382112e80   gmain
0xffff9d039e528000    625      1   0    1   S   0xffff9d039e529500   gdbus
0xffff9d0381131980    596      1   0    0   S   0xffff9d0381132e80   xrdp-sesman
0xffff9d039e410000    597      1   0    2   S   0xffff9d039e411500   unattended-upgr
0xffff9d03815a3300    649      1   0    0   S   0xffff9d03815a4800   gmain
0xffff9d039e421980    628      1   0    0   D   0xffff9d039e422e80   gdm3
0xffff9d039e426600    633      1   0    0   S   0xffff9d039e427b00   gmain
0xffff9d0385d88000    634      1   0    0   S   0xffff9d0385d89500   gdbus
0xffff9d03815a0000    631      1   0    3   S   0xffff9d03815a1500   xrdp
0xffff9d0386bb8000    653      1   0    0   S   0xffff9d0386bb9500   cups-browsed
0xffff9d0385ca3300    680      1   0    0   S   0xffff9d0385ca4800   gmain
0xffff9d0381e26600    681      1   0    3   S   0xffff9d0381e27b00   gdbus
0xffff9d0475b01980    672      1   0    2   S   0xffff9d0475b02e80   kerneloops
0xffff9d0475b08000    678      1   0    3   S   0xffff9d0475b09500   kerneloops
0xffff9d0382688000    749    631   0    0   S   0xffff9d0382689500   xrdp
0xffff9d039df88000    750    628   0    3   S   0xffff9d039df89500   gdm-session-wor
0xffff9d038268e600    751    628   0    3   S   0xffff9d038268fb00   gmain
0xffff9d0382689980    753    628   0    3   S   0xffff9d038268ae80   gdbus
0xffff9d038268b300    755      1   0    3   S   0xffff9d038268c800   systemd
0xffff9d0475b1e600    756    755   0    1   S   0xffff9d0475b1fb00   (sd-pam)
0xffff9d0386f3b300    762    755   0    3   S   0xffff9d0386f3c800   pipewire
0xffff9d039e52e600    799    755   0    0   S   0xffff9d039e52fb00   pipewire
0xffff9d038268cc80    763    755   0    0   S   0xffff9d038268e180   pipewire-media-
0xffff9d0386af1980    779    755   0    2   S   0xffff9d0386af2e80   pipewire-media-
0xffff9d0475b0cc80    764    755   0    0   S   0xffff9d0475b0e180   pulseaudio
0xffff9d0385d89980    821    755   0    1   S   0xffff9d0385d8ae80   null-sink
0xffff9d039d6e0000    841    755   0    1   S   0xffff9d039d6e1500   snapd-glib
0xffff9d039df89980    767    750   0    3   S   0xffff9d039df8ae80   gdm-wayland-ses
0xffff9d039d418000    768    750   0    3   S   0xffff9d039d419500   gmain
0xffff9d039d419980    785    750   0    3   S   0xffff9d039d41ae80   gdbus
0xffff9d039d41e600    769    755   0    0   S   0xffff9d039d41fb00   dbus-daemon
0xffff9d039e413300    770      1   0    0   S   0xffff9d039e414800   rtkit-daemon
0xffff9d039e414c80    771      1   0    3   S   0xffff9d039e416180   rtkit-daemon
0xffff9d039e411980    772      1   0    1   R   0xffff9d039e412e80   rtkit-daemon
0xffff9d039dd43300    780    596   0    1   S   0xffff9d039dd44800   xrdp-sesman
0xffff9d0386f38000    784      1   0    3   S   0xffff9d0386f39500   systemd
0xffff9d039d6c4c80    787    767   0    2   S   0xffff9d039d6c6180   dbus-run-sessio
0xffff9d039d6c0000    788    755   0    3   S   0xffff9d039d6c1500   gvfsd
0xffff9d039d6c1980    796    755   0    2   S   0xffff9d039d6c2e80   gmain
0xffff9d039d6cb300    797    755   0    3   S   0xffff9d039d6cc800   gdbus
0xffff9d0386af4c80    789    787   0    0   S   0xffff9d0386af6180   dbus-daemon
0xffff9d0382129980    790    784   0    1   S   0xffff9d038212ae80   (sd-pam)
0xffff9d0385d8e600    791    787   0    0   S   0xffff9d0385d8fb00   gnome-session-b
0xffff9d039e52b300    810    787   0    3   S   0xffff9d039e52c800   gmain
0xffff9d0381130000    811    787   0    0   S   0xffff9d0381131500   gdbus
```

258

```
0xffff9d039dd40000     812     787   0   1   S   0xffff9d039dd41500   dconf worker
0xffff9d0381661980     801     755   0   3   S   0xffff9d0381662e80   gvfsd-fuse
0xffff9d039df8cc80     805     755   0   2   S   0xffff9d039df8e180   gvfsd-fuse
0xffff9d039d6ce600     806     755   0   0   S   0xffff9d039d6cfb00   gvfsd-fuse
0xffff9d039d6c9980     807     755   0   0   S   0xffff9d039d6cae80   gmain
0xffff9d039d6c6600     808     755   0   2   S   0xffff9d039d6c7b00   gdbus
0xffff9d0475b29980     809     755   0   2   S   0xffff9d0475b2ae80   gvfs-fuse-sub
0xffff9d039dd41980     814     784   0   0   S   0xffff9d039dd42e80   pipewire
0xffff9d039d6e3300     837     784   0   2   S   0xffff9d039d6e4800   pipewire
0xffff9d039dd46600     815     784   0   1   S   0xffff9d039dd47b00   pipewire-media-
0xffff9d039df9e600     834     784   0   0   S   0xffff9d039df9fb00   pipewire-media-
0xffff9d039df96600     816     784   0   0   S   0xffff9d039df97b00   pulseaudio
0xffff9d03a42cb300     878     784   0   2   S   0xffff9d03a42cc800   null-sink
0xffff9d03a4293300     886     784   0   2   S   0xffff9d03a4294800   snapd-glib
0xffff9d039df93300     817     780   0   1   S   0xffff9d039df94800   gnome-session-b
0xffff9d03ba046600    1118     780   0   3   S   0xffff9d03ba047b00   gmain
0xffff9d03b07a1980    1119     780   0   1   S   0xffff9d03b07a2e80   gdbus
0xffff9d03b07a4c80    1120     780   0   3   S   0xffff9d03b07a6180   dconf worker
0xffff9d039df94c80     818     780   0   0   S   0xffff9d039df96180   Xorg
0xffff9d03a7120000     936     780   0   2   S   0xffff9d03a7121500   InputThread
0xffff9d039df9b300     832     784   0   3   S   0xffff9d039df9c800   dbus-daemon
0xffff9d0382ee8000     842     784   0   0   S   0xffff9d0382ee9500   gvfsd
0xffff9d039df98000     848     784   0   3   S   0xffff9d039df99500   gmain
0xffff9d039de00000     850     784   0   3   S   0xffff9d039de01500   gdbus
0xffff9d039df9cc80     843     791   0   3   S   0xffff9d039df9e180   gnome-shell
0xffff9d039de03300     881     791   0   2   S   0xffff9d039de04800   gmain
0xffff9d03a4138000     915     791   0   3   S   0xffff9d03a4139500   gdbus
0xffff9d03a4139980     918     791   0   2   S   0xffff9d03a413ae80   dconf worker
0xffff9d03a4141980     940     791   0   0   S   0xffff9d03a4142e80   llvmpipe-0
0xffff9d03a4148000     941     791   0   3   S   0xffff9d03a4149500   llvmpipe-1
0xffff9d03a414e600     942     791   0   0   S   0xffff9d03a414fb00   llvmpipe-2
0xffff9d03a4149980     943     791   0   0   S   0xffff9d03a414ae80   llvmpipe-3
0xffff9d03a414b300     944     791   0   2   S   0xffff9d03a414c800   gnome-shell
0xffff9d03a414cc80     945     791   0   3   S   0xffff9d03a414e180   gnome-shell
0xffff9d03a4150000     946     791   0   1   S   0xffff9d03a4151500   gnome-shell
0xffff9d03a4156600     947     791   0   3   S   0xffff9d03a4157b00   gnome-shell
0xffff9d03a4154c80     950     791   0   0   S   0xffff9d03a4156180   gnome-s:disk$0
0xffff9d03a7121980     961     791   0   2   S   0xffff9d03a7122e80   gnome-shell
0xffff9d03b0791980     995     791   0   0   S   0xffff9d03b0792e80   JS Helper
0xffff9d03b0793300     996     791   0   0   S   0xffff9d03b0794800   JS Helper
0xffff9d03b0794c80     997     791   0   0   S   0xffff9d03b0796180   JS Helper
0xffff9d03b0790000     998     791   0   0   S   0xffff9d03b0791500   JS Helper
0xffff9d039de04c80     849     780   0   0   S   0xffff9d039de06180   xrdp-chansrv
0xffff9d039de01980     867     780   0   0   S   0xffff9d039de02e80   xrdp-chansrv
0xffff9d039d6e6600     853     784   0   1   S   0xffff9d039d6e7b00   gvfsd-fuse
0xffff9d03a42c8000     860     784   0   1   S   0xffff9d03a42c9500   gvfsd-fuse
0xffff9d03a4131980     861     784   0   2   S   0xffff9d03a4132e80   gvfsd-fuse
0xffff9d03a4133300     862     784   0   3   S   0xffff9d03a4134800   gmain
0xffff9d03a4134c80     863     784   0   3   S   0xffff9d03a4136180   gdbus
0xffff9d03a42c9980     865     784   0   1   S   0xffff9d03a42cae80   gvfs-fuse-sub
0xffff9d03a7101980     882     755   0   0   S   0xffff9d03a7102e80   tracker-miner-f
0xffff9d03a42e3300     889     755   0   1   S   0xffff9d03a42e4800   gmain
0xffff9d03a42e4c80     890     755   0   0   S   0xffff9d03a42e6180   gdbus
0xffff9d03a42e0000     891     755   0   1   S   0xffff9d03a42e1500   dconf worker
0xffff9d03a42e8000     893     755   0   3   S   0xffff9d03a42e9500   pool-tracker-mi
0xffff9d03815a1980    1071     755   0   1   S   0xffff9d03815a2e80   Monitor thread
0xffff9d039d6e1980     885     784   0   3   S   0xffff9d039d6e2e80   tracker-miner-f
0xffff9d03a42ccc80     887     784   0   1   S   0xffff9d03a42ce180   gmain
0xffff9d03a42e1980     888     784   0   3   S   0xffff9d03a42e2e80   gdbus
```

```
0xffff9d03a42e6600    892    784    0    1    S    0xffff9d03a42e7b00    dconf worker
0xffff9d03a42ee600    895    784    0    0    S    0xffff9d03a42efb00    pool-tracker-mi
0xffff9d03a429cc80    1069   784    0    1    S    0xffff9d03a429e180    Monitor thread
0xffff9d03a413cc80    916    755    0    3    S    0xffff9d03a413e180    gvfs-udisks2-vo
0xffff9d03a7116600    919    755    0    1    S    0xffff9d03a7117b00    gmain
0xffff9d038112b300    921    755    0    3    S    0xffff9d038112c800    gdbus
0xffff9d03a42f3300    923    755    0    3    S    0xffff9d03a42f4800    dconf worker
0xffff9d03a7111980    917    784    0    0    S    0xffff9d03a7112e80    gvfs-udisks2-vo
0xffff9d03a413e600    920    784    0    1    S    0xffff9d03a413fb00    gmain
0xffff9d03815a6600    922    784    0    0    S    0xffff9d03815a7b00    gdbus
0xffff9d0382128000    925    784    0    1    S    0xffff9d0382129500    dconf worker
0xffff9d03a4143300    926    755    0    0    S    0xffff9d03a4144800    gvfs-afc-volume
0xffff9d03a4144c80    932    755    0    3    S    0xffff9d03a4146180    gvfs-afc-volume
0xffff9d03a4140000    933    755    0    2    S    0xffff9d03a4141500    gmain
0xffff9d03a42f4c80    935    755    0    0    S    0xffff9d03a42f6180    gdbus
0xffff9d03a7126600    937    755    0    0    S    0xffff9d03a7127b00    gvfs-gphoto2-vo
0xffff9d03a4151980    948    755    0    1    S    0xffff9d03a4152e80    gmain
0xffff9d03a7124c80    951    755    0    0    S    0xffff9d03a7126180    gdbus
0xffff9d03b04b4c80    952    755    0    1    S    0xffff9d03b04b6180    gvfs-goa-volume
0xffff9d03a7106600    954    755    0    3    S    0xffff9d03a7107b00    gmain
0xffff9d03a42ecc80    955    755    0    3    S    0xffff9d03a42ee180    gdbus
0xffff9d03b04b0000    957    755    0    0    S    0xffff9d03b04b1500    goa-daemon
0xffff9d03a7103300    999    755    0    2    S    0xffff9d03a7104800    gmain
0xffff9d03b0521980    1003   755    0    3    S    0xffff9d03b0522e80    gdbus
0xffff9d03b04d4c80    1005   755    0    0    S    0xffff9d03b04d6180    dconf worker
0xffff9d03a42f0000    959    784    0    3    S    0xffff9d03a42f1500    gvfs-afc-volume
0xffff9d03b04b6600    960    784    0    2    S    0xffff9d03b04b7b00    gvfs-afc-volume
0xffff9d03b04b1980    963    784    0    1    S    0xffff9d03b04b2e80    gmain
0xffff9d03a42f6600    965    784    0    3    S    0xffff9d03a42f7b00    gdbus
0xffff9d03b04bcc80    966    784    0    3    S    0xffff9d03b04be180    gvfs-gphoto2-vo
0xffff9d03b04b8000    967    784    0    3    S    0xffff9d03b04b9500    gmain
0xffff9d03a42f1980    969    784    0    3    S    0xffff9d03a42f2e80    gdbus
0xffff9d03b04b9980    970    784    0    3    S    0xffff9d03b04bae80    gvfs-goa-volume
0xffff9d03b04bb300    971    784    0    3    S    0xffff9d03b04bc800    gmain
0xffff9d03b04c3300    972    784    0    3    S    0xffff9d03b04c4800    gdbus
0xffff9d03a429e600    974    784    0    0    S    0xffff9d03a429fb00    goa-daemon
0xffff9d03b0520000    1000   784    0    1    S    0xffff9d03b0521500    gmain
0xffff9d03b04d3300    1004   784    0    0    S    0xffff9d03b04d4800    gdbus
0xffff9d03b0523300    1007   784    0    2    S    0xffff9d03b0524800    dconf worker
0xffff9d0382113300    976    1      0    1    S    0xffff9d0382114800    at-spi-bus-laun
0xffff9d03b04c0000    977    1      0    1    S    0xffff9d03b04c1500    gmain
0xffff9d03b04c6600    978    1      0    3    S    0xffff9d03b04c7b00    dconf worker
0xffff9d03b04d6600    980    1      0    1    S    0xffff9d03b04d7b00    gdbus
0xffff9d03b04d1980    981    976    0    2    S    0xffff9d03b04d2e80    dbus-daemon
0xffff9d03a7110000    1009   755    0    3    S    0xffff9d03a7111500    goa-identity-se
0xffff9d03a7100000    1041   755    0    0    S    0xffff9d03a7101500    gmain
0xffff9d03a42a8000    1043   755    0    2    S    0xffff9d03a42a9500    gdbus
0xffff9d03a42eb300    1012   784    0    0    S    0xffff9d03a42ec800    goa-identity-se
0xffff9d03b0536600    1032   784    0    1    S    0xffff9d03b0537b00    gmain
0xffff9d03b0540000    1034   784    0    3    S    0xffff9d03b0541500    gdbus
0xffff9d03a4298000    1027   755    0    1    S    0xffff9d03a4299500    gvfs-mtp-volume
0xffff9d03a42e9980    1035   755    0    3    S    0xffff9d03a42eae80    gmain
0xffff9d03b7488000    1039   755    0    3    S    0xffff9d03b7489500    gdbus
0xffff9d03b7489980    1031   784    0    3    S    0xffff9d03b748ae80    gvfs-mtp-volume
0xffff9d03a42ce600    1037   784    0    2    S    0xffff9d03a42cfb00    gmain
0xffff9d03b0546600    1040   784    0    3    S    0xffff9d03b0547b00    gdbus
0xffff9d03b0799980    1044   1      0    3    S    0xffff9d03b079ae80    upowerd
0xffff9d03b0541980    1065   1      0    0    S    0xffff9d03b0542e80    gmain
0xffff9d03a42a9980    1066   1      0    3    S    0xffff9d03a42aae80    gdbus
```

```
0xffff9d03b0544c80    1063     843    0    1    S    0xffff9d03b0546180    Xwayland
0xffff9d03814d8000    1070     817    0    3    S    0xffff9d03814d9500    ssh-agent
0xffff9d03b7498000    1088     784    0    2    S    0xffff9d03b7499500    at-spi-bus-laun
0xffff9d03b749cc80    1089     784    0    3    S    0xffff9d03b749e180    gmain
0xffff9d03b749e600    1090     784    0    0    S    0xffff9d03b749fb00    dconf worker
0xffff9d03b07a6600    1092     784    0    3    S    0xffff9d03b07a7b00    gdbus
0xffff9d039e416600    1094    1088    0    3    S    0xffff9d039e417b00    dbus-daemon
0xffff9d03b748e600    1123     784    0    1    S    0xffff9d03b748fb00    gnome-remote-de
0xffff9d03b0524c80    1139     784    0    2    S    0xffff9d03b0526180    gmain
0xffff9d03b0526600    1140     784    0    1    S    0xffff9d03b0527b00    dconf worker
0xffff9d03b748b300    1142     784    0    1    S    0xffff9d03b748c800    gdbus
0xffff9d03b04d0000    1124     784    0    1    S    0xffff9d03b04d1500    gnome-session-c
0xffff9d03ba043300    1131     784    0    2    S    0xffff9d03ba044800    gmain
0xffff9d03ba1f4c80    1138     784    0    3    D    0xffff9d03ba1f6180    gnome-session-b
0xffff9d03a4130000    1143     784    0    1    S    0xffff9d03a4131500    gmain
0xffff9d03a7113300    1144     784    0    3    S    0xffff9d03a7114800    gdbus
0xffff9d0387a5cc80    1148     784    0    2    S    0xffff9d0387a5e180    dconf worker
0xffff9d03b0531980    1153     784    0    0    S    0xffff9d03b0532e80    gnome-keyring-d
0xffff9d03a42be600    1155     784    0    2    S    0xffff9d03a42bfb00    gmain
0xffff9d03a42b9980    1156     784    0    0    S    0xffff9d03a42bae80    gdbus
0xffff9d03a42bb300    1157     784    0    2    S    0xffff9d03a42bc800    timer
0xffff9d03a42bcc80    1166     784    0    0    S    0xffff9d03a42be180    gnome-shell
0xffff9d03b748cc80    1172     784    0    3    S    0xffff9d03b748e180    gmain
0xffff9d03b07ae600    1174     784    0    3    S    0xffff9d03b07afb00    gdbus
0xffff9d03b07a9980    1175     784    0    0    S    0xffff9d03b07aae80    dconf worker
0xffff9d0387a58000    1179     784    0    0    S    0xffff9d0387a59500    llvmpipe-0
0xffff9d0387a5b300    1180     784    0    0    S    0xffff9d0387a5c800    llvmpipe-1
0xffff9d0387a5e600    1181     784    0    0    S    0xffff9d0387a5fb00    llvmpipe-2
0xffff9d0387a59980    1182     784    0    0    S    0xffff9d0387a5ae80    llvmpipe-3
0xffff9d03b07b9980    1183     784    0    0    S    0xffff9d03b07bae80    gnome-shell
0xffff9d03b07bb300    1184     784    0    0    S    0xffff9d03b07bc800    gnome-shell
0xffff9d03b07bcc80    1185     784    0    0    S    0xffff9d03b07be180    gnome-shell
0xffff9d03b07b8000    1186     784    0    0    S    0xffff9d03b07b9500    gnome-shell
0xffff9d03b07be600    1187     784    0    2    S    0xffff9d03b07bfb00    gnome-s:disk$0
0xffff9d03ba044c80    1189     784    0    0    S    0xffff9d03ba046180    JS Helper
0xffff9d03ba041980    1190     784    0    0    S    0xffff9d03ba042e80    JS Helper
0xffff9d03ba061980    1191     784    0    0    S    0xffff9d03ba062e80    JS Helper
0xffff9d03ba063300    1192     784    0    0    S    0xffff9d03ba064800    JS Helper
0xffff9d03a7029980    1986     784    0    0    S    0xffff9d03a702ae80    pool-gnome-shel
0xffff9d03b07b6600    1987     784    0    0    S    0xffff9d03b07b7b00    pool-gnome-shel
0xffff9d03c9deb300    1988     784    0    0    S    0xffff9d03c9dec800    pool-gnome-shel
0xffff9d03c9dd6600    1989     784    0    0    S    0xffff9d03c9dd7b00    pool-gnome-shel
0xffff9d03b07b4c80    1194       1    0    1    S    0xffff9d03b07b6180    xdg-permission-
0xffff9d03b07b0000    1195       1    0    2    S    0xffff9d03b07b1500    gmain
0xffff9d03ba1f6600    1197       1    0    1    S    0xffff9d03ba1f7b00    gdbus
0xffff9d03ba1f1980    1201       1    0    0    S    0xffff9d03ba1f2e80    packagekitd
0xffff9d03b079b300    1209       1    0    3    S    0xffff9d03b079c800    gmain
0xffff9d03b079e600    1211       1    0    0    S    0xffff9d03b079fb00    gdbus
0xffff9d03c4866600    1207       1    0    2    S    0xffff9d03c4867b00    at-spi2-registr
0xffff9d03ba066600    1213       1    0    1    S    0xffff9d03ba067b00    gmain
0xffff9d0386f39980    1218       1    0    2    S    0xffff9d0386f3ae80    gdbus
0xffff9d03b7499980    1208       1    0    3    S    0xffff9d03b749ae80    gjs
0xffff9d03c4860000    1228       1    0    0    S    0xffff9d03c4861500    JS Helper
0xffff9d03c486b300    1229       1    0    2    S    0xffff9d03c486c800    JS Helper
0xffff9d03c486cc80    1230       1    0    2    S    0xffff9d03c486e180    JS Helper
0xffff9d03c4868000    1231       1    0    0    S    0xffff9d03c4869500    JS Helper
0xffff9d03c488e600    1304       1    0    2    S    0xffff9d03c488fb00    gmain
0xffff9d03c4893300    1311       1    0    2    S    0xffff9d03c4894800    gdbus
0xffff9d03c4966600    1219     791    0    3    S    0xffff9d03c4967b00    gsd-sharing
```

```
0xffff9d03ba076600    1226    791    0    2    S    0xffff9d03ba077b00    gmain
0xffff9d03ba071980    1227    791    0    0    S    0xffff9d03ba072e80    dconf worker
0xffff9d03c4873300    1235    791    0    3    S    0xffff9d03c4874800    gdbus
0xffff9d03c4863300    1221    791    0    3    S    0xffff9d03c4864800    gsd-wacom
0xffff9d03c4876600    1246    791    0    1    S    0xffff9d03c4877b00    gmain
0xffff9d03c9dbb300    1251    791    0    0    S    0xffff9d03c9dbc800    dconf worker
0xffff9d03c487b300    1252    791    0    2    S    0xffff9d03c487c800    gdbus
0xffff9d03c4864c80    1224    791    0    3    S    0xffff9d03c4866180    gsd-color
0xffff9d03c9dc4c80    1259    791    0    0    S    0xffff9d03c9dc6180    gmain
0xffff9d03c9dc3300    1264    791    0    3    S    0xffff9d03c9dc4800    gdbus
0xffff9d03c9dcb300    1265    791    0    2    S    0xffff9d03c9dcc800    dconf worker
0xffff9d03c4869980    1234    791    0    1    S    0xffff9d03c486ae80    gsd-keyboard
0xffff9d03c9dc8000    1268    791    0    0    S    0xffff9d03c9dc9500    gmain
0xffff9d03c9dc9980    1270    791    0    1    S    0xffff9d03c9dcae80    dconf worker
0xffff9d03c9dd1980    1271    791    0    1    S    0xffff9d03c9dd2e80    gdbus
0xffff9d03b079cc80    1237    791    0    2    S    0xffff9d03b079e180    gsd-print-notif
0xffff9d03c4879980    1249    791    0    0    S    0xffff9d03c487ae80    gmain
0xffff9d03c487cc80    1254    791    0    2    S    0xffff9d03c487e180    gdbus
0xffff9d03c4971980    1239    791    0    3    S    0xffff9d03c4972e80    gsd-rfkill
0xffff9d03c4870000    1245    791    0    0    S    0xffff9d03c4871500    gmain
0xffff9d03c487e600    1248    791    0    3    S    0xffff9d03c487fb00    gdbus
0xffff9d03c9db9980    1242    791    0    2    S    0xffff9d03c9dbae80    gsd-smartcard
0xffff9d03c4976600    1253    791    0    3    S    0xffff9d03c4977b00    gmain
0xffff9d03c4878000    1255    791    0    2    S    0xffff9d03c4879500    gdbus
0xffff9d03b07ab300    1287    791    0    0    S    0xffff9d03b07ac800    dconf worker
0xffff9d03c4974c80    1244    791    0    1    S    0xffff9d03c4976180    gsd-datetime
0xffff9d03c9dbcc80    1257    791    0    1    S    0xffff9d03c9dbe180    gmain
0xffff9d03c9db8000    1258    791    0    1    S    0xffff9d03c9db9500    gdbus
0xffff9d03c9de3300    1282    791    0    1    S    0xffff9d03c9de4800    dconf worker
0xffff9d03c4970000    1250    791    0    3    S    0xffff9d03c4971500    gsd-media-keys
0xffff9d03cc54e600    1307    791    0    3    S    0xffff9d03cc54fb00    gmain
0xffff9d03cc54b300    1309    791    0    3    S    0xffff9d03cc54c800    dconf worker
0xffff9d03c4894c80    1312    791    0    3    S    0xffff9d03c4896180    gdbus
0xffff9d03c4963300    1256    791    0    1    S    0xffff9d03c4964800    gsd-screensaver
0xffff9d03c9dc6600    1262    791    0    1    S    0xffff9d03c9dc7b00    gmain
0xffff9d03c9dccc80    1266    791    0    1    S    0xffff9d03c9dce180    gdbus
0xffff9d03c4961980    1261    791    0    1    S    0xffff9d03c4962e80    gsd-sound
0xffff9d03c9dd3300    1272    791    0    0    S    0xffff9d03c9dd4800    gmain
0xffff9d03c9dd4c80    1274    791    0    1    S    0xffff9d03c9dd6180    gdbus
0xffff9d03c4888000    1284    791    0    3    S    0xffff9d03c4889500    dconf worker
0xffff9d03a4299980    1267    791    0    1    S    0xffff9d03a429ae80    gsd-a11y-settin
0xffff9d03c488cc80    1276    791    0    0    S    0xffff9d03c488e180    gmain
0xffff9d03cc548000    1296    791    0    1    S    0xffff9d03cc549500    gdbus
0xffff9d03ba060000    1300    791    0    1    S    0xffff9d03ba061500    dconf worker
0xffff9d03c4889980    1273    791    0    0    S    0xffff9d03c488ae80    gsd-housekeepin
0xffff9d03c9dd0000    1277    791    0    1    S    0xffff9d03c9dd1500    gmain
0xffff9d03c9de8000    1293    791    0    1    S    0xffff9d03c9de9500    gdbus
0xffff9d03ba064c80    1298    791    0    1    S    0xffff9d03ba066180    dconf worker
0xffff9d03c488b300    1275    791    0    0    S    0xffff9d03c488c800    gsd-power
0xffff9d03c9de9980    1313    791    0    1    S    0xffff9d03c9deae80    gmain
0xffff9d03c9decc80    1322    791    0    0    S    0xffff9d03c9dee180    gdbus
0xffff9d03b07a8000    1323    791    0    0    S    0xffff9d03b07a9500    dconf worker
0xffff9d03cc4e1980    1299    1    0    0    S    0xffff9d03cc4e2e80    gsd-printer
0xffff9d03ba1f3300    1324    1    0    0    S    0xffff9d03ba1f4800    gmain
0xffff9d03c9de0000    1325    1    0    3    S    0xffff9d03c9de1500    gdbus
0xffff9d03c4891980    1310    784    0    3    S    0xffff9d03c4892e80    xdg-permission-
0xffff9d03cc54cc80    1315    784    0    2    S    0xffff9d03cc54e180    gmain
0xffff9d03cc558000    1319    784    0    0    S    0xffff9d03cc559500    gdbus
0xffff9d03cc4e0000    1318    784    0    0    S    0xffff9d03cc4e1500    gnome-shell-cal
```

```
0xffff9d03b0796600    1328     784   0    1   S   0xffff9d03b0797b00   gmain
0xffff9d03cc4f6600    1332     784   0    0   S   0xffff9d03cc4f7b00   gdbus
0xffff9d03cc4f1980    1334     784   0    3   S   0xffff9d03cc4f2e80   dconf worker
0xffff9d03cc4f3300    1335     784   0    0   S   0xffff9d03cc4f4800   gnome-shell-cal
0xffff9d0482073300    1379     784   0    0   S   0xffff9d0482074800   pool-gnome-shel
0xffff9d03cc4f4c80    1336     784   0    2   S   0xffff9d03cc4f6180   evolution-sourc
0xffff9d03cc4f9980    1342     784   0    1   S   0xffff9d03cc4fae80   gmain
0xffff9d03cc4fb300    1343     784   0    2   S   0xffff9d03cc4fc800   dconf worker
0xffff9d039df90000    1344     784   0    2   S   0xffff9d039df91500   gdbus
0xffff9d0482074c80    1380     784   0    0   S   0xffff9d0482076180   evolution-calen
0xffff9d03cc55b300    1392     784   0    3   S   0xffff9d03cc55c800   gmain
0xffff9d03cc55e600    1393     784   0    3   S   0xffff9d03cc55fb00   gdbus
0xffff9d03cc4f0000    1395     784   0    0   S   0xffff9d03cc4f1500   dconf worker
0xffff9d03cc4f8000    1396     784   0    1   S   0xffff9d03cc4f9500   evolution-calen
0xffff9d03cc608000    1398     784   0    1   S   0xffff9d03cc609500   pool-evolution-
0xffff9d03cc609980    1402     784   0    2   S   0xffff9d03cc60ae80   pool-evolution-
0xffff9d0482071980    1411     784   0    3   S   0xffff9d0482072e80   pool-evolution-
0xffff9d048890b300    1412     784   0    1   S   0xffff9d048890c800   evolution-calen
0xffff9d0482070000    1403     784   0    3   S   0xffff9d0482071500   dconf-service
0xffff9d03cc60b300    1406     784   0    2   S   0xffff9d03cc60c800   gmain
0xffff9d03cc60cc80    1407     784   0    3   S   0xffff9d03cc60e180   gdbus
0xffff9d0482046600    1414     784   0    0   S   0xffff9d0482047b00   evolution-addre
0xffff9d04820db300    1422     784   0    3   S   0xffff9d04820dc800   gmain
0xffff9d04820dcc80    1423     784   0    3   S   0xffff9d04820de180   gdbus
0xffff9d04820de600    1427     784   0    1   S   0xffff9d04820dfb00   dconf worker
0xffff9d04820d9980    1428     784   0    2   S   0xffff9d04820dae80   evolution-addre
0xffff9d0487ee8000    1434     784   0    1   S   0xffff9d0487ee9500   pool-evolution-
0xffff9d0482043300    1430     755   0    3   S   0xffff9d0482044800   xdg-document-po
0xffff9d03c4861980    1433     755   0    0   S   0xffff9d03c4862e80   gmain
0xffff9d03c9de6600    1435     755   0    3   S   0xffff9d03c9de7b00   gdbus
0xffff9d04889a4c80    1446     755   0    0   S   0xffff9d04889a6180   fuse mainloop
0xffff9d0489624c80    1449     755   0    3   S   0xffff9d0489626180   fuse mainloop
0xffff9d0489620000    1450     755   0    3   S   0xffff9d0489621500   fuse mainloop
0xffff9d0482041980    1431     784   0    3   S   0xffff9d0482042e80   xdg-document-po
0xffff9d0386af0000    1436     784   0    2   S   0xffff9d0386af1500   gmain
0xffff9d03cc4fe600    1438     784   0    3   S   0xffff9d03cc4ffb00   gdbus
0xffff9d0482770000    1440     784   0    3   S   0xffff9d0482771500   fuse mainloop
0xffff9d0482771980    1451     784   0    2   S   0xffff9d0482772e80   fuse mainloop
0xffff9d0482773300    1452     784   0    2   S   0xffff9d0482774800   fuse mainloop
0xffff9d04889a6600    1437     755   0    0   S   0xffff9d04889a7b00   xdg-permission-
0xffff9d0487eee600    1442     755   0    2   S   0xffff9d0487eefb00   gmain
0xffff9d04889a1980    1444     755   0    0   S   0xffff9d04889a2e80   gdbus
0xffff9d0482776600    1441    1440   0    2   S   0xffff9d0482777b00   fusermount3
0xffff9d0487eecc80    1447    1446   0    0   S   0xffff9d0487eee180   fusermount3
0xffff9d0489621980    1461     842   0    2   S   0xffff9d0489622e80   gvfsd-trash
0xffff9d0489623300    1462     842   0    1   S   0xffff9d0489624800   gmain
0xffff9d03cc6fcc80    1463     842   0    2   S   0xffff9d03cc6fe180   gdbus
0xffff9d039df91980    1469       1   0    0   S   0xffff9d039df92e80   colord
0xffff9d039d6d9980    1473       1   0    0   S   0xffff9d039d6dae80   gmain
0xffff9d0489626600    1475       1   0    0   S   0xffff9d0489627b00   gdbus
0xffff9d03a4136600    1478     784   0    1   S   0xffff9d03a4137b00   gjs
0xffff9d0488a23300    1485     784   0    1   S   0xffff9d0488a24800   gmain
0xffff9d0488a24c80    1486     784   0    0   S   0xffff9d0488a26180   gdbus
0xffff9d0488a26600    1489     784   0    1   S   0xffff9d0488a27b00   JS Helper
0xffff9d0488a20000    1490     784   0    1   S   0xffff9d0488a21500   JS Helper
0xffff9d0488a21980    1491     784   0    1   S   0xffff9d0488a22e80   JS Helper
0xffff9d0491094c80    1492     784   0    1   S   0xffff9d0491096180   JS Helper
0xffff9d04889bcc80    1481     784   0    3   S   0xffff9d04889be180   at-spi2-registr
0xffff9d03a4294c80    1494     784   0    2   S   0xffff9d03a4296180   gmain
```

```
0xffff9d04910ab300    1495    784    0    0    S    0xffff9d04910ac800    gdbus
0xffff9d04910f8000    1507    784    0    2    S    0xffff9d04910f9500    sh
0xffff9d04889be600    1509    784    0    0    S    0xffff9d04889bfb00    gsd-a11y-settin
0xffff9d049102e600    1513    784    0    1    S    0xffff9d049102fb00    gmain
0xffff9d0491029980    1526    784    0    0    S    0xffff9d049102ae80    gdbus
0xffff9d04971a1980    1548    784    0    0    S    0xffff9d04971a2e80    dconf worker
0xffff9d04889b9980    1511    1507   0    0    S    0xffff9d04889bae80    ibus-daemon
0xffff9d04971e1980    1551    1507   0    3    S    0xffff9d04971e2e80    gmain
0xffff9d04971e0000    1576    1507   0    0    S    0xffff9d04971e1500    gdbus
0xffff9d04889bb300    1512    784    0    3    S    0xffff9d04889bc800    gsd-color
0xffff9d04972acc80    1554    784    0    2    S    0xffff9d04972ae180    gmain
0xffff9d04972a8000    1555    784    0    2    S    0xffff9d04972a9500    dconf worker
0xffff9d049bc5b300    1583    784    0    3    S    0xffff9d049bc5c800    gdbus
0xffff9d03c9dc0000    1515    784    0    0    S    0xffff9d03c9dc1500    gsd-datetime
0xffff9d0497029980    1541    784    0    2    S    0xffff9d049702ae80    gmain
0xffff9d04972a9980    1559    784    0    0    S    0xffff9d04972aae80    gdbus
0xffff9d0497250000    1603    784    0    1    S    0xffff9d0497251500    dconf worker
0xffff9d04889b8000    1517    784    0    3    S    0xffff9d04889b9500    gsd-housekeepin
0xffff9d04910f9980    1520    784    0    1    S    0xffff9d04910fae80    gmain
0xffff9d04912bcc80    1528    784    0    1    S    0xffff9d04912be180    gdbus
0xffff9d04910a9980    1553    784    0    1    S    0xffff9d04910aae80    dconf worker
0xffff9d04912acc80    1518    784    0    3    S    0xffff9d04912ae180    gsd-keyboard
0xffff9d04971a0000    1544    784    0    1    S    0xffff9d04971a1500    gmain
0xffff9d04971a6600    1545    784    0    1    S    0xffff9d04971a7b00    dconf worker
0xffff9d04912b3300    1562    784    0    3    S    0xffff9d04912b4800    gdbus
0xffff9d04912a8000    1519    784    0    3    S    0xffff9d04912a9500    gsd-media-keys
0xffff9d039d41b300    1563    784    0    1    S    0xffff9d039d41c800    gmain
0xffff9d0497328000    1566    784    0    3    S    0xffff9d0497329500    gdbus
0xffff9d0497334c80    1645    784    0    2    S    0xffff9d0497336180    dconf worker
0xffff9d04912ab300    1524    784    0    3    S    0xffff9d04912ac800    gsd-power
0xffff9d04972ab300    1570    784    0    2    S    0xffff9d04972ac800    gmain
0xffff9d0497253300    1596    784    0    3    S    0xffff9d0497254800    gdbus
0xffff9d04972e0000    1651    784    0    3    S    0xffff9d04972e1500    dconf worker
0xffff9d04912b4c80    1529    784    0    1    S    0xffff9d04912b6180    gsd-print-notif
0xffff9d03cc6fe600    1539    784    0    2    S    0xffff9d03cc6ffb00    gmain
0xffff9d04972ae600    1558    784    0    1    S    0xffff9d04972afb00    gdbus
0xffff9d04912b1980    1532    784    0    0    S    0xffff9d04912b2e80    gsd-rfkill
0xffff9d049102b300    1533    784    0    1    S    0xffff9d049102c800    gmain
0xffff9d0491091980    1556    784    0    3    S    0xffff9d0491092e80    gdbus
0xffff9d04895ae600    1534    784    0    3    S    0xffff9d04895afb00    gsd-screensaver
0xffff9d04912b8000    1535    784    0    3    S    0xffff9d04912b9500    gmain
0xffff9d04971e3300    1557    784    0    3    S    0xffff9d04971e4800    gdbus
0xffff9d04895ab300    1537    784    0    0    S    0xffff9d04895ac800    gsd-sharing
0xffff9d03a4291980    1540    784    0    3    S    0xffff9d03a4292e80    gmain
0xffff9d04971e6600    1546    784    0    3    S    0xffff9d04971e7b00    dconf worker
0xffff9d04971e4c80    1561    784    0    3    S    0xffff9d04971e6180    gdbus
0xffff9d03c4890000    1538    784    0    3    S    0xffff9d03c4891500    gsd-smartcard
0xffff9d04971a4c80    1543    784    0    0    S    0xffff9d04971a6180    gmain
0xffff9d0491093300    1560    784    0    3    S    0xffff9d0491094800    gdbus
0xffff9d049bc1b300    1606    784    0    2    S    0xffff9d049bc1c800    dconf worker
0xffff9d049702b300    1542    784    0    2    S    0xffff9d049702c800    gsd-sound
0xffff9d0497028000    1549    784    0    2    S    0xffff9d0497029500    gmain
0xffff9d04972b8000    1577    784    0    2    S    0xffff9d04972b9500    gdbus
0xffff9d04972e6600    1609    784    0    2    S    0xffff9d04972e7b00    dconf worker
0xffff9d049702cc80    1547    784    0    3    S    0xffff9d049702e180    gsd-wacom
0xffff9d04973b9980    1569    784    0    3    S    0xffff9d04973bae80    gmain
0xffff9d0497363300    1624    784    0    0    S    0xffff9d0497364800    gdbus
0xffff9d049702e600    1552    784    0    3    S    0xffff9d049702fb00    gsd-xsettings
0xffff9d04972bcc80    1573    784    0    3    S    0xffff9d04972be180    gmain
```

0xffff9d0497254c80	1597	784	0	1	S	0xffff9d0497256180	gdbus
0xffff9d049bf21980	1647	784	0	2	S	0xffff9d049bf22e80	dconf worker
0xffff9d04973be600	1568	1138	0	3	S	0xffff9d04973bfb00	gsd-disk-utilit
0xffff9d04973e3300	1578	1138	0	3	S	0xffff9d04973e4800	gmain
0xffff9d04972be600	1633	1138	0	3	S	0xffff9d04972bfb00	gdbus
0xffff9d049bc5e600	1587	1138	0	0	S	0xffff9d049bc5fb00	evolution-alarm
0xffff9d03cc549980	1685	1138	0	2	S	0xffff9d03cc54ae80	gmain
0xffff9d049bc59980	1689	1138	0	1	S	0xffff9d049bc5ae80	gdbus
0xffff9d0496004c80	1696	1138	0	3	S	0xffff9d0496006180	dconf worker
0xffff9d0496000000	1697	1138	0	2	S	0xffff9d0496001500	evolution-alarm
0xffff9d03b07a3300	1751	1138	0	2	S	0xffff9d03b07a4800	evolution-alarm
0xffff9d0497366600	1610	1511	0	0	S	0xffff9d0497367b00	ibus-memconf
0xffff9d049732cc80	1623	1511	0	0	S	0xffff9d049732e180	gmain
0xffff9d039d6ccc80	1628	1511	0	0	S	0xffff9d039d6ce180	gdbus
0xffff9d0497361980	1615	1511	0	0	S	0xffff9d0497362e80	ibus-extension-
0xffff9d049bf23300	1655	1511	0	3	S	0xffff9d049bf24800	gmain
0xffff9d049bf24c80	1658	1511	0	0	S	0xffff9d049bf26180	gdbus
0xffff9d0496003300	1695	1511	0	2	S	0xffff9d0496004800	dconf worker
0xffff9d0497364c80	1617	784	0	3	S	0xffff9d0497366180	ibus-x11
0xffff9d03a7028000	1667	784	0	0	S	0xffff9d03a7029500	gmain
0xffff9d03a702e600	1668	784	0	0	S	0xffff9d03a702fb00	gdbus
0xffff9d049bce8000	1629	784	0	3	S	0xffff9d049bce9500	ibus-portal
0xffff9d049bec3300	1638	784	0	0	S	0xffff9d049bec4800	gmain
0xffff9d049bec0000	1640	784	0	3	S	0xffff9d049bec1500	gdbus
0xffff9d04972b9980	1631	784	0	2	S	0xffff9d04972bae80	gsd-printer
0xffff9d04910ae600	1643	784	0	2	S	0xffff9d04910afb00	gmain
0xffff9d049bf26600	1644	784	0	2	S	0xffff9d049bf27b00	gdbus
0xffff9d049bef9980	1641	784	0	0	S	0xffff9d049befae80	xdg-desktop-por
0xffff9d04972e1980	1654	784	0	3	S	0xffff9d04972e2e80	gmain
0xffff9d049bcecc80	1659	784	0	3	S	0xffff9d049bcee180	gdbus
0xffff9d03b0534c80	1830	784	0	0	S	0xffff9d03b0536180	dconf worker
0xffff9d03cc6fb300	1861	784	0	1	S	0xffff9d03cc6fc800	xdg-desktop-por
0xffff9d0382eeb300	1862	784	0	3	S	0xffff9d0382eec800	xdg-desktop-por
0xffff9d04973bcc80	1665	784	0	0	S	0xffff9d04973be180	xdg-desktop-por
0xffff9d03c4973300	1679	784	0	3	S	0xffff9d03c4974800	gmain
0xffff9d03c486e600	1681	784	0	3	S	0xffff9d03c486fb00	gdbus
0xffff9d0383a31980	1730	784	0	1	S	0xffff9d0383a32e80	llvmpipe-0
0xffff9d0383a33300	1731	784	0	1	S	0xffff9d0383a34800	llvmpipe-1
0xffff9d04912b6600	1732	784	0	1	S	0xffff9d04912b7b00	llvmpipe-2
0xffff9d049bc1cc80	1733	784	0	1	S	0xffff9d049bc1e180	llvmpipe-3
0xffff9d049bc18000	1734	784	0	1	S	0xffff9d049bc19500	xdg-desktop-por
0xffff9d049bc1e600	1735	784	0	1	S	0xffff9d049bc1fb00	xdg-desktop-por
0xffff9d0497336600	1736	784	0	1	S	0xffff9d0497337b00	xdg-desktop-por
0xffff9d0497333300	1737	784	0	1	S	0xffff9d0497334800	xdg-desktop-por
0xffff9d0497331980	1738	784	0	1	S	0xffff9d0497332e80	xdg-des:disk$0
0xffff9d03b04b3300	1776	784	0	2	S	0xffff9d03b04b4800	dconf worker
0xffff9d04973b8000	1686	1	0	0	S	0xffff9d04973b9500	gjs
0xffff9d03a42b8000	1691	1	0	3	S	0xffff9d03a42b9500	JS Helper
0xffff9d049befb300	1692	1	0	3	S	0xffff9d049befc800	JS Helper
0xffff9d049bef8000	1693	1	0	3	S	0xffff9d049bef9500	JS Helper
0xffff9d049befe600	1694	1	0	0	S	0xffff9d049beffb00	JS Helper
0xffff9d0383a34c80	1705	1	0	3	S	0xffff9d0383a36180	gmain
0xffff9d0383a36600	1706	1	0	0	S	0xffff9d0383a37b00	gdbus
0xffff9d03b07acc80	1699	784	0	3	S	0xffff9d03b07ae180	gjs
0xffff9d04972e3300	1702	784	0	2	S	0xffff9d04972e4800	gmain
0xffff9d04972bb300	1704	784	0	3	S	0xffff9d04972bc800	gdbus
0xffff9d04912bb300	1707	784	0	0	S	0xffff9d04912bc800	JS Helper
0xffff9d049bcee600	1708	784	0	1	S	0xffff9d049bcefb00	JS Helper
0xffff9d04a1661980	1709	784	0	2	S	0xffff9d04a1662e80	JS Helper

```
0xffff9d04a1663300    1710     784    0    0    S    0xffff9d04a1664800    JS Helper
0xffff9d0482774c80    1768    1511    0    0    S    0xffff9d0482776180    ibus-engine-sim
0xffff9d049329980     1773    1511    0    1    S    0xffff9d049732ae80    gmain
0xffff9d049732e600    1778    1511    0    0    S    0xffff9d049732fb00    gdbus
0xffff9d04910fcc80    1784       1    0    3    S    0xffff9d04910fe180    dbus-launch
0xffff9d04910fe600    1785       1    0    3    S    0xffff9d04910ffb00    dbus-daemon
0xffff9d03a42acc80    1798       1    0    1    S    0xffff9d03a42ae180    at-spi-bus-laun
0xffff9d03a7123300    1799       1    0    3    S    0xffff9d03a7124800    gmain
0xffff9d03a4153300    1800       1    0    3    S    0xffff9d03a4154800    dconf worker
0xffff9d03a4290000    1802       1    0    1    S    0xffff9d03a4291500    gdbus
0xffff9d03a429b300    1804    1798    0    1    S    0xffff9d03a429c800    dbus-daemon
0xffff9d039d6db300    1831     784    0    3    S    0xffff9d039d6dc800    xdg-desktop-por
0xffff9d049102cc80    1832     784    0    2    S    0xffff9d049102e180    gmain
0xffff9d0491028000    1833     784    0    3    S    0xffff9d0491029500    gdbus
0xffff9d0382eecc80    1849     784    0    3    S    0xffff9d0382eee180    dconf worker
0xffff9d04910acc80    1864    1166    0    3    S    0xffff9d04910ae180    gjs
0xffff9d0491096600    1866    1166    0    0    S    0xffff9d0491097b00    gmain
0xffff9d049bceb300    1867    1166    0    0    S    0xffff9d049bcec800    gdbus
0xffff9d039d6e4c80    1868    1166    0    0    S    0xffff9d039d6e6180    JS Helper
0xffff9d039d6c8000    1869    1166    0    0    S    0xffff9d039d6c9500    JS Helper
0xffff9d0386bbe600    1870    1166    0    0    S    0xffff9d0386bbfb00    JS Helper
0xffff9d039d6c3300    1871    1166    0    0    S    0xffff9d039d6c4800    JS Helper
0xffff9d03b749b300    1877    1166    0    2    S    0xffff9d03b749c800    dconf worker
0xffff9d04889a0000    1884     784    0    0    S    0xffff9d04889a1500    snapd-desktop-i
0xffff9d03cc559980    1901     784    0    0    S    0xffff9d03cc55ae80    gvfsd-metadata
0xffff9d0386af3300    1910     784    0    1    S    0xffff9d0386af4800    gmain
0xffff9d04973e1980    1911     784    0    2    S    0xffff9d04973e2e80    gdbus
0xffff9d03cc4e4c80    1942    1884    0    3    S    0xffff9d03cc4e6180    snapd-desktop-i
0xffff9d03c9de1980    1953    1884    0    1    S    0xffff9d03c9de2e80    llvmpipe-0
0xffff9d03c9de4c80    1954    1884    0    1    S    0xffff9d03c9de6180    llvmpipe-1
0xffff9d03cc6f8000    1955    1884    0    2    S    0xffff9d03cc6f9500    llvmpipe-2
0xffff9d03cc6f9980    1956    1884    0    1    S    0xffff9d03cc6fae80    llvmpipe-3
0xffff9d03c9dc1980    1957    1884    0    1    S    0xffff9d03c9dc2e80    snapd-desktop-i
0xffff9d0381136600    1958    1884    0    2    S    0xffff9d0381137b00    snapd-desktop-i
0xffff9d039d6d8000    1959    1884    0    1    S    0xffff9d039d6d9500    snapd-desktop-i
0xffff9d039d6de600    1960    1884    0    2    S    0xffff9d039d6dfb00    snapd-desktop-i
0xffff9d0383a30000    1961    1884    0    1    S    0xffff9d0383a31500    snapd-d:disk$0
0xffff9d03a7114c80    1962    1884    0    1    S    0xffff9d03a7116180    pool-spawner
0xffff9d03cc4fcc80    1963    1884    0    0    S    0xffff9d03cc4fe180    gmain
0xffff9d03c4896600    1964    1884    0    2    S    0xffff9d03c4897b00    gdbus
0xffff9d0497330000    2004     784    0    3    S    0xffff9d0497331500    gnome-terminal-
0xffff9d03b0530000    2005     784    0    3    S    0xffff9d03b0531500    gmain
0xffff9d03b0533300    2006     784    0    3    S    0xffff9d03b0534800    gdbus
0xffff9d039e52cc80    2011     784    0    3    S    0xffff9d039e52e180    dconf worker
0xffff9d04912b9980    2033     784    0    2    S    0xffff9d04912bae80    threaded-ml
0xffff9d03cc4e6600    2034    2004    0    3    S    0xffff9d03cc4e7b00    bash
0xffff9d0385ca6600    2060    1138    0    0    S    0xffff9d0385ca7b00    update-notifier
0xffff9d048890e600    2063    1138    0    3    S    0xffff9d048890fb00    gmain
0xffff9d0488908000    2064    1138    0    3    S    0xffff9d0488909500    gdbus
0xffff9d03b04be600    2068    1138    0    3    S    0xffff9d03b04bfb00    dconf worker
0xffff9d03cc55cc80    2297    2034    0    0    S    0xffff9d03cc55e180    sudo
0xffff9d04912b0000    2298    2297    0    3    S    0xffff9d04912b1500    sudo
0xffff9d0496001980    2299    2298    1    2    R    0xffff9d0496002e80    *echo
0xffff9d03c9dce600    2350       1    0    1    D    0xffff9d03c9dcfb00    (python3)
0xffff9d03c4964c80    2357    1138    0    3    Z    0xffff9d03c4966180    deja-dup-monito
0xffff9d0482044c80    2369       2    0    0    D    0xffff9d0482046180    kworker/0:2
```

8.   We can list the kernel backtrace of any task (thread, process) and make any task current:

```
[2]kdb> btp 2034
Stack traceback for pid 2034
0xffff9d03cc4e6600     2034     2004  0    3    S    0xffff9d03cc4e7b00   bash
Call Trace:
 <TASK>
  __schedule+0x2cb/0x750
 ? queued_spin_unlock+0x9/0x10
  schedule+0x5d/0xf0
  do_wait+0x1c1/0x300
  kernel_wait4+0xaf/0x150
 ? __pfx_child_wait_callback+0x10/0x10
  __do_sys_wait4+0x89/0xa0
 ? sigprocmask+0xb8/0xe0
 ? _copy_to_user+0x25/0x40
 ? __x64_sys_rt_sigprocmask+0x91/0xd0
 ? exit_to_user_mode_prepare+0x49/0x100
 ? syscall_exit_to_user_mode+0x27/0x40
 ? do_syscall_64+0x63/0x80
  __x64_sys_wait4+0x1c/0x30
  x64_sys_call+0x1d4c/0x1ff0
  do_syscall_64+0x56/0x80
 ? exc_page_fault+0x80/0x160
  entry_SYSCALL_64_after_hwframe+0x73/0xdd
RIP: 0033:0x71b10feea45a
RSP: 002b:00007ffeb5bfdbd8 EFLAGS: 00000246 ORIG_RAX: 000000000000003d
RAX: ffffffffffffffda RBX: 00000000000008f9 RCX: 000071b10feea45a
RDX: 000000000000000a RSI: 00007ffeb5bfdc00 RDI: 00000000ffffffff
RBP: 000060aa70292d68 R08: 000060aa71cab570 R09: 0000000000000001
R10: 0000000000000000 R11: 0000000000000246 R12: 000000000000000a
R13: 000060aa71cb0650 R14: 00007ffeb5bfdc00 R15: 0000000000000001
 </TASK>

[2]kdb> pid 2034
KDB current process is bash(pid=2034)

[2]kdb> bt
Stack traceback for pid 2034
0xffff9d03cc4e6600     2034     2004  0    3    S    0xffff9d03cc4e7b00   bash
Call Trace:
 <TASK>
  __schedule+0x2cb/0x750
 ? queued_spin_unlock+0x9/0x10
  schedule+0x5d/0xf0
  do_wait+0x1c1/0x300
  kernel_wait4+0xaf/0x150
 ? __pfx_child_wait_callback+0x10/0x10
  __do_sys_wait4+0x89/0xa0
 ? sigprocmask+0xb8/0xe0
 ? _copy_to_user+0x25/0x40
 ? __x64_sys_rt_sigprocmask+0x91/0xd0
 ? exit_to_user_mode_prepare+0x49/0x100
 ? syscall_exit_to_user_mode+0x27/0x40
 ? do_syscall_64+0x63/0x80
  __x64_sys_wait4+0x1c/0x30
  x64_sys_call+0x1d4c/0x1ff0
  do_syscall_64+0x56/0x80
```

```
 ? exc_page_fault+0x80/0x160
 entry_SYSCALL_64_after_hwframe+0x73/0xdd
RIP: 0033:0x71b10feea45a
RSP: 002b:00007ffeb5bfdbd8 EFLAGS: 00000246 ORIG_RAX: 000000000000003d
RAX: ffffffffffffffda RBX: 00000000000008f9 RCX: 000071b10feea45a
RDX: 000000000000000a RSI: 00007ffeb5bfdc00 RDI: 00000000ffffffff
RBP: 000060aa70292d68 R08: 000060aa71cab570 R09: 0000000000000001
R10: 0000000000000000 R11: 0000000000000246 R12: 000000000000000a
R13: 000060aa71cb0650 R14: 00007ffeb5bfdc00 R15: 0000000000000001
 </TASK>
```

9.   Continue VM execution (**go**), mount the shared folder if necessary, then lunch *kd8*:

```
[2]kdb> go
Catastrophic error detected
kdb_continue_catastrophic=0, type go a second time if you really want to continue

[2]kdb> go
Catastrophic error detected
kdb_continue_catastrophic=0, attempting to continue
```

Note: If the clipboard stops working, launch a different terminal window and continue from there.

```
$ sudo mount -t cifs //172.18.96.1/ALD4 /mnt/c/ALD4 -o
noperm,mfsymlinks,username=coredump,password=<...>
```

```
$ /mnt/c/ALD4/ud8/ud8 &
[1] 3254
```

10.   We see the *kd8* process starts consuming CPU and break-in again:

```
$ top
top - 16:06:27 up  2:46,  0 users,  load average: 1.11, 2.45, 5.92
Tasks: 263 total,   2 running, 261 sleeping,   0 stopped,   0 zombie
%Cpu(s): 26.1 us,  0.2 sy,  0.0 ni, 73.4 id,  0.0 wa,  0.0 hi,  0.2 si,  0.0 st
MiB Mem :   7466.4 total,   4768.1 free,   1697.5 used,   1000.8 buff/cache
MiB Swap:      0.0 total,      0.0 free,      0.0 used.   5446.6 avail Mem

    PID USER      PR  NI    VIRT    RES    SHR S  %CPU  %MEM     TIME+ COMMAND
   3254 coredump  20   0    2640   1024   1024 R 100.0   0.0   1:23.16 kd8
    749 xrdp      20   0   67296  40904  18432 S   2.6   0.5   3:34.32 xrdp
   1166 coredump  20   0 5328520 492552 170452 S   2.0   6.4   4:01.99 gnome-s+
c
```

```
$ sudo echo g >/proc/sysrq-trigger
```

Note: You notice now that only the current terminal window is frozen. Other tasks continue execution and respond to commands.

11.   We now switch to PID **2789** and list its backtrace:

```
Entering kdb (current=0xffff9d04e2fcb300, pid 3262) on processor 3 due to NonMaskable Interrupt
@ 0xffffffffb8621394
[3]kdb> pid 3254
KDB current process is kd8(pid=3254)
```

```
[3]kdb> bt
Stack traceback for pid 3254
0xffff9d04e2fc8000     3254     3237 1    1   R  0xffff9d04e2fc9500  kd8
  Error: no saved data for this cpu
ERROR: Task on cpu 1 didn't stop in the debugger
```

Note: We don't see any kernel backtrace because this thread is currently executing code in user space only:

```
void start_modeling()
{
      while (1)
      {
            sqrt(2); // do some work
      }
}
```

12.   The **btc** command dumps kernel backtraces from all CPUs. The **dumpall** command is useful to see all kernel backtraces from all tasks (it takes some time to dump them all).

13.   Kill PID **3254**:

```
[1]kdb> kill -9 3254
Signal 9 is sent to process 3254.
```

```
[1]kdb> pid 3254
No task with pid=3254
```

14.   Put a breakpoint on the *vfs_rename* function to see what processes attempt to rename files and display registers on function enter:

```
[1]kdb> bp vfs_rename
Instruction(i) BP #0 at 0xffffffffb8870c50 (vfs_rename)
    is enabled   addr at ffffffffb8870c50, hardtype=0 installed=0
```

```
[1]kdb> go
Catastrophic error detected
kdb_continue_catastrophic=0, type go a second time if you really want to continue
```

```
[1]kdb> go
Catastrophic error detected
kdb_continue_catastrophic=0, attempting to continue
```

```
Entering kdb (current=0xffff9d0496001980, pid 3307) on processor 0 due to Breakpoint @
0xffffffffb8870c50
[0]kdb> bt
Stack traceback for pid 3307
0xffff9d0496001980     3307       1 1    0   R  0xffff9d0496002e80 *systemd-journal
CPU: 0 PID: 3307 Comm: systemd-journal Tainted: G        L     6.5.0-1023-azure
#24~22.04.1-Ubuntu
Hardware name: Microsoft Corporation Virtual Machine/Virtual Machine, BIOS Hyper-V UEFI Release
v4.1 04/06/2022
Call Trace:
 <TASK>
 dump_stack_lvl+0x37/0x50
 dump_stack+0x10/0x20
```

```
  kdb_dump_stack_on_cpu+0xb1/0x130
  kdb_show_stack+0x82/0x90
  kdb_bt1+0xc1/0x140
  kdb_bt+0x34b/0x3b0
  kdb_parse+0x2ed/0x560
  kdb_local.constprop.0+0x2ed/0x840
  kdb_main_loop+0xf1/0x220
  kdb_stub+0x1b7/0x400
  kgdb_cpu_enter+0x3a0/0xb60
  kgdb_handle_exception+0xc2/0x120
  __kgdb_notify+0x34/0xd0
  kgdb_ll_trap+0x46/0x60
  do_int3+0x30/0x90
  exc_int3+0x93/0xd0
  asm_exc_int3+0x3a/0x40
 RIP: 0010:vfs_rename+0x0/0xb20
 Code: c6 41 0f 94 c7 45 0f b6 f6 eb b4 66 66 2e 0f 1f 84 00 00 00 00 00 0f 1f 40 00 90 90 90 90
 90 90 90 90 90 90 90 90 90 90 90 90 <0f> 1f 44 00 00 4c 8d 54 24 08 48 83 e4 f0 41 ff 72 f8 55
 48 89 e5
 RSP: 0018:ffffc153434bfd08 EFLAGS: 00000246
 RAX: ffffc153434bfd48 RBX: 0000000000000000 RCX: ffff9d0480ae4580
 RDX: 0000000000000000 RSI: ffff9d0504cdcd80 RDI: ffffc153434bfd90
 RBP: ffffc153434bfe00 R08: 0000000000000000 R09: ffff9d038177c800
 R10: ffff9d0504cdc480 R11: 0000000000000007 R12: ffff9d0504cdcd80
 R13: 0000000000000000 R14: ffff9d04818d4000 R15: 0000000000000000
 ? vfs_rename+0x1/0xb20
 ? do_renameat2+0x58a/0x5d0
 __x64_sys_rename+0x45/0x60
 x64_sys_call+0x1ef9/0x1ff0
 do_syscall_64+0x56/0x80
 ? exit_to_user_mode_prepare+0x49/0x100
 ? syscall_exit_to_user_mode+0x27/0x40
 ? do_syscall_64+0x63/0x80
 ? syscall_trace_enter.constprop.0+0xa3/0x190
 ? exit_to_user_mode_prepare+0x49/0x100
 ? syscall_exit_to_user_mode+0x27/0x40
 ? do_syscall_64+0x63/0x80
 ? syscall_exit_to_user_mode+0x27/0x40
 ? do_syscall_64+0x63/0x80
 ? exc_page_fault+0x80/0x160
 entry_SYSCALL_64_after_hwframe+0x73/0xdd
 RIP: 0033:0x7a14d5a61f2b
 Code: e8 aa 43 0b 00 f7 d8 19 c0 5d c3 0f 1f 40 00 b8 ff ff ff ff 5d c3 66 0f 1f 84 00 00 00 00
 00 f3 0f 1e fa b8 52 00 00 00 0f 05 <48> 3d 00 f0 ff ff 77 05 c3 0f 1f 40 00 48 8b 15 d1 6e 1b
 00 f7 d8
 RSP: 002b:00007fff19333a18 EFLAGS: 00000246 ORIG_RAX: 0000000000000052
 RAX: ffffffffffffffda RBX: 00005736f0e6760a RCX: 00007a14d5a61f2b
 RDX: 0000000007dd6d64 RSI: 00005736f0e67f30 RDI: 00005736f0e41d30
 RBP: 0000000000000000 R08: 0000000000000000 R09: 000000007fffffff
 R10: 0000000000000000 R11: 0000000000000246 R12: 0000000000000000
 R13: 00005736f0e42ac0 R14: 000000000000000a R15: 00005736f0e67609
 </TASK>

[0]kdb> rd
ax: ffffc153434bfd48   bx: 0000000000000000   cx: ffff9d0480ae4580
dx: 0000000000000000   si: ffff9d0504cdcd80   di: ffffc153434bfd90
bp: ffffc153434bfe00   sp: ffffc153434bfd08   r8: 0000000000000000
r9: ffff9d038177c800   r10: ffff9d0504cdc480   r11: 0000000000000007
r12: ffff9d0504cdcd80   r13: 0000000000000000   r14: ffff9d04818d4000
```

```
r15: 0000000000000000  ip: ffffffffb8870c50  flags: 00000246  cs: 00000010
ss: 00000018  ds: 00000018  es: 00000018  fs: 00000018  gs: 00000018
```

15.   Put a breakpoint on the return address from the *vfs_rename* function and display registers on function exit:

```
[0]kdb> mds 0xffffc153434bfd08
0xffffc153434bfd08 ffffffffb8875c6a do_renameat2+0x58a
0xffffc153434bfd10 ffff9d04818d2000    . ......
0xffffc153434bfd18 ffff9d0504cdc480    ........
0xffffc153434bfd20 0000080000000fe0    ........
0xffffc153434bfd28 0000000000000000    ........
0xffffc153434bfd30 0000000200000000    ........
0xffffc153434bfd38 ffffff9cffffff9c    ........
0xffffc153434bfd40 0000000000000000    ........

[0]kdb> bp do_renameat2+0x58a
Instruction(i) BP #1 at 0xffffffffb8875c6a (do_renameat2+0x58a)
    is enabled   addr at ffffffffb8875c6a, hardtype=0 installed=0

[0]kdb> bl
Instruction(i) BP #0 at 0xffffffffb8870c50 (vfs_rename)
    is enabled   addr at ffffffffb8870c50, hardtype=0 installed=0

Instruction(i) BP #1 at 0xffffffffb8875c6a (do_renameat2+0x58a)
    is enabled   addr at ffffffffb8875c6a, hardtype=0 installed=0

[0]kdb> go
Catastrophic error detected
kdb_continue_catastrophic=0, type go a second time if you really want to continue

[0]kdb> go
Catastrophic error detected
kdb_continue_catastrophic=0, attempting to continue

Entering kdb (current=0xffff9d0496001980, pid 3307) on processor 3 due to Breakpoint @
0xffffffffb8875c6a
[3]kdb> bt
Stack traceback for pid 3307
0xffff9d0496001980     3307        1 1    3   R  0xffff9d0496002e80 *systemd-journal
CPU: 3 PID: 3307 Comm: systemd-journal Tainted: G       W    L     6.5.0-1023-azure
#24~22.04.1-Ubuntu
Hardware name: Microsoft Corporation Virtual Machine/Virtual Machine, BIOS Hyper-V UEFI Release
v4.1 04/06/2022
Call Trace:
 <TASK>
 dump_stack_lvl+0x37/0x50
 dump_stack+0x10/0x20
 kdb_dump_stack_on_cpu+0xb1/0x130
 kdb_show_stack+0x82/0x90
 kdb_bt1+0xc1/0x140
 kdb_bt+0x34b/0x3b0
 kdb_parse+0x2ed/0x560
 kdb_local.constprop.0+0x2ed/0x840
 kdb_main_loop+0xf1/0x220
 kdb_stub+0x1b7/0x400
 kgdb_cpu_enter+0x3a0/0xb60
 kgdb_handle_exception+0xc2/0x120
 __kgdb_notify+0x34/0xd0
```

```
 kgdb_ll_trap+0x46/0x60
 do_int3+0x30/0x90
 exc_int3+0x93/0xd0
 asm_exc_int3+0x3a/0x40
RIP: 0010:do_renameat2+0x58a/0x5d0
Code: 89 45 b0 48 8b 85 60 ff ff ff 48 8b 40 18 48 89 45 a8 48 8d 7d 90 48 8d 85 48 ff ff ff 48
89 45 c0 44 89 6d c8 e8 e6 af ff ff <4c> 8b 95 18 ff ff ff 41 89 c7 e9 e2 fd ff ff 4d 39 ec 74
13 41 bf
RSP: 0018:ffffc153434bfd10 EFLAGS: 00000246
RAX: 0000000000000000 RBX: 0000000000000000 RCX: 0000000000000000
RDX: 0000000000000000 RSI: ffff9d038177c800 RDI: ffffc153434bfc90
RBP: ffffc153434bfe00 R08: 0000000000000000 R09: ffff9d03ba10e7f0
R10: ffffc153434bfd10 R11: 0000000000000000 R12: ffff9d0504cdcd80
R13: 0000000000000000 R14: ffff9d04818d4000 R15: 0000000000000000
 ? do_renameat2+0x58b/0x5d0
 __x64_sys_rename+0x45/0x60
 x64_sys_call+0x1ef9/0x1ff0
 do_syscall_64+0x56/0x80
 ? exit_to_user_mode_prepare+0x49/0x100
 ? syscall_exit_to_user_mode+0x27/0x40
 ? do_syscall_64+0x63/0x80
 ? syscall_trace_enter.constprop.0+0xa3/0x190
 ? exit_to_user_mode_prepare+0x49/0x100
 ? syscall_exit_to_user_mode+0x27/0x40
 ? do_syscall_64+0x63/0x80
 ? syscall_exit_to_user_mode+0x27/0x40
 ? do_syscall_64+0x63/0x80
 ? exc_page_fault+0x80/0x160
 entry_SYSCALL_64_after_hwframe+0x73/0xdd
RIP: 0033:0x7a14d5a61f2b
Code: e8 aa 43 0b 00 f7 d8 19 c0 5d c3 0f 1f 40 00 b8 ff ff ff ff 5d c3 66 0f 1f 84 00 00 00 00
00 f3 0f 1e fa b8 52 00 00 00 0f 05 <48> 3d 00 f0 ff ff 77 05 c3 0f 1f 40 00 48 8b 15 d1 6e 1b
00 f7 d8
RSP: 002b:00007fff19333a18 EFLAGS: 00000246 ORIG_RAX: 0000000000000052
RAX: ffffffffffffffda RBX: 00005736f0e6760a RCX: 00007a14d5a61f2b
RDX: 0000000007dd6d64 RSI: 00005736f0e67f30 RDI: 00005736f0e41d30
RBP: 0000000000000000 R08: 0000000000000000 R09: 000000007ffffff
R10: 0000000000000000 R11: 0000000000000246 R12: 0000000000000000
R13: 00005736f0e42ac0 R14: 000000000000000a R15: 00005736f0e67609
 </TASK>


[3]kdb> rd
ax: 0000000000000000  bx: 0000000000000000  cx: 0000000000000000
dx: 0000000000000000  si: ffff9d038177c800  di: ffffc153434bfc90
bp: ffffc153434bfe00  sp: ffffc153434bfd10  r8: 0000000000000000
r9: ffff9d03ba10e7f0  r10: ffffc153434bfd10  r11: 0000000000000000
r12: ffff9d0504cdcd80  r13: 0000000000000000  r14: ffff9d04818d4000
r15: 0000000000000000  ip: ffffffffb8875c6a  flags: 00000246  cs: 00000010
ss: 00000018  ds: 00000018  es: 00000018  fs: 00000018  gs: 00000018
```

16.   Dump the past execution residue (values below the current stack pointer):

```
[3]kdb> mds 0xffffc153434bf000 500
0xffffc153434bf000 0000000000000000   ........
0xffffc153434bf008-0xffffc153434bf0d7 zero suppressed
0xffffc153434bf0d8 0000000000000000   ........
0xffffc153434bf0e0 ffffffffffffffff   ........
0xffffc153434bf0e8 0000000000000000   ........
```

```
0xffffc153434bf0f0 ffffffffffffffff  ........
0xffffc153434bf0f8 6435613631663200  .2f16a5d
0xffffc153434bf100 0000002000000034  4... ...
0xffffc153434bf108 6435613631663262  b2f16a5d
0xffffc153434bf110 24b2887537613134  41a7u..$
0xffffc153434bf118 ffffc153434bf1b0  ..KCS...
0xffffc153434bf120 24b288757b752800  .(u{u..$
0xffffc153434bf128 ffffc153434bf1c0  ..KCS...
0xffffc153434bf130 ffffc153c34bf295  ..K.S...
0xffffc153434bf138 ffffffffb9bb988f  SIGMA2+0xb278f
0xffffc153434bf140 ffffffffb9bb988f  SIGMA2+0xb278f
0xffffc153434bf148 ffffc153434bf298  ..KCS...
0xffffc153434bf150 ffffc153434bf1b0  ..KCS...
0xffffc153434bf158 ffffffffb9364340  vsnprintf+0x2d0
0xffffc153434bf160 0000000000000002  ........
0xffffc153434bf168 000000007fffffff  ........
0xffffc153434bf170 ffffc153434bf296  ..KCS...
0xffffc153434bf178 ffff1020ffffff09  .... ...
0xffffc153434bf180 24b288757b752800  .(u{u..$
0xffffc153434bf188 0000000000000000  ........
0xffffc153434bf190 ffffc153434bf296  ..KCS...
0xffffc153434bf198 0000000000000001  ........
0xffffc153434bf1a0 00007a14d5a61f2b  +....z..
0xffffc153434bf1a8 ffffffffffffffff  ........
0xffffc153434bf1b0 ffffc153434bf210  ..KCS...
0xffffc153434bf1b8 ffffffffb9364716  sprintf+0x56
0xffffc153434bf1c0 ffffc15300000018  ....S...
0xffffc153434bf1c8 ffffc153434bf220  .KCS...
0xffffc153434bf1d0 ffffc153434bf1e0  ..KCS...
0xffffc153434bf1d8 24b288757b752800  .(u{u..$
0xffffc153434bf1e0 ffffc153434bf228  (.KCS...
0xffffc153434bf1e8 0000000000000000  ........
0xffffc153434bf1f0 00007a14d5a61f2b  +....z..
0xffffc153434bf1f8 ffffc153434bf230  0.KCS...
0xffffc153434bf200 ffffc153434bf296  ..KCS...
0xffffc153434bf208 ffff9d0475929e78  x..u....
0xffffc153434bf210 ffffc153434bf270  p.KCS...
0xffffc153434bf218 ffffffffb85e5756  __sprint_symbol.constprop.0+0x106
0xffffc153434bf220 ffffc153434bf326  &.KCS...
0xffffc153434bf228 0000000000000001  ........
0xffffc153434bf230 000000000000001e  ........
0xffffc153434bf238 000000000000001e  ........
0xffffc153434bf240 24b288757b752800  .(u{u..$
0xffffc153434bf248 ffffc153434bf296  ..KCS...
0xffffc153434bf250 ffffffffbbb1bd4a  kdb_buffer+0xa
0xffffc153434bf258 ffffffffbbb1be40  kdb_diemsg
0xffffc153434bf260 ffff0a00ffffff05  ........
0xffffc153434bf268 ffffffffffffffff  ........
0xffffc153434bf270 ffffc153434bf280  ..KCS...
0xffffc153434bf278 ffffffffb85e57e5  sprint_symbol+0x15
0xffffc153434bf280 ffffc153434bf558  X.KCS...
0xffffc153434bf288 ffffffffb9360922  symbol_string+0xa2
0xffffc153434bf290 7830c153434bf2b8  ..KCS.0x
0xffffc153434bf298 3661356434316137  7a14d5a6
0xffffc153434bf2a0 ffffc10062326631  1f2b....
0xffffc153434bf2a8 ffffffffb85e573e  __sprint_symbol.constprop.0+0xee
0xffffc153434bf2b0 0000000000000000  ........
0xffffc153434bf2b8 0000000000000000  ........
0xffffc153434bf2c0 0000000000000073  s.......
```

```
0xffffc153434bf2c8  00000000000000dd       .......
0xffffc153434bf2d0  24b288757b752800       .(u{u..$
0xffffc153434bf2d8  ffffc153434bf326       &.KCS...
0xffffc153434bf2e0  ffffffffbbb1bd41  kdb_buffer+0x1
0xffffc153434bf2e8  ffffffffbbb1be40  kdb_diemsg
0xffffc153434bf2f0  ffff0a00ffffff05       .......
0xffffc153434bf2f8  ffffffffffffffff       .......
0xffffc153434bf300  ffffc153434bf310       ..KCS...
0xffffc153434bf308  ffffffffb85e60f8  sprint_backtrace_build_id+0x18
0xffffc153434bf310  ffffc153434bf5e8       ..KCS...
0xffffc153434bf318  ffffffffb9360922  symbol_string+0xa2
0xffffc153434bf320  6e6534365f4c4c41       ALL_64en
0xffffc153434bf328  435359535f797274       try_SYSC
0xffffc153434bf330  615f34365f4c4c41       ALL_64_a
0xffffc153434bf338  6677685f72657466       fter_hwf
0xffffc153434bf340  3778302b656d6172       rame+0x7
0xffffc153434bf348  3000646478302f33       3/0xdd.0
0xffffc153434bf350  ffffc153434bfc00       ..KCS...
0xffffc153434bf358  0000000000000009       .......
0xffffc153434bf360  00000002434bf409       ..KC....
0xffffc153434bf368  ffffc153434bf558       X.KCS...
0xffffc153434bf370  ffff9d03c9e52200       ."......
0xffffc153434bf378  1ffff3a0793c0043       C.<y....
0xffffc153434bf380  ffff9d0497061bc0       .......
0xffffc153434bf388  00007a14d58e0000       .....z..
0xffffc153434bf390  00007a14d590afff       .....z..
0xffffc153434bf398  ffff9d048228070c       ..(.....
0xffffc153434bf3a0  0000000000000000       .......
0xffffc153434bf3a8  00007a14d57e0fff       ..~..z..
0xffffc153434bf3b0  ffffc153434bf418       ..KCS...
0xffffc153434bf3b8  ffffffffb85a18fd  rcu_nocb_try_bypass+0x5d
0xffffc153434bf3c0  ffff9d0497061bc0       .......
0xffffc153434bf3c8  00007a14d58e0000       .....z..
0xffffc153434bf3d0  00007a14d590afff       .....z..
0xffffc153434bf3d8  ffff9d048887430c       .C......
0xffffc153434bf3e0  00007a14d57e1000       ..~..z..
0xffffc153434bf3e8  24b288757b752800       .(u{u..$
0xffffc153434bf3f0  ffff9d049bf2b208       .......
0xffffc153434bf3f8  ffff9d0483db2a00       .*......
0xffffc153434bf400  ffffffffb93479a0  mt_free_rcu
0xffffc153434bf408  ffff9d0497061bc0       .......
0xffffc153434bf410  00007a14d5930000       .....z..
0xffffc153434bf418  00007a14d5930fff       .....z..
0xffffc153434bf420  ffff9d03c4ab820c       .......
0xffffc153434bf428  00007a14d58db000       .....z..
0xffffc153434bf430  00007a14d59ecfff       .....z..
0xffffc153434bf438  ffff9d0497061bc0       .......
0xffffc153434bf440  00007a14d615e000       .....z..
0xffffc153434bf448  ffff9d0497061bc0       .......
0xffffc153434bf450  00005736ef4e5000       .PN.6W..
0xffffc153434bf458  00005736ef4e5fff       ._N.6W..
0xffffc153434bf460  ffff9d048222010c       ..".....
0xffffc153434bf468  0000000000000000       .......
0xffffc153434bf470  00007a14d570efff       ..p..z..
0xffffc153434bf478  ffff9d04aad18d00       .......
0xffffc153434bf480  0000000000040003       .......
0xffffc153434bf488  ffff9d0497061bc0       .......
0xffffc153434bf490  0000000000000000       .......
0xffffc153434bf498  0000000000002710       .'......
```

```
0xffffc153434bf4a0 0000000000000000    ........
0xffffc153434bf4a8 0000000000002710    .'......
0xffffc153434bf4b0 ffffc153434bf4e0    ..KCS...
0xffffc153434bf4b8 fffffffffb8dda4ce   wait_for_lsr+0x4e
0xffffc153434bf4c0 fffffffffbbc331a0   serial8250_ports
0xffffc153434bf4c8 000000000000000a    ........
0xffffc153434bf4d0 0000000000000000    ........
0xffffc153434bf4d8 fffffffffbbb1be08   kdb_buffer+0xc8
0xffffc153434bf4e0 0000000000000001    ........
0xffffc153434bf4e8 ffffc153434bf558    X.KCS...
0xffffc153434bf4f0 fffffffffb8dc8f31   vt_console_print+0x311
0xffffc153434bf4f8 000000000000000a    ........
0xffffc153434bf500 ffffc153434bf528    (.KCS...
0xffffc153434bf508 fffffffffb8ddb1b7   serial8250_put_poll_char+0x87
0xffffc153434bf510 0000000000000000    ........
0xffffc153434bf518 0000000000002710    .'......
0xffffc153434bf520 ffffc153434bf550    P.KCS...
0xffffc153434bf528 fffffffffb8dda4ce   wait_for_lsr+0x4e
0xffffc153434bf530 0000000000000000    ........
0xffffc153434bf538 0000000000002710    .'......
0xffffc153434bf540 ffffc153434bf570    p.KCS...
0xffffc153434bf548 fffffffffb8dda4ce   wait_for_lsr+0x4e
0xffffc153434bf550 fffffffffbbc331a0   serial8250_ports
0xffffc153434bf558 000000000000000a    ........
0xffffc153434bf560 0000000000000000    ........
0xffffc153434bf568 ffffc153434bf7c0    ..KCS...
0xffffc153434bf570 fffffffffb85e58d3   kallsyms_lookup_names+0xd3
0xffffc153434bf578 ffffc153434bf7d4    ..KCS...
0xffffc153434bf580 0000000000000000    ........
0xffffc153434bf588 000000060002d10f    ........
0xffffc153434bf590 74696e695f544942    BIT_init
0xffffc153434bf598 006d616572745344    DStream.
0xffffc153434bf5a0 0000000000000000    ........
0xffffc153434bf5a8 0000000000002710    .'......
0xffffc153434bf5b0 ffffc153434bf5e0    ..KCS...
0xffffc153434bf5b8 fffffffffb8dda4ce   wait_for_lsr+0x4e
0xffffc153434bf5c0 fffffffffbbc331a0   serial8250_ports
0xffffc153434bf5c8 0000000000000073    s.......
0xffffc153434bf5d0 0000000000000000    ........
0xffffc153434bf5d8 fffffffffbbb1bd50   kdb_buffer+0x10
0xffffc153434bf5e0 0000000000000001    ........
0xffffc153434bf5e8 ffffc153434bf658    X.KCS...
0xffffc153434bf5f0 fffffffffb8dc8f31   vt_console_print+0x311
0xffffc153434bf5f8 0000000000000031    1.......
0xffffc153434bf600 ffffc153434bf628    (.KCS...
0xffffc153434bf608 fffffffffb8ddb1b7   serial8250_put_poll_char+0x87
0xffffc153434bf610 0000000000000037    7.......
0xffffc153434bf618 fffffffffbbc331a0   serial8250_ports
0xffffc153434bf620 fffffffffbbb1bd40   kdb_buffer
0xffffc153434bf628 24b288757b752800    .(u{u..$
0xffffc153434bf630 0000000000000000    ........
0xffffc153434bf638 0000000000002710    .'......
0xffffc153434bf640 ffffc153434bf670    p.KCS...
0xffffc153434bf648 fffffffffb8dda4ce   wait_for_lsr+0x4e
0xffffc153434bf650 fffffffffbbc331a0   serial8250_ports
0xffffc153434bf658 0000000000000020    .......
0xffffc153434bf660 0000000000000000    ........
0xffffc153434bf668 fffffffffbbb1bd53   kdb_buffer+0x13
0xffffc153434bf670 0000000000000001    ........
```

```
0xffffc153434bf678 ffffc153434bf6e8    ..KCS...
0xffffc153434bf680 ffffffffb8dc8f31 vt_console_print+0x311
0xffffc153434bf688 0000000000000020    .......
0xffffc153434bf690 ffffc153434bf6b8    ..KCS...
0xffffc153434bf698 ffffffffb8ddb1b7 serial8250_put_poll_char+0x87
0xffffc153434bf6a0 0000000000000020    .......
0xffffc153434bf6a8 ffffffffbbc331a0 serial8250_ports
0xffffc153434bf6b0 ffffffffbbb1bd40 kdb_buffer
0xffffc153434bf6b8 24b288757b752800    .(u{u..$
0xffffc153434bf6c0 ffffffffba6efec0 vt_console_driver
0xffffc153434bf6c8 0000000000000013    .......
0xffffc153434bf6d0 0000000000000000    .......
0xffffc153434bf6d8 ffffc153434bf6e8    ..KCS...
0xffffc153434bf6e0 ffffffffb8579f5c console_srcu_read_unlock+0x1c
0xffffc153434bf6e8 ffffc153434bf718    ..KCS...
0xffffc153434bf6f0 ffffffffb8625559 kdb_msg_write.part.0+0xa9
0xffffc153434bf6f8 0000000000000000    .......
0xffffc153434bf700 0000000000000000    .......
0xffffc153434bf708 00000000ffffffff    .......
0xffffc153434bf710 0000000000000013    .......
0xffffc153434bf718 ffffc153434bf790    ..KCS...
0xffffc153434bf720 ffffffffb8625a75 vkdb_printf+0x1a5
0xffffc153434bf728 24b288757b752800    .(u{u..$
0xffffc153434bf730 ffffc153434bf828    (.KCS...
0xffffc153434bf738 20ffffffbbb1dd60    `......
0xffffc153434bf740 0000000000000000    .......
0xffffc153434bf748 0000000000000046    F......
0xffffc153434bf750 00002710434bf7c0    ..KC.'..
0xffffc153434bf758 0000000000000050    P......
0xffffc153434bf760 24b288757b752800    .(u{u..$
0xffffc153434bf768 ffffc153434bf768    h.KCS...
0xffffc153434bf770 ffffc153434bf7d8    ..KCS...
0xffffc153434bf778 0000000000000008    .......
0xffffc153434bf780 ffffc153434bf7a8    ..KCS...
0xffffc153434bf788 ffffffffb8755b72 copy_from_kernel_nofault+0x22
0xffffc153434bf790 ffffc153434bf818    ..KCS...
0xffffc153434bf798 ffffc153434bf798    ..KCS...
0xffffc153434bf7a0 ffffc153434bf7a8    ..KCS...
0xffffc153434bf7a8 ffffc153434bf7c8    ..KCS...
0xffffc153434bf7b0 ffffffffb862c365 kdb_getarea_size+0x15
0xffffc153434bf7b8 0000000000000000    .......
0xffffc153434bf7c0 ffffc153434bf7c8    ..KCS...
0xffffc153434bf7c8 ffffc153434bf7f0    ..KCS...
0xffffc153434bf7d0 ffffffffb862c606 kdb_getword+0x86
0xffffc153434bf7d8 0000000000000001    .......
0xffffc153434bf7e0 24b288757b752800    .(u{u..$
0xffffc153434bf7e8 0000000000000008    .......
0xffffc153434bf7f0 ffffc153434bf8c8    ..KCS...
0xffffc153434bf7f8 ffffffffb8627699 kdb_md_line+0x169
0xffffc153434bf800 ffffc153434bf878    x.KCS...
0xffffc153434bf808 0000000100000008    .......
0xffffc153434bf810 0000000100000001    .......
0xffffc153434bf818 0000000000000000    .......
0xffffc153434bf820 0000000000000000    .......
0xffffc153434bf828-0xffffc153434bf847 zero suppressed
0xffffc153434bf848 24b288757b752800    .(u{u..$
0xffffc153434bf850 ffffc153434bf850    P.KCS...
0xffffc153434bf858 ffffc153434bf8c0    ..KCS...
0xffffc153434bf860 0000000000000008    .......
```

```
0xffffc153434bf868  ffffc153434bf890    ..KCS...
0xffffc153434bf870  fffffffffb8755b72   copy_from_kernel_nofault+0x22
0xffffc153434bf878  0000000000000000    ........
0xffffc153434bf880  0000000000000000    ........
0xffffc153434bf888  0000000000000000    ........
0xffffc153434bf890  0000000000000000    ........
0xffffc153434bf898  24b288757b752800    .(u{u..$
0xffffc153434bf8a0  00000000000000e0    ........
0xffffc153434bf8a8  0000000000000000    ........
0xffffc153434bf8b0  0000000000000008    ........
0xffffc153434bf8b8  0000000000000000    ........
0xffffc153434bf8c0  0000000000000001    ........
0xffffc153434bf8c8  ffffc153434bf9a0    ..KCS...
0xffffc153434bf8d0  fffffffffb8629e97   kdb_md+0x417
0xffffc153434bf8d8  00000000000000d9    ........
0xffffc153434bf8e0  0000000000000000    ........
0xffffc153434bf8e8  ffffc153434bf930    0.KCS...
0xffffc153434bf8f0  00000001bbb1c340    @.......
0xffffc153434bf8f8  0000000100000001    ........
0xffffc153434bf900  ffffc153434bf900    ..KCS...
0xffffc153434bf908  0000000800000001    ........
0xffffc153434bf910  00000002bbb1c358    X.......
0xffffc153434bf918  ffffc153434bf918    ..KCS...
0xffffc153434bf920  0000000000000000    ........
0xffffc153434bf928  786c36312e363125    %16.16lx
0xffffc153434bf930  786c36312e363125    %16.16lx
0xffffc153434bf938  ffffc153434b0020    .KCS...
0xffffc153434bf940  24b288757b752800    .(u{u..$
0xffffc153434bf948  24b288757b752800    .(u{u..$
0xffffc153434bf950  000000000000000d    ........
0xffffc153434bf958  0000000000000000    ........
0xffffc153434bf960  000000000000000a    ........
0xffffc153434bf968  0000000000000000    ........
0xffffc153434bf970  24b288757b752800    .(u{u..$
0xffffc153434bf978  0000000000000000    ........
0xffffc153434bf980  fffffffffba5ec948   maintab+0xa8
0xffffc153434bf988  fffffffffbbb1c040   cbuf.8
0xffffc153434bf990  fffffffffba5ec8a0   maintab
0xffffc153434bf998  0000000000000000    ........
0xffffc153434bf9a0  ffffc153434bfa10    ..KCS...
0xffffc153434bf9a8  fffffffffb862a5ad   kdb_parse+0x2ed
0xffffc153434bf9b0  0000001e7b752800    .(u{....
0xffffc153434bf9b8  24b288757b752800    .(u{u..$
0xffffc153434bf9c0  fffffffffbbb1c33f   kdb_nmi_disabled+0x1b
0xffffc153434bf9c8  fffffffffbbb1bb20   kdb_prompt_str
0xffffc153434bf9d0  fffffffffbbb1c340   cmd_cur
0xffffc153434bf9d8  00000000000000c8    ........
0xffffc153434bf9e0  24b288757b752800    .(u{u..$
0xffffc153434bf9e8  fffffffffbbb1c33f   kdb_nmi_disabled+0x1b
0xffffc153434bf9f0  fffffffffbbb1c340   cmd_cur
0xffffc153434bf9f8  fffffffffbbb1d618   cmd_hist+0x11f8
0xffffc153434bfa00  0000000000000017    ........
0xffffc153434bfa08  0000000000000000    ........
0xffffc153434bfa10  ffffc153434bfa48    H.KCS...
0xffffc153434bfa18  fffffffffb862ac0d   kdb_local.constprop.0+0x2ed
0xffffc153434bfa20  ffffc153434bfb28    (.KCS...
0xffffc153434bfa28  0000000000000001    ........
0xffffc153434bfa30  0000000000000003    ........
0xffffc153434bfa38  ffffc153434bfc38    8.KCS...
```
277

```
0xffffc153434bfa40 0000000000000000     .......
0xffffc153434bfa48 ffffc153434bfa78     x.KCS...
0xffffc153434bfa50 ffffffffb862b2b1 kdb_main_loop+0xf1
0xffffc153434bfa58 0000000000000003     .......
0xffffc153434bfa60 0000000000000000     .......
0xffffc153434bfa68-0xffffc153434bfa6f zero suppressed
0xffffc153434bfa70 0000000000000000     .......
0xffffc153434bfa78 ffffc153434bfab0     ..KCS...
0xffffc153434bfa80 ffffffffb862dd07 kdb_stub+0x1b7
0xffffc153434bfa88 ffffc153434bfb28     (.KCS...
0xffffc153434bfa90 ffffc153434bfc38     8.KCS...
0xffffc153434bfa98 0000000000000003     .......
0xffffc153434bfaa0 0000000000000000     .......
0xffffc153434bfaa8 ffff9d0496001980     .......
0xffffc153434bfab0 ffffc153434bfb10     ..KCS...
0xffffc153434bfab8 ffffffffb8621ea0 kgdb_cpu_enter+0x3a0
0xffffc153434bfac0 00000b0fb5bc97cc     .......
0xffffc153434bfac8 0000000000000000     .......
0xffffc153434bfad0 0000000300000064     d.......
0xffffc153434bfad8 0000000000000086     .......
0xffffc153434bfae0 0000000400000001     .......
0xffffc153434bfae8 0000000000000003     .......
0xffffc153434bfaf0 ffffc153434bfb28     (.KCS...
0xffffc153434bfaf8 0000000000000000     .......
0xffffc153434bfb00 ffffc153434bfc38     8.KCS...
0xffffc153434bfb08 0000000000000002     .......
0xffffc153434bfb10 ffffc153434bfb98     ..KCS...
0xffffc153434bfb18 ffffffffb8623232 kgdb_handle_exception+0xc2
0xffffc153434bfb20 ffffe1533fc385b0     ...?S...
0xffffc153434bfb28 0000000500000003     .......
0xffffc153434bfb30 0000000300000002     .......
0xffffc153434bfb38 0000000000000000     .......
0xffffc153434bfb40-0xffffc153434bfb4f zero suppressed
0xffffc153434bfb50 0000000000000000     .......
0xffffc153434bfb58 ffffc153434bfc38     8.KCS...
0xffffc153434bfb60 0000000000000000     .......
0xffffc153434bfb68 24b288757b752800     .(u{u..$
0xffffc153434bfb70 ffffc153434bfbc8     ..KCS...
0xffffc153434bfb78 ffffc153434bfc38     8.KCS...
0xffffc153434bfb80 0000000000000000     .......
0xffffc153434bfb88-0xffffc153434bfb8f zero suppressed
0xffffc153434bfb90 0000000000000000     .......
0xffffc153434bfb98 ffffc153434bfbb8     ..KCS...
0xffffc153434bfba0 ffffffffb849ee84 __kgdb_notify+0x34
0xffffc153434bfba8 0000000000000080     .......
0xffffc153434bfbb0 0000000000000000     .......
0xffffc153434bfbb8 ffffc153434bfbf0     ..KCS...
0xffffc153434bfbc0 ffffffffb849efb6 kgdb_ll_trap+0x46
0xffffc153434bfbc8 ffffc153434bfc38     8.KCS...
0xffffc153434bfbd0 ffffffffb9aecfc8 linux_banner+0x39d708
0xffffc153434bfbd8 0000000000000000     .......
0xffffc153434bfbe0 0000000500000003     .......
0xffffc153434bfbe8 24b288757b752800     .(u{u..$
0xffffc153434bfbf0 ffffc153434bfc08     ..KCS...
0xffffc153434bfbf8 ffffffffb843c460 do_int3+0x30
0xffffc153434bfc00 ffffc153434bfc38     8.KCS...
0xffffc153434bfc08 ffffc153434bfc28     (.KCS...
0xffffc153434bfc10 ffffffffb93d2d43 exc_int3+0x93
0xffffc153434bfc18 0000000000000000     .......
```

```
0xffffc153434bfc20 0000000000000000    .......
0xffffc153434bfc28 ffffc153434bfc39    9.KCS...
0xffffc153434bfc30 ffffffffb9400b9a    asm_exc_int3+0x3a
0xffffc153434bfc38 0000000000000000    .......
0xffffc153434bfc40 ffff9d04818d4000    .@......
0xffffc153434bfc48 0000000000000000    .......
0xffffc153434bfc50 ffff9d0504cdcd80    .......
0xffffc153434bfc58 ffffc153434bfe00    ..KCS...
0xffffc153434bfc60 0000000000000000    .......
0xffffc153434bfc68 0000000000000000    .......
0xffffc153434bfc70 ffffc153434bfd10    ..KCS...
0xffffc153434bfc78 ffff9d03ba10e7f0    .......
0xffffc153434bfc80 0000000000000000    .......
0xffffc153434bfc88-0xffffc153434bfc97  zero suppressed
0xffffc153434bfc98 0000000000000000    .......
0xffffc153434bfca0 ffff9d038177c800    ..w.....
0xffffc153434bfca8 ffffc153434bfc90    ..KCS...
0xffffc153434bfcb0 ffffffffffffffff    .......
0xffffc153434bfcb8 ffffffffb8875c6a    do_renameat2+0x58a
0xffffc153434bfcc0 0000000000000010    .......
0xffffc153434bfcc8 0000000000000246    F.......
0xffffc153434bfcd0 ffffc153434bfd10    ..KCS...
0xffffc153434bfcd8 0000000000000018    .......
0xffffc153434bfce0 ffffffffffffffff    .......
0xffffc153434bfce8 ffffffffb8875c6b    do_renameat2+0x58b
0xffffc153434bfcf0 0000000000000010    .......
0xffffc153434bfcf8 0000000000000246    F.......
0xffffc153434bfd00 ffffc153434bfd10    ..KCS...
0xffffc153434bfd08 0000000000000018    .......
0xffffc153434bfd10 ffff9d04818d2000    . ......
0xffffc153434bfd18 ffff9d0504cdc480    .......
0xffffc153434bfd20 0000080000000fe0    .......
0xffffc153434bfd28 0000000000000000    .......
0xffffc153434bfd30 0000000200000000    .......
0xffffc153434bfd38 fffffff9cfffffff9c  .......
0xffffc153434bfd40 0000000000000000    .......
0xffffc153434bfd48 0000000000000000    .......
0xffffc153434bfd50 ffff9d048023fce0    ..#.....
0xffffc153434bfd58 ffff9d04829e3c00    .<......
0xffffc153434bfd60 ffff9d048023fce0    ..#.....
0xffffc153434bfd68 ffff9d04829e3c00    .<......
0xffffc153434bfd70 0000000fac711b36    6.q.....
0xffffc153434bfd78 ffff9d04818d203d    = ......
0xffffc153434bfd80 0000000705b479a7    .y......
0xffffc153434bfd88 ffff9d04818d403d    =@......
0xffffc153434bfd90 ffffffffba653a80    nop_mnt_idmap
0xffffc153434bfd98 ffff9d048228ee00    ..(.....
0xffffc153434bfda0 ffff9d0504cdcd80    .......
0xffffc153434bfda8 ffffffffba653a80    nop_mnt_idmap
0xffffc153434bfdb0 ffff9d048228ee00    ..(.....
0xffffc153434bfdb8 ffff9d0504cdc480    .......
0xffffc153434bfdc0 ffffc153434bfd48    H.KCS...
0xffffc153434bfdc8 0000000000000000    .......
0xffffc153434bfdd0 24b288757b752800    .(u{u..$
0xffffc153434bfdd8 0000000000000000    .......
0xffffc153434bfde0 ffff9d04818d4000    .@......
0xffffc153434bfde8 00005736f0e41d30    0...6W..
0xffffc153434bfdf0 0000000000000000    .......
0xffffc153434bfdf8 0000000000000000    .......
```

```
0xffffc153434bfe00 ffffc153434bfe20    .KCS...
0xffffc153434bfe08 ffffffffb8875f45 __x64_sys_rename+0x45
0xffffc153434bfe10 ffffc153434bff58  X.KCS...
0xffffc153434bfe18 0000000000000000  .......
0xffffc153434bfe20 ffffc153434bfe30  0.KCS...
0xffffc153434bfe28 ffffffffb84057c9 x64_sys_call+0x1ef9
0xffffc153434bfe30 ffffc153434bff48  H.KCS...
0xffffc153434bfe38 ffffffffb93d1d36 do_syscall_64+0x56
0xffffc153434bfe40 ffffc153434bfe60  `.KCS...
0xffffc153434bfe48 ffffffffb85b0d59 exit_to_user_mode_prepare+0x49
0xffffc153434bfe50 0000000000000000  .......
0xffffc153434bfe58 ffffc153434bff58  X.KCS...
0xffffc153434bfe60 ffffc153434bfe78  x.KCS...
0xffffc153434bfe68 ffffffffb93d7107 syscall_exit_to_user_mode+0x27
0xffffc153434bfe70 ffffc153434bff58  X.KCS...
0xffffc153434bfe78 ffffc153434bff48  H.KCS...
0xffffc153434bfe80 ffffffffb93d1d43 do_syscall_64+0x63
0xffffc153434bfe88 ffffc153434bfec0  ..KCS...
0xffffc153434bfe90 ffffffffb85b0a43 syscall_trace_enter.constprop.0+0xa3
...
```

17.   Finally, we clear all breakpoints and list loaded modules:

```
[3]kdb> bc *
Breakpoint 0 at 0xffffffffb8870c50 cleared
Breakpoint 1 at 0xffffffffb8875c6a cleared
```

```
[3]kdb> lsmod
Module              Size modstruct     Used by
cmac                4096/   4096/     0/   4096 0xffffffffc0b3f140     1  (Live) 0xffffffffc0b3d000/0xffffffffc0cd9000/0x0000000000000000/0xffffffffc0b3f000 [ ]
nls_utf8            4096/   4096/     0/   4096 0xffffffffc0b32100     7  (Live) 0xffffffffc0b30000/0xffffffffc0b34000/0x0000000000000000/0xffffffffc0b32000 [ ]
cifs              573440/ 303104/ 20480/ 512000 0xffffffffc0c02500     2  (Live) 0xffffffffc0b41000/0xffffffffc0c4c000/0xffffffffc0b28000/0xffffffffc0bce000 [ ]
cifs_arc4           4096/   4096/     0/   4096 0xffffffffc0ac1100     1  (Live) 0xffffffffc0abf000/0xffffffffc0ac3000/0x0000000000000000/0xffffffffc0ac1000 [ cifs_arc4 ]
cifs_md4            4096/   4096/     0/   4096 0xffffffffc0b39040     1  (Live) 0xffffffffc0b37000/0xffffffffc0b3b000/0x0000000000000000/0xffffffffc0b39000 [ cifs_md4 ]
fscache           28672/  16384/  4096/ 335872 0xffffffffc0ad1e80     1  (Live) 0xffffffffc0ac6000/0xffffffffc0b21000/0xffffffffc0b26000/0xffffffffc0ace000 [ fscache ]
netfs             20480/   8192/  4096/  28672 0xffffffffc0ab4300     1  (Live) 0xffffffffc0aac000/0xffffffffc0aba000/0xffffffffc0abd000/0xffffffffc0ab2000 [ netfs netfs ]
binfmt_misc         8192/   4096/  4096/   8192 0xffffffffc0aa54c0     1  (Live) 0xffffffffc0aa2000/0xffffffffc0aa8000/0xffffffffc0aaa000/0xffffffffc0aa5000 [ ]
nls_iso8859_1       4096/   4096/     0/   4096 0xffffffffc0a98140     1  (Live) 0xffffffffc0a8f000/0xffffffffc0a9a000/0x0000000000000000/0xffffffffc0a98000 [ ]
crct10dif_pclmul    4096/   4096/     0/   4096 0xffffffffc0a8b280     1  (Live) 0xffffffffc0a89000/0xffffffffc0a8d000/0x0000000000000000/0xffffffffc0a8b000 [ ]
crc32_pclmul        4096/   4096/     0/   4096 0xffffffffc0a9e280     0  (Live) 0xffffffffc0a9c000/0xffffffffc0aa0000/0x0000000000000000/0xffffffffc0a9e000 [ ]
polyval_clmulni     4096/   4096/     0/   4096 0xffffffffc0a94340     0  (Live) 0xffffffffc0a92000/0xffffffffc0a96000/0x0000000000000000/0xffffffffc0a94000 [ ]
polyval_generic     4096/   4096/     0/   4096 0xffffffffc0a27280     1  (Live) 0xffffffffc0a20000/0xffffffffc0a87000/0x0000000000000000/0xffffffffc0a27000 [ polyval_generic ]
ghash_clmulni_intel 4096/   4096/     0/   8192 0xffffffffc0a114c0     0  (Live) 0xffffffffc0a05000/0xffffffffc0a14000/0x0000000000000000/0xffffffffc0a11000 [ ]
sha256_ssse3       16384/   4096/     0/  12288 0xffffffffc0a84180     1  (Live) 0xffffffffc0a7e000/0xffffffffc0a2a000/0x0000000000000000/0xffffffffc0a83000 [ ]
sha1_ssse3         20480/   4096/     0/   8192 0xffffffffc0a1d980     1  (Live) 0xffffffffc0a17000/0xffffffffc0b5000/0x0000000000000000/0xffffffffc0a1d000 [ ]
aesni_intel       331776/   4096/  4096/  16384 0xffffffffc0a092c0     1  (Live) 0xffffffffc0a2c000/0xffffffffc0a0d000/0xffffffffc0a0f000/0xffffffffc0a08000 [ ]
crypto_simd         4096/   4096/     0/   8192 0xffffffffc0a00100     1  (Live) 0xffffffffc09fe000/0xffffffffc0a03000/0x0000000000000000/0xffffffffc0a00000 [ crypto_simd ]
hyperv_drm          8192/   4096/     0/   8192 0xffffffffc0a22580     1  (Live) 0xffffffffc09b7000/0xffffffffc0a25000/0x0000000000000000/0xffffffffc0a22000 [ ]
cryptd              8192/   4096/     0/  12288 0xffffffffc09a8340     2  (Live) 0xffffffffc09a9000/0xffffffffc099d000/0x0000000000000000/0xffffffffc09a8000 [ cryptd cryptd ]
drm_kms_helper     90112/  40960/     0/ 135168 0xffffffffc09d3a00     3  (Live) 0xffffffffc09ba000/0xffffffffc09f3000/0x0000000000000000/0xffffffffc09d1000 [ drm_kms_helper ]
serio_raw           4096/   4096/  4096/   8192 0xffffffffc09ae340     1  (Live) 0xffffffffc09ac000/0xffffffffc09b1000/0xffffffffc09b3000/0xffffffffc09ae000 [ ]
drm_shmem_helper    8192/   4096/     0/  12288 0xffffffffc09a2280     1  (Live) 0xffffffffc099f000/0xffffffffc09a6000/0x0000000000000000/0xffffffffc09a2000 [ drm_shmem_helper ]
joydev             12288/   8192/  4096/   8192 0xffffffffc0973840     0  (Live) 0xffffffffc0963000/0xffffffffc0991000/0xffffffffc0994000/0xffffffffc0973000 [ ]
sch_fq_codel       12288/   4096/     0/   8192 0xffffffffc093e340     5  (Live) 0xffffffffc093a000/0xffffffffc0941000/0x0000000000000000/0xffffffffc093e000 [ ]
hv_sock             8192/   4096/     0/   8192 0xffffffffc0997440     1  (Live) 0xffffffffc0922000/0xffffffffc0976000/0x0000000000000000/0xffffffffc0997000 [ ]
vsock              20480/   8192/     0/  32768 0xffffffffc0985940     5  (Live) 0xffffffffc097f000/0xffffffffc098e000/0xffffffffc09a6000/0xffffffffc0985000 [ vsock ]
ipmi_devintf        8192/   4096/     0/   4096 0xffffffffc0944140     0  (Live) 0xffffffffc095e000/0xffffffffc0961000/0x0000000000000000/0xffffffffc0944000 [ ]
ipmi_msghandler    40960/  12288/  4096/  32768 0xffffffffc09327c0     1  (Live) 0xffffffffc0926000/0xffffffffc0915000/0xffffffffc0919000/0xffffffffc0931000 [ ipmi_msghandler ]
msr                 4096/   4096/     0/   4096 0xffffffffc091e100     0  (Live) 0xffffffffc091c000/0xffffffffc0920000/0x0000000000000000/0xffffffffc091e000 [ ]
parport_pc         20480/  12288/  4096/  16384 0xffffffffc090adc0     0  (Live) 0xffffffffc0904000/0xffffffffc090f000/0xffffffffc0913000/0xffffffffc090a000 [ ]
ppdev               8192/   4096/  4096/   8192 0xffffffffc09784c0     0  (Live) 0xffffffffc0901000/0xffffffffc097b000/0xffffffffc097d000/0xffffffffc0978000 [ ]
lp                 12288/   4096/  4096/  12288 0xffffffffc096c640     0  (Live) 0xffffffffc0967000/0xffffffffc096f000/0xffffffffc0971000/0xffffffffc096b000 [ ]
parport            28672/  16384/  4096/  32768 0xffffffffc094f8c0     3  (Live) 0xffffffffc0946000/0xffffffffc0967000/0xffffffffc095c000/0xffffffffc094e000 [ parport parport parport ]
drm               270336/ 159744/  4096/ 307200 0xffffffffc08960c0     5  (Live) 0xffffffffc084b000/0xffffffffc08da000/0xffffffffc0902000/0xffffffffc088e000 [ drm drm drm ]
i2c_core           36864/  16384/  4096/  61440 0xffffffffc083bf00     2  (Live) 0xffffffffc082f000/0xffffffffc081c000/0xffffffffc0849000/0xffffffffc0839000 [ i2c_core i2c_core ]
efi_pstore          4096/   4096/     0/   4096 0xffffffffc08021c0     0  (Live) 0xffffffffc05e3000/0xffffffffc0804000/0x0000000000000000/0xffffffffc0802000 [ ]
ip_tables          16384/   4096/  4096/  12288 0xffffffffc0827800     0  (Live) 0xffffffffc0822000/0xffffffffc082b000/0xffffffffc082d000/0xffffffffc0827000 [ ]
x_tables           20480/   8192/  4096/  32768 0xffffffffc080de40     1  (Live) 0xffffffffc0807000/0xffffffffc0621000/0xffffffffc0816000/0xffffffffc080d000 [ x_tables ]
autofs4            20480/  12288/  4096/  16384 0xffffffffc07fdb80     2  (Live) 0xffffffffc0607000/0xffffffffc0615000/0xffffffffc05d8000/0xffffffffc07fd000 [ ]
btrfs            1085440/ 253952/  8192/ 569344 0xffffffffc075a9c0     0  (Live) 0xffffffffc0625000/0xffffffffc07bb000/0xffffffffc07fa000/0xffffffffc072f000 [ ]
blake2b_generic     8192/   4096/     0/   8192 0xffffffffc061ca80     0  (Live) 0xffffffffc0619000/0xffffffffc061f000/0x0000000000000000/0xffffffffc061c000 [ ]
xor                12288/   4096/     0/   4096 0xffffffffc0611140     1  (Live) 0xffffffffc060d000/0xffffffffc0613000/0x0000000000000000/0xffffffffc0611000 [ xor ]
raid6_pq           24576/  86016/     0/  16384 0xffffffffc05ecd40     1  (Live) 0xffffffffc05e5000/0xffffffffc05f1000/0x0000000000000000/0xffffffffc05ec000 [ raid6_pq ]
libcrc32c           4096/   4096/     0/   4096 0xffffffffc05c6040     1  (Live) 0xffffffffc05c4000/0xffffffffc05d6000/0x0000000000000000/0xffffffffc05c6000 [ libcrc32c ]
dm_mirror          12288/   4096/     0/   8192 0xffffffffc05da000     0  (Live) 0xffffffffc05c8000/0xffffffffc05e1000/0x0000000000000000/0xffffffffc05de000 [ ]
dm_region_hash      8192/   4096/     0/  12288 0xffffffffc05d01c0     1  (Live) 0xffffffffc05c9000/0xffffffffc05d4000/0x0000000000000000/0xffffffffc05d0000 [ dm_region_hash ]
dm_log              8192/   4096/     0/   8192 0xffffffffc0595240     2  (Live) 0xffffffffc0592000/0xffffffffc05c2000/0x0000000000000000/0xffffffffc0595000 [ dm_log dm_log ]
hid_generic         4096/   4096/     0/   4096 0xffffffffc058e180     0  (Live) 0xffffffffc058c000/0xffffffffc0590000/0x0000000000000000/0xffffffffc058e000 [ ]
hid_hyperv          4096/   4096/     0/   8192 0xffffffffc05cd200     0  (Live) 0xffffffffc059e000/0xffffffffc05a0000/0x0000000000000000/0xffffffffc05cd000 [ ]
hv_netvsc          53248/  20480/  4096/  36864 0xffffffffc05b2c80     0  (Live) 0xffffffffc058c000/0xffffffffc05ba000/0xffffffffc05c0000/0xffffffffc05b0000 [ ]
hyperv_keyboard     4096/   4096/     0/   4096 0xffffffffc059a1c0     0  (Live) 0xffffffffc0598000/0xffffffffc059c000/0x0000000000000000/0xffffffffc059a000 [ ]
hid                65536/  49152/  4096/  49152 0xffffffffc0573f80     2  (Live) 0xffffffffc055f000/0xffffffffc057d000/0xffffffffc058a000/0xffffffffc0570000 [ hid hid ]
```

18.   We continue (go) and close the session.

Exercise KD10

- **Goal:** Learn how to configure and build Linux kernel and use GDB for kernel-level debugging

- **Elementary Diagnostics Patterns:** -

- **Memory Analysis Patterns:** Stack Trace

- **Debugging Implementation Patterns:** Code Breakpoint

- \ALD4\Exercise-Linux-KD10.pdf

Goal: Learn how to configure and build Linux kernel and use GDB for kernel-level debugging.

Memory Analysis Patterns: Stack Trace.

Debugging Implementation Patterns: Code Breakpoint.

1.   Boot *Ubuntu ALD4* VM. We need an uncompressed kernel image with debug symbols:

```
$ sudo apt-key adv --keyserver keyserver.ubuntu.com --recv-keys C8CAB6595FDFF622
```

```
$ codename=$(lsb_release -c | awk '{print $2}')
sudo tee /etc/apt/sources.list.d/ddebs.list << EOF
deb http://ddebs.ubuntu.com/ ${codename}        main restricted universe multiverse
deb http://ddebs.ubuntu.com/ ${codename}-security main restricted universe multiverse
deb http://ddebs.ubuntu.com/ ${codename}-updates  main restricted universe multiverse
deb http://ddebs.ubuntu.com/ ${codename}-proposed main restricted universe multiverse
EOF
```

```
$ sudo apt-get update
```

```
$ sudo apt-get upgrade
```

Reboot the system, install the required image, and copy it to a shared location:

```
$ sudo apt-get install linux-image-$(uname -r)-dbgsym
...
Setting up linux-image-6.5.0-1023-azure-dbgsym (6.5.0-1023.24~22.04.1) ...
```

```
$ sudo mount -t cifs //172.18.96.1/ALD4 /mnt/c/ALD4 -o
noperm,mfsymlinks,username=coredump,password=<...>
```

```
$ sudo cp /usr/lib/debug/boot/vmlinux-6.5.0-1023-azure /mnt/c/ALD4/
```

2.   Quick create another Hyper-V Ubuntu 22.04 LTS VM with the name *Ubuntu GDB*. If you have 16GB of memory on Host, you may want to limit VM memory to 3072 MB and disable dynamic memory before connecting and continuing setup:

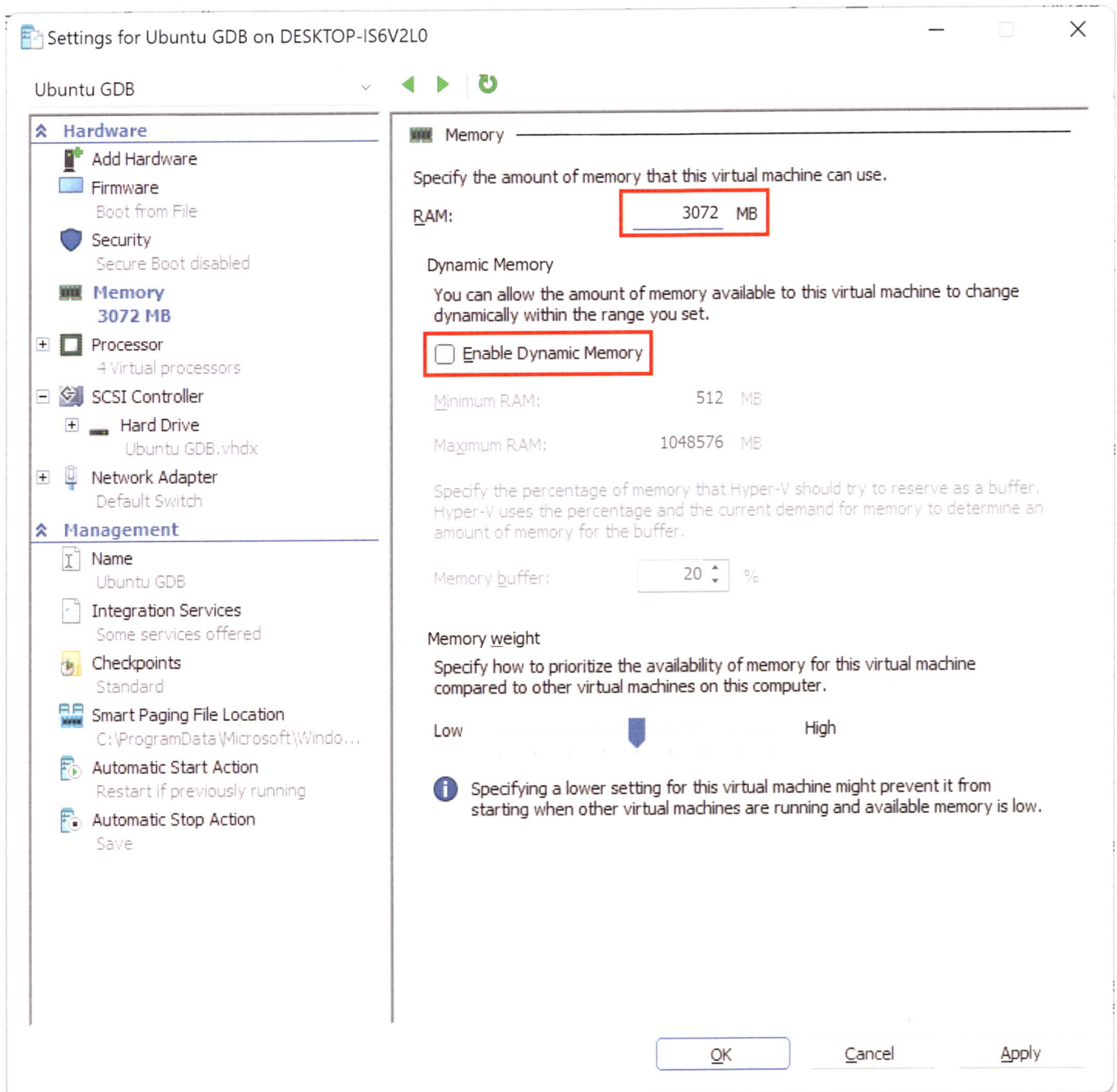

3.   On the Host, open the PowerShell and enable the first serial port for *Ubuntu GDB* VM:

```
PS > Set-VMComPort "Ubuntu GDB" 1 \\.\pipe\kdbpipe

PS > Get-VMComPort "Ubuntu GDB"

VMName        Name   Path
------        ----   ----
Ubuntu GDB COM 1 \\.\pipe\kdbpipe
```

4.	Shut down the *Ubuntu GDB* VM, start it, and connect to it again.

5.	On *Ubuntu GDB* VM, install CIFS:

```
$ sudo apt install cifs-utils
```

6.	On the Host computer, run Command Prompt and note the IP4 address of the *Default Switch* (it may be different and change with every new Hyper-V start after the Host restart):

```
> ipconfig
Windows IP Configuration
[...]
Ethernet adapter vEthernet (Default Switch):
   Connection-specific DNS Suffix  . :
   Link-local IPv6 Address . . . . . : [...]
   IPv4 Address. . . . . . . . . . . : 172.23.112.1
   Subnet Mask . . . . . . . . . . . : 255.255.240.0
   Default Gateway . . . . . . . . . :
[...]
```

7.	On the *Ubuntu GDB* VM, mount the previously created share (Exercise KD0) to the */mnt/c/ALD4* folder:

```
$ sudo mkdir -p /mnt/c/ALD4
```

```
$ sudo mount -t cifs //172.23.112.1/ALD4 /mnt/c/ALD4 -o
noperm,mfsymlinks,username=coredump,password=<...>
```

8.	Then, launch elevated GDB with the previously shared *vmlinux-6.5.0-1023-azure* image:

```
$ sudo gdb /mnt/c/ALD4/vmlinux-6.5.0-1023-azure
GNU gdb (Ubuntu 12.0.90-0ubuntu1) 12.0.90
Copyright (C) 2022 Free Software Foundation, Inc.
License GPLv3+: GNU GPL version 3 or later <http://gnu.org/licenses/gpl.html>
This is free software: you are free to change and redistribute it.
There is NO WARRANTY, to the extent permitted by law.
Type "show copying" and "show warranty" for details.
This GDB was configured as "x86_64-linux-gnu".
Type "show configuration" for configuration details.
For bug reporting instructions, please see:
<https://www.gnu.org/software/gdb/bugs/>.
Find the GDB manual and other documentation resources online at:
    <http://www.gnu.org/software/gdb/documentation/>.

For help, type "help".
Type "apropos word" to search for commands related to "word"...
Reading symbols from /mnt/c/ALD4/vmlinux-6.5.0-1023-azure...
(gdb)
```

9.	Prepare remote debugging over serial port:

```
(gdb) set serial baud 115200
```

```
(gdb) target remote /dev/ttyS0
Remote debugging using /dev/ttyS0
```

10.   On the *Ubuntu ALD4*, set appropriate permissions, enable the kernel debugger over the first serial port again, and trigger the kernel debugger:

```
$ sudo chmod 666 /proc/sysrq-trigger

$ sudo chmod 666 /sys/module/kgdboc/parameters/kgdboc

$ echo "ttyS0" >/sys/module/kgdboc/parameters/kgdboc

$ sudo echo g >/proc/sysrq-trigger
```

11.   On the *Ubuntu GDB*, we see the remote debugging connection:

```
Ignoring packet error, continuing...
warning: unrecognized item "timeout" in "qSupported" response
warning: multi-threaded target stopped without sending a thread-id, using first non-exited
thread
[Switching to Thread 4294967294]
0xffffffff8e821394 in ?? ()
(gdb)
```

Note: If you see GDB disconnected instead, there might have been something wrong with the pipe, so you need to shutdown both VMs and repeat **Set-VMComPort** commands.

12.   However, we don't see any symbolic references in the backtrace (and breakpoints also fail):

```
(gdb) bt
#0  0xffffffff9c621394 in ?? ()
#1  0xffffbebec7aa3ce0 in ?? ()
#2  0xffffffff9c6213e6 in ?? ()
#3  0xffffbebec7aa3d28 in ?? ()
#4  0xffffffff9cdba1be in ?? ()
#5  0xffffbebec7aa3d28 in ?? ()
#6  0xffffffff9ca9735e in ?? ()
#7  0x0000000000000002 in fixed_percpu_data ()
#8  0x0000000000000002 in fixed_percpu_data ()
#9  0xffff9f55fc262b00 in ?? ()
#10 0x00005f42e892c440 in ?? ()
#11 0xffffbebec7aa3e08 in ?? ()
#12 0xffffbebec7aa3d40 in ?? ()
#13 0xffffffff9cdba9d8 in ?? ()
#14 0xffff9f56c28506c0 in ?? ()
#15 0xffffbebec7aa3d60 in ?? ()
#16 0xffffffff9c90ab7e in ?? ()
#17 0xffffffff9d3e4eba in ?? ()
#18 0xffff9f56c0ada000 in ?? ()
#19 0xffffbebec7aa3df8 in ?? ()
#20 0xffffffff9c85d97f in ?? ()
#21 0xffffffff9c7a81cf in ?? ()
#22 0xffffbebec7aa3e50 in ?? ()
#23 0x0400000000000080 in ?? ()
#24 0xffffbebec7aa3df0 in ?? ()
#25 0x000079781fa1ca70 in ?? ()
```

```
#26 0x00000000000007e8 in ?? ()
#27 0x0400000000000000 in ?? ()
#28 0xffffbebec7aa3dc0 in ?? ()
#29 0xffffffff9c7aa17d in ?? ()
#30 0xffffffff9d3e4eba in ?? ()
#31 0x0000000000000000 in ?? ()
```

13.   To quit the GDB kernel debugging session, we need to detach first to resume the debugee properly:

```
(gdb) detach
Detaching from program: /mnt/c/ALD4/vmlinux, Remote target
Ending remote debugging.
[Inferior 1 (Remote target) detached]

(gdb) q
```

14.   We don't see symbolic references because the current Linux kernel on the VM is configured to randomize its start address and various sections:

```
$ grep CONFIG_RANDOMIZE_BASE /boot/config-$(uname -r)
CONFIG_RANDOMIZE_BASE=y

$ grep CONFIG_RANDOMIZE_MEMORY /boot/config-$(uname -r)
CONFIG_RANDOMIZE_MEMORY=y
```

15.   Therefore, we need to change the configuration and re-compile the current kernel version. Make sure you have at least 20GB of free space. Exercise KD0 shows how to increase the size of the partition.

16.   First, we need to edit */etc/apt/sources.list* to uncomment all *#deb-src* entries. Then, we update and install necessary prerequisite packages, including kernel source code.

```
$ sudo apt update

$ sudo apt-get install dpkg-dev

$ sudo apt-get source linux-image-unsigned-$(uname -r)

$ sudo apt-get build-dep linux-image-unsigned-$(uname -r)

$ sudo apt install libncurses-dev bison flex libssl-dev libelf-dev dwarves
```

17.   Next, we change the current configuration to remove the CONFIG_RANDOMIZE_ options.

```
$ cd linux-azure-6.5-6.5.0

$ sudo cp /boot/config-$(uname -r) .config

$ sudo make menuconfig
```

Note: In the *menuconfig* interface, you can type **/** and search for the option location. Both options are located in *Processor types and features*.

18.   Next, we change the current configuration to remove the CONFIG_RANDOMIZE_ options. We unselect (exclude, N) *Randomize the kernel memory sections* and *Randomize the address of the kernel image (KASLR)*.

```
.config - Linux/x86 6.5.13 Kernel Configuration
> Processor type and features
┌─────────────────── Processor type and features ───────────────────┐
│ Arrow keys navigate the menu.  <Enter> selects submenus ---> (or empty │
│ submenus ----).  Highlighted letters are hotkeys.  Pressing <Y>       │
│ includes, <N> excludes, <M> modularizes features.  Press <Esc><Esc> to │
│ exit, <?> for Help, </> for Search.  Legend: [*] built-in  [ ]        │
│   ^(-)──────────────────────────────────────────────────            │
│       [ ]    Require a valid signature in kexec_file_load() syscall   │
│       [*]    Enable bzImage signature verification support            │
│       [*] kernel crash dumps                                          │
│       [*] kexec jump                                                  │
│       (0x1000000) Physical address where the kernel is loaded         │
│       -*- Build a relocatable kernel                                  │
│       [*]    Randomize the address of the kernel image (KASLR)        │
│       (0x200000) Alignment value to which kernel should be aligned    │
│       [ ] Randomize the kernel memory sections                        │
│       [*] Linear Address Masking support                              │
│   v(+)                                                               │
│                                                                     │
│      <Select>     < Exit >     < Help >     < Save >     < Load >     │
└─────────────────────────────────────────────────────────────────────┘
```

288

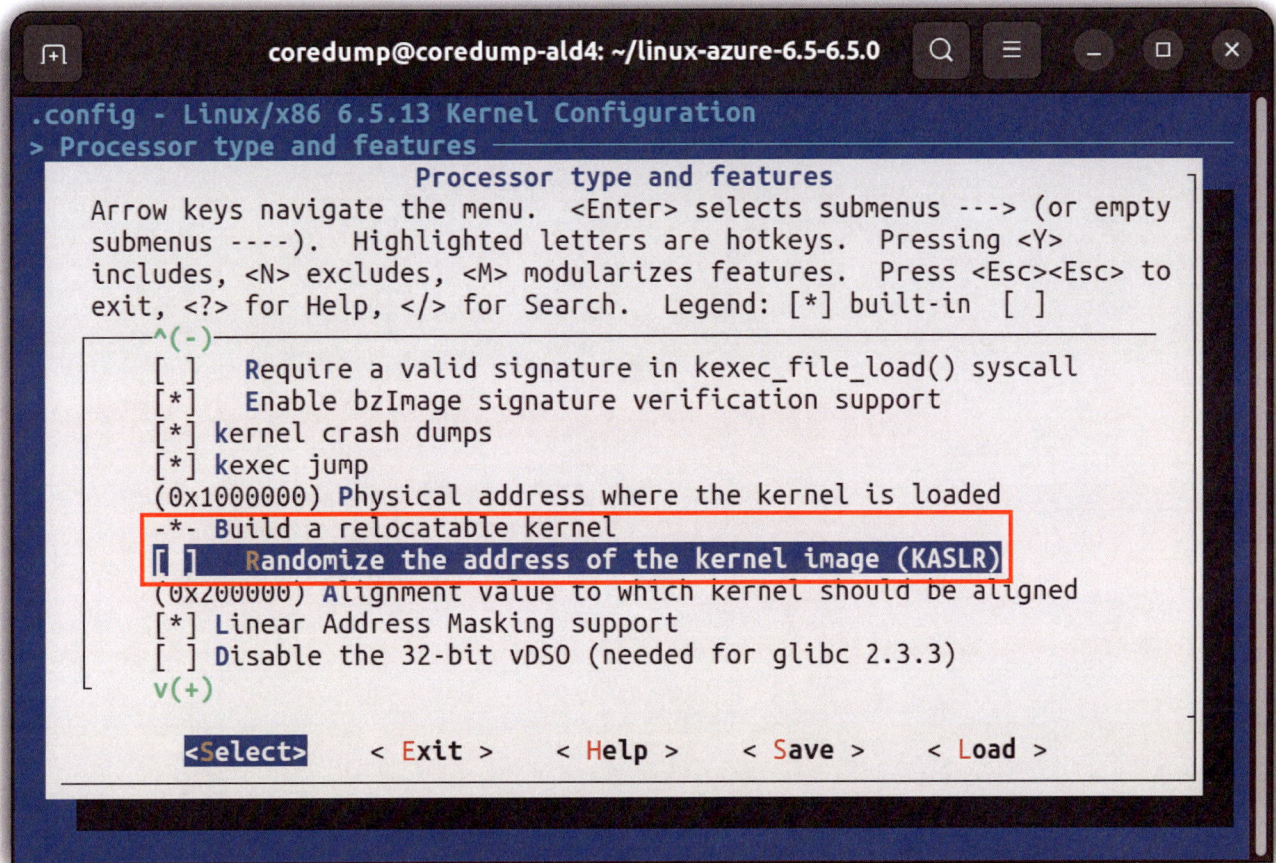

```
.config - Linux/x86 6.5.13 Kernel Configuration
> Processor type and features
                          Processor type and features
    Arrow keys navigate the menu.  <Enter> selects submenus ---> (or empty
    submenus ----).  Highlighted letters are hotkeys.  Pressing <Y>
    includes, <N> excludes, <M> modularizes features.  Press <Esc><Esc> to
    exit, <?> for Help, </> for Search.  Legend: [*] built-in  [ ]
        ^(-)
        [ ]    Require a valid signature in kexec_file_load() syscall
        [*]    Enable bzImage signature verification support
        [*] kernel crash dumps
        [*] kexec jump
        (0x1000000) Physical address where the kernel is loaded
        -*- Build a relocatable kernel
        [ ]    Randomize the address of the kernel image (KASLR)
        (0x200000) Alignment value to which kernel should be aligned
        [*] Linear Address Masking support
        [ ] Disable the 32-bit vDSO (needed for glibc 2.3.3)
        v(+)

            <Select>    < Exit >    < Help >    < Save >    < Load >
```

19.   Now, we are ready to build the kernel. It may take several hours. You may need to increase memory for the Hyper-V VM to at least 6GB if the dynamic memory option was unselected during VM setup.

```
$ sudo make
```

```
$ sudo chmod +x ./debian/scripts/sign-module
```

```
$ sudo make modules_install
```

```
$ sudo make install
```

20.   Finally, we copy the uncompressed kernel image to the shared folder and reboot the VM.

```
$ cp vmlinux /mnt/c/ALD4/
```

```
$ sudo reboot now
```

21.   After reboot, verify that the new kernel was installed and the RANDOMIZE option is not present.

```
$ uname -r
6.5.13
```

```
$ grep CONFIG_RANDOMIZE_BASE /boot/config-$(uname -r)
# CONFIG_RANDOMIZE_BASE is not set
```

22.   On *Ubuntu GDB,* launch elevated GDB with the previously shared *vmlinux* image:

```
$ sudo gdb /mnt/c/ALD4/vmlinux
GNU gdb (Ubuntu 12.1-0ubuntu1~22.04.2) 12.1
Copyright (C) 2022 Free Software Foundation, Inc.
License GPLv3+: GNU GPL version 3 or later <http://gnu.org/licenses/gpl.html>
This is free software: you are free to change and redistribute it.
There is NO WARRANTY, to the extent permitted by law.
Type "show copying" and "show warranty" for details.
This GDB was configured as "x86_64-linux-gnu".
Type "show configuration" for configuration details.
For bug reporting instructions, please see:
<https://www.gnu.org/software/gdb/bugs/>.
Find the GDB manual and other documentation resources online at:
    <http://www.gnu.org/software/gdb/documentation/>.

For help, type "help".
Type "apropos word" to search for commands related to "word"...
Reading symbols from /mnt/c/ALD4/vmlinux...
(gdb)
```

23.   Prepare remote debugging over serial port:

```
(gdb) set serial baud 115200
```

```
(gdb) target remote /dev/ttyS0
Remote debugging using /dev/ttyS0
```

24.   On *Ubuntu ALD4,* set appropriate permissions, enable the kernel debugger over the first serial port again, and trigger the kernel debugger:

```
$ sudo chmod 666 /proc/sysrq-trigger
```

```
$ sudo chmod 666 /sys/module/kgdboc/parameters/kgdboc
```

```
$ echo "ttyS0" >/sys/module/kgdboc/parameters/kgdboc
```

```
$ sudo echo g >/proc/sysrq-trigger
```

25.   On *Ubuntu GDB,* we see the remote debugging connection with symbols:

```
warning: multi-threaded target stopped without sending a thread-id, using first non-exited
thread
[Switching to Thread 4294967294]
kgdb_breakpoint () at kernel/debug/debug_core.c:1222
1222    kernel/debug/debug_core.c: No such file or directory.
(gdb)
```

26.   We also see kernel symbolic references in the backtrace:

```
(gdb) bt
#0  kgdb_breakpoint () at kernel/debug/debug_core.c:1222
#1  0xffffffff812193d6 in sysrq_handle_dbg (key=<optimized out>)
    at kernel/debug/debug_core.c:986
#2  0xffffffff819a26fe in __handle_sysrq (key=103,
    check_mask=check_mask@entry=false) at drivers/tty/sysrq.c:603
```

```
#3  0xffffffff819a2eb8 in write_sysrq_trigger (file=<optimized out>,
    buf=<optimized out>, count=2, ppos=<optimized out>)
    at drivers/tty/sysrq.c:1164
#4  0xffffffff814fc99e in pde_write (ppos=<optimized out>,
    count=<optimized out>, buf=<optimized out>, file=0x67,
    pde=0xffff88810187cd80) at fs/proc/inode.c:340
#5  proc_reg_write (file=0x67, buf=0xffff888103d1f680 "", count=0,
    ppos=0x0 <fixed_percpu_data>) at fs/proc/inode.c:352
#6  0xffffffff814508ff in vfs_write (file=file@entry=0xffff88800a9a1100,
    buf=buf@entry=0x6378c005b440 <error: Cannot access memory at address 0x6378c005b440>,
count=count@entry=2, pos=pos@entry=0xffffc90005123e48)
    at fs/read_write.c:582
#7  0xffffffff81450f47 in ksys_write (fd=<optimized out>,
    buf=0x6378c005b440 <error: Cannot access memory at address 0x6378c005b440>, count=2) at
fs/read_write.c:637
#8  0xffffffff81450ff9 in __do_sys_write (count=<optimized out>,
    buf=<optimized out>, fd=<optimized out>) at fs/read_write.c:649
#9  __se_sys_write (count=<optimized out>, buf=<optimized out>,
--Type <RET> for more, q to quit, c to continue without paging--c
    fd=<optimized out>) at fs/read_write.c:646
#10 __x64_sys_write (regs=<optimized out>) at fs/read_write.c:646
#11 0xffffffff81004f33 in x64_sys_call (regs=regs@entry=0xffffc90005123f58, nr=<optimized out>)
at ./arch/x86/include/generated/asm/syscalls_64.h:2
#12 0xffffffff81fac3b6 in do_syscall_x64 (nr=<optimized out>, regs=0xffffc90005123f58) at
arch/x86/entry/common.c:51
#13 do_syscall_64 (regs=0xffffc90005123f58, nr=<optimized out>) at arch/x86/entry/common.c:81
#14 0xffffffff820000eb in entry_SYSCALL_64 () at arch/x86/entry/entry_64.S:121
#15 0x00007d1f67616a00 in ?? ()
#16 0x00007d1f67617600 in ?? ()
#17 0x00007d1f6761b780 in ?? ()
#18 0x0000000000000002 in fixed_percpu_data ()
#19 0x00006378c005b440 in ?? ()
#20 0x0000000000000002 in fixed_percpu_data ()
#21 0x0000000000000246 in ?? ()
#22 0x0000000000000077 in ?? ()
#23 0x00006378c005b440 in ?? ()
#24 0x0000000000000000 in ?? ()
```

27.   We can also set breakpoints:

```
(gdb) break vfs_rename
Breakpoint 1 at 0xffffffff81462e30: file fs/namei.c, line 4754.

(gdb) c
Continuing.
[New Thread 2034]
[Switching to Thread 1]

Thread 5 hit Breakpoint 1, vfs_rename (rd=rd@entry=0xffffc90000043e50) at fs/namei.c:4754
4754    fs/namei.c: No such file or directory.

(gdb) bt
#0  vfs_rename (rd=rd@entry=0xffffc90000043e50) at fs/namei.c:4754
#1  0xffffffff814689ea in do_renameat2 (olddfd=olddfd@entry=-100, from=<optimized out>,
newdfd=newdfd@entry=-100,
    to=to@entry=0xffff888039e8a000, flags=flags@entry=0) at fs/namei.c:5027
#2  0xffffffff81468cc5 in __do_sys_rename (newname=<optimized out>,
```

```
          oldname=0x56fc440448f0 <error: Cannot access memory at address 0x56fc440448f0>) at
fs/namei.c:5073
#3  __se_sys_rename (newname=<optimized out>, oldname=<optimized out>) at fs/namei.c:5071
#4  __x64_sys_rename (regs=<optimized out>) at fs/namei.c:5071
#5  0xffffffff81005819 in x64_sys_call (regs=regs@entry=0xffffc90000043f58, nr=<optimized out>)
    at ./arch/x86/include/generated/asm/syscalls_64.h:83
#6  0xffffffff81fac3b6 in do_syscall_x64 (nr=<optimized out>, regs=0xffffc90000043f58) at
arch/x86/entry/common.c:51
#7  do_syscall_64 (regs=0xffffc90000043f58, nr=<optimized out>) at arch/x86/entry/common.c:81
#8  0xffffffff820000eb in entry_SYSCALL_64 () at arch/x86/entry/entry_64.S:121
#9  0x00007c3a4e483a58 in ?? ()
#10 0x0000000000000000 in ?? ()

(gdb) delete break 1

(gdb) c
Continuing.
```

28.   On *Ubuntu ALD4*, we break-in again:

```
[New Thread 2050]
[New Thread 2043]
[New Thread 2046]
[New Thread 2048]
[New Thread 2049]

Thread 626 received signal SIGTRAP, Trace/breakpoint trap.
[Switching to Thread 2050]
kgdb_breakpoint () at kernel/debug/debug_core.c:1222
1222    kernel/debug/debug_core.c: No such file or directory.
(gdb)
```

29.   On *Ubuntu GDB*, we can also list the target tasks:

```
(gdb) monitor ps
101 sleeping system daemon (state [ims]) processes suppressed,
use 'ps A' to see all.
Task Addr            Pid    Parent [*] cpu State Thread              Command
0xffff8880205d4c80   2014     2013  1   0   R   0xffff8880205d6180  *echo
0xffff8881002e8000      0        0  1   1   R   0xffff8881002e9500  swapper/1
  Error: no saved data for this cpu
0xffff8881002eb300      0        0  1   2   R   0xffff8881002ec800  swapper/2
  Error: no saved data for this cpu
0xffff8881002e9980      0        0  1   3   R   0xffff8881002eae80  swapper/3
  Error: no saved data for this cpu

0xffff888100279980      1        0  0   1   D   0xffff88810027ae80  systemd
0xffff8881002ecc80     16        2  0   0   R   0xffff8881002ee180  migration/0
0xffff888100adcc80     47        2  0   3   D   0xffff888100ade180  khugepaged
0xffff888100ae3300     52        2  0   2   D   0xffff888100ae4800  kworker/2:1
0xffff8880035d9980     77        2  0   3   D   0xffff8880035dae80  kworker/u8:4
0xffff8880035d8000     80        2  0   1   D   0xffff8880035d9500  kworker/u8:7
0xffff8880f5859980    191        2  0   2   D   0xffff8880f585ae80  jbd2/sda1-8
0xffff8880f48e6600    236        1  0   1   S   0xffff8880f48e7b00  systemd-journal
0xffff888009816600   2015        1  0   1   D   0xffff888009817b00  journal-offline
0xffff888009813300   2016        1  0   3   D   0xffff888009814800  journal-offline
0xffff8880f48acc80    288        1  0   3   S   0xffff8880f48ae180  systemd-udevd
0xffff8880036e9980    410        2  0   0   R   0xffff8880036eae80  kworker/0:4
```

```
0xffff8880f48e4c80    433      1  0    3  S  0xffff8880f48e6180  systemd-oomd
0xffff8880f5864c80    438      1  0    0  S  0xffff8880f5866180  systemd-resolve
0xffff8880f5bb9980    440      1  0    0  S  0xffff8880f5bbae80  systemd-timesyn
0xffff8880f5bb0000    444      1  0    0  S  0xffff8880f5bb1500  sd-resolve
0xffff8880f5bb4c80    465      1  0    2  S  0xffff8880f5bb6180  acpid
0xffff888008c34c80    468      1  0    1  S  0xffff888008c36180  avahi-daemon
0xffff888008c36600    470      1  0    1  S  0xffff888008c37b00  dbus-daemon
0xffff888016f63300    472      1  0    2  S  0xffff888016f64800  NetworkManager
0xffff8880036e8000    534      1  0    2  S  0xffff8880036e9500  gmain
0xffff8880036eb300    535      1  0    0  S  0xffff8880036ec800  gdbus
0xffff8880f48a1980    480      1  0    0  S  0xffff8880f48a2e80  irqbalance
0xffff888020740000    503      1  0    1  S  0xffff888020741500  gmain
0xffff8880f48f8000    485      1  0    0  S  0xffff8880f48f9500  networkd-dispat
0xffff8880f48fb300    488      1  0    2  S  0xffff8880f48fc800  polkitd
0xffff88803ace9980    498      1  0    1  S  0xffff88803aceae80  gmain
0xffff888020743300    528      1  0    2  S  0xffff888020744800  gdbus
0xffff8880f48fe600    490      1  0    1  S  0xffff8880f48ffb00  power-profiles-
0xffff888020746600    509      1  0    2  S  0xffff888020747b00  gmain
0xffff888020741980    527      1  0    1  S  0xffff888020742e80  gdbus
0xffff8880f5860000    491      1  0    1  S  0xffff8880f5861500  rsyslogd
0xffff8880036ee600    540      1  0    3  S  0xffff8880036efb00  in:imuxsock
0xffff888101b54c80    541      1  0    2  S  0xffff888101b56180  in:imklog
0xffff88803ace8000    542      1  0    3  S  0xffff88803ace9500  rs:main Q:Reg
0xffff8880043be600    506      1  0    3  S  0xffff8880043bfb00  snapd
0xffff8880043bb300    510      1  0    0  S  0xffff8880043bc800  snapd
0xffff888016f6cc80    512      1  0    3  S  0xffff888016f6e180  snapd
0xffff888016f6e600    513      1  0    2  S  0xffff888016f6fb00  snapd
0xffff888016f6b300    514      1  0    2  S  0xffff888016f6c800  snapd
0xffff888016f69980    516      1  0    3  S  0xffff888016f6ae80  snapd
0xffff88800bea0000    613      1  0    0  S  0xffff88800bea1500  snapd
0xffff88800bea3300    614      1  0    0  S  0xffff88800bea4800  snapd
0xffff888016e99980    618      1  0    0  S  0xffff888016e9ae80  snapd
0xffff888037413300    620      1  0    1  S  0xffff888037414800  snapd
0xffff88803c09cc80    507      1  0    2  S  0xffff88803c09e180  accounts-daemon
0xffff8880043b8000    550      1  0    3  S  0xffff8880043b9500  gmain
0xffff88803acee600    553      1  0    2  S  0xffff88803acefb00  gdbus
0xffff88803c09e600    508      1  0    1  S  0xffff88803c09fb00  cron
0xffff88803c09b300    517      1  0    2  S  0xffff88803c09c800  switcheroo-cont
0xffff88803ac83300    557      1  0    1  S  0xffff88803ac84800  gmain
0xffff8880f48a4c80    560      1  0    2  S  0xffff8880f48a6180  gdbus
0xffff888003e06600    526      1  0    1  S  0xffff888003e07b00  systemd-logind
0xffff888003e00000    529      1  0    0  S  0xffff888003e01500  udisksd
0xffff8880f5bbcc80    536      1  0    2  S  0xffff8880f5bbe180  gmain
0xffff888016e9cc80    538      1  0    1  S  0xffff888016e9e180  gdbus
0xffff8880011e6600    581      1  0    0  S  0xffff8880011e7b00  probing-thread
0xffff88800bea1980    617      1  0    0  S  0xffff88800bea2e80  cleanup
0xffff8880f48fcc80    530      1  0    2  S  0xffff8880f48fe180  wpa_supplicant
0xffff888016e9e600    543    468  0    2  S  0xffff888016e9fb00  avahi-daemon
0xffff88800be78000    564      1  0    2  S  0xffff88800be79500  cupsd
0xffff88800be79980    566      1  0    1  S  0xffff88800be7ae80  ModemManager
0xffff8880011e3300    602      1  0    3  S  0xffff8880011e4800  gmain
0xffff888016ebcc80    609      1  0    1  S  0xffff888016ebe180  gdbus
0xffff88803ac80000    588      1  0    1  S  0xffff88803ac81500  unattended-upgr
0xffff88801d97cc80    678      1  0    0  S  0xffff88801d97e180  gmain
0xffff88800be96600    589      1  0    1  S  0xffff88800be97b00  xrdp-sesman
0xffff8880011e1980    622      1  0    2  S  0xffff8880011e2e80  gdm3
0xffff88800be91980    639      1  0    2  S  0xffff88800be92e80  gmain
0xffff888016f66600    642      1  0    2  S  0xffff888016f67b00  gdbus
0xffff888016ebe600    630    564  0    1  S  0xffff888016ebfb00  dbus
```
293

```
0xffff888016f60000    633      1   0    3   S   0xffff888016f61500    xrdp
0xffff888059be4c80    635    564   0    1   S   0xffff888059be6180    dbus
0xffff888059be3300    637    564   0    2   S   0xffff888059be4800    dbus
0xffff888016f61980    640    564   0    2   S   0xffff888016f62e80    dbus
0xffff8880f5bb1980    649    564   0    1   S   0xffff8880f5bb2e80    dbus
0xffff888037414c80    650    564   0    1   S   0xffff888037416180    dbus
0xffff8880f48a6600    658      1   0    2   S   0xffff8880f48a7b00    cups-browsed
0xffff88800be93300    684      1   0    1   S   0xffff88800be94800    gmain
0xffff8880f5bb3300    686      1   0    2   S   0xffff8880f5bb4800    gdbus
0xffff88800be90000    666      1   0    3   S   0xffff88800be91500    kerneloops
0xffff888037410000    674      1   0    2   S   0xffff888037411500    kerneloops
0xffff88803acecc80    736    633   0    3   S   0xffff88803acee180    xrdp
0xffff8880043bcc80    737    622   0    2   S   0xffff8880043be180    gdm-session-wor
0xffff88800be7e600    738    622   0    1   S   0xffff88800be7fb00    gmain
0xffff888020416600    740    622   0    1   S   0xffff888020417b00    gdbus
0xffff888016f68000    742      1   0    1   S   0xffff888016f69500    systemd
0xffff88800be7b300    743    742   0    2   S   0xffff88800be7c800    (sd-pam)
0xffff88801d97e600    749    742   0    3   S   0xffff88801d97fb00    pipewire
0xffff888020411980    776    742   0    0   S   0xffff888020412e80    pipewire
0xffff88803aceb300    750    742   0    2   S   0xffff88803acec800    pipewire-media-
0xffff888004124c80    775    742   0    1   S   0xffff888004126180    pipewire-media-
0xffff8880f48ae600    751    742   0    3   S   0xffff8880f48afb00    pulseaudio
0xffff8880f5bd8000    793    742   0    0   S   0xffff8880f5bd9500    null-sink
0xffff8880205a4c80    799    742   0    2   S   0xffff8880205a6180    snapd-glib
0xffff888020414c80    761    737   0    1   S   0xffff888020416180    gdm-x-session
0xffff8880f48ab300    762    737   0    3   S   0xffff8880f48ac800    gmain
0xffff8880f5bdcc80    809    737   0    3   S   0xffff8880f5bde180    gdbus
0xffff8880f5bbb300    763    761   0    3   S   0xffff8880f5bbc800    Xorg
0xffff888059be6600    808    761   0    1   S   0xffff888059be7b00    InputThread
0xffff88801d978000    765      1   0    2   S   0xffff88801d979500    rtkit-daemon
0xffff888020413300    771      1   0    2   S   0xffff888020414800    rtkit-daemon
0xffff888004126600    772      1   0    2   S   0xffff888004127b00    rtkit-daemon
0xffff888037411980    773    742   0    3   S   0xffff888037412e80    dbus-daemon
0xffff888037416600    774    742   0    0   S   0xffff888037417b00    xdg-document-po
0xffff8880011e4c80    777    742   0    1   S   0xffff8880011e6180    gmain
0xffff888016eb8000    778    742   0    2   S   0xffff888016eb9500    gdbus
0xffff8880f48f9980    784    742   0    3   S   0xffff8880f48fae80    fuse mainloop
0xffff8880f585cc80    787    742   0    0   S   0xffff8880f585e180    fuse mainloop
0xffff8880f585e600    788    742   0    0   S   0xffff8880f585fb00    fuse mainloop
0xffff8880011e0000    779    742   0    0   S   0xffff8880011e1500    xdg-permission-
0xffff888016ebb300    780    742   0    0   S   0xffff888016ebc800    gmain
0xffff88800bea4c80    782    742   0    0   S   0xffff88800bea6180    gdbus
0xffff888016e98000    785    784   0    3   S   0xffff888016e99500    fusermount3
0xffff888059be0000    818    761   0    2   S   0xffff888059be1500    dbus-run-sessio
0xffff888008c31980    819    818   0    2   S   0xffff888008c32e80    dbus-daemon
0xffff888020431980    826    818   0    0   S   0xffff888020432e80    gnome-session-b
0xffff8880205a1980    915    818   0    1   S   0xffff8880205a2e80    gmain
0xffff8880205a3300    916    818   0    3   S   0xffff8880205a4800    gdbus
0xffff8880205a6600    917    818   0    0   S   0xffff8880205a7b00    dconf worker
0xffff888020438000    837      1   0    0   S   0xffff888020439500    at-spi-bus-laun
0xffff8880205d6600    839      1   0    2   S   0xffff8880205d7b00    gmain
0xffff8880205d3300    840      1   0    2   S   0xffff8880205d4800    dconf worker
0xffff88802043b300    842      1   0    2   S   0xffff88802043c800    gdbus
0xffff8880205d1980    843    837   0    2   S   0xffff8880205d2e80    dbus-daemon
0xffff8880312dcc80    876    589   0    3   S   0xffff8880312de180    xrdp-sesman
0xffff8880f5bdb300    884      1   0    3   D   0xffff8880f5bdc800    systemd
0xffff8880205de600    892    884   0    1   S   0xffff8880205dfb00    (sd-pam)
0xffff8880205f0000    920    826   0    3   S   0xffff8880205f1500    gnome-shell
0xffff888020434c80    980    826   0    3   S   0xffff888020436180    gmain
```

```
0xffff88803a431980    1019    826    0    2    S    0xffff88803a432e80    gdbus
0xffff88803a43b300    1020    826    0    2    S    0xffff88803a43c800    dconf worker
0xffff888001108000    1052    826    0    2    S    0xffff888001109500    llvmpipe-0
0xffff88800110e600    1053    826    0    0    S    0xffff88800110fb00    llvmpipe-1
0xffff88800110cc80    1054    826    0    1    S    0xffff88800110e180    llvmpipe-2
0xffff88800110b300    1055    826    0    2    S    0xffff88800110c800    llvmpipe-3
0xffff8880f48e3300    1056    826    0    2    S    0xffff8880f48e4800    gnome-shell
0xffff8880312db300    1057    826    0    3    S    0xffff8880312dc800    gnome-shell
0xffff888037734c80    1058    826    0    0    S    0xffff888037736180    gnome-shell
0xffff888037731980    1059    826    0    2    S    0xffff888037732e80    gnome-shell
0xffff88803a438000    1063    826    0    3    S    0xffff88803a439500    gnome-s:disk$0
0xffff88803c258000    1089    826    0    3    S    0xffff88803c259500    JS Helper
0xffff88803c25b300    1090    826    0    2    S    0xffff88803c25c800    JS Helper
0xffff88803c25e600    1091    826    0    2    S    0xffff88803c25fb00    JS Helper
0xffff88803c25cc80    1092    826    0    1    S    0xffff88803c25e180    JS Helper
0xffff88801d979980     923    884    0    3    S    0xffff88801d97ae80    pipewire
0xffff88803a430000     950    884    0    1    S    0xffff88803a431500    pipewire
0xffff888037736600     924    884    0    3    S    0xffff888037737b00    pipewire-media-
0xffff8880205f3300     951    884    0    1    S    0xffff8880205f4800    pipewire-media-
0xffff888037730000     925    884    0    1    S    0xffff888037731500    pulseaudio
0xffff888020430000     994    884    0    2    S    0xffff888020431500    null-sink
0xffff8880f5858000     998    884    0    3    S    0xffff8880f5859500    snapd-glib
0xffff88801d97b300     927    876    0    2    S    0xffff88801d97c800    gnome-session-b
0xffff888024e38000    1164    876    0    1    S    0xffff888024e39500    gmain
0xffff888024e39980    1165    876    0    2    S    0xffff888024e3ae80    gdbus
0xffff888024e3e600    1166    876    0    2    S    0xffff888024e3fb00    dconf worker
0xffff888059be1980     928    876    0    1    S    0xffff888059be2e80    Xorg
0xffff8880f48a8000    1002    876    0    1    S    0xffff8880f48a9500    InputThread
0xffff888001109980     942    884    0    1    S    0xffff88800110ae80    dbus-daemon
0xffff8880f48e1980     962    884    0    3    S    0xffff8880f48e2e80    xdg-document-po
0xffff8880205d9980     968    884    0    0    S    0xffff8880205dae80    gmain
0xffff8880205d8000     969    884    0    3    S    0xffff8880205d9500    gdbus
0xffff8880312d8000     976    884    0    3    S    0xffff8880312d9500    fuse mainloop
0xffff88803a436600     978    884    0    1    S    0xffff88803a437b00    fuse mainloop
0xffff8880312de600     979    884    0    3    S    0xffff8880312dfb00    fuse mainloop
0xffff8880f48e0000     970    884    0    1    S    0xffff8880f48e1500    xdg-permission-
0xffff8880205dcc80     972    884    0    0    S    0xffff8880205de180    gmain
0xffff888008c33300     974    884    0    2    S    0xffff888008c34800    gdbus
0xffff8880205d0000     977    976    0    0    S    0xffff8880205d1500    fusermount3
0xffff88803a433300     995    876    0    2    S    0xffff88803a434800    xrdp-chansrv
0xffff888020439980     999    876    0    3    S    0xffff88802043ae80    xrdp-chansrv
0xffff888037761980    1095    927    0    2    S    0xffff888037762e80    ssh-agent
0xffff888024e3cc80    1137    884    0    3    S    0xffff888024e3e180    at-spi-bus-laun
0xffff888037763300    1138    884    0    3    S    0xffff888037764800    gmain
0xffff888037764c80    1139    884    0    3    S    0xffff888037766180    dconf worker
0xffff88802043e600    1141    884    0    3    S    0xffff88802043fb00    gdbus
0xffff888037760000    1143   1137    0    1    S    0xffff888037761500    dbus-daemon
0xffff88803c263300    1169    884    0    0    S    0xffff88803c264800    gnome-session-c
0xffff888024e3b300    1173    884    0    3    S    0xffff888024e3c800    gmain
0xffff88803c253300    1177    884    0    3    S    0xffff88803c254800    gvfsd
0xffff888020433300    1181    884    0    1    S    0xffff888020434800    gmain
0xffff888008c30000    1182    884    0    2    S    0xffff888008c31500    gdbus
0xffff88803c250000    1186    884    0    0    S    0xffff88803c251500    gvfsd-fuse
0xffff88803a43e600    1189    884    0    1    S    0xffff88803a43fb00    gvfsd-fuse
0xffff88803a439980    1190    884    0    1    S    0xffff88803a43ae80    gvfsd-fuse
0xffff88803a43cc80    1191    884    0    1    S    0xffff88803a43e180    gmain
0xffff88803c261980    1192    884    0    1    S    0xffff88803c262e80    gdbus
0xffff88803c264c80    1193    884    0    2    S    0xffff88803c266180    gvfs-fuse-sub
0xffff88803afe8000    1187    884    0    2    S    0xffff88803afe9500    gnome-session-b
```

```
0xffff88803afeb300    1194    884    0    2    S    0xffff88803afec800    gmain
0xffff88803afe9980    1195    884    0    1    S    0xffff88803afeae80    gdbus
0xffff88802043cc80    1197    884    0    2    S    0xffff88802043e180    dconf worker
0xffff88803c266600    1203    884    0    3    S    0xffff88803c267b00    gnome-keyring-d
0xffff88803c259980    1204    884    0    3    S    0xffff88803c25ae80    gmain
0xffff88803c254c80    1207    884    0    3    S    0xffff88803c256180    gdbus
0xffff888037751980    1210    884    0    3    S    0xffff888037752e80    timer
0xffff88803c206600    1215    884    0    3    D    0xffff88803c207b00    gnome-shell
0xffff88803c200000    1222    884    0    3    S    0xffff88803c201500    gmain
0xffff888037754c80    1224    884    0    1    S    0xffff888037756180    gdbus
0xffff88803c203300    1225    884    0    1    S    0xffff88803c204800    dconf worker
0xffff88803c099980    1229    884    0    2    S    0xffff88803c09ae80    llvmpipe-0
0xffff888037733300    1230    884    0    1    S    0xffff888037734800    llvmpipe-1
0xffff88803ae16600    1231    884    0    1    S    0xffff88803ae17b00    llvmpipe-2
0xffff88803ae10000    1232    884    0    1    S    0xffff88803ae11500    llvmpipe-3
0xffff88803ae13300    1233    884    0    3    S    0xffff88803ae14800    gnome-shell
0xffff8880f2fa3300    1234    884    0    3    S    0xffff8880f2fa4800    gnome-shell
0xffff8880f2fa0000    1235    884    0    3    S    0xffff8880f2fa1500    gnome-shell
0xffff8880f2fa1980    1236    884    0    3    S    0xffff8880f2fa2e80    gnome-shell
0xffff8880f2fa4c80    1237    884    0    2    S    0xffff8880f2fa6180    gnome-s:disk$0
0xffff88803ae04c80    1264    884    0    2    S    0xffff88803ae06180    JS Helper
0xffff88803ae06600    1265    884    0    1    S    0xffff88803ae07b00    JS Helper
0xffff88803ae00000    1266    884    0    1    S    0xffff88803ae01500    JS Helper
0xffff88803ae0cc80    1267    884    0    3    S    0xffff88803ae0e180    JS Helper
0xffff888002594c80    1925    884    0    1    S    0xffff888002596180    pool-gnome-shel
0xffff888002596600    1926    884    0    0    S    0xffff888002597b00    pool-gnome-shel
0xffff888002590000    1927    884    0    0    S    0xffff888002591500    pool-gnome-shel
0xffff888002593300    1928    884    0    0    S    0xffff888002594800    pool-gnome-shel
0xffff88803ae11980    1238    884    0    2    S    0xffff88803ae12e80    snapd-desktop-i
0xffff88803ae0e600    1252    1    0    1    S    0xffff88803ae0fb00    xdg-permission-
0xffff88803ae08000    1253    1    0    1    S    0xffff88803ae09500    gmain
0xffff8880205f6600    1257    1    0    1    S    0xffff8880205f7b00    gdbus
0xffff88803ae03300    1307    1    0    2    S    0xffff88803ae04800    upowerd
0xffff8880f48a9980    1317    1    0    0    S    0xffff8880f48aae80    gmain
0xffff88803ae14c80    1318    1    0    2    S    0xffff88803ae16180    gdbus
0xffff888020436600    1321    1    0    2    D    0xffff888020437b00    geoclue
0xffff8880f100cc80    1333    1    0    3    S    0xffff8880f100e180    packagekitd
0xffff888053856600    1341    1    0    3    S    0xffff888053857b00    gmain
0xffff888053854c80    1342    1    0    3    S    0xffff888053856180    gdbus
0xffff8880f1009980    1336    1    0    2    S    0xffff8880f100ae80    gjs
0xffff8880f2fc0000    1345    1    0    3    S    0xffff8880f2fc1500    JS Helper
0xffff8880f2fc3300    1346    1    0    1    S    0xffff8880f2fc4800    JS Helper
0xffff8880f2fc1980    1347    1    0    0    S    0xffff8880f2fc2e80    JS Helper
0xffff8880f2fc4c80    1348    1    0    0    S    0xffff8880f2fc6180    JS Helper
0xffff888053853300    1361    1    0    1    S    0xffff888053854800    gmain
0xffff888053851980    1363    1    0    1    S    0xffff888053852e80    gdbus
0xffff8880f2facc80    1338    1    0    2    S    0xffff8880f2fae180    at-spi2-registr
0xffff88803ac81980    1349    1    0    2    S    0xffff88803ac82e80    gmain
0xffff8880f2fa6600    1350    1    0    2    S    0xffff8880f2fa7b00    gdbus
0xffff888037753300    1356    826    0    1    S    0xffff888037754800    gsd-sharing
0xffff888016e9b300    1366    826    0    2    S    0xffff888016e9c800    gmain
0xffff888059cfe600    1368    826    0    3    S    0xffff888059cffb00    dconf worker
0xffff888059cf8000    1369    826    0    1    S    0xffff888059cf9500    gdbus
0xffff8880f2fae600    1358    920    0    2    S    0xffff8880f2fafb00    ibus-daemon
0xffff8880f0c28000    1394    920    0    3    S    0xffff8880f0c29500    gmain
0xffff8880f0c2b300    1395    920    0    2    S    0xffff8880f0c2c800    gdbus
0xffff8880f100b300    1359    826    0    1    S    0xffff8880f100c800    gsd-wacom
0xffff88805385cc80    1382    826    0    3    S    0xffff88805385e180    gmain
0xffff888053861980    1386    826    0    0    S    0xffff888053862e80    gdbus
```

```
0xffff888003e03300    1362     826   0   2   S   0xffff888003e04800   gsd-color
0xffff88800c918000    1431     826   0   3   S   0xffff88800c919500   gmain
0xffff88800c91b300    1432     826   0   3   S   0xffff88800c91c800   dconf worker
0xffff8880f0c4cc80    1438     826   0   1   S   0xffff8880f0c4e180   gdbus
0xffff888059cfcc80    1367     826   0   0   S   0xffff888059cfe180   gsd-keyboard
0xffff888059d2e600    1426     826   0   3   S   0xffff888059d2fb00   gmain
0xffff888059d28000    1427     826   0   3   S   0xffff888059d29500   dconf worker
0xffff8880f0dae600    1434     826   0   3   S   0xffff8880f0dafb00   gdbus
0xffff888059cfb300    1370     826   0   0   S   0xffff888059cfc800   gsd-print-notif
0xffff8880f0c2e600    1379     826   0   1   S   0xffff8880f0c2fb00   gmain
0xffff888059d09980    1380     826   0   0   S   0xffff888059d0ae80   gdbus
0xffff888059cf9980    1371     826   0   0   S   0xffff888059cfae80   gsd-rfkill
0xffff88805385b300    1374     826   0   1   S   0xffff88805385c800   gmain
0xffff888053859980    1375     826   0   0   S   0xffff88805385ae80   gdbus
0xffff888037756600    1372     826   0   1   S   0xffff888037757b00   gsd-smartcard
0xffff8880205a0000    1376     826   0   2   S   0xffff8880205a1500   gmain
0xffff88803afee600    1377     826   0   1   S   0xffff88803afefb00   gdbus
0xffff8880f0dab300    1418     826   0   2   S   0xffff8880f0dac800   dconf worker
0xffff888059d08000    1373     826   0   3   S   0xffff888059d09500   gsd-datetime
0xffff888059d1b300    1396     826   0   2   S   0xffff888059d1c800   gmain
0xffff8880f5bb8000    1400     826   0   3   S   0xffff8880f5bb9500   gdbus
0xffff8880f0c40000    1407     826   0   2   S   0xffff8880f0c41500   dconf worker
0xffff888059d0b300    1378     826   0   3   S   0xffff888059d0c800   gsd-media-keys
0xffff8880f0db4c80    1441     826   0   1   S   0xffff8880f0db6180   gmain
0xffff8880f0db6600    1442     826   0   3   S   0xffff8880f0db7b00   gdbus
0xffff8880f0c48000    1450     826   0   2   S   0xffff8880f0c49500   dconf worker
0xffff888059d0cc80    1381     826   0   3   S   0xffff888059d0e180   gsd-screensaver
0xffff888053864c80    1387     826   0   2   S   0xffff888053866180   gmain
0xffff888053860000    1389     826   0   3   S   0xffff888053861500   gdbus
0xffff888059d0e600    1385     826   0   3   S   0xffff888059d0fb00   gsd-sound
0xffff888053863300    1391     826   0   3   S   0xffff888053864800   gmain
0xffff8880f2fc6600    1393     826   0   3   S   0xffff8880f2fc7b00   gdbus
0xffff8880f0da9980    1419     826   0   3   S   0xffff8880f0daae80   dconf worker
0xffff88800be94c80    1390     826   0   3   S   0xffff88800be96180   gsd-a11y-settin
0xffff888059d19980    1399     826   0   3   S   0xffff888059d1ae80   gmain
0xffff888059d1cc80    1401     826   0   3   S   0xffff888059d1e180   gdbus
0xffff888059d24c80    1416     826   0   2   S   0xffff888059d26180   dconf worker
0xffff8880f0da4c80    1392     826   0   1   S   0xffff8880f0da6180   gsd-housekeepin
0xffff8880f0c46600    1406     826   0   3   S   0xffff8880f0c47b00   gmain
0xffff888059d21980    1412     826   0   1   S   0xffff888059d22e80   gdbus
0xffff88800c920000    1443     826   0   2   S   0xffff88800c921500   dconf worker
0xffff8880f0c2cc80    1398       1   0   2   S   0xffff8880f0c2e180   gvfsd
0xffff88800c91cc80    1429       1   0   3   S   0xffff88800c91e180   gmain
0xffff8880f0c44c80    1437       1   0   2   S   0xffff8880f0c46180   gdbus
0xffff8880f0da6600    1402     826   0   2   S   0xffff8880f0da7b00   gsd-power
0xffff88800c928000    1464     826   0   3   S   0xffff88800c929500   gmain
0xffff88800c930000    1467     826   0   0   S   0xffff88800c931500   gdbus
0xffff88800c934c80    1477     826   0   2   S   0xffff88800c936180   dconf worker
0xffff888059d2cc80    1428       1   0   2   S   0xffff888059d2e180   gsd-printer
0xffff888059d29980    1436       1   0   2   S   0xffff888059d2ae80   gmain
0xffff8880f0c4e600    1439       1   0   2   S   0xffff8880f0c4fb00   gdbus
0xffff88800c921980    1446    1358   0   3   S   0xffff88800c922e80   ibus-memconf
0xffff8880f0db9980    1449    1358   0   2   S   0xffff8880f0dbae80   gmain
0xffff8880f0c54c80    1456    1358   0   3   S   0xffff8880f0c56180   gdbus
0xffff88800c933300    1468       1   0   3   S   0xffff88800c934800   ibus-portal
0xffff8880f0c50000    1472       1   0   3   S   0xffff8880f0c51500   gmain
0xffff8880f0c51980    1475       1   0   3   S   0xffff8880f0c52e80   gdbus
0xffff8880f0c56600    1469       1   0   3   S   0xffff8880f0c57b00   colord
0xffff88800ca83300    1479       1   0   2   S   0xffff88800ca84800   gmain
```

```
0xffff88800ca84c80    1481       1   0    3   S   0xffff88800ca86180   gdbus
0xffff8880f0db3300    1484     884   0    3   S   0xffff8880f0db4800   gnome-shell-cal
0xffff88800ca86600    1485     884   0    2   S   0xffff88800ca87b00   gmain
0xffff88803ae19980    1487     884   0    1   S   0xffff88803ae1ae80   gdbus
0xffff88803ae1e600    1488     884   0    3   S   0xffff88803ae1fb00   dconf worker
0xffff88803ae1b300    1489     884   0    3   S   0xffff88803ae1c800   gnome-shell-cal
0xffff88800c92e600    1520     884   0    0   S   0xffff88800c92fb00   pool-gnome-shel
0xffff88803ae18000    1490     884   0    2   S   0xffff88803ae19500   evolution-sourc
0xffff88803ae1cc80    1493     884   0    1   S   0xffff88803ae1e180   gmain
0xffff8880f0db8000    1494     884   0    2   S   0xffff8880f0db9500   dconf worker
0xffff888020744c80    1495     884   0    2   S   0xffff888020746180   gdbus
0xffff888059d20000    1501     884   0    2   S   0xffff888059d21500   goa-daemon
0xffff8880f0dd1980    1534     884   0    3   S   0xffff8880f0dd2e80   gmain
0xffff88800ca91980    1540     884   0    2   S   0xffff88800ca92e80   gdbus
0xffff8880f0dc3300    1543     884   0    1   S   0xffff8880f0dc4800   dconf worker
0xffff8880f2fa8000    1506       1   0    3   S   0xffff8880f2fa9500   gjs
0xffff8880f0da3300    1509       1   0    2   S   0xffff8880f0da4800   JS Helper
0xffff88800c939980    1510       1   0    0   S   0xffff88800c93ae80   JS Helper
0xffff88800c93cc80    1511       1   0    0   S   0xffff88800c93e180   JS Helper
0xffff88800c93e600    1512       1   0    2   S   0xffff88800c93fb00   JS Helper
0xffff88800c92cc80    1527       1   0    3   S   0xffff88800c92e180   gmain
0xffff88800c91e600    1528       1   0    2   S   0xffff88800c91fb00   gdbus
0xffff88800ca94c80    1513    1358   0    2   S   0xffff88800ca96180   ibus-engine-sim
0xffff88800ca96600    1515    1358   0    2   S   0xffff88800ca97b00   gmain
0xffff88800ca90000    1516    1358   0    2   S   0xffff88800ca91500   gdbus
0xffff8880f11d4c80    1514     884   0    3   S   0xffff8880f11d6180   gvfs-udisks2-vo
0xffff88800c938000    1517     884   0    1   S   0xffff88800c939500   gmain
0xffff88800c924c80    1519     884   0    2   S   0xffff88800c926180   gdbus
0xffff88800c936600    1522     884   0    3   S   0xffff88800c937b00   dconf worker
0xffff8880f2fa9980    1521     884   0    2   S   0xffff8880f2faae80   evolution-calen
0xffff88803c098000    1525     884   0    1   S   0xffff88803c099500   gmain
0xffff88803a434c80    1529     884   0    2   S   0xffff88803a436180   gdbus
0xffff88800143cc80    1558     884   0    3   S   0xffff88800143e180   dconf worker
0xffff88800143e600    1559     884   0    2   S   0xffff88800143fb00   evolution-calen
0xffff888001438000    1565     884   0    2   S   0xffff888001439500   pool-evolution-
0xffff8880f0c29980    1570     884   0    2   S   0xffff8880f0c2ae80   pool-evolution-
0xffff8880f0dbb300    1571     884   0    2   S   0xffff8880f0dbc800   evolution-calen
0xffff888001714c80    1576     884   0    0   S   0xffff888001716180   pool-evolution-
0xffff8880f11d6600    1533     884   0    1   S   0xffff8880f11d7b00   gvfs-afc-volume
0xffff8880f0dd4c80    1535     884   0    3   S   0xffff8880f0dd6180   gvfs-afc-volume
0xffff8880f0dd6600    1536     884   0    0   S   0xffff8880f0dd7b00   gmain
0xffff88800ca93300    1539     884   0    1   S   0xffff88800ca94800   gdbus
0xffff8880f0c53300    1546     884   0    0   S   0xffff8880f0c54800   goa-identity-se
0xffff88800ca9e600    1554     884   0    2   S   0xffff88800ca9fb00   gmain
0xffff88800ca9b300    1556     884   0    3   S   0xffff88800ca9c800   gdbus
0xffff888001429980    1547     884   0    2   S   0xffff888001442ae80  gvfs-gphoto2-vo
0xffff88803c204c80    1548     884   0    1   S   0xffff88803c206180   gmain
0xffff88800ca9cc80    1550     884   0    3   S   0xffff88800ca9e180   gdbus
0xffff8880f11d0000    1557     884   0    3   S   0xffff8880f11d1500   gvfs-goa-volume
0xffff8880f0dc4c80    1563     884   0    3   S   0xffff8880f0dc6180   gmain
0xffff88805385e600    1564     884   0    2   S   0xffff88805385fb00   gdbus
0xffff8880f11e4c80    1574     884   0    3   S   0xffff8880f11e6180   dconf-service
0xffff8880205f4c80    1579     884   0    1   S   0xffff8880205f6180   gmain
0xffff888001711980    1580     884   0    3   S   0xffff888001712e80   gdbus
0xffff8880f11e6600    1577     884   0    2   S   0xffff8880f11e7b00   evolution-addre
0xffff888001441980    1588     884   0    0   S   0xffff888001442e80   gmain
0xffff888001444c80    1589     884   0    3   S   0xffff888001446180   gdbus
0xffff8880f11e3300    1591     884   0    0   S   0xffff8880f11e4800   dconf worker
0xffff8880f11e1980    1592     884   0    2   S   0xffff8880f11e2e80   evolution-addre
```

```
0xffff88800145b300    1596     884   0    2   S   0xffff88800145c800   pool-evolution-
0xffff8880f11e0000    1578     884   0    1   S   0xffff8880f11e1500   gvfs-mtp-volume
0xffff88800142b300    1585     884   0    0   S   0xffff88800142c800   gmain
0xffff888001443300    1587     884   0    1   S   0xffff888001444800   gdbus
0xffff888001716600    1616    1177   0    0   S   0xffff888001717b00   gvfsd-trash
0xffff888001710000    1617    1177   0    0   S   0xffff888001711500   gmain
0xffff88800c93b300    1618    1177   0    3   S   0xffff88800c93c800   gdbus
0xffff88800ca8b300    1627     884   0    2   S   0xffff88800ca8c800   gjs
0xffff888001458000    1629     884   0    3   S   0xffff888001459500   gmain
0xffff8880f0c4b300    1635     884   0    2   S   0xffff8880f0c4c800   gdbus
0xffff888001428000    1636     884   0    1   S   0xffff888001429500   JS Helper
0xffff888059d18000    1637     884   0    3   S   0xffff888059d19500   JS Helper
0xffff888001e76600    1638     884   0    1   S   0xffff888001e77b00   JS Helper
0xffff888001e70000    1639     884   0    3   S   0xffff888001e71500   JS Helper
0xffff88803ac86600    1631     884   0    1   S   0xffff88803ac87b00   at-spi2-registr
0xffff88800caa1980    1640     884   0    0   S   0xffff88800caa2e80   gmain
0xffff88800caa0000    1641     884   0    1   S   0xffff88800caa1500   gdbus
0xffff88800c92b300    1644     884   0    2   S   0xffff88800c92c800   sh
0xffff888037750000    1645     884   0    2   S   0xffff888037751500   gsd-a11y-settin
0xffff888001e71980    1651     884   0    1   S   0xffff888001e72e80   gmain
0xffff888001e74c80    1655     884   0    1   S   0xffff888001e76180   gdbus
0xffff888001e78000    1666     884   0    2   S   0xffff888001e79500   dconf worker
0xffff88800caa3300    1647    1644   0    1   S   0xffff88800caa4800   ibus-daemon
0xffff88800caa4c80    1649    1644   0    2   S   0xffff88800caa6180   gmain
0xffff888001459980    1656    1644   0    2   S   0xffff88800145ae80   gdbus
0xffff888001c4e600    1648     884   0    1   S   0xffff888001c4fb00   gsd-color
0xffff888001c96600    1673     884   0    2   S   0xffff888001c97b00   gmain
0xffff888001c90000    1674     884   0    2   S   0xffff888001c91500   dconf worker
0xffff888001c9cc80    1675     884   0    2   S   0xffff888001c9e180   gdbus
0xffff888001733300    1652     884   0    0   S   0xffff888001734800   gsd-datetime
0xffff88800ca8cc80    1672     884   0    0   S   0xffff88800ca8e180   gmain
0xffff88800ca89980    1678     884   0    0   S   0xffff88800ca8ae80   gdbus
0xffff8880f0dbcc80    1691     884   0    0   S   0xffff8880f0dbe180   dconf worker
0xffff888001731980    1653     884   0    2   S   0xffff888001732e80   gsd-housekeepin
0xffff88800caa6600    1663     884   0    2   S   0xffff88800caa7b00   gmain
0xffff888001c91980    1665     884   0    2   S   0xffff888001c92e80   gdbus
0xffff888001c94c80    1669     884   0    2   S   0xffff888001c96180   dconf worker
0xffff888001e7b300    1658     884   0    1   S   0xffff888001e7c800   gsd-keyboard
0xffff888001741980    1693     884   0    3   S   0xffff888001742e80   gmain
0xffff888001744c80    1696     884   0    0   S   0xffff888001746180   dconf worker
0xffff888001740000    1700     884   0    1   S   0xffff888001741500   gdbus
0xffff888001e79980    1660     884   0    2   S   0xffff888001e7ae80   gsd-media-keys
0xffff888001c66600    1705     884   0    0   S   0xffff888001c67b00   gmain
0xffff888001c74c80    1708     884   0    0   S   0xffff888001c76180   gdbus
0xffff888002584c80    1778     884   0    0   S   0xffff888002586180   dconf worker
0xffff888001e7cc80    1662     884   0    3   S   0xffff888001e7e180   gsd-power
0xffff888001c60000    1706     884   0    0   S   0xffff888001c61500   gmain
0xffff888001c76600    1711     884   0    3   S   0xffff888001c77b00   gdbus
0xffff888002581980    1773     884   0    1   S   0xffff888002582e80   dconf worker
0xffff888001e7e600    1668     884   0    2   S   0xffff888001e7fb00   gsd-print-notif
0xffff888001c9e600    1683     884   0    2   S   0xffff888001c9fb00   gmain
0xffff888001c98000    1684     884   0    2   S   0xffff888001c99500   gdbus
0xffff888001e8e600    1670     884   0    2   S   0xffff888001e8fb00   gsd-rfkill
0xffff88803ac84c80    1686     884   0    2   S   0xffff88803ac86180   gmain
0xffff888001746600    1699     884   0    2   S   0xffff888001747b00   gdbus
0xffff888001e88000    1671     884   0    1   S   0xffff888001e89500   gsd-screensaver
0xffff888001e8b300    1676     884   0    1   S   0xffff888001e8c800   gmain
0xffff888001ea4c80    1681     884   0    1   S   0xffff888001ea6180   gdbus
0xffff888001ea3300    1679     884   0    1   S   0xffff888001ea4800   gsd-sharing
```

```
0xffff888001ea0000    1694    884    0    1    S    0xffff888001ea1500    gmain
0xffff8880022d9980    1704    884    0    1    S    0xffff8880022dae80    dconf worker
0xffff8880022de600    1713    884    0    1    S    0xffff8880022dfb00    gdbus
0xffff888001ea1980    1680    884    0    0    S    0xffff888001ea2e80    gsd-smartcard
0xffff88800ca8e600    1685    884    0    3    S    0xffff88800ca8fb00    gmain
0xffff888001c64c80    1695    884    0    1    S    0xffff888001c66180    gdbus
0xffff888001c73300    1715    884    0    2    S    0xffff888001c74800    dconf worker
0xffff888001ea6600    1682    884    0    2    S    0xffff888001ea7b00    gsd-sound
0xffff888001ca4c80    1701    884    0    2    S    0xffff888001ca6180    gmain
0xffff888001ca0000    1703    884    0    3    S    0xffff888001ca1500    gdbus
0xffff8880024ee600    1770    884    0    3    S    0xffff8880024efb00    dconf worker
0xffff8880022d8000    1698    884    0    3    S    0xffff8880022d9500    gsd-wacom
0xffff888001440000    1726    884    0    0    S    0xffff888001441500    gmain
0xffff88800257e600    1749    884    0    1    S    0xffff88800257fb00    gdbus
0xffff8880022db300    1702    884    0    2    S    0xffff8880022dc800    gsd-xsettings
0xffff88803ae01980    1727    884    0    1    S    0xffff88803ae02e80    gmain
0xffff8880022f6600    1731    884    0    3    S    0xffff8880022f7b00    gdbus
0xffff888002301980    1783    884    0    1    S    0xffff888002302e80    dconf worker
0xffff888001743300    1710    884    0    2    S    0xffff888001744800    gsd-printer
0xffff888001ca8000    1750    884    0    1    S    0xffff888001ca9500    gmain
0xffff888001cacc80    1759    884    0    2    S    0xffff888001cae180    gdbus
0xffff8880022dcc80    1712    884    0    3    S    0xffff8880022de180    xdg-desktop-por
0xffff888001c71980    1718    884    0    1    S    0xffff888001c72e80    gmain
0xffff888002574c80    1723    884    0    2    S    0xffff888002576180    gdbus
0xffff888002578000    1843    884    0    3    S    0xffff888002579500    dconf worker
0xffff8880f11d3300    1880    884    0    0    S    0xffff8880f11d4800    xdg-desktop-por
0xffff8880024d1980    1881    884    0    3    S    0xffff8880024d2e80    xdg-desktop-por
0xffff888001439980    1719    1187   0    2    S    0xffff88800143ae80    gsd-disk-utilit
0xffff888001cab300    1757    1187   0    2    S    0xffff888001cac800    gmain
0xffff888001cae600    1761    1187   0    3    S    0xffff888001cafb00    gdbus
0xffff888002573300    1721    1647   0    1    S    0xffff888002574800    ibus-memconf
0xffff888002579980    1728    1647   0    1    S    0xffff88800257ae80    gmain
0xffff88800272b300    1743    1647   0    1    S    0xffff88800272c800    gdbus
0xffff888002571980    1722    1647   0    2    S    0xffff888002572e80    ibus-extension-
0xffff88800272cc80    1763    1647   0    1    S    0xffff88800272e180    gmain
0xffff88800272e600    1764    1647   0    0    S    0xffff88800272fb00    gdbus
0xffff888001c9b300    1795    1647   0    1    S    0xffff888001c9c800    dconf worker
0xffff8880022f4c80    1730    884    0    3    S    0xffff8880022f6180    xdg-desktop-por
0xffff88800258b300    1796    884    0    1    S    0xffff88800258c800    llvmpipe-0
0xffff888002589980    1797    884    0    2    S    0xffff88800258ae80    llvmpipe-1
0xffff888009594c80    1798    884    0    0    S    0xffff888009596180    llvmpipe-2
0xffff888009596600    1799    884    0    1    S    0xffff888009597b00    llvmpipe-3
0xffff888009590000    1800    884    0    1    S    0xffff888009591500    xdg-desktop-por
0xffff888009593300    1801    884    0    0    S    0xffff888009594800    xdg-desktop-por
0xffff888009591980    1802    884    0    0    S    0xffff888009592e80    xdg-desktop-por
0xffff88800959b300    1803    884    0    2    S    0xffff88800959c800    xdg-desktop-por
0xffff888009599980    1804    884    0    1    S    0xffff88800959ae80    xdg-des:disk$0
0xffff88800959e600    1809    884    0    0    S    0xffff88800959fb00    gmain
0xffff8880024e9980    1810    884    0    2    S    0xffff8880024eae80    gdbus
0xffff888002580000    1814    884    0    2    S    0xffff888002581500    dconf worker
0xffff8880022f0000    1733    884    0    1    S    0xffff8880022f1500    ibus-x11
0xffff888002728000    1774    884    0    0    S    0xffff888002729500    gmain
0xffff888002306600    1785    884    0    2    S    0xffff888002307b00    gdbus
0xffff8880024d4c80    1740    884    0    3    S    0xffff8880024d6180    ibus-portal
0xffff8880024d0000    1744    884    0    3    S    0xffff8880024d1500    gmain
0xffff8880024e0000    1747    884    0    3    S    0xffff8880024e1500    gdbus
0xffff8880024e1980    1762    1187   0    1    S    0xffff8880024e2e80    evolution-alarm
0xffff8880027a8000    1812    1187   0    0    S    0xffff8880027a9500    gmain
0xffff8880027a9980    1813    1187   0    2    S    0xffff8880027aae80    gdbus
```

```
0xffff888002303300      1820    1187    0    2    S    0xffff888002304800    dconf worker
0xffff888002729980      1821    1187    0    2    S    0xffff88800272ae80    evolution-alarm
0xffff888001736600      1848    1187    0    2    S    0xffff888001737b00    evolution-alarm
0xffff888002586600      1816     884    0    1    S    0xffff888002587b00    gjs
0xffff888002583300      1818     884    0    0    S    0xffff888002584800    gmain
0xffff8880024e6600      1819     884    0    2    S    0xffff8880024e7b00    gdbus
0xffff8880022f3300      1822     884    0    2    S    0xffff8880022f4800    JS Helper
0xffff8880022f1980      1823     884    0    0    S    0xffff8880022f2e80    JS Helper
0xffff888002741980      1824     884    0    3    S    0xffff888002742e80    JS Helper
0xffff888002744c80      1825     884    0    0    S    0xffff888002746180    JS Helper
0xffff8880024f4c80      1827    1647    0    2    S    0xffff8880024f6180    ibus-engine-sim
0xffff8880024f6600      1830    1647    0    2    S    0xffff8880024f7b00    gmain
0xffff8880027ae600      1840    1647    0    3    S    0xffff8880027afb00    gdbus
0xffff888002743300      1836     884    0    1    S    0xffff888002744800    tracker-miner-f
0xffff888001c99980      1844     884    0    1    S    0xffff888001c9ae80    gmain
0xffff888001734c80      1845     884    0    2    S    0xffff888001736180    gdbus
0xffff8880027b6600      1846     884    0    2    S    0xffff8880027b7b00    dconf worker
0xffff8880027b0000      1847     884    0    2    S    0xffff8880027b1500    pool-tracker-mi
0xffff88800275cc80      1879     884    0    1    S    0xffff88800275e180    Monitor thread
0xffff88803c260000      1853     884    0    2    S    0xffff88803c261500    xdg-desktop-por
0xffff8880027acc80      1865     884    0    1    S    0xffff8880027ae180    gmain
0xffff88800c929980      1866     884    0    3    S    0xffff88800c92ae80    gdbus
0xffff888001ca3300      1878     884    0    2    S    0xffff888001ca4800    dconf worker
0xffff8880024f1980      1889    1215    0    3    S    0xffff8880024f2e80    gjs
0xffff888001c63300      1891    1215    0    2    S    0xffff888001c64800    gmain
0xffff888001713300      1892    1215    0    3    S    0xffff888001714800    gdbus
0xffff88800a8d9980      1893    1215    0    1    S    0xffff88800a8dae80    JS Helper
0xffff88800a8dcc80      1894    1215    0    1    S    0xffff88800a8de180    JS Helper
0xffff88800a8de600      1895    1215    0    2    S    0xffff88800a8dfb00    JS Helper
0xffff88800a8d8000      1896    1215    0    2    S    0xffff88800a8d9500    JS Helper
0xffff88800a8db300      1897    1215    0    1    S    0xffff88800a8dc800    dconf worker
0xffff888002759980      1904     884    0    2    S    0xffff88800275ae80    gvfsd-metadata
0xffff88800257cc80      1905     884    0    1    S    0xffff88800257e180    gmain
0xffff888002758000      1906     884    0    1    S    0xffff888002759500    gdbus
0xffff8880024f3300      1934     884    0    2    S    0xffff8880024f4800    gnome-terminal-
0xffff88800a8c8000      1935     884    0    3    S    0xffff88800a8c9500    gmain
0xffff88800a8cb300      1936     884    0    3    S    0xffff88800a8cc800    gdbus
0xffff88800a8c9980      1937     884    0    2    S    0xffff88800a8cae80    dconf worker
0xffff88800a8ccc80      1955     884    0    3    S    0xffff88800a8ce180    threaded-ml
0xffff8880f5bb6600      1956    1934    0    3    S    0xffff8880f5bb7b00    bash
0xffff88800be7cc80      2012    1956    0    0    S    0xffff88800be7e180    sudo
0xffff888009814c80      2013    2012    0    3    S    0xffff888009816180    sudo
0xffff8880205d4c80      2014    2013    1    0    R    0xffff8880205d6180    *echo
0xffff88800275e600      2017    1187    0    3    D    0xffff88800275fb00    sh
0xffff88800143b300      2019    1187    0    3    D    0xffff88800143c800    sh
0xffff8880f0dc0000      2021    1187    0    2    D    0xffff8880f0dc1500    sh
```

Note: the **monitor** GDB command is the command you can use to execute any KDB commands, for example:

```
(gdb) monitor btp 1956
tack traceback for pid 1956
0xffff8880f5bb6600      1956    1934    0    3    S    0xffff8880f5bb7b00    bash
Call Trace:
 <TASK>
 __schedule+0x3c7/0x1610
 ? __mod_lruvec_state+0x37/0x50
 schedule+0x5d/0xf0
 do_wait+0x1c1/0x300
```

```
 kernel_wait4+0xaf/0x150
 ? __pfx_child_wait_callback+0x10/0x10
 __do_sys_wait4+0x89/0xa0
 ? syscall_exit_to_user_mode+0x27/0x40
 ? do_syscall_64+0x63/0x80
 ? sigprocmask+0xb8/0xe0
 ? exit_to_user_mode_prepare+0x49/0x200
 __x64_sys_wait4+0x1c/0x30
 x64_sys_call+0x1d4c/0x1ff0
 do_syscall_64+0x56/0x80
 ? exc_page_fault+0x80/0x160
 entry_SYSCALL_64_after_hwframe+0x73/0xdd
RIP: 0033:0x7eb2632ea3ea
RSP: 002b:00007ffe595114e8 EFLAGS: 00000246 ORIG_RAX: 000000000000003d
RAX: ffffffffffffffda RBX: 00000000000007dc RCX: 00007eb2632ea3ea
RDX: 000000000000000a RSI: 00007ffe59511510 RDI: 00000000ffffffff
RBP: 00005ad85f41bd68 R08: 00005ad8600e3af0 R09: 0000000000000001
R10: 0000000000000000 R11: 0000000000000246 R12: 000000000000000a
R13: 00005ad8600d80d0 R14: 00007ffe59511510 R15: 0000000000000001
 </TASK>
```

30.   We can print any data as we did in user space debugging exercises:

```
(gdb) p -pretty on -- *(struct task_struct *)0xffff8880f5bb6600
$2 = {
  thread_info = {
    flags = 2,
    syscall_work = 0,
    status = 0,
    cpu = 3
  },
  __state = 1,
  stack = 0xffffc90005044000,
  usage = {
    refs = {
      counter = 1
    }
  },
  flags = 4194304,
  ptrace = 0,
  on_cpu = 0,
  wake_entry = {
    llist = {
      next = 0x0 <fixed_percpu_data>
    },
    {
      u_flags = 48,
      a_flags = {
        counter = 48
      }
    },
    src = 0,
    dst = 0
  },
  wakee_flips = 0,
  wakee_flip_decay_ts = 4294911334,
  last_wakee = 0xffff8880035d8000,
  recent_used_cpu = 1,
```

```
    wake_cpu = 3,
    on_rq = 0,
    prio = 120,
    static_prio = 120,
    normal_prio = 120,
--Type <RET> for more, q to quit, c to continue without paging--c
    rt_priority = 0,
    se = {
      load = {
        weight = 1048576,
        inv_weight = 4194304
      },
      run_node = {
        __rb_parent_color = 1,
        rb_right = 0x0 <fixed_percpu_data>,
        rb_left = 0x0 <fixed_percpu_data>
      },
      group_node = {
        next = 0xffff8880f5bb66a8,
        prev = 0xffff8880f5bb66a8
      },
      on_rq = 0,
      exec_start = 76246782200,
      sum_exec_runtime = 39444900,
      vruntime = 85657887,
      prev_sum_exec_runtime = 39011900,
      nr_migrations = 15,
      depth = 1,
      parent = 0xffff8880f0d3ca00,
      cfs_rq = 0xffff88800a1af200,
      my_q = 0x0 <fixed_percpu_data>,
      runnable_weight = 0,
      avg = {
        last_update_time = 76246781952,
        load_sum = 423,
        runnable_sum = 433152,
        util_sum = 433152,
        period_contrib = 612,
        load_avg = 0,
        runnable_avg = 0,
        util_avg = 0,
        util_est = {
          enqueued = 0,
          ewma = 8
        }
      }
    },
    rt = {
      run_list = {
        next = 0xffff8880f5bb6780,
        prev = 0xffff8880f5bb6780
      },
      timeout = 0,
      watchdog_stamp = 0,
      time_slice = 25,
      on_rq = 0,
      on_list = 0,
      back = 0x0 <fixed_percpu_data>
    },
```

```
dl = {
  rb_node = {
    __rb_parent_color = 18446612686192732080,
    rb_right = 0x0 <fixed_percpu_data>,
    rb_left = 0x0 <fixed_percpu_data>
  },
  dl_runtime = 0,
  dl_deadline = 0,
  dl_period = 0,
  dl_bw = 0,
  dl_density = 0,
  runtime = 0,
  deadline = 0,
  flags = 0,
  dl_throttled = 0,
  dl_yielded = 0,
  dl_non_contending = 0,
  dl_overrun = 0,
  dl_timer = {
    node = {
      node = {
        __rb_parent_color = 18446612686192732168,
        rb_right = 0x0 <fixed_percpu_data>,
        rb_left = 0x0 <fixed_percpu_data>
      },
      expires = 0
    },
    _softexpires = 0,
    function = 0xffffffff81147550 <dl_task_timer>,
    base = 0xffff888103d22580,
    state = 0 '\000',
    is_rel = 0 '\000',
    is_soft = 0 '\000',
    is_hard = 1 '\001'
  },
  inactive_timer = {
    node = {
      node = {
        __rb_parent_color = 18446612686192732232,
        rb_right = 0x0 <fixed_percpu_data>,
        rb_left = 0x0 <fixed_percpu_data>
      },
      expires = 0
    },
    _softexpires = 0,
    function = 0xffffffff81142470 <inactive_task_timer>,
    base = 0xffff888103d22580,
    state = 0 '\000',
    is_rel = 0 '\000',
    is_soft = 0 '\000',
    is_hard = 1 '\001'
  },
  pi_se = 0xffff8880f5bb67b0
},
sched_class = 0xffffffff827f10c0 <fair_sched_class>,
core_node = {
  __rb_parent_color = 18446612686192732312,
  rb_right = 0x0 <fixed_percpu_data>,
  rb_left = 0x0 <fixed_percpu_data>
```

```
    },
    core_cookie = 0,
    core_occupation = 0,
    sched_task_group = 0xffff888102b58500,
    uclamp_req = {{
        value = 0,
        bucket_id = 0,
        active = 0,
        user_defined = 0
      }, {
        value = 1024,
        bucket_id = 4,
        active = 0,
        user_defined = 0
      }},
    uclamp = {{
        value = 0,
        bucket_id = 0,
        active = 0,
        user_defined = 0
      }, {
        value = 0,
        bucket_id = 0,
        active = 0,
        user_defined = 0
      }},
    stats = {
      wait_start = 0,
      wait_max = 0,
      wait_count = 0,
      wait_sum = 0,
      iowait_count = 0,
      iowait_sum = 0,
      sleep_start = 0,
      sleep_max = 0,
      sum_sleep_runtime = 0,
      block_start = 0,
      block_max = 0,
      sum_block_runtime = 0,
      exec_max = 0,
      slice_max = 0,
      nr_migrations_cold = 0,
      nr_failed_migrations_affine = 0,
      nr_failed_migrations_running = 0,
      nr_failed_migrations_hot = 0,
      nr_forced_migrations = 0,
      nr_wakeups = 0,
      nr_wakeups_sync = 0,
      nr_wakeups_migrate = 0,
      nr_wakeups_local = 0,
      nr_wakeups_remote = 0,
      nr_wakeups_affine = 0,
      nr_wakeups_affine_attempts = 0,
      nr_wakeups_passive = 0,
      nr_wakeups_idle = 0,
      core_forceidle_sum = 0
    },
    preempt_notifiers = {
      first = 0x0 <fixed_percpu_data>
```

```
  },
  btrace_seq = 0,
  policy = 0,
  nr_cpus_allowed = 4,
  cpus_ptr = 0xffff8880f5bb6a28,
  user_cpus_ptr = 0x0 <fixed_percpu_data>,
  cpus_mask = {
    bits = {15, 18446744073709551615 <repeats 127 times>}
  },
  migration_pending = 0x0 <fixed_percpu_data>,
  migration_disabled = 0,
  migration_flags = 0,
  trc_reader_nesting = 0,
  trc_ipi_to_cpu = -1,
  trc_reader_special = {
    b = {
      blocked = 0 '\000',
      need_qs = 2 '\002',
      exp_hint = 0 '\000',
      need_mb = 0 '\000'
    },
    s = 512
  },
  trc_holdout_list = {
    next = 0xffff8880f5bb6e40,
    prev = 0xffff8880f5bb6e40
  },
  trc_blkd_node = {
    next = 0xffff8880f5bb6e50,
    prev = 0xffff8880f5bb6e50
  },
  trc_blkd_cpu = 0,
  sched_info = {
    pcount = 112,
    run_delay = 3255000,
    last_arrival = 76246349200,
    last_queued = 0
  },
  tasks = {
    next = 0xffff888001730888,
    prev = 0xffff8880024f3b88
  },
  pushable_tasks = {
    prio = 140,
    prio_list = {
      next = 0xffff8880f5bb6ea0,
      prev = 0xffff8880f5bb6ea0
    },
    node_list = {
      next = 0xffff8880f5bb6eb0,
      prev = 0xffff8880f5bb6eb0
    }
  },
  pushable_dl_tasks = {
    __rb_parent_color = 18446612686192733888,
    rb_right = 0x0 <fixed_percpu_data>,
    rb_left = 0x0 <fixed_percpu_data>
  },
  mm = 0xffff8880205f9600,
```

```
active_mm = 0xffff8880205f9600,
exit_state = 0,
exit_code = 0,
exit_signal = 17,
pdeath_signal = 0,
jobctl = 0,
personality = 0,
sched_reset_on_fork = 0,
sched_contributes_to_load = 0,
sched_migrated = 0,
sched_remote_wakeup = 0,
in_execve = 0,
in_iowait = 0,
restore_sigmask = 0,
in_user_fault = 0,
in_lru_fault = 0,
no_cgroup_migration = 0,
frozen = 0,
use_memdelay = 0,
in_memstall = 0,
in_eventfd = 0,
pasid_activated = 0,
reported_split_lock = 0,
in_thrashing = 0,
atomic_flags = 0,
restart_block = {
  arch_data = 0,
  fn = 0xffffffff810ec2e0 <do_no_restart_syscall>,
  {
    futex = {
      uaddr = 0x0 <fixed_percpu_data>,
      val = 0,
      flags = 0,
      bitset = 0,
      time = 0,
      uaddr2 = 0x0 <fixed_percpu_data>
    },
    nanosleep = {
      clockid = 0,
      type = TT_NONE,
      {
        rmtp = 0x0 <fixed_percpu_data>,
        compat_rmtp = 0x0 <fixed_percpu_data>
      },
      expires = 0
    },
    poll = {
      ufds = 0x0 <fixed_percpu_data>,
      nfds = 0,
      has_timeout = 0,
      tv_sec = 0,
      tv_nsec = 0
    }
  }
},
pid = 1956,
tgid = 1956,
stack_canary = 1112145273383321088,
real_parent = 0xffff8880024f3300,
```

```
      parent = 0xffff8880024f3300,
      children = {
        next = 0xffff88800be7d600,
        prev = 0xffff88800be7d600
      },
      sibling = {
        next = 0xffff8880024f3c70,
        prev = 0xffff8880024f3c70
      },
      group_leader = 0xffff8880f5bb6600,
      ptraced = {
        next = 0xffff8880f5bb6f98,
        prev = 0xffff8880f5bb6f98
      },
      ptrace_entry = {
        next = 0xffff8880f5bb6fa8,
        prev = 0xffff8880f5bb6fa8
      },
      thread_pid = 0xffff888002320500,
      pid_links = {{
          next = 0x0 <fixed_percpu_data>,
          pprev = 0xffff888002320510
        }, {
          next = 0x0 <fixed_percpu_data>,
          pprev = 0xffff888002320518
        }, {
          next = 0x0 <fixed_percpu_data>,
          pprev = 0xffff888002320520
        }, {
          next = 0x0 <fixed_percpu_data>,
          pprev = 0xffff88800be7d670
        }},
      thread_group = {
        next = 0xffff8880f5bb7000,
        prev = 0xffff8880f5bb7000
      },
      thread_node = {
        next = 0xffff88800a982890,
        prev = 0xffff88800a982890
      },
      vfork_done = 0x0 <fixed_percpu_data>,
      set_child_tid = 0x7a7479782f50,
      clear_child_tid = 0x7eb2634eca10,
      worker_private = 0x0 <fixed_percpu_data>,
      utime = 20000000,
      stime = 4000000,
      gtime = 0,
      prev_cputime = {
        utime = 0,
        stime = 0,
        lock = {
          raw_lock = {
            {
              val = {
                counter = 0
              },
              {
                locked = 0 '\000',
                pending = 0 '\000'
```

```
        },
        {
          locked_pending = 0,
          tail = 0
        }
      }
    }
  }
},
vtime = {
  seqcount = {
    sequence = 0
  },
  starttime = 0,
  state = VTIME_INACTIVE,
  cpu = 0,
  utime = 0,
  stime = 0,
  gtime = 0
},
tick_dep_mask = {
  counter = 0
},
nvcsw = 101,
nivcsw = 11,
start_time = 39238451300,
start_boottime = 39238451500,
min_flt = 823,
maj_flt = 4,
posix_cputimers = {
  bases = {{
      nextevt = 18446744073709551615,
      tqhead = {
        rb_root = {
          rb_root = {
            rb_node = 0x0 <fixed_percpu_data>
          },
          rb_leftmost = 0x0 <fixed_percpu_data>
        }
      }
    }, {
      nextevt = 18446744073709551615,
      tqhead = {
        rb_root = {
          rb_root = {
            rb_node = 0x0 <fixed_percpu_data>
          },
          rb_leftmost = 0x0 <fixed_percpu_data>
        }
      }
    }, {
      nextevt = 18446744073709551615,
      tqhead = {
        rb_root = {
          rb_root = {
            rb_node = 0x0 <fixed_percpu_data>
          },
          rb_leftmost = 0x0 <fixed_percpu_data>
        }
```

309

```
          }
        }},
      timers_active = 0,
      expiry_active = 0
    },
    posix_cputimers_work = {
      work = {
        next = 0x0 <fixed_percpu_data>,
        func = 0xffffffff811cbd80 <posix_cpu_timers_work>
      },
      mutex = {
        owner = {
          counter = 0
        },
        wait_lock = {
          raw_lock = {
            {
              val = {
                counter = 0
              },
              {
                locked = 0 '\000',
                pending = 0 '\000'
              },
              {
                locked_pending = 0,
                tail = 0
              }
            }
          }
        },
        osq = {
          tail = {
            counter = 0
          }
        },
        wait_list = {
          next = 0xffff8880f5bb7148,
          prev = 0xffff8880f5bb7148
        }
      },
      scheduled = 0
    },
    ptracer_cred = 0x0 <fixed_percpu_data>,
    real_cred = 0xffff88800a49ce40,
    cred = 0xffff88800a49ce40,
    cached_requested_key = 0x0 <fixed_percpu_data>,
    comm = "bash", '\000' <repeats 11 times>,
    nameidata = 0x0 <fixed_percpu_data>,
    sysvsem = {
      undo_list = 0x0 <fixed_percpu_data>
    },
    sysvshm = {
      shm_clist = {
        next = 0xffff8880f5bb71a0,
        prev = 0xffff8880f5bb71a0
      }
    },
    last_switch_count = 0,
```

```
last_switch_time = 0,
fs = 0xffff88800a7b4bc0,
files = 0xffff8880376efc80,
io_uring = 0x0 <fixed_percpu_data>,
nsproxy = 0xffffffff82e87dc0 <init_nsproxy>,
signal = 0xffff88800a982880,
sighand = 0xffff8880036f39c0,
blocked = {
  sig = {65536}
},
real_blocked = {
  sig = {0}
},
saved_sigmask = {
  sig = {0}
},
pending = {
  list = {
    next = 0xffff8880f5bb7208,
    prev = 0xffff8880f5bb7208
  },
  signal = {
    sig = {0}
  }
},
sas_ss_sp = 0,
sas_ss_size = 0,
sas_ss_flags = 2,
task_works = 0x0 <fixed_percpu_data>,
audit_context = 0x0 <fixed_percpu_data>,
loginuid = {
  val = 1000
},
sessionid = 2,
seccomp = {
  mode = 0,
  filter_count = {
    counter = 0
  },
  filter = 0x0 <fixed_percpu_data>
},
syscall_dispatch = {
  selector = 0x0 <fixed_percpu_data>,
  offset = 0,
  len = 0,
  on_dispatch = false
},
parent_exec_id = 5,
self_exec_id = 6,
alloc_lock = {
  {
    rlock = {
      raw_lock = {
        {
          val = {
            counter = 0
          },
          {
            locked = 0 '\000',
```

```
                              pending = 0 '\000'
                    },
                    {
                      locked_pending = 0,
                      tail = 0
                    }
                  }
                }
              }
            }
          }
        },
        pi_lock = {
          raw_lock = {
            {
              val = {
                counter = 0
              },
              {
                locked = 0 '\000',
                pending = 0 '\000'
              },
              {
                locked_pending = 0,
                tail = 0
              }
            }
          }
        },
        wake_q = {
          next = 0x0 <fixed_percpu_data>
        },
        pi_waiters = {
          rb_root = {
            rb_node = 0x0 <fixed_percpu_data>
          },
          rb_leftmost = 0x0 <fixed_percpu_data>
        },
        pi_top_task = 0x0 <fixed_percpu_data>,
        pi_blocked_on = 0x0 <fixed_percpu_data>,
        in_ubsan = 0,
        journal_info = 0x0 <fixed_percpu_data>,
        bio_list = 0x0 <fixed_percpu_data>,
        plug = 0x0 <fixed_percpu_data>,
        reclaim_state = 0x0 <fixed_percpu_data>,
        io_context = 0x0 <fixed_percpu_data>,
        capture_control = 0x0 <fixed_percpu_data>,
        ptrace_message = 0,
        last_siginfo = 0x0 <fixed_percpu_data>,
        ioac = {
          rchar = 116117,
          wchar = 4974,
          syscr = 235,
          syscw = 96,
          read_bytes = 249856,
          write_bytes = 0,
          cancelled_write_bytes = 0
        },
        psi_flags = 0,
        acct_rss_mem1 = 22750000,
```

```
acct_vm_mem1 = 52058592,
acct_timexpd = 24000000,
mems_allowed = {
  bits = {1, 0 <repeats 15 times>}
},
mems_allowed_seq = {
  seqcount = {
    sequence = 0
  }
},
cpuset_mem_spread_rotor = -1,
cpuset_slab_spread_rotor = -1,
cgroups = 0xffff88800a841c00,
cg_list = {
  next = 0xffff88800be7da78,
  prev = 0xffff88800a841c90
},
closid = 0,
rmid = 0,
robust_list = 0x7eb2634eca20,
compat_robust_list = 0x0 <fixed_percpu_data>,
pi_state_list = {
  next = 0xffff8880f5bb7420,
  prev = 0xffff8880f5bb7420
},
pi_state_cache = 0x0 <fixed_percpu_data>,
futex_exit_mutex = {
  owner = {
    counter = 0
  },
  wait_lock = {
    raw_lock = {
      {
        val = {
          counter = 0
        },
        {
          locked = 0 '\000',
          pending = 0 '\000'
        },
        {
          locked_pending = 0,
          tail = 0
        }
      }
    }
  },
  osq = {
    tail = {
      counter = 0
    }
  },
  wait_list = {
    next = 0xffff8880f5bb7448,
    prev = 0xffff8880f5bb7448
  }
},
futex_state = 0,
perf_event_ctxp = 0x0 <fixed_percpu_data>,
```

```
perf_event_mutex = {
  owner = {
    counter = 0
  },
  wait_lock = {
    raw_lock = {
      {
        val = {
          counter = 0
        },
        {
          locked = 0 '\000',
          pending = 0 '\000'
        },
        {
          locked_pending = 0,
          tail = 0
        }
      }
    }
  },
  osq = {
    tail = {
      counter = 0
    }
  },
  wait_list = {
    next = 0xffff8880f5bb7478,
    prev = 0xffff8880f5bb7478
  }
},
perf_event_list = {
  next = 0xffff8880f5bb7488,
  prev = 0xffff8880f5bb7488
},
mempolicy = 0x0 <fixed_percpu_data>,
il_prev = 0,
pref_node_fork = 0,
numa_scan_seq = 0,
numa_scan_period = 1000,
numa_scan_period_max = 0,
numa_preferred_nid = -1,
numa_migrate_retry = 0,
node_stamp = 0,
last_task_numa_placement = 0,
last_sum_exec_runtime = 0,
numa_work = {
  next = 0xffff8880f5bb74d8,
  func = 0xffffffff8112bf40 <task_numa_work>
},
numa_group = 0x0 <fixed_percpu_data>,
numa_faults = 0x0 <fixed_percpu_data>,
total_numa_faults = 0,
numa_faults_locality = {0, 0, 0},
numa_pages_migrated = 0,
rseq = 0x7eb2634ed0e0,
rseq_len = 32,
rseq_sig = 1392848979,
rseq_event_mask = 7,
```

```
mm_cid = -1,
last_mm_cid = 0,
migrate_from_cpu = 1,
mm_cid_active = 1,
cid_work = {
  next = 0xffff8880f5bb7548,
  func = 0xffffffff8111c400 <task_mm_cid_work>
},
tlb_ubc = {
  arch = {
    cpumask = {
      bits = {0 <repeats 128 times>}
    }
  },
  flush_required = false,
  writable = false
},
splice_pipe = 0x0 <fixed_percpu_data>,
task_frag = {
  page = 0x0 <fixed_percpu_data>,
  offset = 0,
  size = 0
},
delays = 0x0 <fixed_percpu_data>,
nr_dirtied = 0,
nr_dirtied_pause = 32,
dirty_paused_when = 0,
timer_slack_ns = 50000,
default_timer_slack_ns = 50000,
curr_ret_stack = -1,
curr_ret_depth = -1,
ret_stack = 0x0 <fixed_percpu_data>,
ftrace_timestamp = 0,
trace_overrun = {
  counter = 0
},
tracing_graph_pause = {
  counter = 0
},
trace_recursion = 0,
memcg_in_oom = 0x0 <fixed_percpu_data>,
memcg_oom_gfp_mask = 0,
memcg_oom_order = 0,
memcg_nr_pages_over_high = 0,
active_memcg = 0x0 <fixed_percpu_data>,
throttle_disk = 0x0 <fixed_percpu_data>,
utask = 0x0 <fixed_percpu_data>,
sequential_io = 0,
sequential_io_avg = 0,
kmap_ctrl = {<No data fields>},
rcu = {
  next = 0x0 <fixed_percpu_data>,
  func = 0x0 <fixed_percpu_data>
},
rcu_users = {
  refs = {
    counter = 2
  }
},
```

```
    pagefault_disabled = 0,
    oom_reaper_list = 0x0 <fixed_percpu_data>,
    oom_reaper_timer = {
      entry = {
        next = 0x0 <fixed_percpu_data>,
        pprev = 0x0 <fixed_percpu_data>
      },
      expires = 0,
      function = 0x0 <fixed_percpu_data>,
      flags = 0
    },
    stack_vm_area = 0xffff88801da47740,
    stack_refcount = {
      refs = {
        counter = 1
      }
    },
    patch_state = -1,
    security = 0xffff88801da47e80,
    bpf_storage = 0x0 <fixed_percpu_data>,
    bpf_ctx = 0x0 <fixed_percpu_data>,
    mce_vaddr = 0x0 <fixed_percpu_data>,
    mce_kflags = 0,
    mce_addr = 0,
    mce_ripv = 0,
    mce_whole_page = 0,
    __mce_reserved = 0,
    mce_kill_me = {
      next = 0x0 <fixed_percpu_data>,
      func = 0x0 <fixed_percpu_data>
    },
    mce_count = 0,
    kretprobe_instances = {
      first = 0x0 <fixed_percpu_data>
    },
    rethooks = {
      first = 0x0 <fixed_percpu_data>
    },
    l1d_flush_kill = {
      next = 0x0 <fixed_percpu_data>,
      func = 0x0 <fixed_percpu_data>
    },
    rv = {{
        da_mon = {
          monitoring = false,
          curr_state = 0
        }
      }},
    user_event_mm = 0x0 <fixed_percpu_data>,
    thread = {
      tls_array = {{
          limit0 = 0,
          base0 = 0,
          base1 = 0,
          type = 0,
          s = 0,
          dpl = 0,
          p = 0,
          limit1 = 0,
```

```
            avl = 0,
            l = 0,
            d = 0,
            g = 0,
            base2 = 0
          }, {
...
          }, {
            limit0 = 0,
            base0 = 0,
            base1 = 0,
            type = 0,
            s = 0,
            dpl = 0,
            p = 0,
            limit1 = 0,
            avl = 0,
            l = 0,
            d = 0,
            g = 0,
            base2 = 0
          }},
      sp = 18446683600654203992,
      es = 0,
      ds = 0,
      fsindex = 0,
      gsindex = 0,
      fsbase = 139304635385664,
      gsbase = 0,
      ptrace_bps = {0x0 <fixed_percpu_data>, 0x0 <fixed_percpu_data>, 0x0 <fixed_percpu_data>,
0x0 <fixed_percpu_data>},
      virtual_dr6 = 0,
      ptrace_dr7 = 0,
      cr2 = 0,
      trap_nr = 0,
      error_code = 0,
      io_bitmap = 0x0 <fixed_percpu_data>,
      iopl_emul = 0,
      iopl_warn = 0,
      sig_on_uaccess_err = 0,
      pkru = 0,
      fpu = {
        last_cpu = 3,
        avx512_timestamp = 0,
        fpstate = 0xffff8880f5bb7c00,
        __task_fpstate = 0x0 <fixed_percpu_data>,
        perm = {
          __state_perm = 7,
          __state_size = 832,
          __user_state_size = 832
        },
        guest_perm = {
          __state_perm = 7,
          __state_size = 832,
          __user_state_size = 832
        },
        __fpstate = {
          size = 832,
          user_size = 832,
```

```
xfeatures = 7,
user_xfeatures = 7,
xfd = 0,
is_valloc = 0,
is_guest = 0,
is_confidential = 0,
in_use = 0,
regs = {
  fsave = {
    cwd = 895,
    swd = 0,
    twd = 0,
    fip = 0,
    fcs = 0,
    foo = 0,
    fos = 8064,
    st_space = {65535, 0 <repeats 19 times>},
    status = 0
  },
  fxsave = {
    cwd = 895,
    swd = 0,
    twd = 0,
    fop = 0,
    {
      {
        rip = 0,
        rdp = 0
      },
      {
        fip = 0,
        fcs = 0,
        foo = 0,
        fos = 0
      }
    },
    mxcsr = 8064,
    mxcsr_mask = 65535,
    st_space = {0 <repeats 32 times>},
    xmm_space = {0, 0, 0, 0, 4294967295, 4294967295, 4294967040, 4294967295, 0, 0, 0,
0, 3448111207, 23261, 0, 0, 0, 0, 0, 0, 1665248480, 32434, 0, 0, 0, 0, 4294967040, 4294967295,
0, 0, 0, 0, 1868854643, 23040, 0, 0, 0, 0, 0, 0, 0, 0, 0, 2097152, 0 <repeats 20 times>},
    padding = {0 <repeats 12 times>},
    {
      padding1 = {0 <repeats 12 times>},
      sw_reserved = {0 <repeats 12 times>}
    }
  },
  soft = {
    cwd = 895,
    swd = 0,
    twd = 0,
    fip = 0,
    fcs = 0,
    foo = 0,
    fos = 8064,
    st_space = {65535, 0 <repeats 19 times>},
    ftop = 0 '\000',
    changed = 0 '\000',
```

```
            lookahead = 0 '\000',
            no_update = 0 '\000',
            rm = 0 '\000',
            alimit = 0 '\000',
            info = 0x0 <fixed_percpu_data>,
            entry_eip = 0
          },
          xsave = {
            i387 = {
              cwd = 895,
              swd = 0,
              twd = 0,
              fop = 0,
              {
                {
                  rip = 0,
                  rdp = 0
                },
                {
                  fip = 0,
                  fcs = 0,
                  foo = 0,
                  fos = 0
                }
              },
              mxcsr = 8064,
              mxcsr_mask = 65535,
              st_space = {0 <repeats 32 times>},
              xmm_space = {0, 0, 0, 0, 4294967295, 4294967295, 4294967040, 4294967295, 0, 0, 0,
0, 3448111207, 23261, 0, 0, 0, 0, 0, 0, 1665248480, 32434, 0, 0, 0, 0, 4294967040, 4294967295,
0, 0, 0, 0, 1868854643, 23040, 0, 0, 0, 0, 0, 0, 0, 0, 0, 2097152, 0 <repeats 20 times>},
              padding = {0 <repeats 12 times>},
              {
                padding1 = {0 <repeats 12 times>},
                sw_reserved = {0 <repeats 12 times>}
              }
            },
            header = {
              xfeatures = 3,
              xcomp_bv = 9223372036854775815,
              reserved = {0, 0, 0, 0, 0, 0}
            },
            extended_state_area = 0xffff8880f5bb7e80 "\377\377\377\377\377"
          },
          __padding = "\177\003", '\000' <repeats 22 times>, "\200\037\000\000\377\377", '\000'
<repeats 146 times>, "\377\377\377\377\377\377\377\377\000\377\377\377\377\377\377\377", '\000'
<repeats 16 times>...
        }
      }
    }
  }
}
```

31.   We detach from the debugging session to allow the target to continue:

```
(gdb) detach
```

Managed Debugging

Exercise MD9

Now, we have come to managed space debugging of Python scripts. We cover a few techniques and commands here to give you a basic overview in the context of user process space debugging.

Exercise MD9

- **Goal:** Learn how to debug Python code using GDB

- **Elementary Diagnostics Patterns:** Hang

- **Memory Analysis Patterns:** Stack Trace Collection (Unmanaged Space); Stack Trace Collection (Managed Space); Runtime Thread (Python, Linux); Managed Stack Trace (Python); Pointer Cone; Deadlock (Managed Space)

- **Debugging Implementation Patterns:** Break-in

- \ALD4\Exercise-Linux-MD9.pdf

Goal: Learn how to debug Python code using GDB.

Elementary Diagnostics Patterns: Hang.

Memory Analysis Patterns: Stack Trace Collection (Managed Space); Runtime Thread (Python, Linux); Managed Stack Trace (Python); Pointer Cone; Deadlock (Managed Space).

Debugging Implementation Patterns: Break-in.

1. The source code can be found in the *md9* directory:

```
$ git clone https://bitbucket.org/softwarediagnostics/ald4
```

2. We also need to install Python debugging packages (if you use a Red Hat distribution flavor, please check this article: https://developers.redhat.com/articles/2021/09/08/debugging-python-c-extensions-gdb):

```
/mnt/c/ALD4/md9$ sudo apt install python3-dbg
```

3. When we run the *md9.py* script, the process hangs instead of exiting in a few seconds, as expected.

```
/mnt/c/ALD4/md9$ python3 md9.py
```

4. To debug it, we check its PID and attach GDB to it in another terminal:

```
/mnt/c/ALD4/md9$ ps a | grep md9
15330 pts/3     Sl+     0:00 python3 md9.py
15539 pts/7     S+      0:00 grep md9

/mnt/c/ALD4/md9$ gdb -p 15330
GNU gdb (Debian 8.2.1-2+b3) 8.2.1
Copyright (C) 2018 Free Software Foundation, Inc.
License GPLv3+: GNU GPL version 3 or later <http://gnu.org/licenses/gpl.html>
This is free software: you are free to change and redistribute it.
There is NO WARRANTY, to the extent permitted by law.
Type "show copying" and "show warranty" for details.
This GDB was configured as "x86_64-linux-gnu".
Type "show configuration" for configuration details.
For bug reporting instructions, please see:
<http://www.gnu.org/software/gdb/bugs/>.
Find the GDB manual and other documentation resources online at:
    <http://www.gnu.org/software/gdb/documentation/>.

For help, type "help".
Type "apropos word" to search for commands related to "word".
Attaching to process 15330
[New LWP 15331]
[New LWP 15332]
[Thread debugging using libthread_db enabled]
Using host libthread_db library "/lib/x86_64-linux-gnu/libthread_db.so.1".
futex_abstimed_wait_cancelable (private=0, abstime=0x0, expected=0, futex_word=0x7f5680000d50)
at ../sysdeps/unix/sysv/linux/futex-internal.h:205
205     ../sysdeps/unix/sysv/linux/futex-internal.h: No such file or directory.
```

5.   If we look at all threads, we don't see Python script code backtraces, only Python runtime backtraces:

(gdb) **thread apply all bt**

Thread 3 (Thread 0x7f5685d21700 (LWP 15332)):
#0 futex_abstimed_wait_cancelable (private=0, abstime=0x0, expected=0, futex_word=0x1e9b7f0) at
../sysdeps/unix/sysv/linux/futex-internal.h:205
#1 do_futex_wait (sem=sem@entry=0x1e9b7f0, abstime=0x0) at sem_waitcommon.c:111
#2 0x00007f5686e2a988 in __new_sem_wait_slow (sem=0x1e9b7f0, abstime=0x0) at sem_waitcommon.c:181
#3 0x00000000005281f8 in PyThread_acquire_lock_timed (lock=0x1e9b7f0, microseconds=-1000000, intr_flag=1) at
../Python/thread_pthread.h:372
#4 0x000000000061702a in acquire_timed (timeout=<optimized out>, lock=0x1e9b7f0) at ../Modules/_threadmodule.c:61
#5 rlock_acquire (self=0x7f568666ee40, args=<optimized out>, kwds=<optimized out>) at ../Modules/_threadmodule.c:306
#6 0x00000000004d2d34 in _PyMethodDef_RawFastCallKeywords (kwnames=<optimized out>, nargs=<optimized out>,
args=<optimized out>,
    self=<_thread.RLock at remote 0x7f568666ee40>, method=0x87a0a0 <rlock_methods>) at ../Objects/call.c:690
#7 _PyMethodDescr_FastCallKeywords (descrobj=<method_descriptor at remote 0x7f568673d8b8>, args=0x7f568653c4f8,
nargs=<optimized out>,
    kwnames=<optimized out>) at ../Objects/descrobject.c:288
#8 0x000000000054f619 in call_function (kwnames=0x0, oparg=1, pp_stack=0x7f5685d207f0) at ../Python/ceval.c:4593
#9 _PyEval_EvalFrameDefault (f=<optimized out>, throwflag=<optimized out>) at ../Python/ceval.c:3110
#10 0x00000000005d6846 in PyEval_EvalFrameEx (throwflag=0, f=Frame 0x7f568653c388, for file md9.py, line 29, in
thread_func2 ())
    at ../Python/ceval.c:547
#11 function_code_fastcall (globals=<optimized out>, nargs=<optimized out>, args=<optimized out>, co=<optimized out>)
at ../Objects/call.c:283
#12 _PyFunction_FastCallDict (func=<optimized out>, args=<optimized out>, nargs=<optimized out>, kwargs=<optimized
out>) at ../Objects/call.c:322
#13 0x000000000054c9b1 in do_call_core (kwdict={}, callargs=(), func=<function at remote 0x7f568654d158>) at
../Python/ceval.c:4645
#14 _PyEval_EvalFrameDefault (f=<optimized out>, throwflag=<optimized out>) at ../Python/ceval.c:3191
#15 0x00000000005d550c in PyEval_EvalFrameEx (throwflag=0,
    f=Frame 0x7f568659e3d8, for file /usr/lib/python3.7/threading.py, line 865, in run (self=<Thread(_target=<function
at remote 0x7f568654d158>, _name='Thread-2', _args=(), _kwargs={}, _daemonic=False, _ident=140009589053184,
_tstate_lock=<_thread.lock at remote 0x7f56865a2e90>, _started=<Event(_cond=<Condition(_lock=<_thread.lock at remote
0x7f568666d5d0>, acquire=<built-in method acquire of _thread.lock object at remote 0x7f568666d5d0>, release=<built-in
method release of _thread.lock object at remote 0x7f568666d5d0>, _waiters=<collections.deque at remote
0x7f568659f320>) at remote 0x7f5686606630>, _flag=True) at remote 0x7f5686601198>, _is_stopped=False,
_initialized=True, _stderr=<_io.TextIOWrapper at remote 0x7f5686732708>) at remote 0x7f56865fc6d8>)) at
../Python/ceval.c:547
#16 function_code_fastcall (globals=<optimized out>, nargs=<optimized out>, args=<optimized out>, co=<optimized out>)
at ../Objects/call.c:283
#17 _PyFunction_FastCallKeywords (func=<optimized out>, stack=<optimized out>, nargs=<optimized out>,
kwnames=<optimized out>)
    at ../Objects/call.c:408
#18 0x000000000054b72c in call_function (kwnames=0x0, oparg=<optimized out>, pp_stack=0x7f5685d20b30) at
../Python/ceval.c:4616
#19 _PyEval_EvalFrameDefault (f=<optimized out>, throwflag=<optimized out>) at ../Python/ceval.c:3110
#20 0x00000000005d550c in PyEval_EvalFrameEx (throwflag=0,
    f=Frame 0x7f5678000b38, for file /usr/lib/python3.7/threading.py, line 917, in _bootstrap_inner
(self=<Thread(_target=<function at remote 0x7f568654d158>, _name='Thread-2', _args=(), _kwargs={}, _daemonic=False,
_ident=140009589053184, _tstate_lock=<_thread.lock at remote 0x7f56865a2e90>,
_started=<Event(_cond=<Condition(_lock=<_thread.lock at remote 0x7f568666d5d0>, acquire=<built-in method acquire of
_thread.lock object at remote 0x7f568666d5d0>, release=<built-in method release of _thread.lock object at remote
0x7f568666d5d0>, _waiters=<collections.deque at remote 0x7f568659f320>) at remote 0x7f5686606630>, _flag=True) at
remote 0x7f5686601198>, _is_stopped=False, _initialized=True, _stderr=<_io.TextIOWrapper at remote 0x7f5686732708>) at
remote 0x7f56865fc6d8>)) at ../Python/ceval.c:547
#21 function_code_fastcall (globals=<optimized out>, nargs=<optimized out>, args=<optimized out>, co=<optimized out>)
at ../Objects/call.c:283
--Type <RET> for more, q to quit, c to continue without paging--
#22 _PyFunction_FastCallKeywords (func=<optimized out>, stack=<optimized out>, nargs=<optimized out>,
kwnames=<optimized out>)
    at ../Objects/call.c:408
#23 0x000000000054b72c in call_function (kwnames=0x0, oparg=<optimized out>, pp_stack=0x7f5685d20cc0) at
../Python/ceval.c:4616
#24 _PyEval_EvalFrameDefault (f=<optimized out>, throwflag=<optimized out>) at ../Python/ceval.c:3110
#25 0x00000000005d6846 in PyEval_EvalFrameEx (throwflag=0,
    f=Frame 0x7f5686536ac8, for file /usr/lib/python3.7/threading.py, line 885, in _bootstrap
(self=<Thread(_target=<function at remote 0x7f568654d158>, _name='Thread-2', _args=(), _kwargs={}, _daemonic=False,
_ident=140009589053184, _tstate_lock=<_thread.lock at remote 0x7f56865a2e90>,
_started=<Event(_cond=<Condition(_lock=<_thread.lock at remote 0x7f568666d5d0>, acquire=<built-in method acquire of
_thread.lock object at remote 0x7f568666d5d0>, release=<built-in method release of _thread.lock object at remote

```
0x7f568666d5d0>, _waiters=<collections.deque at remote 0x7f568659f320>) at remote 0x7f5686606630>, _flag=True) at
remote 0x7f5686601198>, _is_stopped=False, _initialized=True, _stderr=<_io.TextIOWrapper at remote 0x7f5686732708>) at
remote 0x7f56865fc6d8>)) at ../Python/ceval.c:547
#26 function_code_fastcall (globals=<optimized out>, nargs=<optimized out>, args=<optimized out>, co=<optimized out>)
at ../Objects/call.c:283
#27 _PyFunction_FastCallDict (func=<optimized out>, args=<optimized out>, nargs=<optimized out>, kwargs=<optimized
out>) at ../Objects/call.c:322
#28 0x00000000004d4ca2 in _PyObject_FastCallDict (kwargs=0x0, nargs=1, args=0x7f5685d20e00, callable=<function at
remote 0x7f5686547d90>)
    at ../Objects/call.c:98
#29 _PyObject_Call_Prepend (kwargs=0x0, args=<optimized out>,
    obj=<Thread(_target=<function at remote 0x7f568654d158>, _name='Thread-2', _args=(), _kwargs={}, _daemonic=False,
_ident=140009589053184, _tstate_lock=<_thread.lock at remote 0x7f56865a2e90>,
_started=<Event(_cond=<Condition(_lock=<_thread.lock at remote 0x7f568666d5d0>, acquire=<built-in method acquire of
_thread.lock object at remote 0x7f568666d5d0>, release=<built-in method release of _thread.lock object at remote
0x7f568666d5d0>, _waiters=<collections.deque at remote 0x7f568659f320>) at remote 0x7f5686606630>, _flag=True) at
remote 0x7f5686601198>, _is_stopped=False, _initialized=True, _stderr=<_io.TextIOWrapper at remote 0x7f5686732708>) at
remote 0x7f56865fc6d8>, callable=<function at remote 0x7f5686547d90>)
    at ../Objects/call.c:904
#30 method_call (method=<optimized out>, args=<optimized out>, kwargs=<optimized out>, method=<optimized out>,
args=<optimized out>,
    kwargs=<optimized out>) at ../Objects/classobject.c:309
#31 0x00000000005d8696 in PyObject_Call (callable=<method at remote 0x7f568673bac8>, args=<optimized out>,
kwargs=<optimized out>)
    at ../Objects/call.c:245
#32 0x0000000000616903 in t_bootstrap (boot_raw=boot_raw@entry=0x7f56865a2e18) at ../Modules/_threadmodule.c:994
#33 0x000000000062d7e4 in pythread_wrapper (arg=<optimized out>) at ../Python/thread_pthread.h:174
#34 0x00007f5686e21fa3 in start_thread (arg=<optimized out>) at pthread_create.c:486
#35 0x00007f5686b6906f in clone () at ../sysdeps/unix/sysv/linux/x86_64/clone.S:95

Thread 2 (Thread 0x7f5686522700 (LWP 15331)):
#0  futex_abstimed_wait_cancelable (private=0, abstime=0x0, expected=0, futex_word=0x1e844d0) at
../sysdeps/unix/sysv/linux/futex-internal.h:205
#1  do_futex_wait (sem=sem@entry=0x1e844d0, abstime=0x0) at sem_waitcommon.c:111
#2  0x00007f5686e2a988 in __new_sem_wait_slow (sem=0x1e844d0, abstime=0x0) at sem_waitcommon.c:181
#3  0x00000000005281f8 in PyThread_acquire_lock_timed (lock=0x1e844d0, microseconds=-1000000, intr_flag=1) at
../Python/thread_pthread.h:372
#4  0x000000000061702a in acquire_timed (timeout=<optimized out>, lock=0x1e844d0) at ../Modules/_threadmodule.c:61
#5  rlock_acquire (self=0x7f5686603030, args=<optimized out>, kwds=<optimized out>) at ../Modules/_threadmodule.c:306
#6  0x00000000004d2d34 in _PyMethodDef_RawFastCallKeywords (kwnames=<optimized out>, nargs=<optimized out>,
args=<optimized out>,
    self=<_thread.RLock at remote 0x7f5686603030>, method=0x87a0a0 <rlock_methods>) at ../Objects/call.c:690
--Type <RET> for more, q to quit, c to continue without paging--
#7  _PyMethodDescr_FastCallKeywords (descrobj=<method_descriptor at remote 0x7f568673d8b8>, args=0x7f56866a1370,
nargs=<optimized out>,
    kwnames=<optimized out>) at ../Objects/descrobject.c:288
#8  0x000000000054f619 in call_function (kwnames=0x0, oparg=1, pp_stack=0x7f56865217f0) at ../Python/ceval.c:4593
#9  _PyEval_EvalFrameDefault (f=<optimized out>, throwflag=<optimized out>) at ../Python/ceval.c:3110
#10 0x00000000005d6846 in PyEval_EvalFrameEx (throwflag=0, f=Frame 0x7f56866a1200, for file md9.py, line 24, in
thread_func1 ())
    at ../Python/ceval.c:547
#11 function_code_fastcall (globals=<optimized out>, nargs=<optimized out>, args=<optimized out>, co=<optimized out>)
at ../Objects/call.c:283
#12 _PyFunction_FastCallDict (func=<optimized out>, args=<optimized out>, nargs=<optimized out>, kwargs=<optimized
out>) at ../Objects/call.c:322
#13 0x000000000054c9b1 in do_call_core (kwdict={}, callargs=(), func=<function at remote 0x7f568654d0d0>) at
../Python/ceval.c:4645
#14 _PyEval_EvalFrameDefault (f=<optimized out>, throwflag=<optimized out>) at ../Python/ceval.c:3191
#15 0x00000000005d550c in PyEval_EvalFrameEx (throwflag=0,
    f=Frame 0x7f56867355a0, for file /usr/lib/python3.7/threading.py, line 865, in run (self=<Thread(_target=<function
at remote 0x7f568654d0d0>, _name='Thread-1', _args=(), _kwargs={}, _daemonic=False, _ident=140009597445888,
_tstate_lock=<_thread.lock at remote 0x7f56865a2e40>, _started=<Event(_cond=<Condition(_lock=<_thread.lock at remote
0x7f5686650a80>, acquire=<built-in method acquire of _thread.lock object at remote 0x7f5686650a80>, release=<built-in
method release of _thread.lock object at remote 0x7f5686650a80>, _waiters=<collections.deque at remote
0x7f56865f8048>) at remote 0x7f56865f1b00>, _flag=True) at remote 0x7f56865f1ac8>, _is_stopped=False,
_initialized=True, _stderr=<_io.TextIOWrapper at remote 0x7f5686732708>) at remote 0x7f56865f1a90>)) at
../Python/ceval.c:547
#16 function_code_fastcall (globals=<optimized out>, nargs=<optimized out>, args=<optimized out>, co=<optimized out>)
at ../Objects/call.c:283
#17 _PyFunction_FastCallKeywords (func=<optimized out>, stack=<optimized out>, nargs=<optimized out>,
kwnames=<optimized out>)
    at ../Objects/call.c:408
#18 0x000000000054b72c in call_function (kwnames=0x0, oparg=<optimized out>, pp_stack=0x7f5686521b30) at
../Python/ceval.c:4616
```

```
#19 _PyEval_EvalFrameDefault (f=<optimized out>, throwflag=<optimized out>) at ../Python/ceval.c:3110
#20 0x00000000005d550c in PyEval_EvalFrameEx (throwflag=0,
    f=Frame 0x7f5680000b38, for file /usr/lib/python3.7/threading.py, line 917, in _bootstrap_inner
(self=<Thread(_target=<function at remote 0x7f568654d0d0>, _name='Thread-1', _args=(), _kwargs={}, _daemonic=False,
_ident=140009597445888, _tstate_lock=<_thread.lock at remote 0x7f56865a2e40>,
_started=<Event(_cond=<Condition(_lock=<_thread.lock at remote 0x7f5686650a80>, acquire=<built-in method acquire of
_thread.lock object at remote 0x7f5686650a80>, release=<built-in method release of _thread.lock object at remote
0x7f5686650a80>, _waiters=<collections.deque at remote 0x7f56865f8048>) at remote 0x7f56865f1b00>, _flag=True) at
remote 0x7f56865f1ac8>, _is_stopped=False, _initialized=True, _stderr=<_io.TextIOWrapper at remote 0x7f5686732708>) at
remote 0x7f56865f1a90>)) at ../Python/ceval.c:547
#21 function_code_fastcall (globals=<optimized out>, nargs=<optimized out>, args=<optimized out>, co=<optimized out>)
at ../Objects/call.c:283
#22 _PyFunction_FastCallKeywords (func=<optimized out>, stack=<optimized out>, nargs=<optimized out>,
kwnames=<optimized out>)
    at ../Objects/call.c:408
#23 0x000000000054b72c in call_function (kwnames=0x0, oparg=<optimized out>, pp_stack=0x7f5686521cc0) at
../Python/ceval.c:4616
#24 _PyEval_EvalFrameDefault (f=<optimized out>, throwflag=<optimized out>) at ../Python/ceval.c:3110
#25 0x00000000005d6846 in PyEval_EvalFrameEx (throwflag=0,
    f=Frame 0x7f5686536908, for file /usr/lib/python3.7/threading.py, line 885, in _bootstrap
(self=<Thread(_target=<function at remote 0x7f568654d0d0>, _name='Thread-1', _args=(), _kwargs={}, _daemonic=False,
_ident=140009597445888, _tstate_lock=<_thread.lock at remote 0x7f56865a2e40>,
_started=<Event(_cond=<Condition(_lock=<_thread.lock at remote 0x7f5686650a80>, acquire=<built-in method acquire of
_thread.lock object at remote 0x7f5686650a80>, release=<built-in method release of _thread.lock object at remote
0x7f5686650a80>, _waiters=<collections.deque at remote 0x7f56865f8048>) at remote 0x7f56865f1b00>, _flag=True) at
remote 0x7f56865f1ac8>, _is_stopped=False, _initialized=True, _stderr=<_io.TextIOWrapper at remote 0x7f5686732708>--
Type <RET> for more, q to quit, c to continue without paging--
) at remote 0x7f56865f1a90>)) at ../Python/ceval.c:547
#26 function_code_fastcall (globals=<optimized out>, nargs=<optimized out>, args=<optimized out>, co=<optimized out>)
at ../Objects/call.c:283
#27 _PyFunction_FastCallDict (func=<optimized out>, args=<optimized out>, nargs=<optimized out>, kwargs=<optimized
out>) at ../Objects/call.c:322
#28 0x00000000004d4ca2 in _PyObject_FastCallDict (kwargs=0x0, nargs=1, args=0x7f5686521e00, callable=<function at
remote 0x7f5686547d90>)
    at ../Objects/call.c:98
#29 _PyObject_Call_Prepend (kwargs=0x0, args=<optimized out>,
    obj=<Thread(_target=<function at remote 0x7f568654d0d0>, _name='Thread-1', _args=(), _kwargs={}, _daemonic=False,
_ident=140009597445888, _tstate_lock=<_thread.lock at remote 0x7f56865a2e40>,
_started=<Event(_cond=<Condition(_lock=<_thread.lock at remote 0x7f5686650a80>, acquire=<built-in method acquire of
_thread.lock object at remote 0x7f5686650a80>, release=<built-in method release of _thread.lock object at remote
0x7f5686650a80>, _waiters=<collections.deque at remote 0x7f56865f8048>) at remote 0x7f56865f1b00>, _flag=True) at
remote 0x7f56865f1ac8>, _is_stopped=False, _initialized=True, _stderr=<_io.TextIOWrapper at remote 0x7f5686732708>) at
remote 0x7f56865f1a90>, callable=<function at remote 0x7f5686547d90>)
    at ../Objects/call.c:904
#30 method_call (method=<optimized out>, args=<optimized out>, kwargs=<optimized out>, method=<optimized out>,
args=<optimized out>,
    kwargs=<optimized out>) at ../Objects/classobject.c:309
#31 0x00000000005d8696 in PyObject_Call (callable=<method at remote 0x7f568673bdc8>, args=<optimized out>,
kwargs=<optimized out>)
    at ../Objects/call.c:245
#32 0x0000000000616903 in t_bootstrap (boot_raw=boot_raw@entry=0x7f568666dd00) at ../Modules/_threadmodule.c:994
#33 0x000000000062d7e4 in pythread_wrapper (arg=<optimized out>) at ../Python/thread_pthread.h:174
#34 0x00007f5686e21fa3 in start_thread (arg=<optimized out>) at pthread_create.c:486
#35 0x00007f5686b6906f in clone () at ../sysdeps/unix/sysv/linux/x86_64/clone.S:95

Thread 1 (Thread 0x7f5686a6d740 (LWP 15330)):
#0  futex_abstimed_wait_cancelable (private=0, abstime=0x0, expected=0, futex_word=0x7f5680000d50)
    at ../sysdeps/unix/sysv/linux/futex-internal.h:205
#1  do_futex_wait (sem=sem@entry=0x7f5680000d50, abstime=0x0) at sem_waitcommon.c:111
#2  0x00007f5686e2a988 in __new_sem_wait_slow (sem=0x7f5680000d50, abstime=0x0) at sem_waitcommon.c:181
#3  0x00000000005281f8 in PyThread_acquire_lock_timed (lock=0x7f5680000d50, microseconds=-1000000, intr_flag=1) at
../Python/thread_pthread.h:372
#4  0x0000000000500a45 in acquire_timed (timeout=<optimized out>, lock=0x7f5680000d50) at
../Modules/_threadmodule.c:61
#5  lock_PyThread_acquire_lock (self=0x7f56865a2e40, args=<optimized out>, kwds=<optimized out>) at
../Modules/_threadmodule.c:144
#6  0x00000000004d2d34 in _PyMethodDef_RawFastCallKeywords (kwnames=<optimized out>, nargs=<optimized out>,
args=<optimized out>,
    self=<_thread.lock at remote 0x7f56865a2e40>, method=0x87a1c0 <lock_methods+32>) at ../Objects/call.c:690
#7  _PyMethodDescr_FastCallKeywords (descrobj=<method_descriptor at remote 0x7f568673d630>, args=0x7f568659e730,
nargs=<optimized out>,
    kwnames=<optimized out>) at ../Objects/descrobject.c:288
#8  0x000000000054f619 in call_function (kwnames=0x0, oparg=3, pp_stack=0x7ffd8f826870) at ../Python/ceval.c:4593
#9  _PyEval_EvalFrameDefault (f=<optimized out>, throwflag=<optimized out>) at ../Python/ceval.c:3110
```

325

```
#10 0x0000000000548cd2 in PyEval_EvalFrameEx (throwflag=0,
    f=Frame 0x7f568659e5a0, for file /usr/lib/python3.7/threading.py, line 1048, in _wait_for_tstate_lock
(self=<Thread(_target=<function at remote 0x7f568654d0d0>, _name='Thread-1', _args=(), _kwargs={}, _daemonic=False,
_ident=140009597445888, _tstate_lock=<_thread.lock at remote 0x7f56865a2e40>,
_started=<Event(_cond=<Condition(_lock=<_thread.lock at remote 0x7f5686650a80>, acquire=<built-in method acquire of
_thread.lock object at remote 0x7f5686650a80>, release=<built-in method release of _thread.lock object at remote
0x7f5686650a80>, _waiters=<collections.deque at remote 0x7f56865f80--Type <RET> for more, q to quit, c to continue
without paging--
48>) at remote 0x7f56865f1b00>, _flag=True) at remote 0x7f56865f1ac8>, _is_stopped=False, _initialized=True,
_stderr=<_io.TextIOWrapper at remote 0x7f5686732708>) at remote 0x7f56865f1a90>, block=True, timeout=-1,
lock=<_thread.lock at remote 0x7f56865a2e40>)) at ../Python/ceval.c:547
#11 _PyEval_EvalCodeWithName (_co=<optimized out>, globals=<optimized out>, locals=<optimized out>, args=<optimized
out>, argcount=<optimized out>,
    kwnames=0x0, kwargs=0x7f568661c540, kwcount=<optimized out>, kwstep=1, defs=0x7f5686604c60, defcount=2,
kwdefs=0x0, closure=0x0,
    name='_wait_for_tstate_lock', qualname='Thread._wait_for_tstate_lock') at ../Python/ceval.c:3930
#12 0x00000000005d5802 in _PyFunction_FastCallKeywords (func=<optimized out>, stack=0x7f568661c538, nargs=1,
kwnames=<optimized out>)
    at ../Objects/call.c:433
#13 0x000000000054b72c in call_function (kwnames=0x0, oparg=<optimized out>, pp_stack=0x7ffd8f826af0) at
../Python/ceval.c:4616
#14 _PyEval_EvalFrameDefault (f=<optimized out>, throwflag=<optimized out>) at ../Python/ceval.c:3110
#15 0x0000000000548cd2 in PyEval_EvalFrameEx (throwflag=0,
    f=Frame 0x7f568661c3b8, for file /usr/lib/python3.7/threading.py, line 1032, in join
(self=<Thread(_target=<function at remote 0x7f568654d0d0>, _name='Thread-1', _args=(), _kwargs={}, _daemonic=False,
_ident=140009597445888, _tstate_lock=<_thread.lock at remote 0x7f56865a2e40>,
_started=<Event(_cond=<Condition(_lock=<_thread.lock at remote 0x7f5686650a80>, acquire=<built-in method acquire of
_thread.lock object at remote 0x7f5686650a80>, release=<built-in method release of _thread.lock object at remote
0x7f5686650a80>, _waiters=<collections.deque at remote 0x7f56865f8048>) at remote 0x7f56865f1b00>, _flag=True) at
remote 0x7f56865f1ac8>, _is_stopped=False, _initialized=True, _stderr=<_io.TextIOWrapper at remote 0x7f5686732708>) at
remote 0x7f56865f1a90>, timeout=None)) at ../Python/ceval.c:547
#16 _PyEval_EvalCodeWithName (_co=<optimized out>, globals=<optimized out>, locals=<optimized out>, args=<optimized
out>, argcount=<optimized out>,
    kwnames=0x0, kwargs=0x1e95f80, kwcount=<optimized out>, kwstep=1, defs=0x7f56866064f8, defcount=1, kwdefs=0x0,
closure=0x0, name='join',
    qualname='Thread.join') at ../Python/ceval.c:3930
#17 0x00000000005d5802 in _PyFunction_FastCallKeywords (func=<optimized out>, stack=0x1e95f78, nargs=1,
kwnames=<optimized out>)
    at ../Objects/call.c:433
#18 0x000000000054b72c in call_function (kwnames=0x0, oparg=<optimized out>, pp_stack=0x7ffd8f826d70) at
../Python/ceval.c:4616
#19 _PyEval_EvalFrameDefault (f=<optimized out>, throwflag=<optimized out>) at ../Python/ceval.c:3110
#20 0x00000000005d550c in PyEval_EvalFrameEx (throwflag=0,
    f=Frame 0x1e95df8, for file md9.py, line 42, in main (thread1=<Thread(_target=<function at remote 0x7f568654d0d0>,
_name='Thread-1', _args=(), _kwargs={}, _daemonic=False, _ident=140009597445888, _tstate_lock=<_thread.lock at remote
0x7f56865a2e40>, _started=<Event(_cond=<Condition(_lock=<_thread.lock at remote 0x7f5686650a80>, acquire=<built-in
method acquire of _thread.lock object at remote 0x7f5686650a80>, release=<built-in method release of _thread.lock
object at remote 0x7f5686650a80>, _waiters=<collections.deque at remote 0x7f56865f8048>) at remote 0x7f56865f1b00>,
_flag=True) at remote 0x7f56865f1ac8>, _is_stopped=False, _initialized=True, _stderr=<_io.TextIOWrapper at remote
0x7f5686732708>) at remote 0x7f56865f1a90>, thread2=<Thread(_target=<function at remote 0x7f568654d158>,
_name='Thread-2', _args=(...), _kwargs={}, _daemonic=False, _ident=140009589053184, _tstate_lock=<_thread.lock at
remote 0x7f56865a2e90>, _started=<Event(_cond=<Condition(_lock=<_thread.lock at remote 0x7f568666d5d0>,
acquire=<bu...(truncated)) at ../Python/ceval.c:547
#21 function_code_fastcall (globals=<optimized out>, nargs=<optimized out>, args=<optimized out>, co=<optimized out>)
at ../Objects/call.c:283
#22 _PyFunction_FastCallKeywords (func=<optimized out>, stack=<optimized out>, nargs=<optimized out>,
kwnames=<optimized out>)
    at ../Objects/call.c:408
#23 0x000000000054b590 in call_function (kwnames=0x0, oparg=<optimized out>, pp_stack=<synthetic pointer>) at
../Python/ceval.c:4616
#24 _PyEval_EvalFrameDefault (f=<optimized out>, throwflag=<optimized out>) at ../Python/ceval.c:3124
#25 0x0000000000548cd2 in PyEval_EvalFrameEx (throwflag=0, f=Frame 0x7f56867279f8, for file md9.py, line 46, in
<module> ())
    at ../Python/ceval.c:547
#26 _PyEval_EvalCodeWithName (_co=<optimized out>, globals=<optimized out>, locals=<optimized out>, args=<optimized
out>, argcount=<optimized out>,
--Type <RET> for more, q to quit, c to continue without paging--
    kwnames=0x0, kwargs=0x0, kwcount=<optimized out>, kwstep=2, defs=0x0, defcount=0, kwdefs=0x0, closure=0x0,
name=0x0, qualname=0x0)
    at ../Python/ceval.c:3930
#27 0x000000000054b083 in PyEval_EvalCodeEx (closure=0x0, kwdefs=0x0, defcount=0, defs=0x0, kwcount=0, kws=0x0,
argcount=0, args=0x0,
    locals=<optimized out>, globals=<optimized out>, _co=<optimized out>) at ../Python/ceval.c:3959
#28 PyEval_EvalCode (co=<optimized out>, globals=<optimized out>, locals=<optimized out>) at ../Python/ceval.c:524
```

```
#29 0x0000000000630562 in run_mod (mod=<optimized out>, filename=<optimized out>,
    globals={'__name__': '__main__', '__doc__': None, '__package__': None, '__loader__':
<SourceFileLoader(name='__main__', path='md9.py') at remote 0x7f5686677b00>, '__spec__': None, '__annotations__': {},
'__builtins__': <module at remote 0x7f568677dcc8>, '__file__': 'md9.py', '__cached__': None, 'time': <module at remote
0x7f5686686d18>, 'threading': <module at remote 0x7f56865f44a8>, 'cs1': <_thread.RLock at remote 0x7f568666ee40>,
'cs2': <_thread.RLock at remote 0x7f5686603030>, 'new_feature': <function at remote 0x7f56866f41e0>, 'thread_func1':
<function at remote 0x7f568654d0d0>, 'thread_func2': <function at remote 0x7f568654d158>, 'main': <function at remote
0x7f568654d1e0>},
...
    locals={'__name__': '__main__', '__doc__': None, '__package__': None, '__loader__':
<SourceFileLoader(name='__main__', path='md9.py') at remote 0x7f5686677b00>, '__spec__': None, '__annotations__': {},
'__builtins__': <module at remote 0x7f568677dcc8>, '__file__': 'md9.py', '__cached__': None, 'time': <module at remote
0x7f5686686d18>, 'threading': <module at remote 0x7f56865f44a8>, 'cs1': <_thread.RLock at remote 0x7f568666ee40>,
'cs2': <_thread.RLock at remote 0x7f5686603030>, 'new_feature': <function at remote 0x7f56866f41e0>, 'thread_func1':
<function at remote 0x7f568654d0d0>, 'thread_func2': <function at remote 0x7f568654d158>, 'main': <function at remote
0x7f568654d1e0>}, closeit=1, flags=0x7ffd8f82719c)
    at ../Python/pythonrun.c:988
#31 0x000000000063127f in PyRun_SimpleFileExFlags (fp=0x1ed85e0, filename=<optimized out>, closeit=1,
flags=0x7ffd8f82719c)
    at ../Python/pythonrun.c:429
#32 0x00000000006537ee in pymain_run_file (p_cf=0x7ffd8f82719c, filename=<optimized out>, fp=0x1ed85e0) at
../Modules/main.c:432
#33 pymain_run_filename (cf=0x7ffd8f82719c, pymain=0x7ffd8f827270) at ../Modules/main.c:1632
#34 pymain_run_python (pymain=0x7ffd8f827270) at ../Modules/main.c:2930
#35 pymain_main (pymain=<optimized out>, pymain=<optimized out>) at ../Modules/main.c:3091
#36 0x0000000000653b4e in _Py_UnixMain (argc=<optimized out>, argv=<optimized out>) at ../Modules/main.c:3126
#37 0x00007f5686a9409b in __libc_start_main (main=0x4b5910 <main>, argc=2, argv=0x7ffd8f8273b8, init=<optimized out>,
fini=<optimized out>,
    rtld_fini=<optimized out>, stack_end=0x7ffd8f8273a8) at ../csu/libc-start.c:308
#38 0x00000000005dceaa in _start () at ../Modules/main.c:730
```

We see that all 3 threads are waiting for fast userspace mutexes.

6.   To get Python script backtraces, we use the **py-bt** command:

(gdb) **thread apply all py-bt**

```
Thread 3 (Thread 0x7f5685d21700 (LWP 15332)):
Traceback (most recent call first):
  File "md9.py", line 29, in thread_func2
    cs1.acquire()
  File "/usr/lib/python3.7/threading.py", line 865, in run
    self._target(*self._args, **self._kwargs)
  File "/usr/lib/python3.7/threading.py", line 917, in _bootstrap_inner
    self.run()
  File "/usr/lib/python3.7/threading.py", line 885, in _bootstrap
    self._bootstrap_inner()

Thread 2 (Thread 0x7f5686522700 (LWP 15331)):
Traceback (most recent call first):
  File "md9.py", line 24, in thread_func1
    cs2.acquire()
  File "/usr/lib/python3.7/threading.py", line 865, in run
    self._target(*self._args, **self._kwargs)
  File "/usr/lib/python3.7/threading.py", line 917, in _bootstrap_inner
    self.run()
  File "/usr/lib/python3.7/threading.py", line 885, in _bootstrap
    self._bootstrap_inner()

Thread 1 (Thread 0x7f5686a6d740 (LWP 15330)):
Traceback (most recent call first):
  File "/usr/lib/python3.7/threading.py", line 1048, in _wait_for_tstate_lock
    elif lock.acquire(block, timeout):
  File "/usr/lib/python3.7/threading.py", line 1032, in join
```

327

```
      self._wait_for_tstate_lock()
  File "md9.py", line 42, in main
      thread1.join()
  File "md9.py", line 46, in <module>
      main()
```

Note: Threads #2 and #3 are blocked while acquiring *cs2* and *cs1* Python objects. Because these objects are *RLocks* (Reentrant Locks), we can check their thread ownership without examining the Python script source code. Reentrant locks must keep thread ownership to differentiate between the owner and other threads.

7.   We have the following information about *RLock* addresses from unmanaged backtraces above:

```
Thread 3 (Thread 0x7f5685d21700 (LWP 15332)):
#0  futex_abstimed_wait_cancelable (private=0, abstime=0x0, expected=0, futex_word=0x1e9b7f0) at
../sysdeps/unix/sysv/linux/futex-internal.h:205
#1  do_futex_wait (sem=sem@entry=0x1e9b7f0, abstime=0x0) at sem_waitcommon.c:111
#2  0x00007f5686e2a988 in __new_sem_wait_slow (sem=0x1e9b7f0, abstime=0x0) at sem_waitcommon.c:181
#3  0x00000000005281f8 in PyThread_acquire_lock_timed (lock=0x1e9b7f0, microseconds=-1000000, intr_flag=1) at
../Python/thread_pthread.h:372
#4  0x000000000061702a in acquire_timed (timeout=<optimized out>, lock=0x1e9b7f0) at ../Modules/_threadmodule.c:61
#5  rlock_acquire (self=0x7f568666ee40, args=<optimized out>, kwds=<optimized out>) at ../Modules/_threadmodule.c:306
#6  0x00000000004d2d34 in _PyMethodDef_RawFastCallKeywords (kwnames=<optimized out>, nargs=<optimized out>,
args=<optimized out>,
     self=<_thread.RLock at remote 0x7f568666ee40>, method=0x87a0a0 <rlock_methods>) at ../Objects/call.c:690
...

Thread 2 (Thread 0x7f5686522700 (LWP 15331)):
#0  futex_abstimed_wait_cancelable (private=0, abstime=0x0, expected=0, futex_word=0x1e844d0) at
../sysdeps/unix/sysv/linux/futex-internal.h:205
#1  do_futex_wait (sem=sem@entry=0x1e844d0, abstime=0x0) at sem_waitcommon.c:111
#2  0x00007f5686e2a988 in __new_sem_wait_slow (sem=0x1e844d0, abstime=0x0) at sem_waitcommon.c:181
#3  0x00000000005281f8 in PyThread_acquire_lock_timed (lock=0x1e844d0, microseconds=-1000000, intr_flag=1) at
../Python/thread_pthread.h:372
#4  0x000000000061702a in acquire_timed (timeout=<optimized out>, lock=0x1e844d0) at ../Modules/_threadmodule.c:61
#5  rlock_acquire (self=0x7f5686603030, args=<optimized out>, kwds=<optimized out>) at ../Modules/_threadmodule.c:306
#6  0x00000000004d2d34 in _PyMethodDef_RawFastCallKeywords (kwnames=<optimized out>, nargs=<optimized out>,
args=<optimized out>,
     self=<_thread.RLock at remote 0x7f5686603030>, method=0x87a0a0 <rlock_methods>) at ../Objects/call.c:690
--Type <RET> for more, q to quit, c to continue without paging--
...
```

8.   We dump addresses' memory and check values from the nearby offsets:

```
(gdb) x/4a 0x7f568666ee40
0x7f568666ee40: 0x2       0x87c1c0 <RLocktype>
0x7f568666ee50: 0x1e9b7f0        0x7f5686522700

(gdb) x/4a 0x7f5686603030
0x7f5686603030: 0x2       0x87c1c0 <RLocktype>
0x7f5686603040: 0x1e844d0        0x7f5685d21700
```

Note: We see that thread #3 (0x7f5685d21700) is waiting for the *RLock* 0x7f568666ee40 owned by thread #2 (0x7f5686522700). We also see that thread #2 (0x7f5686522700) is waiting for the *RLock* 0x7f5686603030 owned by thread #3 (0x7f5685d21700). Based on this mutual wait, we hypothesize the deadlock between threads.

9.   We quit GDB (**q**) and kill the *python* process (**^C^C**).

Expected Behavior

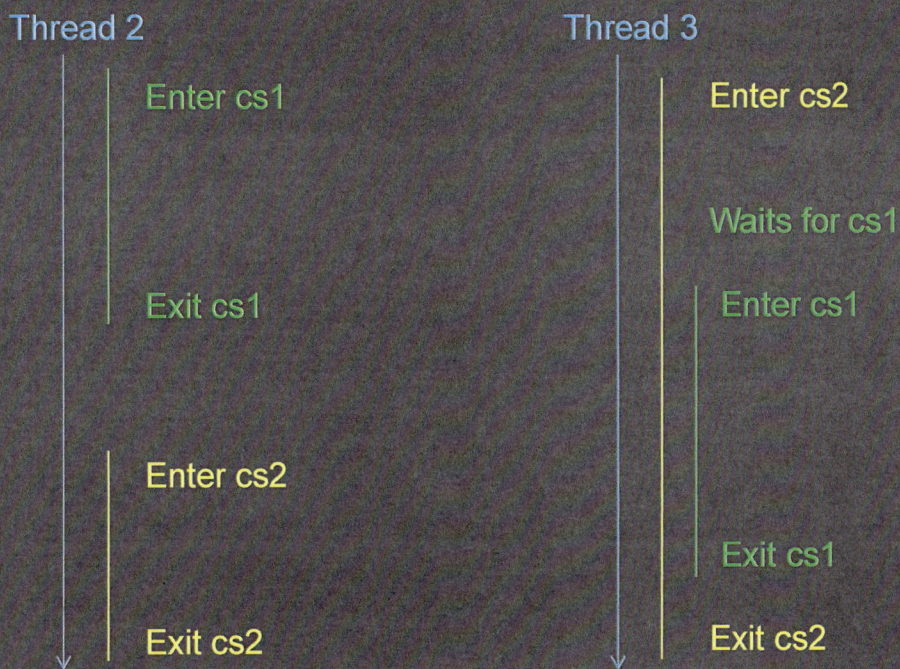

Thread 2	Thread 3
Enter cs1	Enter cs2
	Waits for cs1
Exit cs1	Enter cs1
Enter cs2	
	Exit cs1
Exit cs2	Exit cs2

This is the expected behavior for the *md9* program. The code is supposed to be deadlock-free.

Deadlock

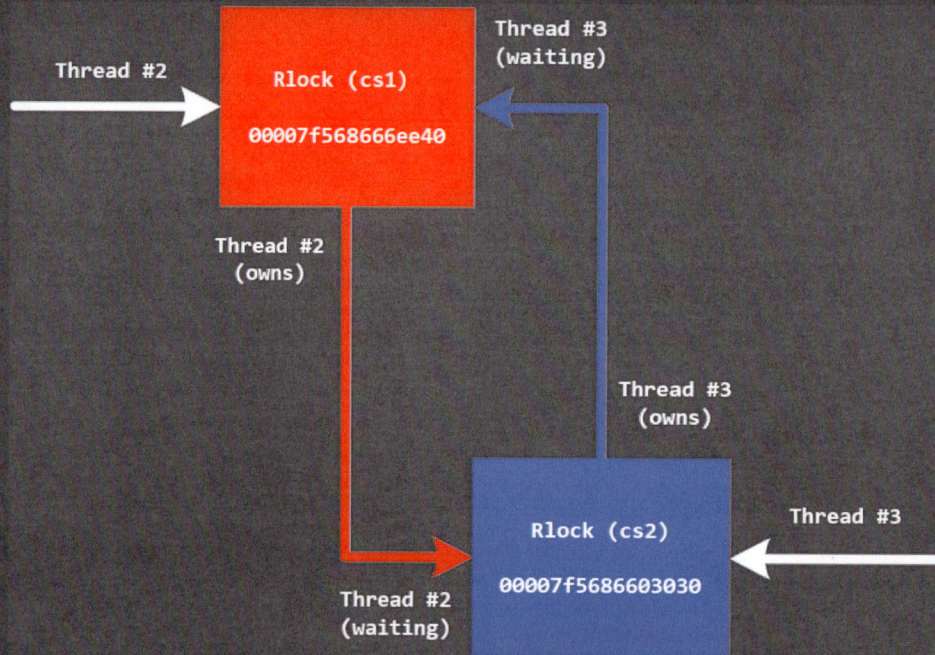

This diagram shows the abnormal behavior of *md9* after a problem new feature was introduced and incorrectly fixed. The data on the diagram corresponds to the exercise transcript and may differ in your debugging system.

Time Travel Debugging

Exercise TD5

Exercise TD5

- **Goal:** Learn how to find hidden exceptions using Time Travel Debugging

- **Elementary Diagnostics Patterns:** Hang

- **Memory Analysis Patterns:** C++ Exception; Hidden Exception (User Space)

- **Debugging Implementation Patterns:** Instruction Trace

- \ALD4\Exercise-Linux-TD5.pdf

Goal: Learn how to find hidden exceptions using Time Travel Debugging.

Elementary Diagnostics Patterns: Hang.

Memory Analysis Patterns: C++ Exception; Hidden Exception (User Space).

Debugging Implementation Patterns: Instruction Trace.

1.   This exercise is based on the previous Exercise UD5. The source code and the *Makefile* to build executables and libraries can be found in the *ud5* directory:

```
$ git clone https://bitbucket.org/softwarediagnostics/ald4
```

2.   Before starting Hyper-V VM (see Exercise KD0 for configuration), open the elevated PowerShell on the host and enable performance monitoring:

```
> Set-VMProcessor "Ubuntu GDB" -Perfmon @("pmu")
```

Note: Please see how to configure your system if it is other than Hyper-V here: https://github.com/rr-debugger/rr/wiki/Building-And-Installing

3.   Start VM and verify the level of access to performance monitoring:

```
$ perf stat -e br_inst_retired.conditional true
Error:
Access to performance monitoring and observability operations is limited.
Consider adjusting /proc/sys/kernel/perf_event_paranoid setting to open
access to performance monitoring and observability operations for processes
without CAP_PERFMON, CAP_SYS_PTRACE or CAP_SYS_ADMIN Linux capability.
More information can be found at 'Perf events and tool security' document:
https://www.kernel.org/doc/html/latest/admin-guide/perf-security.html
perf_event_paranoid setting is 4:
  -1: Allow use of (almost) all events by all users
      Ignore mlock limit after perf_event_mlock_kb without CAP_IPC_LOCK
>= 0: Disallow raw and ftrace function tracepoint access
>= 1: Disallow CPU event access
>= 2: Disallow kernel profiling
To make the adjusted perf_event_paranoid setting permanent preserve it
in /etc/sysctl.conf (e.g. kernel.perf_event_paranoid = <setting>)

$ sudo sysctl kernel.perf_event_paranoid=1
kernel.perf_event_paranoid = 1

$ perf stat -e br_inst_retired.conditional true

 Performance counter stats for 'true':

        133,809      br_inst_retired.conditional
```

```
   0.001432684 seconds time elapsed

   0.001547000 seconds user
   0.000000000 seconds sys
```

4.   Install the *rr* package. You can also build and install the latest version from the *rr* project site: https://rr-project.org/.

```
$ sudo apt-get install rr
```

5.   Mount the shared folder.

```
$ sudo mount -t cifs //172.27.0.1/ALD4 /mnt/c/ALD4 -o
noperm,mfsymlinks,username=coredump,password=coredump2!
```

```
$ cd /mnt/c/ALD4/ud5
```

6.   Run the *ud5a* executable.

```
/mnt/c/ALD4/ud5$ ./ud5a &
```

7.   Start recording the *ud5bv3* execution, wait 1-2 minutes, and break it (**^C**):

```
/mnt/c/ALD4/ud5$ rr record ./ud5bv3
rr: Saving execution to trace directory `/home/coredump/.local/share/rr/ud5bv3-0'.
^C
/mnt/c/ALD4/ud5$
```

8.   Now replay the recorded execution:

```
/mnt/c/ALD4/ud5$ rr replay
GNU gdb (Ubuntu 12.1-0ubuntu1~22.04.2) 12.1
Copyright (C) 2022 Free Software Foundation, Inc.
License GPLv3+: GNU GPL version 3 or later <http://gnu.org/licenses/gpl.html>
This is free software: you are free to change and redistribute it.
There is NO WARRANTY, to the extent permitted by law.
Type "show copying" and "show warranty" for details.
This GDB was configured as "x86_64-linux-gnu".
Type "show configuration" for configuration details.
For bug reporting instructions, please see:
<https://www.gnu.org/software/gdb/bugs/>.
Find the GDB manual and other documentation resources online at:
    <http://www.gnu.org/software/gdb/documentation/>.

For help, type "help".
Type "apropos word" to search for commands related to "word"...
Reading symbols from /mnt/c/ALD4/ud5/ud5bv3...
Really redefine built-in command "restart"? (y or n) [answered Y; input not from terminal]
Remote debugging using 127.0.0.1:5055
Reading symbols from /lib64/ld-linux-x86-64.so.2...
Reading symbols from /usr/lib/debug/.build-
id/41/86944c50f8a32b47d74931e3f512b811813b64.debug...
BFD: warning: system-supplied DSO at 0x6fffd000 has a section extending past end of file
```

```
0x00007c4810b29290 in _start () from /lib64/ld-linux-x86-64.so.2
(rr)
```

9.   Enable catching exceptions and run the recording:

```
(rr) catch throw
Catchpoint 1 (throw)

(rr) c
Continuing.

Catchpoint 1 (exception thrown), 0x00007c48108ae4a1 in __cxa_throw () from /lib/x86_64-linux-
gnu/libstdc++.so.6

(rr) bt
#0  0x00007c48108ae4a1 in __cxa_throw ()
    from /lib/x86_64-linux-gnu/libstdc++.so.6
#1  0x0000627c8fa9b304 in new_feature () at new_feature.cpp:3
#2  0x0000627c8fa9b249 in start_modeling () at ud5bv3.cpp:34
#3  0x0000627c8fa9b1ea in main () at ud5bv3.cpp:18
```

10.   We can go back while skipping function calls via the **reverse-next** command:

```
(rr) reverse-next
Single stepping until exit from function __cxa_throw,
which has no line number information.
new_feature () at new_feature.cpp:3
3               throw 0;

(rr) reverse-next
start_modeling () at ud5bv3.cpp:34
34                       new_feature();

(rr) bt
#0  start_modeling () at ud5bv3.cpp:34
#1  0x0000627c8fa9b1ea in main () at ud5bv3.cpp:18

(rr) reverse-next
30              sleep(10); // some work

(rr) reverse-next
28          sem_wait(sem_b);

(rr) reverse-next
26              if (sem_b == SEM_FAILED) exit(EXIT_FAILURE);

(rr) reverse-next
25          sem_t *sem_b = sem_open("ud5_sem_b", O_CREAT, 0644, 1);

(rr) reverse-next
main () at ud5bv3.cpp:18
```

11.   We can also step back if necessary, instruction by instruction:

```
(rr) reverse-step
0x00007c481049cb52 in __sem_unlink (name=<optimized out>) at ../sysdeps/pthread/sem_unlink.c:46
46      ../sysdeps/pthread/sem_unlink.c: No such file or directory.
```

```
(rr) bt
#0  0x00007c481049cb52 in __sem_unlink (name=<optimized out>)
    at ../sysdeps/pthread/sem_unlink.c:46
#1  0x0000627c8fa9b1e5 in main () at ud5bv3.cpp:16
```

```
(rr) reverse-step
0x00007c481049cb70  43     in ../sysdeps/pthread/sem_unlink.c
```

```
(rr) reverse-finish
Run back to call of #0  0x00007c481049cb70 in __sem_unlink (
    name=<optimized out>) at ../sysdeps/pthread/sem_unlink.c:43
0x0000627c8fa9b1e0 in main () at ud5bv3.cpp:16
16          sem_unlink("ud5_sem_b"); // cleanup in case of previous failures
```

```
(rr) reverse-next
16          sem_unlink("ud5_sem_b"); // cleanup in case of previous failures
```

```
(rr) reverse-next
__libc_start_call_main (main=main@entry=0x627c8fa9b1d5 <main()>, argc=argc@entry=1,
argv=argv@entry=0x7fffd4479e18) at ../sysdeps/nptl/libc_start_call_main.h:58
58      ../sysdeps/nptl/libc_start_call_main.h: No such file or directory.
```

```
(rr) bt
#0  __libc_start_call_main (main=main@entry=0x627c8fa9b1d5 <main()>,
    argc=argc@entry=1, argv=argv@entry=0x7fffd4479e18)
    at ../sysdeps/nptl/libc_start_call_main.h:58
#1  0x00007c4810429e40 in __libc_start_main_impl (
    main=0x627c8fa9b1d5 <main()>, argc=1, argv=0x7fffd4479e18,
    init=<optimized out>, fini=<optimized out>, rtld_fini=<optimized out>,
    stack_end=0x7fffd4479e08) at ../csu/libc-start.c:392
#2  0x0000627c8fa9b11a in _start ()
```

```
(rr) reverse-finish
Run back to call of #0  __libc_start_call_main (
    main=main@entry=0x627c8fa9b1d5 <main()>, argc=argc@entry=1,
    argv=argv@entry=0x7fffd4479e18)
    at ../sysdeps/nptl/libc_start_call_main.h:58
0x00007c4810429e3b in __libc_start_main_impl (main=0x627c8fa9b1d5 <main()>, argc=1,
argv=0x7fffd4479e18, init=<optimized out>, fini=<optimized out>, rtld_fini=<optimized out>,
stack_end=0x7fffd4479e08) at ../csu/libc-start.c:392
392    ../csu/libc-start.c: No such file or directory.
```

```
(rr) bt
#0  0x00007c4810429e3b in __libc_start_main_impl (
    main=0x627c8fa9b1d5 <main()>, argc=1, argv=0x7fffd4479e18,
    init=<optimized out>, fini=<optimized out>, rtld_fini=<optimized out>,
    stack_end=0x7fffd4479e08) at ../csu/libc-start.c:392
#1  0x0000627c8fa9b11a in _start ()
```

```
(rr) reverse-finish
Run back to call of #0  0x00007c4810429e3b in __libc_start_main_impl (
    main=0x627c8fa9b1d5 <main()>, argc=1, argv=0x7fffd4479e18,
    init=<optimized out>, fini=<optimized out>, rtld_fini=<optimized out>,
    stack_end=0x7fffd4479e08) at ../csu/libc-start.c:392
0x0000627c8fa9b114 in _start ()

(rr) reverse-finish
"finish" not meaningful in the outermost frame.

(rr) bt
#0  0x0000627c8fa9b114 in _start ()
```

12.   The rr **help** command is an extension of GDB help, for example:

```
(rr) help
List of classes of commands:

aliases -- User-defined aliases of other commands.
breakpoints -- Making program stop at certain points.
data -- Examining data.
files -- Specifying and examining files.
internals -- Maintenance commands.
obscure -- Obscure features.
running -- Running the program.
stack -- Examining the stack.
status -- Status inquiries.
support -- Support facilities.
text-user-interface -- TUI is the GDB text based interface.
tracepoints -- Tracing of program execution without stopping the program.
user-defined -- User-defined commands.

Type "help" followed by a class name for a list of commands in that class.
Type "help all" for the list of all commands.
Type "help" followed by command name for full documentation.
Type "apropos word" to search for commands related to "word".
Type "apropos -v word" for full documentation of commands related to "word".
Command name abbreviations are allowed if unambiguous.

(rr) help running
Running the program.

List of commands:

advance -- Continue the program up to the given location (same form as args for break command).
attach -- Attach to a process or file outside of GDB.
continue, fg, c -- Continue program being debugged, after signal or breakpoint.
detach -- Detach a process or file previously attached.
detach checkpoint -- Detach from a checkpoint (experimental).
detach inferiors -- Detach from inferior ID (or list of IDS).
disconnect -- Disconnect from a target.
finish, fin -- Execute until selected stack frame returns.
handle -- Specify how to handle signals.
inferior -- Use this command to switch between inferiors.
interrupt -- Interrupt the execution of the debugged program.
jump, j -- Continue program being debugged at specified line or address.
kill -- Kill execution of program being debugged.
kill inferiors -- Kill inferior ID (or list of IDs).
next, n -- Step program, proceeding through subroutine calls.
nexti, ni -- Step one instruction, but proceed through subroutine calls.
queue-signal -- Queue a signal to be delivered to the current thread when it is resumed.
```

```
reverse-continue, rc -- Continue program being debugged but run it in reverse.
reverse-finish -- Execute backward until just before selected stack frame is called.
reverse-next, rn -- Step program backward, proceeding through subroutine calls.
reverse-nexti,
   rni -- Step backward one instruction, but proceed through called subroutines.
reverse-step,
   rs -- Step program backward until it reaches the beginning of another source line.
reverse-stepi, rsi -- Step backward exactly one instruction.
run, r -- Start debugged program.
signal -- Continue program with the specified signal.
start -- Start the debugged program stopping at the beginning of the main procedure.
starti -- Start the debugged program stopping at the first instruction.
step, s -- Step program until it reaches a different source line.
stepi, si -- Step one instruction exactly.
taas -- Apply a command to all threads (ignoring errors and empty output).
target -- Connect to a target machine or process.
target core -- Use a core file as a target.
target ctf -- (Use a CTF directory as a target.
target exec -- Use an executable file as a target.
--Type <RET> for more, q to quit, c to continue without paging--
target extended-remote -- Use a remote computer via a serial line, using a gdb-specific protocol.
target native -- Native process (started by the "run" command).
target record-btrace -- Collect control-flow trace and provide the execution history.
target record-core -- Log program while executing and replay execution from log.
target record-full -- Log program while executing and replay execution from log.
target remote -- Use a remote computer via a serial line, using a gdb-specific protocol.
target tfile -- Use a trace file as a target.
task -- Use this command to switch between Ada tasks.
task apply -- Apply a command to a list of tasks.
task apply all -- Apply a command to all tasks in the current inferior.
tfaas -- Apply a command to all frames of all threads (ignoring errors and empty output).
thread, t -- Use this command to switch between threads.
thread apply -- Apply a command to a list of threads.
thread apply all -- Apply a command to all threads.
thread find -- Find threads that match a regular expression.
thread name -- Set the current thread's name.
until, u -- Execute until past the current line or past a LOCATION.
--Type <RET> for more, q to quit, c to continue without paging--

Type "help" followed by command name for full documentation.
Type "apropos word" to search for commands related to "word".
Type "apropos -v word" for full documentation of commands related to "word".
Command name abbreviations are allowed if unambiguous.
```

13.   Now, we quit *rr* (**q**) and kill the *ud5a* process.

Rust Debugging

Exercise RD11

Exercise RD11

- **Goal:** Learn how WinDbg, GDB, and LLDB can be used to debug Rust applications

- **Elementary Diagnostics Patterns:** Error Message

- **Memory Analysis Patterns:** Stack Trace

- **Debugging Implementation Patterns:** Break-in; Code Breakpoint; Scope; Variable Value; Type Structure

- \ALD4\Exercise-Linux-RD11.pdf

Goal: Learn how WinDbg can be used to debug Rust applications.

Elementary Diagnostics Patterns: Error Message.

Memory Analysis Patterns: Stack Trace.

Debugging Implementation Patterns: Break-in; Code Breakpoint; Scope; Variable Value; Type Structure.

1.   The source code to build the executable can be found in the *rd11* directory:

```
$ git clone https://bitbucket.org/softwarediagnostics/ald4
```

2.   When you run the *rd11* program, it shows an error message after 10 seconds.

```
/mnt/c/ALD4/rd11$ target/debug/rd11
Error
```

3.   Launch the *rd11* executable under the *gdbserver*:

```
/mnt/c/ALD4/rd11$ gdbserver localhost:1234 target/debug/rd11
Process target/debug/rd11 created; pid = 1736
Listening on port 1234
```

4.   Connect WinDbg to the remote debugger:

```
Microsoft (R) Windows Debugger Version 10.0.27553.1004 AMD64
Copyright (c) Microsoft Corporation. All rights reserved.

64-bit machine not using 64-bit API

************* Path validation summary **************
Response                     Time (ms)      Location
Deferred                                    srv*
Symbol search path is: srv*
Executable search path is:
Unknown System Version 0 UP Free x64
System Uptime: not available
Process Uptime: not available
Reloading current modules
ModLoad: 00005555`55554000 00005555`555ad150   /mnt/c/ALD4/rd11/target/debug/rd11
.
ReadVirtual() failed in GetXStateConfiguration() first read attempt (error == 0.)
00007fff`f7fd6090 mov     rdi,rsp
```

5.   First, we put a code breakpoint on the *rd11::main* function (please note, this is Rust rd11 crate's *main*, not C or C++ *main* that may also exist):

```
0:000> lm
start             end               module name
00005555`55554000 00005555`555ad150   rd11        (deferred)
```

```
0:000> x rd11!*main*
Unable to load image /mnt/c/ALD4/rd11/target/debug/rd11, Win32 error 0n2
*** WARNING: Unable to verify timestamp for /mnt/c/ALD4/rd11/target/debug/rd11
00000000`00000000 rd11!main_thread = std::thread::Thread
00005555`555629a0 rd11!rd11::main (void)
00005555`555ad0f8 rd11!std::sys::unix::stack_overflow::imp::MAIN_ALTSTACK::h1249fea233ef7b4a =
<no type information>
00005555`55562a60 rd11!main = <no type information>

0:000> bp rd11!rd11::main
```

6.   We continue execution until the breakpoint is hit (we ignore any intermediate signals, and we use **kL** instead
of **k** to omit Rust runtime source code references):

```
0:000> g
(6c8.6c8): Signal SIGWINCH code 128 at 0x7ffff7fd6090 originating from PID 6c8
First chance exceptions are reported before any exception handling.
This exception may be expected and handled.
00007fff`f7fd6090 mov     rdi,rsp

0:000> k
 # Child-SP          RetAddr           Call Site
00 00007fff`ffffe160 00000000`00000000 0x00007fff`f7fd6090

0:000> g
ModLoad: 00007fff`f7fd3000 00007fff`f7fd3000   linux-vdso.so.1
ModLoad: 00007fff`f7fa8000 00007fff`f7fc1430   /lib/x86_64-linux-gnu/libgcc_s.so.1
ModLoad: 00007fff`f7f9e000 00007fff`f7fa7be0   /lib/x86_64-linux-gnu/librt.so.1
ModLoad: 00007fff`f7f7d000 00007fff`f7f9d4c0   /lib/x86_64-linux-gnu/libpthread.so.0
ModLoad: 00007fff`f7f78000 00007fff`f7f7c110   /lib/x86_64-linux-gnu/libdl.so.2
ModLoad: 00007fff`f7db8000 00007fff`f7f77800   /lib/x86_64-linux-gnu/libc.so.6
ModLoad: 00007fff`f7fd5000 00007fff`f7ffe190   /lib64/ld-linux-x86-64.so.2
Breakpoint 0 hit
rd11!rd11::main:
00005555`555629a0 push    rax

0:000> kL
 # Child-SP          RetAddr           Call Site
00 00007fff`ffffde78 00005555`5555e6cb rd11!rd11::main
01 00007fff`ffffde80 00005555`5555e4ee rd11!core::ops::function::FnOnce::call_once<fn(), ()>+0xb
02 00007fff`ffffdea0 00005555`55561671 rd11!std::sys_common::backtrace::__rust_begin_short_backtrace<fn(), ()>+0xe
03 00007fff`ffffdec0 00005555`55575a7e rd11!std::rt::lang_start::{closure#0}<()>+0x11
04 (Inline Function) --------`-------- rd11!core::ops::function::impls::{impl#2}::call_once<(), (dyn
core::ops::function::Fn<(), Output=i32> + core::marker::Sync + core::panic::unwind_safe::RefUnwindSafe)>+0x3
05 (Inline Function) --------`-------- rd11!std::panicking::try::do_call<&(dyn core::ops::function::Fn<(),
Output=i32> + core::marker::Sync + core::panic::unwind_safe::RefUnwindSafe), i32>+0x3
06 (Inline Function) --------`-------- rd11!std::panicking::try<i32, &(dyn core::ops::function::Fn<(), Output=i32>
+ core::marker::Sync + core::panic::unwind_safe::RefUnwindSafe)>+0x3
07 (Inline Function) --------`-------- rd11!std::panic::catch_unwind<&(dyn core::ops::function::Fn<(), Output=i32>
+ core::marker::Sync + core::panic::unwind_safe::RefUnwindSafe), i32>+0x3
08 (Inline Function) --------`-------- rd11!std::rt::lang_start_internal::{closure#2}+0x3
09 (Inline Function) --------`--------
rd11!std::panicking::try::do_call<std::rt::lang_start_internal::{closure_env#2}, isize>+0x3
0a (Inline Function) --------`-------- rd11!std::panicking::try<isize,
std::rt::lang_start_internal::{closure_env#2}>+0x3
0b (Inline Function) --------`--------
rd11!std::panic::catch_unwind<std::rt::lang_start_internal::{closure_env#2}, isize>+0x3
0c 00007fff`ffffdee0 00005555`5556164a rd11!std::rt::lang_start_internal+0x42e
0d 00007fff`ffffe040 00005555`55562a7e rd11!std::rt::lang_start<()>+0x3a
0e 00007fff`ffffe080 00007fff`f7ddc09b rd11!main+0x1e
0f 00007fff`ffffe090 00005555`5555c8fa libc_so!__libc_start_main+0xeb
10 00007fff`ffffe150 ffffffff`ffffffff rd11!start+0x2a
11 00007fff`ffffe158 00000000`00000000 0xffffffff`ffffffff
```

7. Next, we put code breakpoints on all possible *write* functions:

```
0:000> bm *!*write*
  1: 00005555`5555d8b0 @!"rd11!std::io::Write::write_fmt::{impl#0}::write_str<std::sys::unix::stdio::Stderr>"
  2: 00005555`5555d770
@!"rd11!core::fmt::Write::write_char<std::io::Write::write_fmt::Adapter<std::sys::unix::stdio::Stderr>>"
  3: 00005555`5555d7e0
@!"rd11!core::fmt::Write::write_fmt<std::io::Write::write_fmt::Adapter<std::sys::unix::stdio::Stderr>>"
  4: 00005555`5555d820
@!"rd11!core::fmt::{impl#0}::write_char<std::io::Write::write_fmt::Adapter<std::sys::unix::stdio::Stderr>>"
  5: 00005555`5555d840
@!"rd11!core::fmt::{impl#0}::write_fmt<std::io::Write::write_fmt::Adapter<std::sys::unix::stdio::Stderr>>"
  6: 00005555`5555d880
@!"rd11!core::fmt::{impl#0}::write_str<std::io::Write::write_fmt::Adapter<std::sys::unix::stdio::Stderr>>"
  7: 00005555`5555e7f0 @!"rd11!core::ptr::drop_in_place<&mut
std::io::Write::write_fmt::Adapter<std::sys::unix::stdio::Stderr>>"
  8: 00005555`5555ee50
@!"rd11!core::ptr::drop_in_place<std::io::Write::write_fmt::Adapter<std::sys::unix::stdio::Stderr>>"
  9: 00005555`55561240 @!"rd11!std::io::Write::write_all<std::sys::unix::stdio::Stderr>"
 10: 00005555`55561490 @!"rd11!std::io::Write::write_fmt<std::sys::unix::stdio::Stderr>"
 11: 00005555`555667e0 @!"rd11!alloc::string::{impl#65}::write_char"
 12: 00005555`555630b0 @!"rd11!core::ptr::drop_in_place<&mut std::io::Write::write_fmt::Adapter<alloc::vec::Vec<u8,
alloc::alloc::Global>>>"
 13: 00005555`555635a0
@!"rd11!core::ptr::drop_in_place<std::sync::remutex::ReentrantMutexGuard<core::cell::RefCell<std::io::buffered::linewr
iter::LineWriter<std::io::stdio::StdoutRaw>>>>"
 14: 00005555`555643f0 @!"rd11!core::ptr::drop_in_place<std::io::Write::write_fmt::Adapter<alloc::vec::Vec<u8,
alloc::alloc::Global>>>"
 15: 00005555`55564480 @!"rd11!core::ptr::drop_in_place<std::io::buffered::bufwriter::{impl#0}::flush_buf::BufGuard>"
 16: 00005555`55564590
@!"rd11!core::ptr::drop_in_place<std::io::buffered::linewriter::LineWriter<std::io::stdio::StdoutRaw>>"
 17: 00005555`55562c50 @!"rd11!core::fmt::Write::write_char<std::io::Write::write_fmt::Adapter<alloc::vec::Vec<u8,
alloc::alloc::Global>>>"
 18: 00005555`55562d60
@!"rd11!core::fmt::Write::write_char<std::io::Write::write_fmt::Adapter<std::io::stdio::StdoutLock>>"
 19: 00005555`55562e40
@!"rd11!core::fmt::Write::write_char<std::io::Write::write_fmt::Adapter<std::sys::unix::stdio::Stderr>>"
 20: 00005555`55562f20
@!"rd11!core::fmt::Write::write_fmt<std::io::Write::write_fmt::Adapter<std::io::stdio::StdoutLock>>"
 21: 00005555`55562f60
@!"rd11!core::fmt::Write::write_fmt<std::io::Write::write_fmt::Adapter<std::sys::unix::stdio::Stderr>>"
 22: 00005555`55562fa0 @!"rd11!core::fmt::Write::write_fmt<std::io::Write::write_fmt::Adapter<alloc::vec::Vec<u8,
alloc::alloc::Global>>>"
 23: 00005555`55565a80
@!"rd11!core::fmt::{impl#0}::write_char<std::io::Write::write_fmt::Adapter<std::sys::unix::stdio::Stderr>>"
 24: 00005555`55565b60 @!"rd11!core::fmt::{impl#0}::write_char<alloc::string::String>"
 25: 00005555`55565b70 @!"rd11!core::fmt::{impl#0}::write_char<std::io::Write::write_fmt::Adapter<alloc::vec::Vec<u8,
alloc::alloc::Global>>>"
 26: 00005555`55565b80
@!"rd11!core::fmt::{impl#0}::write_char<std::io::Write::write_fmt::Adapter<std::io::stdio::StdoutLock>>"
 27: 00005555`55565c60 @!"rd11!core::fmt::{impl#0}::write_fmt<std::io::Write::write_fmt::Adapter<alloc::vec::Vec<u8,
alloc::alloc::Global>>>"
 28: 00005555`55565cb0
@!"rd11!core::fmt::{impl#0}::write_fmt<std::io::Write::write_fmt::Adapter<std::sys::unix::stdio::Stderr>>"
 29: 00005555`55565d00
@!"rd11!core::fmt::{impl#0}::write_fmt<std::io::Write::write_fmt::Adapter<std::io::stdio::StdoutLock>>"
 30: 00005555`55565d50 @!"rd11!core::fmt::{impl#0}::write_fmt<alloc::string::String>"
 31: 00005555`55565da0 @!"rd11!core::fmt::{impl#0}::write_str<alloc::string::String>"
 32: 00005555`55565e00
@!"rd11!core::fmt::{impl#0}::write_str<std::io::Write::write_fmt::Adapter<std::io::stdio::StdoutLock>>"
 33: 00005555`55565e10
@!"rd11!core::fmt::{impl#0}::write_str<std::io::Write::write_fmt::Adapter<std::sys::unix::stdio::Stderr>>"
 34: 00005555`55565e20 @!"rd11!core::fmt::{impl#0}::write_str<std::io::Write::write_fmt::Adapter<alloc::vec::Vec<u8,
alloc::alloc::Global>>>"
 35: 00005555`5555b730 @!"rd11!std::sys::unix::locks::futex_rwlock::RwLock::wake_writer_or_readers"
 36: 00005555`5557da70 @!"rd11!std::sys::unix::stdio::{impl#5}::write"
 37: 00005555`5557dad0 @!"rd11!std::sys::unix::stdio::{impl#5}::write_vectored"
 38: 00005555`5557db30 @!"rd11!std::sys::unix::stdio::{impl#5}::is_write_vectored"
 39: 00005555`5555af00
@!"rd11!std::sync::once_lock::OnceLock::initialize<std::sync::remutex::ReentrantMutex<core::cell::RefCell<std::io::buf
fered::linewriter::LineWriter<std::io::stdio::StdoutRaw>>>,
```

std::sync::once_lock::{impl#0}::get_or_init::{closure_env#0}<std::sync::remutex::ReentrantMutex<core::cell::RefCell<st
d::io::buffered::linewriter::LineWriter<std::io::stdio::StdoutRaw>>>, std::io::stdio::stdout::{closure_env#0}>, !>"
  40: 00005555`5555af50
@!"rd11!std::sync::once_lock::OnceLock::initialize<std::sync::remutex::ReentrantMutex<core::cell::RefCell<std::io::buf
fered::linewriter::LineWriter<std::io::stdio::StdoutRaw>>>,
std::sync::once_lock::{impl#0}::get_or_init::{closure_env#0}<std::sync::remutex::ReentrantMutex<core::cell::RefCell<st
d::io::buffered::linewriter::LineWriter<std::io::stdio::StdoutRaw>>>, std::io::stdio::cleanup::{closure_env#0}>, !>"
  41: 00005555`55577c30 @!"rd11!std::io::Write::write_all<std::sys::unix::stdio::Stderr>"
  42: 00005555`55577cf0 @!"rd11!std::io::Write::write_all_vectored<alloc::vec::Vec<u8, alloc::alloc::Global>>"
  43: 00005555`55578010 @!"rd11!std::io::Write::write_all_vectored<std::sys::unix::stdio::Stderr>"
  44: 00005555`55578220 @!"rd11!std::io::Write::write_fmt<std::sys::unix::stdio::Stderr>"
  45: 00005555`55578320 @!"rd11!std::io::Write::write_fmt<alloc::vec::Vec<u8, alloc::alloc::Global>>"
  46: 00005555`55578420 @!"rd11!std::io::Write::write_fmt::{impl#0}::write_str<std::io::stdio::StdoutLock>"
  47: 00005555`555784d0 @!"rd11!std::io::Write::write_fmt::{impl#0}::write_str<std::sys::unix::stdio::Stderr>"
  48: 00005555`55578630 @!"rd11!std::io::Write::write_fmt::{impl#0}::write_str<alloc::vec::Vec<u8,
alloc::alloc::Global>>"
  49: 00005555`55577060 @!"rd11!std::io::impls::{impl#11}::write<alloc::alloc::Global>"
  50: 00005555`555770d0 @!"rd11!std::io::impls::{impl#11}::write_vectored<alloc::alloc::Global>"
  51: 00005555`55577270 @!"rd11!std::io::impls::{impl#11}::is_write_vectored<alloc::alloc::Global>"
  52: 00005555`55577280 @!"rd11!std::io::impls::{impl#11}::write_all<alloc::alloc::Global>"
  53: 00005555`555766c0 @!"rd11!std::io::buffered::bufwriter::BufWriter::flush_buf<std::io::stdio::StdoutRaw>"
  54: 00005555`5555add0 @!"rd11!std::io::buffered::bufwriter::BufWriter::write_all_cold<std::io::stdio::StdoutRaw>"
  55: 00005555`555773a0 @!"rd11!std::io::stdio::{impl#13}::write_fmt"
  56: 00005555`55577580 @!"rd11!std::io::stdio::{impl#14}::write_all"
  57: 00005555`5555bc70
@!"rd11!std::sys_common::once::futex::Once::call<std::sync::once::{impl#2}::call_once_force::{closure_env#0}<std::sync
::once_lock::{impl#0}::initialize::{closure_env#0}<std::sync::remutex::ReentrantMutex<core::cell::RefCell<std::io::buf
fered::linewriter::LineWriter<std::io::stdio::StdoutRaw>>>,
std::sync::once_lock::{impl#0}::get_or_init::{closure_env#0}<std::sync::remutex::ReentrantMutex<core::cell::RefCell<st
d::io::buffered::linewriter::LineWriter<std::io::stdio::StdoutRaw>>>, std::io::stdio::stdout::{closure_env#0}>, !>>>"
  58: 00005555`5555bee0
@!"rd11!std::sys_common::once::futex::Once::call<std::sync::once::{impl#2}::call_once_force::{closure_env#0}<std::sync
::once_lock::{impl#0}::initialize::{closure_env#0}<std::sync::remutex::ReentrantMutex<core::cell::RefCell<std::io::buf
fered::linewriter::LineWriter<std::io::stdio::StdoutRaw>>>,
std::sync::once_lock::{impl#0}::get_or_init::{closure_env#0}<std::sync::remutex::ReentrantMutex<core::cell::RefCell<st
d::io::buffered::linewriter::LineWriter<std::io::stdio::StdoutRaw>>>, std::io::stdio::cleanup::{closure_env#0}>, !>>>"
  59: 00005555`55589dc0 @!"rd11!core::fmt::{impl#0}::write_char<rustc_demangle::SizeLimitedFmtAdapter<&mut
core::fmt::Formatter>>"
  60: 00005555`55589eb0 @!"rd11!core::fmt::{impl#0}::write_fmt<rustc_demangle::SizeLimitedFmtAdapter<&mut
core::fmt::Formatter>>"
  61: 00005555`55589f00 @!"rd11!core::fmt::{impl#0}::write_str<rustc_demangle::SizeLimitedFmtAdapter<&mut
core::fmt::Formatter>>"
  62: 00005555`55594e10 @!"rd11!core::fmt::write"
  63: 00005555`55595790 @!"rd11!core::fmt::Formatter::write_str"
  64: 00005555`555957a0 @!"rd11!core::fmt::Formatter::write_fmt"
  65: 00005555`55594490 @!"rd11!core::fmt::builders::{impl#2}::write_str"
  66: 00005555`55595b40 @!"rd11!core::fmt::{impl#10}::write_char"
  67: 00005555`55594b90 @!"rd11!core::fmt::Write::write_char<core::fmt::builders::PadAdapter>"
  68: 00005555`55594c70 @!"rd11!core::fmt::Write::write_fmt<core::fmt::builders::PadAdapter>"
  69: 00005555`55594cb0 @!"rd11!core::fmt::{impl#0}::write_str<core::fmt::builders::PadAdapter>"
  70: 00005555`55594cc0 @!"rd11!core::fmt::{impl#0}::write_char<core::fmt::builders::PadAdapter>"
  71: 00005555`55594da0 @!"rd11!core::fmt::{impl#0}::write_fmt<core::fmt::builders::PadAdapter>"
  72: 00005555`555953d0 @!"rd11!core::fmt::{impl#9}::pad_integral::write_prefix"
Unable to load image /lib/x86_64-linux-gnu/libdl.so.2, Win32 error 0n2
*** WARNING: Unable to verify timestamp for /lib/x86_64-linux-gnu/libdl.so.2
Unable to load image /lib/x86_64-linux-gnu/libpthread.so.0, Win32 error 0n2
*** WARNING: Unable to verify timestamp for /lib/x86_64-linux-gnu/libpthread.so.0
Unable to load image /lib/x86_64-linux-gnu/librt.so.1, Win32 error 0n2
*** WARNING: Unable to verify timestamp for /lib/x86_64-linux-gnu/librt.so.1
Unable to load image /lib/x86_64-linux-gnu/libgcc_s.so.1, Win32 error 0n2
*** WARNING: Unable to verify timestamp for /lib/x86_64-linux-gnu/libgcc_s.so.1
Unable to load image linux-vdso.so.1, Win32 error 0n2
*** WARNING: Unable to verify timestamp for linux-vdso.so.1
Unable to load image /lib64/ld-linux-x86-64.so.2, Win32 error 0n2
*** WARNING: Unable to verify timestamp for /lib64/ld-linux-x86-64.so.2

8.   We continue execution until a breakpoint is hit:


```
0:000> g
Breakpoint 39 hit
rd11!std::sync::once_lock::OnceLock::initialize<std::sync::remutex::ReentrantMutex<core::cell::RefCell<std::io::buffer
ed::linewriter::LineWriter<std::io::stdio::StdoutRaw>>>,
```

```
std::sync::once_lock::{impl#0}::get_or_init::{closure_env#0}<std::sync::remutex::ReentrantMutex<core::cell::RefCell<st
d::io::buffered::linewriter::LineWriter<std::io::stdio::StdoutRaw>>>, std::io::stdio::stdout::{closure_env#0}>, !>:
00005555`5555af00 sub     rsp,28h


0:001> kL
 # Child-SP          RetAddr               Call Site
00 00007fff`f7db4b08 00005555`55577b96
rd11!std::sync::once_lock::OnceLock::initialize<std::sync::remutex::ReentrantMutex<core::cell::RefCell<std::io::buffer
ed::linewriter::LineWriter<std::io::stdio::StdoutRaw>>>,
std::sync::once_lock::{impl#0}::get_or_init::{closure_env#0}<std::sync::remutex::ReentrantMutex<core::cell::RefCell<st
d::io::buffered::linewriter::LineWriter<std::io::stdio::StdoutRaw>>>, std::io::stdio::stdout::{closure_env#0}>, !>
01 (Inline Function) --------`--------
rd11!std::sync::once_lock::OnceLock::get_or_try_init<std::sync::remutex::ReentrantMutex<core::cell::RefCell<std::io::b
uffered::linewriter::LineWriter<std::io::stdio::StdoutRaw>>>,
std::sync::once_lock::{impl#0}::get_or_init::{closure_env#0}<std::sync::remutex::ReentrantMutex<core::cell::RefCell<st
d::io::buffered::linewriter::LineWriter<std::io::stdio::StdoutRaw>>>, std::io::stdio::stdout::{closure_env#0}>,
!>+0x6e
02 (Inline Function) --------`--------
rd11!std::sync::once_lock::OnceLock::get_or_init<std::sync::remutex::ReentrantMutex<core::cell::RefCell<std::io::buffe
red::linewriter::LineWriter<std::io::stdio::StdoutRaw>>>, std::io::stdio::stdout::{closure_env#0}>+0x6e
03 (Inline Function) --------`--------        rd11!std::io::stdio::stdout+0x6e
04 (Inline Function) --------`--------        rd11!std::io::stdio::print_to<std::io::stdio::Stdout>+0x96
05 00007fff`f7db4b10 00005555`555629f5        rd11!std::io::stdio::_print+0xd6
06 00007fff`f7db4bd0 00005555`555629cd        rd11!rd11::bar+0x25
07 00007fff`f7db4c10 00005555`5555e52d        rd11!rd11::foo+0x1d
08 00007fff`f7db4c20 00005555`5555e50e        rd11!rd11::start_modeling::{closure#0}+0xd
09 00007fff`f7db4c30 00005555`5556273a
rd11!std::sys_common::backtrace::__rust_begin_short_backtrace<rd11::start_modeling::{closure_env#0}, ()>+0xe
0a 00007fff`f7db4c50 00005555`5556122e
rd11!std::thread::{impl#0}::spawn_unchecked_::{closure#1}::{closure#0}<rd11::start_modeling::{closure_env#0}, ()>+0xa
0b 00007fff`f7db4c60 00005555`5555de89        rd11!core::panic::unwind_safe::{impl#23}::call_once<(),
std::thread::{impl#0}::spawn_unchecked_::{closure#1}::{closure_env#0}<rd11::start_modeling::{closure_env#0}, ()>>+0xe
0c 00007fff`f7db4c80 00005555`5555dffb
rd11!std::panicking::try::do_call<core::panic::unwind_safe::AssertUnwindSafe<std::thread::{impl#0}::spawn_unchecked_::
{closure#1}::{closure_env#0}<rd11::start_modeling::{closure_env#0}, ()>>, ()>+0x29
0d 00007fff`f7db4cc0 00005555`5555dd9a        rd11!_rust_try+0x1b
0e 00007fff`f7db4ce0 00005555`5555dd5a        rd11!std::panicking::try<(),
core::panic::unwind_safe::AssertUnwindSafe<std::thread::{impl#0}::spawn_unchecked_::{closure#1}::{closure_env#0}<rd11:
:start_modeling::{closure_env#0}, ()>>>+0x3a
0f 00007fff`f7db4d40 00005555`55562591
rd11!std::panic::catch_unwind<core::panic::unwind_safe::AssertUnwindSafe<std::thread::{impl#0}::spawn_unchecked_::{clo
sure#1}::{closure_env#0}<rd11::start_modeling::{closure_env#0}, ()>>, ()>+0xa
10 00007fff`f7db4d50 00005555`5555e68e
rd11!std::thread::{impl#0}::spawn_unchecked_::{closure#1}<rd11::start_modeling::{closure_env#0}, ()>+0x1b1
11 00007fff`f7db4e60 00005555`5557de05
rd11!core::ops::function::FnOnce::call_once<std::thread::{impl#0}::spawn_unchecked_::{closure_env#1}<rd11::start_model
ing::{closure_env#0}, ()>, ()>+0xe
12 (Inline Function) --------`--------        rd11!alloc::boxed::{impl#45}::call_once<(), dyn
core::ops::function::FnOnce<(), Output=()>, alloc::alloc::Global>+0x8
13 (Inline Function) --------`--------        rd11!alloc::boxed::{impl#45}::call_once<(), alloc::boxed::Box<dyn
core::ops::function::FnOnce<(), Output=()>, alloc::alloc::Global>, alloc::alloc::Global>+0xf
14 00007fff`f7db4e80 00007fff`f7f84fa3        rd11!std::sys::unix::thread::{impl#2}::new::thread_start+0x25
15 00007fff`f7db4ec0 00007fff`f7eb106f        libpthread_so!start_thread+0xf3
16 00007fff`f7db4f80 ffffffff`ffffffff        libc_so!clone+0x3f
17 00007fff`f7db4f88 00000000`00000000        0xffffffff`ffffffff
```

9.   We see that *std::io::stdio::_print* was called from the *bar* function. Let's clear all other breakpoints and put the breakpoint on the return address to see whether that call was printing the error message:

```
0:001> bc *

0:001> bp 00005555`555629f5

0:001> g
Breakpoint 0 hit
rd11!rd11::bar+0x25:
00005555`555629f5 add     rsp,38h
```

```
0:001> kL
 # Child-SP          RetAddr           Call Site
00 00007fff`f7db4bd0 00005555`555629cd rd11!rd11::bar+0x25
01 00007fff`f7db4c10 00005555`5555e52d rd11!rd11::foo+0x1d
02 00007fff`f7db4c20 00005555`5555e50e rd11!rd11::start_modeling::{closure#0}+0xd
03 00007fff`f7db4c30 00005555`5556273a
rd11!std::sys_common::backtrace::__rust_begin_short_backtrace<rd11::start_modeling::{closure_env#0}, ()>+0xe
04 00007fff`f7db4c50 00005555`5556122e
rd11!std::thread::{impl#0}::spawn_unchecked_::{closure#1}::{closure#0}<rd11::start_modeling::{closure_env#0}, ()>+0xa
05 00007fff`f7db4c60 00005555`5555de89 rd11!core::panic::unwind_safe::{impl#23}::call_once<(),
std::thread::{impl#0}::spawn_unchecked_::{closure#1}::{closure_env#0}<rd11::start_modeling::{closure_env#0}, ()>>+0xe
06 00007fff`f7db4c80 00005555`5555dffb
rd11!std::panicking::try::do_call<core::panic::unwind_safe::AssertUnwindSafe<std::thread::{impl#0}::spawn_unchecked_::
{closure#1}::{closure_env#0}<rd11::start_modeling::{closure_env#0}, ()>>, ()>+0x29
07 00007fff`f7db4cc0 00005555`5555dd9a rd11!__rust_try+0x1b
08 00007fff`f7db4ce0 00005555`5555dd5a rd11!std::panicking::try<(),
core::panic::unwind_safe::AssertUnwindSafe<std::thread::{impl#0}::spawn_unchecked_::{closure#1}::{closure_env#0}<rd11:
:start_modeling::{closure_env#0}, ()>>>+0x3a
09 00007fff`f7db4d40 00005555`55562591
rd11!std::panic::catch_unwind<core::panic::unwind_safe::AssertUnwindSafe<std::thread::{impl#0}::spawn_unchecked_::{clo
sure#1}::{closure_env#0}<rd11::start_modeling::{closure_env#0}, ()>>, ()>+0xa
0a 00007fff`f7db4d50 00005555`5555e68e
rd11!std::thread::{impl#0}::spawn_unchecked_::{closure#1}<rd11::start_modeling::{closure_env#0}, ()>+0x1b1
0b 00007fff`f7db4e60 00005555`5557de05
rd11!core::ops::function::FnOnce::call_once<std::thread::{impl#0}::spawn_unchecked_::{closure#1}<rd11::start_model
ing::{closure_env#0}, ()>, ()>+0xe
0c (Inline Function) --------`-------- rd11!alloc::boxed::{impl#45}::call_once<(), dyn
core::ops::function::FnOnce<(), Output=()>, alloc::alloc::Global>+0x8
0d (Inline Function) --------`-------- rd11!alloc::boxed::{impl#45}::call_once<(), alloc::boxed::Box<dyn
core::ops::function::FnOnce<(), Output=()>, alloc::alloc::Global>, alloc::alloc::Global>+0xf
0e 00007fff`f7db4e80 00007fff`f7f84fa3 rd11!std::sys::unix::thread::{impl#2}::new::thread_start+0x25
0f 00007fff`f7db4ec0 00007fff`f7eb106f libpthread_so!start_thread+0xf3
10 00007fff`f7db4f80 ffffffff`ffffffff libc_so!clone+0x3f
11 00007fff`f7db4f88 00000000`00000000 0xffffffff`ffffffff
```

Note: If we look at the terminal, we see that the error message was indeed printed upon the return.

10.   Let's now switch to the main thread and look at the local variables inside the *start_modeling* function:

```
0:001> ~0s
libpthread_so!_GI___pthread_timedjoin_ex+0x1d5:
00007fff`f7f86495 mov     edx,dword ptr [rbx+2D0h] ds:00007fff`f7db59d0=0000287e
```

```
0:000> kL
 # Child-SP          RetAddr           Call Site
00 00007fff`ffffdc50 00005555`5557df1d libpthread_so!_GI___pthread_timedjoin_ex+0x1d5
01 00007fff`ffffdcc0 00005555`55561728 rd11!std::sys::unix::thread::Thread::join+0xd
02 00007fff`ffffdd20 00005555`5556195c rd11!std::thread::JoinInner<()>::join<()>+0x18
03 00007fff`ffffde00 00005555`55562a3c rd11!std::thread::JoinHandle<()>::join<()>+0x1c
04 00007fff`ffffde20 00005555`555629a6 rd11!rd11::start_modeling+0x3c
05 00007fff`ffffde70 00005555`5555e6cb rd11!rd11::main+0x6
06 00007fff`ffffde80 00005555`5555e4ee rd11!core::ops::function::FnOnce::call_once<fn(), ()>+0xb
07 00007fff`ffffdea0 00005555`55561671 rd11!std::sys_common::backtrace::__rust_begin_short_backtrace<fn(), ()>+0xe
08 00007fff`ffffdec0 00005555`55575a7e rd11!std::rt::lang_start::{closure#0}<()>+0x11
09 (Inline Function) --------`-------- rd11!core::ops::function::impls::{impl#2}::call_once<(), (dyn
core::ops::function::Fn<(), Output=i32> + core::marker::Sync + core::panic::unwind_safe::RefUnwindSafe)>+0x3
0a (Inline Function) --------`-------- rd11!std::panicking::try::do_call<&(dyn core::ops::function::Fn<(),
Output=i32> + core::marker::Sync + core::panic::unwind_safe::RefUnwindSafe), i32>+0x3
0b (Inline Function) --------`-------- rd11!std::panicking::try<i32, &(dyn core::ops::function::Fn<(), Output=i32>
+ core::marker::Sync + core::panic::unwind_safe::RefUnwindSafe)>+0x3
0c (Inline Function) --------`-------- rd11!std::panic::catch_unwind<&(dyn core::ops::function::Fn<(), Output=i32>
+ core::marker::Sync + core::panic::unwind_safe::RefUnwindSafe), i32>+0x3
0d (Inline Function) --------`-------- rd11!std::rt::lang_start_internal::{closure#2}+0x3
0e (Inline Function) --------`--------
rd11!std::panicking::try::do_call<std::rt::lang_start_internal::{closure_env#2}, isize>+0x3
0f (Inline Function) --------`-------- rd11!std::panicking::try<isize,
std::rt::lang_start_internal::{closure_env#2}>+0x3
10 (Inline Function) --------`--------
rd11!std::panic::catch_unwind<std::rt::lang_start_internal::{closure_env#2}, isize>+0x3
```

```
11 00007fff`ffffdee0 00005555`5556164a    rd11!std::rt::lang_start_internal+0x42e
12 00007fff`ffffe040 00005555`55562a7e    rd11!std::rt::lang_start<()>+0x3a
13 00007fff`ffffe080 00007fff`f7ddc09b    rd11!main+0x1e
14 00007fff`ffffe090 00005555`5555c8fa    libc_so!_libc_start_main+0xeb
15 00007fff`ffffe150 ffffffff`ffffffff    rd11!start+0x2a
16 00007fff`ffffe158 00000000`00000000    0xffffffff`ffffffff


0:000> .frame 4
04 00007fff`ffffde20 00005555`555629a6    rd11!rd11::start_modeling+0x3c [/mnt/c/ALD4/rd11/src/main.rs @ 28]


0:000> dv /i /V
prv local  00007fff`ffffde28 @rsp+0x0008                        s = rd11::S
prv local  00007fff`ffffde60 @rsp+0x0040                        w = 0xa


0:000> dt rd11::S
   +0x000 wait             : Uint8B


0:000> dt s
Local var @ 0x7fffffffde28 Type rd11::S
   +0x000 wait             : 0xa


0:000> dx s
s                  [Type: rd11::S]
    [+0x000] wait               : 0xa [Type: u64]
```

11.   We now continue execution (**g**) until the program exits and WinDbg is disconnected, and then quit WinDbg.

Goal: Learn how GDB can be used to debug Rust applications.

Elementary Diagnostics Patterns: Error Message.

Memory Analysis Patterns: Stack Trace.

Debugging Implementation Patterns: Break-in; Code Breakpoint; Scope; Variable Value; Type Structure.

1.   The source code to build the executable can be found in the *rd11* directory:

```
$ git clone https://bitbucket.org/softwarediagnostics/ald4
```

2.   When you run the *rd11* program, it shows an error message after 10 seconds.

```
/mnt/c/ALD4/rd11$ target/debug/rd11
Error
```

3.   Launch the *rd11* executable under GDB:

```
/mnt/c/ALD4/rd11$ gdb target/debug/rd11
GNU gdb (Debian 8.2.1-2+b3) 8.2.1
Copyright (C) 2018 Free Software Foundation, Inc.
License GPLv3+: GNU GPL version 3 or later <http://gnu.org/licenses/gpl.html>
This is free software: you are free to change and redistribute it.
There is NO WARRANTY, to the extent permitted by law.
Type "show copying" and "show warranty" for details.
This GDB was configured as "x86_64-linux-gnu".
Type "show configuration" for configuration details.
For bug reporting instructions, please see:
<http://www.gnu.org/software/gdb/bugs/>.
Find the GDB manual and other documentation resources online at:
    <http://www.gnu.org/software/gdb/documentation/>.

For help, type "help".
Type "apropos word" to search for commands related to "word"...
Reading symbols from target/debug/rd11...done.
warning: Missing auto-load script at offset 0 in section .debug_gdb_scripts
of file /mnt/c/ALD4/rd11/target/debug/rd11.
Use `info auto-load python-scripts [REGEXP]' to list them.
(gdb)
```

4.   First, we put a code breakpoint on the *rd11::main* function (please note, this is Rust rd11 crate's *main*, not C or C++ *main* that may also exist):

```
(gdb) break rd11::main
Breakpoint 1 at 0xe9a1: file src/main.rs, line 12.
```

5.   We continue execution until the breakpoint is hit:

```
(gdb) r
Starting program: /mnt/c/ALD4/rd11/target/debug/rd11
[Thread debugging using libthread_db enabled]
```

```
Using host libthread_db library "/lib/x86_64-linux-gnu/libthread_db.so.1".

Breakpoint 1, rd11::main () at src/main.rs:12
warning: Source file is more recent than executable.
12          start_modeling();

(gdb) bt
#0  rd11::main () at src/main.rs:12
```

6.   Next, we put a code breakpoint on the *write* syscall (we can see it if we trace the program under *strace*):

```
(gdb) catch syscall write
Catchpoint 2 (syscall 'write' [1])

(gdb) info breakpoints
Num     Type           Disp Enb Address            What
1       breakpoint     keep y   0x00005555555629a1 in rd11::main at src/main.rs:12
        breakpoint already hit 1 time
2       catchpoint     keep y                       syscall "write"
```

7.   We continue execution until a breakpoint is hit:

```
(gdb) c
Continuing.
[New Thread 0x7ffff7db5700 (LWP 19311)]
[Switching to Thread 0x7ffff7db5700 (LWP 19311)]

Thread 2 "rd11" hit Catchpoint 2 (call to syscall write), __libc_write (nbytes=6,
buf=0x555555599600, fd=1) at ../sysdeps/unix/sysv/linux/write.c:26
26      ../sysdeps/unix/sysv/linux/write.c: No such file or directory.

(gdb) bt
#0  __libc_write (nbytes=6, buf=0x555555599600, fd=1) at ../sysdeps/unix/sysv/linux/write.c:26
#1  __libc_write (fd=1, buf=0x555555599600, nbytes=6) at ../sysdeps/unix/sysv/linux/write.c:24
#2  0x00005555555776f9 in std::sys::unix::fd::FileDesc::write () at library/std/src/sys/unix/fd.rs:247
#3  <std::sys::unix::stdio::Stdout as std::io::Write>::write () at library/std/src/sys/unix/stdio.rs:43
#4  std::io::Write::write_all () at library/std/src/io/mod.rs:1558
#5  <std::io::stdio::StdoutRaw as std::io::Write>::write_all () at library/std/src/io/stdio.rs:142
#6  <std::io::buffered::linewritershim::LineWriterShim<W> as std::io::Write>::write_all () at
library/std/src/io/buffered/linewritershim.rs:260
#7  <std::io::buffered::linewriter::LineWriter<W> as std::io::Write>::write_all () at
library/std/src/io/buffered/linewriter.rs:206
#8  <std::io::stdio::StdoutLock as std::io::Write>::write_all () at library/std/src/io/stdio.rs:746
#9  0x0000555555578436 in <std::io::Write::write_fmt::Adapter<T> as core::fmt::Write>::write_str () at
library/std/src/io/mod.rs:1687
#10 0x0000555555595003 in core::fmt::write () at library/core/src/fmt/mod.rs:1278
#11 0x0000555555577455 in std::io::Write::write_fmt () at library/std/src/io/mod.rs:1698
#12 <&std::io::stdio::Stdout as std::io::Write>::write_fmt () at library/std/src/io/stdio.rs:726
#13 0x0000555555577b83 in <std::io::stdio::Stdout as std::io::Write>::write_fmt () at library/std/src/io/stdio.rs:700
#14 std::io::stdio::print_to () at library/std/src/io/stdio.rs:1018
#15 std::io::stdio::_print () at library/std/src/io/stdio.rs:1095
#16 0x00005555555629f5 in rd11::bar () at src/main.rs:21
#17 0x00005555555629cd in rd11::foo (s=0x7ffff7db4c20) at src/main.rs:17
#18 0x000055555555e52d in rd11::start_modeling::{{closure}} () at src/main.rs:28
--Type <RET> for more, q to quit, c to continue without paging--
#19 0x000055555555e50e in std::sys_common::backtrace::__rust_begin_short_backtrace (f=...)
    at /rustc/90c541806f23a127002de5b4038be731ba1458ca/library/std/src/sys_common/backtrace.rs:134
#20 0x000055555556273a in std::thread::Builder::spawn_unchecked_::{{closure}}::{{closure}} ()
    at /rustc/90c541806f23a127002de5b4038be731ba1458ca/library/std/src/thread/mod.rs:526
#21 0x000055555556122e in <core::panic::unwind_safe::AssertUnwindSafe<F> as
core::ops::function::FnOnce<()>>::call_once (self=...)
    at /rustc/90c541806f23a127002de5b4038be731ba1458ca/library/core/src/panic/unwind_safe.rs:271
#22 0x000055555555de89 in std::panicking::try::do_call (data=0x7ffff7db4cf0 "\n")
    at /rustc/90c541806f23a127002de5b4038be731ba1458ca/library/std/src/panicking.rs:485
```

```
#23 0x000055555555dffb in __rust_try () at library/std/src/panicking.rs:469
#24 0x000055555555dd9a in std::panicking::try (f=...) at
/rustc/90c541806f23a127002de5b4038be731ba1458ca/library/std/src/panicking.rs:449
#25 0x000055555555dd5a in std::panic::catch_unwind (f=...) at
/rustc/90c541806f23a127002de5b4038be731ba1458ca/library/std/src/panic.rs:140
#26 0x0000555555562591 in std::thread::Builder::spawn_unchecked_::{{closure}} ()
    at /rustc/90c541806f23a127002de5b4038be731ba1458ca/library/std/src/thread/mod.rs:525
#27 0x000055555555e68e in core::ops::function::FnOnce::call_once{{vtable-shim}} ()
    at /rustc/90c541806f23a127002de5b4038be731ba1458ca/library/core/src/ops/function.rs:250
#28 0x0000555555557de05 in <alloc::boxed::Box<F,A> as core::ops::function::FnOnce<Args>>::call_once () at
library/alloc/src/boxed.rs:1973
#29 <alloc::boxed::Box<F,A> as core::ops::function::FnOnce<Args>>::call_once () at library/alloc/src/boxed.rs:1973
#30 std::sys::unix::thread::Thread::new::thread_start () at library/std/src/sys/unix/thread.rs:108
#31 0x00007ffff7f84fa3 in start_thread (arg=<optimized out>) at pthread_create.c:486
--Type <RET> for more, q to quit, c to continue without paging--
#32 0x00007ffff7eb106f in clone () at ../sysdeps/unix/sysv/linux/x86_64/clone.S:95
```

Note: We see that *std::io::stdio::_print* was called from the *bar* function. Let's clear all other breakpoints and put the breakpoint on the return address to see whether that call was printing the error message:

```
(gdb) delete break
Delete all breakpoints? (y or n) y

(gdb) break *0x00005555555629f5
Breakpoint 3 at 0x5555555629f5: file src/main.rs, line 22.

(gdb) c
Continuing.
Error

Thread 2 "rd11" hit Breakpoint 3, rd11::bar () at src/main.rs:22
22      }
```

Note: Upon the return, the error message was indeed printed.

8.   Let's now switch to the main thread and look at the local variables inside the *start_modeling* function:

```
(gdb) thread 1
[Switching to thread 1 (Thread 0x7ffff7db7240 (LWP 17832))]
#0  0x00007ffff7f86495 in __GI___pthread_timedjoin_ex (threadid=140737351735040,
thread_return=0x0, abstime=0x0, block=<optimized out>)
    at pthread_join_common.c:89
89      pthread_join_common.c: No such file or directory.

(gdb) bt
#0  0x00007ffff7f86495 in __GI___pthread_timedjoin_ex (threadid=140737351735040,
thread_return=0x0, abstime=0x0, block=<optimized out>)
    at pthread_join_common.c:89
#1  0x0000555555557df1d in std::sys::unix::thread::Thread::join () at
library/std/src/sys/unix/thread.rs:263
#2  0x0000555555561728 in std::thread::JoinInner<T>::join (self=...)
    at /rustc/90c541806f23a127002de5b4038be731ba1458ca/library/std/src/thread/mod.rs:1425
#3  0x000055555556195c in std::thread::JoinHandle<T>::join (self=...)
    at /rustc/90c541806f23a127002de5b4038be731ba1458ca/library/std/src/thread/mod.rs:1558
#4  0x0000555555562a3c in rd11::start_modeling () at src/main.rs:28
#5  0x00005555555629a6 in rd11::main () at src/main.rs:12

(gdb) frame 4
#4  0x0000555555562a3c in rd11::start_modeling () at src/main.rs:28
28          let _ = thread::spawn(move || { foo(&s) }).join();
```

```
(gdb) info locals
s = rd11::S {wait: 10}
w = 10

(gdb) ptype rd11::S
type = struct rd11::S {
  wait: u64,
}

(gdb) p s
$1 = rd11::S {wait: 10}
```

9.   We now continue execution (**c**) until the program exits and then quit GDB.

Exercise RD11 (LLDB)

Goal: Learn how LLDB can be used to debug Rust applications.

Elementary Diagnostics Patterns: Error Message.

Memory Analysis Patterns: Stack Trace.

Debugging Implementation Patterns: Break-in; Code Breakpoint; Scope; Variable Value; Type Structure.

1.   The source code to build the executable can be found in the *rd11* directory:

```
$ git clone https://bitbucket.org/softwarediagnostics/ald4
```

2.   When you run the *rd11* program, it shows an error message after 10 seconds.

```
/mnt/c/ALD4/rd11$ target/debug/rd11
Error
```

3.   Launch the *rd11* executable under GDB:

```
/mnt/c/ALD4/rd11$ lldb target/debug/rd11
(lldb) target create "target/debug/rd11"
Current executable set to 'target/debug/rd11' (x86_64)
```

4.   First, we put a code breakpoint on the *rd11::main* function (please note, this is Rust rd11 crate's *main*, not C or C++ *main* that may also exist):

```
(lldb) break set -name rd11::main
Breakpoint 1: where = rd11`rd11::main::haddbaaee7b3ad775 + 1 at main.rs:12, address =
0x000000000000e9a1
```

5.   We continue execution until the breakpoint is hit:

```
(lldb) r
Process 22761 launched: '/mnt/c/ALD4/rd11/target/debug/rd11' (x86_64)
Process 22761 stopped
* thread #1, name = 'rd11', stop reason = breakpoint 1.1
    frame #0: 0x00005555555629a1 rd11`rd11::main::haddbaaee7b3ad775 at main.rs:12
   9    }
   10
   11   fn main() {
-> 12       start_modeling();
   13   }
   14
   15   fn foo(s: &S) {
```

```
(lldb) bt
error: need to add support for DW_TAG_base_type '()' encoded with DW_ATE = 0x7, bit_size = 0
* thread #1, name = 'rd11', stop reason = breakpoint 1.1
  * frame #0: 0x00005555555629a1 rd11`rd11::main::haddbaaee7b3ad775 at main.rs:12
    frame #1: 0x000055555555e6cb
rd11`core::ops::function::FnOnce::call_once::h050406f74728a5c1((null)=(rd11`rd11::main::haddbaa
ee7b3ad775 at main.rs:11), (null)=<unavailable>) at function.rs:250
```

```
    frame #2: 0x000055555555e4ee
rd11`std::sys_common::backtrace::__rust_begin_short_backtrace::hbae218fc706a333e(f=(rd11`rd11::
main::haddbaaee7b3ad775 at main.rs:11)) at backtrace.rs:134
    frame #3: 0x0000555555561671
rd11`std::rt::lang_start::_$u7b$$u7b$closure$u7d$$u7d$::h25784916792c723e at rt.rs:166
    frame #4: 0x0000555555575a7e rd11`std::rt::lang_start_internal::h76f3e81e6b8f13f9 [inlined]
core::ops::function::impls::_$LT$impl$u20$core..ops..function..FnOnce$LT$A$GT$$u20$for$u20$$RF$
F$GT$::call_once::hb1327dc2ef3fecdf at function.rs:287
    frame #5: 0x0000555555575a7b rd11`std::rt::lang_start_internal::h76f3e81e6b8f13f9 [inlined]
std::panicking::try::do_call::h4044173225fe83dd at panicking.rs:485
    frame #6: 0x0000555555575a7b rd11`std::rt::lang_start_internal::h76f3e81e6b8f13f9 [inlined]
std::panicking::try::hd8a722c09d156a53 at panicking.rs:449
    frame #7: 0x0000555555575a7b rd11`std::rt::lang_start_internal::h76f3e81e6b8f13f9 [inlined]
std::panic::catch_unwind::hd2ca07971cf0119b at panic.rs:140
    frame #8: 0x0000555555575a7b rd11`std::rt::lang_start_internal::h76f3e81e6b8f13f9 [inlined]
std::rt::lang_start_internal::_$u7b$$u7b$closure$u7d$$u7d$::h26d89d595cf47b70 at rt.rs:148
    frame #9: 0x0000555555575a7b rd11`std::rt::lang_start_internal::h76f3e81e6b8f13f9 [inlined]
std::panicking::try::do_call::hf47aa1aa005e5f1a at panicking.rs:485
    frame #10: 0x0000555555575a7b rd11`std::rt::lang_start_internal::h76f3e81e6b8f13f9
[inlined] std::panicking::try::h73d246b2423eaf4e at panicking.rs:449
    frame #11: 0x0000555555575a7b rd11`std::rt::lang_start_internal::h76f3e81e6b8f13f9
[inlined] std::panic::catch_unwind::hbaaeae8f1b2f9915 at panic.rs:140
    frame #12: 0x0000555555575a7b rd11`std::rt::lang_start_internal::h76f3e81e6b8f13f9 at
rt.rs:148
    frame #13: 0x000055555556164a
rd11`std::rt::lang_start::h1fca1d97916de92a(main=(rd11`rd11::main::haddbaaee7b3ad775 at
main.rs:11), argc=1, argv=0x00007fffffffe158, sigpipe='\0') at rt.rs:165
    frame #14: 0x0000555555562a7e rd11`main + 30
    frame #15: 0x00007ffff7ddc09b libc.so.6`__libc_start_main(main=(rd11`main), argc=1,
argv=0x00007fffffffe158, init=<unavailable>, fini=<unavailable>, rtld_fini=<unavailable>,
stack_end=0x00007fffffffe148) at libc-start.c:308
    frame #16: 0x000055555555c8fa rd11`_start + 42
```

6.   Next, we put a code breakpoint on the __libc_write syscall:

```
(lldb) break set -name __libc_write
Breakpoint 2: 4 locations.

(lldb) c
Process 25400 resuming
Process 25400 stopped
* thread #2, name = 'rd11', stop reason = breakpoint 2.2
    frame #0: 0x00007ffff7f8e460 libpthread.so.0`__libc_write(fd=1, buf=0x0000555555599600,
nbytes=6) at write.c:26

(lldb) bt
error: need to add support for DW_TAG_base_type '()' encoded with DW_ATE = 0x7, bit_size = 0
error: need to add support for DW_TAG_base_type '()' encoded with DW_ATE = 0x7, bit_size = 0
* thread #2, name = 'rd11', stop reason = breakpoint 2.2
  * frame #0: 0x00007ffff7f8e460 libpthread.so.0`__libc_write(fd=1, buf=0x0000555555599600, nbytes=6) at write.c:26
    frame #1: 0x00005555555776f9
rd11`_$LT$std..io..stdio..StdoutLock$u20$as$u20$std..io..Write$GT$::write_all::h85a5785ee005e6e5 [inlined]
std::sys::unix::fd::FileDesc::write::hc94ccc2880dddb80 at fd.rs:247
    frame #2: 0x00005555555776d2
rd11`_$LT$std..io..stdio..StdoutLock$u20$as$u20$std..io..Write$GT$::write_all::h85a5785ee005e6e5 [inlined]
_$LT$std..sys..unix..stdio..Stdout$u20$as$u20$std..io..Write$GT$::write::h6e4419e483bb752b at stdio.rs:43
    frame #3: 0x00005555555776d2
rd11`_$LT$std..io..stdio..StdoutLock$u20$as$u20$std..io..Write$GT$::write_all::h85a5785ee005e6e5 [inlined]
std::io::Write::write_all::hfd2337e71c1345b5 at mod.rs:1558
```

```
        frame #4: 0x000055555557768f
rd11`_$LT$std..io..stdio..StdoutLock$u20$as$u20$std..io..Write$GT$::write_all::h85a5785ee005e6e5 [inlined]
_$LT$std..io..stdio..StdoutRaw$u20$as$u20$std..io..Write$GT$::write_all::h416948dc593d50ca at stdio.rs:142
        frame #5: 0x000055555557768f
rd11`_$LT$std..io..stdio..StdoutLock$u20$as$u20$std..io..Write$GT$::write_all::h85a5785ee005e6e5 [inlined]
_$LT$std..io..buffered..linewritershim..LineWriterShim$LT$W$GT$$u20$as$u20$std..io..Write$GT$::write_all::h0fe8d69e39d
a1803 at linewritershim.rs:260
        frame #6: 0x00005555555775b7
rd11`_$LT$std..io..stdio..StdoutLock$u20$as$u20$std..io..Write$GT$::write_all::h85a5785ee005e6e5 [inlined]
_$LT$std..io..buffered..linewriter..LineWriter$LT$W$GT$$u20$as$u20$std..io..Write$GT$::write_all::h5dadc124f2ed787b at
linewriter.rs:206
        frame #7: 0x00005555555775b7
rd11`_$LT$std..io..stdio..StdoutLock$u20$as$u20$std..io..Write$GT$::write_all::h85a5785ee005e6e5 at stdio.rs:746
        frame #8: 0x0000555555578436
rd11`_$LT$std..io..Write..write_fmt..Adapter$LT$T$GT$$u20$as$u20$core..fmt..Write$GT$::write_str::h6ecb79d3a89ade81 at
mod.rs:1687
        frame #9: 0x0000555555595003 rd11`core::fmt::write::h9ffde816c577717b at mod.rs:1278
        frame #10: 0x0000555555577455
rd11`_$LT$$RF$std..io..stdio..Stdout$u20$as$u20$std..io..Write$GT$::write_fmt::hcfaa1e02134d824a [inlined]
std::io::Write::write_fmt::h98103a99e9ea3d02 at mod.rs:1698
        frame #11: 0x0000555555577430
rd11`_$LT$$RF$std..io..stdio..Stdout$u20$as$u20$std..io..Write$GT$::write_fmt::hcfaa1e02134d824a at stdio.rs:726
        frame #12: 0x0000555555577b83 rd11`std::io::stdio::_print::h1de311987873daa6 [inlined]
_$LT$std..io..stdio..Stdout$u20$as$u20$std..io..Write$GT$::write_fmt::h0cd57de824858bb9 at stdio.rs:700
        frame #13: 0x0000555555577b6b rd11`std::io::stdio::_print::h1de311987873daa6 [inlined]
std::io::stdio::print_to::h888da167aadac7d0 at stdio.rs:1018
        frame #14: 0x0000555555577b00 rd11`std::io::stdio::_print::h1de311987873daa6 at stdio.rs:1095
        frame #15: 0x00005555555629f5 rd11`rd11::bar::h62a8ba746f6b18d4 at main.rs:21
        frame #16: 0x00005555555629cd rd11`rd11::foo::hde7d4530a7169060(s=0x00007ffff7db4c20) at main.rs:17
        frame #17: 0x000055555555e52d rd11`rd11::start_modeling::_$u7b$$u7b$closure$u7d$$u7d$::h2ec80ac3a69a7407 at
main.rs:28
        frame #18: 0x000055555555e50e
rd11`std::sys_common::backtrace::__rust_begin_short_backtrace::hfe0b8a27f5b59993(f={closure_env#0} @
0x00007ffff7db4c40) at backtrace.rs:134
        frame #19: 0x000055555556273a
rd11`std::thread::Builder::spawn_unchecked_::_$u7b$$u7b$closure$u7d$$u7d$::_$u7b$$u7b$closure$u7d$$u7d$::h72d267c5edd2
7278 at mod.rs:526
        frame #20: 0x000055555556122e
rd11`_$LT$core..panic..unwind_safe..AssertUnwindSafe$LT$F$GT$$u20$as$u20$core..ops..function..FnOnce$LT$$LP$$RP$$GT$$G
T$::call_once::h66703ec694841d90(self=AssertUnwindSafe<std::thread::{impl#0}::spawn_unchecked_::{closure#1}::{closure_
env#0}<rd11::start_modeling::{closure_env#0}, ()>> @ 0x00007ffff7db4c70, (null)=<unavailable>) at unwind_safe.rs:271
        frame #21: 0x000055555555de89 rd11`std::panicking::try::do_call::h7d7b14966a0a2392(data="\n") at panicking.rs:485
        frame #22: 0x000055555555dffb rd11`__rust_try + 27
        frame #23: 0x000055555555dd9a
rd11`std::panicking::try::h2e777fa24c7de2ba(f=AssertUnwindSafe<std::thread::{impl#0}::spawn_unchecked_::{closure#1}::{
closure_env#0}<rd11::start_modeling::{closure_env#0}, ()>> @ 0x00007ffff7db4d08) at panicking.rs:449
        frame #24: 0x000055555555dd5a
rd11`std::panic::catch_unwind::h8245e685544ea367(f=AssertUnwindSafe<std::thread::{impl#0}::spawn_unchecked_::{closure#
1}::{closure_env#0}<rd11::start_modeling::{closure_env#0}, ()>> @ 0x00007ffff7db4d40) at panic.rs:140
        frame #25: 0x0000555555562591
rd11`std::thread::Builder::spawn_unchecked_::_$u7b$$u7b$closure$u7d$$u7d$::hdbf5efdf03776566 at mod.rs:525
        frame #26: 0x000055555555e68e
rd11`core::ops::function::FnOnce::call_once$u7b$$u7b$vtable.shim$u7d$$u7d$::ha99cb9c96439fd35((null)=0x00005555555ae92
0, (null)=<unavailable>) at function.rs:250
        frame #27: 0x000055555557de05 rd11`std::sys::unix::thread::Thread::new::thread_start::h33b6dae3e3692197 [inlined]
_$LT$alloc..boxed..Box$LT$F$C$A$GT$$u20$as$u20$core..ops..function..FnOnce$LT$Args$GT$$GT$::call_once::ha1f2224656a778
fb at boxed.rs:1973
        frame #28: 0x000055555557ddfd rd11`std::sys::unix::thread::Thread::new::thread_start::h33b6dae3e3692197 [inlined]
_$LT$alloc..boxed..Box$LT$F$C$A$GT$$u20$as$u20$core..ops..function..FnOnce$LT$Args$GT$$GT$::call_once::haa29ed9703f354
b7 at boxed.rs:1973
        frame #29: 0x000055555557ddf6 rd11`std::sys::unix::thread::Thread::new::thread_start::h33b6dae3e3692197 at
thread.rs:108
        frame #30: 0x00007ffff7f84fa3 libpthread.so.0`start_thread(arg=<unavailable>) at pthread_create.c:486
        frame #31: 0x00007ffff7eb106f libc.so.6`__GI___clone at clone.S:95
```

Note: We see that *std::io::stdio::_print* was called from the *bar* function. Let's clear all other breakpoints and put the
breakpoint on the return address to see whether that call was printing the error message:

```
(lldb) break delete
About to delete all breakpoints, do you want to do that?: [Y/n] Y
All breakpoints removed. (2 breakpoints)
```

```
(lldb) break set -address 0x00005555555629f5
Breakpoint 3: where = rd11`rd11::bar::h62a8ba746f6b18d4 + 37 at main.rs:22, address =
0x00005555555629f5

(lldb) c
Process 25400 resuming
Error
Process 25400 stopped
* thread #2, name = 'rd11', stop reason = breakpoint 3.1
    frame #0: 0x00005555555629f5 rd11`rd11::bar::h62a8ba746f6b18d4 at main.rs:22
   19
   20   fn bar() {
   21       println!("Error");
-> 22   }
   23
   24   fn start_modeling() {
   25       let w: u64 = 10;
```

Note: Upon the return, the error message was indeed printed.

7.   Let's now switch to the main thread and look at the local variables inside the *start_modeling* function:

```
(lldb) thread select 1
* thread #1, name = 'rd11'
    frame #0: 0x00007ffff7f86495
libpthread.so.0`__GI___pthread_timedjoin_ex(threadid=140737351735040,
thread_return=0x0000000000000000, abstime=0x0000000000000000, block=true) at
pthread_join_common.c:89

(lldb) bt
error: need to add support for DW_TAG_base_type '()' encoded with DW_ATE = 0x7, bit_size = 0
* thread #1, name = 'rd11'
  * frame #0: 0x00007ffff7f86495 libpthread.so.0`__GI___pthread_timedjoin_ex(threadid=140737351735040,
thread_return=0x0000000000000000, abstime=0x0000000000000000, block=true) at pthread_join_common.c:89
    frame #1: 0x000055555557df1d rd11`std::sys::unix::thread::Thread::join::hb66f760ed5120703 at thread.rs:263
    frame #2: 0x0000555555561728 rd11`std::thread::JoinInner$LT$T$GT$::join::h77990fdede9af11c(self=<unavailable>) at
mod.rs:1425
    frame #3: 0x000055555556195c rd11`std::thread::JoinHandle$LT$T$GT$::join::h1e3777d827101072(self=<unavailable>) at
mod.rs:1558
    frame #4: 0x0000555555562a3c rd11`rd11::start_modeling::h728217ad27eee427 at main.rs:28
    frame #5: 0x00005555555629a6 rd11`rd11::main::haddbaaee7b3ad775 at main.rs:12
    frame #6: 0x000055555555e6cb
rd11`core::ops::function::FnOnce::call_once::h050406f74728a5c1((null)=(rd11`rd11::main::haddbaaee7b3ad775 at
main.rs:11), (null)=<unavailable>) at function.rs:250
    frame #7: 0x000055555555e4ee
rd11`std::sys_common::backtrace::__rust_begin_short_backtrace::hbae218fc706a333e(f=(rd11`rd11::main::haddbaaee7b3ad775
at main.rs:11)) at backtrace.rs:134
    frame #8: 0x0000555555561671 rd11`std::rt::lang_start::_$u7b$$u7b$closure$u7d$$u7d$::h25784916792c723e at
rt.rs:166
    frame #9: 0x000055555557a7e rd11`std::rt::lang_start_internal::h76f3e81e6b8f13f9 [inlined]
core::ops::function::impls::_$LT$impl$u20$core..ops..function..FnOnce$LT$A$GT$$u20$for$u20$$RF$F$GT$::call_once::hb132
7dc2ef3fecdf at function.rs:287
    frame #10: 0x000055555557a7b rd11`std::rt::lang_start_internal::h76f3e81e6b8f13f9 [inlined]
std::panicking::try::do_call::h4044173225fe83dd at panicking.rs:485
    frame #11: 0x000055555557a7b rd11`std::rt::lang_start_internal::h76f3e81e6b8f13f9 [inlined]
std::panicking::try::hd8a722c09d156a53 at panicking.rs:449
    frame #12: 0x000055555557a7b rd11`std::rt::lang_start_internal::h76f3e81e6b8f13f9 [inlined]
std::panic::catch_unwind::hd2ca07971cf0119b at panic.rs:140
    frame #13: 0x000055555557a7b rd11`std::rt::lang_start_internal::h76f3e81e6b8f13f9 [inlined]
std::rt::lang_start_internal::_$u7b$$u7b$closure$u7d$$u7d$::h26d89d595cf47b70 at rt.rs:148
    frame #14: 0x000055555557a7b rd11`std::rt::lang_start_internal::h76f3e81e6b8f13f9 [inlined]
std::panicking::try::do_call::hf47aa1aa005e5f1a at panicking.rs:485
```

```
    frame #15: 0x0000555555575a7b rd11`std::rt::lang_start_internal::h76f3e81e6b8f13f9 [inlined]
std::panicking::try::h73d246b2423eaf4e at panicking.rs:449
    frame #16: 0x0000555555575a7b rd11`std::rt::lang_start_internal::h76f3e81e6b8f13f9 [inlined]
std::panic::catch_unwind::hbaaeae8f1b2f9915 at panic.rs:140
    frame #17: 0x0000555555575a7b rd11`std::rt::lang_start_internal::h76f3e81e6b8f13f9 at rt.rs:148
    frame #18: 0x000055555556164a rd11`std::rt::lang_start::h1fca1d97916de92a(main=(rd11`rd11::main::haddbaaee7b3ad775
at main.rs:11), argc=1, argv=0x00007fffffffe158, sigpipe='\0') at rt.rs:165
    frame #19: 0x0000555555562a7e rd11`main + 30
    frame #20: 0x00007ffff7ddc09b libc.so.6`__libc_start_main(main=(rd11`main), argc=1, argv=0x00007fffffffe158,
init=<unavailable>, fini=<unavailable>, rtld_fini=<unavailable>, stack_end=0x00007fffffffe148) at libc-start.c:308
    frame #21: 0x000055555555c8fa rd11`_start + 42

(lldb) frame select 4
frame #4: 0x0000555555562a3c rd11`rd11::start_modeling::h728217ad27eee427 at main.rs:28
   25          let w: u64 = 10;
   26          let s = S { wait: w };
   27
-> 28          let _ = thread::spawn(move || { foo(&s) }).join();
   29      }

(lldb) frame variable
(unsigned long) w = 10
(rd11::S) s = (wait = 10)

(lldb) p s
(rd11::S) $0 = (wait = 10)

(lldb) type lookup rd11::S
struct S {
    unsigned long wait;
}
```

8.   We now continue execution (**c**) until the program exits and then quit LLDB.

Postmortem Debugging

- Accelerated Linux Core Dump Analysis, Third Edition (PDF book + Recording)

- Accelerated Linux Core Dump Analysis (Educative course)

A few words about postmortem debugging using core dumps: most of the time, memory analysis patterns are the same. However, crash and hang memory dump analysis is also used to analyze abnormal software behavior when we don't have the source code, and we need to analyze multiple processes and their relations because we don't know who caused the problem.

Accelerated Linux Core Dump Analysis, Third Edition (PDF book + Recording)

https://www.patterndiagnostics.com/accelerated-linux-core-dump-analysis-book

Accelerated Linux Core Dump Analysis (Educative course)

https://www.educative.io/courses/accelerated-linux-core-dump-analysis

Additional Training for Debugging

- Accelerated Linux API for Software Diagnostics

- Accelerated C & C++ for Linux Diagnostics

- Accelerated Linux Disassembly, Reconstruction and Reversing, Second Edition

- Memory Thinking for Rust

- Foundations of Linux Debugging, Disassembling, and Reversing

- Debugging, Disassembly & Reversing in Linux for x64 Architecture (Educative course)

- Foundations of ARM64 Linux Debugging, Disassembling, and Reversing

- Foundations of Linux ARM64: Debug, Disassemble, and Reverse (Educative course)

© 2024 Software Diagnostics Services

Accelerated Linux API for Software Diagnostics

https://www.patterndiagnostics.com/accelerated-linux-api-book

Accelerated C & C++ for Linux Diagnostics

https://www.patterndiagnostics.com/accelerated-c-cpp-linux-diagnostics

Accelerated Linux Disassembly, Reconstruction and Reversing, Second Edition

https://www.patterndiagnostics.com/accelerated-linux-disassembly-reconstruction-reversing-book

Memory Thinking for Rust

https://www.patterndiagnostics.com/memory-thinking-rust

Foundations of Linux Debugging, Disassembling, and Reversing

https://link.springer.com/book/10.1007/978-1-4842-9153-5

Debugging, Disassembly & Reversing in Linux for x64 Architecture (Educative course)

https://www.educative.io/courses/debugging-disassembly-reversing-in-linux-x64-architecture

Foundations of ARM64 Linux Debugging, Disassembling, and Reversing

https://link.springer.com/book/10.1007/978-1-4842-9082-8

Foundations of Linux ARM64: Debug, Disassemble, and Reverse (Educative course)

https://www.educative.io/courses/foundations-of-linux-arm64-debug-disassemble-and-reverse

Resources

- [DumpAnalysis.org](#) / [SoftwareDiagnostics.Institute](#) / [PatternDiagnostics.com](#)
- [Debugging.TV](#) / [YouTube.com/DebuggingTV](#) / [YouTube.com/PatternDiagnostics](#)
- [Software Diagnostics Library](#)
- [Pattern-Driven Software Problem Solving](#)
- [Encyclopedia of Crash Dump Analysis Patterns, Third Edition](#)
- [Memory Dump Analysis Anthology (Diagnomicon)](#)

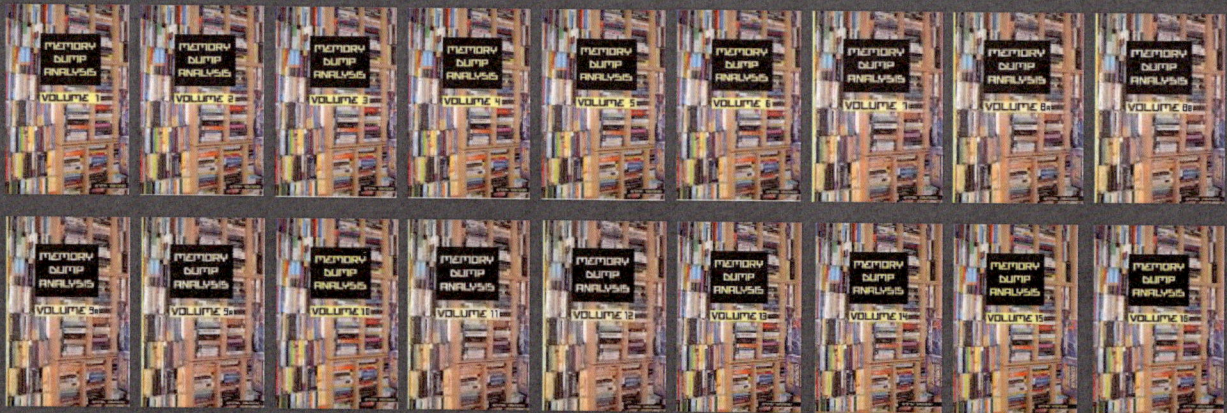

Software Diagnostics Institute
https://www.dumpanalysis.org/

Debugging.TV / DebuggingTV YouTube Channel
http://www.debugging.tv/
https://www.youtube.com/DebuggingTV

Software Diagnostics Library
https://www.dumpanalysis.org/blog/

Pattern-Driven Software Problem Solving
https://www.dumpanalysis.org/pattern-driven-software-problem-solving

Encyclopedia of Crash Dump Analysis Patterns, Third Edition
https://www.patterndiagnostics.com/encyclopedia-crash-dump-analysis-patterns

Memory Dump Analysis Anthology (Diagnomicon)
https://www.dumpanalysis.org/advanced-software-debugging-reference

9 781912 636716